The Informed Student Guide to
MARKETING

Dedication

Dedicated to Diane and Anne, the unacknowledged contributors to this book.

The Informed Student Guide to MARKETING

Edited by Philip J. Kitchen and Tony Proctor

Australia • Canada • Mexico • Singapore • Spain • United Kingdom • United States

Prelude

The Informed Student Guide to Marketing aims to provide an authoritative guide to the subject of marketing as it is located within the overarching field of business and management.

The *study* of marketing can be radically different from the *practice* of marketing. This text is perceived as adding to the marketing armoury of those studying the subject, in other words developing a knowledge base in this discipline. It is also suitable as a source of ready reference – or an aide-memoire – in the diverse topics represented. The practice element – or skills base – develops as and when marketing is applied in a specific set of contextual circumstances. In terms of the practice of marketing, questions undoubtedly arise. The answers, both creative and managerial, vary from firm to firm and from market to market owing to different contexts, circumstances, competitive positions and market needs. In other words, there are no 'pat' or 'easy' answers. But finding an approach toward answers or solutions is the essence of this text. What we as editors and the various contributors have sought to do is to provide a series of bases, definitions and explanations of the different areas represented under the heading of 'marketing'. The result should be informed and enquiring students in this expansive and global subject.

While there are some interesting and erudite synopses of definitions and articles on the subject of marketing available already, the aim of this book is to draw upon the opinions, views and conceptualizations about various elements of marketing from a large number of authors and writers teaching marketing across the European community. The various sections represent individual viewpoints concerning specific areas within marketing. Notably, the individual views do not always agree in terms of their definitions, or in terms of contextualization. And that is fine, as marketing – at least in terms of application – invariably is a balancing act between organizational resource and contextual circumstance. Our role as editors was to strive to ensure some uniformity in terms of style and form.

The book provides comprehensive coverage of the subject with the latest definitions:

- Short, easy to read entries of approximately 300 words for each subject.
- Where necessary the entries contain a number of key references.

What we have sought to do as editors is to ensure that:

- readers' needs are kept in mind
- entries are kept concise and to the point
- each entry can be read independently
- a small number of key references of relevance to the individual entry are provided
- each reader should be able to start from scratch with a topic and finish in a position to go on to more specialized enquiry, be they students or professional managers.

This book thus provides an authoritative reference guide for undergraduate students who wish to have definitional material to hand concerning marketing. It should also act as support or adjunct material to students undertaking marketing courses and provide a source of reference for postgraduate students and marketing practitioners.

This book is needed. At a time when courses in marketing are multiplying, it is time for a good quality student reference guide to be made available in order to satisfy demand. There is also a determination to use the latest definitions. We trust that readers and users will find the text informative and a valuable source of reference to the marketing discipline.

Philip J. Kitchen and Tony Proctor
January 2001

List of contributors

AJN – Andrew Newman
BF – Bram Foubert
BZE – B. Zafer Erdogan
CTG – Colin Gilligan
CV – Claudio Vigneli
DM – Danny Moss
DWP – David Pickton
EG – Els Gijsbrechts
GL – Geoff Lancaster
IPD – Ioanna Papasolomou-Doukakis
JWDB – Jim Blythe
JDH – Joeri De Haes
KC – Keith Crosier
KCa – Katia Campo
KP – Ken Peattie

LdeC – Leslie de Chernatony
MJE – Martin Evans
MJT – Michael Thomas
PBB – Peter Betts
PJK – Philip Kitchen
RAA – Ruth A. Ashford
RAS – Ruth A. Schmidt
RM-R – Rosmimah Mohd-Roslin
RMSW – Richard M.S. Wilson
SFX – Stephen Brown
SP – Stephen Parkinson
SR – Stuart Roper
TP – Tony Proctor
WvW – Walter van Waterschoot
WGD – Bill Donaldson

Ruth A. Ashford is a Senior Lecturer at Manchester Metropolitan University and the Senior Examiner for the Chartered Institute of Marketing (CIM) Certificate in Marketing. She is also the Senior Examiner for the newly launched joint award with the Chartered Institute of Bankers and CIM. Her previous experience includes over 12 years in marketing and purchasing, working within the NHS for over eight years. She has published in the area of consumer behaviour, concentrating on perceived risk and health services, public relations and enterprise education.

Peter Betts is Senior Lecturer in Marketing at Manchester Metropolitan University and Visiting Fellow at Manchester Business School. He is also marketing consultant for MAP plc, a medium sized advertising agency in Manchester where he works on marketing and advertising strategies for a wide range of regional and national clients.

Jim Blythe is a former company director and marketing consultant. He has been an academic for ten years and is author of 12 papers and four textbooks, as well as contributing to other edited works. Jim is a Senior Lecturer at the University of Glamorgan.

Stephen Brown is Professor of Marketing Research at the University of Ulster, Jordanstown. He has written or co-edited ten books, including *Postmodern Marketing*, *Postmodern Marketing Two* (both Thomson Learning) and *Imagining Marketing* (forthcoming from Routledge). His papers have been published in many journals, including *Journal of Marketing*, *Journal of Advertising*, *Journal of Retailing* and *Journal of Macromarketing*.

Katia Campo has a degree in Applied Economic Sciences, and a PhD in Marketing Modelling from the University of Antwerp. She was granted a Postdoctoral

Fellowship by the Fund for Scientific Research-Flanders (Belgium). She is now Senior Manager Modelling and Analytics at Accuris Group Belgium, and part-time Marketing Professor at the University of Antwerp.

Keith Crosier is Honorary Research Fellow in the Department of Marketing at the University of Strathclyde, where he was previously Director of the Honours Programme and Director of Teaching. A former advertising manager in London and New York, he has kept in touch with the marketing communications business via four years as a freelance journalist and periodic consultancy. He holds the CAM Diploma (Communications Advertising and Marketing Education Foundation), is Assistant Editor of *Marketing Intelligence and Planning*, and has contributed to a variety of encyclopaedias, dictionaries and textbooks.

Leslie de Chernatony is Professor of Brand Marketing and Director of the Centre for Research in Brand Marketing at the Business School at the University of Birmingham. With a doctorate in Brand Marketing and a previous career in the marketing departments of blue chip organisations he combines rigorously grounded research with a pragmatic orientation. He has published in numerous American and European journals and is a regular presenter at international conferences. Lead author of the popular text, *Creating Powerful Brands*, he has had several books published. Leslie is a Fellow of the Chartered Institute of Marketing.

Joeri de Haes is both teaching assistant and doctoral student at the University of Antwerp (University Faculties Saint-Ignatius).

Bill Donaldson BA PhD MCIM Chartered Marketer is Director, Marketing and a Senior Lecturer at the University of Strathclyde, Graduate School of Business. He is also a Senior Examiner for the UK Institute of Professional Sales and author of *Sales Management: Theory and Practice* 2nd edition (Macmillan, 1998). He has also had a number of publications published in the areas of customer service, sales and relationship marketing.

B. Zafer Erdogan is Assistant Professor of Marketing, Dumlupinar University, Turkey. He holds a PhD from the University of Strathclyde, UK and an MBA from the University of Hartford, USA. His current teaching and research interests are developments in marketing communications, branding, social marketing and research methods.

Martin Evans BA, MA, MIDM, MMRS, FCIM is Royal Mail/Mail Marketing Professor of Marketing and Director of the Bristol Business School Marketing Research Unit (CReM: Customer Knowledge: Research and Management). His industrial experience was with Hawker Siddeley and then as a consultant to a variety of organisations for over 25 years. He has published more than 100 papers plus eight books, including *Exploring Direct Marketing* (with Lisa O'Malley and Maurice Patterson, Thomson Learning).

Bram Foubert graduated in Applied Economic Sciences at the University of Antwerp (Belgium). He did research in the area of production management at the University of Leuven, and is now working as a PhD student in Marketing and Quantitative Methods at the University of Antwerp. His current research interests are pricing and product bundling.

Els Gijsbrechts has a degree in Applied Economic Sciences, and obtained a PhD in Marketing Modelling at the University of Antwerp. She was a Lecturer at the Catholic University of Leuven, and a Visiting Professor at the University of California, Los Angeles. She is now a Full Marketing Professor at the University of Antwerp and the Catholic University of Mons.

Colin Gilligan is Professor of Marketing at Sheffield Business School. He is the author or co-author of ten books on marketing including, with Professor Richard

M.S. Wilson, the best-selling *Strategic Marketing Management: Planning, Implementation and Control*. He acts as a consultant to a wide variety of organisations in both the private and the public sectors, providing advice on marketing planning, marketing strategy and customer care.

Philip Kitchen is the Martin Naughton Professor of Business Strategy, specialising in marketing, at the School of Management and Economics, Queen's University, Belfast. He teaches and carries out research in marketing management, marketing communications, corporate communications, promotion management, and international communications management. He is Founding Director of the Executive MBA programme. A graduate of the CNAA (BA[Hons]) initially, he received Masters degrees in Marketing from UMIST (MSc) and Manchester Business School (MBSc) respectively, and his PhD from Keele University. Since 1984 he has been active in teaching and research in the communications domain. He is founding editor of the *Journal of Marketing Communications* (Routledge Journals, 1995) and editor of *Public Relations: Principles and Practice* (Thomson Learning, 1997) and *Marketing Communications: Principles and Practice* (1999). He has recently co-authored – with Don Schultz of Northwestern University – *Communicating Globally: An Integrated Marketing Approach* (NTC Business Books, Chicago and Macmillan, London, 2000) and he and Don and are co-writing and co-editing: *Raising the Corporate Umbrella* (Macmillan, 2001).

Geoff Lancaster is Professor of Marketing at the University of North London and Visiting Professor of Marketing at Macquarie University, Sydney. He is Chairman of Durham Associates, a corporate communications group with offices in Castle Eden, Durham, Bahrain, Iran, Saudi Arabia, Dubai, Oman and Zambia, engaged in video production, e-commerce, PR, compugraphics, strategic planning and business education and training. The company was awarded the Queen's Award for Export Achievement in 1999.

Rosmimah Mohd-Roslin is a Senior Lecturer at MARA University of Technology in Malaysia and is currently the Coordinator of Research at the Bureau of Research and Consultancy at the university. She received her PhD in Marketing from Keele University in UK and holds an MBA from Western Illinois University and a BSc from Indiana University, USA. Her research and teaching interests are management of marketing channels, distribution channel relationships, retailing and purchasing, and supply chain management.

Danny Moss is Senior Research Fellow in Public Relations at Manchester Metropolitan University where he developed and now directs the MA in Public Relations. He has written and published widely in the field of public relations and consistently presents papers on this topic around the world.

Andrew Newman is a Lecturer in Retailing at the Department of Textiles, UMIST, where he teaches marketing, retailing and research in consumer behaviour. His research interests lie in the impact of the physical setting or built environment on customer behaviour, retail store design and the use of e-commerce in retailing. Before 1993, Andrew worked for British Airways in areas of marketing and customer service and has travelled extensively throughout the world.

Ioanna Papasolomou-Doukakis holds a BA in business studies from Philip's College in Cyprus, an MBA, an MPhil in Marketing Public Relations, and a PhD in Internal Marketing from Keele University. Her research and teaching interests include internal marketing, services marketing and marketing management. She is a Lecturer in Marketing at Chester Business School.

Stephen Parkinson is Professor of Business Strategy and Director of the Graduate School of Management, University of Ulster. He has published widely in a range of international journals and is the author of six books on marketing and marketing strategy. He is also actively involved as a consultant in marketing strategy and sales management with a range of major international companies.

Ken Peattie is Professor of Marketing and Strategy at the Cardiff Business School, where he has worked since 1986. He lectures and researches in subjects including marketing, strategic management and environmental management and marketing. Before becoming an academic, he worked in marketing and information systems for Kimberly-Clark Ltd, and also spent two years as a corporate planner in the UK electronics industry. He has published two books and more than 40 academic articles, mainly focusing on innovations in marketing communication and on the environmental challenge for management and marketing.

David Pickton has worked on 'both sides of the fence' for clients and agencies alike in marketing, advertising and PR in the public and private sectors. He has been a DTI registered marketing consultant, has run his own consultancy business and is currently a Chartered Marketer with the CIM. He is Deputy Head of Marketing at De Montfort University, in one of the largest marketing departments in the UK and his teaching and research is focused towards marketing communications, competitive marketing intelligence and the management of marketing.

Tony Proctor is Professor in Marketing at Chester Business School. He holds the CIM Diploma in Marketing, an MA in Marketing Education from Lancaster University, an MPhil in Industrial and Business Studies from Warwick University and a PhD in Business Administration from Manchester University. Formerly Senior Lecturer in Marketing and Head of Department of Management at Keele University, he is a regular contributor to *Management Decision* and *Creativity and Innovation Management*. He is author of *Strategic Marketing* (Routledge, 2000), *Creative Problem solving for Managers* (Routledge, 1999), *Marketing Management* (Thomson Learning, 1996), *The Essence of Management Creativity* (Prentice Hall, 1995) and *Essential Marketing* (Collins Educational, 1992).

Stuart Roper is a Senior Lecturer in Marketing in the Department of Retailing and Marketing at Manchester Metropolitan University. His research interests are in the area of branding, specifically corporate branding and brand personality. Stuart is a CIM examiner on the Diploma's Integrated Marketing Communications paper.

Ruth A. Schmidt is a Principal Lecturer in the Department of Retailing and Marketing at Manchester Metropolitan University. Before going into teaching she was a self-employed market trader and she obtained all her academic qualifications, including a master's degree, as a part-time student. She particularly enjoys working with commercially sponsored mature students.

Michael Thomas is President of the Market Research Society, former Chairman of the Chartered Institute of Marketing and Professor Emeritus of Marketing at Strathclyde University. He is a Chartered Marketer and was awarded the OBE last year for his services to management education and training in Poland. He is the author of numerous books and articles in learned journals, and is editor of *Marketing Intelligence and Planning*.

Claudio Vigneli is the Editor of *Management Case Quarterly* and regularly guest edits for the *British Food Journal*. He has published widely and has texts in strategy and international marketing pending publication. He is presently a Senior Lecturer at Manchester Metropolitan University (MMU) and course leader for the Retail Management Development Programmes.

Walter van Waterschoot is Professor of Marketing at the University of Antwerp (University Faculties Saint-Ignatius). He is co-author of and/or contributor to numerous marketing books and articles.

Richard M.S. Wilson is Professor of Business Administration at Loughborough

University Business School, having previously held chairs at Keele University, the Queen's University of Belfast and Nottingham Business School. He is a Chartered Marketer who holds the Diploma in Marketing (with distinction) of the Chartered Institute of Marketing (of which he is a Fellow) and the Diploma of the Market Research Society (of which he is a Full Member).

Actual product

The actual product includes those items and services that go to support the core product or service in a direct way, and they form part of the total marketing package. This definition includes criteria such as performance, style and design, packaging, quality, durability and the brand name. The actual product relates to what consumers 'feel' or think about when they relate to the product and this includes this broader definition. **GL**

References
Kotler, P. (1994) *Marketing Management, Analysis, Planning, Implementation and Control*, 8th edn, New Jersey: Prentice Hall, pp. 432–436.

Added value

Added value is the monetary value of the components or goods that the company manufactures, less the value of the materials or services it has purchased from other companies. For instance, if a car manufacturer buys components and materials for £10 000 and then manufactures a car that sells to the trade for £15 000, the value added by the car manufacturer is £5 000. This added value is simply the difference between the two figures; it does not mean that £5 000 profit has been made. It does not include the cost of labour or other overheads to make this added value possible. The calculation is simply based upon the total price received less the total price paid. **GL**

References
Kotler, P. (1994) *Marketing Management, Analysis, Planning, Implementation and Control*, 8th edn, New Jersey: Prentice Hall, pp. 432–436.

Adoption and diffusion

Adoption and diffusion is the process by which products are accepted into the marketplace. An understanding of this process is important to marketing communicators as it helps in the selection of target audiences, media and promotional messages. From the work of Everett Rogers (1983), it is clear that some people have a predisposition to adopt new ideas and products more quickly than others. These he has called 'innovators'. Acceptance by the wider market (diffusion) tends only to occur after this initial adoption has been achieved. Through research, Rogers has modelled this process and he has been able to identify five distinct adopter types or categories: innovators, early adopters, early majority, late majority and laggards. Each type is linked to its own personalities and behavioural tendencies. Innovators are likely to be more adventurous, willing to explore and seek out new things to try. Laggards, at the other end of the scale, are reluctant to change or adopt new ideas but may do so when the product has already been well accepted in the market. By this stage, the innovators may well have moved on to new things. Newness and novelty appeal to innovators and early adopters, something well established and trustworthy to the late majority and laggards.

Given a sufficiently large potential market, the figure below shows how Rogers has mapped adopter types onto a normal distribution curve and through this it is possible to estimate (statistically) the proportion of the market that is likely to fit into each category.

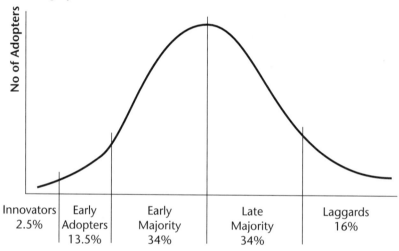

Time of adoption of innovations

Figure: **Rogers' adopter types**

As products are accepted and diffused in the market, messages and media need to change to meet the needs of the different adopter types. The nature of the process, of course, is made more complicated in markets where truly new products are few and where claims for new improved versions are made. Although applied directly to consumer markets, the principle applies equally to industrial and organizational markets in which companies fall into the different adopter categories. **DWP**

Reference
Rogers, E.M. (1983), *Diffusion of Innovations*, 3rd edn, New York: Macmillan.

Advertisers

British advertisers collectively spent £11 599 000 000 on media space and time alone in 1997. Since the cost of advertising is normally recovered in the price of the advertised brand, this represents in effect a levy of £473 per household, for which they should in theory be compensated by the benefits of competition among those advertisers. Only in Switzerland and the USA is per capita spending on advertising higher. The UK figure corresponds to 1.7 per cent of Gross National Product, compared with 1.5 per cent in 1993 and 1.4 per cent in 1983. The table below shows the half-dozen currently highest-spending product categories and individual advertisers.

Table: **Allocation of total UK advertising expenditure in 1998**

	% of total		% of total
Retail	18.9	Unilever	2.0
Motors	10.9	Procter & Gamble	1.5
Food	10.8	BT	1.1
Financial	8.3	Dixons	0.9
Toiletries and cosmetics	6.2	General Motors (Vauxhall + Saab)	0.9
Office equipment	6.1		
Sub-Total	61.2	Sub-Total	7.5

Source: Advertising Association (1999)

Advertisers typically organize the function in one of two ways. The traditional model was to set up an Advertising Department headed by a specialist *advertising manager*, whose role was essentially to support the sales function. As the marketing orientation generally supplanted the focus on selling, specialists tended to be replaced by generalist *brand managers*, whose operational responsibilities included advertising. It may help to visualize these as respectively vertical and horizontal arrangements. Recently, 'vertical' managers have reappeared in response to rapid and radical changes in the advertising environment. The current emphasis on 'integrated marketing communications' means they are typically responsible for the whole marketing communications mix, not just advertising. Such titles as 'marketing communications manager' reflect that development. **KC & BZE**

References

Advertising Association (1999) *Marketing Pocket Book 2000*, Henley-on-Thames: NTC Publications.

Crosier, K. (1999) 'The relationship among advertisers, agencies, media and target audiences' in P.J. Kitchen (ed.) *Marketing Communications: Principles and Practice*, London: Thomson Learning, ch. 24.

Advertisers and audiences

The theoretical frameworks described in 'Advertising, how it works' implicitly take a micro-level view of the advertiser-audience relationship, describing the response of single individuals to the words and symbols in an advertising message (except, potentially, for semiotics). This ignores the obvious fact that advertising is normally directed via mass media at audiences rather than individuals and is typically consumed in a social context rather than in private. A macro focus would clearly be more appropriate. Furthermore, the most popular models of advertising effect imply that advertising is a unilateral force applied to passive 'consumers', which works if the advertiser manages to get the formulae right. This is inconsistent with the concept of 'consumer sovereignty', practitioners' anxieties about channel hopping during commercial breaks and many other pieces of contrary evidence.

A more realistic view is that 'people use or process messages: the results are not always what the advertiser wants, but are decided by the recipient' (Broadbent, 1997). The question of whether advertising is in fact a strong or a weak force was discussed at length in a journal article that has so far had more impact on academics than on practitioners (Jones, 1990). The theory of advertising effect will remain deficient until a transactional paradigm with a macro focus replaces the prevailing unilateral micro-models. A priority for the new century should be to search for transferable principles of mass communication and propaganda.

It is sometimes suggested by journalists, social commentators, politicians and non-marketing academics that one social influence on the individual's response to advertisements is that advertising is more or less generally disliked. On the contrary, there has been no evidence to support that position in any of nine large-scale public-opinion surveys commissioned from independent market research companies on the industry's behalf in Britain since 1961. In the most recent (Advertising Association, 1996), only 3 per cent of the sample chose advertising, from a list of a dozen general social topics, as one they felt strongly about. One in six took the opportunity to register a negative opinion when invited to rate their approval or disapproval on a five-point scale. Asked about the concrete manifestations of an abstract concept, one in five expressed a dislike for television commercials, one in eight for posters and one in ten for press advertisements. The survey report concluded that ordinary people accept the existence of an advertising industry and seldom object to its output, though it does warn that advertisers 'should never become complacent about public attitudes ... advertising is far too much in the public eye (and in its ears) for the industry to let its standards fall'.

Despite the generally supportive social climate, a formal system of direct legislation, statutory regulation and self-regulation pro-actively defends advertisers' audiences against attempts to manipulate their consumption choices by means of unduly devious messages and images. It comprises two statutory authorities and one independent authority voluntarily financed by the industry itself, the latter collectively operating three formal codes of practice, plus over 100 potentially relevant Acts of Parliament. Details can be found at the 'advertising control' entry in Baker (1998). **KC & BZE**

References

Advertising Association (1996) *Public Attitudes to Advertising 1996*, London: Advertising Association.

Baker, M.J. (ed.) (1998) *Macmillan Dictionary of Marketing and Advertising*, 3rd edn, Basingstoke: Macmillan.

Broadbent, S. (1997) *Accountable Advertising*, Henley-on-Thames: Admap Publications.

Jones, J.P. (1990) 'Advertising: strong force or weak force? Two views an ocean apart', *International Journal of Advertising*, 9:233–246.

Advertisers and media owners

It is generally accepted that only about 20 per cent of all advertising expenditure in the UK passes direct from advertisers to media owners, i.e. not via advertising agencies or specialist media-buying agencies. However, that small proportion is spread among a relatively large number of advertisers. Those are mainly smaller and less sophisticated but include many retailers of all shapes and sizes, who often need to modify their messages and media bookings almost instantaneously and are unwilling to risk time delays caused by working through an intermediary. Such advertisers may rely on media owners' internal services to lay out their print advertisements, write their radio scripts, or even produce their television commercials. This results in a reduction of control over the way in which they present themselves to their audiences, potentially more severe than that risked by others who *do* use advertising agencies.

Given the complexity of media pricing and the hard-bargaining ethos of media sales, as described in the previous section, it is hardly surprising that small advertisers who deal directly with the media owners generally buy package deals rather than building a specific media schedule from the details of a formal plan. This relationship is thus rather one-sided, and there is little more that can be said about it. **KC & BZE**

Reference

Crosier, K. (1999) 'The relationship among advertisers, agencies, media and target audiences' in P.J. Kitchen (ed.) *Marketing Communications: Principles and Practice*, London: Thomson Learning, ch. 24.

Advertising

Advertising is unique among other forms of 'marketing communications' in being an integral part of the average citizen's daily life. People generally find their jobs and houses by way of advertisements in newspapers. They can usually call to mind advertisements for the breakfast cereal they ate that morning, the brand of toothpaste they used afterwards and the car they then drove to work. If they need to dispose of an outdated PC or an old bike, they may well place a 'small ad' in a newspaper or magazine. Consequently, everyone has a good idea what 'advertising' is and does not normally ask for it to be formally defined.

Nevertheless, formal definitions of advertising have multiplied alongside advancements in management science, media technology and economic development, reflecting the communications, marketing, economic or social perspectives of their authors. Bernstein (1974) memorably said '*adv*ertising is *adv*ocacy', to which one might add that it gives *adv*ice, albeit biased. Two rather more typical textbook definitions are 'the activity that involves any paid form of non-personal presentation and promotion of ideas, goods or services by an identified sponsor' (Alexander, 1960) and 'a form of mass communication, which is non-personal and paid for by an identified sponsor.' (DeLozier, 1979). The four defining and de-limiting characteristics of an advertiser's output were thereby formalized during the early days of marketing as a quasi-science: it is a *non-personal* message, *promoting* something, which is formally *paid for* by an *identifiable* originator. From those, we derive the following test to distinguish advertising from related forms of mass communication, such as publicity, sales promotion, teleselling or – beyond the sphere of marketing – propaganda. It always consists of:

- a recognizable *advertisement*
- appearing in definable *advertising media*
- which guarantee delivery of an unmodified *message*
- to a specified *audience*
- on payment of published *rate* for the space or time used.

An organized advertising business has existed in Britain for three centuries, since newspapers began to feature advertisements that would be readily recognized as such today. It is characterized by five main organizational elements, formally described as: advertisers; advertising agencies; media owners; various providers of ancillary services, such as market research agencies, design studios, typesetters, printers and so on; and trade bodies and professional associations. **KC & BZE**

References

Alexander, R. (1960) *Marketing Definition: A Glossary of Marketing Terms*, Chicago: American Marketing Association, p. 9.
Bernstein, D. (1974) *Creative Advertising*, Harlow: Longman.
DeLozier, M.W. (1979) *The Marketing Communications Process*, 2nd edn, New York: McGraw-Hill.

Advertising account planning

One of the services offered by many 'full-service advertising agencies' is to bring a form of research and development to bear on the process of converting guidelines in the client's brief into a formal creative strategy. This activity is generically described as 'account planning'. The prefix 'account' is misleading in two ways. First, it has nothing to do with financial accounts, but is explained by the fact that advertising agencies have always used it to describe one discrete project handed over by a client: 'the Fairy Liquid account', for example. Second, the focus of planning is not the account itself but development of an advertising campaign. It is therefore no surprise that the description is nowadays more usually just 'planning'.

(Account) planners are, so to speak, the intellectual wing of the business. Their goal is to understand consumers, audiences, markets and society, and to use that knowledge as a basis for the development of effective advertising messages. They do not play any part in the craft of converting those messages into the words and images that make up actual advertisements, but are generally responsible for any comparative pre-tests of alternative treatments. In practice, even that modest level of involvement in the creative process can bring them into conflict with key people in the agency's creative department, who may maintain that making advertisements is an intuitive skill, not amenable to design by committee and only inhibited by research-based theorizing. But for that, the most logical job description would in fact be 'creative planning', clearly complementing the long-established 'media planning' discipline.

(Account) planning seems to be in prolonged adolescence at the turn of the century, not yet really widespread in smaller or less sophisticated advertising agencies. It originated in London, and remains something of a British specialization. The Account Planning Group – the professional common-interest group for planners – has published a handbook (now in its second edition) (Cooper, 1997) and a series of case histories of planning in action (Account Planning Group, 1993, 1995, 1997). *Admap* is effectively a house journal for the discipline. **KC & BZE**

References

Account Planning Group (1993, 1995, 1997) *Creative Planning > Outstanding Advertising*, volumes 1–3, London: Account Planning Group.

Cooper, A. (ed.) (1977) *How to Plan Advertising*, 2nd edn, London: Cassell.

Advertising agencies

It is generally agreed that roughly 80 per cent of total UK advertising expenditure passes from advertisers to advertising media via advertising agencies. By 1800, proliferation of media options had spawned entrepreneurs who advised advertisers on media selection and handled their media bookings, for a fee. These 'agents' were in due course joined by 'brokers', who first bought advertising space speculatively and re-sold it to advertisers at a marked-up price, but later negotiated a fixed discount from the 'media owners'. By charging their clients the published list price, they could offer them a free service. In due course, they began to prepare their clients' advertising as well as placing it. The 'commission' discount subsidized this extra service initially, but additional 'top-up fees' became necessary as technical sophistication developed. The early agents and brokers are together the ancestors of the present-day advertising agency. Legal cases in 1917 and 1957 established that agencies do not in fact act as 'agents' to their 'clients' but are 'principals' in the contract with the media owner. The important ramifications of their complex history are taken up in other sections to do with advertising. In the 1970s, media brokers reappeared in the guise of media independents, planning and buying media for their clients but offering none of the ancillary services performed by full-service advertising agencies.

British advertising agencies are collectively represented by a thriving professional association, the Institute of Practitioners in Advertising, which organizes biannual IPA Effectiveness Awards. Media independents can join the Association of Media and Communication Specialists (AMCO). The table below lists the 10 largest firms in either category in the UK and shows the considerable sums they spend on their clients' behalf ('billings'). The dominance of media independents is reversed in the remainder of the top 20.

Table: **Highest-spending advertising agencies and media independents in 1998**

Agency name	Status	Total annual billings £ million
Zenith Media	Media independent	563.1
Carat Group UK	"	494.1
Abbott Mead Vickers BBDO	Advertising agency	356.1
Mindshare Media UK	Media independent	347.5
MediaVest UK	"	321.6
CIA Medianetwork UK	"	318.0
Initiative Media	"	306.5
BMP OMD	"	305.9
Universal McCann	"	305.3
Saatchi & Saatchi	Advertising agency	267.5

Source: Advertising Association (1999)

The organizational structure of a typical advertising agency comprises six main functions. The creative and media departments convert the client's brief into the two key components of overall campaign strategy. Account planning and media planning are 'thinking' disciplines that back up those 'doing' functions. The traffic department operates a control system ensuring that the large number of often complex operations between initial planning and the eventual campaign are efficiently coordinated. Though always low-profile, this function is in fact crucial: the mortar that makes a wall from a pile of bricks. Account handling is the client-service function, 'account' being the word traditionally used to define one piece of business given to an agency by its client. Though often disparaged as 'bag carriers' or 'suits', account handlers play a pivotal role in the whole agency-client working relationship. **KC & BZE**

References

Advertising Association (1999) *Advertising Statistics Yearbook 1999*, Henley-on-Thames, NTC Publications.

Crosier, K. (1999) 'The relationship among advertisers, agencies, media and target audiences' in P.J. Kitchen (ed.) *Marketing Communications: Principles and Practice*, London: Thomson Learning, ch. 24.

Advertising agencies and media owners

Once an advertiser has approved an agency's media plan, media buyers have the task of converting it into a cost-effective media schedule, consisting of spaces, sites and slots in a variety of media vehicles over a period. In so doing, they deal with media sales representatives, who deploy an array of facts and figures extracted from industry-wide research programmes by in-house research managers. Typically, they are practised exponents of the hard sell, working under the constant pressure of quotas and bonuses.

The price structure in media owners' rate cards is notoriously complex. There are surcharges for fixed dates, special positions and the like, and discounts for series bookings and sheer volume. Furthermore, the state of supply and demand at a given time can result in prices substantially different from the figures on paper. In the particular case of television, rate cards are a statutorily required departure point for what becomes in effect an open auction. Firm bookings can be 'pre-empted' by better offers up to the eleventh hour. Given the breadth and depth of the UK media mix, described under 'Media owners', media buyers tend to specialize, particularly in the case of television.

Effective media buying thus requires innate numeracy combined with the haggling skills of the souk. In contrast to the normally collaborative client-agency working relationship, this one is often adversarial.

A rigorously observed convention affecting this working relationship is that media owners do not make sales pitches to advertisers without informing the advertising agency handling the account, and that advertisers with agencies do not place orders direct. The rationale is to protect the right to the media commission, which accounts for almost three quarters of a typical advertising agency's total income throughout Europe (see 'The commission system'). **KC & BZE**

Reference

Crosier, K. (1999) 'The relationship among advertisers, agencies, media and target audiences' in P.J. Kitchen (ed.) *Marketing Communications: Principles and Practice*, London: Thomson Learning, ch. 24.

Advertising agencies and remuneration

Advertising agencies first developed as organizations that sold advertising space on behalf of media owners. They were, essentially, agents of the media owners and were paid commission on all the space they sold, a feature that still exists today. The agencies, however, soon realized that if they offered extra services to advertisers, such as designing advertisements and arranging for artwork and production, they were more likely to sell more space and so earn more money. Advertising agencies, therefore, became agents for their advertising clients rather than for the media owners and would place advertising anywhere they felt best for their clients' business.

Although traditionally advertising agency revenue (known as 'billings') comes from media commission, this has come under a great deal of criticism, which has caused agencies to review their approach. Competition has led to 'commission rebating', in which agencies sometimes give part of their commission back to their clients. Agencies also charge fees for their work, particularly if their client's media spend is limited and does not cover all the work the agency undertakes such as the production of leaflets and other sales promotions. More recently, during the 1990s, remuneration schemes have included payments-by-results, in which remuneration is linked to the effectiveness of the agency's campaigns.

The range of services offered by advertising agencies varies significantly. Some agencies are 'full service' and offer a range of services from initial advice and the development of campaigns to media planning and buying and production. They also involve themselves in necessary research work to ensure that their campaigns are effective. They take the work from start to finish, undertake not just advertising but also other forms of promotion, and sub-contract to other agents and freelance workers (such as designers, artists, film producers, printers and researchers) where necessary. Key members of the agency include the creatives (art directors and copywriters), account handlers (who form the principal liaison between clients and the agency), account planners (who are responsible for understanding the client's market, much of the research and overall planning activity), media planners and buyers, production staff and traffic (staff responsible for progress chasing).

By contrast, some advertising agencies specialize in particular areas of advertising such as financial or recruitment advertising and others – such as 'boutiques' or 'creative hot shops' – offer only a limited range of services with emphasis on creative ideas and development.

As well as advertising agencies, the industry is also serviced by a range of other agencies specializing in their own areas of marketing communications: PR, sales promotion, media planning and buying, direct marketing, new media and the Internet, telemarketing, exhibitions, packaging, corporate identity, merchandising, store design, brand naming, and so on. It becomes a challenge to orchestrate all their

activities in an attempt to integrate the total marketing communications package.
DWP

References
Kitchen, P.J. (1999) *Marketing Communications: Principles and Practice*, London: Thomson
Learning, chs 24 and 25.
Pickton, D.W. and Broderick, A. (2001) *Integrated Marketing Communications* London: Financial
Times Prentice Hall, ch. 16.

Advertising agencies, selection process

In other entries relating to advertising we can see that most advertisers delegate campaign planning to advertising agencies, that the working relationship between the
two typically lasts less than 10 years, and that the most realistic role for advertising
is long-term brand building. It follows that a high priority for advertising managers
(or brand managers) is to minimize the risk of a premature rift with their agency.
One way to do so is to choose wisely in the first place, so the figure below suggests
a framework for a properly systematic approach to this key task.

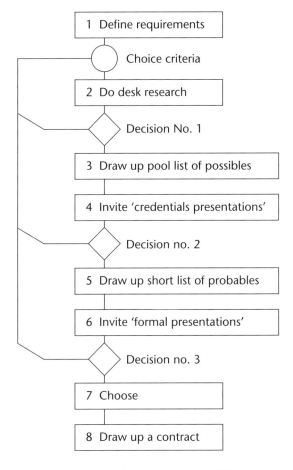

Figure: **A systematic procedure for selecting an advertising agency**

Step 1 yields the decision criteria needed at three points in the selection process,
but can fall victim in practice to a human preference for doing over thinking. It is
also the obvious starting point for the eventual working relationship. *Step 2* exploits

the range of facts and opinions to be culled from the agencies' own professional association, the Institute of Practitioners in Advertising (IPA), various directories, the trade press, the World Wide Web and the informal grapevine within the business. Videos, prepared by agencies to a standard specification, can be viewed anonymously at the premises of the Advertising Agency Register.

The advertiser is now in a position to take *Steps 3 and 4* by using the criteria derived from Step 1 to compile a list of 'possibles' and inviting their credentials presentations. These typically provide a 'philosophy statement', staff profiles, a client list, 'showreels' of television and cinema commercials, 'radio reels', dossiers of print work and some case histories. Other agencies will undoubtedly make approaches, as the grapevine and the trade press spread the word. The decision criteria can then be applied to *Steps 5 and 6*, drawing up a final shortlist and inviting formal presentations from those 'probables', who will more graphically describe the process as 'pitching' for the business. At *Step 7*, the criteria are used for the last time, to make the choice.

Step 8 is all too often no more than the kind of 'gentlemen's agreement' common in the true professions, but can significantly reduce the likelihood of damaging arguments and messy partings at a later stage. The IPA can provide a useful pro forma.
KC & BZE

Reference
Crosier, K. (1999) 'The relationship among advertisers, agencies, media and target audiences' in P.J. Kitchen (ed.) *Marketing Communications: Principles and Practice*, London: Thomson Learning, ch. 24.

Advertising and marketing communications

Advertising is one of the best known and recognized areas of the marketing communications mix. Unfortunately, it is a term widely used, mistakenly so, to refer to all types of marketing communications. To avoid confusion with other promotional tools, it is best to limit its definition to highlight its essential features, which are that it is paid for, non-personal and uses the mass media (TV, radio, cinema, press, posters and the Internet).

Crosier (1999) describes it as: 'communication via a recognizable advertisement placed in a definable advertising medium, guaranteeing delivery of an unmodified message to a specified audience in return for an agreed rate for the space or time used.' ('Agreed rate' has replaced Crosier's 'published rate' as there is often a difference between the rates published by the media and the rate actually paid.)

Advertising is also known as above-the-line promotion because it uses the mass (or above-the-line) media. It is a phrase used because the mass media pay published commission rates to advertising agencies and these are seen as being 'above-the-line' in contrast to all other forms of promotion in which the mark-ups are unknown or 'below-the-line'.

How advertising actually works is something that is hotly debated, some believing that it has a direct effect on sales ('strong effect' – Jones, 1995) and others who believe that the effect is significant but more subtle by primarily influencing awareness and pre-dispositions. In this way, sales are achieved by advertising working with the other elements of the marketing communications mix ('weak effect' – Ehrenberg *et al.*, 2000). Farr (2000) emphasizes that it is best to think of advertising as having a number of roles and effects and working differently in each. He simplifies them to three: persuasion (to take action, to buy), publicity (to make familiar and remind), and association (to increase the perceived value through semiotic associations).
DWP

References

Crosier, K. (1999) 'Advertising', in Kitchen, P.J. *Marketing Communications*, London: Thomson Learning.

Ehrenberg, A.S.C., Scriven, J.A. and Bernard, N.R. (2000), 'Advertising established brands: an international dimension', in S. Moyne *The Handbook of International Marketing Communications*, Oxford: Blackwell.

Farr, A. (2000), *Linking Sales to Advertising*, Proceedings Monitoring Advertising Performance Conference, Admap and the Advertising Association, January.

Jones, J.P. (1995) *When Ads Work: New Proof That Advertising Triggers Sales*, NJ: Simon and Schuster.

Advertising commission system

This description is shorthand for the *system of remunerating* (American usage prefers 'compensating') *advertising agencies by commission from media owners*, which is an anachronism with remarkable powers of survival. Ignorance of its complicated workings would result in a seriously incomplete understanding of the working relationship between advertisers and their agencies.

Nineteenth-century media owners, recognizing the ancestors of present-day advertising agencies as the primary customers for their advertising space, allowed them a standard discount on the list price. Agencies could thereby provide their clients with a free service for which they had hitherto charged a fee. Independent directories soon followed, allowing advertisers to verify that they were indeed being charged no more than they would have had to pay the media owners. History thus explains the anomalous present-day situation that agencies are remunerated by a third party, being actually sales agents to media owners rather than service agents to advertisers. The full description of the system makes that clear, but the usual contracted version does not.

Early agencies absorbed the cost of designing and producing advertisements in their commission. Increasing sophistication of proliferating advertising media has since obliged advertisers to accept the necessity for separate charges to cover costly items such as television production, though there is surprisingly little agreement about what should be included on such a list.

The media commission system was declared a restrictive practice in Britain in the 1970s, and in America 20 years earlier. It nevertheless remains the norm in both countries, despite uninformed assertions to the contrary. A field study in an unspecified number of European countries has shown that commission discounts still account, on average, for 71 per cent of an advertising agency's total income (European Association of Advertising Agencies, 1994). This robustness is due to the system's straightforwardness and consistency, and to vested interests. Media owners prefer relatively few large and regular customers to very many sporadic smaller ones. Advertisers can put pressure on agencies to absorb costs and subsidize extra services out of their commission, and suspect that a properly calculated direct fee would cost them more. Only the agencies at the centre of the whole system are disadvantaged.
KC & BZE

References

European Association of Advertising Agencies (1994) *Client/Advertising Agency Partnerships in the New Europe*, Henley-on-Thames: NTC Publications.

Advertising commission system, bad debts and cash-flow problems

The cases of *Tranter* vs *Astor* 1917 and *Emmett* vs *DeWitt* 1957 established that a British advertising agency is not legally an agent to anyone, but an independent principal. Crucially, this means that when it places media orders on its client's behalf, in order to benefit from the 15 per cent commission discount, it enters into a contract with the media owner. If the client subsequently fails to reimburse that up-front expenditure, for whatever reason, the agency has acquired a bad debt. In the event of a client's bankruptcy, it will normally stand low in the list of creditors. Insurance against these not altogether uncommon occurrences is available but expensive, and typical agencies operate on net profit margins of between 1 and 5 per cent, according to the Institute of Practitioners in Advertising.

When an advertising agency receives a media invoice for time or space, there is a strong incentive to pay up promptly. If it does not settle by the due date, which, in the case of television, can be two weeks before the advertising actually begins, the media owner will impose a progressive reduction in the commission discount. Given the net profit margins just mentioned, it would be rash to delay deliberately. On the other hand, it would be unreasonable to expect the agency's clients to accept any charge until they see evidence that their advertising has appeared as planned. Thereafter, the collection period for the agency is likely to be the norm for a typical British company, which a survey by Experian Ltd found to be 74 days in late 1999 despite the recent Late Payment Act. Pressing for payment too firmly or frequently would only risk antagonizing a valuable client, and the system thus virtually guarantees a time lag between payment and reimbursement. Agencies consequently live under constant threat of a cash-flow crisis.

Running an advertising agency is clearly a very risky business. One can only assume that sheer enthusiasm for the craft is why sane people continue to want to do so, year in and year out. **KC & BZE**

Reference
Crosier, K. (1999) 'The argument for advertising agency remuneration' in P.J. Kitchen (ed.) *Marketing Communications: Principles and Practice*, London: Thomson Learning, ch. 25.

Advertising, full fee system

The earliest 'advertising agents' offered their services to advertisers for a fee, but that arrangement was later swamped by the media commission system of remuneration. During the 1990s, commentators repeatedly asserted that the 'full fee' arrangement was making a comeback and the commission system was 'dying'.

Payment by fee is certainly the more logical of the two, reflecting the pragmatic reality of the working relationship between an advertising agency and client, rather than the legal technicality that the agency is in fact a principal in contractual relationships with media owners. However, the commission system has a historical pedigree, is a uniform standard, is understood throughout the business, and is easy to put into practice. Furthermore, we have already seen that both advertisers and media owners have a vested interest in its retention. If an agency nevertheless wants to work with its clients on a fee basis, several practical obstacles present themselves:

- media owners will still deduct the commission discount
- it would therefore have to be subtracted from the fee
- separate fee calculations would be needed for each client
- that would require careful forecasting of costs or the fee would have to be received in arrears
- re-negotiation would be necessary at every new budget period
- clients would exert strong downward pressure
- the agency would get into price wars.

The net outcome is considerable inertia in the system. Surveys in the 1960s, 80s and 90s show the proportion of income derived from fees falling rather than rising. In

1993, it averaged 18 per cent across Europe (European Association of Advertising Agencies, 1994). In France, a parliamentary bill of 1992 proposed that media owners would pay commission direct to advertisers, so agencies would have to set up alternative financial arrangements with their clients. A year later, new legislation reprieved the commission system, but required it to become more transparent in various ways. Reports of its death have, as they say, been exaggerated. **KC & BZE**

Reference
European Association of Advertising Agencies (1994) *Client/Advertising Agency Partnerships in the New Europe*, Henley-on-Thames: NTC Publications.

Advertising, how it works

Our definition of advertising takes it as read that its aim is to persuade the target audience to revise negative opinions or renew positive ones, and ultimately act accordingly. The very existence of a large and thriving advertising business implies a belief that this can be achieved, at least widely enough to make the considerable investment of effort and money worthwhile. To explain how advertisements do, or fail to do, this remains a continuously challenging topic, three-quarters of a century after the first formal attempt.

The very people who execute advertising campaigns are the least likely to provide an answer. As a professional guide to best practice remarks, they 'may follow very varied "mental models" but they too seldom articulate them' (Broadbent, 1995). When they do, the model will probably belong to a family of verbal paradigms proposing that advertisements trigger a progressive sequence of behavioural responses in the individual, from cognitive via affective to conative: think-feel-do. In the marketing communications context, this is called the 'hierarchy of effects' (Lavidge and Steiner, 1961). The most frequently cited variant, by practitioners and textbooks alike, is the venerable 'AIDA' (Strong, 1925), originally offered as a guide to the effective delivery of a sales pitch but soon transferred to the formulation of advertising strategy. Its title is an acronym composed of the initial letters of four progressive stages, from attention, through interest and desire, to action. This 'model' has the obvious appeal of being an intuitively reasonable representation of a presumed cause-and-effect relationship. On the other hand, it clearly describes rather than explains, and has in fact been subject to continuous theoretical criticism over the past 40 years by, among others, Palda (1966), Ray (1973) and Ehrenberg (1988).

One might expect that its theoretical shortcomings would by now have inhibited its use as the basis for strategic decision making. On the contrary, case histories repeatedly couch campaign objectives in all-too-familiar terms. Therefore, one has to acknowledge that AIDA and its kin remain the implicit conceptual underpinning of present-day advertising strategy, and concede that a deficient but codified framework is better than none at all. This must remain the case until marketing academics are able to produce a better model that practitioners can understand and are willing to use. Alas, two authoritative reviews commissioned by the Advertising Association (McDonald, 1992; Frantzen, 1994) provide ample evidence that this state of affairs is little closer than it ever has been. If progress is to be made in the 21st century, the impetus is likely to originate in the 'planning' discipline within advertising agencies. The new paradigm will no doubt combine existing models with information-processing theory (Sternthal and Craig, 1982), discourse analysis (Cook, 1992), applied linguistics (Myers, 1994) and semiotics (Dyer, 1982). It should also treat the response of individuals in a target audience as their personal reactions modulated by their membership of a culture and a society, as well as a 'market segment': in other words, at the macro rather than micro level. This caveat is taken up in 'Advertisers and audiences'. **KC & BZE**

References

Broadbent, S. (1995) *Best Practice in Campaign Evaluation*, London: Institute of Practitioners in Advertising.

Cook, G. (1992) *The Discourse of Advertising*, London: Routledge.

Dyer, G. (1982) *Advertising as Communication*, London: Routledge, ch. 6.

Ehrenberg, A.S.C. (1988) *Repeat Buying: Facts, Theory and Applications*, 2nd edn, London: Charles Griffin.

Frantzen, G. (1994) *Advertising Effectiveness: Findings from Empirical Research*, Henley-on-Thames: NTC Publications.

Lavidge, R.J. and Steiner, G.A. (1961) 'A model for predictive measurements of advertising effectiveness', *Journal of Marketing*, 25(October): 59–62.

McDonald, C. (1992) *How Advertising Works: A Review of Current Thinking*, Henley-on-Thames: NTC Publications.

Myers, G.(1994) *Words in Ads*, London: Edward Arnold.

Palda, K.S. (1966) 'The hypothesis of a hierarchy of effects: a partial evaluation', *Journal of Marketing Research*, 3(Feb): 13–24.

Ray, M.L. (1973) 'Marketing communications and the hierarchy of effects', in P. Clarke (ed.), *New Models for Mass Communication Research*, Volume II, Beverly Hills, CA: Sage Publications, pp. 147–176.

Sternthal, B. and Craig, C.S. (1982) *Consumer Behavior: An Information-Processing Perspective*, Englewood Cliffs: Prentice Hall.

Strong, E.K. (1925) *The Psychology of Selling*, New York: McGraw-Hill.

Advertising, mark-up fees

The increasing costs of media production, which produced the top-up fee convention, had another significant consequence. Agencies could hardly be expected, on the basis of anticipated usage, to invest in machinery capable of printing enormous posters or pay the salary of a top flight commercials director. For exactly the same reason that their clients employed them, they in turn subcontracted the most costly work. Simultaneously, logical extension of the full-service ideal led to agencies buying-in on their clients' behalf non-advertising services such as market research or corporate identity design.

Another convention duly evolved whereby agencies were entitled to recover the cost of finding the most suitable subcontractors and managing the project. Rather than doing so by means of individually negotiated handling fees, they would *mark up* the actual cost at a rate that left them in the same financial position as if the providers had given a 15 per cent discount on the list price. In other words, the mark-up mimics media commission. But a different figure is required to make the actual mark-up on their selling price equivalent to the hypothetical discount on their buying price.

Suppose that client ABC instructs agency XYZ to supply promotional calendars. XYZ finds a capable supplier at a favourable price, and places the order. The supplier delivers the goods and charges XYZ £850. We can see, using the worked example in 'Advertising, rebating' and moving the decimal point, that the eventual charge has to be £1 000. Our calculator will tell us that the required £150 mark-up is 17.647058 per cent of £850. To double check this equation, rounding off: $(0.1765 \times 850) + 850 = 1000.025$, which is near enough. So XYZ renders an invoice to ABC for £1 000.03 (no doubt ignoring the three pence), which reimburses the price paid on ABC's behalf and compensates it for the work done in arranging and delivering this full-service extra.

The European Association of Advertising Agencies (1994) confirms that 'it is normal practice for all production and other outside purchases which are billable to be charged at cost plus 17.65 per cent': this is universally and routinely applied, even to the second place of decimals. **KC & BZE**

Reference
European Association of Advertising Agencies (1994) *Client/Advertising Agency Partnerships in the New Europe*, Henley-on-Thames: NTC Publications, p. 21.

Advertising, message delivery

About 80 per cent of all advertising expenditure in the UK passes from advertisers to advertising media via advertising agencies. Thus, the process of message delivery typically begins when a 'client brief' is passed to an agency, where it is distilled into a *creative brief* and a *media brief* – the frameworks for developing the respective plans. The corresponding functional divisions ultimately combine their solutions into a single strategy for delivering the required message to the specified audience.

The creative brief yields a plan that eventually becomes words and images conveyed to the audience via print advertisements or radio, television and cinema commercials. Authoritative descriptions of the decision-making processes are elusive, but we have elsewhere offered a basic framework for the development and implementation of a creative plan (Crosier, 1999). That should be a team operation, involving 'account managers' (the client-liaison people), 'account planners' (creative planners in all but name) and the 'creatives', who write and design the actual advertisements. The outcome is text and images believed to be capable of communicating the required message, but it has yet to be delivered.

Meanwhile, the media brief is refined into a 'media plan', specifying the 'media vehicles' to be used for the purpose, and a 'media schedule', setting out the timing of individual advertisements during the campaign. The only authoritative description of this decision-making process in the British context was published when the media landscape was radically different (Broadbent and Jacobs, 1984). The general principles remain valid, however, and are a major ingredient of a decision-making framework we have proposed elsewhere (Crosier, 1999). Media planning is another team effort, involving the same account managers, plus media planners and media buyers. The outcome is a media schedule for the cost-effective delivery of the message to the target audience.

It would be natural to wonder which should come first, the creative plan or the media plan. On the one hand, even the best of creative strategies cannot deliver the message efficiently unless advertisements are placed where they can do their work to best effect. On the other, the most skilful media strategy will be ineffective if the creative execution fails to evoke the required response. Thus, the two plans are completely interdependent, and both crucial to successful message delivery. **KC & BZE**

References
Broadbent, S. and Jacobs, B (1984) *Spending Advertising Money*, 4th edn, London: Business Books.
Butterfield, L. (ed.) (1997) *Excellence in Advertising: The IPA Guide to Best Practice*, Oxford: Butterworth-Heinemann, chs 4, 7 and 8.
Cooper, A. (ed.) (1977) *How to Plan Advertising*, 2nd edition, London: Cassell, chs 4, 5 and 6.
Crosier, K. (1999) 'Advertising', in P.J. Kitchen (ed.) *Marketing Communications: Principles and Practice*, London: Thomson Learning, pp. 278–280.

Advertising, professional associations

In Britain, the interests of advertising agencies are represented by the *Institute of Practitioners in Advertising* (IPA). It was established in 1917, partly to press for a standard rate of 'media commission' and to lobby against the prevalent practice of 'commission rebating', which became an issue again 60 years later. In 1999, just over 200 agencies were incorporated members of the IPA, entitled to style themselves Incorporated Practitioners *in* (not 'of') Advertising. They account for only about 10 per cent of the advertising agencies in the UK, but collectively handle more than 80 per cent of all advertising placed in UK media. The IPA provides specialist services to member agencies, is represented on most industry-wide committees and working parties, commissions research surveys, produces handbooks and occasional papers, publishes reports on aspects of the advertising business and runs the biennial IPA Advertising Effectiveness Awards.

The interests of agencies' clients are represented by the *Incorporated Society of British Advertisers* (ISBA), set up in 1900 to press the media owners of the day for reliable circulation figures. Forced by inaction to publish its own estimates, it was taken to court for suggesting a sixteenth of the real figure in one case, but won the action on principle. The ultimate outcome was the independent body which today publishes audited ABC Circulations for almost all British newspapers and magazines. ISBA organizes professional-development courses and publishes a wide range of guides and reference booklets.

The *Advertising Association* (AA) is the umbrella professional association for the whole industry. It was founded in 1924 to monitor compliance with the general spirit of 'truth in advertising' and draw up a tentative code of ethics. In 1962, that remit passed to the Advertising Standards Authority. The present-day AA states its aims as: promoting public confidence in advertising; safeguarding the common interest of the business; encouraging the development of education for advertising and theoretical research into its effect; maintaining professional standards; fostering good relations with interested parties in business, the professions, the media; and public service. It sponsors and co-publishes many publications, from textbooks to pamphlets, including the definitive Advertising Statistics Yearbook. **KC & BZE**

References

Advertising Association (2000) *Annual Review 1999–2000*, London: The Advertising Association.

Incorporated Society of British Advertisers (2000) *Annual Report & Accounts 2000*, London: Incorporated Society of British Advertisers.

Institute of Practitioners in Advertising (2000) *Annual Report 2000*, London: The Institute of Practitioners in Advertising.

Advertising, rebating

Given that typical advertising agencies derive almost three quarters of their income from the fixed 15 per cent media commission and an unknown further proportion from the equally standard 17.65 per cent mark-up on subcontracted services, they would seem to be restricted to non-price competition with one another. However, some do offer *commission rebating* deals, as a ploy to win new business or because of pressure from existing clients. Commentators regularly describe this as 'cutting commission' or 'handing back' a portion of it to the client. In fact, these are both impossible. They cannot cut a discount given to them automatically by the media owners, and that would not in any case benefit the advertiser in any way. Nor can they hand something back to a party who never handed it over in the first place. The actual mechanism is as follows.

Suppose that agency XYZ offers a 3 per cent commission rebate to client ABC, then buys advertising time costing £10 000 on its behalf. Receiving an invoice from the media owner for £8 500, XYZ bills ABC for £10 000 – 3% = £9 700. Its profit on the deal is thus £9 700 – £8 500 = £1 200 instead of 15 per cent of £1 500 = £1 500. The rebate is in fact a second discount in the transaction, which has the effect of reducing the agency's commission, while its discount from the media owners in fact remains intact.

This practice is perennially controversial. Proponents argue that the time and effort put into a £10 million television campaign is not a thousand times more than would be demanded by a £10 000 local newspaper campaign, yet that is the ratio of the corresponding commission amounts. Agencies should therefore be prepared to accept a pro rata reduction in remuneration as spending increases. Opponents point out that the apparently small rebates actually cut agency margins drastically. In the example, the 3 per cent discount XYZ gives to ABC is a fifth of the 15 per cent it receives from the media owner. ABC will need to make up the loss by cutting corners somewhere else or loading on unnecessary extras and XYZ has joined in a game of swings and roundabouts. The debate is likely to continue. **KC & BZE**

Reference

Crosier, K. (1999) 'The argument for advertising agency remuneration' in P.J. Kitchen (ed.) *Marketing Communications: Principles and Practice*, London: Thomson Learning, ch. 25.

Advertising, regulatory bodies

British advertising is regulated by direct legislation, statutory control and self-regulation. Informed opinion, at home and abroad, is generally that this 'tripartite' system works well in practice.

More than 100 pieces of legislation can affect advertisers in some way, but control is mainly exercised via statutory and self-regulatory bodies. Acts of Parliament charge the *Independent Television Commission* (ITC) with the duty to publish a code of standards, devise a mechanism for enforcing it, prevent television commercials from being broadcast until they have passed its scrutiny and respond to any public complaints about those which are cleared. The ITC Code of Advertising Standards and Practice states that 'television advertising should be legal, decent, honest and truthful', spelling out the details in 40 rules and five appendices. It is enforced by mandatory pre-clearance of every proposed commercial by the *Broadcast Advertising Clearance Centre* (BACC). In 1998, the ITC received 7855 complaints about 2560 commercials, 122 of which it upheld. The *Radio Authority* has a parallel statutory duty. Its Advertising and Sponsorship Code states the same general principle, elaborated in 32 rules and seven appendices. Pre-clearance is carried out by individual stations if proposed commercials are to be broadcast only locally but by the central *Radio Advertising Clearance Centre* in the case of national campaigns. In 1998, 336 complaints about surviving commercials were received and 72 upheld.

The self-regulatory *Advertising Standards Authority* (ASA) is financed by a 0.1 per cent levy on the cost of advertising space, collected on its behalf by the media owners. It exercises control over non-broadcast advertising of all kinds via a Code of Advertising, stating the familiar principle that 'all advertisements should be legal, decent, honest and truthful'. Pre-clearance of 30 million separate advertisements per year is clearly not practical, so control is mainly retrospective. Fairly high public awareness of the ASA' s regulatory role resulted in 12 217 complaints about 8343 advertisements during 1998. Every case was publicized in monthly reports to the news media and consumer-protection organizations. In 623 instances, the ASA required modification or withdrawal, backed by the sanctions of future rejection by media owners and eventual referral to the Office of Fair Trading.

The European Union has concerned itself with the harmonization of advertising regulation in member states, issuing Directives concerning Misleading Advertising in 1984 and Transfrontier Television in 1991. **KC & BZE**

References

Advertising Standards Authority (1999) *The British Codes of Advertising and Sales Promotion*, London: The Advertising Standards Authority.
Independent Television Authority (1997) *The ITC Code of Advertising Standards and Practice; The ITC Code of Programme Sponsorship*, London: The Independent Television Commission.

Radio Authority (1997) *The Radio Authority Advertising and Sponsorship Code*, London: The Radio Authority.

Advertising research

Often used interchangeably with 'advertising testing', this term in fact embraces formative research, developmental research, concept testing, pre-testing and post-testing. It is not generally taken to include the quite separate discipline of 'media research'.

The first of those five operations happens before the generation of a thematic concept has even begun, to establish the necessary background knowledge about the ways in which the target audience might use or abuse the messages and images in the eventual advertisements. The second relates to the progressive development of the concept after it has been generated. Together, these are very much the province of an advertising agency's *advertising account planning* function, described in an earlier entry. The outcome is typically a number of contenders for translation into the main campaign concept. Concept testing sorts out the winners from the losers, which are then converted into finished advertising by the process described in 'Creative strategy'. At that stage, they may be pre-tested under conditions approximating to the eventual campaign.

Ideally, pre-testing and post-testing should follow a methodical, standard procedure: *criteria* of effectiveness are derived from advertising *objectives* set at the planning stage; a suitable *measuring instrument* is chosen; field test results are recorded; effectiveness is assessed by *comparison* with the criteria. This is precisely the approach advocated by one well known model of advertising effect: 'Dagmar' = defining advertising goals for measured advertising results (Colley, 1962). In practice, alas, objectives are too often so loosely defined, in the headlong rush to create the advertising, that criteria have to be invented or the task avoided. Bespoke measurement methods are replaced by surrogate off-the-peg tests, concisely and authoritatively reviewed by Brierley (1995). There is no doubting their variety and the methodological sophistication of some, but only by good luck will the outcomes they test coincide with the implicit criteria for the advertising being evaluated. 'Effectiveness' may thus be claimed without actually being proved. **KC & BZE**

References
Brierley, S. (1995) *The Advertising Handbook*, London: Routledge, ch. 13.
Colley, R.H. (1962) 'Squeezing the waste out of advertising', *Harvard Business Review*, 40 (September/October): 76–88.

Advertising spending

The scope of an advertising campaign is limited by the financial resources available, particularly for allocation to the buying of media space and time. In an ideal world, the sum required would be decided by those responsible for spending it; in practice, they compete with others for their share of finite marketing funds. Research studies in Britain and America simultaneously found that a notably hierarchical process typically took place (Rees, 1977; Dhalla, 1977). Heads of each major function within the marketing division negotiated among themselves, the outcome was scrutinized at board level, where vested interests might result in further negotiation, the chief executive made the decisions, and they were transmitted down the organization to the budget-holders. The political nature of the process was confirmed a decade later in Britain by Piercy (1987), and there is no reason to believe that it has changed significantly since then.

The amount to be spent in a fixed period, generally a year, is formally defined as the *advertising appropriation*, reflecting the fact that it has been appropriated from a larger fund. It is informally called the 'budget', though that is actually a complete control mechanism, rather than just a sum of money, which specifies future sources and uses of funds and sets standards for their cost-effective application to pre-determined objectives.

With those various provisos, a number of appropriation-setting techniques have been described under a variety of names. In fact, they can be grouped into five categories:

- executive judgement
- internal ratios
- external ratios
- modelling and experimentation
- 'objective-and-task'.

Executive judgement ('notional sum' or 'all you can afford') may seem an unacceptably vague and risky approach to such an important decision. However, the other options can be disturbingly illogical and highly inflexible, despite the attraction of quantification. Consequently, the accumulated wisdom and intuition of experienced practitioners may be as useful as any other approach to the task. The 'objective-and-task' method attracts support on the grounds that it is more logical, in starting with objectives and then costing the tasks required to achieve them rather than fixing a sum and then deciding what to do with it. However, 'estimating the required expenditures' is a sting in the tail of practical guides, which can in practice result in nothing more precise than the application of executive judgement. More details of the other procedures can be found in Crosier (1999); for an authoritative account of modelling and experimentation see Broadbent (1997).

A survey of practice in the USA, Canada, Britain and a number of other European countries has shown that three of the six general options dominate practice: objective-and-task, one particular internal ratio (advertising-to-sales) and executive judgement, in descending order of popularity (Synodinos *et al.*, 1989). **KC & BZE**

References

Broadbent, S. (1997) *Accountable Advertising*, Henley-on-Thames: Admap Publications, ch. 8.

Crosier, K. (1999) 'Advertising', in P.J. Kitchen *Marketing Communications: Principles and Practice*, London: Thomson Learning, pp. 273–275.

Dhalla, N.K. (1977) 'How to set advertising budgets', *Journal of Advertising Research*, 17 (October): 11.

Piercy, N. (1987) 'Advertising budgeting; process and structure as explanatory variables', *Journal of Advertising*, 16 (2):59–65.

Rees, R.D. (1977) *Advertising Budgeting and Appraisal in Practice*: Research Study No.11, London: Advertising Association.

Synodinos, N.E., Keown, C.F. and Jacobs, L.W. (1989), 'Transnational advertising practice: a survey of leading brand advertisers in fifteen countries', *Journal of Advertising Research*, 29(2):43–50.

Advertising strategy and the five-step model

A five-step model is a programme of inquiry undertaken to ensure that all relevant information is collected before an advertising strategy is developed.

The first step is to specify *key facts*. The key fact refers to a statement requiring the marketer to clarify from the customers' point of view why they are or are not purchasing or considering the marketers' brands, products or services. Specifying the key facts here ensures that the marketer understands the problem from the consumers' perspectives.

The next step is to state the *marketing problem*. Extending from the key facts, the problem is now assessed from the marketer's point of view. The problem may pertain to the product itself, such an as image problem or a positioning problem, or it may be related to competitive pressures.

Once this has been stated precisely, the next step in the model is to develop *communications objectives*. These should be a precise statement of what the marketing communications are intended to achieve. If advertising aims to create awareness, then the communications objectives must be stated to achieve awareness.

The fourth step is to develop the *creative message strategy*. Based on the communications objectives, the messages must now be developed in line with the objectives. The creative messages are essentially the core of the advertising strategy because developing these requires the marketer to define precisely the target market and the main competitors, and then select the statement or the promise to make in the message and the supporting facts to back up the message.

Once the message has been created, the final step is to take into account any *mandatory requirements* that must accompany the advertising message. This would include regulatory requirements such as health warnings on cigarette packaging or corporate slogans of the marketers. **RM-R**

Reference

Shimp, T.A. (1997) *Advertising, Promotion, and Supplemental Aspects of Integrated Marketing Communications*, Florida: The Dryden Press.

Advertising system

The figure below illustrates the working relationships among the four parties comprising this system: *advertisers*, the *media owners* who provide them with their channel of communication to *target audiences*, and the *advertising agencies* (or similar intermediaries) whose services they typically use in the process.

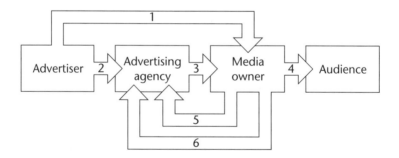

Figure: **The structure of the advertising business**

The omission of an arrow linking advertiser directly to audience is deliberate. Elsewhere in this text, we argue that three criteria in particular distinguish advertising from other ingredients of the marketing communications mix: the message is contained in what would universally be recognized as an advertisement; it is delivered via definable advertising media; and a standard rate is paid for the space or time used in the process. So, every instance of that direct communication link must properly be located elsewhere in the mix, for sloppy terminology risks costly tactical errors.

Arrow 1 implies an unusual decision, for only about 20 per cent of all advertising expenditure passes to media owners from advertisers who do all the work in-house. Arrow 2 symbolizes the normal practice of delegating campaign development to a professional intermediary. The quid pro quo is that some control is sacrificed as expertise is acquired. Arrow 3 reflects the fact that the orders for media time and space are placed by the agencies, not the advertisers themselves, who are rewarded with a standard 'commission' discount on the list price. Arrow 4 raises the issue that messages transmitted in this way are bound to be mediated, to some extent, by audiences' feelings about the intervening media. A little more control is thereby sacrificed. Arrows 5 and 6 symbolize an unwritten code of professional conduct: because advertising agencies depend on media commission for about two thirds of their total income, media owners make their sales pitches to agencies, not advertisers. In practice, they present to both, of course, but are careful to observe the correct priority. **KC & BZE**

Reference

Crosier, K. (1999) 'Promotion', in M.J. Baker (ed.) *The Marketing Book*, 4th edn, Oxford: Butterworth-Heinemann, ch. 17, esp. pp. 398–400.

Advertising, top-up fees

In the late 19th century, an advertising agency in America added creative services to the media planning and buying which had been its raison d'être, subsidizing the cost from its media commission. This set a troublesome precedent for the 'full-service' advertising agencies that followed its lead, as poster sites became bigger, cinemas offered more than static projections of print advertisements, magazines and then newspapers began to print in colour and, finally, television arrived. Agencies had to meet escalating production costs out of a 15 per cent discount on media prices that were rising only in pace with general price inflation or persuade their clients to spend ever increasing sums on advertising. Meanwhile, their creative people expected greater rewards for their increasingly specialized skills. It was obvious that successful agencies with ambitious clients could no longer survive on media commission alone.

A new convention duly evolved that certain on-costs could be charged direct to clients. That would include studio fees, for example, but also many grey areas. A report on the situation in an unspecified number of Europe countries is far from precise on the subject: 'The range of services provided at no charge will depend on each individual relationship. Where non-commissionable agency services are charged (work done within the agency), this is normally done on the basis of a prior estimate' (European Association of Advertising Agencies, 1994). Such vagueness presents an unfortunate opportunity for advertisers to haggle, and sow the seeds of disharmony in a crucial working relationship. **KC & BZE**

Reference

European Association of Advertising Agencies (1994) *Client/Advertising Agency Partnerships in the New Europe*, Henley-on-Thames: NTC Publications, p. 12.

Advertising, what it can and cannot do

Popular opinion often credits advertising with a wider range of effects than is reasonable. In fact its key characteristic, that it delivers messages via advertising media, means it has a more distant relationship with its target audience than do several of its relatives in the marketing communications mix. As a result, it is unlikely to be able to clinch a sale, except in the special case of direct-response advertisements. A more realistic role is longer-term brand-building, which it can do by:

- building awareness
- conveying information
- telling a story
- establishing an identity
- creating a predisposition.

These are, of course, generalized common aims; more specific objectives must be set for individual advertising campaigns. In practice, those all too often include the requirement to 'increase sales' within the period of the campaign, which is normally comparatively short-term. Such an objective typically places an unfair burden on advertising management and advertising agencies by ignoring: (i) the crucial gap between responding favourably to an advertisement and being persuaded to take up the product, (ii) the time lag between being convinced and deciding to act accordingly, (iii) the concurrent positive or negative effects of the advertiser's decisions about other elements of the marketing mix, such as price and (iv) entirely external determinants, such as personal economics, social norms or the activities of the advertiser's competitors.

If we imagine ourselves a brand manager or advertising manager called in by the marketing director for a roasting about the failure of the advertising campaign to produce the expected upturn in the sales graph, would we be likely to accept responsibility meekly? Or would we point out the complicity of those who made unhelpful decisions about sales strategy, distribution policy, pricing and so on? The development of creative and media strategies demands the guidelines provided by formal objectives, and assessment of campaign effectiveness depends upon calibrated criteria derived from them. The key issue is that those objectives must, in the first place, take account of what advertising can be expected to do in general, and what the campaign should be expected to achieve in the particular current circumstances. **KC & BZE**

Reference
Crosier, K. (1999) 'Advertising', in P.J. Kitchen (ed.) *Marketing Communications: Principles and Practice*, London: Thomson Learning, ch. 16.

Advertising, what it is and is not

Advertising is one ingredient of the 'marketing communications mix' (sometimes called the 'promotional mix'). There are almost as many opinions about the other ingredients as there are authors writing on the subject. We propose:

- advertising
- publicity
- direct marketing (communications)
- sponsorship
- exhibitions
- packaging
- point-of-sale merchandising
- sales promotion
- personal selling.

Advertising is thus one of a choice of routes to a common goal: communicating persuasively for a marketing purpose.

Although three major world languages use *publicité*, *publicidad* and *publicidade* to describe advertising, and it is *pubblicità* in a fourth European language, in English the distinction between the 'publicity' and 'advertising' is vital. Commentators who routinely describe publicity as 'free advertising', in contrast to 'paid advertising', are carelessly ignoring a crucial strategic distinction between these two marketing communications methods. While advertising is 'the placing of an advertisement in chosen advertising media, guaranteeing delivery of an unmodified message to a known target audience, in return for a standard rate for the time or space used' (plus the cost of producing the advertisement, of course), publicity depends on 'the delivery of a news release to chosen news media, resulting, if newsworthiness earns an editorial mention, in exposure to a specified target audience at no charge' (except the cost of producing and distributing the release). To opt for a publicity initiative as part of a marketing communications campaign thus introduces the significant risk that the message will receive an editorial 'spin', not necessarily either favourable or neutral. That cannot happen to an advertisement. Sloppy vocabulary, obscuring the fact that 'paid' advertising buys the control 'free' publicity sacrifices, could result in a very risky tactical decision.

It is often assumed that publicity can be bought for the price of simultaneous advertising. On the contrary, a strong professional etiquette maintains clear boundaries between the editorial and advertising functions. For instance, *Cosmopolitan* once formally contradicted a marketing manager's apparent 'assumption that spending a significant amount on advertising gives the right to demand editorial coverage ... [which is] judged purely on its relevance and interest to our magazine's 2.3 million readers.'

We single out this particular confusion of terminology because it is frequently encountered and can have damaging consequences. The distinction between advertising and other ingredients of the marketing communications mix can be easily established by applying the test described in 'Advertising'. **KC & BZE**

Reference

Crosier, K. (1999) 'Promotion', in M.J. Baker (ed.), *The Marketing Book*, 4th edn, Oxford: Butterworth-Heinemann, ch. 17, esp. pp. 379–385.

Advertising, working relationships

The abstract 'advertising system' described earlier is in fact a set of working relationships among three parties (that with the audience being of a rather different kind). *Advertising managers* or brand managers brief advertising agency *account executives*, who respond with advice from planning colleagues and, in due course, specific plans developed in their creative and media departments. Meanwhile, agency *media buyers* negotiate with media owners on behalf of advertisers for use of an intangible commodity, advertising space or time. *Media sales representatives* will already have been making periodic speculative calls on both agencies and advertisers. While campaigns are running, *account executives* maintain regular contact with their clients, until changes of plan set the whole process in motion again, or an entirely new campaign is launched.

A key feature of this system is delegation of campaign planning and execution to a third party, and the consequent risk of reduced control over outcomes. However, setting up a self-sufficient in-house advertising operation would cost the substantial salaries needed to lure creative and media experts from their natural habitat in advertising agencies. It would furthermore be hard to keep them motivated, once denied the stimulation of working on diverse campaigns for a variety of clients. Moreover, that very breadth of experience allows agencies to apply lateral thinking to strategy development, free from the insider's preconceptions. In short, it makes sense for an advertiser to buy a 'timeshare' in a pool of independent experience and expertise that is managed and motivated by someone else.

All this bears the hallmarks of a service industry. It is a truism that those are 'people businesses', but it reminds us that one crucial factor among many that determine the effectiveness of an advertising campaign will always be the quality of the interpersonal service-delivering relationships just described. **KC & BZE**

Reference

Crosier, K. (1999) 'The relationship among advertisers, agencies, media and target audiences' in P.J. Kitchen (ed.) *Marketing Communications: Principles and Practice*, London: Thomson Learning, ch. 24.

After sales service

When the sale has been completed it is important that purchasers are supported in order to persuade them to become loyal customers. The burgeoning subject of customer care is testament to the importance that companies now place on customer retention. It has been proved that it is far more economical to retain regular customers than to seek new ones.

After sales service can start by a simple follow-up call to enquire if the buyer is satisfied with the product that they have purchased and that it was received on time and in a satisfactory condition. After sales service is, of course, much more than this, for it includes physical service, warranty work and the general way in which customers are cared for once they have purchased their product or service. **GL**

Reference

Lancaster, G. and Reynolds, P. (1998) *Marketing*, Basingstoke: Macmillan pp. 225–226.

Analysis and marketing communications planning

Analysis is the first part of the marketing communications planning process. Before any decisions can be made about what form marketing communications should take, there needs to be a detailed understanding of the situation and the factors and trends affecting that situation. This involves collating both internal and external information. Data might be collected continuously or for a specific project. The important thing is that information is available when needed. Research reports may be purchased, research companies commissioned or research undertaken by the organization itself. The development of marketing information and database systems is a fundamental facility to all marketing managers whatever their particular areas of responsibility. But, for the process of analysis to be meaningful, the collection of information is only the first step. Analysis requires the ability to understand, evaluate and use the information collected.

Analysis of the many environmental factors that impinge on marketing communications planning is an early step in the analytical process. Pickton and Wright (1998) suggest the use of PRESTCOM analysis. This involves evaluation of the **p**olitical, **r**egulatory, **e**conomic, **s**ocial, **t**echnological, **c**ompetitive, **o**rganizational and **m**arket environments. Undertaking such analysis results in a better appreciation of the market forces that impact on marketing communications. This includes a clear understanding of what has been done before, what the competition is doing, influences on customer and consumer behaviour within the target market, the role of the trade, media opportunities, trends in the market, evaluation of previous campaigns and so on.

The quality of subsequent marketing communication decisions is strongly affected by the quality of analysis that first takes place. Although analysis may be identified as the first task, analysis and evaluation are carried out on an on-going basis throughout campaigns to arrive at initial decisions and to determine what will work, what is working and what has worked. Analysis and evaluation, monitoring and control represent a cycle or loop of activity. **DWP**

Reference

Pickton, D.W. and Wright, S. (1998) *Improved Competitive Strategy Through Value Added Competitive Intelligence'*, Proceedings, Third Annual European Conference, Society of Competitive Intelligence Professions, Berlin.

Art of marketing

For more than 50 years marketing academics have debated the artistic and/or scientific status of the subject area. Certainly most of this argument revolves around marketing's scientific credentials. Some say it *is* a science; others contend that it is *not*; and yet others maintain that it might eventually become a science. Of late, however, academic attention has turned to marketing's artistic side, partly out of growing disillusion with 'big' science *per se* and partly on account of marketing science's failure to deliver on its extravagant post-war promises. True, this latter-day concern with aesthetic matters is not exactly new, as the late-19th century controversy over 'advertising art' bears eloquent witness, but the emergence of postmodern-mediated critiques has forced it back on the marketing agenda (Bogart, 1995; Brown, 1996)

These days, nevertheless, the debate has moved far beyond the banalities of 'art versus science' to discussions concerning the kind of art that marketing is, the precise nature of the relationship between art and marketing and, not least, the character-cum-status of attendant academic commentary (Brown e*t al.*, 1998). Obviously, marketing contains important visual, tactile, aural and narratological components (ads, packaging, jingles, storylines and so on), which imply parallels with fine art, sculpture, music and drama, to say nothing of movies, video and photography. Marketing, moreover, frequently appropriates the icons of high art for commercial purposes (Benson & Hedges' surrealism, Absolut Picasso etc.); cinematic auteurs often earn their stripes in television commercials (Ridley Scott, Tony Kaye); the line between museum and shopping mall is becoming increasingly blurred (World of Coca-Cola, The Museum Store); and there is a burgeoning literature on marketing the arts, as well as the marketing practices of major artists such as Warhol, Koons and Hirst (Brown and Patterson 2000).

Of all the arts, however, literature is proving the most productive for academic marketing purposes. This predilection is primarily due to the literary nature of scholarly discourse – books, papers, research reports and the like – but it is also attributable to postmodernism's tendency to treat everything as a 'text', whether it be a haircut, a holiday or a hockey match. The upshot is a steadily growing body of academic research that either culls the literary canon for marketing insights (consumer behaviour in sex 'n' shopping novels, for example) or applies the tools and techniques of literary criticism to marketing 'texts' (department stores, service encounters, advertising campaigns *et al.*). It has even been suggested that the marketing literature itself is amenable to literary criticism, though that's stretching things a bit! **SFX**

References

Bogart, M.H. (1995) *Artists, Advertising and the Borders of Art*, Chicago: University of Chicago Press.

Brown, S. (1996) 'Art or science?: Fifty years of marketing debate', *Journal of Marketing Management* 12 (4), 243–267.

Brown, S. and Patterson, A. (eds) (2000) *Imagining Marketing: Art, Aesthetics and the Avant-Garde*, London: Routledge.

Brown, S., Doherty, A.M. and Clarke, W. (eds) (1998) *Romancing the Market*, London: Routledge.

Attitude measurement

Attitudes are mental states used by individuals to structure the way they perceive their environment and guide the way they respond to it (Kumar, Aaker and Day, 1999). It refers to positive or negative feelings or evaluative judgements an individual has towards some person, object or issue. Basically, attitudes are learned, are relatively enduring and can influence behaviour. That is why attitudes are useful constructs for marketers to understand. They are regarded as the essence of the human change agent that all marketers strive to influence. By conducting attitudinal research and measuring attitudes, marketers hope to obtain useful information capable of inducing target consumers towards purchasing or using their products or services. Attitudes can generally be divided into cognitive or knowledge component, affective or liking component, and intention or action component. Each of these represents a person's attitude towards a particular object or someone, or towards some issues.

The way to measure attitudes is by using the appropriate attitudinal scales. When a researcher develops questionnaires, scales are used to assess the attitudinal level of respondents. Those most commonly used to measure attitudes are the Likert scale and semantic differential scales. The Likert scale provides respondents with a list of variables that are anchored on a scale ranging from 'strongly disagree', 'disagree' and 'neither disagree nor agree' to 'agree' and 'strongly agree'. The respondents indicate the extent to which they agree or disagree to a variety of statements which are then summated. Semantic differential scales use bipolar attributes to indicate respondents' attitudes toward a particular individual, object, or event. The bipolar adjectives could represent such factors as 'good–bad' or 'strong–weak'. Essentially, they can be used to assess respondents' attitudes towards a particular brand, advertisements, likes and dislikes, on various dimensions. **RM-R**

References
Chisnall, P. (1992) *Marketing Research*, 4th edn, London, McGraw-Hill.
Kumar, V., Aaker, D.A. and Day, G.S. (1999) *Essentials of Marketing Research*, New York: John Wiley & Sons.

Audience

Defining the audience is an extremely important marketing communications task. Unless the right audience is identified and reached, marketing communications cannot be effective. Research and analysis is used to identify and develop an understanding of audiences. Messages and media are then chosen to reach selected targets effectively and efficiently.

The most obvious target audiences are customers, but these should not be thought of as the only targets. Consumers are another group. Whereas customers are buyers, consumers are users and, as such, influence the decision to buy. Sometimes they may be the same people, but often they are not. In industrial purchases, this is typically the case. In family situations, the mother may make many household purchases, but do so for other members of the family. In situations where trade intermediaries are used (e.g. wholesalers and retailers), both trade customers and the end customers/consumers will need to be targeted. Promotional strategies are known as push (promoting to the trade) and pull (promoting to end buyers and users) strategies.

A third category of target audience is other *influencers*. These, alongside customers and consumers, are the principal members of the 'decision making unit' (DMU), any one or combination of whom may be selected as targets. Such a group might come together formally, as in industrial markets, or informally, as in many consumer purchase decisions. Influencers for a child's toy, for example, might include the child, friends, teachers, relatives, parents and the media. If marketing communications are used to 'influence the influencers', more favourable outcomes may occur. For this reason, opinion leaders and the media may be specifically targeted when new products are being launched.

It is wise to consider a range of target audiences (both 'push' and 'pull') when planning marketing communications and their specification should be as precise as possible. The most widely quoted approach is use of the social grading system. It uses 'occupation of the head of household' as the basis of the A B C1 C2 D E classification system familiar to so many people. The groupings roughly equate to social classes. Although the social grading approach remains popular, it is best used in conjunction with other approaches. Today, there are many other and more powerful

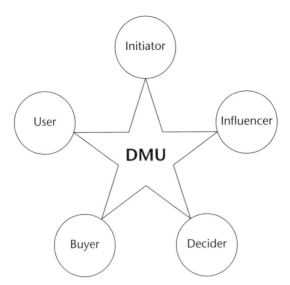

Figure: **The decision making unit**

measures that can be used, including those using other demographic, geodemographic, psychographic, mediagraphic, buyer behaviour and life-stage variables. For example, research into people's lifestyles reveals telling differences between audience groups. Douglas Coupland (1991) first coined the now widely accepted term 'Generation X' to describe the 25-35 year-old generation who reject the typical career ethic and urban consumer lifestyle. Advertising agency BMP DDB Needham's sponsored research has proposed seven youth audiences: Bill and Teds, Conservative Careerists, Moral Fibres, Blairites, New Modernists, Corporate Clubbers, and Adolescent Angsts (Armstrong, 1996). Such lifestyle groupings are constantly changing and require continuing research to track them if marketing communications is to be able to 'speak' to its audiences. **DWP**

References
Armstrong, S. (1996) 'Catch 'em young', *The Sunday Times* 12 May, Culture Supplement, p12.
Coupland, D. (1991) *Generation X, Tales for an Accelerated Culture,* London: Abacus.

Augmented product

The augmented product refers to services and other activities that support the marketing of the main (or core) product. This definition is wider than the mere provision of after sales services and warranty backup which form part of this definition; it also includes sales persons, service personnel, transportation and, where appropriate, assembly or construction of the product at the customer's home or workplace. It also includes all aspects of the commercial transaction of the purchase itself and the provision of credit when required.

In many modern marketing situations, the value of the augmented product is often deemed to be at least as important as the core product. **GL**

Reference
Kotler, P. (1994) *Marketing Management, Analysis, Planning, Implementation and Control*, 8th edn, New Jersey: Prentice Hall pp. 432–436.

Barnumarketing

P.T. Barnum, the superlative American showman of the late 19th century, is rarely mentioned in mainstream marketing textbooks. If he is name-checked at all, it is as an exemplar of how-not-to-do-it. Despite a long and brilliantly successful career – he was the Richard Branson with-knobs-on of his day – Barnum is mistakenly remembered for a remark that he didn't actually make. Namely, 'there's one born every minute'. Along with 'buyer beware', 'never give a sucker an even break' and 'you can have any colour as long as it's black', his alleged aphorism is redolent of rip offs, the hard sell, price gouging and egregious customer exploitation. The kind of disreputable practices, in short, that 'real' marketers, 'proper' marketers, 'get your loyalty card here' marketers have long since renounced.

To be sure, the fact that Barnum didn't utter the dread words doesn't mean that he was a customer-hugger at heart. *Au contraire*, the self-styled 'Prince of Humbugs' firmly believed in ripping people off and, to add insult to injury, he subsequently boasted about the deception. Not to put too fine a point on it, Barnum was a chiseler, a charlatan, a cheat, a chancer, a con-artist, no less, who revelled in his con-artistry. In fact, he used to go on huge speaking tours of America and Europe, where he expounded the Principles of Barnumarketing and bragged about his customer-cozening activities. The really curious thing, however, is that he was such a sublime scam-monger that people literally flocked to have their hard earned money misappropriated and hear how he did it.

Clearly, this poses a conceptual problem for conventional (Kotlerite) approaches to marketing. How, after all, is it possible for a self-confessed con man to make good when total customer-orientation is the key to marketing success? All sorts of 'explanations' can be posited (long time ago; once bitten, twice shy; he was a marketer in disguise; and so on) but none of these holds water. The fact of the matter is that he ripped people off – time and time again – and they loved him for it. The possibility therefore arises that Barnum knew more about marketing than today's academic marketing authorities and that there is still much to learn from the greatest sham on earth (see Brown, 1998; Vitale, 1998). **SFX**

References

Brown, S. (1998) 'The unbearable lightness of marketing: a neo-romantic, counter-revolutionary recapitulation', in S. Brown *et al.* (eds), *Romancing the Market*, London: Routledge, pp. 255–277.

Vitale, J. (1998) *There's a Customer Born Every Minute: P.T. Barnum's Secrets to Business Success*, New York: American Management Association.

Behavioural sciences

'Behavioural sciences' is essentially a collective term identifying a number of disciplines that study human behaviours. These include psychology, sociology, economics, anthropology and history. Although there are distinct similarities between them there are also noted differences in the way the behaviour of humans is studied, the focus of human behaviours, and the behavioural concepts, as well as the unit of analysis. Nevertheless, the understanding from all these disciplines contributes towards enhancing our understanding of human behaviours.

Behavioural sciences have contributed significantly to our understanding of consumer buying behaviours. For example, economics' theory of production, exchange and consumption of goods and services is the basis of many marketing principles such as the satisfaction of consumer wants and needs and the consumer buying model. In addition to this, marketers have also adopted the principles of psychology to a large extent in understanding consumer behaviours. Social psychology assesses how individuals influence and are influenced by group pressures whilst organizational psychology looks at the functioning of the individuals within the organizational setting. These are important considerations to marketers in the course of assessing whether a sufficient number of individuals display similar characteristics that may form the focus of specific marketing efforts. A good example of this is when marketers develop segmentation analysis. Indeed, the disciplines in behavioural sciences have contributed significantly to understanding the behaviours of consumers and in helping marketing decision makers to develop ways of tackling their wants and needs effectively. **RM-R**

References
Williams, K.C. (1984) *Behavioural Aspects of Marketing*, Oxford: Heinemann Professional Publishing.
Schiffmann, L.G. and Kanuk, L.L. (1983) *Consumer Behavior*, 2nd edn, Englewood Cliffs, NJ: Prentice Hall.

Benefits of brands

Brands benefit producers, distributors and consumers.

Brands, if successfully managed, act as a guarantee of a long term future income stream. One of the reasons why Nestlé paid such a high premium buying Rowntree Mackintosh was because of the large portfolio of brands that had stood the test of time and had considerable consumer goodwill. Brands such as Polo, Kit Kat and Quality Street had been nurtured to generate healthy long term cash flows.

A powerful brand has a strong reputation in consumers' minds, which acts as a barrier, protecting the brand against competitors. In the luxury perfume market Chanel has built such a strong reputation that new entrants find it hard to dislodge it from its pedestal of status, high quality and sophistication.

Brand producers benefit from brands because they provide legal protection against imitators. Organizations take care over correctly registering their brands.

Powerful brands make it difficult for distributors to negotiate lower prices and make it easier for brand owners to choose between competing distributors when seeking exclusive distributors.

Distributors value brands, because specific brands reinforce their image. They find it easier to sell leading brands and welcome the marketing support provided. Brands help intermediaries build stronger relationships with their customers and reduce operating costs.

Consumers benefit from brands for a variety of reasons. Brands guarantee a particular quality level, which will be consistently delivered. Consumers perceive minimal risk purchasing well known brands.

In an era of increasing choice, brands simplify consumers' purchase decisions. They facilitate rapid recognition. A brand name enables a consumer rapidly to recall information from long term memory, and by remembering its characteristics to facilitate purchase decision making.

Consumers value brands because they make personality statements about themselves. For conspicuous branded goods, for example cars and clothing, consumers value brands because they help project either an actual or an aspirational aspect of their personality. Through their symbolic nature, brands help consumers mix with particular social groups, since having a particular brand makes a statement about commonality of beliefs within the group. **LdeC**

References

Biel, A. (1991) 'The brandscape: converting brand image into equity', *ADMAP* 26 (10):41–44.
de Chernatony, L. and McDonald, M. (1998) *Creating Powerful Brands in Consumer, Service and Industrial Markets*, Oxford: Butterworth-Heinemann.
Elliott, R. (1994) 'Exploring the symbolic meaning of brands' *British Journal of Management* 5 (June): 131–144.
Solomon, M. (1983) 'The role of products as social stimuli: a symbolic interactionism perspective', *Journal of Consumer Research* 10 (December): 319–329.

Brand

Interest in brands was fuelled during the late 1980s when organizations began to value their brands and debate arose about including them on balance sheets. A good way of understanding brands is from the definition – a successful brand is an identifiable product, service, person or place, augmented in such a way that the buyer or user perceives relevant, unique added values which match their needs most closely; furthermore, its success results from being able to sustain these added values in the face of competition.

As the definition indicates, brands act as efficient differentiating devices. However, to conceive brands primarily in terms of their differentiating ability misses their strategic importance. Brands differ from their core commodity form because they have 'added values'. In other words, something extra added which customers particularly appreciate. For example, garages, as commodities, offer car servicing. However, a branded garage not only has a differentiating name, but also takes the car owner, who daily commutes to London, to the station in the morning, then collects the car owner from the station in the evening in their newly serviced car. This example shows how brands can have functional values. However, successful brands are an amalgam of functional and emotional values. In the banking market, one of the factors differentiating the Cooperative Bank is its emotional value of adhering to ethical principles. It is more difficult for a competitor to emulate another brand's emotional rather than functional values.

Brands are particularly common in product sectors, with Interbrand in 1999 recording Coca Cola as the most valuable global brand at US$83.9 bn. They are increasingly prevalent in services, for example Microsoft in 1999 was the second most valuable global brand, valued at US$56.7 bn. In business to business markets managers are striving to move beyond brands as differentiating devices. In the not for profit sector, managers are acutely aware of the values their brands stand for and portray these to stakeholders such as donors and volunteers. **LdeC**

References

de Chernatony, L. and McDonald, M. (1992) *Creating Powerful Brands in Consumer, Service and Industrial Markets*, Oxford: Butterworth-Heinemann.

Hart, S. and Murphy, J. (eds) (1998) *Brands, The New Wealth Creators*, Basingstoke: Macmillan.
Kapferer, J-N. (1997) *Strategic Brand Management*, London: Kogan Page.

Brand equity

Brand equity describes the way that the differential attributes of a brand give increased value to a firm's balance sheet. It has been argued that brand equity can be nurtured over time. For example, in the early days of a new brand, there is little inherent brand equity and managers seek to increase awareness, then associate their brand with a unique set of associations. With increasing consumer trial, if the equity is to grow consumers need to have a favourable perception of the brand's quality, consistency and value.

Young and Rubicam have a model about growing brand equity which is based on four brand elements. The first, brand differentiation, represents the start point, enabling consumers to distinguish the brand from competitors. Then, to attract and retain consumers, it needs to convince them that the brand is relevant to their needs. The third element is ensuring consumers have high regard and esteem for the brand's capabilities. Ultimately its success will depend on its familiarity in terms of whether the brand is well known and is part of consumers' everyday lives.

However, while the Young and Rubicam model is most insightful, because of its proprietary nature, it can only be employed by Young and Rubicam. A more generalised perspective is proposed by Feldwick (1996). As the differential attributes of a brand give rise to the brand's strength and thus to its balance sheet value, brand equity can be assessed by monitoring these three components. When evaluating the brand's differential attributes an organization is concerned with appreciating its awareness, image, perceived quality, perceived value and personality and, if its brand name draws on the corporation's name, any organizational associations. To evaluate the brand's strength, issues that should be considered are its market share and distribution, its price premium, the degree of consumer loyalty and the extent to which the brand is technologically or socially innovative within its category. To complete the picture about the brand's equity, its balance sheet value needs auditing. The three blocks of differential attributes, strength and valuation not only provide a detailed picture of a brand's equity, but by benchmarking these against competitors, indications about new branding activity are provided. **LdeC**

References
Aaker, D. (1996) 'Measuring brand equity across products and markets', *California Management Review* 38(3):102–120.
de Chernatony, L. and McDonald, M. (1998) 'Creating powerful brands' in *Consumer, Service and Industrial Marketing*, Oxford: Butterworth-Heinemann.
Young and Rubicam (1994) *Brand Asset Valuation*, London: Young and Rubicam.
Feldwick, P. (1996) 'What is brand equity anyway and how do you measure it?', *Journal of the Market Research Society* 38(2):85–104.
Gordon, G., di Benedetto, A. and Calantone, R. (1994) 'Brand equity as an evolutionary process', *The Journal of Brand Management* 2(1):47–56.

Brand image

Brand image is the perception of the brand held by the market – what is thought and felt about the brand, real and imagined (see 'Image building'). The product brand may be linked to the corporate brand, as it is for many companies such as Coca Cola, Virgin, IBM, Ford, Cadbury, McDonald, Microsoft and Marks and Spencer. Other companies prefer to separate the company or corporate brand from the product brand so that individual products stand or fall on their own, although the separation is not always complete, it is a matter of extent. Companies adopting more of this stance include Sara Lee, Mars, Unilever and Proctor & Gamble, who own thousands of product brands not associated with the companies themselves.

One of four basic strategies can be pursued in building brand images.

- *Corporate umbrella branding* – the organization's brands fall under the same corporate name, for example, Heinz.
- *Family umbrella branding* – the organization has a corporate brand and a separate brand (or brands) for its products, for example, Marks and Spencer's St. Michael brand.
- *Range branding* – a number of related products are grouped together under one brand name, for example, Lean Cuisine's range of low calorie foods.
- *Individual branding* – each product is branded separately, for example, Penguin chocolate bars.

Whereas 'brand image' tends to be a term reserved for the product brand, when the organization as a whole is branded, this tends to be referred to as 'corporate image'. In both cases, however, the process is one of 'branding'. **DWP**

References

de Chernatony, L. and McDonald, M. (1998) *Creating Powerful Brands in Consumer, Service and Industrial Markets*, Oxford: Butterworth-Heinemann.

Brand loyalty

There are numerous definitions of brand loyalty. One of the most comprehensive is that of Jacoby and Chestnut, who define brand loyalty as 'the biased, behavioural response expressed over time by some decision making unit with respect to one or more alternative brands out of a set of brands and is a function of psychological processes'. A considerable amount of research has been undertaken by Ehrenberg and his team, who found that it is indeed rare to find consumers who are 100 per cent loyal to a particular brand. Instead, consumers have a small number of brands (a repertoire) in a category that they use more regularly. Their work showed that high market share brands are bought within the repertoire more frequently than smaller brands. Furthermore a brand's most loyal consumers are the least valuable as they buy the category infrequently and a brand's best consumers are mostly competitors' consumers who occasionally buy it.

One reason for these results is because brands in the same category satisfy different needs. Wendy Gordon introduced the term 'need-state' to describe the way a brand reflects a consumer's need in a particular context. This can best be appreciated from someone buying yoghurts during a week. Preparing for a dinner party, on Friday they buy 'Real Greek yoghurt', not only to complete the recipe's ingredients, but to meet their need-state of being a sophisticated host. To ease their feelings of guilt at the children having to stay upstairs during the dinner party, they also buy a pack of Mr Men yoghurts, which the children regard as a treat. Two days later, concerned about putting on weight after the party, they buy a diet yoghurt. As Thursday approaches, with the weekly pay, the person wishes to satisfy their need state of living within a budget and for lunch chooses a cheaper, own label yoghurt. **LdeC**

References

de Chernatony, L. and McDonald, M. (1998) *Creating Powerful Brands in Consumer, Service and Industrial Marketing*, Oxford: Butterworth-Heinemann.

Ehrenberg, A. (1993) 'If you're so strong why aren't you bigger?' *ADMAP* (October): 13–14.

Gordon, W. (1994) 'Taking brand repertoires seriously', *Journal of Brand Management* 20(1):25–30.

Jacoby, J. and Chestnut, R. (1978) *Brand Loyalty Measurement and Management*, New York: John Wiley.

Brand management

Brand management entails protecting the brand against competitors and ensuring growth targets are met. One way of doing this is using the de Chernatony – McWilliam matrix shown below.

Representationality

	Low	High
High		
Low		

Functionality

Figure: **The de Chernatony-McWilliam matrix**

As de Chernatony and McWilliam (1990) argued, since a brand is a cluster of functional and emotional values, it can be categorized by the degree to which it emphasizes functional values and the extent to which it draws on emotional values to represent something about the consumer's personality. Once an organization is clear about the quadrant in which it wants its brand to reside it can be managed following the strategies below.

- *High representationality – high functionality.* A creative strategy that reinforces consumers' lifestyle requirements is needed, possibly drawing on reference group endorsement. A continuous promotional presence is essential, ensuring that the brand's symbolic meaning is communicated to the consumer's peer group. High standards of quality control are crucial. Availability should be restricted to quality distributors.
- *Low representationality – high functionality.* These brands are bought because of high utilitarian needs. Continuous R & D investment is critical to ensure competitive functional advantage over competitors. The promotional support should communicate the brand's functional benefits, possibly using 'product as hero' in the advertising.
- *High representationality – low functionality.* These brands satisfy consumers looking for symbolic devices without too much concern about functionality. The role of advertising is either to gain their acceptability as part of a culture or to reinforce a lifestyle. More reliance needs placing on the results of branded, rather than blind, product testing against competition.
- *Low representationality – low functionality.* The development of Spar, 7-11 and other convenience stores reflect these brands. These brands need wide distribution and to be price competitive. Competing on price entails being an efficient producer, avoiding marginal customers, having long production runs and continually monitoring overheads. 'Fighting brands' are often launched to complete a range, as an offensive attack against a particular competitor, or as part of a segmented approach to markets. **LdeC**

References

de Chernatony, L. and McDonald, M. (1998) *Creating Powerful Brands in Consumer, Service and Industrial Markets,* Oxford: Butterworth-Heinemann.

de Chernatony, L. and McWilliam G. (1990) 'Appreciating brands as assets through using a two dimensional model', *International Journal of Advertising*, 9(2):111–119.

Park, W., Jawarski, B. and MacInnis, D. (1986) 'Strategic brand concept-image management', *Journal of Marketing* 50(October): 135–145.

Sheth, J., Newman, B. and Gross, B. (1991) 'Why we buy what we buy: a theory of consumption values', *Journal of Business Research* 22(2):159–170.

Brand naming

A name is a powerful asset as it facilitates brand recognition and evokes associations about the brand. There are guidelines that organizations consider when developing brands' names.

The name should be short, easy to pronounce and quickly understood. People have finite mental capacities and find it easier to encode short words in memory. This is one of the reasons why consumers contract names with four or more syllables. Another is because they get emotionally closer to a brand, for example Merc rather than Mercedes.

Brand names that communicate consumer benefits are particularly valuable. Brands such as Xpelair and Lean Cuisine need little explanation, enabling marketing communication to build the brand's personality, rather than convey the brand's functional capabilities.

Marketers are cautious about creating new words, rather than adapting existing ones, since significant promotional budgets are needed to establish awareness. Over the years, brands such as Xerox and Kodak have had notable levels of support to register their brands in consumers' minds, yet these brands would require vast sums of money to create awareness were they to start again.

Some organizations are striving to develop names that can travel across continents. Brands such as Coca Cola or Microsoft have no linguistic impediments to global expansion. However the car brand Nova was handicapped in Spanish speaking zones because of its translation as 'doesn't go'.

Many firms seek to draw on positive associations with their corporate brand names and strongly tie their new brand with the corporation, for example Heinz Baked Beans and Heinz Tomato Ketchup. The goodwill that has been built in the corporate brand name can facilitate consumer acceptance, through greater confidence. There are instances where the values of the individual brand are distinct from those of its parent and, for this reason, it will be launched without strong corporate associations. For example KLM's budget airline has such a different set of associations that it was decided to name it Buzz, just as British Airways did with its budget airline, Go. **LdeC**

References:

de Chernatony, L. and McDonald, M. (1998) *Creating Powerful Brands in Consumer, Service and Industrial Marketing*, Oxford: Butterworth-Heinemann.

Keller, K. (1998) *Strategic Brand Management*, Upper Saddle River: Prentice Hall.

Shipley, D., Hooley, G. and Wallace, S. (1988) 'The brand name development process', *International Journal of Advertising* 7(3):253–266.

Brand personality

Brands can be conceived as clusters of functional and emotional values. Rather than consumers thinking about these (which they infrequently do), they use the concept of brand personality to appreciate the brand's characteristics in terms of the type of personality it radiates. The visual cues associated with a brand plus communication help establish a brand's personality.

Particularly for conspicuously consumed brands, consumers use brands to communicate an aspect of their personality through the brand's personality. This is only effective if the consumer's peer group is also aware of the brand's personality. In some situations, the brand personality can become a particularly important selection criteria. Barclaycard may project a personality of being middle class and easy to get on with while American Express could be conceived as being a sophisticated, well travelled and relatively well off personality. When a successful consultant has a lunch meeting with a client and pays the bill, they may select their American Express card to reinforce their personality.

People choose brands just as they do their friends; they like to feel comfortable with what they stand for. People have a perception about their actual personality, the personality they would like to have (ideal) and also the personality they like to portray in the company of others (social self). According to the extent to which the brand is conspicuously consumed and whether a consumer is with other people, so their brand choice is influenced by these three perceptions of their self.

A clear brand personality leads the consumer to anticipate a particular type of relationship with the brand. Brand marketers have the opportunity to influence consumers' views about a brand through its personality, but they need to ensure this leads to a valued relationship. For example, an airline may have worked hard to develop its brand personality as knowledgeable, innovative and forward thinking, yet some travellers may shun it as they may perceive their relationship with the cabin crew during the flight might make them feel intimidated. **LdeC**

References

Blackston, M. (1992) 'A brand with an attitude: a suitable case for treatment', *Journal of the Market Research Society*, 31(3):231–241.

de Chernatony, L. and McDonald, M. (1998) *Creating Powerful Brands in Consumer, Service and Industrial Markets*, Oxford: Butterworth-Heinemann.

Elliott, R. (1994) 'Exploring the symbolic meaning of brands', *British Journal of Management*, 5(June): 131–144.

Brand positioning

Markets are becoming increasingly competitive and consumers are being bombarded with large numbers of brand messages. Good positioning facilitates instant appreciation of the brand's functional capabilities to the extent that the consumer recognizes what the brand does better than competing brands. Thus some might argue that Volvo is positioned as safe cars and BMW as high performance cars.

If a brand positioning is to be effective it should:

- communicate what the brand is particularly good at
- capture the understanding of consumers
- act as a purchasing stimulus
- differentiate the brand from competitors
- provide direction for staff.

Marketers face the problem of 'overpositioning', where consumers may have too narrow a perception of what the brand stands for. As a high quality jewellery retailer, consumers may perceive that Tiffany does not stock rings costing less then £3 000, yet this is far from the case.

Some organizations use brand positioning to communicate that they are striving to strengthen the brand. Avis is famous for its positioning of being the number two car hire firm, majoring upon 'we try harder'.

Over time markets change and thus firms 're-position' their brands, to fit new circumstances. For example, the RAC has repositioned itself from being a breakdown service to a company that helps people stay on the road. Its web site (www.rac.co.uk)

provides considerable information about road conditions and suggested travel routes.

There are numerous positioning alternatives. One is to major upon a particular consumer benefit, for example Sony stands for innovation, yet Bang and Olufsen stands for design. Another option is to position against a key competitor, as Pepsi does against Coca Cola. Yet another alternative is to position with respect to a particular product class, for example 'I Can't Believe It's Not Butter'. **LdeC**

References

Aaker, D. (1996) *Building Strong Brands*, New York: The Free Press.

de Chernatony, L. and McDonald, M. (1998) *Creating Powerful Brands in Consumer, Service and Industrial Marketing*, Oxford: Butterworth-Heinemann.

Rossiter, J. and Percy, L. (1996) *Advertising Communications and Promotion Management*, New York: McGraw-Hill.

Trout, J. and Steve, R. (1995) *The New Positioning*, New York: McGraw-Hill.

Brand strategy decisions

Brand strategy decisions in essence entail answering the following questions.

- What envisioned future does the brand wish to bring about?
- What is the brand's purpose?
- What values will the brand be true to?

An envisioned future should be about 10 years ahead. This stops incremental thinking and encourages scenario thinking. Microsoft envisions a future in which there will be a PC on every desk and as a result is striving to overcome barriers to make this become a reality. The Orange mobile telephone envisions a future when all people will have a phone number that goes with them wherever they are, so there are no barriers to communication. Their future is a wirefree environment in which you call people, not places.

Brand purpose is about the brand's reason for existing. It is taken for granted that the brand has to make a profit since profits, like oxygen, food and water, are necessary conditions for existence. A good example of a brand's purpose is from Federal National Mortgage Company whose brand exists to strengthen the social fabric by continually democratizing home ownership. A powerful brand purpose guides and inspires staff and is the response to the question 'why don't we sell this brand off?'

The third question – what values will this brand be true to? – entails corporate soul searching. This necessitates identifying the type of behaviour the brand would condone. The Cooperative Bank has as one of its core values ethical banking and does not associate itself with countries or organizations that have acted in an immoral way. The Virgin corporation has being a challenger as one of its values. One of its criteria for entering a new market is whether it considers consumers are getting a fair deal and if not can Virgin challenge the existing status quo to improve consumers' well-being? **LdeC**

References

Collins, J. and Porras, J. (1996) *Built to last*, London: Century.

de Chernatony, L. (1998) 'Developing an effective brand strategy', in C. Egan, and M. Thomas (eds) *The CIM Handbook of Strategic Marketing*, Oxford: Butterworth-Heinemann.

de Chernatony, L. (1999) 'Brand management through narrowing the gap between brand identity and brand reputation', *Journal of Marketing Management*, 15(1–3):157–180.

Hamel, G. and Prahalad, C. (1994) *Competing for the future*, Boston: Harvard Business School Press.

Brand values

Brands can be considered as being clusters of values. Effective brand differentiation is about building a cluster of values unique to a particular brand and ensuring these are relevant and welcomed by consumers. One of the most widely accepted definitions is that from Rokeach (1973), i.e. a value is an enduring belief that a specific mode of conduct or end-state of existence is personally or socially preferable to an opposite or converse mode of conduct or end-state of existence.

Virgin's values include quality, innovation, value for money, fun and sense of challenge. By contrast, the values of British Airways include safety, honesty and being innovative, responsible, team-spirited and caring. From these brand values these organizations have developed integrated brand strategies, aiming to ensure that at every point of contact, staff's behaviour should be consistent with the brand values. A clear example of this is the different philosophies these two airlines have about the in-flight service.

There are different ways of categorizing a brand's values, one of which is functional versus emotional values. With advances in technology it is more difficult to sustain a brand's functional values.

Values influence behaviour. By making staff aware of their brand's values, organizations help staff appreciate how they should act to project the brand's values. This is particularly important in the case of brands relating to services rather than products, where the customer-facing staff is seen as being the brand and yet, because of the variability of human nature, it is difficult to ensure consistent staff behaviour. By continually enabling staff to understand their brand's values, they can decide how they should act in different situations when resolving consumers' problems.

When considering issues such as 'can the brand be stretched to encompass a new product?' (for example extending the brand from cameras to photocopiers) organizations look at the values of the parent brand and the proposed brand extension, and if there is tension between the two sets of values, they would devise a new brand name. **LdeC**

References

de Chernatony, L. and McDonald, M. (1998) *Creating Powerful Brands in Consumer, Service and Industrial Marketing*, Oxford: Butterworth-Heinemann.

Durgee, J., O'Connor, G. and Veryzer, R. (1996) 'Translating values into product wants' *Journal of Advertising Research*, 36(6):90–99.

Reynolds, T. and Gutman, J. (1988) 'Laddering theory, method, analysis and interpretation' *Journal of Advertising Research*, 28(February–March): 11–31.

Rokeach, M. (1973) *The Nature of Human Values*, New York: The Free Press.

Branding

This is the establishment and formal registration of a product or service name, usually with a distinctive logotype (logo), which can include a brand mark or trade mark or trade name. This is done in order to preserve the brand's distinctive identity and differentiate it from similar products or services on the market.

The extent to which the brand name is recognized by potential buyers is termed 'brand awareness', which means that the manufacturer or service provider must make the brand stand out through some kind of product or service attribute or promotional activity. Companies seek to establish positive brand attitudes in order that customers will prefer the promoted brand to competing brands. The purpose of branding is to signify and maintain consistency of quality and service, and the goal is to attempt to make consumers 'brand loyal' so they make repeat purchases. Branding is a tangible service or product characteristic containing verbal cues. This can help customers to identify the product or service and influence their choice.

Without branding, product or service choice would be indiscriminate, because purchasers would have no conviction that they were purchasing what they really needed. Branding also assists when judging quality, as a strong brand name conveys confidence that it is backed up by what is perceived to be a large organization. It is also helpful when launching a new product that carries the same brand name as purchasers will already be familiar with the name.

'Manufacturer brands' are those brands that are owned and controlled by manufacturers. 'Private brands', or 'own label brands' are owned by retailers or wholesalers. These brands are goods bearing the retail group's specific logo. 'Generic brand' is a term that signifies the product or service category, not a specific company. These are sometime called 'economy brands' as they appear in stark lettering and do not carry any promotional support, with the basis of consumer appeal being low price. **GL**

Reference

Kotler, P. (1994) *Marketing Management, Analysis, Planning, Implementation and Control*, 8th edn, New Jersey: Prentice Hall pp. 444–446.

Budget allocation for promotion

Budget allocation is the process of assigning costs and incomes to specific activities or areas of activity. Budgets can be calculated in at least three ways: the objective and task approach, the competitive parity approach and the percentage of sales approach. The objective and task approach begins by deciding what is to be achieved and then goes on to calculate what expenditure will be necessary to reach the goal. In the competitive parity approach the budget is set at a level which matches competitors' spending on the activity. This method is often used for setting promotional budgets. The percentage of sales (or percentage of margin) approach, which sets the budget according to a percentage of the firm's sales (Blasko and Patti 1984).

The percentage of sales approach is regarded as dangerous because it reverses the logic of promotional spending; the implication is that sales will cause promotion, rather than the other way round. The effect is that falling sales will lead to falling spending, which in turn further depresses sales.

Competitive parity has the advantage of maintaining the status quo between the firm and its competitors, but suffers from the drawback that the firm is allowing its competitors to decide its budgets.

The objective and task method is probably the most customer-orientated of the approaches, since it involves deciding what will need to be done if the firm is to succeed in the marketplace, rather than relying on competitors' views of what is currently happening in the marketplace, or on passively waiting for the marketplace to dictate the budget. The difficulty lies in deciding how the objectives can be reached, and in being sure that the budget is sufficient to cover the tactical costs of reaching the objective. A further difficulty often lies in persuading company accountants to accept this method; many accountants feel uneasy about agreeing to such apparently open-ended arrangements. **JWDB**

Reference

Blasko, V.J., and Patti C.H. (1984) 'The advertising budgeting practices of industrial marketers' *Journal of Marketing*, 48(Fall): 104–110.

Budgeting and resource allocation

A budget is a quantitative plan of action that aids in coordinating and controlling the acquisition, allocation and utilization of resources over a defined time period.

The marketing budget reflects the integration of the various marketing interests into a programme that all have agreed is workable in attempting to attain marketing objectives.

Budgetary control works through the formal organization, viewing it as a series of responsibility centres and attempting to isolate the performance measurement of each centre from the effects of the performance of others.

Budgeting is more than just forecasting: it involves the planned manipulation of the key variables that determine marketing performance in an effort to arrive at some preferred future position. In this way budgets help give form to alternative courses of action by measuring (predominantly in financial terms) the inputs and outputs of specific marketing strategies. A project or activity may begin as someone's bright idea but this cannot be implemented unless there is a clear specification of the inputs required to bring the idea to fruition and the outputs that may be expected to follow. The budget is a means whereby the inputs and outputs associated with a future course of action can be expressed with reasonable precision in financial terms.

Other analytical techniques to help in allocating marketing resources include marketing experimentation and mathematical programming. One particular form of experimentation that can be used in conjunction with marketing budgets is sensitivity analysis. This indicates the extent to which outcomes are sensitive (i.e. subject to change) in response to variations in particular inputs, and which inputs can be varied with little impact on outputs. Mathematical programming is a form of analytical modelling which seeks to determine the optimum allocation of effort (i.e. resources) in situations involving clear objectives and specified constraints. **RMSW & CTG**

References

Duffy, M.F. (1989) 'ZBB, MBO, PPP and their effectiveness within the planning/marketing process', *Strategic Management Journal*, 10:163–173.

Mantrala, M.K., Sinha, P. and Zoltners, A.A. (1992) 'Impact of resource allocation rules on marketing investment-level decisions and profitability', *Journal of Marketing Research*, 29:162–175.

Piercy, N.F. (1986) *Marketing Budgeting*, London: Croom Helm.

Sevin, C.H. (1965) *Marketing Productivity Analysis*, New York: McGraw-Hill.

Stasch, S.F. (1972) *Systems Analysis for Marketing Planning and Control*, Glenview, Ill: Scott, Foresman.

Wilson, R.M.S. (1999) *Accounting for Marketing*, London: Thomson Learning.

Business to business direct marketing

On the one hand business markets can be thought of as being easier to target than consumer markets because there are fewer businesses than there are consumers. The Standard Industrial Classification database provides lists of companies in the type of business that might be relevant for some sort of direct contact. Other databases can also be used, such as KOMPASS, which lists companies according to SIC code, size, number of employees and so on.

On the other hand the direct marketer also needs to know about the buyers, influencers, decision makers and users within the organization's buying behaviour 'decision making unit' (DMU). The type of purchase category needs to be investigated as well: is it a repeat purchase of a 'nuts and bolts' nature, a modified rebuy in the sense of some change in specification or a completely 'new task' purchase. Clearly more people will be involved in the purchasing process as the category of purchase moves towards 'new task'. Also, more information will be needed by those involved in the process so there are opportunities for business to business marketers to develop a relationship marketing strategy that might last beyond the immediate, complex purchase, increasing the likelihood of the subsequent routine buying of supplies from the same company.

To develop these relationships, every contact should be used to add more to the database in terms of personal details and preferences of each DMU member. Even non-task information will be useful, such as eating preferences (which will smooth the way at business lunches and supplier organized conferences).

Electronic Data Interchange (EDI) already makes routine buying simpler because stock levels are automatically communicated to suppliers and delivery details can be similarly automated. The Internet is adding momentum to this approach but also providing new relational opportunities between buyers and sellers. Indeed, some of the origins of the new relationship marketing paradigm were in organizational buyer and seller networks.

A final consideration is strategic integration of buying and selling organizations, such as the sharing of consumer loyalty card database information between super-markets and their fast moving consumer goods (fmcg) suppliers, in order for synergy to lead to growing categories of product, not just specific brand or product lines. **MJE**

Reference
McDonald, W. (1998) *Direct Marketing: An Integrated Approach*, Irwin: McGraw-Hill, ch. 15.

Buying behaviour

In order to understand the buying behaviour of consumers, there is a need to explore the factors that affect the buying process. How consumers make decisions to buy a product or service will determine their buying behaviours. Consumer decisions on what to acquire, when to acquire, how much to acquire and from whom are factors influencing their buying behaviours. Consumers' usage and disposition decisions are also key issues to consider. These decisions are influenced by psychological, cultural and social factors. When a consumer wants to purchase a product or service, his or her buying decisions will depend on the motivation, ability and opportunity to purchase. These factors influence what information consumers are exposed to, how they perceive things, how they receive and interpret information, how they form and change their buying attitudes, and how much they remember and retrieve information that may affect their future purchase decisions.

Buying behaviour can be a complex process because it involves psychological, social, and cultural elements, which interact and integrate to influence consumers' decisions. It is important to recognize the existence of a multitude of factors influencing buying behaviours, which have to be dealt with effectively because such knowledge can provide useful inputs to marketing strategies and guide marketing decisions on product, pricing, distribution and promotions. **RM-R**

Reference
Assael, H. (1998) *Consumer Behavior and Marketing Action*, Cincinnati, Ohio: South-Western College Publishing.

Buying process

The buying process that consumers go through is influenced by a multitude of factors, including psychological and cultural ones. The first step is the consumer recognizing that there is a need that has to be satisfied or a consumption problem that requires a buying solution. This leads the consumer to seek information that will enable him or her to determine where to go, how much to spend and when to buy. Such information search may lead the consumer to consult many information sources. He or she may talk to friends, reads magazines, newspapers, or books, consult expert advisers, or even watch TV or listen to the radio. The consumer will also assess his or her financial situation.

Based on the information that has been gathered, the consumer will then judge the viability of the purchase. The decision on whether or not to buy may be taken within a short period or the consumer may take a long time before deciding. This will depend on the type of products or services being considered, and other external and internal factors that may influence the purchase. For example, the consumer's psychological state, such as his or her attitudes and perception will influence the decision. External factors in the form of cultural influences, e.g. ethnicity and religious values, will also affect the buying decision. Once a buying decision has been made, the consumer will evaluate whether the outcome has met his or her expectations and led to satisfaction or whether the decision was a wrong one. This evaluation will influence future buying decisions. The buying process is described in the figure below. **RM-R**

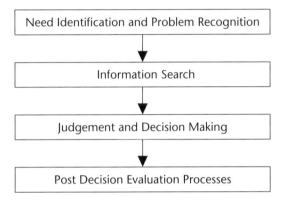

Figure: **Buying process**

References
Assael, H. (1998) *Consumer Behavior and Marketing Action*, Cincinnati, Ohio: South-Western College Publishing.
Solomon, M.R. (1996) *Consumer Behavior*, Englewood Cliffs, NJ: Prentice Hall Inc.

Campaigns

Campaigns are collections of marketing communications activities focused to achieve specific goals. In essence, marketing communications tend to be implemented around a succession of campaigns. A campaign may feature a particular marketing communications element such as an advertising campaign or a public relations campaign or it may be an integration of elements. The campaign will feature a common theme or message; frequently it will be based around the short to medium term of up to a year, but there is no reason why a campaign could not be planned over an extended period. Campaigns may run in parallel, each achieving its own goals, and as one campaign ends another will be planned to take its place so that marketing communications will be continuous (see 'Marketing communications planning'). **DWP**

Reference
Pickton, D.W. and Broderick, A. (2001) *Integrated Marketing Communications*, London: Financial Times Prentice Hall, chs 4, 5 and 6.

Catalogue selling

In catalogue selling the retailer uses an illustrated book rather than an in-store display as the vehicle for conveying product information and facilitating the customer choice process. The catalogue's layout, presentation and design are devised to attract attention and encourage browsing. It also has to give sufficient detail to ensure accurate ordering and minimize the likelihood of product returns. Catalogues may be made available within showroom type stores, via direct mail or through a system of agents.

In the UK the *agency* catalogue sector is dominated by the 'Big Five', namely GUS, Littlewoods, Freemans, Grattan and Empire. Their catalogues are more than a 1000 pages and feature a relatively homogeneous product mix, with around one third women's fashion. A 14 days free returns policy is the norm and on average approximately 30 per cent of goods are returned. *Direct mail order* catalogues, such as Next Directory and the Marks and Spencer catalogue have formed an entry point for branded retailers into catalogue selling as a parallel channel to existing store operations. This segment is growing as it meets the needs of skilled professional convenience-oriented consumers. The competitive response from the agency sector has been the introduction of a wide range of designer and branded goods, as illustrated by the example of Littlewoods, who entered a joint venture with Arcadia to make High Street fashion available via its catalogue. Fifty per cent of the Littlewoods catalogue pages now feature branded goods.

There are substantial price differences between the different channels. Agency catalogue prices, which are set to include a bundle of benefits such as interest free credit and free delivery and returns of unwanted items, are least competitive, with levels often 15-20 per cent higher than equivalent High Street prices and up to 30 per cent more than direct books. Consequently the market for the 'big books' is relatively static. Traditionally aimed at the lower socio-economic groups, they are underperforming the market as a whole, as the emphasis is shifting towards the more upmarket, financially sophisticated and time-pressed consumer. **RAS**

References

Baron, S., Davies, B. and Swindley, D. (1991) *Macmillan Dictionary of Retailing*, Macmillan Reference Books, London: Macmillan.

Corporate Intelligence on Retailing (1998) *Home Shopping in the UK*, London: CIR.

Mintel (1998) *Home Shopping, Special Report*, London: Mintel International Group.

Channel design

In recruiting intermediaries, the manufacturers are essentially selecting their channel partners, who are going to participate in distributing their goods and services. This is the vital ingredient in creating a channel design. A channel design can be defined as those decisions involving the development of new marketing channels or as alterations to existing channel structures. It is quite common to equate channel design with the term 'channel structure' although designing distribution channels is concerned with the decision making tasks when appropriate channel partners are selected.

In designing the distribution channel, it is important to consider specific needs of the target market and develop appropriate distribution objectives to meet those needs. Only then can channel strategies be developed and specific channel structures and channel partners be selected. When developing possible channel structures, the channel decision maker needs to consider the number of distribution levels, the intensity of distribution coverage and the types of intermediaries to be used at each level of the distribution channel. The number of distribution levels may vary from two to four. In a two-level channel, the manufacturer is going direct to the customers without using any intermediaries. A three-level channel is when the manufacturer decides to use one intermediary, while a four-level channel is when two intermediaries are used. The decision on the number of distribution levels may be influenced by factors such as the nature and size of the market, availability of intermediaries and financial constraints.

The intensity of distribution coverage refers to the number of intermediaries at each level of the distribution channel. This may range from intensive coverage to exclusive coverage. When extensive distribution is required, a large number of intermediaries will be involved in the distribution activities. On the other hand, if the channel strategy calls for selective distribution, then only a few qualified distributors will be selected to participate. The selection of the types of intermediaries to use is dependent on their different functions. Wholesalers, for example, may perform various wholesaling tasks and some may specialize in specific distribution functions. Limited function wholesalers such as jobbers and mail order wholesalers offer only specific functions. Full function wholesalers, on the other hand, may provide various services ranging from delivery to financing of the goods they are distributing. As such, in designing the channel structure, the channel decision maker has to consider several strategic factors. **RM-R**

References

Bowersox, D.J. and Cooper, M.B. (1992) *Strategic Marketing Channel Management*, Singapore: McGraw-Hill International Editions.

Little, R.W. (1970) 'The marketing channel: who should lead this extra-corporate organisation?', *Journal of Marketing*, 34(January): 31–38.

Channel functions

A distribution channel operates through the execution of several basic functions, which include carrying of inventory, physical distribution, ordering and selling, financing and promotional functions. Each function has to be performed either by the manufacturers themselves or by one or more of the channel intermediaries. There may be situations when the same functions are performed at more than one level of the marketing channel. Manufacturers and wholesalers, as well as retailers, for example, may carry inventory. It is important to ensure that duplication of channel functions will not lead to an excessive increase in distribution. It is, however, viable to have duplication of functions if it can be shown that this will ensure that goods and services can be delivered to target segments at the right quantity, time and place.

It is common to associate channel functions with the movement of activities in distribution channels. Functions that are performed in sequence by channel members are termed as 'flows'. All the flows or functions in a distribution channel are indispensable where at least one channel intermediary within the channel structure must assume responsibility for each of them. The use of specific channel intermediaries to carry out these functions is related to the concept of specialization, where individual intermediaries are more likely to excel in the implementation of specific tasks through their experience, contacts or economies of scale. It is therefore pertinent that there is coordination among channel members so that functions and flows performed by different channel members will be carried out consistently and move the members towards achieving common distribution objectives. **RM-R**

References

Mallen, B.E. (1973) 'Functional spin-off: a key to anticipating change in distribution structure', *Journal of Marketing*, 37 (July): 18–25.

Stern, L.W., El-Ansary, A.I. and Brown, R.J. (1989) *Management in Marketing Channels*, New Jersey: Prentice Hall International Editions.

Channel intermediaries

Channel intermediaries may comprise a multitude of organizations, including wholesalers, retailers, logistic companies, transport agencies, financial institutions, advertising agencies and other relevant organizations that play important roles in ensuring the movement of goods or services through the distribution channel. These intermediaries have specific functions to perform and they are often dependent on one another to carry out the distribution activities. The interdependency between channel intermediaries is a distinctive characteristic of many distribution channel structures. Because of this interdependency, many distribution channels are often viewed as systems where sets of interrelated and interdependent components are engaged in producing an output. It is easy to look at distribution channels as comprising two subsystems – commercial and consumer. It is the commercial subsystem upon which channel intermediaries are located. In the commercial subsystem, firms involved in the distribution tasks are vertically aligned in moving the products or services into the consumer subsystem.

Intermediaries perform several important functions that contribute to increasing the efficiency of the exchange process between manufacturer and consumer. The number of intermediaries and how they are arranged within a channel structure are dependent upon the functional requirements of the distribution channel as well as economic factors. The existence of channel intermediaries helps in adjusting the quantities and assortments produced by the manufacturer to those required by the consumers. The existence of wholesalers, for example, helps in breaking bulk where large quantities of the products purchased from the manufacturers are broken into smaller units as required by the consumers. In addition, assortments are created when retailers offer a number of different manufacturers' products in their retail outlets. In essence, intermediaries help in facilitating the exchange process between buyers and sellers and in so doing, they increase the likelihood of channel efficiency.

Although it is stressed that channel intermediaries should function as an integrated distribution system, it is common to see channel intermediaries acting independently of one another. This is often the case in conventional channels, where isolated and independent firms perform traditionally defined sets of marketing functions. In a conventional distribution channel, intermediaries are often more concerned with the transactions that take place between them and their direct channel partners or with firms that are located immediately adjacent to them. In such cases, channel intermediaries are acting independently without much consideration to the overall channel performance. **RM-R**

References

Berman, B. (1996) *Marketing Channels*, New York: John Wiley & Sons.

Dwyer, R., Schurr, P.H. and Oh, S. (1987) 'Developing buyer-seller relationships', *Journal of Marketing*, 51(April): 11–27.

Stern, L.W., El-Ansary, A.I. and Brown, J. (1989) *Management in Marketing Channels*, New Jersey: Prentice Hall International Editions.

Channel pricing

In channel pricing, a company tries to account for price decisions at different channel levels simultaneously. This may be done in different ways, depending on channel structure, the allocation of power, the level of coordination and the availability of information on other members' price reactions. In integrated channels, prices at different levels will be set in concert and in the interest of the whole channel. In the absence of such complete coordination between the channel members, a company may still anticipate the other members' price reactions or deliberately influence their price setting (Lee and Staelin, 1997). For instance, a manufacturer can decide on the price he or she will charge to the retailer and at the same time formulate a 'suggested' retail price for the end consumer. Vice versa, a retailer may influence the manufacturer's price by extorting guaranteed profit margins, irrespective of the retail price (Krishnan and Soni, 1997).

In independent channels, there is often a conflict of interest. An example of such 'channel miscoordination' is the problem of double marginalisation. When a retailer with some monopoly power sets a high price to maximize his or her own profit and the manufacturer also seeks high profit, the margin for the entire channel – and thus the end prices to consumers – can become excessive. As a result, consumers who would be profitable clients for the integrated channel may be excluded (see Gerstner and Hess, 1995). In situations where such conflicts are important, improving channel coordination may constitute a relevant pricing objective. Specific pricing strategies may be required to overcome or attenuate these conflicts and lead to a fair allocation of profit within the channel. For instance, 'targeted pull' strategies, where the manufacturer offers a discount directly to price-sensitive consumers who then ask the retailer for the product, are a way to overcome double marginalisation (Gerstner and Hess, 1995). Profit sharing arrangements constitute another example of a conflict-resolving strategy. **KCa, BF, EG**

References

Gerstner, E. and Hess, J. (1995), 'Pull promotions and channel coordination', *Marketing Science*, 14(1):82–104.

Krishnan, T. V. and Soni, H. (1997) 'Guaranteed profit margins: a demonstration of retailer power', *International Journal of Research in Marketing*, 14:35–56.

Lee, E. and Staelin, R. (1997) 'Vertical strategic interaction: implications for channel pricing strategy', *Marketing Science*, 16(3):185–207.

Nagle, T.T. and Holden, R.K. (1995), *The Strategy and Tactics of Pricing: A Guide to Profitable Decision Making*, Englewood Cliffs, NJ: Prentice Hall.

Channel strategy

Planning a distribution channel requires a creative, well-executed strategy. A well-planned marketing channel can become a competitive advantage for a company and can enhance its ability to compete in the domestic as well as international market. Channel strategy is concerned with the overall process of planning, setting up and managing the operations of selected firms that are responsible for achieving the distribution objectives of the product or service.

In developing a channel strategy, channel decision makers commonly concentrate on relationships with their channel partners as well as the requirements of the target markets. Channel strategy that focuses on building long-term relationship with channel partners is likely to lead to a firm competitive advantage for the company. Such an advantage has long-term viability since building the relationships is a long process and is not a strategy that can be copied easily by competitors. Strong channel relationships can lead to better channel planning, as channel partners are more likely to collaborate on strategic issues and implementation of the strategies.

It is also important for channel decision makers to consider the wants and needs of target markets when developing channel strategies. Such a focus has been termed 'customer intimacy', where target markets are segmented precisely and distribution offerings are then tailored to match exactly the demands of the target segment. Channel strategy that is capable of capturing the exact requirements of target markets and of getting the right support from channel partners is more likely to succeed in achieving distribution objectives. **RM-R**

References

Treacy, M. and Wiersema, F. (1993) 'Customer intimacy and other value disciplines', *Harvard Business Review*, 71 (January–February) 84–93.

McCalley, R.W. (1992) *Marketing Channel Development and Management*, Westport, CT: Quorum Books.

Channels, evolution of

The evolvement of distribution channels is characterized by the rationale of having intermediaries as channel partners within the distribution structure. The emphasis here is on the economic rationale for distribution channels. Essentially, channels evolve through the need for specialized channel functions, which can be performed more efficiently by channel intermediaries. By breaking down a complex distribution task into smaller, less complex functions, and dividing them between intermediaries who specialize in particular functions, there is likely to be greater efficiency in the total distribution channel. The existence of specialization and division of labour among appropriate channel participants reflects the contribution of intermediaries in the evolution of distribution channels. In addition, channel intermediaries are responsible for facilitating the flow of goods and services as they move along the distribution structure. Through the execution of specialized functions, it is possible to increase efficiency through the development of routine activities. This enables manufacturers to maximize productivity through better planning of inventory, purchasing, warehousing and, ultimately, the execution of marketing tasks through the distributors. **RM-R**

References

Stern, L.W. and Brown, J.W. (1969) 'Distribution channels: a social systems approach', in L.W. Stern (ed.) *Distribution Channels: Behavioural Dimensions*, Boston: Houghton Mifflin Company.

West, A. (1988) 'Manufacturer/retailer relationships', in A. West (ed.) *Handbook of Retailing*, Aldershot, England: Gower.

Channels management

Marketing channels evolve through the participation of different intermediaries with varying functions. Coordinating these different functions to ensure the achievement of distribution objectives can be overwhelming. This is, however, a necessary task and the channel manager is responsible for managing the activities of all the different intermediaries within a distribution channel. Channel management can therefore be defined as the administration of a distribution channel to ensure the coordination and cooperation of all channel members to achieve the firm's established distribution objectives.

As distribution channels are made up of different firms with a tendency towards diverging objectives, it becomes necessary for the channel manager to have some set of controlling factors to make the distribution channel function smoothly and generate the maximum possible performance levels.

Managing the distribution channel requires a channel manager who is able to lead and motivate channel members. The channel leader should stress the interdependency of the channel network and how important it is to focus on relationship building. This is an important requirement in motivating channel members where the establishment and maintenance of firm relationships among channel members are stressed. Managing the distribution channel therefore builds on the channel planning process where decisions on the administrative patterns are made. For example, a channel manager needs to decide whether to have a tighter control of the distribution network through vertical marketing systems or to depend on loose distribution coalitions in the forms of conventional channels or administered channels. In vertical marketing systems the whole distribution network is operated by one firm thus rendering total control to that firm and ensuring unity of objectives. In the case of conventional channels there are individual firms with differing channel objectives. Administered channels exist when independent distribution intermediaries allow some form of control by the firm considered to be the channel leader through some distribution programmes essential in carrying out the distribution tasks.

Whichever administered patterns are selected, the main task of the channel leader in managing the distribution channels is to ensure that coordination and cooperation are maintained consistently. **RM-R**

References

Little, R.W. (1970) 'The marketing channel: who should lead this extra-corporate organization?', *Journal of Marketing*, 34(January): 31–38.

Mallen, B.E. (1969) 'A theory of retailer-supplier conflict, control and cooperation', in L.W. Stern (ed.) *Distribution Channels: Behavioural Dimensions*, Boston: Houghton-Mifflin Company.

Stern, L.W., El-Ansary, A.I. and Coughlan, A. (1996) *Marketing Channels*, 5th edn, New Jersey: Prentice Hall International Editions.

Checkout scanning and automated information capture

Scanning devices are used at the checkout counters of many retail outlets. Retailers that have scanner checkouts are able to record purchases made by their customers by using this laser scanner. This device reads the information that is embedded in the Universal Product Code (UPC), which is attached to a package or a product. The scanner will read this information as it is processed at the retailers' checkout, thus providing an automatic information capture. Scanner data includes information on all transactions including size, price and style of the product. All the scanner data on the purchase is stored in the retailers' computer and can be accessed instantly for analysis. Apart from information on prices, the scanner also registers and retains information on coupon use so that retailers can measure consumer response to using coupons. It can also include in-store information such as special displays. Information about shelf space and displays can be retained on these scanners, which can then be measured with respect to their impact on sales, turnover and net contribution. With scanners, it is now possible for retailers to obtain quick information about item movement for any particular period. This data is useful to control inventory, to determine the response to advertised specials, to assess changes in demand and to determine the sales effect brought about by altering shelf spaces. **RM-R**

Reference

Lusch, R.F. and Dunne, P. (1990) *Retail Management*, Ohio: South-Western Publishing.

Client and ad agency

It is generally accepted that about 80 per cent of all advertising expenditure in the UK passes to media owners via advertising agencies or specialist media-buying agencies. However, it does not follow that responsibility for campaign development and execution has been delegated in four cases out of every five, for the other 20 per cent is accounted for by a large number of small advertisers. It does indicate, nevertheless, that the client-agency working relationship is a major feature of the advertising business.

The onus for maintaining that relationship in good working order falls mainly on agency 'account handlers', the generic term for people in what is in effect the client-service function. They help their clients to refine the brief for a new campaign and interpret it from the agency perspective, and play a major role in translating it into separate briefs for the creative and media departments. In due course, they have the task of delivering the agency's campaign proposal to the client and justifying its rationale. There is no survey evidence to tell us how many iterations of the process take place before everything is agreed, but the probability of periodic tension is obviously high. Maintenance of a healthy working relationship depends on account handlers' skill in dividing time and loyalty between the agency that pays their salary and the client that employs the agency. One of them memorably summed this up to a class of students: 'Whenever I'm at the client's office, I must be the agency's man; back at the agency, I have to be the client's man.' The most effective exponents are thus diplomats, negotiators, facilitators, coordinators, organizers – and more besides. Only the worst actually deserve the routine disparaging descriptions, 'suits' and 'bag carriers'. A well known writer who was once a senior executive in the business gives an entertainingly anarchic yet balanced account of the relationship (Mayle, 1990).

The client-agency working relationship tends to have a shorter life than equivalents in other professions. Briggs (1993) reports evidence that more than three quarters last less than ten years. **KC & BZE**

References

Briggs, M. (1993) 'Why ad agencies must change', *Admap*, (January): 22.

Mayle, P. (1990) *Up the Agency: The Snakes and Ladders of the Advertising Business*, London: Pan Books.

Cognitive information processing

Psychologists over the years have sought to understand and model cognitive information processing and this has led to a greater understanding of how we make sense of the world around us. Marketing communications work only in that the audience, the receivers of the communication, is able to process the message. This is the 'decoding' activity referred to as part of the marketing communications process (see 'Marketing communications process'), it is how receivers make sense of the communication.

A large part of that sense making involves understanding the message through cognitive information processing, interpreting incoming stimuli through thinking and reasoning, through the 'mind'.

This view of 'people as thinkers' tended to dominate consumer behaviour research from its early beginnings to the late 1960s. Emphasis was given to the role of verbal information processing to the exclusion of the other senses (Holbrook, 1985). But this can be contrasted with comprehension that comes about through other means, through emotions and feelings, through the 'heart' rather than the 'head'. In reality, it is most likely that audiences respond to marketing communications as a mixture of both logic and emotion (Shimp, 1997) and marketing communications can be designed to make the most of appropriate appeals.

Research into cognitive information processing has allowed marketing communicators to understand the importance of certain attributes of the communication. For example, attention to the communication and how well it stands out not only affects *whether* it is noticed but also *how well* it is remembered (Webb, 1979). An understanding of selective perception of messages has revealed how important it is to make messages relevant and novel (Shimp, 1997). They are also more believable if delivered by personalities that the audience think of as trustworthy and credible (Perloff, 1993). Research has also shown that marketing communications have subconscious as well as conscious effects and messages are more likely to be believed if they are consistent with existing thoughts, experiences and preconceptions (Zimbardo and Leippe, 1991). **DWP**

References

Holbrook, M.B. (1985*) Consumer Research – Introspective Essays on the Study of Consumption*, CA: Sage.

Perloff, R.M. (1993) *The Dynamics of Persuasion,* NJ: Lawrence Erlbaum.

Shimp, T.A. (1997) *Advertising and Promotion and Supplemental Aspects of Integrated Marketing Communications*, 4th edn, Fort Worth: Dryden Press.

Webb, P.H. (1979) 'Consumer initial processing in a difficult media environment', *Journal of Consumer Research,* 6(December): 225–236.

Zimbardo, P.G. and Leippe, M.R. (1991) *The Psychology of Attitude Change and Social Influence*, New York: McGraw-Hill.

Collaborative strategies

A collaborative strategy is one in which two or more organizations or divisions of an organization work together to develop a mutually beneficial strategic outcome. Organizations may choose to collaborate with others for a number of reasons: to pool the resources needed to enter a particular market or to compete with an established powerful competitor, to exploit complementary technologies or competences or to realize significant cost savings through streamlining combined operations.

Collaborative strategies are often the product of formal strategic alliances between companies such as GEC Alsthom, which is a joint venture company set up to compete more effectively with Asea Brown Boveri (ABB), the world's largest electrical engineering group. Similar alliances have been formed between a wide range of companies to exploit complementary capabilities, technologies or market positions. Thus, for example, Sony and Apple Computer have formed a new joint multi-media company to develop miniaturized wire-less personal communication devices. Similarly, Motorola, IBM, Siemens and Toshiba have formed an alliance to develop the next generation of computer chips. The high cost and complexity of such research and development has been spread across the partners in this alliance. A further example of such collaborative ventures is the alliance between Guinness and LVMH, who have developed a series of distribution joint ventures around the world that have led to significant efficiency savings and marketing advantages for both companies.

Perhaps one of best examples of the value of collaborative strategies is the Japanese 'Keiretsu' economic grouping of firms that are organized around trading companies and or banks. Keiretsu are organized on the basis of common loyalty, reciprocity and complementarity. Their members may collaborate to help each other with procurement of cheap raw materials, share technology and market intelligence, and provide mutual financial support. Keiretsu may also pool resources to help the lead or front-line member company compete more effectively in their markets.

The development of successful collaborative strategies does, of course, require commitment by all parties. Without the commitment of sufficient management time, trust and respect, such collaborative ventures are likely to fail. Equally, successful longer-term collaboration may require a degree of flexibility as, if circumstances change, the objectives or priorities of the partners may change.

While collaborative strategies are intended to yield mutual benefits to the parties involved, they may also require sacrifices on all sides. Here again, unless there is a clear recognition of the commitment required and what each party wants from the agreement, there is a danger of the collaborative strategy breaking down. On the other hand, when managed effectively, collaborative strategies can result in significant synergies, particularly where organizations have complementary competences and resources which, when combined, can provide a significant source of competitive advantage. **DM**

References

Badarocco, J.L (1991) *The Knowledge Link: How Firms Compete through Strategic Alliances*, Boston, MA: Harvard Business School Press.

Jarillo.J.C. (1988) 'On strategic networks', *Strategic Management Journal*, 9(1):31–41.

Ohmae, K (1989) 'The global logic of strategic alliances', *Harvard Business Review*, March/April.

Thompson, J.L (1997) *Strategic Management: Awareness and Change*, London: Thomson Learning.

Commodities

Commodities can be defined as goods that are used in conjunction with, or in support of, more tangible products. They are items that are used in some kind of supporting capacity and, although not made by the same manufacturing process, the commodity is a natural complement to the main product in question. The commodity can be made by an original equipment manufacturer or by another company. An example is a print cartridge, which is the commodity in support of the main printer product. **GL**

Reference

Lancaster, G. and Reynolds, P. (1999) *Introduction to Marketing*, London: Kogan Page, pp. 179–181.

Competition

Competition is the result of firms attempting to offer similar bundles of benefits to the same target market.

Frequently managers take too narrow a definition of competition; competitive pressure can arise from firms who are not in the same industry, but do offer the consumer a similar bundle of benefits. For example, a cinema owner might correctly identify other cinemas as competition, but might easily fail to identify as competition a local pub that offers live entertainment. From the viewpoint of the consumer, both are offering an evening's entertainment, and therefore both are competing for the same expenditure. The consumer cannot spend the same evening (or the same money) in both the pub and the cinema, so a competitive conflict arises.

Types of competition are as follows.

- *Perfect competition.* There are a large number of suppliers, all selling almost identical products, and everyone in the market has full knowledge of what the other market members are doing. Such competition is extremely rare – one of the few examples is the international money market.
- *Monopolistic competition.* One major firm has a large share of the market, but other firms are able to enter. An example is the soft drinks market, which is dominated by Coca Cola, but not to the exclusion of other firms.
- *Oligopoly.* A few firms control the market almost entirely, either by direct collusion or by tacit agreement. This usually happens when cost of entry is high, as in the petroleum industry or the aircraft industry.
- *Monopoly.* A single firm has a product with no close substitutes. This is extremely rare, because this situation is often abused and government regulatory authorities try to prevent monopolies. In some countries government monopolies on electricity generation, telephone systems and railway systems do exist.

Monopolistic competition is probably the most common form of competition. In such markets, the lead firm's most effective approach is to try to increase the size of the total market; expanding market share by competing with smaller firms is usually much more difficult. From the viewpoint of the smaller firms, expansion of the total market will bring obvious benefits, but taking market share from the other small firms is also an effective strategy. Competing with the largest firm in the industry is difficult because of differing levels of available resources. **JWDB**

Reference
Hamel, G., Doz, Y., and Prahalad, C.K. (1989) 'Collaborate with your competitors – and win', *Harvard Business Review.*

Competition research

Information that is collected about competitors is commonly termed as 'competition research'. This type of research often falls under the category of a problem identification research and provides an important input in planning the marketing strategy. Quantitative facts about competitors, such as the size of their market, control of the market and sales data can be used to assess threats and opportunities that are present in the market. Often the marketing intelligence system of a firm, which is part of the marketing information system, collects information about competitors, which can be obtained through competitors' annual reports, press releases and advertisements. It is also possible to learn about competitors from watching what they do. By buying and analysing competitors' products, it is possible to determine the strength and weaknesses of their brands. Also, monitoring their sales and assessing what others say about them in business publications or at trade shows can provide marketers with pertinent information about competitors. **RM-R**

References
Porter, M.E. (1985) *Competitive Advantage: Creating and Sustaining Superior Performance*, New York: The Free Press.
Procter, T. (2000) *Strategic Marketing*, London: Routledge.

Competitive advantage

The aim of corporate, marketing or any other form of business strategy is to gain a 'competitive advantage'. The advantage over one's competitors may be within a market segment as with a niche or focus strategy or within the entire industry, e.g. by cost leadership. A competitive advantage allows a company to earn returns on its investment that are consistently above the industry average.

There are many ways in which a competitive advantage may be gained. The core competencies of the company are a possible source. The organization may excel in manufacturing techniques or through innovative research and development. Philips is an innovative organization and secures competitive advantage through its history of developing exciting new products, e.g. the compact disc and the DVD player. The competencies that provide advantage need to be nurtured to ensure they survive. In this way, they become part of the culture of the organization. Competitive advantage is gained not only through tangibles such as product quality, but through intangibles such as innovative marketing, e.g. Nike.

It is vital for success that competitive advantage is sustainable. The company may be able to offer something unique to the customer that provides it with an advantage or its internal processes may provide the advantage. In order to be sustainable it is important that competitors are not able to copy the source of competitive advantage. Where products or services within a market are homogeneous it may still be possible to gain competitive advantage through marketing communications strategy or via excellent customer service. Richer Sounds is an independent hi-fi retailer that claims competitive advantage because of its knowledgeable and friendly staff. The internal culture of the organization is geared to rewarding excellent customer service. Many organizations claim that they have a competitive advantage. Lynch (2000) provides three tests to measure whether it has been achieved. The advantage should be sufficiently significant to make a difference, sustainable against environmental change and competitor attack and be recognizable and linked to customer benefits. **SR**

References
Lynch, R., (2000) *Corporate Strategy*, 2nd edn, Harlow: Financial Times/Prentice Hall.
Porter, M.E., (1980) *Competitive Strategy*, New York: The Free Press.
Porter, M.E., (1985) *Competitive Advantage*, New York: The Free Press.

Competitive advantage matrix

As identified by many academics and practitioners, the purpose of any competitive strategy is to achieve a sustainable competitive advantage; one way of measuring whether the advantage is sustainable is through market share. The marketer must know what competitive strategies are open to the organization.

Porter (1980) put forward his competitive advantage matrix, which identified generic strategies, which he believes helps firms to achieve industry success by helping them to develop a market strategy that establishes their competitive position in the market.

This model provides a framework for the marketer when devising competitive strategy as it combines the target that the marketer has chosen – namely narrow or broad – and the competitive scope – i.e. low cost or differentiation.

Overall cost leadership strategy is where the business works hard to achieve lower

		Low Cost	Differentiation
Competitive Scope	**Broad Target**	Cost Leadership	Differentiation
	Narrow Target	Cost Focus	Differentiation Focus

Figure: **Competitive advantage matrix**
Source: Porter, M. (1985)

costs of production and distribution, so that the company must be good at engineering, purchasing, manufacturing, etc. Only one firm in a product market can follow this strategy successfully, e.g. Aldi, Netto.

Differentiation strategy is where the business concentrates on achieving superior performance in some important customer benefit area valued by the market as a whole. It can strive to be the service leader, the quality leader or technology etc. but not all of these. A company that has pursued this broad target strategy is the supermarket chain Sainsbury's.

The focus strategy is where the business targets on one or more narrow market segment rather than going after the whole market. The firm gets to know the needs of the segments and pursue either cost leadership or some form of differentiation within the target segment. Companies that have pursued this narrow target strategy include Morgan Cars and Land Rover.

Dangers arise when the company fails to pursue one of these strategies and instead is forced or drifts into a 'middle-of-the-road' position where the message to the market is confused and the likelihood of a successful competitive attack is increased. **CV**

References

Porter, M, (1979) 'How competitive forces shape strategy', *Harvard Business Review*, March–April.

Porter, M. (1980) *Competitive Strategy: Techniques for Analyzing Industries and Competitors*, New York: The Free Press.

Porter, M. (1985) *Competitive Advantage: Creating and Sustaining Superior Performance*, New York: The Free Press.

Competitive factors

Competitive factors are those issues that arise from the activities of other firms in the same industry, or those who are targeting the same market segment. In some cases competitive factors may represent threats, in others they can be turned to advantage; much depends on the definition of competition.

Competitive factors manifest themselves in the following ways.

- *Price setting*. Many firms use competitive pricing, in other words they price the products using the competitors' prices as a benchmark. This does not necessarily mean that the firm sets a lower price – since consumers often use price as a surrogate for judging quality, many firms will deliberately set their prices higher than their competitors in order to imply that the product is of a higher quality.
- *Product features and benefits*. Firms usually try to ensure that their products offer a

unique selling proposition (USP). This is an aggregate of the features that distinguish the product or the firm from its rivals by offering extra benefits to a specific target group of consumers.

- *Promotional activities*. Aggressive campaigns by competitors can make inroads into market share, so firms often need to make a rapid response to such campaigns. Sales promotions can be particularly damaging in the short term.
- *Creative approaches to distribution*. The advent of telephone banking (pioneered by First Direct) has forced other banks to respond in kind (Blythe, 2000).

Although firms should not allow their competitors to dictate policy, responses to competitive pressures are an inevitable part of maintaining market share; proactive attacks on competitors' market share are equally part of the marketer's brief, and are an unavoidable way of expanding business in situations where markets are stable or in decline.

Competitive factors are of lesser importance in growing markets; in rapidly-growing markets competition will often bring positive benefits, as competitor activities help in growing the overall market, to the benefit of all other firms in the market. JWDB

Reference
Blythe, J. (2000) *Marketing Communications*, London: Financial Times Prentice Hall.

Competitive strategy

Organizations need to develop competitive strategies to enable them to compete effectively in the industries or markets in which they operate. Here competitive strategy is sometimes referred to as 'business level' or 'business unit' strategy. Two dominant schools of thought have emerged as to how organizations can best develop effective competitive strategies – the 'positioning approach' and the 'resource-based or distinctive competences approach'.

The positioning approach dominated thinking during the 1980s and takes the organization's external environment as the starting point when determining strategies. Here the aim is to analyse the external environment to identify attractive market opportunities that the organization can successfully exploit and defend. Once such a superior market position has been attained it can provide a source of sustained profitability. However, such positions are rarely easy to attain, requiring careful analysis of the market and the mobilizing of strategic resources to secure and sustain a superior market position and thereby achieve competitive advantage. Here, it has been argued that there are only two routes to sustainable competitive advantage – through becoming the lowest cost producer in an industry or by differentiating products or services in ways valued by customers to a degree where they are willing to pay a premium price to acquire them. A third so-called 'generic strategy' can be adopted in that low cost leadership or differentiation can be applied on a broad industry-wide basis or to a narrow market segment, thus leading to a 'focused' low cost or differentiation strategy.

An alternative resource-based or distinctive competences school of thought has emerged during the 1990s, focusing not on the external market opportunities, but on the organization's internal strengths and resources. Here the route to sustainable competitive advantage is seen to lie in exploiting the difficult-to-imitate competences/capabilities or assets that organizations possess. Building up such distinctive competences can be a lengthy process but once acquired, they can be extremely difficult for competitors to imitate. Distinctive competences can be based around unique sets of skills, processes or knowledge that an organization has acquired, or access to particular assets that an organization owns. One danger with such competence-based strategies is that it may be difficult for organizations to switch to other competences if those they possess are no longer in demand. Hence, from this perspective, it is advisable first to develop the unique competence and then find or create a suitable market for them, rather than attempting to follow the whims of the market. In short, the approach is that of selecting the market position to fit with the organization's resource base. **DM**

References

Porter, M.E. (1980) *Competitive Strategy: Techniques for Analyzing Industries and Competitors*, New York: Free Press.

Porter, M.E. (1985) *Competitive Advantage: Creating and Sustaining Superior Performance*, New York: Free Press.

Prahalad, C.K. and Hamel, G. (1990) 'The core competence of the corporation', *Harvard Business Review*, May/June: 79–91.

Stalk, G., Evans, P, and Schulman, L.E. (1992) 'Competing on capabilities: the new rules of corporate strategy', *Harvard Business Review* March/April: 57–69.

Consumer behaviour, future developments in

The area of consumer buying behaviour has been expanded over the years to include several different types of consumers. It is no longer appropriate to focus solely on end-users when other types of consumers have distinct preferences that should also be given due consideration. There is a need to expand understanding of consumer buying behaviours to include suppliers, environmental groups, government organizations and the marketers' own employees. The focus towards establishing firm relationships among channel partners implies that marketers have to be sensitive to the needs of all relevant groups within the marketing channel structures. By establishing closer relationships with these different groups, the marketer will be prepared and more able to identify and respond to the changes in the environment, both internally and externally.

Recent developments in the use of advanced technology in marketing products and services have prompted marketers to re-evaluate the focus on consumer buying behaviours. How consumers react to the use of e-commerce and the Internet as a buying medium should be given emphasis because of its implications for consumer buying behaviours. Are consumers likely to behave differently when shopping through the Internet? Indeed, the Internet is seen as a powerful marketing tool that is likely to transcend various marketing boundaries.

The focus on environmental issues in marketing is also likely to be given greater emphasis in understanding consumer buying behaviours. Social and environmental changes are contributing to the growth of consumer movements with strong social principles now influencing consumption patterns. It will be difficult for marketers to ignore the impact of such strong views by the new breed of consumers seeking more than just basic satisfaction of needs. This is indeed a challenge that marketers of today have to face in understanding the many groups of consumers and their distinctive buying behaviours. **RM-R**

References

Solomon, M.R. (1996) *Consumer Behavior*, Englewood Cliffs: Prentice Hall Inc.

Consumer behaviour models

A model of consumer behaviour traces the relationship between the marketers and the consumers. Consumer decision making involves the process of evaluating, assessing and deciding about brand choice. This process is influenced by marketing strategies developed by business organizations. Consumer buying choices are influenced by both internal and external factors. The individual consumer or group of consumers has specific needs that have to be satisfied, and demographic characteristics, lifestyles, and personality characteristics may influence brand choice. In addition, environmental influences in terms of culture, social influences and marketing organizations will also play important roles in influencing consumer buying choices. Essentially, the consumer behaviour model outlines the characteristics of the consumers and the influences, either internal or external, that affect consumer buying responses. A simple model of consumer behaviour is presented in the figure below.

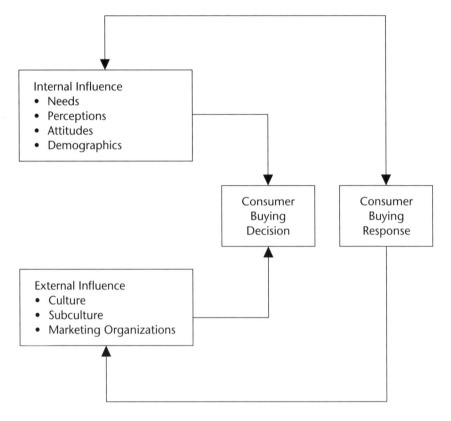

Figure: **Model of consumer behaviour**

Another, more complex model relates consumer behaviour outcomes with the process of buying decisions and the influence of psychological and cultural factors. This model is presented below.

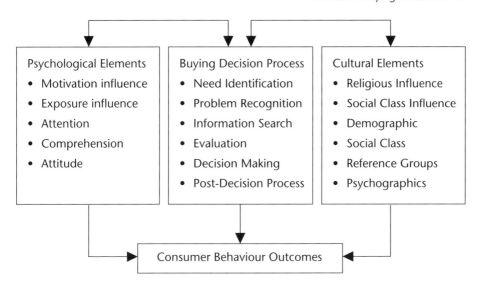

Psychological Elements	Buying Decision Process	Cultural Elements
• Motivation influence • Exposure influence • Attention • Comprehension • Attitude	• Need Identification • Problem Recognition • Information Search • Evaluation • Decision Making • Post-Decision Process	• Religious Influence • Social Class Influence • Demographic • Social Class • Reference Groups • Psychographics

Consumer Behaviour Outcomes

Figure: **Consumer behaviour model 2**

There may be other models that look at consumer behaviours but essentially the focus of most of them is to look at both internal and external elements affecting consumer buying responses. What is most important is to understand how these elements interact and the impact they have in influencing consumer buying decisions. **RM-R**

Reference
Solomon, M.R. (1996) *Consumer Behavior*, Englewood Cliffs, NJ: Prentice Hall Inc.

Consumer buying behaviour

Consumer buying behaviour looks at the processes involved when individuals or groups assess information, select, acquire, use and then dispose of products or services that meet their needs and wants. This behaviour involves more than just purchasing or acquiring a product or service. The processes of using and disposing of the product or service are also important considerations. The whole process of selecting, purchasing, consuming and disposing can occur over time in a dynamic sequence. A product that has been selected and acquired will be used and then disposed of when there is no longer a need for it. This then will set the stage for another sequence of future buying behaviour.

Consumer buying behaviour often involves many people who may have different roles in the process. For example, in purchasing a personal computer, one or more family members might take the role of information gatherer and collect as much relevant information as possible about possible brands to purchase. Other family members might be the ones who influence the outcome of the decision. The purchaser may be another family member while the user could be another person or more than one member of the family. Finally, several family members may be involved in disposing of the computer when it is no longer needed.

What can be gathered from the consumer buying process is that different people may be involved in the process. The purchaser and user of a product need not necessarily be the same person, and the decision maker and purchaser may be different individuals. It is critical for a marketer to understand not only the different processes involved but also the different 'actors' who are playing different roles in the processes. Appropriate marketing strategies must be planned taking into consideration these processes and the people involved in them. **RM-R**

References

Hoyner, W. and MacInnis, D. J. (1997) *Consumer Behavior*, Boston: Houghton Mifflin Company
Solomon, M.R. (1996) *Consumer Behavior*, Englewood Cliffs, NJ: Prentice Hall Inc.

Consumer loyalty and sales promotion

Over the last 20 years there has been a steady and measurable decrease in our loyalty to specific brands. Several reasons have been suggested for this, including a narrowing of the actual and perceived differences between leading brands and a significant increase in the quality and credibility of retailers' own-brands. Sales promotion has been blamed for decreasing brand loyalty, by critics who argue that customers can become conditioned to buy only those goods which are on 'special offer'. It is equally easy to argue that sales promotion growth is simply a symptom, rather than a cause, of declining consumer loyalty. If brand loyalty is not enough to motivate consumers to purchase, then offering them 'something extra' can clinch a sale. The effect of a promotion on consumer loyalties will vary among customers and according to the nature of the promotion and the market. There are some consumers who will regularly switch brands to take advantage of different promotions. This has led to the emergence of concepts such as the 'Deal-prone consumer' and the 'Coupon-prone consumer'.

Critics of sales promotion tend to concentrate on price-based, value-increasing promotions and their ability to erode consumer loyalty, but not create it. However, a number of promotions are clearly geared towards generating loyalty. This could be as simple as including 'money off next purchase' coupons on packages, or something much more complex, such as offers requiring the accumulation of tokens, or clubs such as Marriott Hotel's 'Honored Guest' scheme, or frequent flier schemes. Value adding promotions often encourage consumers to collect things, either for themselves or for others to create repeat purchases. In South America, Savoy Brands issued 700 million character milk bottle caps for children to collect during 1995-1996. In the UK, Sainsbury's 1999 School Rewards campaign saw 758 000 customers register to collect points for 20 000 participating schools. **KP**

References

Davies, S., Inman, J.J. and McAlister, L. (1992) 'Promotion has a negative effect on brand evaluations – or does it? Additional disconfirming evidence', *Journal of Marketing Research*, 29(1):143–148.
Grover, R. and Srinivasam, V. (1992), 'Evaluating the multiple effects of retail promotions on brand loyalty and brand switching segments', *Journal of Marketing Research*, 29(1):76–89.

Consumer tracking studies

The impact of a marketing campaign carried out by a firm is often monitored by means of a consumer tracking study, whose main purpose is to evaluate and assess the advertising campaign. The study tries to understand why an advertising campaign may be working well or may not be effective. It evaluates the effectiveness of the campaign especially in terms of awareness, preferences and usage patterns. It is common for most tracking studies to trace aspects of advertisement awareness, brand awareness, beliefs about brand attributes, brand image, occasions of use and brand preference. Marketers are especially interested in knowing how the campaign is affecting their brands.

It is quite common for marketers to conduct tracking studies by using survey research methods or customized tests that are specifically developed to ascertain the effectiveness of the marketing campaign. The assessment can be carried out in the period before and after the campaign. Information generated from tracking studies will enable marketers to evaluate their promotional strategies and, if necessary, to take corrective actions to improve the campaign. **RM-R**

Reference
Kumar, V., Aaker, D.A. and Day, G.S. (1999) *Essentials of Marketing Research*, New York, John Wiley & Sons.

Consumerism

Consumerism is a belief (accompanied by action) in the need to establish the consumer as the principle force in company activities. The term also refers to the growth in consumer power in markets.

Consumerism began in the late 1950s and early 1960s in the United States, initially in response to a series of accidents involving dangerous products. The view expressed at the time was that firms were putting profits ahead of safety, and therefore the shareholders and directors were being advantaged at the expense of consumers. Consumerism has since become established as one of the driving forces behind the marketing concept; consumers expect to be treated fairly, given good value for money and not to be sold dangerous or defective goods. (Bloom and Greyser 1981)

The principal mechanisms through which consumerism manifests its influence are as follows.

- Lobbying governments to encourage the passing of laws protecting the consumers from dishonest or dangerous practices by firms (the UK government has a Minister for Consumer Affairs whose role is apparently to champion consumers).
- Public debate through the newspapers and television.
- Legal action through pressure groups and watchdogs to compel firms to change their behaviour.
- Radio and TV programmes and press columns devoted to consumer affairs.

Consumerism is often seen as essentially adversarial, and being concerned with forcing companies to comply against their will; in fact, the idea of giving consumers value for money and meeting their needs is central to the marketing concept. The result of 40 years of consumerism has been a welter of legislation and regulation of companies' activities, but at the same time there has been a raising of corporate consciousness about the importance of looking after consumers. **JWDB**

Reference
Bloom, P.N. and Greyser, S.A. (1981) 'The maturing of consumerism', *Harvard Business Review*, (November–December): 130–139.

Convenience goods

These are commonly needed purchases where buying takes little effort or thought on the part of the buyer. They are everyday necessities, of which the purchaser has prior knowledge, that are bought on a regular basis. Advertising is important for marketers as they must attempt to persuade customers to purchase their particular brand rather than just purchase the generic product. Examples are toothpaste, washing detergent, coffee and potato crisps.

Staple convenience goods are products that are required for daily consumption, and here it is more difficult for marketers to differentiate between brands. Examples are milk and sugar which, unlike coffee, are used in a greater variety of cooking and drink-making processes. **GL**

Reference

Lancaster, G. and Reynolds, P. (1999) *Introduction to Marketing*, London: Kogan Page, pp. 179–181.

Convenience stores

A convenience store is a small shop – less than 3000 sq. ft – trading seven days a week, for extended opening hours and selling a wide assortment of goods to meet immediate consumer needs.

Convenience stores were first developed in the USA by the Southland Corporation, who during the 1930s developed the 7-Eleven concept. The term encompasses various types of small shops serving the needs of a local community, such as traditional corner shops, historically CTN (i.e. confectionery, tobacco, newsagents) or off-license based shops, as well as some petrol forecourt shops. In the UK convenience shops are largely used for occasional distress purchases and for regular purchases of conventional 'CTN' products, i.e. confectionery, lottery tickets, newspapers and cigarettes. Men use convenience stores more frequently than women.

During the 1990s UK convenience retailing has undergone a transition, with the previously dominant independents losing out to multiples who are able to gain cost advantages from the economies of scale available from operating a network of stores. This has been accompanied by increasing affiliation of independents to 'symbol groups' such as Spar and Londis, who offer similar advantages through shared fascias and economies of bulk buying whilst allowing independent store owners to remain self-employed. Mostly because of consumer concerns about high prices, limited product range and poor quality of fresh foods, traditional convenience stores have failed to attract consumers' secondary shopping expenditure. However, this may be overcome by creating a distinct selling proposition and the sector remains highly attractive, as illustrated by the rapid growth of Alldays, which by 1998 was the largest UK convenience retailer, the heavy investment of the larger cooperative societies and experiments by the dominant grocery retailers in this sector (e.g. Tesco Express and Sainsbury's Local). Partnerships, such as the BP/Safeways petrol station supermarkets and the Alldays/Victoria Wine line-up, are another promising development for the sector. **RAS**

References

Barnes, S. and Dadomo, S. (1996) *Convenience Retailing: Profiting From Growth*, Watford: IGD Business Publications.

Baron, S., Davies, B. and Swindley, D. (1991) *Macmillan Dictionary of Retailing*, London: Macmillan Reference Books, Macmillan.

Corporate Intelligence on Retailing (1996) *Convenience Stores in the UK*, London: CIR.

Mintel (1999) *Convenience Retailing*, London: Mintel International Group.

Cooperative societies

Founded in 1844 with a store opened by the Rochdale Pioneers and since then expanded worldwide, the cooperative movement is governed by the principles of a cooperative ethos, including democratic control and the distribution of surplus profits to members. Cooperatives form an important element of retail trade in several European countries, e.g. Switzerland, Finland and Denmark.

In the UK growth for the sector stopped after World War II and, following consolidation via a series of mergers, in the late 1990s there were 51 cooperative societies operating in 10 main product sectors – food, funerals, garages, household, milk, travel agents, farms, insurance, household goods and optical/chemist.

Cooperative retailers hold approximately 4 per cent (and declining) share of UK retail sales, and mostly operate on a regional basis. Fifty per cent of the sector is in the hands of the two main societies, the Co-operative Wholesale Society (CWS) and Co-operative Retail Services (CRS). Both operate nationwide, with their core business in food retailing.

During the 1990s a number of cooperative societies, such as the CWS and CRS, heavily invested in convenience stores, hoping to capitalize on the community appeal of the cooperative concept and philosophy. However, they were disadvantaged by archaic structures, resulting in duplication of effort, ineffective marketing, overall underperformance and a disjointed retail offering. This caused positioning problems. Reputed to have failed to keep pace with retail developments, coops are commonly viewed as catering to the older or disadvantaged consumer. Competitive developments include the recent rationalization of the CWS achieved by selling off factories and the packaging business. The CWS has also been proactive in its trials of a dividend loyalty card, which capitalizes on own brands by linking generous rewards exclusively to 'co-op' branded purchases. The proposed merger between CWS and CRS would facilitate the creation of a single brand, supported by a streamlined structure with a view to shedding superstores and acquiring additional convenience outlets, thus enhancing competitiveness. **RAS**

References
Baron, S., Davies, B. and Swindley, D. (1991) *Macmillan Dictionary of Retailing*, London: Macmillan Reference Books, Macmillan.
Birchall, J. (1994) *Co-op: The People's Business*, Manchester: Manchester University Press.
Davis, P. and Donaldson, J. (1998) *Cooperative Management: A Philosophy for Business*, Cheltenham: New Harmony Press.
Institute of Grocery Distribution (1999) *CWS, Account Management Series*, Watford: IGD.

Core product

The core product refers to the package of benefits that the purchaser expects from a product or service. For instance, a lunchtime sandwich is normally purchased for nutritional reasons, but its taste is equally important to the consumer so this also is part of the core benefit. This core benefit does not include packaging as this does not satisfy the need of hunger or the psychological requirement for a tasty sandwich. **GL**

Reference
Lancaster, G. and Reynolds, P. (1999) *Introduction to Marketing*, London: Kogan Page, pp. 179–181.

Corporate image

Corporate image is the perception of a company held by its audiences. This may not be a single image as it may differ between its various stakeholders or publics. Employees may perceive the company differently to its customers, who may see it differently to its investors and shareholders. Corporate image will have an impact on brand images and vice versa.

Corporate image should not be confused with corporate identity even though the terms are used interchangeably (see 'Image building'). Unlike corporate identity, corporate image is not changed easily. It is the perception left in the minds' of the audience and may be affected not only by what the company does but also by a host of other factors that lie outside its control. 'The reality is that images 'belong' to the observers, not to the 'owners'' (Crosier, 1990).

Corporate identity is about the use of 'cues' that lie in the company's control (although they may not always be used well) to influence its image. This is very much the remit of corporate and marketing communications and involves a variety of communication 'tools' such as signage and livery, letterheading and company stationery, corporate advertising, public relations activities, internal communications, annual reports, logos and slogans. Corporate identity practitioners are quick to counsel managers that identity programmes should accurately reflect the corporate personality if a credible corporate image is to be achieved. Simple cosmetic changes are unlikely to be effective, especially in the longer term. **DWP**

Reference
Crosier, K. (1990) 'Corporate image' in M.J. Baker *Macmillan Dictionary of Marketing and Advertising*, 2nd edn, London: Macmillan.

Creative organizations

One can divide the characteristics of organizational creativity into four distinct elements (the four Ps of creativity).

- *People* – teams or individuals
  The creative process is very dependent on social interaction, which takes the form of face-to-face encounters. The make up of teams, the various roles and responsibilities that are assigned to members and the various experiences they can bring to bear are therefore critical factors influencing the creative output. The most significant insights (e.g. those that lead to innovative new products or uses for new technology) are often characterized by a synthesis of information from multiple domains, which can be both as far apart as physics is from social anthropology, or as close as neighbouring branches of psychology.
  Those involved need to possess a strong interest in the subject matter, curiosity and intrinsic motivation.

- *Processes* – how ideas are developed and innovation accomplished
  Strands of thought need to be synthesized, which means that there has to be:
  - a thorough knowledge of one or more domains
  - a thorough immersion in a field that practices the domain
  - attention on a problematic area of the time
  - free time for incubation that allows insights to emerge
  - ability to recognize an insight as one that helps to resolve the problematic situation
  - evaluation and elaboration of the insight in ways that are valuable to the field or domain.

  In addition it is important to provide opportunities for testing insights, to develop their consequences.

- *Place* – creative environment
  Perhaps this is the one to receive the least attention. An organization concerned with creating a climate that influences effective creative activity should provide at least the following:
  Resources: these should be appropriate and sufficient.
  Security: adequate salary and security of job tenure
  Trust: allow for mistakes;
  Reward/recognition: feedback, recognition and reward.

- *Product* – the output of the creativity
  This can take many forms, ranging from products and processes to new ideas or insights into problems.
  One cannot treat each one of the four Ps in isolation from the other. They are inter-dependent. **TP**

Reference

Ford, C.M. and Gioa, D. A. (eds) (1995) *Creative Action in Organizations*, London: Sage.

Creative strategies in distribution

The evolution of distribution channels is a widespread phenomenon. Traditional retailers are developing new channels such as different store formats for different occasions, experimenting with home-shopping and direct delivery and developing their customer focus. At the same time, many manufacturers are looking for the opportunity to develop a dialogue with the consumer through direct sales, dedicated stores and other retailing concepts.

The trend is towards making a shopping trip an experience to savour. The latest stores in the United States aim to offer the customer experiences that are so vivid that retailers could probably charge admission for them. This contrasts strongly with the traditional view of supermarkets that has been the norm in both Europe and the USA for the past 40 years. For decades, grocers have assumed that good design means helping shoppers get in to and out of a market as quickly as possible. The accent has been not only on one stop convenience shopping but on getting it done as quickly as possible. Long aisles placed side by side, grocers have argued, make it easy for customers to find what they came for and then head speedily to the cash registers. The new trend, however, involves having no aisles. Instead, merchandise runs along a single path that winds through the building. Despite a few escape routes along the way, shoppers have little choice but to walk past every section of the store. One organizational benefit of this layout is that it allows more shelf space than a standard layout and brings to the attention of the customers all the goods that the supermarket has to offer.

Distribution is often regarded as the Cinderella of the marketing mix elements but it does offer considerable scope for creative thinking to improve its effectiveness. TP

Reference

Evans, M. and Moutunho, L. (1999) *Contemporary Issues in Marketing*, London: Macmillan.

Creative strategy

The formulation of creative strategy is a matter of arriving at a set of words and images capable of communicating an advertising message to a specified target audience. Authoritative descriptions of the process by which that happens are elusive. Interesting expert discussions of advertising creativity are to be found in two edited collections of papers from the Institute of Practitioners in Advertising (Butterfield, 1997) and the Account Planning Group (Cooper, 1977), but they do not collectively define the means to the end. This shortfall contrasts markedly with an abundance of literature dealing with the outcomes of creative planning, such as edited collections of winning submissions for the Creative Planning Awards in Britain (Account Planning Group, 1993, 1995, 1997). These can at least yield some insights into the processes involved.

Creative strategy development begins with clarification of communication objectives, key messages and target audiences. It is likely that the creative planning team will next 'apply lateral, disruptive thinking to the problem', in the words of a partner in a prominent London advertising agency. This somewhat mystical activity does not feature at all in the advertising literature, but will probably include 'brainstorming', 'blue skies groups' and various other techniques commonly applied to new-product development process (Kotler, 1997). The raw results may then be subjected to the discipline of scrutiny against a research-based analysis of probable audience responses, typically contributed by the 'account planner' on the planning team. The survivors are refined into more precise communication concepts, then converted into creative executions. Evans (1988) provides an expert description of the craft, which produces the words and pictures, and melds them into finished advertisements and commercials.

The planning team may take the precaution of pre-testing these on a sample of the target audience, or may decide to trust the creative development process and back their own judgement. Once the campaign has run, it would be extremely unusual not to conduct a post-test of effectiveness, the findings of which can be held as an input to the next cycle of creative strategy development. **KC & BZE**

References

Account Planning Group (1993, 1995, 1997) *Creative Planning > Outstanding Advertising*, vols 1–3, London: Account Planning Group.

Butterfield, L., (ed.) (1997) *Excellence in Advertising: The IPA Guide to Best Practice*, Oxford, Butterworth-Heinemann, chs 4, 7 and 8.

Cooper, A., (ed.) (1977) *How to Plan Advertising*, 2nd edn, London: Cassell, chs 4, 5 and 6.

Evans, R.B. (1988) *Production and Creativity in Advertising*, London: Pitman.

Kotler, P. (1997) *Marketing Management, Analysis, Planning, Implementation and Control*, 9th edn, Englewood Cliffs, NJ: Prentice Hall, pp. 313–315.

Creative thinking, blocks and barriers of

Individual blocks arise from personal bias. Jones (1987) identified four types of blocks.

- *Strategic*: one right answer approaches, inflexibility in thinking.
- *Value*: over-generalized rigidity influenced by personal values.
- *Perceptual*: over-narrow focus of attention and interest.
- *Self-image*: poor effectiveness through fear of failure, timidity in expressing ideas, etc.

This approach has resulted in training applications that centre on personal feedback and counselling, including suggestions for the most appropriate mechanisms for developing improved skills. Strategic blocks can be challenged through creative problem solving training. Values, however, are a more difficult problem – but creating an awareness of personal values in the individual offers some respite. Perceptual blocks can be freed through observation and self-image blocks can profit from assertiveness training.

Some of the organizational blocks are:

- emphasis on managerial control
- short range thinking – a tendency to give priority to quick returns with financially measurable results
- analysis paralysis – ideas are often overanalysed and time is lost along with any competitive advantage
- rigid hierarchical structures – an unpredictable environment requires a responsive organizational structure
- tendency to look for one project that is likely to generate a big payoff, rather than a number of smaller projects with small to medium payoffs; good small projects can thus often be overlooked
- market versus technology-driven product planning – an over-emphasis on market research
- pressure to achieve and do more with fewer resources
- lack of a systematic approach to innovation
- the belief that some people are creative and others are not.

Ways of dealing with such blocks include:

- encouraging prudent risk taking
- freedom of thought – some degree of autonomy
- linking rewards with specific performance
- encouraging different viewpoints on problems
- positive involvement of top management
- continual flow of ideas
- responding positively to new ideas. **TP**

References

Jones, L.J. (1987) 'The development and testing of a psychological instrument to measure barriers to effective problem solving', unpublished MBSc dissertation, Manchester Business School.

Proctor, T. (1999) *Creative Problem Solving for Managers*, London: Routledge, ch. 2.

Creativity

Creativity occurs when we are able to organize our thoughts in such a way that readily leads to a different and even better understanding of something. If we try to do things in the same way as they have always been done in the past this can lead to difficulties in a business environment that is experiencing rapid cultural, economic or technological change. Change is an ever-present phenomenon to which businesses of all kinds are forced to respond if they want to stand the best chance of survival and prosperity. The rapid growth of competition in business and industry is often given as a reason for wanting to understand more about the creative process. Many firms experience pressure continually to enhance old systems, processes and products. Growth and survival can be related directly to an organization's ability to produce (or adopt) and implement new products or services, and processes. Marketers need to discover ways to solve new problems that have few or no precedents and hence fewer tried and tested ways of approaching them with the anticipation of reaching a successful outcome.

Creative thinking benefits all areas and activities of marketing. It is required to dream up better ways of marketing goods, to find new ways to motivate people, and so on. Typical marketing problems requiring creative thinking are:

- how to employ staff time more effectively in the pursuit of marketing activities
- how to improve a product's appeal to customers
- how to appeal to customers' wants and needs
- how to identify new and profitable product-market opportunities.

Problems that require creative thinking are 'open-ended' problems for which there is not just one solution. They are to be found in all aspects of marketing and especially in relation to setting policies and decisions with respect to the marketing mix. **TP**

Reference

Proctor, T. (1999) *Creative Problem Solving for Managers*, London: Routledge.

Creativity and innovation

To remain competitive in the business world firms need to keep abreast of innovation. Innovation applies to both products and processes and each one is inextricably bound to the other. Organizations need to be constantly on the lookout for new products and services and more efficient and effective ways of delivering them. Technology plays a large role in enabling organizations to achieve this end. Underpinning the innovative process is creativity and in particular the ability to come up with original inventions and practical ideas.

Innovation requires vision, change, risk and upheaval and is not performed for its own sake. There has to be a driving force compelling the organization to develop the systems, resources and culture needed to support innovation. In today's environment of rapid change that driver is survival. The purpose of innovation is to find better ways to satisfy customers while meeting the needs of all other stakeholders associated with the organization and creating a financially viable organization.

Innovative thinking needs to permeate an organization and it is a skill needed by every member of the enterprise. It comprises the ability constantly to look for new possibilities, generate ideas, think productively, make sound decisions and gain the commitment needed for rapid and effective implementation of ideas. Innovation considers the whole system for creating solutions to problems. It needs a diverse, information and interaction-rich environment: people with different perspectives working together toward a common objective, with accurate, up-to-date information and the proper tools are the only source of innovation. It benefits from a risk-tolerant environment since the creation of anything new involves risk and the possibility of failure. It involves and rewards every member of the organization.

Innovation is an on-going process and it requires a continuous scan of future trends and a preparedness to learn. It is only by creating an environment where every member of the organization is continuously learning more about its products, services, processes, customers, technologies, industry and environment that an organization can continuously innovate in a successful manner. **TP**

Reference
Rickards, T. (1999) *Creativity and the Management of Change*, Oxford: Blackwell.

Creativity in marketing communications

Integrated marketing communications and an increased reliance on highly targeted communication methods such as direct mail, speciality interest magazines, cable TV, sponsorship of events, and alternative media such as video cassettes, CD-ROM and messages via the Internet lead to a greater demand for creative thinking in marketing communications. There is also a constant need to find new ways of stimulating consumer interest in a brand and this often demands considerable effort in terms of creative thinking.

Virtually every situation where marketing communications are employed demands the use of stereotyping. The creative challenge is to devise stereotypes that lead to positive evaluation of the message by the majority of the audience. Not only is accurate stereotyping an important dimension to any marketing communications but the nature of the message must have unique properties. The communicator has to work out what to say to the target audience to produce the desired response. Many marketers advocate promoting only one benefit to the market. One view is that a company should develop a unique selling position for each brand and stick to it. Not everyone agrees that single-benefit positioning is always best. Double benefit positioning may be necessary if two or more firms are claiming uniqueness or being the best on the same attribute. And there are even examples of triple attribute positioning. All of this calls for creative thinking, which benefits from good marketing research information.

Developing a message strategy means taking the basis of the competitive edge and communicating it to prospects in the most forceful way possible. Once a message strategy has been decided upon, the next step is developing an audience strategy. The 'message strategy' has to do with *what* to say while the audience strategy has to do with *how* to say it. It is in this area of audience strategy that creative thinking comes to the fore. **TP**

Reference
Proctor, T. (1999) 'The need for research into creativity in marketing', *Creativity and Innovation Management*, 8(4):281–285.

Creativity in marketing research

Data mining is the new buzzword in market research. In making use of what is traditionally viewed as secondary sources of information, the researchers analyse direct marketing company records to build up an in-depth picture of the lifestyles of millions of consumers. In the course of doing this new ways of segmenting markets based on lifestyles and attitudes are being discovered, and ways of translating market research into market action are being implemented more quickly and effectively. The speed of analysing such research enables market researchers to offer high-quality tailored research packages to small firms that previously could not have afforded professional market research.

Another area where market research is being revolutionized is through the Internet. The use of this medium can improve both response rates and the speed of response. On one Web-based project 160 out of 400 respondents replied to an e-mail survey within three hours. It would have taken days or even weeks to obtain this kind of response using a more traditional approach, for example, normal postal services. An additional advantage is that such surveys cost around one-third of the price of telephone surveys. Currently most of this research is being conducted in the United States, where more people are connected to the Internet than is the case in Europe, but eventually Web-based research is expected to outperform all other methods of conducting surveys.

The relatively new activity of category management has also thrown up new challenges for market researchers. What this means in practice is that manufacturers and retailers need to cooperate in managing certain product categories, rather than concentrating solely on brands. Increasingly, the business community is becoming more information-orientated. In a constantly-changing world, the need for up-to-date and accurate information is more important than ever before, and market researchers are using (and seeking) new tools for collecting and analysing that information. **TP**

Reference
Nuttall, C. (1996) 'Research needs more creativity', *Marketing Week*, 29(April): 32.

Creativity in products

The virtual world of cyberspace and the pseudo worlds of theme parks, hotels and heritage centres typify 'hyperreality'. It involves the creation of consumption sites and marketing phenomena at any geographic place that are more than real. The Valley of the Kings, for example, might be recreated in a theme park near a European capital city. In some respects this would be superior to the real thing since the negative aspects of the original would be absent – extreme heat for example. Hyperreality offers the customer previously new, creative and innovative experiences. While at the turn of the century such opportunities are relatively limited in scope there seems little doubt that they can be developed in all kinds of different ways in the future. The whole concept of shopping may be adapted to the needs of providing a 'hyperreal' experience. For example, if one wants to try out the experience of the bazaars in the Near East, why should it be necessary to travel all the way to places such as Istanbul?

Reversed production and consumption reflects consumers' loyalty to images and symbols that they produce while they consume. Because symbols keep shifting, consumer loyalties cannot be established. Consumers become relatively unpredictable in their behaviour and this becomes the issue as far as providing goods and services to satisfy the wants and needs of customers. The shifting nature of the symbolism of consumer wants and needs promotes the belief that marketers might conclude that consumers do not know what they want but only what they do *not* want. What is symbolic today may not be symbolic tomorrow or if it is it may symbolize something that is undesirable as far as consumers are concerned. Marketers need to be able to predict what will be a fashionable symbol tomorrow and, equally important, when tomorrow will be. The saying that tomorrow never comes is not something that marketers should accept unchallenged. **TP**

References

Brown, S. (1999) 'Postmodernism: the end of marketing', in D. Brownlie, D.M. Saren, R. Wensley, and R. Whittington *Rethinking Marketing*, London: Sage, pp. 27–57.

Proctor, T. (2000) *Strategic Marketing*, London: Routledge.

Rogers, E. (1995) *Creating Product Strategies*, London: Thomson Learning.

Critical success factors

Critical success factors are those elements in the marketing plan that will determine whether the objectives will be reached. There may be other elements that will help the process along or contribute towards other aims or objectives, but failure to achieve one or other of the critical success factors will mean that the plan itself will fail.

Identifying the critical success factors is therefore a necessary part of all marketing planning and implementation. Sometimes the critical factors will be interdependent, in which case the firm may need to draw up a critical path analysis, to show the order in which objectives need to be achieved.

Critical success factors can be determined by examining customer needs. For example, in product design one critical success factor is that the core product must meet the consumer's basic needs. The augmented product must meet needs that are currently unmet by competing products in the same market, and so forth. **JWDB**

Reference

Kotler, P., Armstrong, G., Saunders, J. and Wong, V. (2000) *Principles of Marketing*, 2nd European Edn, Harlow: Prentice Hall, p. 96.

Cultural and social factors

Cultural and social factors are those issues relating to the shared beliefs, values and behaviours of a recognizable group of people. Cultural factors relate to aspects such as religion, language, institutions, beliefs and customs which are shared by members of a society. Social factors are about the ways people relate to each other within the overall cultural umbrella: family structures, expectations and obligations between friends, and accepted ways of behaving.

Culture is important to marketers because it helps in predicting how particular groups of individuals will behave in a given set of circumstances. Examples of marketing mistakes caused by cultural insensitivity are legion: using brand names which are humorous or obscene in the foreign language, products which offend against local religions, inappropriate use of colours on products (in Japan, the colour of mourning is white, for example).

Marketers often try to do business in countries where there is a degree of psychological proximity – British firms often seek to do business in the United States despite the fact that France is much nearer, largely because the UK and USA are culturally more similar than the UK and France. For the same reason, Spanish firms often prefer to do business in Latin America.

Marketers need to be wary of ethnocentrism – the tendency to believe that one's own culture is the 'right' one, and everybody else's is either a poor imitation of the 'right' one or is actually mistaken in its beliefs. (Shimp and Sharma, 1987) **JWDB**

Reference

Shimp, T. and Sharma, S. (1987) 'Consumer ethnocentrism: construction and validation of CETSCALE', *Journal of Marketing Research*, 24(August): 280–9.

Culture and sub-culture

Culture is defined as shared patterns of behaviour embedded in shared values, beliefs, meaning and understanding of a given group of people (Meyerson and Martin, 1987; Bate, 1984). It is essentially a set of socially acquired values that society accepts and which is then transmitted to its members through language and symbols (Assael, 1998). These values may have a very strong impact on members' consumption patterns. In a number of Asian countries, for example, cultural values dictate the importance of the extended family, which in turn influences the purchasing and consumption pattern of households. A typical Asian household may consist of a father, mother, children and the grandparents all under one roof. Therefore, it is common for marketers to plan their marketing strategies to include such extended family units.

Within a culture, there may be a broad group of people with similar values that distinguish them from society as a whole. This is called a 'subculture'. Subcultures can be delineated in terms of age, region, religious affiliation or ethnic identity (Assael, 1998). For instance, ethnicity can be considered a subculture when we divide the British society into English, Asians and Africans. Each of these ethnic groups has distinct consumption patterns, which may be different from one another. It is important for marketing organizations to define these subcultures precisely and develop marketing strategies capable of meeting the needs of each. **RM-R**

References

Assael, H. (1998) *Consumer Behavior and Marketing Action*, Cincinnati, Ohio: South-Western College Publishing.

Bate, P. (1984). 'The impact of organizational culture on approaches to organizational problem-solving', *Organization Studies*, 5, (1):43–66.

Meyerson, D. and Martin, J. (1987) 'Cultural change: an integration of three different views', *Journal of Management Studies*, 24(6)(November): 623–647.

Customer acquistion

Although it usually costs more to acquire a new customer than to retain an existing one, organizations can't rely on existing customers staying with them for ever, new customers are also needed. Acquisition strategies include:

- using promotional media such as direct response TV, radio and press, which have some form of response mechanism, to encourage potential customers to make contact, either for further details or to make a purchase
- using an 'identikit' approach. Here, the characteristics of existing (best) customers are determined by profiling the customer database. For example, a mail order wine business could profile its best customers (according to recency, frequency and monetary value of their purchases) and profile these on the basis of (say) geodemographics. Perhaps four geodemographic categories are found to be especially prominent and the wine company can then provide a mailing list of others within these categories, either nationally or within a more concentrated geographical location.

It is possible to calculate how much can be devoted to acquiring new customers.

Suppose the selling price of a directly distributed computer is £1 000, its cost of production is £600, order handling is £40, p&p is £20 and the desired profit is £250. Costs total £660 so the 'contribution' is £340. If the selling price is £1 000 and the sum of costs and profit for the average sale is £910 (£660 costs + £250 profit) then the allowable cost to acquire a customer is £90 (£1 000 – £910).

If the mailing costs are £26 000 and we allow £90 per order, we then need to get 289 sales (26 000 ÷ 90). If the mailshot is to 28 000 people a response rate of 1.03 per cent will be required. With a 'contribution' of £340 we can divide this into the cost of the promotion (£26 000) to identify the break-even point (76 orders in this case). This analysis can be done for different selling prices and different promotional campaigns and shows again how direct marketing can be measurable and accountable (O'Malley *et al.*, 1999). **MJE**

Reference

O'Malley L., Patterson M. and Evans, M. (1999) *Exploring Direct Marketing*, London: Thomson Learning, ch. 4.

Customer focus

At the heart of the marketing orientation is customer focus, which is demonstrated when the organization recognizes that the central driving force behind its activities is the customer. Marketing orientation needs to be adopted at a strategic level and become an organization's driving strategy. Organizational top management should support customer-orientated views and integrate marketing and customer focus into the strategic planning process. Achievement of customer orientation and integration of marketing throughout the organization require internal commitment.

Piercy and Morgan (1990) suggest that marketing should not be confined to the external market of customers but must be practised internally within the organization in order to make the external marketing strategies work. The key rationale is the creation of an internal environment in which customer consciousness becomes an organizational imperative. The foundation of an internal marketing programme is the belief that the creation of happy customers is dependent on the satisfaction of employee needs. Based on that, the two programmes should be closely related and the internal marketing programme should parallel and match the external marketing programme.

The core aim of traditional marketing is to match the needs and wants of an organization to those of the environment within which it has to operate. Internally, the marketing function is responsible for the promotion and selling of customer-orientation throughout the organization (Kotler and Andreasen 1991). In doing that it deals with internal and external markets where the success in the latter is dependent on success in the former. **IPD**

References

Kotler, P. and Andreasen, A.R. (1991) *Strategic Marketing for Non-Profit Organizations*, Englewood Cliffs, NJ: Prentice Hall.

Piercy, N. and Morgan, N. (1990) 'Internal marketing: making marketing happen', *Marketing Intelligence and Planning*, 24:82–93.

Customer satisfaction

At the heart of the marketing orientation are customer orientation and satisfaction. The marketing concept suggests that organizations should focus their operations and efforts on identifying customer needs and profitably satisfying them. Kotler (1997) defines satisfaction as: '... a person's feelings of pleasure or disappointment resulting from comparing a product's perceived performance (or outcome) in relation to his or her expectations).

Clearly, satisfaction is a function of perceived performance and expectations. Different factors influence customers' expectations, for example their past buying experience, their friends' opinions and marketers' information. Customers' expectations, perceived organizational performance, competitors' performance and customer satisfaction become the focus of measuring and monitoring efforts. More and more organizations recognize that customer satisfaction contributes to building and sustaining a competitive advantage. It can be used as a marketing tool in order to improve an organization's position in the market place. Customer focused organizations aim at achieving customer satisfaction in order to create customer loyalty.

In achieving customer satisfaction, it is paramount that the organization's staff practise a strong customer orientation. There is a need to motivate and train employees to recognize the external customers' needs and undertake the necessary actions to satisfy them (Irons, 1997). Satisfied employees make for satisfied customers (Zeithaml and Bitner, 1996; George, 1977; Kotler and Armstrong, 1996). The rationale is that satisfied people will perform better.

The focus on internal customers and internal customer satisfaction has been labelled 'internal marketing' (Ballantyne, 1996). Many organizations have recognized that the needs of internal customers must be fulfilled before the needs of external customers can be satisfied.

Internal customer satisfaction is especially important to the success of a service organization since very often the service provider becomes part of the service delivered to the external customers. Tansuhaj *et al.* (1991) argue that service organizations are in a better position to satisfy their external customers by designing internal products that satisfy the needs of their internal customers. If employees are viewed and treated as internal customers this will lead to high quality service to external customers through effective marketing behaviour by customer oriented people. **IPD**

References

Ballantyne, D. (1996) 'Internal networks for internal marketing', 4th International Colloquium in Relationship Marketing, Swedish School of Economics, Helsinki, Finland, pp. 1–27.

George, W.R. (1977) 'The retailing of services – a challenging future', *Journal of Retailing*, Fall: 91.

Irons, K. (1997) *The World of Superservice: Creating Profit through a Passion for Customer Service,* London: Addison-Wesley Publications.

Kotler, P. (1997) *Marketing Management: Analysis, Planning, Implementation, and Control*, 9th edn, New Jersey: Prentice Hall International Editions.

Kotler, P. and Armstrong, G. (1996) *Principles of Marketing*, New Jersey: Prentice Hall International Editions.

Tansuhaj, P., Randall, D. and McCullough, J. (1991) 'Applying the internal marketing concept within large organizations: as applied to a credit union', *Journal of Professional Services Marketing*, 6(2):193–202.

Zeithaml, V.A. and Bitner, M.J. (1996) *Services Marketing*, Singapore: McGraw-Hill International Editions.

Customer services

There has been an increasing awareness of the importance and value of providing customer services in order to instil strong customer relationships. Jobber (1995) posits that a key method of building relationships is by providing customer services. As organizations recognize the importance of treating trusted suppliers as strategic partners, there has been a considerable increase in the resources invested for improving the quality of their service and hence, customer satisfaction. Shipley (1991) identifies the following forms of customer services that help establish strong buyer-seller relationships.

- Technical support, where the supplier can offer after-sales service or training to the customer's personnel.
- Providing expertise to the customer.
- Resource support, where suppliers extend credit facilities, give low interest loans and cooperate with the customer in promoting the products/services in an attempt to reduce the financial burden for the customer.
- Improving service levels by providing reliable service and fast delivery and setting up computerized reorder systems.
- Risk reduction by offering free demonstrations, product and delivery guarantees and product trials.

According to Payne (1993), the key elements of customer service are the following.

- Pre-transaction elements such as processes supporting service objectives, technical support and back up.
- Transaction elements such as demonstrations and convenience of acquisition.
- Post-transaction elements such as complaints handling, service recovery programmes and service blueprinting to correct problems.

Many suppliers of goods and services for industrial and consumer markets emphasize the quality and responsiveness of their service operations. The customer service function has become the focus of manufacturing and service organizations' efforts for the achievement of superior performance. Lovelock (1996) stipulates that: 'Customer service ... should be designed, performed, and communicated with two goals in mind: customer satisfaction and operational efficiency.'

Organizations recognize that after-sales service and customer care are key means for remaining competitive. Woodruffe (1996) suggests that after-sales service is vital in ensuring the long-term credibility of an organization through the quality of routine installation, maintenance and repair services. Particular emphasis is placed on the development and launch of customer care programmes that nourish the need for instilling a customer and marketing orientation throughout the organization. The core element of customer care programmes is customer care training. Other activities are likely to accompany customer care programmes in an attempt to improve the quality of customer service, for example incentive schemes, staff appraisals and staff and customer surveys.

As competition intensifies in both consumer and industrial markets, the only form of long-term differentiation between suppliers is the quality of service provided and the standard of customer care. The increasing emphasis on relationship marketing highlights the importance of investing in improving the quality of service and the standard of customer care in order to create customer satisfaction and loyalty. **IPD**

References

Jobber, D. (1995) *Principles and Practice of Marketing*, Maidenhead: McGraw-Hill.

Lovelock, C.H. (1996) *Services Marketing*, 3rd edn, New Jersey: Prentice Hall International Editions.

Payne, A. (1993) *The Essence of Services Marketing*, New Jersey: Prentice Hall International Editions.

Shipley, D. (1991) 'Key Customer Services', *Management Decision*, 32(8):17–20.

Woodruffe, H. (1995) *Services Marketing*, London: M and E Pitman Publishing.

Data fusion and mining

Now that transactional data is at the heart of many databases, overlaid with a multitude of profile data, we have moved into the era of 'biographics' – the fusion of profile and transaction data (Evans and Moutinho, 1999). The ability to match names, addresses, purchasing behaviour, and lifestyles all together onto one record allows companies to build a picture of someone's life. Another example of data fusion is linking a geographical information system (GIS) with neighbourhood groups database to target as narrowly as a newspaper round! A round usually consists of 150-200 households and, by linking transactional data with lifestyle, geodemographics and panel data, a very accurate picture of individual buying patterns emerges. The newspaper round – or milk round – can be used for door drops or direct mail as well as for local catchment area analysis. This has been rather more formalized by Unigate who have advertised a door-step delivery service based on MOSAIC geodemographic profiles at local level. In addition to product delivery they offered a delivery service for samples and vouchers and a delivery and collection service for questionnaires.

Data mining is concerned with extracting information that can be actioned from what sometimes appear to be incomprehensible mountains of data. There are two approaches that data mining can adopt. The first is verification-driven; where information is extracted according to some preconceived model; the second approach refers to digging around in databases in a relatively unstructured way with the aim of discovering links between customer behaviour and almost any variable that might potentially be useful.

Direct marketers have tried a variety of unusual or unexpected areas in which to mine. For example some have examined consumers' individual biorhythms and star signs as predictors of their purchasing patterns (Mitchell and Haggett, 1997) and others have linked their transactional and profile data with meteorological databases to predict, perhaps months ahead, what demand there might be for ice cream or woolly sweaters! **MJE**

References
Evans, M. and Moutinho, L. (1999) *Contemporary Issues in Marketing*, Macmillan pp. 66–74.
Mitchell, V.W. and Haggett, S. (1997) 'Sun-sign astrology in market segmentation: an empirical investigation', *Journal of Consumer Marketing*, 14, (2):113–131.

Data gathering

Data gathering is one of the main tasks in carrying out research. It may take the form of a simple observation or may entail a complex survey involving large corporations located in different geographical areas. Essentially, the method of research that has been identified will determine the extent of data gathering. Some of the more common methods include face-to-face interviews, telephone interviews and questionnaire surveys that are either mailed or administered personally to the identified respondents.

The purpose of data gathering is to ensure that the right information required to answer the research objectives is effectively collected. However, capturing the right data may be quite complicated. Changes that have taken place over a period will alter the validity of particular data. People's opinions, attitudes and preferences may vary from one milieu to another and with the passage of time. For example, the consumption patterns of consumers differ from one decade to another. As such, designing the right method of gathering data is crucial to ensure that relevant data is captured in line with the need of the research.

The advancement of technology is playing a key role in shaping future data gathering methods. Modern technology is currently facilitating computer surveys as well as the preparation and administration of questionnaires. Questionnaires that are sent through e-mails can sometimes provide quick responses, although there are some disadvantages associated with this method. The choice of data gathering methods depends on the facilities available, the extent of accuracy required, the expertise of the researcher, the time span of the study and other costs and resources. **RM-R**

References

Cooper, D.R. and Schindler, P.S. (1998) *Business Research Methods*, 6th edn, Singapore: McGraw-Hill.

Sekaran, U. (1996) *Research Methods for Business*, 2rd edn, New York: John Wiley & Sons.

Data interpretation

Data that has been gathered must be transformed into useful information. Raw data has little use in management decision making – managers need information rather than just raw data with no specific meaning. The process of analysing data essentially involves interpreting it into useful information. Interpretation of data transforms it into information, which managers can use for decision making purposes.

The raw data obtained from the data gathering procedure must undergo preliminary preparation before it can be analysed using statistical techniques. The major data preparation techniques including data editing, coding and statistically adjusting the data if necessary. The main aim of data editing is to identify omissions, ambiguities and errors in the responses. The process of coding then takes place, in which response values are entered into a computer file. Sometimes there is a need to adjust the data statistically in order to enhance the quality of the data interpretation. This involves statistical procedures relevant to the need of the data.

Data interpretation or data analysis involves reducing accumulated data to a manageable size and then developing relevant summaries. These summaries are further analysed to identify distinct patterns, and by applying relevant statistical techniques, the data will be transformed into more meaningful information. This information can be used to test the hypotheses that have been developed in the research or to answer the research questions. Researchers interpret the data in light of the research questions or determine if the results are consistent with the hypotheses or theories set out at the initial stage of the research. **RM-R**

References
Cooper, D.R. and Schindler, P.S. (1998) *Business Research Methods*, 6th edn, Singapore: McGraw-Hill.
Kumar, V., Aaker, D.A. and Day, G.S. (1999) *Essentials of Marketing Research*, New York: John Wiley & Sons.

Database analysis: recency, frequency and monetary value (RFM) and longtime values (LTVs) and allowable costs

Marketers are more interested in a customer who has purchased recently than someone who was a customer many years ago. A one-off purchase may also make a customer less attractive than a frequent purchaser. Marketers are increasingly concentrating on their 'better' customers – those who have the highest monetary value (and frequency) of purchase – and on those who bring greater returns. RFM analysis means that transactional data must be tracked by the database because actual purchase history is needed.

'Lifetime' value is often quoted by the industry but is perhaps a little of an overstatement – it doesn't mean the lifetime of the customer, but rather a designated period of time during which they are a customer of your organization. Depending on the type of products or services on offer, 'lifetime' might be as little as six months (as in purchases for baby products) or as long as 10 years (as in the automotive market). Essentially, different sectors have worked out the probable lifetime value of the 'average' customer and calculate accordingly. If a car company is only concerned with acquiring customers and does nothing to retain them, there is a fair chance that each customer who buys one of their cars this year will go on to buy another make next time. The value of the sale might be £10 000 but subtracting acquisition, production and other costs could mean a net profit of a just a few pounds.

With a more dedicated retention programme the company could expect that customer to buy one of their cars every third year for, perhaps, 12 years – not just at £10 000 but as they progress through their life stages they may be able to buy more expensive models (say, £2 000 more each time). So, with the lower costs of retaining a customer than acquiring him/her in the first instance, together with repeat buying and the prospect of up-selling over a period, the sales value could be as high as, say, £70 000 (£10k + £12k + £14k + £16k +£18k) (O'Malley *et al.*, 1999). **MJE**

Reference
O'Malley, L., Patterson, M. and Evans, M. (1999) *Exploring Direct Marketing*, Thomson Learning, ch. 4.

Databases

Information on a database is usually structured on the basis of files, records and fields. The database is the equivalent of the manual filing system: individual files are the filing cabinets, records are the suspension files (which might pertain to individual customers) and fields the different pieces of information held within those files. Files could hold information on all customers, products or transactions. These files are composed of a series of 'records'. Each record contains data about someone or something, for example a customer or potential customer. Each record is then further divided into 'fields,' which store particular data items such as post code, name, age and sex.

'Field' data is held separately because a marketer may want to extract those customers in a particular age category, or of a particular sex for analysis or targeting purposes.

Relational databases are currently the dominant database 'architecture' (or design) for systems developments (O'Malley *et al.*, 1999). Relational databases store data in two-dimensional tables of rows and columns. A single row represents all attributes (data) for a given entity (such as a customer), while a column represents the same attribute for all records. Thus, routes of access are independent of the data and files can easily be joined in new logical structures. The tables are linked by a common key, such as a customer number. This link allows users to create dynamic views of data and to add new data with minimum difficulty. Relational databases have provided a huge boost for direct marketing applications.

Think of a mail order business operating in the book market. A relational database allows records to communicate with each other so that stock levels can be checked and updated as the sale is made. The customer record is also updated so we now have a field containing purchased books against each customer, from which a pattern of their reading preferences can be analysed, together with whatever other data is being stored – quantities purchased, time of year when orders are usually placed, profile characteristics, method of payment and so on. **MJE**

References
O'Malley, L., Patterson, M. and Evans, M. (1999) *Exploring Direct Marketing*, London: Thomson Learning, ch. 4.

Deductive research

Deductive research is research that draws conclusions through logical reasoning. It need not necessarily be true in reality but it is logical. With deductive research, the researcher accepts or rejects hypotheses by means of logical reasoning. This acceptance and rejection help the researcher to explain and predict. The researcher understands a theory and looks at the consequences of the theory. Deduction involves gathering facts to confirm or disprove hypothesized relationships among variables that have been deduced from earlier theories or propositions.

Essentially, hypothesis testing is called deductive research. Through hypothesis testing, conclusions are derived by interpreting the meaning of the results of the data analysis. Generally, deductive research involves several steps, starting with observation, followed by preliminary data gathering, theory formulation, hypothesizing, scientific data collection, data analysis and finally deduction. The deduction is the conclusion that follows from the reasons given that represent the relevant proof. **RM-R**

References
Ghauri, P. Gronhaug, K. and Kristianlund, I. (1995) *Research Methods in Business Studies*, New York: Prentice Hall.
Sekaran, U. (1996) *Research Methods for Business*, 2nd edn, New York: John Wiley & Sons.

Demographics

Demographic information consists of such information as age, educational level, income and marital status. It is a collection of information on human factors in terms of size, location, age, sex, race, occupation and other statistics. Essentially, demographics involve information about people and, because people make up markets, this becomes an important source of information to marketers. Demographic information is often required by marketers to help in profiling customers. With demographics, marketers are able to segment markets more precisely and develop specific marketing strategies to meet the requirements of each target segment.

The changes that are constantly taking place in the markets, including changing family structures, geographic population shifts, more educated groups in the population, increasing ethnic and racial diversity, are all important information of which marketers have to be aware. To plan marketing strategies effectively, marketers use these types of information. In demographic segmentation, marketers divide the markets into groups based on variables such as age, sex, family size, income, occupation, education and race. This is the most common form of segmentation because consumer needs, wants and usage patterns are often closely related to demographic variables. Demographic variables are also very useful and much easier to measure and often provide richer information about the markets and their needs than many other marketing variables. **RM-R**

References

Kotler, P. and Armstrong, G. (1996) *Principles of Marketing*, 7th edn, Englewood Cliffs, NJ: Prentice Hall.

Malhotra, N.K. (1993) *Marketing Research: An Applied Orientation*, Englewood Cliffs, NJ: Prentice Hall.

Demographics and psychographics

Demographic criteria include dimensions such as age, sex, family factors and social grade and have long been used in segmentation, not least because of their simplicity in terms of identification and research.

Current 'age' issues include an increasingly ageing population. Indeed, in the USA, a baby boomer will turn 50 every 6.8 seconds in 2001, suggesting that they will remain important to marketers for some time to come. Research also suggests that the current over-45s are less tolerant of direct mail and telemarketing than their younger counterparts (Evans and Moutinho, 1999). Some younger segments have been found to be especially 'street-wise' and cynical about marketing activity: they reject the hard sell and patronizing approaches in favour of humour based, participative marketing communications.

Sex is a long established segmentation variable and is used mostly on the basis of stereotyping messages. Recent research suggests another dimension worth considering, namely that male and female brains process information differently (Evans *et al.*, 2000).

Although social grade has been a long-standing segmentation base in marketing, it is now criticized as being too generalized (there are only six categories and differentiation is based on just one variable: the occupation of the chief income earner in the household). Nevertheless, it easy to use and buying behaviour in some markets appears to reflect social grade differences.

Many direct marketers use family life cycle as a segmenting base. As people move through stages (such as 'bachelor', 'couple', 'with children', empty nesters') their requirements change considerably. This has especially been used as a segmentation base by financial services direct marketers and some supermarket loyalty schemes.

Although reasons for buying behaviour can be inferred from demographics these dimensions are largely profiling methods.

Psychographics (Evans, 1999) attempt to explore what consumers do rather than the nature of their characteristics. One of the main forms of this approach employed by direct marketers is 'lifestyle'. to use structured questionnaires to ask consumers which products, services and brands they buy. The data is not anonymized as in traditional market research so the value to the direct marketer is that a database is compiled of the claimed interests of named individuals, who can then be targeted personally. **MJE**

References

Evans, M. (1999) 'Market segmentation', in M.J. Baker (ed.) *The Marketing Book*, 4th edn, Oxford: Butterworth-Heinemann, pp. 209–236.

Evans, M. and Moutinho, L. (1999) *Contemporary Issues in Marketing*, London: Macmillan pp. 37–40.

Evans. M., Nairn, A. and Maltby, A. (2000) 'The hidden sex life of the male and female shot', *International Journal of Advertising*, 19(1) (February).

Department and variety stores

Department and variety stores are large retail shops operating on more than one floor and selling a wide and deep range of predominantly non-food household items.

Variety stores traditionally sell to a chiefly undifferentiated mass market. This incorporates a very wide range of retailers competing in vast array of markets. Overall the market is dominated by Marks and Spencer, Boots and Argos, who between them have 70 per cent market share. The recent quest for differentiation has taken various forms, such as investment in innovative store design, as exemplified by BhS, the development of customer cards, such as Marks and Spencer's store card, the Boots Advantage loyalty card and the wedding list service introduced by M&S and Argos, and outperforming comparable department store lists. In addition variety store retailers have increasingly diversified into making use of new non-store channels in parallel to existing physical outlets, such as catalogue selling and home-shopping via the Internet and direct sell television.

Department stores concentrate on the core product areas of quality clothing, toiletries/cosmetics and houseware. They are distinguished from variety stores by the presence of concessions – 'shop-within-shop' retailers renting space and operating their own outlets within the store, typically selling products such as perfumes, cosmetics or designer goods. Department stores increasingly practise lifestyle marketing, and designer labels in particular were a rapidly growing product category throughout the 1990s.

Both department and variety stores serve as anchors in new shopping developments. Store sales have benefited from the growth of singles households, the rising number of women in employment and the rise of the upmarket, sophisticated consumer segment. Retail sales through department stores were growing throughout the 1990s. Department store numbers were static, with underperforming and independent store closures counterbalanced by extensive developments by multiple operators such as Debenhams. The variety sector also experienced growth throughout the 1990s, but was tailing off at the end of the millennium with Marks and Spencer in particular experiencing declining profitability. **RAS**

References

Baron, S., Davies, B. and Swindley, D. (1991) *Macmillan Dictionary of Retailing*, Macmillan Reference Books, Macmillan: London.
Corporate Intelligence on Retailing (1998) *Department Stores in the UK*, CIR: London.
Lancaster, B. (1995) *The Department Store*, Leicester University Business Press: Leicester.
Mintel (1998) *Department Stores*, Mintel International Group: London.
Mintel (1998) *Variety Stores Retailing*, Mintel International Group: London.

Direct mail

Direct mail has a longer history within direct marketing than most media. Indeed, catalogue and other mail order methods existed before the telephone was even invented. Consumers have begun to turn to alternative media such as the telephone and the Internet but still trust the mail, even if they can be frustrated by the relative slowness in comparison with these other two media.

A major benefit to consumers of direct mail shopping is convenience, especially for those who can't easily get to stores because of a rural location or time constraints. Another benefit concerns the ability to search through large catalogues that sometimes include more extensive ranges than entire shopping centres. With the availability of many catalogues – general and the more specialized 'specialogues' – the consumer can have vast product assortments from which to choose from the comfort of their living room. Ordering might be moving increasingly to telephone and the Internet but delivery will still be via the postal services.

However, there are some disadvantages too, for example, there is an element of risk in not knowing if what has been ordered is appropriate. Catalogue pictures can deceive and garment fabrics, for instance, may disappoint when they are delivered. For this reason, some fashion catalogues include fabric swatches as a compromise. Generous exchange facilities are becoming normal policy in order to overcome the disappointment problem. Other dimensions of risk include untimely delivery, breakages during transit and even theft between order picking and delivery.

Direct mail allows videos and large brochures to be received, more than a press advertisement could cover for example. The medium can be used as a regular form of contact with customers, not only in terms of sales material but also through customer magazines to foster relationships. Some recipients are often bombarded with large quantities of direct mail and if they do not perceive it to be relevant and timely it goes in the bin as 'junk mail'.

Before this stage is reached, mail is a good method for prospecting, for using mailing lists or geodemographic lists of people who match what previous analysis suggests to be a relevant profile.

Other forms of direct mail include 'statement stuffers'. For example, utility bills or credit card statements include direct mail material, addressed to the individual. Here, there are significant economies because the mailing is going out in any case and there can be a high degree of targeting. MJE

Reference

O'Malley, L., Patterson, M. and Evans, M. (1999) *Exploring Direct Marketing*, London: Thomson Learning, ch. 8.

Direct marketing

Direct marketing is not a new concept. A book catalogue was published by Aldus Manutius in Venice in 1498 and a gardening catalogue was published by William Lucas in England in 1667.

The American Direct Marketing Association defines direct marketing as : 'An interactive system of marketing which uses one or more advertising media to effect a measurable response and/or transaction at any location'.

Another useful definition is provided by Bauer and Miglautsch (1992): 'A relational marketing process of prospecting, conversion and maintenance that involves information feedback and control at the individual level by using direct response advertising with tracking codes'.

Direct marketing can be thought of in promotional terms but also as a distribution channel, reflecting its mail order origins. Today it is contributing to the paradigm shift in marketing itself, from transactional to relationship marketing. This is based on fuller knowledge of customers as individuals and also because it is easier to facilitate personalized interaction between buyer and seller.

Reasons for the recent growth of direct marketing (Evans *et al.*, 1996; Evans 1998) include changes in market behaviour and in the effectiveness of traditional media. In terms of markets, fragmentation has taken place and markets have become demassified. Families, for example, are not eating together as often and family members have TV and sound systems in their own rooms. The increase in the number of working women means more women have joined their male counterparts in seeking time-saving purchasing methods, such as direct mail and telemarketing. The divorce rate has risen and with it the number of small and single households – affecting both sexes.

In promotional terms, companies have become disillusioned with more traditional media. Market fragmentation has resulted in diminishing audiences for individual media, media costs have soared and consumers are experiencing clutter. Audiences are fragmenting as more TV channels appear (on satellite and cable) along with more newspapers and magazines – all with advertising space to fill. These trends have created a *demand* for more effective targeting. The *supply* side, on the other hand, is concerned with changes in information about customers (such as personalized lifestyle surveys and transactional data) and also on technological improvements, which have facilitated the collection and analysis of huge amounts of detailed and personalized information, via data fusion and mining within marketing databases (see 'Data fusion and mining'). **MJE**

References

Bauer, C. L. and Miglautsch, J. (1992) 'A conceptual definition of direct marketing', *Journal of Direct Marketing*, 6(2):7–17.

Evans, M. (1998) 'From 1086 and 1984: direct marketing into the millennium' in special issue of *Marketing Intelligence and Planning on Direct Marketing*, 16(1):56–67.

Evans, M., O'Malley, L. and Patterson, P. (1996) 'Direct marketing communications in the UK: a study of growth, past, present and future', *Journal of Marketing Communications*, 2(1).

Direct marketing and marketing communications

Direct marketing is a broad term that literally refers to all marketing activities undertaken by the manufacturer or original service provider without going through intermediaries. In this way, marketing is direct to end customers and consumers. For obvious reasons, therefore, a great deal of emphasis is placed on marketing communications.

Initially, direct marketing was most closely associated with the use of catalogues and the mail order business, direct mail being a primary direct marketing tool. But the close association that many have between direct marketing and direct mail is no longer appropriate, 'In modern business, direct marketing is far more than merely a few tactical mailshots to back up an advertising campaign' (Tapp, 2001). Today, technological changes have changed the face of direct marketing and the focus of marketing itself.

In the past, intermediaries (wholesalers, retailers, etc.) grew to fulfil a need in the marketplace to facilitate the distribution and availability of products. Today products can be made readily available through other means. Postal systems are highly advanced and next day delivery can be assured for mail and parcels if necessary. Retailing today does not have to rely on the High Street and shopping centres. Even the retailers themselves are willing to provide goods direct to your door. Choice, ordering and payment is facilitated through the Internet, digital television, CD-ROM/DVD, over the phone and through credit and banking services. Amazon was one of the early companies to exploit the Internet for this purpose when it set up its virtual bookstore.

Behind the growth of direct marketing lies the development of very sophisticated information services. These are facilitated by developments in computers, the most notable of which is a marketing and management database which is used to capture customer information. The database can be used to track customer data and interface internal information with other external information sources. The result is a powerful management tool that can be used for (amongst other things) precise customer targeting. **DWP**

Reference

Tapp, A. (2001), 'Direct marketing communications', in D. Pickton, and A. Broderick *Integrated Marketing Communications,* London: Financial Times Prentice Hall, ch. 28.

Direct marketing creative

Direct marketing 'creative' can healthily draw from buying behaviour theory. The direct marketer should strive truly to understand the needs of his/her market in order to convert the product/service features into benefits that are more likely to satisfy these needs. Using Maslow's hierarchy of needs, direct campaigns for life assurance, especially covering family members, might relate to concerns for loved ones (i.e. social needs) and to more personal esteem needs (our self esteem can be enhanced by feeling we are looking after those for whom we have some responsibility) (Maslow, 1954).

Another useful framework is based on 'sequential' models of customer response to marketing. For example, customers first become aware, then understand, remember and become interested in the message; purchase is another stage in the sequence, followed by post-purchase reaction.

The direct marketer can use many techniques to gain attention, including movement. Video cassettes, which allow the use of movement, are becoming more popular for communicating direct messages, as is direct communication via the Internet. Envelopes for direct mail can be triangular or adorned with coloured graphics and pictures to arrest attention.

Encouraging participation in the message on the part of the recipient can be effective in securing more enduring understanding and memory of the message. One Oxfam mailing, for example, included a tape measure which could be used to measure whether one's child's arm was small enough to be classified as suffering from malnutrition.

In order to facilitate purchase, there needs to be a response mechanism. Unfortunately, many are poorly designed and make it difficult for the target audience to respond (e.g. coupons that are too small to fill out completely or direct response TV advertisements that do not provide ample time for the telephone number to be recorded).

Post-purchase activities can be understood with reference to cognitive dissonance theory, which is a kind of psychological tension resulting from how positive and negative cognitions might conflict. For example, a consumer might have bought a car after an extensive pre-purchase search and evaluation of alternatives, and although they might be delighted with the car, if their next door neighbour then says the manufacturer has a poor repair record, the purchaser experiences this conflict between cognitions. Car companies often promote after-sales' warranties in order to reduce this sort of post-purchase dissonance. Direct charity marketers often draw attention to the downside of, for example, parting with one's hard earned money but for a very good cause. The direct marketer might also emphasize how many satisfied customers there are, in order to shift the balance of positive and negative cognitions. For example, in the mid 1990s a satellite broadcaster, in direct response advertising, used the copy headline 'half a million people can't be wrong'.
MJE

References

Maslow, A. (1954) *Motivation and Personality*, New York: Harper & Row.
O'Malley, L., Patterson, M. and Evans, M. (1999) *Exploring Direct Marketing*, London: Thomson Learning, ch.10.

Direct marketing research and testing

The direct marketing industry is able to conduct experiments by selecting samples from different lists and monitoring response rates in order to identify those that perform best (Evans and Middleton, 1998). Different 'creative' can be tested on sub samples and the version that produces stronger response rates can be rolled out.

The database has probably changed marketing research for ever. It allows marketers to study actual buying patterns via analysis of transactional data and to evaluate the effects of different campaigns in terms of response rates. Statistical principles can be used to determine appropriate sample sizes for the results to be within specified levels of confidence.

On the other hand there should be a clear role for both qualitative and quantitative market research – not least to explore reasons for different response rates in order to increase the likelihood of even stronger and more sustainable responses. Testing per se might identify better performing approaches but cannot provide more insightful explanations of why some are more effective.

As a result some direct marketers are linking their databases with market research data. In this way, for example, consumer panels are linked with geodemographic or lifestyle databases in 'T-Groups'. The 'T' means that 'horizontal' database data provides tremendous breadth of data over millions of consumers but the 'vertical', from market research (e.g. panels), provides greater depth of information over a period, because panels are continuous data sources.

However, a related issue is raised by Fletcher and Peters (1996) with respect to the use of market research data to populate databases. The main problem is one of using marketing research data for selling purposes (selling under the guise of research; 'SUGGING'). The market research society has long outlawed this practice but has now compromised over the issue by having dual codes of conduct for the two 'reasons' for data collection. The concerns will not go away, however, and the direct marketing and marketing research industries probably have more work to do to resolve these conflicts. **MJE**

References

Evans, M. and Middleton, S. (1998) 'Testing and research in direct mail: the agency perspective', *Journal of Database Marketing*, 6(2):127–144.

Fletcher, K. and Peters, L. (1996) 'Issues in consumer information management', *Journal of the Market Research Society*, 38(2):145–160.

Direct response media

Rather than individualized direct media such as mail, the Internet or telephone contact, direct response media involve placing messages in what are usually the more traditional mass promotional media but which also provide a mechanism for contacting the company. This might be a telephone number, web site or postal address. Media used include television, radio, press and outdoor advertising and a large proportion of advertisements communicated through these traditional media now include a response mechanism.

The purpose of some direct response campaigns might be selling per se; that is, to advertise products and provide a contact device for the placement of orders. Others, however, aim to gather data by encouraging requests for brochures or further information. The profile of those responding can lead marketers to understand more about the types of people who are more likely to be interested in their products, as well, of course, as targeting the actual responders with individualized marketing.

Kiosk marketing involves interaction between potential customers and an organization via touch screen technology in a store or a shopping mall. Customers can browse catalogues, check answers to 'frequently asked questions' and follow up via response mechanisms to store or non store purchasing.

There is also a new range of media: 'ambient media'. These involve the use of those locations that the unsuspecting consumer doesn't normally think of as providing advertising, such as supermarket trolleys, floor tiles in shopping centres or petrol pump nozzles. Again, contact devices are provided and the range of ambient media appears almost limitless. However, the novelty might wear off, with familiarity leading to lower attention levels. On the other hand, the placement of messages in this way is very inexpensive and, especially while they hold novelty values, their impact can be cost effective. This form has certainly seen a higher than average growth rate amongst outdoor media. **MJE**

Reference
O'Malley, L., Patterson, M. and Evans, M. (1999) *Exploring Direct Marketing*, London: Thomson Learning, ch. 8.

Discounters

A discounter is a retailer whose strategy is based on gaining high volume sales by charging low prices. In order to counterbalance the resulting low margins, discounters often aim for cost leadership by creating a highly cost effective infrastructure through their store networks and supply chain management. Discount stores typically concentrate on selling a limited range of popular goods, have low staffing levels and a high level of self-service and basic shop fittings.

In the UK discounting is particularly strong in grocery retailing, but has also been growing in the furniture, carpet and electrical sectors, DIY retailing and the chemist and drugstore market. Whereas the non-food sectors often make use of special sales periods to attract the price-conscious consumer, in the grocery sector price comparisons, typically featuring the comparative price of a shopping basket, are of a more ongoing nature. This is partly because of the presence of continental discounters – ALDI, Lidl and NETTO – whose arrival in the early 1990s coincided with a period of relative economic uncertainty and put price firmly back on the competitive agenda. The leading grocery multiples succeeded in diffusing much of the threat posed by the newcomers through the introduction of budget own brands, which are now regularly bought by half the adult population. However, nearly a quarter of all adults also regularly shop at a grocery discount store and by 1997 the discounters had captured a 5.6 per cent market share. Whereas in the early 1990s most discount shoppers were driven by economic necessity, this is no longer the case, and consumers have come to trust discounter house brands in terms of value for money.

Historically, discounting has been particularly prevalent in the USA, the home of Walmart, which is the world's largest and fastest growing retailer and well known for its 'every-day-low-pricing' policy. Walmart's entry into the UK via ASDA may be the start of a new wave of discounting. **RAS**

References
Berry, C. and Holmes, S. (1993) *Discount Grocery Retailing: Fashion or Philosophy?*, Watford: Institute of Grocery Distribution Business Publication.
Humphries, G. (1995) *Prospects for Food Discounters and Warehouse Clubs: Growth or Decline?* London: Pearson Professional.
Mintel (1998) *Discounting and Price Promotion in Retailing*, Special Report, London: Mintel International Group.
Sampson, S.D. and Tigert, D.J. (1994) 'The impact of warehouse membership clubs: the wheel of retailing turns one more time', *The International Review of Retail, Distribution and Consumer Research*, 4(1):33–59.
Schmidt, R.A., Segal, R. and Cartwright, C. (1994) 'Two-shop shopping or polarization – with-

er UK grocery shopping?' *International Journal of Retail and Distribution Management*, 22(1):12–19.

Distribution centres

Distribution centres are central locations from which finished goods that are stored are distributed to identified customers. Privately-owned warehouses are forms of distribution centres used by specific companies.

Distribution centres are distinguished from conventional private warehouses by the fact that they are carrying out major centralized warehousing operations. The main aim of establishing distribution centres is to facilitate speedy movements of goods rather than use as storage facilities. They act as main terminals where finished goods from the manufacturers are placed and swiftly disbursed to appropriate customers.

Although most distribution centres are set up by individual firms as part of their warehousing facilities they operate as distribution terminals rather than as storage facilities. The rationale underlying the development of distribution centres is to ensure that the finished products from the manufacturer move efficiently and in a constant flow from the time they are taken out of the production plant until the time they reach the intended destination. Today, large companies are setting up distribution centres as an integral part of their distribution system. **RM-R**

References

Ballou, R.H. (1992) *Business Logistics Management*, 3rd edn, Englewood Cliffs, NJ: Prentice Hall.
Bowersox, D.J. and Cooper, M.B. (1992) *Strategic Marketing Channel Management*, Singapore: McGraw-Hill International Editions.

Distribution channels: simple and complex

Distribution channels may vary in terms of the number of intermediaries involved in carrying out specific distribution activities, the number of distribution levels and the extent of specialization of functions performed. When a distribution channel comprises a single or very few intermediaries, it is regarded as a 'simple' channel. A simple channel may be required for distributing products or services where manufacturers require more control over distribution matters. Distributing to markets, as in the distribution of industrial products, may also specify the need for simpler channel structures where manufacturers can move directly to potential buyers. For example, a manufacturer may opt to have their own sales offices rather than use independent intermediaries or agents as distributors of their industrial products. In setting up their own sales offices, the manufacturer may have more control over matters such as pricing, special product features required by customers, provision of technical assistance and decisions on promotions.

A 'complex' channel structure is one where a number of intermediaries exist between the manufacturer and the final consumers. The more intermediaries there are in the distribution structure whose functions are very specialized, the more complex will be the distribution channel. Specialization of individual functions leads to complex channel structures because channel intermediaries become more dependent on one another in carrying out distribution tasks. A number of channel intermediaries exist to perform numerous distribution activities to ensure that the products are made available to consumers. The complexity of distribution channel structures is also a reflection of the competitive environment where it is common to see channel intermediaries competing aggressively. The proliferation of retail merchandise lines, for example, has resulted in similar items being sold at many different retail types and locations within the same market area. This ensures the availability of the products and increases the competitive pressures between channel intermediaries performing similar functions. **RM-R**

References

Bowersox, D. J. and Cooper, M.B. (1992) *Strategic Marketing Channel Management*, Singapore : McGraw-Hill International Editions.

Robicheaux, R.A.and Coleman, J.E. (1994) 'The structure of marketing channel relationships', *Journal of the Academy of Marketing Science*, 22(1):38–51.

Diversification

Diversification is a strategy that may be adopted by a company that wishes to increase the size of its market(s). It is the final segment of the classic product/market expansion matrix devised by Ansoff (1957). The other segments are 'market penetration', 'market development' and 'product development'. Within Ansoff's matrix diversification is the strategy that is considered most risky as it involves developing new products or services and selling them to new markets. The company is therefore moving out of its normal field of expertise. It may need to invest in new manufacturing equipment and develop knowledge of new customer segments. This makes the strategy time-consuming and expensive. On a more positive note, a diversification strategy may spread risk by ensuring that a company does not become too reliant on a particular product or market.

Two main types of diversified growth exist. *Concentric* diversification occurs where there is some link or harmony between the old and new set of activities. For example a new product may be introduced by an organization but be sold through the same outlets as the company's existing portfolio. Marks & Spencer (M&S) have diversified into the financial services market but used their database of M&S charge card holders to establish their customer base.

Conglomerate diversification occurs when the organization undertakes completely new activities without any link to existing business. An example would be Virgin's move away from music into airlines, soft drinks and mobile phones. Each move takes them into a new marketplace with a new product or service.

The R.J. Reynolds Tobacco Company is responding to the decline in its traditional cigarette market, caused by health concerns, by diversifying. It uses its famous Camel brand on a range of leisurewear. Not only is this market not subject to the constraints of the cigarette market but it also provides brand support for its cigarettes which owing to legal restrictions face tough advertising controls. **SR**

Reference

Ansoff, H.I. (1957) 'Strategies for diversification', *Harvard Business Review*, 25(5):113–125.

Divestment

The opposite of investment, divestment can be the sale of part of a company, (e.g. assets, product lines, divisions, brands) to a third party, or can also be seen as internal, where a company closes part of its operation, (e.g. manufacturing plant) as a rationalization programme. Divestment can occur after a period of harvesting, where despite every effort, the business or product continues to lose money. The inability to turn a potentially loss making situation into a profitable one is an obvious reason to divest part of the business. Companies, however, divest parts of the business for reasons other than pure profit.

Attempting to refocus a company on its core business can lead to significant divestment of those parts of the company which are not seen as being central to the core activity. In 1997 ICI, the UK chemicals company, shed its bulk chemicals and explosives businesses whilst purchasing National Starch and Quest. The result is a business which now focuses on paint, perfume and flavourings. Similarly, a company may feel that it has too diverse a business portfolio. In order to concentrate on fewer core activities it will divest itself of non-core businesses. A company may also acknowledge that it doesn't have the management expertise, marketing capability or financial strength to compete in certain markets and will therefore divest those parts of the business where it believes it operates at a significant disadvantage to its main competitors.

The decision to get out of a particular market or business should never be taken lightly.

Supposedly uneconomic business units may provide an invaluable input to other parts of the company. Divestment may therefore seriously impede the company's ability to trade effectively in other sectors, especially where skills and knowledge are shared across different industry sectors. **PBB**

References

Davis, J.V. (1974) 'The strategic divestment decision', *Journal of Long Range Planning*, (February)
Harrigan, K.R. (1980) *Strategies for Declining Businesses,* London: Heath & Co.

Dynamic pricing

Price determinants are not static, but change in a more or less predictable and uniform way along the product life cycle (PLC). In dynamic pricing, these evolutions are explicitly taken into account, which leads to an (optimal) price path, rather than one (optimal) price level (for a discussion on dynamic pricing models, see Simon, 1989 and Gijsbrechts, 1993).

Some pricing strategies capitalize on demand dynamics. In *price skimming*, a company introduces a product at a high price in order to 'skim' the high willingness to pay of innovators and early adopters, and gradually lowers the price in later stages of the PLC. Alternatively, a company adopting *penetration pricing*, charges low prices in the introduction stage in order to secure a solid customer base before competitors enter the market in later stages, where the company will charge higher prices. This especially makes sense in markets characterized by high risk aversion, high loyalty and/or network externalities (i.e. when the value of a product increases with the number of people that have that product, e.g. fax machines). Most of the models that capture demand dynamics are based on the diffusion model developed by Bass (1980) or some adaptive reference price model (e.g. Greenleaf, 1995; Kopalle *et al.*, 1996).

Dynamic pricing can also be effective in generating and exploiting cost advantages (vis-à-vis future competitors). In *experience curve pricing*, the company charges low initial prices in order to realize high sales volumes and reduces costs as a result of experience. Also, more external dynamic processes, like technological evolutions, may influence cost structure and thus price setting.

Finally, price setters should account for dynamics in the competitive environment. As indicated above, a company can anticipate possible competitive entries (cf. experience curve and penetration pricing) in deciding upon its price path. Moreover, it could include competitive price reactions in its pricing decisions. Price wars, which usually occur in markets with little or no product differentiation, are an extreme example of the price interactions between competitors. The dominant approach to modelling dynamic competitive behaviour is based on game theory (e.g. Eliashberg and Jeuland, 1986; Nascimento and Van Honacker, 1988; Coughlan and Mantrala, 1992). **KCa, BF, EG**

References

Bass, F. M. (1980) 'The relationship between diffusion rates, experience curves, and demand elasticities for consumer durable technological innovations', *Journal of Business*, 53(2)2:s51–s67.

Coughlan, A. and Mantrala, M. (1992) 'Dynamic competitive pricing strategies', *International Journal of Research in Marketing*, 9(1):91–108.

Eliashberg, J. and Jeuland, A. P. (1986) 'The impact of competitive entry in a developing market upon dynamic pricing strategies', *Marketing Science*, 5(1):20–36.

Gijsbrechts, E. (1993) 'Prices and pricing research in consumer marketing: some recent developments', *International Journal of Research in Marketing*, 10(2):115–151.

Greenleaf, E. A. (1995) 'The impact of reference price effects on the profitability of price promotions', *Marketing Science*, 14(1):82–104.

Kopalle, P.K., Rao, A.G. and Assunçao, J.L. (1996) 'Asymmetric reference price effects and dynamic pricing policies', *Marketing Science*, 15(1):60–85.

Nagle, T.T. and Holden, R.K. (1995), *The Strategy and Tactics of Pricing: A Guide to Profitable Decision Making*, Englewood Cliffs, NJ: Prentice Hall.

Nascimento, F. and Vanhonacker, W. (1988), 'Optimal strategic pricing of reproducable consumer products', *Management Science*, 34(8):921–937.

Simon, H. (1989) *Price Management*, Amsterdam: Elsevier.

Ecological factors

Ecological factors (or 'green issues') are those issues which are concerned with the preservation and restoration of the natural environment. Green marketing has been defined as 'The management process responsible for identifying, anticipating and satisfying the requirements of customers and society, in a profitable and sustainable way.' (Peattie, 1992).

Ecological issues have been a cause for scientific concern for much of the 20th century, but it is only since the early 1980s that environmentalism has impinged on the public consciousness. Public concern about environmentalism has led to the following effects on businesses.

- There is a public relations issue, which revolves around ensuring that the public is aware of the firm's environmental credentials.
- Changes in business practice have had to be implemented in order to comply with pressure group influence (for example, protests by Friends of the Earth or Greenpeace).
- Some consumers have become suspicious of companies' claims to be environmentally friendly.
- Conceptually, marketers now feel the need to go beyond satisfying the consumer's immediate needs and wants; marketers are focusing more on the longer-term implications and are developing societal marketing which looks at the long-term needs and wants of society as a whole. This means that marketing (and business) has to become more sustainable for the future (O'Connor, 1994).

Three dimensions of a business determine its environmental impact. First, its technology, which might be wasteful of resources or might cause damage to the environment through pollution. Sometimes these impacts can be reduced by re-engineering to reduce waste or to cut polluting emissions. Secondly, the economic impact of the business. This covers issues such as employment, creating unrealistic expectations among customers and sourcing of raw materials. Thirdly, the managerial style of the company, which is sometimes geared towards profit considerations or towards the management's personal aims rather than being environmentally-centred. **JWDB**

References
Peattie, K. (1992) *Green Marketing*, London: Pitman.
O'Connor, J (1994) 'Is sustainable capitalism possible?', in M. O'Connor (ed.) *Is Capitalism Sustainable?* New York: The Guildford Press.

E-commerce and the Internet

Not only does the Internet enable marketers to communicate with individuals in both consumer and organizational markets but it also allows potential buyers to do their own research into different suppliers' prices, delivery charges, catalogues and so on quickly and easily. In this way, buyers are finding they have somewhat greater control over buyer-seller interactions than was often the case previously. They certainly do not have perfect knowledge in economists' terms, but more than might have been the case.

In addition, the Internet provides an extra dimension of participation; people can 'surf', exchange information about different companies and products with like minded people and enter into games and competitions that companies might provide in order to encourage a relationship with them (Frost *et al.*, 1999). Some market segments, for example the so-called generation X, are thought to seek greater interaction with marketing material and welcome opportunities to participate rather than be passive recipients of messages.

Many organizations are finding it relatively inexpensive to market via the Internet and at the same time reach widely geographically dispersed markets. However, although the Internet allows individual targeting, its use in any uniform sense across borders should be cognisant of geographic market segments becoming more heterogeneous at regional and even local level. It is dangerous to assume that the same Internet marketing approach will be applicable, accepted or even legal in different countries.

Another implication of cost structures is that 'doing business' via the Internet (e-commerce) is cheaper than supporting a retail branch network. A financial transaction at a bank branch might cost around 68p, whereas via the Internet it can be as low as 7p. One result is the closure of branches in favour of e-commerce but this could exclude some disadvantaged market segments that don't and won't have Internet access. The question could be asked whether this is just good for profits and shareholders but not entirely socially responsible. **MJE**

References
Frost, F. and Evans, M. (1999) 'The use of the Internet in relationship marketing in consumer markets', in Backhaues *Contemporary Developments in Marketing*, Paris: ESKA, pp. 385–397.
Frost, F., Matthews, B. and Evans, M. (1999) 'Responses to general enquiries via the Internet: targeting the organizational decision maker', *Journal of Targeting, Measurement and Analysis for Marketing* 7(4).

Economic determinants

Economic determinants relate to factors that affect the buying power of organizational and consumer purchasers, as well as to their respective purchasing and spending patterns. In a market based economy it is ultimately consumer demand that pulls organizational (especially industrial and retail, but less so institutional) demand through the system. This process is termed *derived demand*. Consumer buyers purchase for a variety of reasons, ranging from logical to illogical criteria, and this is well documented under consumer buying behaviour. Organizational buyers make their purchases in order to fulfil the needs and requirements of their respective organizations and do not engage in impulse purchasing. Decisions are thus based more upon logical commercial reasons than personal reasons.

The general state of the economy and levels of employment will determine how consumers purchase. In times of economic downturn, consumers will put off luxury and non-essential purchases or trade down to less expensive purchases. Conversely, in times of economic boom there is a greater demand for luxury products and consumers will often trade up to better grades of merchandise. These economic conditions and the consumer purchasing patterns associated with them will, in turn, ultimately work their way through to organizational purchases. **GL**

Reference
Lancaster, G. and Massingham, L. (1999) *Essentials of Marketing*, 3rd edn, Maidenhead: McGraw-Hill, pp. 34–35.

Economic factors

Economic factors are those issues relating to the demand cycle and to exchanges between firms and consumers or customers. Macroeconomic factors are concerned with the overall economic climate of the country and the world: such issues as overall demand in the economy, levels of unemployment, levels of inflation and taxation. The trends behind these issues are part of the macroeconomic climate. Microeconomics deals with exchanges at the level of the firm and its customers and consumers, and is concerned with such issues as pricing, level of competition and elasticity of demand.

Only the largest of firms are able to influence macroeconomic factors; the most notable examples are major multinationals, who are able to manipulate money markets in order to influence government policy (Kotler, 1986). Management of demand in the economy is generally considered to be a responsibility of government, and in practice many governments are more concerned about inflation and unemployment than they are about individual firms.

Microeconomics is a way of modelling business activities in order to understand some of the processes that are operating. Some of the main issues which microeconomics addresses are explained below.

- *Pricing* – prices are determined by supply and demand; as supply increases, the price will fall unless demand increases alongside it. Likewise if demand rises without a corresponding increase in supply, prices will rise.
- *Elasticity of demand* – for most goods, price rises cause a fall in demand. Elasticity refers to the degree to which a price rise will affect demand; inelastic products (such as salt) are hardly affected at all by price rises, whereas elastic products (such as borrowed money) are affected strongly by price rises.
- *Competition* – the more competitive the market, the greater the elasticity of demand. In other words, if there are many close substitutes for a product, price becomes a key issues for consumers when choosing between products. **JWDB**

Reference
Kotler, P. (1986) 'Megamarketing' *Harvard Business Review*, (March–April): 117–124.

Elaboration likelihood

The elaboration likelihood model of persuasion was first proposed by Petty and Cacioppo in 1983. Underlying it is an understanding of cognitive information processing which recognizes that individuals are sometimes willing to think very carefully about a piece of marketing communication and sometimes hardly think about it at all. The degree or amount of thoughtful consideration in these circumstances is called *elaboration*. It represents the amount of effort the recipient is willing to put in for themselves and, in this way, add to the communication by bringing in their own thoughts, attitudes, feelings and experiences. Simply, it is about the relationship receivers have with a piece of communication and how they embellish or elaborate on it. The nature and amount of elaboration will have an impact on the persuasiveness of the communication. Elaboration can take many forms and involve searching for more information, consulting others, thinking, exploring feelings, and so forth.

Elaboration likelihood is concerned with the amount of elaboration that is likely to take place, recognizing that it forms a continuum from extremely high to very little or none. Research has indicated that the levels of motivation, ability and predisposition to enter into elaboration vary between people and will be affected by the nature of the communication. Petty and Cacioppo, whose work gained wide acceptance because it helped to consolidate many of the apparent contradictory findings of other research that had existed in the field of cognitive information processing (Greenwald, 1968), described two principal routes in the elaboration likelihood process. The first, a 'central' route, is typified by 'a person's careful and thoughtful consideration of the true merits of the information presented in support of an advocacy' (Petty and Cacioppo, 1986). The second, a 'peripheral' route, is where there is little elaboration. In this case, the persuasiveness of the message relies on peripheral cues such as the perceived credibility of the sender, familiarity with the message or product, how much the communication is liked and the reactions of others to the communication. **DWP**

References

Greenwald, A.G. (1968) 'Cognitive learning, cognitive response to persuasion, and attitude change', in A. Greenwald, T. Brock and T. Ostrom (eds) *Psychological Foundations of Attitudes*, New York: Academic Press, pp. 148–170.

Petty, R.E. and Cacioppo, J.Y. (1983) 'Central and peripheral routes to persuasion: application to advertising' in L. Percy and A. Woodside (eds) *Advertising and Consumer Psychology*, MA: Lexington Books, pp. 3–23.

Petty, R.E. and Cacioppo, J.Y. (1986) *Communication and Persuasion: Central and Peripheral Routes to Attitude Change*, New York: Springer-Verlag.

Empowerment

There are different definitions of employee empowerment. Sutherland and Canwell (1997) propose that: 'If an individual employee is allowed to control their contribution to the organization, complete tasks and attain targets independently without reference to management, then this is an example of empowerment.'

Thorlakson (1996) defines employee empowerment as: '...getting workers to do what needs to be done rather than doing what they're told, and that involves delegation, individual responsibility, autonomous decision making, and feelings of self-efficacy.'

The process of employee empowerment can only take place in an environment where it is allowed and promoted. Managers play a pivotal role in creating an environment that nourishes empowerment. It is thus important for managers to encourage their staff to change and to take risks and ensure that they stand by their staff even when they fail. However, managers may refuse to empower their subordinates because of their own personal insecurities, need for control and fear of delegating power and authority (Gilmore and Carson 1995).

The organization's structure may inhibit or assist employee empowerment. A risk-averse bureaucratic culture makes empowerment difficult because by allowing individual initiatives it raises the possibility of making errors. French and Bell (1995) propose that participation is an effective form of employee empowerment, and that participation enhances empowerment.

Empowered employees are more productive, competent, committed, satisfied and innovative, and create higher quality products and services than their non-empowered employees in other places of employ. Organizations are more effective when they empower their workforce. Bateson (1995) and Bowen and Lawler III (1995) stipulate that empowered employees are more customer-focused, interact with customers with more warmth and enthusiasm, and are a great source of ideas about how best to serve the customer. Such employees are much quicker in responding to customer needs, are more likely to respond positively to service failures, and tend to feel better about their jobs and themselves.

Despite the many benefits that an organization can gain from empowering employees, there are also drawbacks, for example, greater monetary investment in selection and training, slower or inconsistent service delivery, bad decisions made by employees (Bowen and Lawler III 1995), and overconfidence and misjudgements on the part of subordinates (Conger and Kanungo 1989). **IPD**

References

Bateson, J.E.G. (1995) *Managing Services Marketing: Text and Readings*, 3rd edn, Orlando: The Dryden Press.

Bowen, D.E. and Lawler III, E.E. (1995) 'Organising for service: empowerment or production line?', in W.J. Glynn and J.G. Barnes (eds) *Understanding Services Management,* Chichester: John Wiley & Sons.

Conger, J.A. and Kanungo, R.N. (1989) 'The empowerment process', *Academy of Management Review*, 13.

French, W.L. and Bell Jr, C.H. (1995) *Organisational Development* 5th edn, New Jersey: Prentice Hall International Editions.

Gilmore, A. and Carson, D. (1995) 'Managing and marketing to internal customers', in W.J. Glynn and J.G. Barnes (eds) *Understanding Services Management*, Chichester: John Wiley & Sons.

Sutherland, J. and Canwell, D. (1997) *Organisation, Structures and Processes*, London: Pitman Publishing.

Thorlakson, A.J.H. (1996) 'An empirical study of empowerment in the workplace', *Group and Organization Management,* 21(21):67.

Environment for marketing communication

The environment is the context in which marketing communications take place. It affects how messages are received. It can work positively to their benefit or negatively and detract from their effectiveness. The environment may be the wider 'macro' marketing communications environment (things going on in society in general), or the narrower, more focused 'micro' marketing communications environment (things happening at the time and place of the communication). It is constantly changing.

Commonly, the macro environment is assessed in terms of PEST analysis (Political, Economic, Social and Technological factors). However, a more comprehensive breakdown for marketing communications purposes would be the PRESTCOM analysis (Pickton and Wright, 1998) which proposes that the macro environment should be analysed by determining what is happening in the Political, Regulatory, Economic, Social, Technological, Competitive, Organizational (i.e. within the organization) and Market environments. Changes in these areas profoundly affect target audiences and the nature of marketing communications. For example, major developments are taking place in telecommunications. The Internet, digital and mobile communications and computing power are revolutionizing the way business is conducted and how we communicate. Media is fragmenting as new media opportunities are developed with the creation of new television stations – satellite, digital and cable – more commercial radio stations, new magazines, video, CD-ROM and DVD. Social norms and social acceptance are shifting, social demographics and lifestyles are affecting attitudes, values, interests, expectations and spending. Concerns over 'green' issues and social responsibilities are playing greater roles. Increased internationalization is widening markets but bringing with it new marketing communication challenges. The macro environment is dynamic and challenging.

The marketing communications 'micro' environment directly affects how marketing communications messages are received. Every item of communication is sensed – seen, heard, felt, tasted or smelled – in a context. Something else is always happening at the same time. The editorial environment and other advertising affect a newspaper or magazine advertisement. Television commercials are seen within and between programmes and with other advertisements. We are distracted by what else is going on while we are watching. The shopping environment at the point of sale, shelf displays, posters, packaging, special offers, smells from the bakery and so on, all affect how we perceive the shopping experience and how we react to the marketing communications that surround it. All of this represents 'noise' to our marketing communications, and usually detracts from its effectiveness. If managed well, however, the micro environment can offer opportunities for positive reinforcement of communications messages. **DWP**

Reference
Pickton, D.W. and Wright, S. (1998) *Improved competitive strategy through value added competitive intelligence'*, proceedings, Third Annual European Conference, Society of Competitive Intelligence Professions, Berlin.

Evaluating strategies

Marketing managers and strategists need to evaluate the choice of strategies to ensure the most appropriate decision is made. There is a range of general evaluation criteria, which relates to the following areas.

- *Suitability* – analysis should be undertaken to assess the extent to which a strategy fits the organization's aims and objectives, considering the resource constraints.
- *Feasibility* – the feasibility in terms of the successful implementation of the strategy will need to be considered. Therefore, funds flow analysis and break-even analysis should be undertaken to consider the financial implications. Resource deployment analysis should also be assessed by identifying the key resources for each strategy.
- *Acceptability* – this is related to internal and external expectations. Analysis should be undertaken to ascertain stakeholder perceptions towards the proposed strategies.

More specifically, however, quantitative analysis needs to be undertaken to ensure that each strategic option is evaluated appropriately. This can include:

- *Portfolio analysis* – the balance of the portfolio in relation to the BCG (Boston Consultancy Group) matrix.
- *Life cycle analysis* – the life cycle portfolio matrix, which was developed by Arthur D. Little, (Wright, 1974), can be used to establish the suitability of strategies in relation to the stage of the industry maturity and the competitive position of the organization.
- *Return* – financial analysis in relation to profitability, cost/benefit and shareholder value analysis (SVA) should also be considered. This may include the forecast for the return on capital employed (ROCE), the payback period and the discounted cash flow. The earnings potential is also an important indicator.
- *Risk and control* – this will also need to be evaluated to assess the risk which the company may face in pursuing a strategy. Financial ratio projections can be

analysed as a measure of risk. Sensitivity analysis in testing how sensitive the predicted outcome is for each strategy can also be undertaken. Simulation models can be used to assess each strategy, where the overall degree of uncertainty in undertaking a strategy is mathematically assessed by combining the uncertainties within each of the elements of the strategic option.

- *Stakeholder expectations* – stakeholder analysis should identify the suitability of each strategy. This includes the assessment of the stakeholders' reaction to the strategy in relation to share issues, maintenance activities and power struggles.

It must be remembered, however, that strategy evaluation cannot account for or anticipate all of the issues that may be considered when a new strategy is embarked upon. **RAA**

References

Day, G. (1986) *Analysis for Strategic Market Decisions,* USA: West Publishing Company.

Porter, M. (1980) *Competitive Strategy: Techniques for Analysing Industries and Competitors,* New York: Free Press.

Proctor, R. A. and Hassard, J. S. (1990) 'Towards a new model for product portfolio analysis', *Management Decision,* 28(3):14–17.

Wright, R. (1974) *A System for Managing Diversity,* Cambridge MA: Arthur D. Little Inc.

Evolution of marketing

Marketing maturity is the result of an evolutionary process and is achieved when the organization fully adopts the marketing concept. Business has evolved through lower stages of development to a sophisticated stage where customer satisfaction is the principal goal of all commercial activity. Companies have realized that of all business stakeholders, the customer is the most important, for it is from customer satisfaction that all stakeholder needs are satisfied.

Although this is clear common sense, in a situation where demand outstrips supply, the primary purpose of business might be seen to be production. In such 'suppliers' markets' this is known as *production orientation*. This philosophy contends that customers will prefer products or services that are affordable, and that management should focus on improving distributive and productive efficiency. This concept is closely related to the *product concept*, which holds that customers will prefer products offering the best quality, features and performance. The organization should then devote its energies to making continuous product improvements.

Sales orientation is where business begins to realize that in a highly competitive environment it is simply not enough to produce goods efficiently. This realization dawns when goods are not taken up automatically by the market place. The reality is that this is the period when supply begins to outstrip demand and manufacturers are left with unsold stocks. The sales department is the automatic place to which business turns in order to boost sales, with the emphasis being upon pushing the organization's products or services towards the market place. Some of the tactics used in sales orientation are dubious and it often involves high pressure selling, misleading advertising and many similar techniques that have emphasized the darker side of marketing. Sales orientation was prevalent in Europe in the 1960s, but it was shortlived because companies realized that customer satisfaction through *marketing orientation* was the key to long lasting business success. **GL**

Reference

Lancaster, G. and Massingham, L. (1999) *Essentials of Marketing,* 2nd edn, Maidenhead: McGraw-Hill, pp. 354–355.

Exhibitions

Exhibitions and trade shows provide a temporary forum for sellers to exhibit and demonstrate their products. Some exhibitions exist as marketplaces at which products are bought and sold. Others, such as the Motor Show, exist purely for promotional purposes with no actual selling taking place (although less directly, sales leads may be generated). Some are business-to-business only, others are open to the public. Exhibitions present a quite unique situation in which prospects and competitors are brought together under one roof.

A significant feature of exhibitions is the presumption that those attending are active, rather than passive, seekers and are, as such, prime prospects ready to receive marketing communications. That exhibitions are selling opportunities is emphasized by most of the research and literature on the subject. Research by Herbig *et al.* (1994) indicates that managers allocate resources in relation to the level of sales leads they anticipate, while Sharland and Balogh (1996) define exhibition effectiveness in terms of sales leads generated. Of particular benefit is the low cost per contact made when compared with cold calling in the field.

Exhibitions are perceived to have other benefits and the table below is an adaptation of the findings from research conducted on managers by Shipley *et al.* (1993). Thirteen reasons for exhibiting have been identified. **DWP**

Table: **Reasons for exhibiting**

Objective	UK Companies Rank	Overseas Companies Rank
Meet new customers	1	1
Enhance company image	2	2
Interact with customers	3	4
Promote existing products	4	3
Launch new products	5	5
Get competitor intelligence	6	6
Get edge on non-exhibitors	7	9
Keep up with competitors	8	8
Enhance personnel morale	9	13
Interact with distributors	10	7
General market research	11	11
Take sales orders	12	12
Meet new distributors	13	10

References

Herbig, P., O'Hara, B. and Palumbo, F. (1994) 'Measuring trade show effectiveness: an effective exercise?' *Industrial Marketing Management*, 23:165–170.

Sharland, A. and Balogh, P. (1996) 'The value of non-selling activities at international trade shows', *Industrial Marketing Management*, 25:59–66.

Shipley, D., Egan, C. and Wong, K.S. (1993) 'Dimensions of trade show exhibiting management', *Journal of Marketing Management*, 9(1).

Experiments

A form of research method which is carried out to establish cause-effect relationships between variables either within the natural environment or by creating an artificial one is called experimental research. Studies that are conducted to establish cause-effect relationships using the same natural environment in which the subject of interest normally functions are called *field experiments*. In this experiment, the researcher interferes with the natural flow of events by manipulating specific variables.

Another form of experimental research is when the research setting is created artificially in a laboratory to represent the natural setting. This is called a *lab experiment* and is often carried out to identify cause-effect relationships between variables within an artificial, contrived environment in which all the extraneous factors are strictly controlled. Subjects are carefully chosen by the researcher to respond to certain manipulated stimuli.

Both types of experimental research are meant to collect information which could be useful in assessing events within a real situation. These are scientific research methods where the findings of the research are likely to be precise, objective and can be generalized to apply to a real situation. The information obtained from experimental research is often used as inputs for decisions by decision makers. **RM-R**

Reference

Sekaran, U. (1996) *Research Methods for Business*, 2nd edn, New York: John Wiley & Sons.

Exporting

It is possible that the very word 'exporting' is obsolete in the context of global trade developments. Is the owner of a web site offering goods for sale through the Internet an exporter, a global marketer, or what?

Traditionally it is the small business that we associate with exporting. We associate exporting with the first stage of internationalization. It is the low entry cost, low risk approach to global business. Time horizons are relatively short, with sales the principal objective. As the least cost approach it may be appropriate to a cautious exploration of the learning curve.

The problem is that our perception of what constitutes a small firm is changing. Silicon Valley is replete with small firms if you focus on number of employees, even on revenue. But in terms of profitability and global reach some of them are world players.

The reasons for failure in exporting are as revealing as any list of success factors. Here is my top ten.

1. Failure to obtain good advice and to develop a marketing plan.
2. Insufficient commitment by top management to financial requirements for exporting.
3. Insufficient care in selection of agent/distributors.
4. Chasing orders around the world instead of concentrating on a few potentially profitable markets.
5. Neglecting export business when the home market is buoyant.
6. Failure to treat overseas distributors as you treat domestic counterparts.
7. Assuming that a marketing formula that has worked in the home market will work overseas.
8. Unwillingness to modify products to meet local requirements in use, and local regulations.
9. Failure to communicate in local languages, including warranty and instructions.
10. Failure to provide adequate servicing. **MJT**

References

London Chamber of Commerce and Industry (1994) *The Export Handbook: A Complete Guide and Reference Source for International Traders*, London: Kogan Page.

Noonan, C. (1996) *The CIM Handbook of Export Marketing: A Practical Guide to Opening and Expanding Markets Overseas*, Oxford: Butterworth-Heinemann.

Extending past behaviour

Extending past behaviour is a forecasting technique which uses previous experience as a guide to future outcomes. Past behaviour is analysed and an extrapolation made in order to develop a forecast.

The problem with this concept is that it assumes that all other factors will remain the same; that the past is a good guide to the future. In fact this is unlikely to be the case, since the environment within which firms operate is changing rapidly, and almost continuously.

The main techniques used in extending past behaviour are as follows (Lancaster and Jobber 1997):

- *Time series analysis* – this involves using time as the only variable; it is useful in industries such as the toy industry in which there is pronounced seasonality. The drawback with this approach is that it ignores possible wider changes in the market.
- *Causal techniques* – here it is assumed that there is a relationship between a measurable independent variable and the forecasted dependent variable. For example, a manager may predict that each salesperson will generate a certain average level of sales, so that increasing the number of salespeople will increase the overall level of sales.

Extending past behaviour can be used as a check against the usefulness of more complex techniques; if past behaviour provides as accurate a prediction as, say, expensive market research, then past behaviour might be used instead (Makridikas and Wheelwright 1977). **JWDB**

References

Lancaster, G. and Jobber, D. (1997) *Selling and Sales Management,* 4th edn, London: Pitman Publishing.

Makridikas, S. and Wheelwright, S. (1977) 'Forecasting: issues and challenges for marketing management', *Journal of Marketing* 41(October): 30.

Fast moving consumer goods

'Fast moving consumer goods', commonly abbreviated to 'FMCGs', are everyday necessities of a relatively low unit value with which we are all familiar. Unlike the purchase of organizational goods, where logical economic and performance factors determine purchases, more irrational motives surround FMCG buying and generally little pre-planning goes into their purchase. In fact the FMCG classification also includes convenience goods, although FMCG categorization is somewhat broader as it includes a whole range of products that are used by the general public, but are more durable in nature. These categories are sometimes called 'shopping goods' and here the purchase frequency is longer.

FMCG producers tend to put a lot of promotion behind their products, whose purpose is to make consumers 'brand loyal' so they will automatically choose the same brand again and again. This is known as using a 'pull' strategy of promotion, whereby consumers are pre-sold on the brand through advertising and sales promotion. The expectation is that the product will be offered for sale in most outlets, as retailers cannot afford to ignore the power of demand built up through advertising. Some manufacturers of FMCGs use a 'push' strategy of promotion, whereby they promote the product through the trade by offering price incentives and discounts. This is in the expectation that agents, wholesalers and retailers will push the products towards consumers and display them in retail outlets where buyers will have the opportunity to see the products on display and hopefully make their purchases. GL

Reference
Lancaster, G. and Massingham, L. (1999) *Essentials of Marketing*, 3rd edn, Maidenhead: McGraw-Hill, pp. 36 and 343.

Fiscal issues

Fiscal issues are those revolving around the firm's money situation: cash flow, return on capital, income generation and so forth.

It has often been said that the marketing department is the only department that generates income; all other departments only *spend* money. This view ignores the interconnectivity of the firm's activities: marketers would be unable to generate income if they had no products to sell, and would be unable to collect the money if there were no finance department to send out the invoices. Nevertheless, the burden of attracting and retaining customers (and hence their money) rests firmly with marketing.

Fiscal constraints also prevent marketers from being able to spend money as freely as they might wish; this is the driving force behind segmentation, since marketers have to direct limited resources towards the most productive segments of the overall market.

Credit control issues can sometimes impinge on marketers, since the finance department will not wish to continue to supply bad payers. Since giving credit can have a serious effect on the firm's cashflow, it is important that only those customers who can be relied on to pay up on time (or at least within a reasonable time) are supplied. This places a burden on the salesforce since they will need to raise the sensitive issue of creditworthiness when they find a new customer; in some firms, the salesforce is also given the unpleasant task of chasing bad debt. Writing off bad debt is tantamount to giving away supplies, so firms are naturally reluctant to do this and will seek to pursue debtors. Since the salesforce usually has the closest relationships with the customers, they are the natural candidates for the job. **JWDB**

Reference
Brassington F., and Pettitt, S. (2000) *Principles of Marketing* 2nd edn, Harlow: Financial Times Prentice Hall, pp. 582–585.

Focus strategy

Porter (1985) says that in order to succeed every business must adopt one of the three generic strategies: cost leadership, differentiation or focus. Focus involves selecting a narrow target and focusing on a niche within the marketplace. Owing to the costs of pursuing a differentiation strategy or the economies of scale necessary to adopt a cost leadership strategy, focus is the generic strategy that is most easily implemented by small as well as large companies. A company adopting a focus strategy develops products or services specifically targeted at a market segment (or small number of segments) to the exclusion of other segments. In this way it is possible for even a very small company to hold a competitive advantage within a targeted market segment.

The Blackpool car manufacturer TVR has continued to prosper despite the decline of the generic British car industry because it follows a clear focus strategy. A small company that builds sports cars by hand rather than by using a production line, TVR satisfies a small yet profitable niche of wealthy and discerning customers. Customers are prepared to wait for two years for delivery of their car, such is the individuality of the TVR product.

In an increasingly global marketplace, companies are choosing to specialize in order to compete in a narrower competitive environment. Advertising agencies used to offer a 'full service', but now there are few full service agencies remaining. Instead the industry is sub-divided into specialisms e.g. media buying or creative, and even within this into agencies specializing in radio advertising or direct marketing.

Focus can be combined with the other generic strategies to produce a 'cost focus' strategy whereby a company looks for a cost advantage in its target segment only, or a 'differentiation focus' whereby a firm seeks differentiation in its target segment only. **SR**

Reference
Porter, M.E., (1985) *Competitive Advantage*, New York: The Free Press.

Forecast accuracy

Forecast accuracy is the degree of conformity between predicted results and actual outcomes. Predicting the future is certainly possible, and most people do it as a matter of routine but with varying degrees of accuracy; judging the level and type of inaccuracy which is likely to result from a forecast is often fraught with difficulty.

Forecasting will be more accurate when there are patterns of repetition in events, or where there are persistent trends whose direction can be predicted. Accuracy increases when the time frame is short, when the data from which the forecast is extrapolated is plentiful and when the forecast is arrived at from different directions (Floes and White, 1988). For example, two forecasts that use different data, compiled by different individuals, which arrive at the same conclusion will be more likely to lead to a high degree of accuracy than would one forecast alone. Long-range forecasting is notoriously difficult and is frequently inaccurate.

Forecasts may also become accurate when they are self-fulfilling. For example, a sales forecast may become self-fulfilling because the sales manager and the sales force become committed to its achievement. Much depends on the extent to which the forecast becomes part of the corporate plan.

Exactitude is probably not feasible, so forecasts almost always deal with probabilities. **JWDB**

Reference

Flores, B.E. and White, E.M. (1988) 'A framework for the combination of forecasts', *Journal of the Academy of Marketing Science*, 16(Fall): 95–103.

Franchises

A franchise is a contractual arrangement whereby one person or business organization (the *franchisor*) authorizes another person (the *franchisee*) to use the franchisor's business system and trade name in exchange for financial rewards, both initial and recurring. There are different types of franchise arrangements to accommodate partnerships between manufacturing, wholesale and retail organizations. In the retail and service sector *business format franchising* is the most common form. Here a uniform business format is used in order to create a clearly defined retail brand image in the eyes of the consumer. Sourcing, branding and advertising strategies are shared, thus offering economies of scale. Typically there is a strong central steer, with the franchisor guiding administration and management. Training and assistance before and after opening are provided, and there is a network of fellow franchisees. At the same time franchising offers the investment opportunity, independence and responsibility of self-employment. The greater security of franchising is illustrated by the fact that, whilst a quarter of independent new business start-ups fail in the first year, around 90 per cent of franchises survive. However, disadvantages may result where franchisees are contractually bound to accept exclusive supplies from the franchisor, as this may mean above market prices, thus depressing profit margins.

Business format franchising was developed in the USA after the Civil War and became popular in the UK in the 1960s through the Wimpy Hamburger chain and is now strong in retail and services, especially in the dairy delivery market. Since 1977 the industry has been represented by the British Franchise Association. Between 1986 and 1996 total turnover from UK franchises grew from £1.9bn to £6.4bn, with further strong growth projected for the sector. Franchising is an important vehicle for retail internationalization. Well known franchises include McDonald's, Dunkin' Donuts, the Body Shop, Tie Rack and Benetton. **RAS**

References

Forward, J. and Fullop, C. (1993) *Issues in Franchising: an Analysis of the Literature*, London: NatWest Centre for Franchising Research.

Key Note (1997) *Franchising*, Hampton: Key Note Ltd.

Mendelsohn, M. (1999) *The Guide to Franchising*, 6th edn, London: Cassell.

Schmidt, R.A. and Oldfield, B.M. (1998) 'Dunkin' Donuts – the birth of a new distribution and franchising concept', *The British Journal of Food*, 100(2):119–124.

Franchising

A franchise system is a form of a contractual vertical market network since firms that are part of a franchise are tied by specific contractual agreements. The contractual agreement may be in the form of a licensing agreement, where an entire business format may be licensed by the owner (the franchisor) to other firms (the franchisees) who agree to market and operate the business that has been developed by the franchisor. In such a case, the franchisee is entitled to use the franchisor's trade names, trademarks, business methods and service marks. In return, the franchisor expects specific payments to be made in the forms of franchise fees. This may range from an initial franchise fee for new franchisees, royalty fees which are commission based on the gross value of a franchisee's sales volume, licence fees for the use and display of the franchisor's trademark and management fees for consultation services provided by the franchisor.

Depending on the types of franchise systems, many franchises offer an alternative form of marketing channel organization with several distinct advantages such as equity expansion. For a supplier, a franchise system offers capital advantages since funds for business expansion can be acquired without necessarily losing ownership to the business. Initial franchise fees provided by the franchisees become a major source of working capital to the franchisor without a need for borrowing. In addition, franchisees' royalty payments often go toward promotional programmes or cooperative advertising which reduce the franchisor's promotional costs.

The high costs of maintaining company-owned distribution networks in many geographical locations is encouraging the formation of franchises since franchising reduces distribution costs. If a firm relies on company-owned distribution networks, it will be burdened with fixed overhead expenses. Franchisees who share in the profits of the business are more likely than company paid managers to be motivated in making substantial profits.

Franchising, however, can be saddled with several disadvantages. Finding the right channel partners to be part of the franchise system can be quite difficult. The need to be very selective is crucial in ensuring the success of the franchise systems. In addition, franchise systems can be more inflexible than other types of distribution structures.

Since many franchise agreements are long-term, terminating poor franchisees or selling off a weak franchise system can be quite difficult. Controlling the marketing functions of a franchise system may prove to be more difficult than corporate vertical networks. The existence of channel conflict is sometimes more apparent in franchise systems since franchisees often view the franchisor suspiciously because of their need to have control over the business operations. Despite these drawbacks, franchise systems appear to be lucrative for some form of businesses, especially fast food operators. **RM-R**

References

Hunt, S. D. (1977) 'Franchising: promise, problems, prospects', *Journal of Retailing*, 53(3)(Fall): 78.

Izraeli, D. (1972) *Franchising and the Total Distribution System*, London: Longman.

Geodemographics

From the 1981 UK census, some 40 census variables were cluster analysed and the emerging clusters of households led to the creation of 39 neighbourhood types in the first geodemographic system in the UK (ACORN – A Classification of Residential Neighbourhoods, developed by CACI – Consolidated Analysis Centres Incorporated). The marketing industry suddenly had access to census data for all 24 million UK households. Names and addresses cannot be revealed from the census, but the statistics for enumeration districts can. Such data can be linked with the postcode database (there is one postcode for approximately 15 households) and, with the electoral register (another database), it is possible to identify individual households and their characteristics.

The basic rationale behind the use of geodemographics is that 'birds of a feather flock together' (Leventhal, 1995), a criticism being that 'I'm not like my neighbour'. However, geodemographics have proved to be useful differentiators of consumer behaviour and therefore have uses in profiling retail catchment areas for profiling, segmenting and targeting via marketing databases.

There are 'me-toos' of the original ACORN system. Richard Webber, who created ACORN, set up one of the competitors after he left CACI to join CCN (now Experian, following the link with the American company of that name) and developed MOSAIC which analyses the census data in conjunction with a variety of data sources including County Court Judgments on bad debt (CCJs), electoral roll and Royal Mail data. Similar systems operate in many other developed countries.

A limitation of census data relates to the difficulties associated with updating information, particularly because in the UK the census is only carried out every 10 years. Also, as sophisticated as geodemographics are, certainly compared with the simplicity of age, sex and occupation (the main variables of the demographic alternative) the approach is essentially the same, that is it 'profiles' people. It does not in itself explain why people behave as they do and neither does it provide individualized information on what people buy (Evans, 2000). **MJE**

References

Evans, M. (2000) 'Marketing research and the new biographics', in M. Crimp and L.T. Wright Pearson *The Marketing Research Process*, Harlow: Prentice Hall.

Leventhal, B. (1995) 'Evaluation of geodemographic classifications', *Journal of Targeting, Measurement and Analysis for Marketing*, 4(2):173–183.

Geographic pricing

Geographic pricing, or spatial pricing, is a pricing strategy adopted by firms serving different geographic markets, where transportation cost is an important component of transaction cost. Prices to be charged in various regions depend on competitive conditions in those regions and on consumer valuation of transaction costs and prices. Two basic (and opposite) geographic strategies are *delivered pricing* and *non-delivered pricing*. Under delivered pricing the company delivers the products and incurs the transportation cost. In single-zone (or uniform) delivered pricing, the product is delivered in all markets at the same ultimate price, while multiple-zone delivered pricing requires that various prices be associated with pre-specified geographic areas. Non-delivered pricing implies that the customer is responsible for the transportation of the goods from the point of origin (factory, warehouse, etc.) and bears the freight cost (Tellis, 1986; Hanna and Dodge, 1997).

Companies may also opt for an in-between strategy. Menu plans allow (some) consumers to choose from different options. They are a combination of delivered and non-delivered prices: consumers within a designated area are offered a delivered price but get a discount if they transport themselves. Outside the zone only non-delivered prices are valid. In a menu plan, the choice of the geographic area affects both the market served and the market share and margins within that served area (Basu and Mazumdar, 1995).

In an international setting, sales contracts typically stipulate not only who is in charge of transportation costs, but also when product ownership and other responsibilities are transferred from seller to buyer. This gives rise to a range of alternative trade terms (Incoterms) and agreements, such as free-on-board (FOB) and cost-insurance-freight (CIF) (see Ramberg, 1999). **KCa, BF, EG**

References

Basu, A. K. and Mazumdar, T. (1995) 'Using a menu of geographic pricing plans: a theoretical investigation', *Journal of Retailing*, 71(2):173–202.
Hanna, N. and Dodge, H.R. (1997) *Pricing: Policies and Procedures*, London: Macmillan Press.
Monroe, K. (1990) *Pricing: Making Profitable Decisions*, New York: McGraw-Hill International Editions.
Ramberg, J. (1999) *ICC Guide to Incoterms 2000*, Paris: ICC Publishing.
Tellis, G.J. (1986) 'Beyond the many faces of price: an integration of pricing strategies', *Journal of Marketing*, 50(October): 46–60.

Globalization

Globalization, already galloping, will dominate the 21st century, as will the Internet and e-commerce. No business, indeed no person, anywhere in the world will be untouched by it.

Continuously, since the founding of the General Agreement on Tariffs and Trade (GATT) and the successor World Trade Organisation (WTO), world trade has expanded. The composition of this trade has moved from being predominantly primary products and natural resources to finished goods and services. The period since 1946 has seen a dramatic increase in the number of global corporations – these, the largest multinationals, excluding banking and finance, constitute 40 to 50 per cent of all cross border assets.

The 20th century may be said to have been the Atlantic century, since world trade was dominated by activity originating in North America and Western Europe. Crudely stated, that was the developed world, or most of it.

The 21st century will see a shift in the balance of power to the Pacific Rim, as China and India join other East Asian countries on the road to full development. The Pacific Rim will create huge market opportunities.

Globalization and information technology are changing the rules of the game. The drivers of globalization may be portrayed as follows.

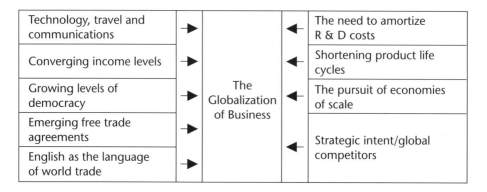

Figure: **The globalization process**

All these factors are at work, touching every corner of our lives. For the majority of companies, a global presence will be necessary for survival. If you presently have customers, then your (global) competitors will be eyeing them enviously and in a predatory way. Though niche markets may prosper, there are many companies eyeing niche market opportunities. But it is the 'Big Brands' and the global corporations that will make life uncomfortable. They have scale and experience to work with, they have brand power, and they will seek customers wherever they are found to be.
MJT

Reference
Hakensen, S. (1998) *Global Marketing*, Hemel Hempstead: Prentice Hall.

Globalization debate

The world, according to the 'globalization thesis', is rapidly becoming a single socio-economic system, thanks to the increasing interdependence of countries and trading blocs, dramatic improvements in communications technology and the development of supra-national institutions, attitudes, relationships and lifestyles (Lechner and Boli, 2000). Certainly, there is no shortage of corroborative evidence. The shelves of our neighbourhood supermarkets are stocked with the produce of far-flung farmers, the principal shopping streets of our cities are lined with the same array of luxury goods outlets and, thanks to the Internet, it is easier to buy an Australian CD from an American e-tailer, than to patronize a local record store (which won't have the CD in stock, in any event). Globalization, of course, is not new. The process started several centuries ago with the voyages of discovery, the associated development of long-distance trade routes and the West's scramble for colonies in the 19th century. However, it has intensified in recent years, especially in the aftermath of Communism's dramatic collapse and subsequent surrender to American-style free-market ideology (albeit many Third World countries have paid a heavy economic price to join the global party).

Within marketing, the globalization 'debate' dates from Ted Levitt's (1983) famous contention that today's increasingly homogeneous markets are conducive to global marketing strategies, where standardized goods and services can be sold on a worldwide basis. The economies of scale accruing to companies purveying the same wares in the same way, regardless of superficial regional and cultural differences, gives them a powerful competitive advantage. Small, locally-focused organizations and old-style multinationals, which adapt their products to national tastes or preferences, are sure to be swept away by gigantic, globally-orientated conglomerates. To be sure, Levitt's characteristically extravagant vision resonated with many megalo-maniacal marketing managers. Saatchi and Saatchi actually attempted to implement his thesis and only just survived to tell the tale. But, as with so many of the great guru's predictions, one-size-fits-all globalization never really came to pass. Survey after survey has shown that there are comparatively few truly global brands – Coke, Benetton, Disney etc – and even these organizations are inclined to think-global-act-local, by adapting their offerings to the idiosyncratic characteristics of individual markets.

If anything, indeed, the tub-thumping rhetoric of globalization has given rise to a countervailing discourse of difference, heterogeneity and uniqueness. Strategists emphasize how local clusters of industry-specific expertise underpin the competitive advantage of nations; companies are exhorted to think-local-act-global, as in the case of the ersatz Irishness sold by theme pub operators and the producers of *Riverdance*; marketers' attempt to develop one-on-one relationships with their customers by means of dedicated databases, loyalty card schemes *et al.*, or remain content to farm out their production facilities, distribution arrangements, call centres and all the rest to cadres of foreign suppliers, conveniently situated in perniciously low-cost locations. On a larger socio-economic scale, moreover, the rise of 'McWorld' has called forth a sectarian, xenophobic, anti-American mindset. Termed 'jihad' by Barber (1995), this not only refers to religious fundamentalism and ethnic conflict, but also to the anti-globalization, anti-consumption, anti-Third World exploitation attitudes that found expression in London's Carnival against Capitalism of June 1999 and December 1999's anti-WTO riots in Seattle. It is striking that the latter began with attacks on branches of customer-orientated organizations such as McDonald's, Starbucks and Niketown. So much for the much-lauded marketing concept. **SB**

References

Barber, B.J. (1995) *Jihad vs. McWorld: How Globalism and Tribalism are Reshaping the World*, New York: Ballantine Books.
Lechner, F.J. and Boli, J. (eds) (2000) *The Globalisation Reader*, Oxford: Blackwell.
Levitt, T. (1983) 'The globalization of markets', *Harvard Business Review*, reprinted in *Levitt on Marketing*, Boston, MA: Harvard Business Review Press, 39–49.

Glocalization

An ugly word, but for some companies it may be salvation. The pressures for globalization, for global integration, have already been cited: global customers, global competitors, customers with similar needs (segmentation), pressures for cost reduction and exploiting economies of scale, investment intensity, technology intensity.

At the same time, pressures for local responsiveness exist, because of differences in customer needs, channels of distribution, availability of local substitutes, market structure and host government demands and regulations.

These factors may impede global integration and may protect some local producers. What they tell us is that, while you must think global, you must still be prepared to act local in order to respond appropriately to local customer demand.

The fact is, however, that the rules of the game are changing. The pressure for local responsiveness is being eroded. McDonalds and Coca Cola are symbols of the problem, for consumers all over the world seem to be ready to consume the products of global businesses that grew up in the USA but which are now universal symbols of what we have in common.

E-commerce and the Internet are merely accelerating the process of global integration. Ironically, the Internet provides every company with the opportunity to respond on a one-to-one basis with any and every networked customer, reducing most government influence and removing channel barriers at the stroke of a keyboard.

What will emerge? More minnows (successful niche players) and more giants. More global provision. More customized content and service. More communities of culture. More perfect competition? More global peace and understanding? Let us hope so.

Before concluding I wish to point out the downside of the situation described in the preceding sections.

- The global economy does not embrace the whole planet. A visitor from outer space would easily observe large sections of the planet – much of Africa, the land we now call Russia, Central America, i.e. the Third or Developing World as opposed to the First or Developed World – still in the grip of poverty, where the majority of the population lives hand to mouth, with virtually no discretionary income to spend. We may not care to show our visitor the Fourth World either, the world of exclusion from the excess of consumption that surrounds them: Tower Hamlets in London, the South Bronx in New York, the barrios of South America.
- The company of the future will be unlike the companies of our past. Virtual reality companies may have global reach but employ few people directly, hence forecasts about purchasing power may be much more difficult to make in the future as secure employment is replaced with contract employment.
- Social polarization and social exclusion may produce the nightmare Pareto world of 80 per cent of the world's wealth being commanded by 20 per cent of the world's population.
- The oligopoly of the world of the media may result in the homogenization of demand – everyone will be the same in the global village, glued to CNN and vacationing only in Disneyworld, Coke from McDonalds clutched in their hands.
- Politics and political processes will become soap opera, motivated by greed, betrayal, sex, violence and spin doctors.

Do not be depressed, but think about these things: the 21st century will be either globalized or glocalized. **MJT**

References

Paliwoda, S.J. and Thomas, M.J., (1998) *International Marketing* 3rd edn, Oxford: Butterworth-Heinemann.

Thomas, M.J., (1999) 'The information age and the death of distance', Proceedings of the First International Conference on Critical Management Studies, Manchester School of Management, (July): 14–16.

Newman, B.I., (1999) *The Mass Marketing of Politics: Democracy in an Age of Manufactured Images*, London: Sage Publications.

Goods and services

Unlike physical goods with which people can immediately associate, services are intangible and it is more difficult to relate to them. However, when they are marketed, services are often associated with tangible items (e.g. the service of a flight requires an aeroplane and a car hire service requires a car, but it is essentially the service to which the customer relates). There are no special 'rules' for the marketing of a service, except that because of intangibility, characteristics of the service itself must be highlighted to satisfy customers.

Manipulation of the marketing mix, which includes the 4 Ps (see 'Marketing mix'), is the means through which goods and services are sold to the public. The nature of services means that special efforts must be made to attempt to persuade customers to associate the service with more tangible items and these are highlighted through the 7 Ps of service marketing, the three extra Ps being people, process and physical evidence (see also 'Marketing mix').

Services are intangible so it is not possible for customers to taste, feel, hear or smell services before they purchase. The marketing company must, therefore, emphasize the benefits to be derived from the service rather than describe the service itself.

It is not possible to separate services from the seller and some are created and dispensed at the same time (e.g. a meal in a restaurant). This is termed *inseparability* and, because many people are involved at the same time with production, delivery and consumption of the service, efforts must be made to create the best impression in the minds of customers, so they will make repeat purchases. Using the restaurant analogy, it is not only the quality of the food that should impress customers, but also the ambience of the restaurant and standard of service.

Heterogeneity is another criterion and in this context it refers to the difficulty of standardizing a service. For example, service tasks on a car will differ from task to task and marketers must try to ensure consistency in an attempt to make all service offerings as good as each other.

The final criterion is *perishability*, which relates to the fact that service items cannot be stored. When a restaurant is not busy it is not making money for the owner. Fluctuating demand is a facet of services and the creative marketer must offer specific deals such as lower priced meals during off peak times to attract customers. **GL**

Reference
Lancaster, G. and Reynolds, P. (1999) *Introduction to Marketing*, London: Kogan Page, pp. 179–181.

Growth strategies

The development of growth strategies is an important element of the marketing planning process. A business may choose one or more competitive strategies summarized within Ansoff's competitive strategy matrix, which focuses upon the product and the market place.

	Current products	**New products**
Current markets	Market penetration strategy	Product development strategy
New markets	Market development strategy	Diversification strategy

Figure: **Ansoff's competitive strategy matrix**
Source: Ansoff (1988) p.83

Intense growth is where current products and current markets have the potential for increasing sales or market share. The three main strategies are market penetration, market development and product development.

- *Market penetration strategy* is where increased market share is developed in existing markets with current products. This could involve penetration pricing policies cutting existing prices to compete with competitors, increased promotion, including personal selling, sales promotion and advertising in the trade press.

- *Market development strategy* develops growth by entering new markets with existing products. Research would be necessary to establish any new markets which would be viable for the product. An example of this is the recent development of Haagen-Dazs ice cream, where the brand was developed across Europe with the '100 per cent perfection' strapline, which aimed to position the brand, introducing irony and humour.
- *Product development strategy* encourages growth by introducing new or improved products to existing markets. Expertise and skills to change and develop the product are required to sell to the market already established. Boots the Chemist in the UK recently lunched six own-label 'power brands' as part of its new strategy to drive growth through its core retail business. These brands were part of its 'differentiation-led' strategy where a self-diagnosis kit and interactive unit helped customers to select the right products for their lifestyle and hair type.
- *Diversified growth strategy* involves growing by introducing a completely new product and moving into a new market. This can be described as horizontal diversification, concentric diversification or conglomerate diversification. This strategy is often employed to allow firms to spread their risk across a number of markets and it is often developed through joint ventures or mergers and acquisitions.

The management decisions are influenced by the product life cycle and the current state of the company's product portfolio and resources. **RAA**

References

Ansoff, H.I. (1988) *The New Corporate Strategy,* New York: Wiley & Sons: New York.

Wilson, R.M.S. and Gilligan, C. (1997) *Strategic Marketing Management: Planning, Implementation and Control,* Oxford: CIM/Butterworth-Heinemann, pp. 221–225.

H

Harvesting

Harvesting is also referred to as 'milking'. The term 'harvesting' can be directly applied in two specific situations. First, it is often referred to in the context of a company harvesting part of its product range. A company may be faced with falling demand and sales for its product. This could be due to increased competition, changing fashion and trends and/or improvements in technology, which would all impact upon the ability to sell the product. When faced with a slowdown in sales growth and consequently profits, a company may attempt to harvest the product. Therefore the company would attempt to maintain the existing profit levels of the product by reducing the amount of marketing expenditure invested in it. If the company believed that it was unlikely that sales would begin to rise again in the future, then a harvesting strategy would be adopted up to the point where profits were at an acceptable level. Beyond this point, the company would consider deleting the product from the range and diverting resources into other profitable areas.

Secondly, harvesting is also referred to where companies adopt the same strategy, but within a distinct business area, (e.g. a strategic business unit). The company would aim to improve overall performance of the business unit by harvesting those areas which were proving to be unattractive in terms of long term sales and profit growth. The company may have no intention of selling the business unit or closing it down, but would try and improve its profits and performance by concentrating its resources in more attractive markets. However, in some instances, such a strategy can ultimately lead to the business unit being divested from the company if it no longer fits within the overall portfolio.

The main focus of any harvesting strategy is to ensure tight control over the costs and to maintain an adequate profit margin for the business. A company following such an approach will also have to maintain a certain degree of demand and customer base. **PBB**

References
Day, G.S. (1977) 'Diagnosing the product portfolio', *Journal of Marketing*, 41(2):29–38.
Kotler, P.C. (1978) 'Harvesting strategies for weak products' *Business Horizons*, 21(4):15–22.

Haulage and storage

One important component of a distribution system is transportation, since the product must be moved in the right quantity at a specific time to a specific place. Haulage in a distribution channel refers to the transportation system that has been selected to move goods physically through the distribution network. Selecting the appropriate transportation mode is critical in the accomplishment of distribution objectives. Inadequate transportation service and inconsistent delivery schedules can result in an increase in inventory costs since a company may be forced to hold inventory much longer than necessary. As such, a distribution manager needs to decide on the most efficient and reliable haulage system to transport the goods so that they can be delivered to the right place at the right time in the correct quantity as required by the customers.

Finished goods that are awaiting transportation may need to be stored before they are delivered to the appropriate locations. Storage facilities in the form of warehouses are necessary to store finished goods inventories. The storage function occurs when distribution managers add goods to stock, or when they store seasonally produced items, or when there is a need to preserve perishable products. The presence of inventories and the need to keep inventories in ensuring continuity of supply dictates the need for storage. Although distribution managers often try to minimize total inventory costs, there is still a need to maintain an adequate amount of inventory. As such, storage facilities are part and parcel of warehousing and inventory management. **RM-R**

References

Ballou, R.H. (1992) *Business Logistics Management*, 3rd edn, Englewood Cliffs, NJ: Prentice Hall.
Bowersox, D.J. and Cooper, M.B. (1992) *Strategic Marketing Channel Management*, Singapore: McGraw-Hill International Editions.

Hedonic experiential model

The cognitive information processing model of how people make sense of the world represents people as thinkers. In contrast, the hedonic experiential model (HEM), emphasizes the major influence that past experiences, emotions and feelings have in communication and consumption behaviour. 'This experiential perspective is phenomenological in spirit and regards consumption as a primarily subjective state of consciousness with a variety of subjective meanings, hedonic responses and aesthetic criteria', (Hirschman and Holbrook, 1982). Shimp (1997) recognizes that much marketing communication is a composite of the two and that individuals are motivated by both emotional and cognitive stimulation although, as researchers point out, responses to each are personal (Lofman, 1991) and vary by gender, ethnicity and culture (Hirschman, 1982; Hirschman and Holbrook, 1982; Lacher, 1994; Lacher and Mizerski, 1994).

It is easy to see that much marketing communication activity is intended to appeal to emotions. This has resulted in the growth in emphasis on branding and brand imagery, so strongly advocated by the renowned David Ogilvy, founding partner of one of the world's largest advertising agencies, Ogilvy and Mather. Marketing communications are used in this instance to help build emotional and psychological associations and extensive use is made of symbolism. Whereas a cognitive style of presentation will feature information, reason and logic, the hedonic style highlights brand values, symbolism and experiential features. **DWP**

References

Hirschman, E.C. (1982) 'Ethnic variation in hedonic consumption', *Journal of Social Psychology* 118(2):225–234.

Hirschman, E.C. and Holbrook, M.B. (1982) 'Hedonic consumption: emerging concepts, methods and propositions', *Journal of Marketing*, 46(3):92–101.

Lacher, K.T. (1994) 'An investigation of the influence of gender on the hedonic responses created by listening to music', *Advances in Consumer Research*, 21(September): 354–359.

Lacher, K.T. and Mizerski, R. (1994) 'An exploratory study of the responses and relationships involved in the evaluation of, and intention to purchase new rock music', *Journal of Consumer Research*, 21(September): 366–381.

Lofman, B. (1991) 'Elements of experiential consumption: an exploratory study', *Advances in Consumer Research*, 18:729–735.

Shimp, T.A. (1997) *Advertising and Promotion and Supplemental Aspects of Integrated Marketing Communications*, 4th edn, Fort Worth: Dryden Press.

Home shopping

Home shopping involves the ordering of goods or services directly from domestic premises through agents, mail, telephone or electronic channels without having to visit business premises. Product information is typically provided through catalogues, direct selling or adverts.

Home shopping consists of six segments: agency mail order, direct mail order, direct response, direct selling, catalogue shops and electronic shopping. Agency mail order, direct selling and direct mail order all make use of catalogues; in the first two there are agents involved who earn a commission, in the third the consumer deals directly with the retailer. Direct response makes use of newspaper and magazine adverts. For catalogue shops most purchases are made in the retailer's showroom. Electronic shopping utilizes the Internet, interactive cable and digital TV and CD-ROM catalogues.

In 1997 the UK home shopping market was valued at £9.58bn (ex-VAT), the equivalent of 5.9 per cent of retail sales. The market is highly concentrated. In 1997 the top two operators, GUS/Argos and Littlewoods/Index together held a 51.2 per cent market share. Agency mail order has traditionally dominated the market with the catalogues of the 'Big Five', i.e. GUS, Littlewoods, Freemans, Grattan and Empire. In terms of the product mix women's wear has traditionally had the highest percentage of total home shopping turnover, with sales concentrated in the agency and direct mail segments. Home shopping has also held more than 20 per cent of the market share for jewellery, household textiles/soft furnishings, housewares/home decor and toys/nursery products. There are clear differences in target segments for traditional home shopping channels (women in the lower socio-economic groups) and the current profile of Internet users (male and from the higher socio-economic groups). The current trend for the dominant players to move their offering upmarket by investing in the direct channels is set to continue. The sector as a whole is set to grow, driven by the predicted growth of electronic shopping, direct mail and catalogue shops, with an accompanying decrease in agency sales. **RAS**

References
Baron, S., Davies, B. and Swindley, D. (1991) *Macmillan Dictionary of Retailing*, London: Macmillan Reference Books, Macmillan.

Corporate Intelligence on Retailing (1998) *Home Shopping in the UK*, London: CIR.

Pioch, E.A. and Brook, P. (1996) 'The strange case of homeshopping in the Single European Market', *Journal of Retailing and Consumer Services*, 3(3):175–182.

Household decision making

The process of making buying decisions is affected by household influences. There are many instances when acquisition, consumption and disposition are made by households rather than individuals. A household may not be a family unit because it includes a single person living alone or a group of individuals who live together in a common dwelling, regardless of whether they are related (Hoyer and MacInnis, 1997). An important aspect of households is that more than one person may be involved in the process of acquiring and consuming the product or service. Different household members may perform different roles. When making a purchase, one or more household members may be performing the role of the information gatherer. Other members may be the influencers, whilst still others may perform the role of decider. Yet another household member or members may actually do the buying. The user could be just one member of the household or the whole household may be using the product or service.

A key point here is that each role can be performed by different household members, by a single individual or the entire household. There may be instances when buying decisions are made jointly. This is most common for decisions where the perceived risk associated with the buying decision is high or when the buying decision is very important and directly involves more than one household member. It is very important for marketers to recognize that household decision making exists and there is a need to develop marketing strategies that appeal to different household members who perform different buying roles. Extending marketing efforts to include the entire household is sometimes necessary to ensure that messages will reach the appropriate target audience. **RM-R**

References
Hoyner, W. and MacInnis, D.J. (1997) *Consumer Behavior*, Boston: Houghton Mifflin Company.
Solomon, M.R. (1996) *Consumer Behavior*, Englewood Cliffs, NJ: Prentice Hall.

Human resources

Between 1985 and 1998 the number of people employed in retailing, catering and services grew by 28 per cent, making up half the UK work force by the year 2000. Over the same period there were large decreases in the areas of raw materials extraction, manufacturing and agriculture. These figures indicate a strong and continuing shift towards a service economy, accompanied by a strong growth of female and part-time employment. In a move towards a 24/7 society, working patterns have become more flexible in general. The legalization of Sunday trading and advent of 24 hour store opening has meant shift patterns of work for many store-based retail employees. For non-store personnel there have been experiments with working from home. However, retail employees do work increasingly long and family-unfriendly hours and have above average vulnerability to work-related stress. Recent regulations of working times ensure that staff are not forced to work more than 48 hours a week.

Retailing is dominated by part-time staff and staff scheduling is an important management task focusing on one of the cost elements controllable at store level. The recent imposition of the National Minimum Wage Act may have increased this cost element further. Also, an increasing emphasis on the service offering as a differentiating factor in retail marketing has had implications for staff training and development, placing greater emphasis on interpersonal skills and customer perceptions. The growth of the 'grey' market segment has prompted a number of retailers (e.g. DIY retailer B&Q) to experiment with employing pensioners on a part-time basis, thus utilizing their experience and reliability.

The 1990s saw the development of retail marketing as an academic discipline, and at the turn of the century there were over 25 distinct retailing oriented degree programmes, with a number of retailers having developed in-house retailing qualification programmes in collaboration with universities. This may help change the traditionally poor image of retailing as a professional career. **RAS**

References

Liff, S. and Turner, S. (1999) 'Working in a corner shop: are employee relations changing in response to competitive pressures?' *Employee Relations*, 21(4):418–429.
McGoldrick, A. (ed.) (1996) *Cases in Human Resource Management*, London: Pitman Publishing.
Spilsbury, M. (1993) 'Occupation and skill change in the European retail sector: a study for CECD', IMS report 247, Brighton: Institute of Manpower Studies.

Hypermarkets

A hypermarket is very large store, usually over 50 000 square feet, typically on one level and selling a wide range of food and non-foods products. Hypermarkets are usually located on the edge of town or in retail parks.

The first hypermarket was developed by French retailer Carrefour in 1963. The concept quickly spread within France and throughout Europe through the internationalization efforts of French operators, who were sharing their expertise and establishing joint ventures. At the end of the 1980s the share of food sales through hypermarkets was estimated as approximately 20 per cent for the UK, however, a changing focus in UK planning regulation meant a move away from large out-of-town developments, thus inhibiting the growth of hypermarket sales. As a result Key Note (1999) estimated hypermarket sales in the grocery sector as stable at approximately 8 per cent for much of the 1990s.

Hypermarkets remain an important feature in French food retailing. Despite recent legislation aimed at restricting the growth of hypermarkets, 58 per cent of grocery sales and 31 per cent of speciality retailing is commanded by supermarkets and hypermarkets. The sector is highly concentrated, and in 1997 the leading three hypermarket groups (i.e. Leclerc, Carrefour and Auchan-Mammouth-Docks) achieved nearly 75 per cent of overall hypermarket sales. Originally strongly price-focused, the leading hypermarket chains have responded to the advent of pan-European hard discount formats and the introduction of new pricing laws which prohibit loss leader prices, thus inhibiting deep discounting, by turning to geographical expansion into rural areas. Hypermarket operators have also continued to internationalize (e.g. Promodes, who are active throughout Europe and Carrefour, who have expanded to other European locations, as well as South America and Asia). In recent years, French hypermarkets changed their marketing approach and started to make individual departments look like local shops to break up the scale of the store, which can otherwise be perceived as intimidating. **RAS**

References

Baron, S., Davies, B. and Swindley, D. (1991) *Macmillan Dictionary of Retailing*, London: Macmillan Reference Books.
Gray, D. (1999) *Hypermarkets and Supermarkets in Europe*, London: Financial Times Business.
Key Note (1999) *Supermarkets and Superstores*, 16th edn, Hampton: Key Note Ltd.
Sternquist, B. (1998) *International Retailing*, New York: Fairchild Publications.

Hyperreality

Exemplified by the virtual worlds of cyberspace and the pseudo worlds of theme parks, heritage centres and television spectaculars, hyperreality involves the creation of marketing environments that are 'more real than real'. The distinction between reality and fantasy is momentarily blurred, as in the back lot tour of 'working' movie studios in Universal City, Los Angeles. In some respects, indeed, hyperreality is superior to everyday mundane reality, since the aversive side of 'authentic' consumption experiences – anti-tourist terrorism in Egypt, muggings in New York, dysentery in Delhi – magically disappears when such destinations are recreated in Las Vegas, Busch Gardens, Walt Disney World and countless variants on the theme park theme.

Ironically, however, the perceived superiority of the fake is predicated on an often unwarranted stereotype of reality and the reality of the fake (e.g. the queues in Disneyland) may be much worse than anything the average visitor would actually experience in Egypt, New York, Delhi or wherever (Eco, 1986; Firat and Venkatesh, 1995).

Hyperreality, nevertheless, is an especially common hybrid of postmodern marketing and retro marketing, a kind of retro pomo combo. There's hardly a High Street in Britain without its quota of 'Victorian' theme pubs (complete with plastic horse brasses and electric gas fittings), phoney 30s tea shoppes (white-aproned waitresses and triple-decker cake stands akimbo), fake 50s diners (all chrome counter-seating and red gingham table cloths) and sham 70s discotheques (platform shoes, acrylic tank top and flared trousers, a go-go). The suburbs, similarly, are suffused with pseudo rococo shopping malls (whose 'gallerias' convey a homeopathic, one-part-per-million hint of Milan's immortal Vittorio Emanuele II), seen-one-seen-em-all heritage centres (working smithy, weaving demonstration, costumed attendants, souvenir tea-towels etc.) and naff neo-Georgian entertainments complexes featuring even-better-than-the-real-thing tribute bands such as Bjorn Again, Dread Zeppelin, Illegal Eagles, Australian Pink Floyd and the one and only Gabba Gabba Hey (a postmodern cross between Abba and the Ramones, whose set climaxes with 'Gimme, Gimme, Gimme, Shock Treatment at Midnight'). **SFX**

References
Eco, U. (1986) *Travels in Hyperreality*, London: Picador.
Firat, A.F. and Venkatesh, A. (1995) 'Liberatory postmodernism and the reenchantment of consumption', *Journal of Consumer Research*, 22 (December): 239–267.

Ideas evaluation

Methods of evaluation range from simple checklists to complex weighted scoring systems. It is, however, often quite useful to adopt a more qualitative approach. One such approach is *reverse brainstorming* – a group method for discussing all possible weaknesses of an idea or what might go wrong when the idea is implemented. It is almost identical to brainstorming, except that criticisms rather than ideas are generated.

Imagine the problem was 'how to counteract declining sales' and that the following potential ideas for solutions were generated by classical brainstorming or some other ideation method:

- new advertising strategy
- offer discounts
- door to door sales
- change or improve packaging
- find new markets.

The first step is to suggest criticisms for the first of these ideas – new advertising strategy. Criticisms developed might be:

- too expensive
- unable to target the specific areas required.

After exhausting criticisms for the first idea the group begins criticizing the second idea and the process continues until all the ideas have been criticized.

Using brainstorming the group then re-examines the ideas to generate possible solutions for each weakness that has been identified. For example, in the case of the second idea, 'offer discounts', the criticisms might be that people could perceive the quality of the product to be poor as a result of offering discounts. In the case of 'door to door selling' it might be that unacceptable training and added costs would be incurred because of the need to employ more sales staff. Other criticisms will no doubt be found for the other ideas. It may be felt that there aren't any solutions to these criticisms in, say, the case of 'a new advertising strategy', however, with 'door to door selling' it may be felt possible to employ part-time workers in order to lower the cost.

The idea with the fewest weaknesses and that will be most likely to solve the problem is usually selected for implementation. Of course, one does also have to bear in mind the comparative seriousness of any unresolved criticisms. **TP**

Reference
Proctor, T. (1999) *Creative Problem Solving for Managers*, London: Routledge.

Ideas implementation

Getting new ideas off the ground can meet considerable opposition. Blocks to implementing ideas reflect such things as:

- a lack of adequate resources to implement ideas
- a lack of commitment and motivation in those required to implement ideas
- resistance to change
- procedural obstacles
- perceived risk associated with implementing ideas
- political undercurrents
- lack of cooperation in the organization.

The important thing is to uncover the nature of and the reasons for the resistance. With this information one can then look for ways of implementing ideas so that the resistance can be reduced.

The key to effecting change is to involve people in the process early, to consult with them and to get them to take ownership of the new ideas. To sustain a programme of change it is essential to understand the culture of the organization in which new ideas are to be introduced. New ideas that run counter to the traditional values of an organization are those that are most difficult to introduce. Organizational culture is the pattern of shared values and norms that distinguishes the organization from all others. One also needs to create a readiness for change within an organization. One needs to think of the organization as an internal market for change initiatives where ideas have to be marketed. This means that opinions and attitudes have to be assessed and potential sources of resistance identified. Commitment to change can be instigated by helping people to develop a shared diagnosis of what is wrong in an organization and what can and must be improved.

Good communication ensures that successful change can take place. It helps to overcome ambiguity and uncertainty and it provides information and power to those who are the subject of change. It enables them to have control over their destiny and understand why change is necessary and it provides the suppressant to fear. Through open communication channels people can express their doubts about the effectiveness of proposed changes and can understand the necessity for new ideas. Relying on an attempt to implement ideas only from the top is likely to meet with difficulties. Grassroots change is the only way to ensure that process becomes firmly embedded. It is natural for people to resist change, and by anticipating, identifying and welcoming resistance it is converted into a perceived need for change. **TP**

Reference
Proctor, T. (1999) *Creative Problem Solving for Managers*, London: Routledge.

Image building

Products are composites of physical and aesthetic features. They are a bundle of attributes that the market place does not necessarily separate. Rather, products are perceived as a 'gestalt', a whole. The overall image held of a product or a company is an important aspect of this 'gestalt'. Indeed, impressions of companies and their products are usually intertwined.

Image building is about building perceptions in the areas of corporate branding and product branding either as an integrated activity or as separate activities. Bernstein (1984), has usefully identified three elements in the image building process.

Personality ⟶ Identity ⟶ Image

Figure: **Three dimensions of image building**

Just as people have personalities so, too, do brands. The personality is the underlying 'essence' of the brand, corporate or product, 'It is the soul, the persona, the spirit, the culture .... manifested in some way' (Olins, 1990). Identity is the means by which personality is projected, it is the set of 'cues' used to communicate the brand's personality, and identity should reflect the brand's personality if confusion is to be avoided. Image is the impression or perception created in the minds of the audience. Images are perceptions held by the market and image building is the process of creating those perceptions or impressions through use of the identity cues (colours, symbols, messages, creative themes, names, slogans, logos, associations) used in marketing communications. 'Identity means the sum of all the ways a company chooses to identify itself to all its publics. Image, on the other hand, is the perception of the company (and its products) by these publics' (Margulies, 1977). **DWP**

References
Bernstein, D. (1984) *Company Image and Reality: A Critique of Corporate Communications*, London: Holt Rinehart and Winston.
Margulies, W.P. (1977) 'Make the most of your corporate identity', *Harvard Business Review*, July–August.
Olins, W. (1990) *The Corporate Personality*, London: The Design Council.

Impactory factors

Impactory factors are those events or actions that affect the implementation of the marketing plan during its lifetime. Some impactory factors are negative, for example a change in competitive activity, while others are positive, for example an easing of legislative restrictions or the advent of a new opportunity for the firm.

Impactory factors cannot always be foreseen; by their nature they are unexpected events. It is not therefore possible to include them in any contingency plans. On the other hand, contingency plans need to exist for the redrawing of the original plan if the unexpected does happen. **JWDB**

Reference
Kotler, P., Armstrong, G., Saunders, J. and Wong V. (2000) *Principles of Marketing* 2nd European Edn, Harlow: Prentice Hall, ch3.

Impulse purchasing

Impulse purchasing occurs when a consumer experiences a sudden urge to buy a product or service which he or she cannot resist. The decision to buy is usually unplanned. Impulse purchases are characterized by strong feelings of attraction towards a product or service that are difficult to resist. The presence of external stimuli such as in-store displays, colourful packaging and attractive merchandising enhance impulse buying. Items that are less involving, often called 'impulse' products, including chocolates, sweets, and magazines, are often placed near check-out counters to instigate impulse buying. Impulse products are purchased with little search effort and usually without prior planning. These products are usually widely available and are placed in strategic areas of the retail stores.

Impulse purchases are important to marketers because if products are placed strategically in the store, sales are likely to increase dramatically. The way merchandises are organized and placed in the store can help to boost sales because store customers can be induced to move through aisles and are likely to be attracted by eye-catching displays and attractive product packaging. Ease of payment for purchases through credit cards, debit cards and the existence of automatic tellers have made it more convenient for consumers to indulge in impulse purchases. **RM-R**

References

Assael, H. (1998) *Consumer Behavior and Marketing Action*, Cincinnati, Ohio: South-Western College Publishing.

Kotler, P. and Armstrong, G. (1996) *Principles of Marketing*, 7th edn, Englewood Cliffs, NJ: Prentice Hall.

Independents and multiples

Many retail sectors have an oligopolistic and highly concentrated structure, with continuing merger and acquisition activity. In the 1990s approximately 1000 village shops, 500 post offices and 150 bank or building society branches closed down, and in 1999 30 per cent of UK villages had no shop.

Independents are hindered in their marketing activities by lack of finance, expertise and time. The owner/manager is often involved in fulfilling all business functions, and this may result in a lack of clear strategic direction. Competitive pressures on the independent sector increased with the end of resale price maintenance, the expansion of supermarkets and out-of-town superstores, the growth of retailer own brands and the increase in costs brought about by introduction of the minimum wage.

In the grocery sector UK consumers use multiples almost exclusively for their primary shopping, but utilize independents for top-ups. Thus the move of multiples into the convenience market traditionally dominated by independents proves a further challenge (e.g. Tesco Metro and Sainsbury Local). The recent Walmart entry may pose an additional threat as Walmart often sells merchandise identical to that on sale through independents, but at much lower prices.

Current UK government measures to support independents include a reduction of corporation tax starting rate and the facilitation of mentoring schemes, where multiples support independents, as illustrated by Sainsbury's initiative to allow rural shopkeepers to purchase own brand products for resale at a higher price. Also in 1999 a Competition Commission investigation of profits and margins in grocery retailing was launched.

Self-help initiatives include the growth in franchising, increased participation in voluntary groups and the formation of 'farmers' markets' where producers and growers sell directly to the consumer. Many independents strive to enhance their service offering and to establish a unique selling proposition via specialization. Expansion of the geographical target market via the Internet is also popular, with independents showing the fastest growth rate in the area of e-commerce. **RAS**

References

Baron, S., Leaver, D., Oldfield, B.M. and Cassidy, K. (1999) *Economic and Social Trends and the Non-Affiliated Independent Retailer*, report by the Manchester Metropolitan University Small Retail Skills Forecasting Unit, Manchester: MMU.

Davies, G. and Harris, K. (1990) *Small Business, The Independent Retailer*, Basingstoke: Macmillan Education.

Inductive research

Inductive research begins with ideas and facts that lead the researcher to develop propositions, theories and predictions. When a researcher utilizes observed facts in generating a theory consistent with these facts, they are doing induction. Induction is essentially a process of observing facts to generate a theory. It is often seen as a first step in scientific research methods. Inductive research can also be described as a 'hypothesis generation' research. Unlike deductive research in which hypotheses are tested, inductive research generates hypotheses based on the data obtained.

Inductive research is the opposite of deductive research since it proceeds in the opposite direction as the researcher begins with the data in hand and generates hypotheses and the theory from the ground up. Induction occurs when the researcher observes the fact in hand and asks 'why?' by generating the appropriate hypotheses. The hypothesis is plausible if it explains the fact that prompted the question. **RM-R**

References
Ghauri, P., Gronhaug, K. and Kristianlund, I. (1995) *Research Methods in Business Studies*, New York: Prentice Hall.
Sekaran, U. (1996) *Research Methods for Business*, 2nd edn, New York: John Wiley & Sons.

Industrial products

Industrial products refer to those goods that are needed by a company in the manufacture of other products or installations, or to be used in the operations of the organization. Business in this context is often referred to as 'business to business marketing'.

Industrial buyers in large firms often specialize in purchasing a particular class or category of product. The task of the buyer is to select suppliers who can offer the best price, quality and standard of service including delivery. There is a tendency in industrial buying to purchase direct from other manufacturers rather than through wholesalers or agents.

Often the term 'industrial products' is mistakenly quoted as meaning 'organizational products'. The term 'organizational products' has a wider meaning as it includes industrial products as well as organizational products, which include goods and services needed for public sector organizations such as the police force, the armed forces, the fire service and local authorities. Organizational products also include products that are bought for resale by independent shops, multiple chains, catalogue operators and other forms of retailers. **GL**

Reference
Lancaster, G. and Reynolds, P. (1999) *Introduction to Marketing*, London: Kogan Page.

Industry life cycles

The industry life cycle is the process of introduction, growth maturity and eventual decline which entire industries are thought to follow. Like the product life cycle, the industry life cycle is technology-dependent; as a simple example, the decline and eventual demise of the horse-drawn carriage manufacturing industry was a direct result of the invention of the automobile.

In the introduction phase of a new industry, technology is rapidly improving and corporate strategy is uncertain; regulation of the industry is likely to be minimal. Costs tend to be high, as are profit margins, and access to raw materials, skilled labour and distribution channels is difficult. Existing industries that are likely to be threatened by the new technology may try to strangle the fledgling industry, but companies within the new industry are likely to cooperate in building the initial market presence. The competitive response is likely to emphasize partnerships of all kinds; small firms allying with established firms in the dying industry, groups of new firms banding together to fight competition (Gross *et al.* 1993).

As the industry matures, the strategic emphasis shifts towards internal competition, cost reductions and the battle for market share. Expansion is likely to be by acquisition rather than by competition in the market place, and regulation of the industry is likely to be introduced, either by the industry itself or by government legislation.

In the decline phase, the industry is threatened by newcomers. Competitive pressures may lead to efforts to destroy the new industry or to attempts to absorb the newcomers and access their technology. In many cases the firm's original *raison d'être* will disappear in favour of switching to the new technology; in other cases the industry will shrink to a few large, highly cost-efficient firms who still satisfy the dwindling band of customers, before finally disappearing. **JWDB**

Reference
Gross, A.C., Banting, P.M., Meredith, L.N., and Ford, I.D. (1993) *Business Marketing*, Boston: Houghton Mifflin.

Information acquisition

The acquisition of information in organizational buying decisions can range from extensive, in the case of a large expensive purchase such as a new piece of capital equipment, to minimal, in the case of a frequently purchased inexpensive item.

New-buy decisions involve the purchase of an item or service which the organization has not made before. For example, if the company was thinking about investing in a new piece of capital equipment, then production engineers, purchasing, finance and general management could all be involved in collecting information. This could come from a wide range of formal sources, including press, catalogues and brochures, trade shows and exhibitions, visits to potential suppliers and visits to companies which were already using the equipment. The information acquisition process could take a long time to complete.

Modified re-buy decisions are typically repeat purchase decisions. The company has bought the product before (e.g. desks or chairs). The main difference may be that the company is changing supplier, or making some change to product specification. Information search and evaluation may be less extensive and involve fewer people.

Finally, straight re-buy decisions involve no changes. For example, the company may have an approved source of supply for paper. There will be little or no attempt to collect further information in these circumstances. The company is likely to place a straightforward re-purchase order from the same supplier.

It is very important in industrial marketing situations to understand how information is used to make buying decisions. By understanding the different sources of information and their usefulness the supplier can make an informed decision about how to supply information in the most appropriate format. In many business-to-business markets this is now increasingly being influenced by e-commerce, which makes information about suppliers readily available to a wide range of potential customers. **SP**

References
Gilliland, D.I. (1997) 'Toward a model of business-to-business marketing communications effects' *Industrial Marketing Management*, 26(1):15–30.
Heide, J.B., Weiss, A.M (1995) 'Vendor consideration and switching behavior for buyers in high-technology markets', *Journal of Marketing*, 59(3):30–44.

Information management and retail marketing

With the convergence of technologies, the UK is moving towards a 24/7 society. Information management issues are affecting interactions with both consumers and suppliers.

All leading grocers have moved into Internet ordering and home delivery (except for Waitrose@Work, who target the workplace). Growth is likely as customers build their confidence in interacting with the technology. The advent of interactive TV shopping channels may prove a breakthrough. With a 95 per cent degree of penetration of UK households TV is a mainstream medium commanding a high degree of consumer familiarity. Shopping for higher value non-food items may become a global activity as consumers make use of intelligent search engines to hunt for bargains.

Historically, UK retailers were among the first to invest extensively in bar code scanning, and electronic point of sale systems (EPoS). Recently, Safeway has introduced self-scanning, the use of touch screens and do-it-yourself checkouts to reduce queues. Loyalty cards have produced a wealth of customer data across the industry. This enables purchase-based segmentation of customer groupings and individual profiling, leading to clearly targeted marketing campaigns and promotions.

On the supply side, the trend is towards retailer/manufacturer partnerships based on knowledge sharing and the alignment of processes and practices. The underlying business philosophy is known as efficient consumer response (ECR). Knowledge flow is managed through electronic data interchange (EDI) or the less expensive use of extranets, which utilize a secure part of the Internet for information exchanges. Sharing of stock data is used to facilitate automated ordering and continuous replenishment, thus cutting supply chain costs. The Institute of Grocery Distribution acted on behalf of the grocery industry in compiling industry cost data to develop spreadsheet-based direct product costing systems, which help shift the focus from individual products onto category management. **RAS**

References

Dadomo, S. and Soars, B. (1999) *A Guide to E-Commerce – Business to Consumer*, Watford: Institute of Grocery Distribution Business Publication.

De Kare-Silver (1999) *e-Shock 2000, The Electronic Shopping Revolution*, Basingstoke: Macmillan Business.

Fernie, J. (ed.) (1998) *The Future for UK Retailing: Change, Growth and Competition*, London: Financial Times Business.

Mintel (1998) *Customer Loyalty in Retailing*, special report, London: Mintel International Group

Mintel (1999) *Online Shopping*, London: Mintel International Group.

Ody, P. (1998) *Non-Store Retailing: Exploiting Interactive Media and Electronic Commerce,* London: Financial Times Retail and Consumer.

Information, need for

The need for information is enormous. When managers are required to make decisions, they often need relevant information to guide them in making the right ones. Research is often undertaken in business organizations to serve the information needs of both strategic and operational functions in the organizations. The operational aspect is concerned with manufacturing, marketing, finance and other relevant functions in running the business. The strategic element of a business is concerned with long-run decisions including activities such as long-range planning and research and development. The information collected through research becomes the necessary input for decision making. Hence, the role of marketing research is twofold. First, it is part of the marketing intelligence feedback process where decision makers are provided with the necessary data to assess the current marketing mix strategies. Secondly, marketing research provides decision makers with a clearer view on existing opportunities in the marketing environment.

Good information from strong research is essentially the raw material used by marketing managers in deciding the company's marketing strategies and day-to-day operations. It is through this information that marketing strategies can be planned and implemented effectively. Effective research is essentially required in all phases of marketing. It is often seen as the guiding tool to assist the marketing efforts of organizations. Unless business organizations undertake forms of research in gathering marketing information, it is unlikely that marketing managers would be able to make sound decisions and effective product, pricing, distribution and promotional strategies for the firms. **RM-R**

Reference

Lehmann, D., Gupta S. and Steckel, J. (1998) *Marketing Research*, Massachusetts: Addison-Wesley.

Insights and ideas

In terms of creativity and creative problem solving we might prefer to think of 'insights' rather than ideas. The gaining of insights into a problem can lead to a restructuring of that problem and development of further insights into the solution of the problem. There may not be a perfect solution to a problem but only different solutions, more acceptable solutions and often, only further insights into a problem.

Many insights appear to arise by chance. Westinghouse discovered the concept of the air-brake when he casually read in a journal that compressed air power was being used by Swiss engineers in tunnel building. Insights appear to arise by chance only when people are actually looking for them. It does not happen to people who are not curious or inquiring or who are not engaged in a hard search for opportunities, possibilities, answers or inventions. Immersion in one's subject matter can be an important factor in gaining creative insights. Creative insights appear to be easiest to gain in fields where we have considerable prior knowledge and experience and in relation to problems that we know a great deal about.

Motivation plays an important role in the ability to be creative. Creative work demands both a passionate interest on the part of the thinker and a degree of detachment from the work and ideas. Creative thinking does not appear to occur where the individual's interest in the subject matter is relatively low. There is a delicate balance whereby the creative thinker has to remain sufficiently detached from the work so as to be able to examine it critically and if necessary reject or even destroy the work. **TP**

Reference

Proctor, T. (1999) *Creative Problem Solving for Managers*, London: Routledge.

Insights generation

There are many different techniques for generating insights. Two which are very relevant to marketing are brainstorming and morphological analysis.

- *Brainstorming* helps to overcome the restrictive nature of evaluation that takes place in most business meetings. One of the most popular forms of brainstorming takes the form of a group activity. The aim is to generate as many ideas as possible – the wilder the ideas the better. Ideas are never evaluated during the generation process. By being able to see other people's ideas recorded individuals are able to find new combinations or 'hitchhike or freewheel' on those ideas to produce new insights.
- *Morphological analysis* is a technique that can help generate a vast number of ideas. Ideally, the problem should have two or three dimensions to permit the construction of two or three dimensional grids. First, possible dimensions are list-

ed that describe the problem or system being studied. No more than three dimensions can be represented in diagram form and they must be relevant and have a logical inter-relationship. For example, if an organization decides to alter its product in response to changing environmental requirements it may consider product shape and material out of which the product can be made as two such dimensions. In this case the dimensions would be represented on a two-dimensional grid (or cube for three dimensions) and a list of attributes is then generated under each dimension. Freewheeling and off-beat ideas are encouraged. The next step is to examine combinations of attributes across the dimensions, however unusual or impractical they may seem. For example, a cross may be put in a box if the combination is used at present and a nought if it is potentially one which is worth pursuing. Promising ideas are then subsequently evaluated for their suitability.

Example
A publisher wants to extend its range into more specialized and unusual products. In this case the axes used were 'type '– the type of publication used by people – and 'age group' – the age range that might use the publication.

Age group	Type of publication						
	Book	Video	Magazine	CD	Newspaper	Internet	Journal
Baby	○	○				○	
Toddler	○	○				○	
Pre-school	✖	○		○		○	
Child	✖	○	○	○		○	
Adolescent	✖	○	○	○	○	○	
Adult	✖	○	○		✖		○

In this example we can see that the publisher identifies many new categories for publications. The next step would involve selecting some of them for more detailed morphological analysis. **TP**

Reference
Proctor, T. (1999) *Creative Problem Solving for Managers*, London: Routledge.

Integrated marketing communications

Integration has become recognized as an important function in the management of marketing communications. Its benefits may generally be described as 'synergistic', but have been reported more specifically by Kitchen (1999) and Linton and Morley (1995). These are shown jointly in the table below in a form that emphasises the communications and the management benefits that accrue from integration.

Table: **Benefits of integrated marketing communications**

Communications benefits

- Greater communications consistency
- Greater impact from creative ideas
- Improves creative integrity
- Improves use of media
- Increases overall impact
- Underlines increased importance of brand image
- Improves marketing precision

Management benefits

- Enables greater client control over marketing communications
- Helps eliminate misconceptions between multiple agencies
- Provides more client control over parties involved
- Provides client with greater professional expertise
- Necessitates fewer meetings
- Improves operation efficiency
- Enables client consolidation of responsibilities
- Reduces cost of marketing communications programmes
- Provides method for effective measurement
- Agency can provide faster solutions
- Creates opportunity for greater agency accountability

The most obvious task of integration is to bring together the various elements of the marketing communications mix, something that has been referred to as 'orchestration' by the advertising agency Ogilvy and Mather. It is this aspect of integration that is most easily recognized. But this is only one part of the total task, as all aspects of marketing communications need to be managed in an integrated fashion if greatest value is to be achieved. Pickton and Broderick (2001) have attempted to provide a comprehensive, if somewhat cumbersome, definition of 'integrated marketing communications' (a shortened version of which is given below), which Pickton and Hartley (1998) propose has nine clearly identifiable dimensions as shown in the table below.

'Integrated marketing communications is a process that involves the management and organization of all 'agents' in the analysis, planning, implementation and control of all marketing communications contacts, media, messages and promotional tools focused at selected target audiences to achieve pre-determined marketing communications objectives.' (adapted from Pickton and Broderick, 2001)

Table: **Dimensions of integrated marketing communications**

- Promotional mix integration
- Promotional mix with marketing mix integration
- Creative integration
- Intra-organizational integration
- Inter-organizational integration
- Information and database systems integration
- Target audience integration
- Corporate and brand integration
- Geographical integration

The question arises: 'if integration is so beneficial, why has it not been adopted more widely?'. The simple answer is that it is extremely difficult to attain and requires a great deal of effort to overcome barriers to its achievement. However, the benefits far outweigh the difficulties and integration is something that should be continually sought. **DWP**

References

Kitchen, P.J. (1999) *Marketing Communications: Principles and Practice*, London: Thomson Learning.

Linton, I. and Morley, K. (1995) *Integrated Marketing Communications*, Oxford: Butterworth Heinemann.

Pickton, D.W. and Broderick, A. (2001) *Integrated Marketing Communications*, London: Financial Times Prentice Hall.

Pickton, D.W. and Hartley, B. (1998) 'Measuring integration: an assessment of the quality of integrated marketing communications', *International Journal of Advertising* 17(4):447–465.

Intermediary recruitment

It is essential for manufacturers to decide which types of intermediaries are suitable for delivering their goods and services to the target market. The intermediaries themselves need to decide whether products from the manufacturers are best suited for their customers and how much channel support they are willing to provide to the manufacturers. There must be mutual agreement between manufacturers and intermediaries in terms of the execution of channel tasks and the amount of support that both parties are willing to give.

Often, manufacturers use credit rating and financial position to evaluate potential wholesalers and retailers. Intermediaries with good credit ratings and financial capabilities are more likely to be selected as channel members as this will assure manufacturers of their credit worthiness. Manufacturers also assess other intermediaries' qualities such as the capabilities of their sales force, their reputation in the market, their sales performance, and their existing product lines. Generally, manufacturers do not like to select intermediaries whose existing merchandise lines may be in direct competition with their own.

Intermediaries are also concerned with selecting the right suppliers. Retailers and wholesalers want to select suppliers or manufacturers whose products or services are potentially lucrative. Also, suppliers who are willing to provide promotional support and financial assistance and who have supportive sales representatives are more likely to be selected as channel partners. Thus, the selection of channel partners is very much a matter of establishing and maintaining supportive relationships between suppliers and distributors. **RM-R**

References

McCalley, R.W. (1992) *Marketing Channel Development and Management*, Westport, CT: Quorum Books.

Rosenbloom, B. (1985) ' The influence of manufacturer organizational structure on marketing channel management', in *Proceedings of the Second World Marketing Congress*, Stirling, Scotland, pp. 733–744.

Internal marketing

Internal marketing promotes the central role of employees in achieving organizational effectiveness. It is an umbrella term covering different ideas, theories and frameworks, aimed at inspiring employees to be committed to different organizational goals including customer-consciousness and service-orientation. Internal marketing is recognized as a necessary precondition for effective services marketing leading to its wide adoption by different service organizations.

Despite the fact that the term 'internal marketing' has only been in vogue since the 1980s its ideas are by no means new. Varey (1996) claims that there is evidence to suggest that associated attitudes and methods are noted in the early marketing management literature. Gilmore and Carson (1995) and Sargeant and Asif (1998) propose that internal marketing emerged from the services marketing literature. In recent years the concept has been noted in service management and industrial literature.

As yet there has not been a unanimously agreed 'internal marketing' definition; this causes disagreement in academic circles concerning the underlying principles of internal marketing, which results in a variety of implementation formats adopted by practitioners. There is a plethora of different definitions including: 'Viewing employees as internal customers, viewing jobs as internal products, and endeavouring to offer internal products that satisfy the needs and wants of these internal customers while addressing the objectives of the organization.' (Berry, 1981, p. 34) and 'Internal marketing is the process for achieving internal exchanges between the organization and its employee groups as a prerequisite for successful exchanges with external markets.' (George, 1990)

Several criticisms are targeted at the internal marketing concept. For example, Gilmore and Carson (1995) criticize the reliance on techniques and concepts designed for the implementation of external marketing programmes, which may be inappropriate for the internal markets. Rafiq and Ahmed (1993) claim that internal marketing is highly incompatible in striving to meet the requirements of both internal and external customers.

The growing internal marketing literature is of a descriptive nature, with limited work carried out in the context of implementation. This is an important issue for the legitimacy of the concept. **IPD**

References

Berry, L.L. (1981) 'The employee as customer', *Journal of Retail Banking*, 3(1):33–40.

George, W.R. (1990) 'Internal marketing and organizational behaviour: a partnership in developing customer-conscious employees at every level', *Journal of Business Research*, 20(1)(January): 63–70.

Gilmore, A. and Carson, D. (1995) 'Managing and marketing to internal customers', in W.J. Glynn and J.G. Barnes (eds) *Understanding Service Management*, Chichester: Wiley Publications, pp. 295–321.

Rafiq, M. and Ahmed, P.K. (1993) 'The scope of internal marketing: defining the boundary between marketing and human resource management' *Journal of Marketing Management*, 9:219–232.

Sargeant, A. and Asif, S. (1998) 'The strategic application of internal marketing – an investigation of UK banking', *International Journal of Bank Marketing*, 16(2):66–79.

Varey, R.J. (1996) 'A broadened concept of internal marketing' PhD thesis, UMIST.

International market entry

One of the most significant decisions any company has to resolve is the method by which it will enter new international markets. Establishing a presence in another international market is usually driven by the need to expand the business out of its indigenous market. Entering an international market can vary from being a relatively low investment decision that might involve simple direct exporting to one which involves significant amounts of investment if the company is wishing to establish its wholly owned operations. The extent to which a company will commit vast sums of investment will vary between the degree of control the company requires and the degree of risk it will encounter in entering a foreign market. Normally speaking, the higher the degree of investment, the higher the degree of risk particularly if the company is attempting to enter the market alone through building its own operations.

However, companies can enter new markets with the cooperation of companies already in the market. Developing strategic alliances and licensing agreements can allow entry to a market which would otherwise have been either expensive or very difficult. Many of the European and US based brewers have entered the UK market through licensing agreements, since distribution into the market has been limited and building brewing operations seen as expensive and unnecessary. Similarly, many of the world's leading pharmaceutical companies have entered international markets through strategic alliances and acquisitions.

Clearly, the method by which to enter a new market is dependent upon a number of criteria. These will include the extent of the company's existing international operations, nature of competition in the market, the potential barriers to entry, the degree of control required by the company, availability of financial resources and the company's objectives in wishing to enter the market. **PBB**

References
Lowe, R. and Doole, I. (1999) *International Marketing Strategy*, London: Thomson Learning.
Stern, L.W., El-Ansary, A.I. and Coughlan, A.T. (1996), *Marketing Channels*, 5th edn, Englewood Cliffs, NJ: Prentice Hall International.

International market segmentation

International market segmentation is defined as the pursuit of the best prospects in any given market. This targeted, rifle approach contrasts sharply with the scattergun or shotgun approach which is not focused, but which hopes to catch customers within the more general market. Segmentation analysis is about making homogeneity out of heterogeneity. Using it, the marketer hopes to improve understanding of the nature of the individuals who are buying within the product field or buying particular brands. Having segmented the market, the marketer can then target the offering directly, i.e. provide information which will directly identify the vehicles by which sub-groups can be reached (to assist media scheduling, sales promotion activity, choice of distribution channels, price, etc).

The ability to perform segmentation analysis is governed by the availability of information, i.e. good market research is the sine qua non of segmentation. This is because segmentation is a feasible strategy only if the following conditions can be met.

- *Measurability* – the target segment must be capable of some form of measurement.
- *Size* – the target segment has to be large enough to make the 'focused' marketing effort financially viable.
- *Accessibility* – the targeted segment must be accessible by promotion and distribution. The great potential of e-commerce is that it facilitates one to one promotion and distribution (via intermediaries such as FedEx).
- *Responsiveness* – the targeted segment must demonstrate that they respond to the marketing mix on offer (orders, sales, hits).

It follows from the above that there are five areas of consumer activity that must be researchable.

1. *Consumer demographics* – typically focus would be on social grade, sex, age, stage in the life-cycle, disposable income, occupation, household composition. SAGACITY is a proprietary classification available commercially.
2. *Geographic* – analysis by country and by region. ACORN (geodemographic classification) and MOSAIC are proprietary products available.
3. *Consumer behaviour* – more detailed data on consumer behaviour such as use occasion, weight of purchase, degree of loyalty.
4. *Consumer attitudes* – various psychosociological measures, such as psychographics, capable of yielding insights into attitudes towards different brands.

5. *Consumer situation* – within a given segment, the specifics of the buying situation may be investigated, i.e. gifts versus purchases for own use. **MJT**

References
Birn, R. (1999) *The Effective Use of Market Research*, 3rd edn, London: Kogan Page.
Birn, R. (2000) *A Handbook of Market Research Techniques*, London: Kogan Page.
Martin, D, (1995) 'The role of research in international marketing', in M.J.Thomas (ed.) *The Handbook of Marketing*, 4th edn, Aldershot, Hants: Gower.
Tonks, D. (1998) 'Exploring the principles of market segmentation', in C. Egan and M.J. Thomas (eds) *The CIM Handbook of Strategic Marketing*, Oxford: Butterworth Heinemann.

International marketing

The Chartered Institute of Marketing defines marketing as 'The management process which seeks to identify, anticipate and satisfy customer requirements profitably'. The American Marketing Association defines marketing as 'The process of planning and executing the conception, pricing, promotion and distribution of ideas, goods and services to create exchanges that satisfy individual and organizational objectives'.

We could be glib and say that both definitions would satisfy us by merely adding the word 'internationally' to each! That would, however, hide more than it would reveal.

The exchange process is clearly at the heart of marketing. What is the difference between the exchange process in the domestic market and the 'international' exchange process? If we can answer that question, we will perhaps have defined international marketing.

One approach is to differentiate the 4Ps of domestic marketing from the 6Ps of international marketing.

The familiar 4Ps are product, price, promotion and place (distribution). It is argued that, to encompass the international environment, to differentiate domestic marketing from international marketing, marketers must be aware of political power and public opinion formation. In other words, the environment has to be managed, in addition to managing the traditional marketing mix. This is one way to view international marketing, because it forces the marketing manager to recognize that international marketing, if it is to be managed successfully, is not merely an extension of domestic marketing abroad (i.e. exporting) but is a radically different approach to the marketing task. Marketers have traditionally regarded the (domestic) environment as a given, governed by forces outside the control of the business. In international marketing, the manager has the choice of which markets to enter. That, in one sense, gives the manager control. However, how this choice is made, how international markets are targeted, is one of the learnt skills of the international marketing manager.

In the international marketing environment, no assumptions can be made about product or market maturity – each market will have to be examined independently, no assumptions can be made about the nature of competition, no assumptions can be made about the political environment, and the purchasing power of the population. **MJT**

References
Fahy, J. (1998) 'Global marketing', in C. Egan and M.J. Thomas (eds) *The CIM Handbook of Strategic Marketing*, Oxford: Butterworth Heinemann.
Paliwoda, S.J. and Thomas, M.J. (1998) *International Marketing*, 3rd edn, Oxford: Butterworth Heinemann.
Usunier, J-C. (2000) *Marketing Across Cultures*, 3rd edn, London: Financial Times/Prentice Hall.

International marketing, importance of

We have entered the age of e-mail and e-commerce. The first decade of the 21st century will see the growth of international trade and marketing at an unprecedented rate. Every networked consumer will have the world in which to shop; every company will have the world as its potential market.

Barriers to trade will reduce, at least that is the message coming from the World Trade Organisation (WTO). Globalization will encourage firms to produce wherever it is efficient to do so, thus factor endowment, the old rationale for the Theory of Comparative Advantage will no longer dictate who will be able to supply (and demand) in any particular national market. Technology will be the catalyst for change. Free trade and integration will move nations and companies through a hierarchy, as they try to compete in an increasingly competitive global market – from customs unions, to common markets, to monetary (and political) union. The European Union will compete with the North American Free Trade Area, and with the Association of South-East Asian Nations and vice versa.

Companies will go international for a number of reasons: not least because they have found the home market to be mature, with no room for growth, or because they think that overseas competition may be less exacting, or because they have excess capacity that needs to be utilized, or because they think that geographical expansion may be easier than product diversification. Companies will go international because they have done what good marketing companies should do: they have done marketing opportunity analysis, have seen by that analysis that population and purchasing power potential will provide opportunity to pull global customers into their served market. How to exploit those opportunities still requires the highest marketing skills. 'Act Global, Think Local' is a useful starting point. Product, price, channels and communications will all need tuning to local market conditions. But if you are not out there, some other company will be. **MJT**

Reference
Paliwoda, S.J. and Thomas, M.J., (1998) *International Marketing*, 3rd edn, Oxford: Butterworth Heinemann.

International opportunities

I hold a radical view of marketing in the Information Age. Never before has the volume and value of international trade been as large as it is today, nor the speed of international communication so instant. We are witnessing what I have called 'the death of distance'.

Location is irrelevant. Any company can potentially reach any customer anywhere in the world. Any company can move its production base anywhere in the world if factor costs require it. Size is irrelevant, the smallest company can set up a web site. If it produces goods or services that someone out there in the world values, it can become a international marketer. Niche markets will potentially prosper and suppliers will customize content as required. Brands become more powerful, because brands represent a powerful marketing tool – universal symbols such as Coca Cola or Nike demonstrate the power of the brand.

It may be easier to visualize the changing nature of the global economy by contrasting the old economy with the new economy. **MJT**

Table: **The changing nature of the global economy**

Old economy	New economy
Standardized output Assembly line production	Customized goods and services Increased variety and bundling of services
In-house production	Networking, outsourcing, interlinking
Local, national markets	Internationalization of both production and competition
Vertical integration Large corporations	Vertical disintegration Small firms, large transnational conglomerates, virtual corporations
Rigid technology	Flexible production modes JIT manufacturing – multiple sourcing, Supply chain management
Material inputs Material outputs	Human resource investment Knowledge based inputs Non-material investment
Blue collar and White collar workers	Knowledge workers
Sectoral regulation	WTO regulation?

Reference

Doyle, P., (1998) 'Looking at the future: marketing in the twenty-first century', in C. Egan and M.J. Thomas (eds) *The CIM Handbook of Strategic Marketing*, Oxford: Butterworth Heinemann.

International pricing

Companies operating in an international market can adopt standard pricing, adaptive pricing or an in-between strategy. In a *standard pricing strategy*, the same base price is charged in each market. Companies following an *adaptive pricing strategy*, in contrast, set prices in accordance with local demand, costs and competitive characteristics (Hanna and Dodge, 1997). International companies may also opt for an *in-between strategy*, allowing for minor adjustments to the base price in view of differences in costs or competitive situation. For instance, in 'dual pricing', prices in the export markets account for additional export costs.

Several factors affect the appropriateness of these strategies. Standard pricing may become less attractive if costs in the export markets are driven up substantially by transportation costs or import duties. When production is (partially) moved to the foreign markets, local production and labour costs and the transfer prices of the parts imported from the parent company come into play. Standard pricing can also be hindered by differences in the company's competitive position across the foreign markets, like its degree of control over distribution channels, and its knowledge and experience vis-à-vis the local competition (Dahringer and Mühlbacher, 1991; Toyne and Walters, 1993). Further, differences in customers' willingness to pay across the foreign markets will favour a more differential strategy, albeit that the emergence of the Euro- and global consumer encourages price harmonization. Other important factors influencing the choice of an international pricing strategy are the presence of barriers that obstruct parallel imports from low to higher price markets (cf. services versus commodities), the stability of the exchange rate and government regulations (e.g. penalizing dumping) (see also Dolan and Simon, 1996; Hanna and Dodge, 1997). **KCa, BF, EG**

References

Dahringer, L.D. and Mülbacher, H. (1991*) International Marketing: A Global Perspective*, Reading, MA: Addison-Wesley Publishing Company.

Dolan, R. J. and Simon, H. (1996) *Power Pricing: How Managing Price Transforms the Bottom Line*, New York, NY: The Free Press.

Hanna, N. and Dodge, H.R. (1997) *Pricing: Policies and Procedures*, London: Macmillan Press.

Monroe, K. (1990) *Pricing: Making Profitable Decisions*, New York: McGraw-Hill International Editions.

Toyne, B. and Walters, P.G.P. (1993) *Global Marketing Management: A Strategic Perspective*, Englewood Cliffs, NJ: Prentice Hall.

Internationalization

Retail internationalization involves the transfer of an existing retail format to another country or the management of another retail format in a different country. Observable factors of international retailers are geographic scope, entry mode, operating strategy and cultural spread, as well as marketing approach and management style used when entering new markets.

Retailers may enter new geographical markets via new start-ups, franchising, joint venture, acquisition, concession or licensing, or through virtual retailing via the Internet. Cultural differences in consumer and staff behaviour can be a major risk factor in retail internationalization and cultural zoning can be used to evaluate potential target markets. In this Hofstede's work on national cultures may form a starting point, utilizing the factors of power distance, uncertainty avoidance, individualism/collectivism, femininity/masculinity and long-term versus short-term orientation. However, some cultural affinities and lifestyles can also be seen as spanning national boundaries.

The terms 'international', 'multinational', 'global' and 'transnational' have been used to describe different stages in the internationalization ladder of development. For the international retailer, there is some cautious experimentation in new geographic markets, often within a similar cultural zone, and culturally and managerially the focus is ethnocentric, i.e. on the home market. The multinational retailer has a polycentric orientation, which is based on an appreciation of the different operating contexts. The global and transnational retailer both have a fully global strategy, with the former maximizing benefits obtainable from economies of scale in product standardization, sourcing and marketing and the latter having an adaptable geocentric approach, which allows them to think globally and act locally.

Traditionally size was a prerequisite for retail internationalization. Whilst retailers such as Walmart are amongst the largest companies in the world retail internationalization is still a rather limited activity for most retailers. However, the growth of electronic shopping is opening up opportunities for small retailers to access geographically remote markets. **RAS**

References

Harris, P. and McDonald, F. (eds) (1994) *European Marketing Case Studies*, London: Paul Chapman Publishing.

Helfferich, E. , Hinfelaar, M. and Kasper, H. (1997) 'Towards a clear terminology on international retailing', *The International Review of Retail, Distribution and Consumer Research*, (July): 287–307.

Hofstede, G. (1980) *Culture's Consequences: International Differences in Work-Related Values*, Beverley Hills, CA and London: Sage.

McGoldrick, P. and Davies, G. (eds) (1995) *International Retailing: Trends and Strategies*, London: Pitman.

Schmidt, R.A. and Pioch, E. (1996) 'Serving the euro-consumer: A marketing challenge or a case for intervention?' *Marketing Intelligence and Planning*, 14(5):14–19.
Sternquist, B. (1998) *International Retailing*, New York: Fairchild Publications.

Internationalization of marketing

It is important to recognize that international marketing was not invented by Coca Cola and McDonalds. Companies and states have exchanged goods and services for most of recorded history. Do not tell the Trobriand Islanders or the Phoenicians that you have discovered something new. What we do observe at this time is the very rapid growth of international trade – never before has the volume and value of international trade been as large as it is today. I have explored this phenomenon under the title 'the death of distance'.

Modern transport and modern communications methods have created a truly global village. The result – globalization – decouples the firm from the factor endowment of its home nation. Factors of production can be shifted around the globe making comparative advantage in terms of factor costs relatively temporary. In particular, capital, labour and entrepreneurship are almost totally mobile. Technology can also transform factors of production, and technology transfer is easily facilitated.

At the beginning of the 21st century, the reality facing *all* companies and organizations is the following.

- Money has no nationality and follows all market opportunities.
- Dynamic competition is found in all markets exhibiting economic growth.
- There is a global market place for all products (and services) displaying high added value.
- Portfolio and foreign direct investment (FDI) lubricates the growth and the dynamics of global growth and competition.
- Global reach and local provision is the key to future market success. Product adaptation is still necessary even though it is possible to argue that global tastes are becoming homogenized.
- New product diffusion increasingly occurs on a global scale (Ford launches many new models on a global scale, as do VW, Honda and Daewoo).
- Instant international communication has caused the death of distance – e-mail and fax facilitates instant message transfer.
- The development of new trading regions merely accelerates the progress of the globalization of trade. MJT

Reference
Czinkota, M.R. and Ronkainen, I.A., (1996) *Global Marketing*, Fort Worth: The Dryden Press.

Internationalization of marketing and e-commerce

Traditionally, internationalization is seen as a process, beginning with exporting on an irregular basis, leading to regular exporting, either indirectly, or directly via overseas agents. Stage 3 would see the establishment of at least one overseas sales subsidiary and finally stage 4, the most mature stage, would see the establishment of production overseas. E-commerce is a radical innovation, which may make redundant the traditional model, because e-commerce holds out the possibility of any company becoming a global marketer without any sort of progressing through the traditional stages.

What may be helpful is to contrast exporting with international marketing, because this will highlight the difference in psychological commitment and resource allocation.

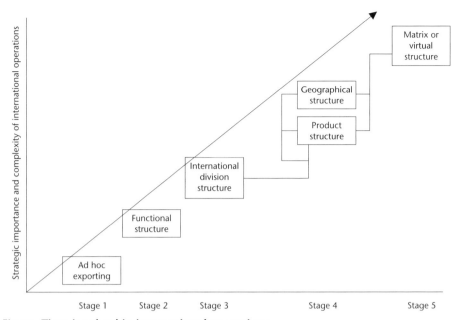

Figure: **Time involved in international operations**

Table: **Exporting and international marketing contrasted**

	Exporting	International marketing
Time horizon Target markets	Short run Ad hoc Unsystematic Reactive not proactive	Long run (at least 3-5 years) Selection based on analysis of market potential
Dominant objective	Immediate sales	Establish permanent market presence
Resource commitment	Enough to obtain the sale	What is required to establish a permanent presence
Entry mode	Indirect or direct, usually using agents or distributors	What is appropriate to reach defined objective, usually requiring foreign direct investment
New product development (NPD)	Home market products focus only	NPD for both home and overseas markets
Product adaptation	Usually only mandatory adaptation (legal/technical) of home products	Foreign buyers' preferences, income and use conditions determine NPD
Channels	No or little control	Distribution controlled
Price	Cost plus	Determined by demand and local competition
Promotion	Personal selling	Advertising, sales promotion and personal selling mix to achieve marketing objectives

E-commerce holds out the possibility that any company or organization can become an international marketer from the day of its establishment. A web site holds the possibility of reaching a worldwide audience – always provided that what is on offer will excite potential buyers. **MJT**

Reference
Paliwoda, S.J. and Thomas, M.J., (1999) *International Marketing*, 3rd edn, Oxford: Butterworth Heinemann.

Internet

The Internet is virtually revolutionizing business and marketing communications. It brings together the potential for immediacy, interactivity, global communications, direct communications, use by all, and, increasingly, cheap, easy access. Some people have referred to the use of the Internet for marketing purposes as 'cybermarketing' (Keeler, 1995).

The Internet is, in essence, a computer network or, more accurately, a collection of inter related networks that span the globe. It was born out of a research project in the late 1960s, but its phenomenal growth only occurred in the 1990s when a ban on its use for commercial purposes was lifted. It is currently closely associated with the PC but this will not remain so as mobile telecommunications develop the capacity to link with the Internet. The World Wide Web is a part of the Internet that permits the greatest opportunity for multimedia applications. This has resulted in an explosion of business and personal web sites that use text, colour, graphics, sound and video. The 'addressing' system, 'browsers' and 'hypertext links' facilitate the easy movement around the Web, or 'surfing' as it has become known.

Keeler *(*1995) has suggested that the use of the Internet for marketing and communications are fivefold:

- sending messages (e-mail)
- transferring files
- monitoring news and opinions (including bulletin boards)
- searching and browsing
- posting, hosting and presenting information.

Keeler's list can be expanded since his publication to make explicit the use of the Internet for:

- advertising
- public relations and sponsorship
- sales promotions
- direct sales
- exhibitions
- market research
- developing closer links with customers and other groups
- intranets and extranets (parts of the internet that are accessible only by closed user groups, from within the organization (intranet) or outside it (extranet). **DWP**

Reference
Keeler, L. (1995) *Cybermarketing*, New York: Amacom.

Internet and connectivity

One key to understanding the Internet is the concept of 'connectivity'. This involves building networks that connect people and organizations. Within a company, they are termed 'intranets', and are termed 'extranets' when they connect an organization with its suppliers or distributors. The 'Internet describes how users are connected via the World Wide Web or information superhighway' (Kotler, 2000). As we neared the end of the 20th century, estimates of e-commerce were nearing £65 billion (*Economist*, 1997), and the potential death of traditional shopping was being prophesied (*The European*, 1998).

Green and Browder (1998), citing Forrester Research, have given the following estimates for year-end 2002.

Table: **Estimates of e-commerce by end-2002**

Type	Estimate $ billion
• Durable goods	99
• Wholesale office supplies, electronic goods, scientific equipment	89
• Travel	7
• Consumer purchases of computer hardware and software	4
• Books, music and entertainment	4

Connectivity attaches PCs and computer users. The most expensive and largest computer is still of little value when used as a stand-alone. When networked to other PCs, it becomes a very powerful communication and information search vehicle. The greatest potential for the Internet is the movement of control of information into the hands of customers and consumers (existent and potential). It draws attention to the fact that consumers can now decide which information to access, when, and for what purposes. They are no longer strapped to the rigid linear information control exhibited by traditional forms of marketing. The promise of interconnectivity has extended from computers to telecoms, cable and satellite television systems, and ultimately the integration and interaction associated with the blending of telecoms, television, and computer technology. **PJK**

References
Economist, The (1997) 'Electronic commerce survey', 10 May.
European, The, (1998) 'Retailing: the death of the shop' 24–30 August, pp. 18–19.
Green, H. and Browder, S. (1998) 'Cyberspace windows: how they did it', *Business Week*, June 22, pp. 82–85.
Kotler, P. (2000) *Marketing Management*, 10th edn, New Jersey: Prentice Hall International.

Internet and marketing communications

This section examines the ways in which marketing communications might be used on the Internet and the development of a 'digital mindset' needed to inculcate success. Effective Internet marketing communications (marcoms) goes well beyond simply designing and developing a web site. Despite the field of dreams analogy it is not enough to have the mentality of 'build it and they will come'. The Internet, however, is not a mass media advertising or sales medium. It is a communications, informational, entertainment, distribution, and marketing medium – and it can be any or all of these things depending on why the medium is being accessed or used. Proactive use of tools such as e-mail and the proper use of usenet and listserv groups are essential to building electronic relationships and will lead toward effective marketing communications. Product, production and sales orientations do not work well in cyberspace. The mindset required emphasizes mutual help, support, and the establishment of relationships. A unified relationship marketing approach is best.

Various modes of marketing communications are facilitated by the Internet and can help improve relationships with national, international and global customers – both existing and potential. These modes include e-mail, usenet/newsgroups, list-serv, internet relay Chat, MOOS and MUDS, video conferencing and interactive web sites. The first three are the workhorses of effective Internet marketing communications.

- *E-mail* – widely used and best known form. Offers significant advantages over traditional modes of communication (i.e. telephone, letter, fax). It is cost effective, and does not rely on real-time presence. Users can transfer graphics as well as text-based material, and these are easily downloaded as attachments.
- *Usenet/newsgroups* – online discussion forums on specific topics or range of subjects. Most are serious, some are trivial. Readers access a string of messages which they can read, reply to, or commence a new avenue of discussion. Usenet newsgroups are important as a source of information and a channel of information. They can be an excellent source of market research data, and form a sample frame for further research. Specific groups can be seen as a way of promoting the company and its products and services.
- *Listserv* – a combination of e-mail and newsgroups. On a listserv, messages are automatically e-mailed to all subscribers. Newsgroup subscribers may visit occasionally. Listservs can be moderated or unmoderated. In the former, someone has responsibility to review postings to ensure they fit with the group's scope. In 1999 over one million individuals were known to subscribe to listserv groups, coverage a diverse and expansive range of topics.

These three tools or modes equate to a radically different environment in which marketing communication can be deployed. The differences are caused by the following.

- The Internet is a hypermedia, computer-mediated environment (CME) (Hoffman and Novak, 1995a &b).
- The Internet is an interactive environment (it is not one-way or linear)
- Consumers and customers can interface directly with organizations. Informational control is passing from manufacturers and distributors to consumers.
- Computer-mediated environments are created and experienced by participants.
- In the CME mode, traditional marcoms are transformed – that is they have to be reconstructed to suit the dynamic in which transmissive interaction takes place
- The Internet impacts significantly on seller-to-buyer relationships and has a profound impact on business to business marketing.
- The question of whether new marketing paradigms are required to explore this new dimension is being taken seriously around the world. **PJK**

References

Hoffman, D.K. and Novak, T.P. (1995a) 'Marketing in hypermedia computer-mediated environments: conceptual foundations', working paper, Vanderbilt University. http://www2000.ogsm.vanderbilt.edu/cmepaper.revision.july11.1995/cmepaper.html

Hoffman, D.K. Novak, and Chatterjee, P. (1995b) 'Commercial scenarios for the Web: opportunities and challenges', *Journal of Computer-Mediated Communication*, 1(3), December. Available at: http://www.ascusc.org/jcmc/vol1/issue3/hoffman.html

Internet and marketing development

The interactive marketplace is still in the introduction stage of its own explosive and expansive life cycle. The new marketspace is radically different in form and style to that which has gone before. Importantly, it places informational power in the hands of customers and consumers (existent, swingers and non-customers). From a marketing perspective, these are not negative developments. The marketplaces of yesterday are still with us, the marketspaces of today and tomorrow are still emergent. The advent of the Internet has immeasurably expanded markets, and should be greeted with acclaim by marketers who for decades now have proclaimed that the customer or consumer is king. Well, the crowning ceremony is not far away. Customer and consumers, in market after market and industry after industry, now have radically different alternatives that enable them to fulfil their needs and wants at their convenience and under their own conditions (Schultz and Kitchen, 2000).

Undoubtedly, marketing has actually to become demand or response-driven, not product or service driven. Manufacturers and channels of distribution will now have to respond to the needs, wants, desires and wishes of customers and consumers. This, if anything, represents a coming of age for marketing – as an academic discipline and as a business practice. While it would be unfair to say that marketing has been 'hoisted by its own petard', there is undoubtedly a feeling that the Internet provides the modus operandi whereby it finally has to deliver that which it has ostensibly promised for nearly half a century.

Admittedly, the above scenario is not here – *yet*. But, with the Internet as the primary vehicle of choice, the marketplace of tomorrow is on its way – powerful, inexorable and irresistible. **PJK**

Reference

Schultz, D.E. and Kitchen, P.J. (2000) *Communicating Globally: An Integrated Marketing Approach,* London: Macmillan Business.

Internet demographics

In 1995 – almost light years ago in Internet terms – Troiano indicated that users tended to be male (65-90 per cent), 18-35 years of age, college/university educated (60-80 per cent), white collar employed (50-60 per cent), and affluent (average income between $65 and $85k). Vassos (1996) stated that: 'the Internet is not about mass marketing and mass markets. It's about people – individuals with unique aspirations, needs, desires and cultural backgrounds. It's not so much a mass market of 60 million people as it is 60 million individual markets, each containing one person'.

By 2000 the estimate is between 200 and 500 million people, all connected, all on-line. The Internet is growing on average at over 60 per cent per annum and the demographics of Internet users are changing rapidly. In 1999, the major change was toward female and older users. In 2000 more and more young people around the world are also connected and/or growing up with Internet as a communications, informational and entertainment medium. In the USA between 10 and 15 million new customers began shopping online in 1999. Most of the rush occurs at peak seasons when customers rush to place orders for the first time. Notably, the Internet is only one form of electronic commerce – credit cards, cash points, telephone banking, electronic data interchange (EDI) and other forms of commercial services add to a world where dealing electronically is moving alongside more traditional forms of buyer behaviour.

Rapid Internet growth has walked hand in hand with use of online Internet Demographic Surveys. Numerous surveys have been published in recent years. These are growing in popularity both from a commercial/organizational perspective and in terms of customer/consumer surveys. There is, however, a problem from a firm perspective and that is that many web sites are not that interactive in terms of content. Very few make any serious attempt to gather information about their users, and fewer than 5 per cent (Strassel, 1997; Kierzkowski *et al* 1996) allow any user-to-user communications. **PJK**

References

Kierzkowski, A., McQuade, S. , Waitman, R. and Zeisser, M. (1996) 'Marketing to the digital consumer', *The McKinsey Quarterly*, 3:5–21.

Strassel, K.A. (1997) 'Wait and see: European firms are treading warily on the Internet', *The Wall St Journal, Europe*, 3 June, p. 12.

Troiano, M. (1995) in *Campaign*, 7 July, p. 30.

Vassos, T. (1996) *Strategic Internet Marketing*, London: QUE Books. The author's web site is at: http://www.weWGDiamonds.com and the book web site at http://www/mcp.com/que/desktop os/int market/

Internet, origins, growth and evolution

The origins of the Internet go beyond 1983, in fact, to over a quarter of a century ago in the mid-1970s, when the US Defense Agency established the Advanced Research Projects Agency (ARPAnet) to join, or link, military and research institutions. The important achievement was not just the linkage between disparate institutions but the development of a protocol that allowed different computer systems to communicate with each other. This protocol was known as TCP (transmission control protocol, or Internet protocol). This remains the basis of common usage on the Internet today. Later, during the late 1980s the National Science Foundation used the ARPAnet technology to expand its own NSFNET – a high speed backbone network linking universities and research centres to NSF's supercomputers (Hamill and Kitchen, 1999). Readers, please note that Internet design and technology arose from outside the marketing discipline. Originally the preserve of 'geeks' and 'nerds' the Internet is the new technology on the marketing block. Its growth is exponential.

It is important to note that the Internet is not just a channel for marketing communication – it is an information source, a communication channel, a transaction vehicle and a distribution vehicle. Unlike supermarkets and other retail stores, it is open 24 hours day, every day, and is available in every corner of the planet. Thus timeliness and access, coupled with sound user-friendly marketing, have catapulted e-businesses to the top of stock markets, even though proof of usage is still embryonic or emergent (Gronstedt, 2000).

The Internet is a global medium. Admittedly, while the greatest number of users reside in the USA, exponential growth is also taking place in Europe and the Pacific Rim. While complaints of 'gridlock' leading to clogged telephone lines and snail-like download times are evident, these are being dealt via massive telecommunication investment infrastructure. Witness Tony Blair's recent goal to provide everyone in the UK with their own e-mail address. **PJK**

References

Gronstedt, A. (2000) *The Customer Century*, London: Routledge, p. 211.

Hamill, J. and Kitchen, P.J. (1999) 'The Internet', in P.J. Kitchen *Marketing Communications*, London: Thomson Learning, ch. 22.

Interviews

One of the most common methods of primary data collection is interviewing. Interviews can be structured or unstructured and can be carried out face-to-face with respondents or by telephone. Unstructured interviews are carried out when the interviewer does not have a planned sequence of questions and will normally start the interview with broad open-ended questions. It is sometimes referred to as the 'informal conversational interview' since respondents are urged to talk freely and the interviewer maintains flexibility by pursuing information in the appropriate direction. The main purpose of an unstructured interview is to explore areas that may be crucial or central to the broad problem area. It may lead to the identification of other possible deep-rooted problems. Responses from unstructured interviews can be probed further by means of structured interviews.

Structured interviews involved the use of an interview guide, where the interviewer has a predetermined list of questions, which are likely to be those relating to issues identified during the unstructured interview sessions. To ensure that meaningful responses have been obtained, the interview must relate the questions to the purpose and objective of the research. When enough information has been collected from the interviews, the next step is to tabulate the responses and analyse them appropriately. **RM-R**

References
Patton, M.Q. (1990) *Qualitative Evaluation and Research Methods*, Newbury Park: Sage Publications.
Sekaran, U. (1996) *Research Methods for Business*, 2nd edn, New York: John Wiley & Sons.

Joint decision making – buying centres

Organizational buying decisions are rarely made by one person; typically several people can be involved in the buying process. For example, in the purchase of a personal computer this group could include the user, their manager and representatives from the purchasing department, the information technology department, and finance. Each participant plays a different role in the buying decision.

The user is primarily responsible for defining the requirement in terms of the specification. The purchase may have to be approved by the manager against a departmental budget. This is a gatekeeping role. Purchasing department may have a list of approved suppliers, which they review on a regular basis. They will be responsible for ensuring that the purchase is made as economically as possible within the overall budget and specification. The IT department may be asked to provide a technical specification for the personal computer. They are important specifiers and information providers. If a supplier cannot meet the specification then the company would not consider purchase.

Each of the members of this buying centre could play a critical role in the decision to buy the personal computer. From a marketing point of view it is important to identify the potential members of the buying centre and anticipate their impact on the final purchase. The computer user may be interested in the technical performance of the machine in terms of the work they have to do. However, they are far less likely to be interested in the technical specification or the ease of service support. This is more likely to be the responsibility of the IT department. The purchasing department is more likely to be concerned with the overall cost of the product including maintenance contracts and payment terms. Effective marketing communication needs to take each of these interests into account. **SP**

References

Katrichis, J.M. (1998) 'Exploring departmental level interaction patterns in organizational purchasing decisions', *Industrial Marketing Management*, 27(2):135–147.

McWilliams, R.D., Naumann, E., Scott, S. (1992) 'Determining buying center size', *Industrial Marketing Management*, 21(1):43–50.

Joint ventures

The modern term 'joint venture' most likely stems from the historical practice of spreading risk by distributing stock ownership. As far back as 1602 the Dutch East India Company created a system of 'joint stock' ventures. These were entities or companies in which members held shares entitling them to a proportion of the profits, while narrowing the level of risk for the participants. A traditional joint venture is thus a commercial enterprise undertaken jointly by two or more parties otherwise retaining their separate identities. The consequence of the traditional joint venture is that each company in the venture takes an equity stake in a newly formed entity – this sets the joint venture apart from the strategic alliance which itself is more of a coalition or collaboration. There is, however, another type of joint venture that has non-equity terms or agreements between partners. Both types foster greater co-operation through the setting up of a new entity, which is a key reason for the popularity of joint ventures.

Firms can gain significant competitive advantages by finding a suitable partner and forming a new incorporated company. In the Far East, for example, certain countries discourage or exclude foreign ownership but may accept market entry if one or more of the partners is from the host country. Joining forces in this manner can access good business and government contacts and the market knowledge and skills of the host. Frequently, entry seekers possess technical or production skills. For example, the Nissan Motor Company holds a minority stake in a joint venture with Thai die maker Sammitra Motor Group, the China International Trust and Investment and the Zhengzhou truck factory. The plan is to build trucks in China's Henan province. It is common to see this form of technology transfer at the centre of production-based joint ventures. **AJN**

References

Harris, P. and McDonald, F. (1994), *European Business and Marketing Strategic Issues*, London: Paul Chapman Publishing Ltd., ch. 5.

Reitman, V. (1996), 'Nissan Motor gets toehold in China via truck venture', *The Wall Street Journal*, 9 April, p. A15.

Zahra, S. (1994), 'The strategic management of international joint ventures', *European Management Journal,* 12(1):83–93.

Just in time management

The just in time (JIT) system is a form of logistics management that emphasizes the efficient flow of materials for manufacturing purposes. According to this approach, material resources should flow through the logistics system at the time they are to be used. In essence, JIT calls for the right materials in the right quantities at the right time without the need for keeping inventories. This concept focuses on the active movement of all materials as work-in-process (WIP) without any stoppage in the entire operation. As such, the JIT system requires the integration and coordination of all departments involved in the development and processing of the goods. The engineering, purchasing, manufacturing, materials management and marketing systems need to work together efficiently to ensure the achievement of the JIT system. The main aim of the JIT system is to promote the efficient flow of materials through the logistics system where waste is eliminated from all areas of the production and delivery systems.

The importance of coordinating all the relevant functions within the system emphasizes the involvement of several pertinent functions, including purchasing, transportation, warehousing, inventory control, production, quality control and data processing. These functional linkages serve as a necessary component of the JIT system. The advancement of technology, however, has helped to ensure the effective coordination of all these functions to enable JIT to be achieved, computer link-ages between relevant firms within the network have enabled its effective implementation. In general, JIT works best in repetitive manufacturing situations where there are significant levels of inventory to begin with and accurate forecasts of demand, and where production is possible and suppliers are within easy reach. Essentially, JIT is successfully implemented when there is high degree of cooperation and coordination by all relevant firms within the network. **RM-R**

References

Frazier, G., Spekman, R. and O'Neal, C. (1988) 'Just-in-time exchange relationships in indus-trial markets', *Journal of Marketing*, (October): 53.

Lambert, D.M. and Stock, J.R. (1993) *Strategic Logistics Management*, 3rd edn, Homewood, Illinois: Richard D. Irwin.

Key account selling

Key account selling is sales effort with customers of strategic importance to the business. Their importance is usually because they account for a significant proportion of existing and potential business, they form part of a supply chain with high levels of interdependence, or extensive technical or service support is required in the relationship. Arguably, the most important asset a company has is its relationship with its customers. Selling is no longer about selling to customers: it is doing business with customers. As a result there is a need to view buyers and sellers in new and different ways. Rather than viewing selling as an independent activity, there is a need to understand relationships by studying interactions between buyers and suppliers and vice versa.

The centralization of buying units, the changing structure of major retailers, distributors and others, means that for many companies certain customers are of strategic importance. These key accounts must be given the attention and service they deserve. Further, since these are normally large organizations with buying groups, a more customized approach is appropriate. Where an organization is attempting to open a new account a different approach may be required. Special skills are needed in key account selling where it is vital to keep these customers loyal by customizing the product-service-information mix and such people require competencies in a number of different areas of strategic formulation and implementation, systems and process design and relationship building.

Key account selling requires greater openness and freer communications between buyer and supplier but they are not mutual admiration societies and often involve extensive negotiation, conflict and the desire for favourable outcomes, a process of negotiation. The salesperson, as an inter-organizational link, is more rather than less important in this process. This is likely to be reflected in a change of title from 'salesperson' to 'account manager' and this is more than semantic. These trends will continue. The field sales force of the firm lies at the intersection between the firm and its customers and is a prime communication vehicle between the two but, in the past, the main driving force behind sales management efforts to improve the performance of the firm has been in 'closing the sale'. Key account selling implies this has been replaced by relationship selling, interactive communication of the salesperson with customers and customer specialization. **WGD**

Reference

McDonalds, M. and Rogers, B. (1998) *Key Account Management: Learning from supplier and customer perspectives* Oxford: Butterworth Heinemann.

L

Legal factors

Legal factors are those issues arising from government legislation, which is debated by the elected representatives of the country's people, and from case law as decided by judges and magistrates. Case law is often the greater part of the law, since judges must interpret legislation in ways that will fit actual cases brought before them. The judges' decisions then become precedents for similar cases in the future; the intention is that cases will be decided in a more or less equal manner. Laws are often passed in order to control business dealings, to prevent abuses of power by large firms, or to give new rights to consumers, employees or shareholders.

Sometimes uncertainty exists about new legislation until after it has been tested in the courts. In the first instance, a judge may find an unexpected way of interpreting the law in order to ensure a fair outcome in the particular case before him or her. In the second instance, case law does not depend on the political colour of the government of the day. During the 1980s considerable doubt existed about the meaning of UK company law, because a great many changes had happened in a short time, most of which had not been tested in the courts.

Within the European Union, a further complication arises because of EU law, which now takes precedence over national laws on many issues. This makes it increasingly difficult to be sure what the law actually says, and also makes it difficult to predict what changes might occur, since both case law and EU law are not dependent on the national government. This adds considerably to the existing problems of dealing with differing national laws when trading across borders (Stern, 1991). **JWDB**

References
STERN (1991) *The media scene in Europe*, 3, Hamburg: STERN.

Legal implications of direct marketing

The Data Protection Act 1998 is the dominant piece of legislation affecting direct marketing and came into force on 1 March 2000. Some of its components were phased in after this date.

The legislation is composed of eight principles.

1. Personal data shall be obtained and processed fairly and lawfully. It is considered

unfair if the individual is not fully informed as to what use may be made of the information, including further sale of their data.

2. Personal data shall be obtained only for lawful purposes and shall not be further processed in any incompatible manner.
3. Personal data shall be adequate, relevant and not excessive in relation to the purpose for which they are processed.
4. Personal data shall be accurate and kept up to date.
5. Personal data shall not be kept longer than is necessary.
6. Personal data shall be processed in accordance with the rights of data subjects (individuals who are the subject of personal data).
7. Appropriate technical and organizational measures shall be taken against unauthorized or unlawful processing of personal data and against accidental loss or destruction of, or damage to, personal data.
8. Personal data shall not be transferred to a country or territory outside the EEA (Austria, Belgium, Denmark, Finland, France, Germany, Greece, Holland, Iceland, Ireland, Italy, Liechtenstein, Luxembourg, Norway, Portugal, Spain, Sweden, United Kingdom) unless that country or territory ensures an adequate level of protection for the rights and freedoms of data subjects in relation to the processing of personal data.

Although there are some exceptions, an individual is entitled to be supplied with a copy of all personal information relating to themselves. If any such information is inaccurate (financial details for credit provision, for example) an individual can apply to the Court or Data Protection Commissioner for an order that this be corrected or erased and might be entitled to compensation for any resulting loss or distress. Individuals also have the right to prevent personal information about them being used for direct marketing purposes.

The Telecommunications (Data Protection and Privacy) Regulations Act 1999 also came into force on 1 March 2000. This bans unsolicited faxes to individuals unless they have consented. Outbound telephone calls to individuals are also illegal if they have registered their objection to these with the Telephone Preference Service. **MJE**

References
The Data Protection Act 1998, London: The Stationery Office.
The Telecommunications (Data Protection and Privacy) Regulations Act 1999, London: The Stationery Office.

Less developed countries

The less developed countries (LDCs) or 'third world markets' as they are often referred to, are not uniform, not homogeneous.

Four categories can be readily identified.

1. High volume, low value raw material exporters, with an infrastructural base.
2. High volume, low value raw material exporters, with little infrastructure base.
3. Low value, low volume traditional exporters, with an infrastructural base.
4. Least developed nations, largely subsistence economies.

The growth in global trade that has characterized the last 40 years has in general not greatly benefited the less developed nations. These nations are generally not attractive to marketers. The dice of globalization are stacked against LDCs.

LDCs represent political risk, lack of political stability, perhaps hostility towards foreign enterprise (the scars of colonial exploitation have in many cases not yet healed), social unrest, terrorism, corruption and local vested interests. All militate against normal trade and exchange.

Market access may be difficult because of lack of infrastructure and non-tariff barriers and, most importantly, lack of purchasing power may make the market unattractive. The global market is divided between the rich and the poor, applying to both people and nations. It is no surprise therefore, that the 100 largest international enterprises are based in the world's rich countries, and that most of their business is with rich countries.

What is deeply worrying is that recent developments in international trade suggest that the rich are getting richer and the poor poorer. The e-commerce revolution hardly touches the LDCs, where only tiny elites have access to computers.

Efforts are made to improve the trading possibilities between developed and developing economics. The European Union has the 'Lome' convention, agreements between the European Community and 71 African, Caribbean and Pacific countries, involving both commercial and financial assistance, but Lome and the Americans are at loggerheads over bananas. The LDCs are victims, not beneficiaries, the needs and future of the LDCs is one of the great unanswered questions for International Marketing. **MJT**

Reference
Porter, M.E. (1996) *The Competitive Advantage of Nations*, London: Macmillan.

Logistics

Logistics refers to the tasks of moving materials and finished goods from the point of origin to the final point of consumption. It is a term which reflects the management of the supply chain, where a network of suppliers and customers interact in carrying out distribution tasks. The logistics system ensures that the right products are moved in the right quantity at the right time to identified locations in the most efficient manner. Designing a logistics system that is suitable to meet the needs of a firm is not an easy task since a host of factors have to be considered in meeting customer demands. Essentially, the output of most logistics systems is customer service because the efficiency with which goods are delivered to customers is used as a yardstick to measure the effectiveness of the logistics systems.

The basic components of a logistics systems are transportation, inventory control, and warehousing. The most fundamental element in the logistics systems is transportation since products must be physically moved from one location to another in the most efficient manner. Selecting the appropriate mode of transportation to achieve customer service requirements is essential in any logistics system. The warehousing or storage component of the logistics system is concerned with the holding of finished goods until they are ready to be sold. Occasionally, inventories need to be kept to ensure a continuity of supply to customers. This requires an effective management of the third component of the logistics system, the inventory control.

Inventory control refers to the attempt of the logistics manager to hold the lowest level of invenry that will still be able to meet customer demand. Put together, these three tocomponents reflect the importance of managing the logistics system in the most cost efficient manner since changes in one component are likely to affect the other two. **RM-R**

References
Ballou, R.H. (1992) *Business Logistics Management*, 3rd edn, Englewood Cliffs, NJ: Prentice Hall.
Christopher, M. (1986) *The Strategy of Distribution Management*, London: Heinemann.
Christopher, M. (1997) *Marketing Logistics*, Oxford: Butterworth Heinemann.

Logistics and supply chain management

'Logistics' involves the distribution of goods, from the point of raw materials acquisition to the point of sale to the consumer. Store-based retailers form part of a 'supply chain', which consists of the successive organizations involved in producing and distributing consumer goods, i.e. manufacturers, wholesalers and transport providers. Logistics and supply chain management are concerned with the allocation of resources and coordination of processes and associated costs of a wide range of activities, including forecasting, stockholding and inventory handling, space utilization, customer service levels and transport costs, as well as information flow.

Increasingly efficient consumer response (ECR) is used to create a supply chain driven by consumer demand. The principles of just in time (JIT) management and business process re-engineering are applied to maximize efficiency for the whole supply chain, rather than for individual organizations. Retailer and manufacturer objectives and processes are aligned. The trade-off concept is applied to identify how overall improvements can be achieved by investing in one area of the supply chain to achieve greater cost savings in another area, simultaneously adding customer service and value. Category management (recognizing that consumers shop for categories (e.g. cereals) rather than products (e.g. cornflakes) and activity based costing (looking at the cost of processes rather than products) are used. Inter-organizational electronic links are created for information sharing, joint demand forecasting and computer assisted ordering. The flow of goods is enhanced and stock levels are reduced through transport consolidation, often making use of third party logistics providers.

In the UK ECR initiatives are usually led by large retail organizations and can result in substantial cost savings. The movement was originally led by grocery retailing, however with the grocers' move into many non-food areas, their approach towards supply chain management is moving with them. Therefore in recent years there has been a shift away from competition between companies towards competition between supply chains, resulting in a growth of retailer – manufacturer partnerships and cooperation in both operational and marketing activities. **RAS**

References

Baron, S., Davies, B. and Swindley, D. (1991) *Macmillan Dictionary of Retailing*, Macmillan Reference Books, London: Macmillan.

Fernie, J. (ed.) (1998) *The Future for UK Retailing: Change, Growth and Competition*, London: Financial Times Business.

Fernie, J. and Sparks, L. (1998) *Logistics and Retail Management: Insights into Current Practice and Trends*, London: Kogan Page.

Jarvis, M. and Woolven, J. (1999) *Category Management in Action*, Watford: Institute of Grocery Distribution Business Publication.

Mintel (1997) *Efficient Consumer Response*, Special Report, London: Mintel International Group.

Market analysis

Market analysis is the process of identifying, categorizing and quantifying the elements that drive a market.

In general, these elements will be contained within the SWOT (strengths, weaknesses, opportunities and threats) analysis and the marketing audit (for more on these, see 'Swot analysis' and 'Marketing audit'). Analysing all the elements that contribute to creating a market can be a long-drawn-out and complex activity; it is sometimes more cost-effective to leave out some of the more detailed analyses and concentrate on the more obvious and immediate elements.

External analysis involves learning as much as possible (or at least, as much as is reasonable) about the markets in which the firm intends to operate. *Internal analysis* involves learning as much as is reasonable about the firm's capacity to service and compete in those markets.

The following areas should be examined.

- *Environmental factors* – economic conditions, social changes, government policies and regulation, costs and availability of raw materials, availability of skilled manpower, availability of energy, environmental (green) policies and regulations.
- *Market conditions* – consumer needs, size of market, growth rate, geographic location, market potentials and forecasts, market shares of the firm and its competitors, market segments.
- *Customers* – present and prospective customers, buying processes, size of orders, rates of product use, purchasing policies and procedures, motives and influences on buying behaviour.
- *Channels* – present channel relationships, channel options, motivations of channel intermediaries, needs of channel intermediaries, costs of channel options, physical distribution characteristics, legal aspects of dealing with intermediaries.
- *Competitors* – number and location of competitors, primary and secondary competitors, competitive strengths and weaknesses, research and development commitment, engineering capabilities, purchasing capabilities.

(Haas and Wotruba, 1983)

Unlike the marketing audit, which is an activity intended to give an instant picture of the firm's status at a given moment, market analysis should be conducted on an ongoing basis. **JWDB**

Reference

Haas, R.W. and Wotruba, T.R. (1983) *Marketing Management*, Plano, TX: Business Publications Inc.

Market challenger

A 'market challenger' is a firm that has a smaller market share in a particular market than the 'market leader'. It is in a position, however, to be a serious threat to the leader. The market challenger may wish to develop its strategies based on the ambition to become the market leader itself. In order to do this a challenger will need to display a significant competitive advantage in order to challenge the dominance of the market leader. Alternatively it may decide that there is too much risk in such a strategy and may seek to gain greater returns from its existing market position, perhaps by reducing its cost base. The challenger may gain ground on the leader by attacking similar sized or smaller competitors. The nature of the competitive rivalry within the industry will help shape strategy. For example, where there is low growth overall an individual firm will only be able to grow by taking market share from its competitors. Pepsi Cola is possibly the most famous example of a market challenger as it constantly battles to win market share from the market leader, Coca-Cola. It does this by using high profile celebrities in its advertising campaigns and by taking to the streets and inviting consumers to take the 'Pepsi Challenge' taste test.

Attacking strategies for market challengers often take their names from military strategy. A 'frontal attack' involves attacking the leader's strengths, whereas a 'flanking attack' involves challenging the leader's weaknesses. An 'encirclement attack' involves attacking from all directions; a 'bypass attack' is where the challenger attacks easier markets i.e. through diversification. Finally, a 'guerrilla attack' may be used by a smaller firm against a much larger one, e.g. Easyjet's challenge to the established airlines. **SR**

Reference

Kotler, P., Armstrong, G., Saunders, J. and Wong, V. (1999) *Principles of Marketing*, 2nd European edn, London: Prentice Hall Europe.

Market coverage

Market coverage in distribution channels refers to the intensity of distribution required by the manufacturer. The number of intermediaries required in a specific geographical area influences the market coverage or market exposure strategy. A manufacturer may opt to have intensive distribution, selective distribution or exclusive distribution coverage for its products or services.

Intensive coverage is adopted when many intermediaries are used at each level of the channel. This is typical of consumer convenience goods distribution where as many different outlets as possible are used. On the other hand, *exclusive coverage* refers to a highly selective pattern of distribution where only a single selected intermediary is involved in distributing the goods or service in a specific geographical area. In this situation, customers are willing to search for the product or services extensively. Speciality goods are often distributed in this manner. In between intensive and exclusive coverage lies *selective coverage*, which refers to a distribution strategy where a few selected intermediaries are used in the distribution channel. This is typical in the distribution of consumer convenience goods.

A key factor influencing which market coverage strategy to adopt is the extent of distribution saturation. For instance, when there are too few intermediaries distributing within a market area, the manufacturer may lose out on potential sales and market share growth. In contrast, with too many distributors, competition may be so great that conflict may be more significant. Manufacturers need to decide on the right level of saturation appropriate for achieving its distribution objectives. **RM-R**

References
Little, R.W. (1970) 'The marketing channel: who should lead this extra-corporate organisation?', *Journal of Marketing*, 34(January): 31–38.
Stern, L.W., El-Ansary, A.I. and Coughlan, A. (1996) *Marketing Channels*, 5th edn, New Jersey: Prentice Hall International Editions.

Market drivers

Market drivers are those factors which create and control the growth of a market. Although drivers can vary from one industry to another, the list is likely to include the following:

- demand for the product category
- general levels of demand in the economy
- the rate of technological change
- rate of change of competitive activity and competitive levels
- social changes which affect demand.

These factors are generally considered to be part of the marketing environment, but apply to a specific market rather than to the general business climate. As with other environmental factors, some market drivers can be controlled (or at least influenced) by marketing activities, while others are beyond the control of the firm. **JWDB**

Reference
Kotler P., Armstrong G., Saunders J., and Wong V. (2000) *Principles of Marketing* 2nd European edn, Harlow: Prentice Hall, pp. 142–179.

Market follower

A firm usually competes in a marketplace with other firms. Within the marketplace individual firms will make competitive moves with the objective of seeking an advantage. The competitive environment may be made up of a 'market leader', the firm with the largest market share, and a 'market challenger' with the second largest market share whose aim may be to directly challenge and overtake the leader. A Market follower is a firm that would have a smaller, yet still significant share of the market e.g. 10 per cent. Such a firm may not have the financial resources nor the inclination to aspire to be the market leader. Instead of directly challenging the leading company and its other competitors the market follower is happy to maintain its current position in the marketplace. It can be an expensive and potentially dangerous business strategy to act aggressively towards one's competitors. Such a move may result in a hostile reaction from the market leader and lead to a reduced market share for the follower. Many firms are happy to plod along doing what they are good at and to pursue a slow and steady growth or simply to maintain the status quo.

Market followers often adopt a 'me too' strategy, which involves shadowing the developments of the leaders. First Direct took the lead in implementing telephone banking in the UK and once this strategy was proved to be effective it was followed by the High Street banks, who set up their own direct banking operations. The followers have avoided the huge expense of developing a new service from scratch. A market follower may develop its strategy in order to become a market challenger, but this will necessitate a more innovative approach.

Being a follower does not mean having no strategy. A firm will still have to defend its markets and win new customers; it merely seeks not to introduce strategies that lead to retaliation from other players. **SR**

Reference

Kotler, P., Armstrong, G., Saunders, J. and Wong, V. (1999) *Principles of Marketing*, 2nd European edn, London: Prentice Hall Europe.

Market growth

Market growth is concerned with the rate at which the demand for a product class rises over a given period. If a market is growing, it means that demand for the product is rising: this may be due to increased consumption by existing consumers, or (more likely) an increased number of consumers using the product.

In markets which are growing at a low rate, it is difficult and costly to increase market share. This is because any share increase has to be obtained by winning customers over from competitors, whereas in a fast-growing market new customers are entering the market frequently, so that the firm that presents the most attractive package will have little difficulty in attracting the extra business. An example of this is the Japanese motorcycle industry. At a time when the motorcycle market was growing rapidly, the Japanese captured most of the new customers entering the market. At the same time, the British motorcycle industry maintained its output, but did not increase its sales; eventually, the Japanese controlled the market, and when the market growth rate levelled out the British firms were unable to increase their share and were eventually squeezed out.

If the market is growing at a high rate, firms within the market may be tempted to take the 'easy option' of reducing expenditure on promotion and be content to accept rates of sales growth lower than the rate of market growth. This will, in the long run, lead to the problems outlined above – when the growth rate slows or the market shrinks, the complacent firms will be squeezed out. This very commonly happens during recessions. Ultimately the cost advantages go to the firms with the biggest market shares.

The Boston Consulting Group Matrix offers a way of viewing the relationship between market share, market growth and product portfolio.

		Relative market share	
		High	**Low**
	High	Star	Problem child
Market growth	**Low**	Cash cow	Dog
	Negative	War horse	Dodo

Figure: **Expanded Boston Consulting Group Matrix**
Source: Barksdale and Harris, 1982, pp. 74-82

The matrix shows that if growth is high and market share is high, the product will be a star performer; if growth is low but share is high, the product will generate cash for the company, without much need for high promotional expenditure. If the market is shrinking, but the share is high, the product will be a war-horse – still strong, but doomed in the long run. If growth is high, but share is low, the product presents problems – is it right for the market? Can it be saved? If share is low and growth is low, the product is probably not worth keeping. If share is low and growth is negative, the product is probably already heading for extinction. **JWDB**

Reference
Barksdale, H.C. and Harris, C.E. (1982) 'Portfolio analysis and the plc', *Long Range Planning*, 15(6):74–83.

Market leader

Most industries are able to acknowledge the presence of a market leader. The market leader is recognized as the company that enjoys the largest market share within the industry. Whilst market share may be deemed to be the clearest signal of market leadership, market leaders often exhibit other characteristics that set them apart from their main competitors. With a large market share, they usually enjoy the benefits of significant buying power, which reduces the cost of purchases. They may also be seen to be the leaders in terms of product innovation (note how Kellogg's continually seeks to introduce new products into the cereals market). Brand dominance can be another benefit enjoyed by the market leader, for example, Nike is the market leader in the sports apparel and footwear market, with the most recognized brand and clear leadership in product innovation. Market leaders also have links into a wide and extensive distribution network, which gives them the ability to gain market access for existing and new products. It should be noted, however, that the term 'market leadership' is dependent upon how the term 'market' is defined. For example, BMW enjoys a larger market share of the luxury sports car market than General Motors, but the latter has a larger market share of the world car market in total.

Market leaders are clear targets for many of their competitors. New product innovations, technology and simple complacency can all contribute to the demise of the market leader, if they do not maintain close contact with the market. Consequently, if a market leader aims to retain its position as number one it needs to develop a range of strategies. This may involve attempting to build total demand for the product category; defending market share against keen and smaller competitors and/or gaining market share at the expense of market competitors. **PBB**

References
Buzzell, D.R., Gale, T.B. and Sultan, G.M. (1975) 'Market share, the key to profitability', *Harvard Business Review*, Jan–Feb.
Woo, C.Y. and Cooper, A.C. (1984) 'Market leadership, not always so good', *Harvard Business Review*, Jan–Feb.

Market opportunity analysis

Market opportunity analysis (MOA) could more appropriately be called market research and, in addition to this section, the reader should consult other sections as needed.

Opportunity analysis requires information and international market research is about just that. We usually require three types of information.

- The international macro-environment:
  - demographic trends
  - economic trends
  - lifestyle trends
  - technological trends
  - political/regulatory trends.

- Task environments:
  - consumer information
  - collaborator/business partner information
  - competitor information.
- Company environment:
  - company sales and market share
  - company orders and order history
  - company costs
  - customer profitability.

The macro environment will usually be a country, although in the future it may be a trading zone or an economic region. Which countries to choose will be related to stage of economic development in many cases.

Consumer information is critical in marketing opportunity analysis. Use the following framework.

- Who are our potential customers?
- What do they need and want?
- What objectives are they trying to satisfy?
- Who participates in the buying decision?
- How do consumers make their buying decisions?
- When do consumers seem ready to buy?
- Where do consumers prefer to buy?

Collaborators/business partners may be defined as middlemen, suppliers, marketers, agencies – advertising agencies, direct mail firms and logistics agencies – transportation companies, warehouses and expediters. **MJT**

Reference
Douglas, S. and Craig, C.A. (1995) *Global Marketing Strategy*, New York: McGraw-Hill.

Market penetration

Market penetration is one of the intensive growth opportunities identified by Ansoff (1988) in the product/market expansion grid. It is one of the strategic approaches that aims to increase the current product's share in the current market in order to achieve growth. It is also one of the intensive growth opportunities that many organizations consider as among the less risky approaches to increasing sales.

The marketing decision relating to market penetration for the launch of new products must consider either a rapid-penetration strategy or a slow-penetration strategy. If undertaking a rapid market penetration strategy a marketer must launch the product at a low price and spend heavily on promotion, and it is generally effective when the market is large, most buyers are price-sensitive but there is little knowledge about the product. A slow penetration strategy is where the company launches the product at a low price and low levels of promotion with the objective of encouraging rapid product acceptance, but allowing profits to build. This is most effective where the demand for the product is highly sensitive to price but minimally sensitive to promotion, which is usually found in large markets where consumers are highly aware of the product and there is potential competition.

Marketers considering market penetration as a growth strategy for existing products need to concentrate on encouraging frequency of purchase and increasing the amount of product purchased. The adaptation of pricing policies by cutting prices, undercutting competitors' prices or using promotional pricing will help to achieve this approach. Marketers can also increase communications and promotional spend in an effort to encourage further trial, repeat purchases, loyalty and customer retention. Indeed, the marketer is likely to use more effective relationship marketing techniques to encourage such market penetration.

Boots the Chemist has recently launched a loyalty card aimed at men, as their current 'Advantage Card' loyalty scheme was proving to be too effeminate for its male customers. This has been devised to improve penetration of the male grooming market which is currently worth over £700 million in the UK and is reported to be growing by around 8 per cent per year. **RAA**

References
Ansoff, H.I. (1988) *The New Corporate Strategy*, New York: Wiley and Sons, p. 83.

Kotler, P., (1997) *Marketing Management: Analysis, Planning, Implementation and Control*, London: Prentice Hall International, pp. 72–74; 77–80.

Wilson, R.M.S. and Gilligan, C. (1997) *Strategic Marketing Management: Planning, Implementation and Control*, Oxford: CIM/Butterworth-Heinemann, pp. 221–226.

Market research

Research that is conducted to assess the market situation is called 'market research'. A market is the set of actual and potential buyers or consumers who have specific needs and wants that require satisfaction. The size of a market is dependent on the number of people who are considered as potential buyers for a product or service. Marketers are interested to collect information about these potential buyers and the size of the market for their products or services. When marketers are developing a marketing plan, an assessment of the current marketing situation requires them to have a good description of the market. This means that the market for their products or services has to be defined precisely by indicating the market size. Only when this information is available can marketers develop a clearer picture of potential threats and opportunities that exist in the market and then go on to develop their strategies.

A market research can also be used to evaluate the demand for a product or service. When a company identifies a potentially attractive market, it needs to identify the market's current size and future potential. This information can only be gathered through appropriate research, which normally is generated through marketing information systems of the marketing organization. It is quite important for the information system in the company to have a pool of information that can distinguish various levels of market, including potential market, available market, served market and penetrated market. **RM-R**

Reference
Kotler, P., Armstrong, G., Saunders, J. and Wong, V. (1996) *Principles of Marketing – The European Edition*, London: Prentice Hall.

Market segmentation

Market segmentation is the process of identifying groups of customers or consumers with similar needs. The object of the exercise is to ensure that marketing efforts are targeted in the most appropriate way to achieve marketing objectives and that resources are directed in the most efficient manner.

In the past, firms were able to produce standardized products for mass markets. Because mass production enabled firms to produce very cheap goods, consumers were prepared to accept that the products were less than perfect, and did not entirely fit their needs. As time has moved on, two factors have militated against this approach. First, consumers have become more demanding and more prepared to pay a little extra for products that more closely suit their needs rather than products that fulfil only a basic function. Secondly, global marketing has produced markets which are large enough so that even a small segment of the market is big enough to support a more tailored approach (Chee and Harris, 1993).

Segmentation can be carried out in many different ways, examples are geographical segmentation, behavioural segmentation and psychographic segmentation. For example, a clothing firm would produce warm clothing for cold countries and lighter clothing for hot countries. This would be an example of geographical segmentation. An example of behavioural segmentation would be targeting car drivers to buy air fresheners. The firm does not need to know how old the drivers are or their sex, the fact that they are driving cars is sufficient to make them a target market. An example of psychographic segmentation might be aiming a product at people who like to dress smartly.

In order to be viable for the firm, a segment must have the following characteristics.

- It must be substantial, in other words there must be enough people in it to justify producing a product especially for them.
- It must be measurable and definable. There must be some way of identifying the members of the segment and counting them.
- It must be congruent. Members must have close agreement on their needs.
- It must be accessible. There must be some way of targeting the segment with marketing messages and products.
- It must be stable. The nature and membership of the segment must be reasonably constant. **JWDB**

Reference
Chee, H. and Harris, R. (1993) *Marketing: A Global Perspective*, London: Pitman.

Market share

Market share is the proportion of the total customer base that the firm supplies and services. Firms seek to maximize their market share in two ways: by seeking out new customers for the product class, thus expanding the total market, or by taking existing customers for the product class away from their competitors. In general, larger firms have most to gain by expanding the total market and smaller firms have most to gain from winning customers over.

One of the difficulties in calculating market share lies in determining the overall size of the market. This stems from the difficulty of defining product categories and competition. For example, a cinema chain might calculate market share by comparing its own number of customers against overall national cinema attendances; on the other hand, the same chain might assume that it is in the entertainment business, and compare its total revenue against the total national expenditure on entertainment. The problem here is that many products have close substitutes; in the consumer's mind the products offer very similar benefits, even if there is no similarity from the producer's viewpoint.

Relatively few organizations track their market share (Mercer, 1999). If the market is expanding, it is quite possible for a firm to have rising sales (which would, of course, be viewed positively) but at the same time have a falling market share. This will have a severe impact on the firm if the market begins to shrink. The market share needs to be tracked against the following:

- overall market share
- segment share (share of the targeted segment)
- relative share, in relation to the market leaders or main competitors. **JWDB**

Reference
Mercer, D. (1999) *Marketing*, 3rd edn, Oxford: Blackwell Publishing.

Market signals

If marketers are to plan effective marketing strategies, it is important to recognize the market signals which need to be analysed. This analysis will allow the marketer to recognize either the potential of entering a new market or the achievement of a strategy within a particular existing market.

There is a range of market signals that should be researched and interpreted before strategic decisions can be evaluated. Indeed, these can be related to the main macroeconomic data relating to geographic areas and include data relating to:

* recession or economic boom
* changes in interest rates and exchange rates
* price and wage inflation
* changes in unemployment
* changes in income distribution.

Changes in any one of these macroeconomic variables will have an effect on the rest. For example, if there is a sharp increase in the rate of inflation in the UK then the Bank of England would have to raise interest rates and the pound would appreciate against other currencies. This would result in imports increasing and exports decreasing. This would in turn have an effect on investment and consumer demand because of the higher cost of borrowing. Thus economic growth would probably slow down and there would most likely be a rise in unemployment.

Other political factors or signals, such as a change in national government or the level of the national minimum wage, may also have an impact on a country's economic state. Further signals are often as important to assess, such as demographic changes or changes in social attitudes towards issues such as environmental protection.

Therefore, the analysis of the market signals will allow the strategist to be assured of confidence in the forecasts relating to a proposed strategy. The following references relate to Internet sites which will help to identify such information for certain countries. **RAA**

References
Euromonitor – www.euromonitor.com
OECD – www.oecd.org
The Economist Intelligence Unit – www.eiu.com
The European Commission – www.europa.eu.int
The World Bank – www.worldbank.org
United Nations – www.un.org

Marketing and economic development

Although the term 'marketing' is relatively new, its philosophy has been practised since the beginnings of the exchange or trade system. Trade has existed ever since humankind has been capable of producing a surplus. This surplus was usually agricultural produce, which was often traded for manufactured goods such as implements, textiles or earthenware. Such exchange brought into existence venues such as village fairs and local markets that facilitated trade. This emergence of trade allowed people to specialize in producing particular goods and services that could be exchanged in markets for other goods that they needed.

Between 1760 and 1830 the UK economy was transformed during the Industrial Revolution, and the country moved away from a dependence on agricultural produce. Industrialization meant huge gains in productivity, and manufacturing became geographically concentrated. Manufacturing firms produced in volume in purpose-built premises near to supplies of raw materials initially for national and then for international markets. This also meant a move of the population away from rural to urban environments.

In order that producers could manufacture goods and services that would appeal and sell in widely separated markets, companies had to analyse and interpret the needs and wants of customers so that products could be manufactured that would match these needs and wants. This matching process originally amounted to 'sensing' what the market needed, and this was usually the task of the business entrepreneur, based upon personal judgement. It was not until much later that a scientific means of matching customer needs to the production process, principally through medium of marketing research, came into existence. **GL**

Reference

Lancaster, G. and Massingham, L. (1999) *Essentials of Marketing*, 3rd edn, Maidenhead: McGraw-Hill, pp. 3–50.

Marketing and the Internet

Rapid technological change, especially in digitization, information technology, intellectual property and communication systems (Schultz and Kitchen, 2000) is having a revolutionary effect on the study and practice of marketing in the new 21st century interactive globalized marketplace. Many of the straightforward and traditional tenets associated with marketing are being questioned and new models, techniques, systems and approaches are being developed under the heading of 'e-commerce' or 'e-business'.

One example of this is the move from retailing to e-tailing. The Internet appeared on the scene back in 1983 with an admittedly research-centric usage. By 1991, as the commercial opportunities became apparent, full commercial connections were extended. Since 1991 the Internet, also known as 'cyberspace' or the 'information superhighway', has swept around the planet, transforming many traditional marketplaces into 'marketspaces', operating alongside, but not necessarily supplanting, the earlier markets (Rayport and Sviokla, 1994). The Internet is at minimum 'a global web of computer networks' which has 'made instantaneous and decentralized global communication possible' (Kotler, 2000). A more simplistic definition is that the Internet is a network of inter-linked computers operating on a standard protocol that allows data (or marketing information from our context) to be transferred between different machines. The word itself literally means 'network of networks'. It is the network, abbreviated to the 'Net,' that allows consumers, customers, channels, companies, governments and all forms of organizations to transmit data. Transmission includes text, graphics, video, software, voice etc. Back in 1996, the number of computers linked to the Internet was estimated at 10 million. By 2000, the estimate had risen to in excess of between 200 and 500 million and is rising year-on-year (Hamill and Kitchen, 2000).

All marketers (existent and wannabes) have to ensure that they understand the strategic import of the Internet, familiarize themselves with the range of tools available, develop the hands-on skills (not just to 'surf the Net', though this may act as a mode of learning) to help design and use web sites for commercial user-oriented marketing purposes. **PJK**

References

Hamill, J. and Kitchen, P.J. (1999) 'The Internet', in P.J. Kitchen *Marketing Communications*, London: Thomson Learning, ch.22.
Kotler, P. (2000) *Marketing Management*, 10th edn, Prentice Hall International: New Jersey.

Rayport, J.R. and Sviokla, J.J. (1994) 'Managing in the marketspace', *Harvard Business Review*, November/December: 75–85.
Schultz, D.E. and Kitchen, P.J. (2000) *Communicating Globally: An Integrated Marketing Approach*, Macmillan Business: London.

Marketing audit

Performance in the marketplace is typically influenced by three factors:

- the organization's current market position
- the nature of the environmental threats and opportunities that it faces
- the ability of the management team to cope with the demands of the environment.

The marketing audit is designed to provide the marketing manager with a clear understanding of each of these areas and to provide a firm foundation for the development of strategy.

The marketing audit is a comprehensive, systematic, independent and periodic examination of a company's – or business unit's – marketing environment, objectives, strategies and activities with a view to determining problem areas and opportunities and recommending a plan of action to improve the company's marketing performance. It is therefore a measure both of environmental opportunities and threats and of the organization's marketing capability.

The audit consists of three principal steps, which involve a review of:

- the organization's environment and the opportunities and threats that emerge from this
- the strengths and weaknesses of its marketing system and the organization's overall level of marketing capability
- its marketing activities.

In conducting the audit, the planner typically begins with an examination of the external factors. The internal audit then builds upon this by assessing the extent to which the organization, its structure and resources relate to the environment and have the capability of operating effectively within the constraints that the environment poses. Taken together, these highlight the potential benefits to the organization of marketing auditing.

- The analysis of the external environment and internal situation.
- The evaluation of past performance and present activities.
- The identification of future opportunities and threats. **CTG & RMSW**

References
Brownlie, D., (1996) 'Marketing audits and auditing: diagnosis through intervention', *Journal of Marketing Management*, 12(1–3):99–112.
Kotler, P, Gregor, W.T. and Rodgers, W.H. (1989) 'The marketing audit comes of age', *Sloan Management Review*, 30(3), winter: 49–62.
Wilson, A. (1982) Marketing Audit Check Lists, London: McGraw-Hill.

Marketing audit activities

The marketing audit is a checklist used for analysing the current state of marketing activities within the firm. It evaluates the effectiveness of the organization in implementing the 7Ps of marketing – products, price, place, promotion, people, processes and physical evidence (Booms and Bitner 1981).

The marketing audit encompasses but goes beyond SWOT and STEP analyses, and covers the following categories of activity (Kotler, 1997).

- *The marketing environment* – economic, technological, politico-legal, cultural and ecological factors affecting the firm.
- *The task environment* – markets, customers, competitors, distribution, suppliers, facilitators, and publics.
- *Marketing strategy* – business mission, marketing objectives, corporate strategy.
- *Marketing organization* – formal and informal structures, functional efficiency, interface efficiency.
- *Marketing systems* – information systems, planning systems, control systems, new product development.
- *Marketing productivity* – profitability analysis, cost-effectiveness analysis.
- *Marketing function* – product portfolio, pricing policy, distribution policy, promotion, salesforce management.

The marketing audit is the marketing equivalent of the balance sheet; it offers a snapshot of what is currently happening within the organization, with the primary objective of identifying strengths and weaknesses and areas where improvement is possible. This means that the audit should be carried on a regular basis, within the limits of time and money available for the task. **JWDB**

References
Booms B.H. and Bitner, M.J. (1981) ' Marketing strategies and organization structures for service firms', in J. Donnelly and W.R. George (eds) *Marketing of Services,* Chicago: American Marketing Association Proceedings.

Kotler, P. (1997) *Marketing Management, Analysis, Planning and Control,* 9th edn, Englewood Cliffs NJ: Prentice Hall.

Marketing communications

Marketing communications, which is another term for promotion, is just one part of marketing, one of the famous 4Ps of the marketing mix. It is, of course, not a single entity but, rather, involves a wide range of activities that have at their heart the need to convey marketing messages to target audiences. It is this area of marketing that is best known by the general public because its effects are all around us. Marketing communications shout from televisions, cinemas and radios; adorn newspapers, magazines, poster sites, buildings and shop fronts; drop through letterboxes; surround shoppers in high streets, malls, arcades and supermarkets; leap from packaging; talk to us face-to-face and over the phone; flash on our computer screens; assail all our senses. At work and at play, marketing communications are part of our everyday lives. They are vital to marketing in extending communications to a myriad of audiences: customers, consumers, the trade, investors, employees, the media, the government and a host of other possible groups. Managing marketing communications is a creative, challenging and rewarding career in an industry worth multi-billions of pounds each year in media sales, research, sales promotions, fees and remuneration. **DWP**

Reference
Pickton, D.W. and Broderick, A. (2001) *Integrated Marketing Communications,* London: Financial Times Prentice Hall, ch. 1.

Marketing communications mix

Marketing communications comprise a range of activities called the 'marketing communications mix', itself just one part of the overall marketing function. This mix is also referred to as the 'promotional mix' or 'promotions mix'. Various authors (e.g. Shimp, 1997) have attempted to categorize the mix so that it is easy to remember, unfortunately, no approach has found favour with everybody. The simplest system is to classify the mix under the headings of 'advertising', 'public relations', 'sales promotions' and 'personal selling'. These headings will overlap so that some activities thought of as advertising might also be placed under public relations and so on. The actual choice of heading is somewhat arbitrary.

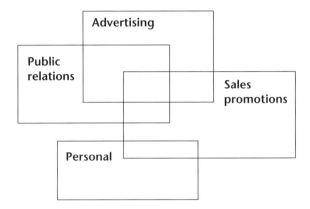

Figure: **The marketing communications mix**

To complicate matters further, some activities may be combined so that, for example, an advertisement might include a sales promotion offer, or a public relations event might include some personal selling and sales promotions. In fact, because public relations is such a wide and varied range of activities, not all of which are directly relevant to marketing, some authors now prefer to use the term 'marketing public relations' to emphasize the sub-set of public relations most relevant to marketing communications. The two areas that do not overlap are personal selling and advertising as these are two quite distinct areas of marketing communications. All of the main elements of the marketing communications mix are described more fully in their own entries, these should be referred to for more information.

By way of an overview to illustrate the range of marketing communications mix activities, the figure provides a list of examples under each main category heading. **DWP**

Advertising	Public relations	Sales promotions	Personal selling
Corporate Ads	Corporate PR	Premium/Money	Telemarketing
Product Ads	Marketing PR	Offers	Sales Assistance
Direct Response	Internal	Competitions	Door-to-Door
Ads	Marketing PR	Banded Packs	Selling
Joint Ads	Sponsorship	Merchandising	Canvassing
	Exhibitions	Point of Sale	Counter Sales
Advertisements	Press Releases	Displays	Trade Selling
in or on the:	Press Relations	Exhibitions	Consumer Selling
Press	Events	Promotional Gifts	Negotiating
TV	Hospitality	Discounts	Sales
Cinema	Lobbying	Tie-in Promotions	Management
Radio	Publicity	Buy One Get One	Customer Service
Poster	Corporate	Free	
Direct Mail	Identity	Catalogues	
Internet	Product	Leaflets	
	Placement	Coupons/Vouchers	

Figure: **Examples of marketing communications mix activities**

Reference

Shimp, T.A. (1997) *Advertising, Promotion, and Supplemental Aspects of Integrated Marketing Communication*, Orlando: The Dryden Press.

Marketing communications: organizational context

The marketing communications industry is people-driven with a high reliance on personnel. Creativity is actively encouraged and valued. Stress is placed on managing people and projects that must be completed to exacting time deadlines and financial constraints. Management is about motivation, leadership and meticulous attention to detail if advertisements are to appear when scheduled, if catalogues and brochures are to be printed and delivered on time, if competitions are to be organized, if trade and consumer promotions are to be coordinated, and a myriad of tasks are to be completed successfully.

It would be nice to think of marketing communications as a simple and harmonious blend of common interests, but the fact is that they take place in a complex organizational environment in which no single manager has complete control. Many marketing communications activities are carried out across departmental boundaries and involve numerous people, internal and external to the organization. Responsibilities for different aspects of marketing communications fall to different managers. Networks of staff and external agencies are needed to bring marketing communications to fruition (see 'Figure: Marketing communications networks' opposite). Internally, staff need to liaise between departments and at different levels of the management hierarchy. Externally, a network of suppliers is needed, from various promotional agencies, media owners and printers to freelancers, consultancies and research companies, all overseen by regulators, professional bodies and consumer groups.

The marketing communications business is typified by fragmented specialisms (Duncan and Everett, 1993) and conflicting interests. Elitist attitudes are commonplace (Robbs and Taubler, 1996), and Gonring (1994) and Schultz (1993) note the problems of 'turf battles and 'functional silos' in which individuals are protective of their own specialization and interests. In this environment, the task of integrating marketing communications is made all the more difficult yet, daily, it is an industry of impressive achievements. **DWP**

References

Duncan, T.R. and Everett, S.E. (1993) 'Client perceptions of integrated marketing communications', *Journal of Advertising Research*, May/June: 30–39.

Gonring, M.P. (1994) 'Putting integrated marketing communications to work today', *Public Relations Quarterly*, 39(3):5–48.

Robbs, B. and Taubler, D. (1996), 'Will creatives prevent agencies from adopting integrated marketing communications?', *Marketing News*, 23rd September, 30(20):4.

Schultz, D.E. (1993), 'How to overcome the barriers to integration', *Marketing News*, 19th July, 27(15):16.

Marketing communications planning

Marketing communications planning involves consideration of alternative courses of action, decision making and the production of plans. Ultimately, plans are statements of what should be done. As successful plans invariably concern many people, it is argued that the planning process should encourage involvement and be produced in written form so that plans can be shared and understood. In practice, this does not always happen and many managers have criticized the 'normative' (see below) model of how planning should be carried out as just not reflecting the realities of their work experience – planning is not always efficient or organized and

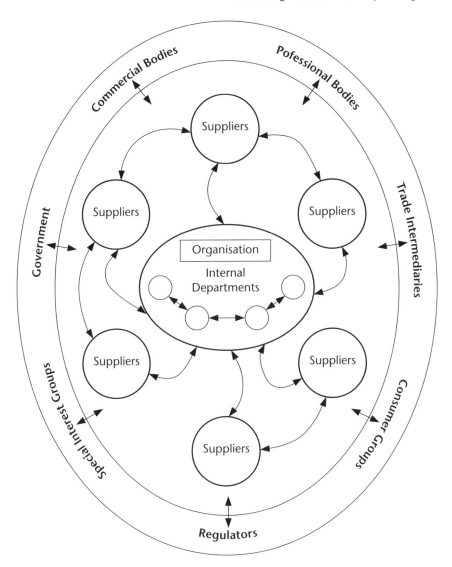

Suppliers include:

- Advertising agency
- PR agency
- Sales promotions agency
- Research companies
- Printers

- Corporate design consultants
- Packaging consultants
- Brand name consultants
- Telemarketing agency

- Production companie
- Designers
- Freelancers
- Photographers
- Finished artists

Figure: **Marketing communications networks**

sequential, nor are plans always committed to paper. Objectives are not always as detailed as they might be and evaluation is not always objective or comprehensive.

A typical normative (i.e. a proposal of what 'should' be done) planning sequence is given in the figure below, where the major areas involved in planning are identified. In marketing communications, plans are usually developed around campaigns, they tend to be produced annually although they can be for shorter or longer terms or can incorporate a group of campaigns or integration of a range of marketing communications.

- *Analysis* – involves the collection, interpretation and use of all relevant information and assessment of the situation, competitive position and the market.
- *Objectives* – the determination of what the plan is intended to achieve.
- *Target audience(s)* – statement of the audiences to be reached.
- *Budget and budget allocations* – the total budget, and allocation of budgets to different marketing communications elements and tasks.
- *Strategy and tactics* – broad description of the strategy (e.g. push and pull, competitive positioning, creative and media) and more detailed description of the tactical use of the marketing communications mix elements.
- *Evaluation, monitoring and control* – how the plan and its elements will be checked, first to determine if the concepts used are likely to work (pre-testing) and later, during implementation, to monitor progress to check that plans are working or have been successful (tracking and post-testing). **DWP**

Figure: **A marketing communications planning framework**

Reference
Pickton, D.W. and Broderick, A. (2001) *Integrated Marketing Communications*, London: Financial Times Prentice Hall, chs. 15–22.

Marketing communications process

At its most basic, marketing communications is the process of passing messages from a sender to receivers (target audiences). This is the area of marketing best known as 'promotion' – one of the 4Ps of the marketing mix. Although the terms 'promotions' and 'marketing communications' tend to be used interchangeably, marketing communications messages may not always be promotional, they may merely try to convey information and may be targeted towards audiences other than customers. It is often better, therefore, to use the more general term, 'marketing communications', instead of 'promotion'.

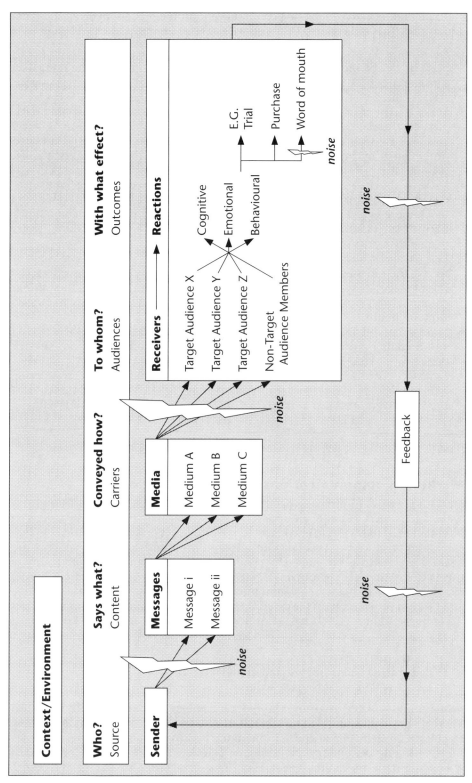

Figure: **The marketing communications process**

To produce effective marketing communications, the process involved should be understood. This is illustrated in the above figure and briefly described below.

- *Environment* – this is the 'context' in which marketing communications take place. It can be the wider environment (macro-environment) or the immediate surroundings of the communication (micro-environment).
- *Sender* – the source of the message, a person or organization.
- *Message* – the message requires to be understood. A process of 'encoding' takes place to 'translate' what the sender wishes to communicate into the signs, words and sounds used in the marketing communications. This will then be 'decoded' (interpreted) by the receiving audience. The study of these messages is called 'semiotics'.
- *Media* – the means by which messages are transmitted to target audiences. Usually thought of in terms of the mass media such as television, media can be much more varied and include anything that can carry marketing communications messages such as packaging, leaflets and even personal clothing, which frequently carries brand names and logos.
- *Receivers/target audiences* – receivers are the audiences whom senders wish to receive their messages. Typically, some non-target audience members will receive the messages as well. Audience reactions may be cognitive (what they think), emotional (what they feel) and/or behavioural (what they do and say to others – word of mouth).
- *Noise* – the 'interference' or distraction that can take place during the encoding and decoding processes, thereby reducing marketing communication effectiveness.
- *Feedback* – this is important to see if marketing communications are working. This can be direct or indirect (Hunt and Grunig, 1994). Noise can interfere with the feedback process just as it can with the original communication. **DWP**

Reference
Hunt, T. and Grunig, J.E. (1994) *Public Relations Techniques*, New York: Harcourt Brace.

Marketing communications, roles and functions

Marketing communications bridge the gap between the sender of marketing communications messages and the receivers. The sender may merely wish to convey information or may wish to encourage some form of action such as attendance at an exhibition or purchase. This range of response from unawareness to action is frequently referred to as the 'hierarchy of effects' and one common way of identifying this is to use the AIDA acronym – Awareness, Interest, Desire and Action (Strong, 1925). The roles of marketing communications can be mapped onto such a model and this can provide a basis for determining marketing communications objectives. Accordingly, Shimp (1997) has identified three principal marketing communications roles:

- to inform (make aware)
- to persuade (generate interest and desire)
- to induce action (to encourage action).

While this is suitable as an overview, other more specific roles can be identified. These might include developing a brand image, ensuring common understanding, reaching a diversity of audiences, overcoming negative communications and objections, changing perceptions and attitudes, counteracting competitive promotions, enhancing trade marketing, encouraging favourable word of mouth and recommendation, encouraging brand involvement, encouraging favourable press comment, reminding, encouraging immediate purchase, etc.

To fulfil such roles, marketing communications has an 'armoury' of activities or functions, which are called the 'marketing communications mix'. Each function (or combination of functions) works towards the achievement of marketing communications objectives. In simple classification terms, the functions or elements of the marketing communications mix are 'advertising', 'public relations', 'sales promotions' and 'personal selling'. Of course, under these headings a host of more specific activities can be identified (see 'Marketing communications mix'). **DWP**

References

Shimp, T.A. (1997) *Advertising and Promotion and Supplemental Aspects of Integrated Marketing Communications*, 4th edn, Fort Worth: Dryden Press.

Strong, E.K. (1925) *The Psychology of Selling*, New York: McGraw-Hill.

Marketing competencies

Marketing competencies are the skills which exist in-house for handling issues relating to customers and publics.

The marketing audit needs to address the issue of marketing competencies since these form part of the firm's resource base. The intellectual resources represented by the marketing competencies may be the most expensively-obtained resources within the firm; salaries and training costs are high, and experience tends to be even more expensive. Competencies need to be developed over many years, and form a part of the corporate culture; the individual's knowledge and experience is passed on within the organization. **JWDB**

Reference

Kotler P., Armstrong G., Saunders J., and Wong V. (2000) *Principles of Marketing* 2nd European edn, Harlow: Prentice Hall, pp. 114–115.

Marketing concept

The marketing concept is the key to achieving organizational goals and it rests on market focus, customer orientation, coordinated marketing and profitability. In not for profit organizations, profitability is substituted by criteria such as 'maximum social benefit'.

Marketing came to prominence in Europe around the mid 1960s and during the early 1950s in the USA. These dates were the respective times that each of these countries found themselves with surplus capacity following the Second World War. A realization then dawned upon companies that production and sales were no longer the key to prosperity, growth and survival. Instead, they realized that the identification, quantification and satisfaction of consumer needs was an essential pre-requisite to business success. Rather than make products and then look for markets, a marketing orientated philosophy holds that it is better to find out market requirements and then produce goods to fulfil these needs. It was recognized that without satisfied customers there would be no long term business.

The marketing concept is thus the underlying philosophy that actuates the practice of marketing throughout an organization with the avowed goal of satisfying the needs of customers. **GL**

Reference

Lancaster, G. and Massingham. L. (1999) *Essentials of Marketing*, 3rd edn, Maidenhead: McGraw-Hill, pp. 3–20.

Marketing concept, adoption of

The marketing concept has proved successful in helping companies to stay in business and produce goods and services that people really want. Information that companies need from the market place in order to apply this concept is assembled through a company's marketing information system (MkIS). The function of the MkIS is to gather regular information from within and outside the business. This system receives inputs from:

- marketing research
- the company's internal accounting system (i.e. how it analyses its sales data over time, by customer type, by product type and by geographical areas covered
- market intelligence (that is, gathered principally from the field sales force).

This information is collected in a computer based decision support system that outputs into the strategic marketing plan, and this plan is one element of the corporate planning system. As the strategic marketing plan is actioned and it unfolds over the planning period, so information can be fed back into the MkIS. By doing this, deviations from the plan can be analysed and corrective action taken. The marketing concept thus relies upon strategic marketing planning in its implementation.

Put simply, products may be viewed as 'bundles of benefits' and customers choose those products that give the best value and the most satisfaction. Companies which adopt the marketing concept go to extreme lengths to understand customer requirements through a variety of research techniques. They train company personnel to view customer needs as the dominating force within the business, and from this the notion of the 'part-time marketer', which holds that everybody in the organization has responsibility for marketing, has been suggested by Gummesson (1991). Products and services are developed to satisfy customer needs and wants and it must be seen that these give value and satisfaction to ensure repeat business. This helps to build long-term customer relationships, from which the term 'relationship marketing' has been coined. **GL**

References
Gummesson, E. (1991) 'Marketing orientation revisited: the crucial role of the part time marketer', *European Journal of Marketing*, 25:60–75.

Lancaster, G. and Massingham, L. (1999) *Essentials of Marketing*, 3rd edn, Maidenhead: McGraw-Hill, pp. 3–20.

Marketing control

Given that control is a process whereby management ensures that the enterprise is achieving desired ends, marketing control can be defined as a set of organized, adaptive actions directed towards achieving specified marketing goals in the face of constraints. To bring about particular future events, it is necessary to influence the factors that lie behind those events and this ability is the essence of control. Marketing control itself is a process and not an event. The idea of control is synonymous with such notions as adaptation, influence, manipulation and regulation, but it is not synonymous with coercion. Nor does it have as its central feature the detailed study of past mistakes in order to attribute blame, but rather the focusing of attention on learning from the past in order to ensure that future activities are carried through in ways which lead to the attainment of desired ends. It reflects an organization's culture.

The existence of a marketing control process enables management to know from time to time where the organization stands in relation to a predetermined future position. This requires that progress can be observed, measured and re-directed if there are discrepancies between the actual and desired positions.

Control and planning are complementary, so each should logically presuppose the existence of the other. Planning presupposes objectives (i.e. ends), and objectives are of very limited value in the absence of facilitating plans (i.e. means) for their attainment. In the planning process management must determine the enterprise's future course of action by reconciling corporate resources with specified marketing objectives. This will usually involve a consideration of various alternative courses of action and the selection of the one which is seen to be best in the light of the specified objectives. **RMSW & CTG**

References

Agarwal, S. (1996) 'Consequences of marketing controls among sales and non sales marketing personnel', *Industrial Marketing Management*, 25:411–420.

Jaworski, B.J. (1988) 'Toward a theory of marketing control: environmental context, control types, and consequences', *Journal of Marketing*, 52(3)July: 23–39.

Jaworski, B.J., Stathakopoulos, V. and H.S. Krishnan, H.S. (1993) 'Control combinations in marketing: conceptual framework and empirical evidence', *Journal of Marketing*, 57(1) January: 57–69.

Ramaswami, S.N. (1996) 'Marketing controls and dysfunctional employee behaviors: a test of traditional and contingency theory postulates', *Journal of Marketing*, 60(2) April: 105–120.

Wilson, R.M.S. (ed.) (2000) *Marketing Controllership*, Aldershot: Dartmouth/Ashgate.

Wilson, R.M.S. and C.T. Gilligan (1997) *Strategic Marketing Management: Planning, Implementation and Control*, 2nd edn, Oxford: Butterworth-Heinemann.

Marketing cost analysis

Marketing cost analysis is the process of identifying and allocating sources of marketing expenditure, in order to calculate the profitability of different brands or product lines within the firm's product portfolio.

In some ways, cost analysis can be more difficult than sales analysis, because many costs (particularly those attached to marketing activities) are shared with other products, other brands and other departments within the firm. For example, the sales manager's salary is spread across every product handled by the sales force, but there may be particular brands or product lines which demand more management attention than others.

Variance analysis can be used to identify those factors that cause differences between actual and targeted costs. Managers need to compare factors such as price per unit, production cost per unit, selling cost per unit, profit contribution and market share to find out where the discrepancies have arisen. By comparing budgeted and actual expenses the marketing manager can identify those activities which contribute to significant variances in costs (Cooper and Kaplan, 1991).

The first step in cost analysis is to determine the cost structure of the marketing activities. Activity-based costing will often give a more realistic picture than the rules laid down by the accounting profession, which often relate more to calculating end-of-year figures than to management of the business. **JWDB**

Reference

Cooper, R. and Kaplan, R.S. (1991) *The Design of Cost Management Systems*, New York: Prentice Hall.

Marketing defined

The UK Chartered Institute of Marketing (CIM) defines marketing as: 'The management process responsible for identifying, anticipating and satisfying customer requirements profitably'.

The American Marketing Association (AMA) defines marketing as: 'The process of planning and executing the conception, pricing, promotion and distribution of ideas, goods and services to create exchanges that satisfy individual and organizational objectives'.

Both definitions are correct. The CIM definition is more succinct and describes the true role of marketing, whereas the AMA definition is the more technical one. Although the CIM definition emphasizes profitability, marketing is also applicable in not for profit organizations.

Marketing holds an important place in business and commerce alongside the functions of production, finance, human resource management, research, design and development (R, D&D), purchasing and management services (or the information technology (IT) function that manages information, including the organization's management information system). The importance of marketing has only been recognized relatively recently and its rise to prominence in the UK has been a post 1970 phenomenon.

Marketing comprises what E. Jerome McCarthy described as the '4Ps': product, price, place and promotion. A fifth 'P' – 'people'– has since been added and two extra 'Ps' – 'process' and 'physical evidence' – have been added for service marketting to give the '7Ps of service marketing'. These four, five and seven Ps notions are now part of the regular vocabulary of marketing.

Put succinctly, marketing covers decisions on:

- pricing
- product
- place, or more correctly, distribution, which includes the logistics of getting the goods or services into the hands of consumers and channels, including the various means through which goods or services are sold, such as direct channels through sales representatives and indirect methods such as agents or distributors
- promotion, or more correctly, communications, which include the elements of advertising, sales promotion, public relations and selling
- buyer behaviour, which includes consumer buying and organizational buying
- market segmentation, targeting and positioning
- sales forecasting
- marketing research.

Added to the above, which might be said to be the 'nuts and bolts' of the subject, marketing is also a planned activity. A routine exists that covers strategic marketing planning, fits into overall corporate planning and utilizes the marketing information system as its principal source of information. Marketing also takes place in an international environment and this aspect of marketing has separate theories and concepts. Marketing must also display social responsibility and this, too, has spawned a separate discipline of societal marketing. The subject of marketing is thus dynamic and developing, and its knowledge base is being continually expanded. **GL**

References
Lancaster, G. and Massingham, L. (1999) *Essentials of Marketing*, 3rd edn, Maidenhead: McGraw-Hill, pp. 3–20.
McCarthy, E.J. (1960) *Basic Marketing: A Managerial Approach*, Homewood, Ill: Irwin.

Marketing functions, performance of

The simplest form of organizational structure for marketing is one based upon the different functions of marketing – advertising and sales promotion, marketing research, selling, new product development, marketing and sales office administration. These individual functions come under the overall direction of marketing management.

The type of structure that is adopted will depend upon the nature of the product or service and the structure of the market to be serviced. The structure just described is common in business to business marketing and the likelihood is that the sales function will be by far the most important sub-function.

For fast moving consumer goods (FMCGs), where advertising and sales promotion feature heavily, it is often more appropriate to have a dual structure, where individual brands are managed by product or brand managers and sales management is separate. The responsibility of brand management is to develop marketing plans for individual product lines that include overseeing marketing research, product development plans, sales promotion and advertising. Selling is managed by sales management, generally operating on a geographically based structure. Sales management and brand management each work in close liaison under the overall control of marketing management.

A market based structure is another alternative, where marketing is organized around customers or markets rather than around products or functions. The basis for this kind of structure is that different groups of customers will have different requirements. For example, if a company markets both to retailers and to the public sector their needs might be sufficiently diverse to make this kind of split desirable.

The reality is that a number of companies, with relatively diverse products and markets, design a matrix type of structure that incorporates some kind of permutation of the alternatives just described. **GL**

Reference
Kotler, P. (1994) *Marketing Management, Analysis, Planning, Implementation and Control*, 8th edn, New Jersey: Prentice Hall, pp. 741–766.

Marketing information system

A marketing information system (MkIS) is a system that utilizes people, equipment and procedures to gather, sort, analyse, evaluate and distribute accurate and timely information that is required by marketing decision makers. It is important that a formal information system be formulated so that information can be gathered accurately and disseminated in accordance with the needs of marketing decision makers. The different information needs require a careful analysis of the requirements that the system is expected to satisfy. It is important that long term objectives are clearly set that reflect the ultimate scope and size of the system. In addition, decisions have to be made regarding the allocation of responsibilities for designing and implementing the system, deciding on how sophisticated it should be, the type of information to store, the origin and source of the information and how the information will be accessed.

It should be recognized that a marketing information system will be sharing data with other subsystems within the context of a larger management information system. Therefore, the possibilities of integrating marketing information with other sub-systems in developing the MkIS is necessary and should be well considered in developing the system. Developments in information technology have resulted in a revolution with regards to the distribution of information. With the advent of computers and telecommunications, most information can be readily accessible from any location. As such, the MkIS is likely to be more flexible in meeting the demands and the different levels of sophistication of users as well as in handling different forms of information used for decision making. **RM-R**

Reference
Fletcher, K. (1990) *Marketing Management and Information Technology*, New York: Prentice Hall.

Marketing management

This is defined as the process of analysing, planning, implementing and controlling marketing activities in order to build and facilitate exchanges with target customers so as to fulfil the company's organizational objectives.

From this description it can be seen that the modern view of marketing management is that it is strategic in nature; a full description of how this strategic activity is conducted is contained under 'Marketing strategy' and 'Marketing plan characteristics'.

This is not to say that the function of marketing management is solely strategic, because strategic plans must be translated into tactics in order that these strategies can be implemented in a practical manner to realize company objectives. Overseeing and implementing these tactics is also the responsibility of marketing management. Tactics relate to advertising, sales promotions, public relations, sales activities, logistics, pricing and other elements of the marketing mix and a fuller description of this detail is given under 'Marketing mix'. **GL**

Reference
Lancaster, G. and Reynolds, P. (1998) *Marketing*, Basingstoke: Macmillan, pp. 16–19.

Marketing management organization

Organizing is concerned with the structuring and positioning choices faced by management in locating marketing responsibilities. Its importance has increased significantly over the past decade, moving from a focus on the internal arrangements for administering marketing activities to a broader concern for the role of marketing as an attitudinal issue within a customer-driven organization (which includes both intra-organizational relationships and inter-organizational alliances, plus crucial boundary-spanning environmental interfaces).

The traditional approach to organizing for marketing management focused on four broad categories of organizational form:

- *functional* (in which functional marketing specialists, such as sales managers and advertising managers, report to a marketing director)
- *product* (in which product managers are given responsibility for coordinating functional activities targeted on particular products)
- *markets* (in which market managers are given responsibility for coordinating functional activities targeted on specific groups of customers)
- *matrix* (in which functional managers and product or market managers work together on projects related to particular products or markets, or both).

A contemporary approach to organizing for marketing management must recognize the range of organizational structures that can be adopted for implementing marketing activities, identify the likely impact of particular structures on marketing performance and accommodate those contingent environmental factors likely to impact on structure and performance.

Organizational change in marketing is being driven by such factors as strategic alliances, self-managed teams, flattening hierarchies, re-engineering, global competition, customer service requirements, the development of the learning organization and the need for greater flexibility and speed. Some of these factors are internal, but reflect responses to external pressures.

The marketing organization is crucial for providing coordinating mechanisms for implementing marketing strategies, (e.g. in the field of new product development it is evident that R&D, operations, marketing and logistics need to be managed in a holistic manner). **RMSW & CTG**

References

Achrol, R.S. (1991) 'Evolution of the marketing organisation: new forms for turbulent environments', *Journal of Marketing*, 55(4) (October):77–93.

Alson, E.M., O.C. Walker, Jr and R.W. Ruekert (1995) 'Organising for effective new product development: the moderating role of product innovativeness', *Journal of Marketing*, 59(1)(January): 48–62.

Piercy, N.J. (1985) *Marketing Organisation: An Analysis of Information Processing, Power and Politics*, London: Allen and Unwin.

Workman J.P. Jr, Homburg, C., and Gruner, K. (1998) 'Marketing organisation: an integrative framework of dimensions and determinants', *Journal of Marketing* 62(3)(July): 21–41.

Marketing management process

The marketing management process embraces four main activities: the analysis, planning, implementation and control of the marketing effort. In doing this, the marketing manager focuses upon the identification of customers' needs, the definition of target market segments and, through the elements of the marketing mix, the development – and exploitation – of competitive advantage.

At a strategic level, the marketing management process needs to address three fundamental questions.

- In which markets should the organization operate?
- What products or services should the organization sell? (This is sometimes referred to in terms of 'what solutions can we provide the customer with?')
- What will be the basis of the organization's selling proposition and competitive advantage?

Throughout the marketing management process, a primary consideration for the marketing manager is the achievement of a degree of differentiation and the development and exploitation of competitive advantage. To do this, the marketing manager manipulates each of the elements of the marketing mix within the constraints and opportunities imposed by the external environment and with the needs of different target groups in mind. The marketing management process should not, however, be seen to be a wholly externally focused activity. Instead, it is one which also involves a strong internal focus in terms of setting market-related values and operating procedures and ensuring that they are then adhered to. As such, the marketing management process involves a focus upon three areas.

- *External marketing*, which involves the management of the 4Ps of the marketing mix (product, price, place and promotion).
- *Internal marketing,* which is concerned with the development and communication to the staff of the organization's values and priorities.
- *Interactive marketing*, which is concerned with the ways in which staff interact with the customer base. **CTG & RMSW**

References

Dibb, S., Simkin, L., Pride, W.M. and Ferrell, O.C. (1997) *Marketing Concepts and Strategies*, 3rd European edn, Boston: Houghton Mifflin.

Kotler, P. (2000) *Marketing Management: Analysis, Planning, Implementation and Control*, 10th edn, Upper Saddle River: Prentice Hall.

Jobber, D.G. (1998) *Principles and Practice of Marketing*, 2nd edn, London: McGraw-Hill.

Marketing management, strategy and tactics

Definitions and perceptions of marketing – and therefore of the nature and role of marketing management – have developed in a variety of ways over the past 20 years. From the early days, in which marketing was viewed as a largely functional activity concerned essentially with the development and (tactical) management of the 4Ps of the marketing mix, it is now seen to be a managerial orientation or way of doing business that needs to pervade the entire organization. The implications of this for marketing management have been considerable and highlight its role today as that part of the managerial process responsible for the management of the interface between the organization and its markets. In doing this, marketing staff are concerned with managing the nature of the relationship with customers, competitors and the distribution network, as well as with the other stakeholders – both internal and external – with whom the organization interacts. The way and the extent to which it does this more effectively than its competitors is a major determinant of marketing success.

Given this, marketing management focuses upon the creation and management of demand. This involves the development of market-related organizational objectives such as sales growth, market positioning, market share and the development and management of the marketing mix at both a tactical and a strategic level, together with the means by which these objectives might best be achieved. As such, marketing management has a responsibility for developing and implementing an approach to business in which customer satisfaction and competitive positioning are paramount. **CTG & RMSW**

References

Doyle, P. (1998) *Marketing Management and Strategy*, 2nd edn, Hemel Hempstead: Prentice Hall.

Kotler, P. (1999) *Kotler on Marketing: How to Create, Win and Dominate Markets*, Upper Saddle River: Prentice Hall.

Wilson, R.M.S. and Gilligan, C.T. (1997) *Strategic Marketing Management: Planning, Implementation and Control*, 2nd edn, Oxford: Butterworth-Heinemann.

Marketing mix

The term 'marketing mix' was coined in 1953 by Neil Borden in his presidential address to the American Marketing Association. It can be defined as 'the set of controllable demand-impinging elements that can be combined into a marketing programme for use by an organization to achieve a certain level and type of response from its target market' (van Waterschoot and Van den Bulte, 1992).

Since 1960 the marketing mix has been associated with McCarthy's 4Ps. The development of a particular marketing mix is an integral part of selecting a target market since the elements of the mix, when linked to the target market, make up the marketing strategy for securing that market. Thus, in terms of McCarthy's 4Ps:

- *product* must be the right one for the target market
- the product must be available in the right *place* for the target market
- the *price* of the product must be set at the right level for the target market
- *promotion* must communicate to the target market that the right product is available in the right place at the right price.

The original marketing mix was developed for manufacturing enterprises and is insufficiently comprehensive for service marketing. To suit this latter context the original 4Ps need to be supplemented by the following:

- *people* – i.e. those who deal directly with customers and who actually perform a service (e.g. hairdresser, bank cashier)
- *physical evidence* – i.e. the physical environment (e.g. furnishing, colour scheme, noise) and facilitating goods (e.g. hire cars, packaging of dry-cleaned clothes) which relate to the provision of services
- *process* – i.e. the way in which these services are delivered (e.g. policies and pro-

cedures adopted, amount of discretion on the part of staff, the booking system in use for appointments). **RMSW & CTG**

References

Booms, B.H. and M.J. Bitner (1981) 'Marketing strategies and organization structures for service firms', in J. Donnelly and W. R. George (eds) *Marketing of Services*, Chicago: American Marketing Association, pp. 44–51.

Kent, R. (1986) 'Faith in 4Ps: an alternative', *Journal of Marketing Management*, 2(2)(winter): 145–154.

McCarthy E.J. (1960) *Basic Marketing: a Managerial Approach*, Homewood, Illinois: Irwin.

van Waterschoot, W. and Van den Bulte, C. (1992) 'The 4P classification of the marketing mix revisited', *Journal of Marketing*, 56(4)(October): 83–93.

Marketing mix: a functional classification

As mix instruments exist because of their contribution to marketing mix functions, the primary function that instruments fulfil represents a logical basis by which to classify them (van Waterschoot and Van den Bulte, 1992, p.86). The four generic functions of the marketing mix, in combination with the situational or promotional function, make up a positively defined classification without the typical unjustified overlaps, blanks or negatively defined categories of pragmatic classifications (see the table below).

The four columns of the table define and group instruments according to the generic marketing mix function they primarily fulfil. The product-mix in the first column groups these instruments that primarily contribute to the need fulfilment function. The price mix in the second column groups instruments primarily contributing to the pricing function. The distribution-mix in the third column groups instruments primarily contributing to the availability function. The communication mix in the fourth column groups instruments primarily contributing to the communication function of the marketing mix. The communication mix is further divided on the basis of two criteria: whether the ultimate message is fully under control of the marketer and whether the instrument relies on personal or non-personal communication.

Vertically the table is divided into two major sections. The upper section, on the left hand page contains the instruments belonging to the basic or regular composition of the marketing mix. The lower section, on the right contains those primarily fulfilling a complementary, situational or promotional function. They are defined as a supplementary group of instruments, which mainly aim at inducing immediate overt behaviour by strengthening the basic marketing mix during relatively short periods (van Waterschoot and Van den Bulte, 1992). Together they form the promotion mix. The promotion instruments spread out over all major classes of marketing mix instruments. As a result there is a set of promotion sub-mixes corresponding with the sub-mixes of the basic mix.

It should be stressed that many instruments typically belong to a particular cell in the table, but not necessarily so. Take, for instance, the packaging of a product, which typically belongs to the (basic) product mix. Its principal secondary functions are typically the communication and availability function. But depending on the context, the primary function of the packaging could become communication, for example when it would not be vital to protect the product, but would mainly serve to create or sustain brand awareness. **WvW & JDH**

Reference

Van Waterschoot, W. and Van Den Bulte, C. (1992), 'The 4P classification of the marketing mix revisited', *Journal of Marketing*, 56(October): 83–93.

Table: **An improved classification of the marketing mix**

Marketing mix	Product mix	Price mix	Distribution mix	Communication mix		
				Mass communication mix	Personal communication mix	Publicity mix
Basic mix	*Basic product mix* Instruments that mainly aim at the satisfaction of the prospective exchange party's needs	*Basic price mix* Instruments that mainly fix the size and the way of payment exchanged for goods or services	*Basic distribution mix* Instruments that mainly determine the intensity and manner of how the goods or services will be made available	*Basic mass communication mix* Non-personal communication efforts that mainly aim at announcing the offer or maintaining the awareness and knowledge about it: evoking or maintaining favourable feelings and removing barriers to wanting	*Basic personal communication mix* Personal communication efforts that mainly aim at announcing the offer or maintaining awareness and knowledge about it: evoking or maintaining favourable feelings and removing barriers to wanting	*Basic publicity mix* Efforts that aim at inciting a third party (persons and authorities) to favourable communication about the offer
	e.g. product characteristics, options, assortment, brand name, packaging, quantity, factory guarantee.	e.g. list price, usual term of payment, usual discounts, term of credit, long-term savings campaigns..	e.g. different types of distribution channels, density of the distribution system, trade relation mix (policy of margins, terms of delivery, etc.), merchandising advice.	e.g. theme advertising in various media, permanent exhibitions, certain forms of sponsorship.	e.g. amount and type of selling, personal remuneration.	e.g. press bulletins, press conferences, tours by journalists.

Table: An improved classification of the marketing mix

Promotion mix	Product promotion mix	Price promotion mix	Distribution promotion mix	Mass communication promotion mix	Personal communication promotion mix	Publicity promotion mix
	Supplementary group of instruments that mainly aim at inducing immediate overt behaviour by strengthening the basic product mix during relatively short periods	Supplementary group of instruments that mainly aim at inducing immediate overt behaviour by strengthening the basic price mix during relatively short periods	Supplementary group of instruments that mainly aim at inducing immediate overt behaviour by strengthening the basic distribution mix during relatively short periods	Supplementary group of instruments that mainly aim at inducing immediate overt behaviour by strengthening the basic mass communication mix during relatively short periods	Supplementary group of instruments that mainly aim at inducing immediate overt behaviour by strengthening the basic personal communication mix during relatively short periods	Supplementary group of instruments that mainly aim at inducing immediate overt behaviour by strengthening the basic publicity mix during relatively short periods
	e.g. economy packs, 3-for-the-price-of-2 deals, temporary luxury options on a car at the price of the standard model.	e.g. exceptionally favourable price, end-of-season sales, exceptionally favourable terms of payment and credit, short-term savings campaigns, temporary discounts, coupons.	e.g. extra point of purchase material, trade promotions such as buying allowances or sales contests, temporary increase of the number of distribution points.	e.g. action advertising, contests, sweepstakes, samples, premiums, trade shows or exhibitions.	e.g. temporary demonstrations, sales force promotions such as sales force contests.	e.g. all measures to stimulate positive publicity about a sales promotion action.

Marketing mix, criticism of

In spite of its widespread acceptance, the marketing mix concept has been criticized in several respects (Van den Bulte, 1991). First, it has been accused of applying to micro issues only. More particularly, it is said to take the stance of only one exchange party, namely that of the seller and not that of the consumer or society at large. The concept would, moreover, imply a mechanistic and rational-economic neo-classical view of customer behaviour. The typical expression of this view is market response curves that allow optimization of mix instruments and compositions without taking into consideration many interactions between the market and the decision maker. As a result, the institutional and social supports to market processes, such as attraction, trust, friendship, power and interdependency, would be excluded.

Logically, for the same reason, the concept would lead to myopic concentration on isolated exchanges instead of on relationships, and on customers and dealers at the expense of other publics. Moreover, it would lump buyers together into markets of homogeneous respondents. Further criticism concerns vital insight and research about interactions between mix variables. The concept is criticized because hypotheses about marketing mix interactions cannot be derived from it. The concept is also accused of a lack of relevance to internal tasks necessary to plan and implement the marketing (mix) function(s). Finally, the mix concept implies a self-reliant mixer. Bridging strategies such as bargaining, cooption, joint programmes and licensing would not be taken into account.

Some of the so-called criticism of the marketing concept uses the metaphor of the cake mixer, such as the suggestion of the self-reliant mixer. Most of the criticism summarized above rightly or wrongly concerns the actual traits of marketing theory and practice and not the marketing mix concept itself, however (van Waterschoot 1999). Marketing theory has mainly concerned the consumer, with an eye to influencing him or her in favour of the marketer. Marketing practice has probably concentrated too much on isolated transactions. Hardly any of the previous criticism, however, seems to concern the marketing mix concept itself. Critics seem to have unrealistic expectations about a basic, necessary and powerful but at the same time limited concept. The usefulness of a properly defined and classified set of demand-impinging instruments is applicable to any exchange situation, not just to 'channel captain applications'. Also, in defence of the mix concept it should be emphasized that it fits both stimulus-response and interactive views of market behaviour. The mix concept in no way conflicts with the idea of relationships. An exchange relationship, for instance, supposes a more pronounced quality and service emphasis than a mere one-time exchange. Also, marketing theory and practice may have put too much emphasis on the consumer, but there is no logic in blaming the mix concept for this. This basic, but by its very nature limited, concept is a factual device in any market approach – market oriented or not. It also neither implies nor excludes differentiated, undifferentiated and concentrated segmentation approaches. A well-defined marketing mix concept and classification are also prerequisites for the study of marketing mix interactions. Nonetheless, the inventory of a set of instruments cannot be supposed to provide, in itself, a theory about the interactions among the instruments. Similarly, the mix concept and classification may be helpful devices in delineating and planning marketing tasks, but cannot possibly provide theories, approaches or bridging strategies. This does not mean that it would exclude them nor that such strategies would not profit from a clear concept and classification. **WvW & VdB**

References

Van den Bulte, C. (1991) 'The concept of the marketing mix revisited: a case analysis of metaphor in marketing theory and management', Research paper, Ghent: The Vlerick School of Management, University of Ghent.

van Waterschoot, W. (1999) 'The marketing mix' in M.J. Baker (ed.) *The IEBM Encyclopaedia of Marketing*, London: Thomson Learning pp. 327–329.

Marketing mix, expanded

Many textbooks erroneously state that the marketing mix is E. Jerome McCarthy's '4Ps'. This is too narrow a view and a better view was put forward by Neil Borden, who coined the term 'marketing mix'. He stated that the marketing mix is those controllable variables that the company can blend together to produce the response it desires from its target market.

The elements of the marketing mix are the following.

- *Product*
- *Price*
- *Place* or, more correctly, *placement*. This covers channels of distribution or the outlets and methods by and through which the company's products are sold. It also covers logistics which relates to the physical warehousing and transportation of goods from the manufacturer to the end customer.
- *Promotion* or, better in terms of being a more correct description, *communications*. Communications has its own sub-mix, whose elements are:
  - advertising (or above-the-line promotion)
  - sales promotion (or below-the-line promotion)
  - public relations
  - selling.
- *Segmentation, targeting and positioning*. This is not one of the '4Ps', but it is a controllable variable that the company can manipulate to produce the response it requires from the target market. The marketer decides which segments to target and then determines a positioning strategy.
- *People,* which relates to the people who are involved directly and indirectly in the marketing process.
- *Process* concerns service marketing in particular. The example of telephone services serves to illustrate this point. As this is intangible unlike, say, the purchase of a hi-fi unit, it is important to highlight matters such as the standard of service received and service options available especially as this is a high contact service.
- *Physical evidence* again relates particularly to the intangibility of services. Managing physical evidence means examining all criteria by which customers judge a particular service and then ensuring that their needs are fulfilled through paying to attention to such matters as the ambience of a restaurant as well as to the quality of its food. **GL**

Reference

Borden, N. (1964) 'The concept of the marketing mix', *Journal of Advertising Research* 4(June)2–7.

Marketing mix: explications and extensions

The mix metaphor gained usage spectacularly quickly as a result of its expressiveness, liveliness, compactness and therefore memorability (van Waterschoot, 1999, p.329). McCarthy's 4Ps classification also received acceptance speedily and easily. Presumably as a result of its strong mnemonic appeal and in spite of its shortcomings.

Throughout the years a number of alternative marketing mix classifications have been formulated. Ironically, they did not challenge McCarthy's mnemonic. On the contrary, the pragmatic P mnemonic was typically extended as a means of explication of submixes or in order to draw attention to marketing aspects that were not always mix issues (van Waterschoot, 1999). The aid of memory, instead of playing a subordinate role, began to play an obligatory, dominant and therefore unjustified role. A communication gimmick led logical thinking instead of the other way around. Let us look at two examples. Both belong to the field of service marketing.

Sometimes a separate fifth 'P' was added to McCarthy's mnemonic to denote 'people', or 'personnel' or 'personal selling'. In this way a collective noun was provided each time to stress the importance of all sorts of selling and servicing efforts carried out by any person within the organization (van Waterschoot, 1999). In applications where sales efforts are of a typically high strategic value – for instance in service marketing – no fundamental objection can be made against such an explication. The explication can even be defended on pedagogical grounds. On the other hand there is no conceptual necessity for an explication since the provision of services primarily belongs to the product mix (instruments primarily contributing to need fulfilment) and sales efforts typically belong to the communication mix.

A 'P' has also often been added in service marketing to indicate 'participants' (Booms and Bitner, 1981). The participants in a service marketing situation can indeed significantly improve or harm the quality of the execution of service (van Waterschoot, 1999). However, the activities of the personnel carrying out the service conceptually belong to the product mix. Insofar as the clients are meant by participants, the addition becomes conceptually incorrect, since the marketing mix groups *controllable* demand impinging elements and not the *actual* demand constituting elements. **WvW & JDH**

References

Booms, B.H. and Bitner, M.J. (1981) 'Marketing strategies and organisation structures for service firms', in J.H. Donnelly and W.R. George (eds), *Marketing of Services*, Chicago: American Marketing Association Proceedings.

van Waterschoot, W. (1999) 'The marketing mix', in M.J. Baker (ed.) *The IEBM Encyclopaedia of Marketing*, London: Thomson Learning.

Marketing mix: functions

To understand and apply the marketing mix it is useful to have insight into its fundamental functions. These follow from the exchange situation (Kotler, 1972) implicit in the realization of demand. In particular they follow directly from the basic conditions for exchange to take place (van Waterschoot and Van den Bulte, 1992).

For exchange not just to be possible, but actually to take place, each party will have to determine exactly what it will offer, which services it is prepared to offer and what inconveniences it is prepared to undergo to be of service to the other party. We could call this the *need fulfilment function* of the marketing mix.

The second generic function for the marketer consists of determining which benefits, services, sacrifices and the like that they would like to receive from the other party (or cause it to undergo) in exchange for their offering. This is the *pricing function* of the marketing mix.

The third generic function consists of informing the market about their existence and offering. This function also encompasses the creation of positive feelings and of a preference. It may be called the *communication function* of the marketing mix.

Finally, for exchange to take place delivery must take place. The marketers must determine where, when and how they will make their product available to the market. This will be called the *distribution function* of the marketing mix.

These four functions are generic in the sense that they cannot be avoided. They need to be fulfilled somehow for exchange to come about. If any of them is not be carried out, no exchange would take place. No demand would be created, fulfilled or maintained (van Waterschoot and Van den Bulte, 1992).

As well as these four generic functions, there is also a complementary function, which we will call the *situational* or *promotional* marketing mix function (van Waterschoot and Van den Bulte, 1992, p.88). The reason for its existence is the fact that the generic functions lead to exchanges 'sooner *or* later', whereas the marketer might prefer to elicit exchanges 'sooner *than* later'. This situational function consists of immediate inducement or immediate provocation. It leads to immediate exchange or, more generally, to forms of visible exchange related behaviour. It tackles 'barriers to acting' such as physical and psychological inertia barriers, risk barriers or competitive barriers from close substitutes (Beem and Shaffer, 1981).

Suppose, for example, that the customer's inertia keeps them loyal to their current brand although they do not really favour it. They are simply not very much interested and act out of routine. In this case the promotional function may try to overcome this inertia, for example by offering temporary price reductions. This provocation of immediate exchanges implies that the promotional function is situational in the sense that it is carried out on a non-routine basis during short periods (van Waterschoot, 2000). If in the previous example the customer were not convinced of the temporary nature of the price reduction, it would be less likely to provoke an immediate brand switch. **WvW & JDH**

References

Beem, E. and Schaffer, R.H. (1981) *Triggers to Action: Some Elements in a Theory of Promotional Inducement*, Report no. 81–106, Cambridge : Marketing Science Institute.

Kotler, P. (1972) 'A generic concept of marketing', *Journal of Marketing* 36(April): 46–54.

van Waterschoot, W. (2000) 'The marketing mix as a creator of differentiation', in K. Blois (ed.) *The Oxford Textbook of Marketing*, Oxford: Oxford University Press.

van Waterschoot, W. and Van den Bulte, C. (1992) 'The 4P classification of the marketing mix revisited', *Journal of Marketing* 56(October): 83–93.

Marketing mix: influencing demand

By definition marketing mix instruments impinge more or less directly on demand. Demand refers to a number of exchanges of a certain type that would occur under certain conditions in a certain environment in a certain period (Kotler, 1999). For example, under favourable economic conditions and under current trade practices roughly 2.25 million new cars would be sold in Great Britain in one year.

Marketing mix instruments more or less directly affect demand. This means exerting a straight influence on demand without any intermediate condition, stage, person, institution, etc. Car prices, for example, may directly affect demand for cars. Many marketing mix instruments, however, affect demand indirectly. Some typical ways are briefly described.

Unlike demand resulting from Economic Man's completely rational and conscious mind – that of attaining optimal choices instantly without being hampered by perceptual, learning or processing phenomena, delays or decays – real demand originates within a certain behavioural context. Demand related behaviour refers to both visible and invisible behaviour that logically or psychologically precedes actual purchasing behaviour, coincides with it, follows it or follows from it. Examples are active or passive learning about a brand and its features, enjoying or undergoing consumption experiences, favouring a brand, being negatively or positively loyal to a brand, spreading rumours about it. The marketing mix may affect this 'demand related behaviour' and indirectly affect demand in the strict sense of the word. For example, a manufacturer of light bulbs might create brand awareness, resulting in some people picking the brand out from a number of competing brands on a supermarket shelf. Those customers may not bother too much about this kind of purchase but vaguely prefer the only brand they (also vaguely) know.

The marketing mix may be aimed at some people or organizations with an eye on indirect impingement upon some other target group. A traditional example is the effort directed at journalists to make them write favourably about one's company and its offerings. Other traditional examples are margins granted to middlepeople so that they would push a company's offering.

The indirect creation of demand for one's own offering may also take place via the impact exerted on demand for complementary products. A legendary example is the French tyre producer Michelin fostering tourism by selling tourist guides, with an eye on increased car use that would in turn increase its tyre sales. A more modern example would be the sponsoring of mountain bike races to foster the sales of energy bars.

The effect of marketing mix instruments most typically concerns demand for one's own offering. However, depending on the circumstances and on the approach, marketing mix elements may not only affect demand for the organization's own offering (secondary or selective demand) but also, to a greater or lesser extent for (the totality of) similar offerings (primary demand). In an extreme situation primary demand would be affected mostly, and secondary demand only indirectly. This, probably rarely pursued, type of influence could be the dreadful situation of the innovator of non-alcoholic beer, who sees their competitors enjoying the results of their efforts to educate the market.

At the limit, demand impingement may refer to the creation of or contribution to circumstances that allow the origination of demand. For example, contributing to children's education may ultimately help sell computers, such as when Microsoft donates its software, together with PCs, to schools. Even political lobbying leading to the disclosure of markets may fall under this category. However, these examples concern borderline cases since, by definition, some genuine influence on demand must be exerted or exertable for an instrument to belong to the marketing mix.

It should also be stressed, however, that the meaning of the term 'demand' has become less strict as a consequence of the extension of the marketing concept to non profit organizations (Kotler and Levy, 1969). As a result, demand may also refer to forms of behaviour that show some similarity with demand, without literally following from exchanges. Examples would be the creation of good driving or drinking habits among car drivers by anti-alcohol-organizations. In such instances demand should often be put equal to 'demand related behaviour'.

The last point applies even more strongly to the extension of the marketing concept to non-traditional target groups. Marketing mix instruments may provoke favourable reactions with groups such as the press, investors and the general public. The creation of goodwill with the general public, for example, shows at best resemblance with the creation of 'demand-related-behaviour'. **WvW & JDH**

References
Kotler, P. (1999) *Kotler on Marketing: How to Create, Win and Dominate Markets*, Upper Saddle River: Prentice Hall.
Kotler, P. and Levy, S.J. (1969) 'A new form of marketing myopia – rejoinder to Professor Luck', *Journal of Marketing* 33(July): 5–57.

Marketing mix instruments

The marketing mix refers to a set of elements impinging upon demand that are under the control of the marketer, which are therefore called 'instruments'. This distinguishes the marketing mix from demand impinging elements not under the control of the marketer, an example of which would be a county's birth rate (van Waterschoot, 2000). A high birth rate favourably affects the sales of baby clothes.

However, it is not controllable by the marketer. Lack of control, however, does not necessarily mean complete lack of influence. For example, company lobbying could persuade the government to take measures such as increasing birth premiums that would in turn affect the birth rate.

Another limitation in delineating mix instruments is that marketing instruments, which only contribute to the creation or fine-tuning of mix instruments, are not considered mix instruments themselves (van Waterschoot, 2000). For example, marketing research could lead to improved mix compositions, but is not itself a mix instrument. The same holds for the choice of a competent advertising agency. The effect of advertising money may differ tremendously depending on the quality of the campaign. The amount of advertising money, the choice of the theme and the message are mix instruments. The analyst who decides on the budget is not a mix element. The same holds for the advertising agency developing the creative side of the campaign.

The near-synonym of marketing mix variables is often used to indicate marketing mix instruments. This synonym is warranted when the instrument can take on numerous numerically expressible values. Advertising budgets are a typical example. In other instances several choices are available that cannot be expressed numerically, which would make the synonym much less appropriate. An example would be the available choices between different messages or media.

The multi-faceted nature of demand suggests that marketing mix instruments may exert multiple effects. They may, for example, at the same time create awareness, determine a brand image, make people search for information and buy instantaneously. Marketing mix instrument typically exert multiple effects. This is a fundamental trait.

Mix instruments not only produce multiple effects, these effects may also range from very weak to very strong and from immediate to delayed. Energy consumption by private households may well illustrate this (van Waterschoot, 2000). Electricity prices do not affect household demand drastically in the short run. If prices go up, there would be not be a sudden drop in the number of hours of television watching. Neither would washing machines and refrigerators be turned off. Longer term effects of price changes, however, could be more substantial. For example, electrical heating might compare unfavourably on a cost basis with oil heating. As a result significantly fewer people might favour electrical heating in spite of its superior convenience and safety.

Next to being stronger or weaker, taking place sooner or later, marketing mix effects may affect primary or secondary demand or both. Another example related to energy consumption is illustrative (van Waterschoot, 2000). Changes in car petrol prices hardly affect long term driving habits, as people are very much dedicated to the comfort of driving a private car. Many, however, are very keen on economizing on the operating costs without changing their driving habits. Deviating national price agreements on car petrol prices in Holland and Belgium have occasionally led to price differences between the two countries. As a result, small price differences of a few Belgian francs or Dutch guilders sometimes cause marked regional shifts in demand in the border regions between the two countries.

Marketing mix effects may be visible and/or invisible. An advertising campaign announcing spectacular temporary price discounts for baby nappies may lead to massive instant purchases. Theme advertisements for baby clothes, on the other hand, may create and sustain brand awareness, leading to some increased sales over a longer period.

Marketing mix instruments are most typically used to increase demand. However, they can be used not only to encourage demand but also to discourage it. This approach is called 'demarketing' (Kotler and Levy, 1971). In Belgium, for example, a continuous oversupply of qualified medical practitioners led organizations of

Belgian doctors throughout the nineties to visit secondary schools in order to discourage school-leavers, or at least some of them, from studying medicine (van Waterschoot, 1999). Still more generally, marketing mix elements can be used to affect demand in a way favoured by the marketer. An example would be to soften seasonality by using price schemes that would make demand match production possibilities more closely, for example with ferry services.

Last but not least, the effects of marketing mix instruments can be economically warranted or not. They can be desirable or undesirable. They can be so in the short and/or medium and/or long term. **WvW & JDH**

References

Kotler, P. and Levy, S.J. (1971) 'Demarketing, yes, demarketing', *Harvard Business Review* 49(November–December): 74–80.

van Waterschoot, W. (2000) 'The marketing mix as a creator of differentiation', in K. Blois (ed.) *The Oxford Textbook of Marketing*, Oxford: Oxford University Press.

Marketing mix planning

Marketing mix planning is the process of developing strategy and tactics for the implementation, monitoring and control of the firm's products, pricing, promotion, distribution, personnel, physical evidence and service provision processes.

Planning the marketing mix is like following a recipe; the ingredients need to be added at the right times and in the right quantities, one ingredient cannot substitute for another. The planner needs to monitor the process at each stage to ensure that the mix is ready for the next ingredient and ensure that enough time is allowed for the mixture to work properly.

The basis of the marketing mix plan is the establishment of achievable marketing objectives. Objectives should state what is to be achieved and when results are to be accomplished; they do not state *how* the results are to be achieved (Quinn, 1980). To be achievable, objectives need to be measurable; a statement that the firm wants to 'maximize market share' is not achievable, since there is no way of knowing what the maximum achievable market share is. A statement that the firm wants to 'increase market share by 10 per cent' is achievable because it is measurable.

Planning the mix will usually involve drawing up a calendar of events, this ensures that all those who have responsibility for the various elements of the mix will know when they need to schedule their activities. The calendar should not be a straitjacket, however, the organization needs to be able to respond to changes in the marketplace and to new initiatives from within the firm, while keeping sight of the overall objectives of the plan. **JWDB**

Reference

Quinn, J.B. (1980) *Strategies for Change: Logical Incrementalism*, Homewood Ill.: Irwin.

Marketing mix: pragmatic classifications

The making of listings and taxonomies was one of the first tasks in the development of a new body of thought, such as marketing throughout the 20th century. Several pragmatic marketing mix classifications were developed, some of which were rough classifications to help practitioners in quickly acquiring a feel for major categories. Known elements, supposedly belonging to the family of marketing mix instruments, were inventoried and intuitively put together into groups, not so much on the basis of theoretical insight, but rather on the basis of their apparent or supposed similarity (van Waterschoot, 1999). As a result the categories were not explicitly defined and it was not certain that they would cover all instruments. It was also uncertain that there was no unjustified overlap between categories.

In 1956, Albert Frey divided the marketing mix instruments into two main categories. The first category he called 'the offering', which included product characteristics, packaging, brand name, price and service. The second category he called 'methods and tools', which grouped distribution channels, personal selling, advertising, sales promotion and publicity (Frey, 1956). In 1962, William Lazer and Eugene Kelley distinguished three categories: the goods and service elements, the distribution elements and the communication elements (Lazer and Kelley, 1962). In 1960 Jerome McCarthy discerned four classes: product, price, place and promotion (McCarthy, 1960). This classification became known as the memory-friendly '4Ps-classification'. Probably because of the easy-to-remember and intuitively appealing description of some undeniable basic principles, McCarthy's 4Ps became the most often used classification of the marketing mix.

One problem with the McCarthy typology is, as with other pragmatic typologies, that he labelled the classes, but did not define them. Another problem is that the fourth category 'promotion' is a hybrid made up predominantly of communication instruments and only to a lesser extent of promotion instruments. Still another important problem is that the promotion instruments are defined in a negative, residual way. Every instrument that would belong neither to one of the 'first three Ps', nor to one of the other categories (advertising, personal selling and publicity) making up the 'fourth P' would (rightly or wrongly) be called and grouped as 'sales promotion' (van Waterschoot and Van den Bulte, 1992, p.85). **WvW & JDH**

References

Frey, A.W. (1956*) The Effective Marketing Mix : Programming for Optimum Results,* Hanover, NH: The Amos Tuck School of Business Administration, Dartmouth College.

Lazer, W. and Kelley, E.J. (1962*) Managerial Marketing: Perspectives and Viewpoints: A Sourcebook,* Homewood, Ill.: Irwin.

McCarthy, E.J. (1960) *Basic Marketing: A Managerial Approach*, Homewood, Ill.: Irwin.

van Waterschoot, W. (1999) 'The marketing mix', in M.J. Baker (ed.) *The IEBM Encyclopaedia of Marketing*, London: Thomson Learning.

Van Waterschoot, W. and Van Den Bulte, C. (1992) 'The 4P classification of the marketing mix revisited', *Journal of Marketing*, 56(October): 83–93.

Marketing mix: the origins of the metaphor and the concept

The term 'marketing mix' is probably one of the most frequently used terms of the discipline. Any novice is almost immediately introduced to it or inevitably runs into it. Any seasoned practitioner or academic cannot do other than keep using the term and the corresponding concept and classification. In spite of its popularity and strong intuitive appeal it is worthwhile getting a formal, explicit introduction to the concept behind this existing metaphor. The same goes for the marketing mix classification.

The metaphor goes back as far as 1949 when James Culliton pictured the marketing executive as someone combining different ingredients. It was his metaphor that inspired Neil Borden to use the expression 'marketing mix' in 1953 in his presidential address to the American Marketing Association (Borden, 1964). The expression referred to the combination of instrumental ingredients used to provoke a certain response from a target market. The term 'marketing mix' can be compared to the use of the word 'mix' in expressions such as salad mix, alcohol mix or grill mix. In all these cases a number of ingredients out of a wider range can be more or less successfully combined into numerous amalgamations with widely differing tastes and effects. In a similar way, the marketing mix metaphor implies that marketing executives have a whole range of instruments at their disposal, which can be combined in numerous ways to influence the demand for their offering. The marketing mix metaphor also suggests that different combinations of instruments may produce largely differing outcomes – both wished and unwished for.

The concept of the marketing mix can more formally be defined as 'the set of controllable demand-impinging instruments that can be combined into a marketing programme used by a firm (or any other organization) to achieve a certain level and type of response from its target market' (van Waterschoot and Van den Bulte, 1992, p. 88). **WvW & JDH**

References

Borden, N. (1964) 'The concept of the marketing mix', *Journal of Advertising Research* 4(June): 2–7.

van Waterschoot, W. and Van den Bulte, C. (1992) 'The 4P classification of the marketing mix revisited', *Journal of Marketing* 56(October): 83–93.

Marketing: organizational role

Relationships within marketing include levels of responsibility and authority that are needed to conduct business in a satisfactory manner. At a broader level, how marketing co-ordinates with other departments is important. How these relationships are co-ordinated and managed can positively or negatively affect the effectiveness of the organization. The key is to balance the degree of authority that is needed to fulfil the responsibility, but there can be problems when a mismatch occurs.

In a decentralized structure, marketing is given authority and responsibility for making strategic decisions. This system is more democratic and encourages creative thinking. Marketing is generally closer to customers, but its major drawback is in having difficulty maintaining a focused strategy. In a centralized structure, marketing's role is reduced to one of carrying out the directives delegated by top management. Here there is often a problem of lack of responsiveness to customer needs, but on the plus side there is a greater clarity of strategic control and direction.

How marketing relates to other functions is best described by looking at a simple hypothetical commercial transaction. A customer places an order that directly or indirectly involves sales. This order might have been generated through advertising or through the salesperson's own means or a combination. How the product was developed might have come from R&D in conjunction with information from marketing research, who provided the development brief from a consumer survey. Production manufactures the order from material that has been acquired by the purchasing department. Finance manages the commercial transaction, including paying for raw materials and invoicing the customer for the finished product. At a more indirect level, human resource management is responsible for recruiting and training personnel who provide the expertise to make this commercial transaction possible. Management services is the department that provides the information infrastructure to ensure that all of this transaction is coordinated in an effective manner. **GL**

Reference

Lancaster, G. and Reynolds, P. (1998) *Marketing*, Basingstoke: Macmillan, pp. 16–19.

Marketing performance measurement

Performance measurement systems seek to identify (and explain) exceptions or variations between actual and planned performance. The aim is to facilitate learning in order to improve future performance: if something has been done right, with beneficial results, it is important to know how this was achieved in order to do more of it. (Conversely, of course, if something was being done wrong, with damaging consequences, it is important to learn the cause of this in order to do less of it.)

Performance measurement presupposes a standard of comparison or 'bench mark'. Desirable performance may be characterized by either a single criterion or by multiple criteria. Taking the former first, the single criterion may be financial or non-financial. Examples include the following.

Financial	Non-financial
Liquidity	Sales volume
Cash generation	Market share
Value-added	Growth rate
Earnings per share	Competitive position
Shareholder value	Consumer franchise
Share price	Risk exposure
Profit	Reliance on new products
Profitability	Customer satisfaction and levels of loyalty
Cost leadership	Sustainable competitive advantage
	Image/reputation

Turning to multiple criteria approaches to benchmarking, those which attract most support include:

- the balanced scorecard
- the marketing performance assessment model
- critical success factors
- core competences.

Single criterion approaches, whilst widely employed, lack the richness of the multiple criteria approaches.

Whilst the focus of performance measurement will often be on specific marketing activities such as product line performance, it will regularly be the performance of marketing managers which is being measured (and evaluated). This can have significant behavioural consequences since managers tend not to be indifferent over approaches taken to assessing their performance. **RMSW & CTG**

References
Ambler, T. and Kokkinaki, F. (1997) 'Measures of marketing success', *Journal of Marketing Management*, 13(7)(October): 665–678.
Bonoma, T.V. and Clark, B.H. (1988) *Marketing Performance Assessment*, Boston, Mass.: Harvard Business School Press.
Buzzell, R.D. and Gale, B.T. (1987) *The PIMS Principles*, New York: The Free Press.
Hamel, G. and Prahalad, C.K. (1994) *Competing for the Future*, Boston, Mass.: Harvard Business School Press.
Kaplin, R.S. and Norton, D.P. (1996) *The Balanced Scorecard*, Boston, Mass.: Harvard Business School Press.
Stathakopoulos, V. (1997) 'Effects of performance appraisal systems on marketing managers', *Journal of Marketing Management*, 13(8)(November): 835–852.
Wilson, R.M.S. and Gilligan, C.T. (1997) *Strategic Marketing Management, Planning, Implementation and Control*, 2nd edn, Oxford: Butterworth-Heinemann.

Marketing plan

This is the blueprint for the marketing element of the corporate planning process. At a general level it comprises three major elements:

- *planning* – including situational analysis, setting goals, selection of strategies and tactics
- *implementation* – that involves organizing staffing and directing
- *evaluation* – that compares actual performance with goals.

A detailed marketing plan is the blueprint for a period of activity (normally one year) in relation to a specific strategic business unit (SBU) or product group, and it consists of a number of headings that take the plan from the general to the specific, ending up with a detailed costed budget. The structure of marketing plans can differ slightly according to different products or SBUs and the market segments being targeted. However, the following general structure can be adapted for individual SBU circumstances.

Strategic company planning

- Define the organizational mission.
- Conduct a situational analysis (the 'company audit').
- Set organizational objectives.
- Select appropriate strategies.

Although this is not strictly speaking part of the marketing plan, it is needed in order that the marketing plan can be developed in detail.

Strategic marketing planning

- Conduct a situational analysis (the 'marketing audit', which looks at external factors under: Socio-cultural, Technological, Economic, Environmental, Political, Legal and Environmental (steeple) issues and then looks at internal company factors that impact on marketing).
- Develop marketing objectives.
- Determine positioning and differential advantage.
- Select target markets and measure market demand through sales forecasting.
- Design a strategic marketing mix.
- Plan in detail for individual elements of the marketing mix.
- Budget and timetable for the individual elements identified in the previous point.
- Control and evaluate the marketing plan.

The plan should have a number of feedback points in order that corrections can be made if the plan does not proceed as anticipated. **GL**

Reference

Lancaster, G. and Massingham, L. (1999) *Essentials of Marketing*, 3rd edn, Maidenhead: McGraw-Hill, pp. 347–358.

Marketing plan characteristics

The marketing plan is the central instrument for directing and controlling the marketing effort (Kotler, 1997). It is usually a formal written document, and is the tangible result of the marketing planning process.

Generally, marketing plans are used as guides rather than as rigid rulebooks. This is because market conditions change, or new opportunities or threats present themselves; it would be foolish to insist that the firm remains committed to a plan that has become obsolete. Most marketing plans are relatively short-term; typical marketing plans last one year, although some might run for three to five years.

Typically, marketing plans will have the following characteristics.

- The plan contains measurable objectives.

- The details of the plan are unambiguous, in order to facilitate implementation and control.
- The plan is flexible enough to allow for unforeseen events.
- The plan sets out both the responsibility for its completion and the authority to do so.
- The plan includes the time frame within which objectives must be reached and events must occur.

In most firms the marketing manager is responsible for drawing up the marketing plan, but this is not usually done in isolation; it is obviously sensible to consult fully with those who will have responsibility (and authority) for implementing the plan. **JWDB**

Reference
Kotler, P. (1997) *Marketing Management, Analysis, Planning and Control* 9th edn, Englewood Cliffs NJ: Prentice Hall.

Marketing planning

At a strategic level, marketing planning involves the identification and prioritization of the target markets in which the organization will operate, its market positioning and competitive stance, and the formulation of the organization's marketing strategy. At a tactical level, marketing planning is concerned with a series of decisions relating to the ways in which the strategy will be implemented. In essence, therefore, marketing planning is concerned with the development and coordination of marketing activity. In doing this, it contributes to and takes its lead from the organization's overall corporate plan.

Marketing planning involves the evaluation or assessment of marketing opportunities and resources, the development of the marketing objectives, the identification of the ways in which these objectives will be achieved, and the creation of the marketing mix for the implementation and control of the strategy and tactics. Marketing planning also determines when and how marketing activities will be performed and by whom. As such, it involves a focus upon both the present and the future shape of the organization. A key output of marketing planning is therefore the marketing plan, detailing the requirements for the organization's marketing activities.

Traditionally, organizations operated with three types of plan: a short-term plan that covered a period of up to one year, a medium-term plan covering two to five years, and a long-term plan for the period beyond this. Because of the volatility of many market environments, the nature of marketing planning has changed significantly over the past few years. Whereas at one time it was the case that plans were typically very formal and highly structured, many marketing planners today deliberately develop plans that are far less highly structured and which incorporate a much greater degree of contingency thinking. **CTG & RMSW**

References
De Kare-Silver, A. (1997) *Strategy in Crisis: Why Business Urgently Needs a New Approach*, Basingstoke: Macmillan.

Dibb, S., Simkin, L. and Bradley, J. (1996) *The Marketing Planning Workbook*, London: Thomson Learning.

Ferrell, O.C., Hartline, M.D., Lucas, G.H. and Luck, D., (1999) *Marketing Strategy*, Orlando: Harcourt Brace.

McDonald, M.H.B. (1999) *Marketing Plans: How to Prepare Them, How to Use Them*, 4th edn, Oxford: Butterworth-Heinemann.

Marketing public relations

Public relations at its simplest is 'The management of communications between an organization and its publics' (Hunt and Grunig, 1994). The use of the word 'between' in this definition suggests the importance of two-way communication with a variety of publics, or what management authors prefer to call stakeholders. The Institute of Public Relations extends this definition to include the nature and outcome of the communication: 'Public relations practice is the planned and sustained effort to establish and maintain goodwill and mutual understanding between an organization and its publics.'

While many have viewed public relations as a sub-element of marketing (one of the principal areas of the marketing communications mix), these definitions draw attention to how the public relations function incorporates broader, organization-wide issues that some argue lie beyond marketing. Since the 1980s, the confusion concerning the boundaries between PR and marketing has been somewhat reduced with the growing acceptance of the term 'marketing public relations' (MPR), which encapsulates the overlap between the two functions. Shimp (1997) describes marketing public relations as: 'The marketing-oriented aspect of public relations .... the narrow aspect of public relations involving an organization's interactions with consumers and other publics regarding marketing matters.'

Kotler (1988) lists the following ways in which MPR can contribute to and support marketing communications and the table identifies some of the activities most closely associated with MPR:

- assist in launching new products
- assist in repositioning existing products
- build interest in the product category
- influence specific target groups
- defend products that have suffered public problems
- build corporate image to reflect favourably on its products.

Table: **Activities closely associated with marketing public relations**

• Publicity, press/media releases	• Lobbying
• Publications – newsletters, reports, corporate and product videos, in-house and customer magazines, corporate literature	• Sponsorship
	• Product placement
	• Events management and publicity 'stunts'
• Corporate identity materials	• Crisis management
• Company web site	• PR related advertising and advertorials

The area of marketing public relations that tends to receive widest attention is 'publicity', which may be generated by numerous means. It is often evaluated in terms of advertising equivalent expenditure. This is a measure of how much it would cost to gain an equivalent amount of media exposure if the space and time were to be bought at advertising rates. Often publicity is thought of as 'free advertising', which is somewhat misleading in that publicity is rarely free and is usually accompanied by a great deal of effort if positive results are to be achieved, or if damaging effects are to be minimized in cases of negative publicity. The notion of free publicity comes from the fact that the actual editorial space in the press or news time on TV that it takes up is not paid for. **DWP**

References
Hunt, T. and Grunig, J.E. (1994), *Public Relations Techniques*, New York: Harcourt Brace.
Kotler, P. (1988), *Marketing Management*, Englewood Cliffs: Prentice Hall.

Shimp, T.A. (1997), *Advertising and Promotion and Supplemental Aspects of Integrated Marketing Communications*, 4th edn, Fort Worth: Dryden Press.

Marketing research

Marketing research has generally been defined as the 'systematic and objective identification, collection, analysis, and dissemination of information'. The purpose of the marketing research process is to improve decision making to aid problem solving. The definition focuses on the *systematic process* of conducting research. Marketing research should be seen as a systematic process of identifying, collecting, analysing, and integrating information for the purpose of solving a marketing problem or as a guide for making effective decisions. Marketing research takes some of the risk out of marketing decisions by providing information that can be used to form the basis of decision making. The marketing information obtained from research can be used as the raw data to aid management decision making. Essentially, a systematic approach offered by marketing research is a necessary reinforcement in aiding managers to make important decisions.

In marketing, identifying customer needs and being able to satisfy those needs effectively is paramount in ensuring the success of the firm. Marketing managers are required to make numerous decisions at the strategic as well as the tactical level. They need to select the right target segments to market their products or services and they need to plan and implement effective marketing programmes. In order to make these decisions, they have to take into consideration several factors that may not be within their immediate control. For example, environmental factors such as economic conditions, technological changes, policies and regulations affecting their firms and the products or services they are marketing, competitive factors, as well as social and cultural influences are all aspects which the marketing managers have to look into. Research helps them to link the marketing variables, including marketing mix variables, with environmental factors and customer information. It is information gathered by marketing research that aids managers in making the most viable decisions for the implementation of their marketing programmes. **RM-R**

Reference
Proctor, T. (1997) *Essentials of Marketing Research*, London: Pitman Publishing.

Marketing strategy

Marketing strategy is the method by which the company or a product line or brand or an individual strategic business unit (SBU) within the company expects to achieve its marketing objectives. This distinction is made, because separate plans will be appropriate for individual SBUs if there are different marketing strategies for different product lines or SBUs. This planning consists of detailed strategies for targeting predetermined market segments by manipulating various elements of the marketing mix within predetermined levels of expenditure.

It covers the goals and strategies for the organization's marketing efforts. This is coordinated with company wide strategic corporate planning, which is the process of developing and maintaining a strategic fit between the organization's capabilities and its ever changing marketing opportunities. In this corporate context strategic marketing planning is one of five planning horizons, the others being:

- production planning
- human resource planning
- financial planning
- distribution planning.

Its place within marketing planning is best summed up through the acronym 'MOST' that stands for:

- *mission* – or a general statement that acknowledges the business the company is in
- *objectives* – which state what the company wants to accomplish
- *strategy* – which states in overall terms how the company is going to do the job
- *tactics* – which state in specific terms how the job is going to be accomplished.

In general terms a marketing strategy might involve issues like those suggested by Ansoff:

- new products into new markets (or diversification)
- new products into existing markets (or product development)
- existing products into new markets (or market development)
- existing products into existing markets (or market penetration).

Strategies can also involve methods to take away market share from competitors, and some terms borrowed from the military include: frontal attack, flanking attack, encirclement attack, bypass attack and guerrilla attack. **GL**

Reference

Lancaster, G. and Massingham, L. (1999) *Essentials of Marketing*, 3rd edn, Maidenhead: McGraw-Hill, pp. 347–358.

Maslow and motivational theory

One of the factors influencing a consumer's buying decisions is his or her motivational level. The person's motivation plays a very important role in whether that person buys a product or service. Each individual has many needs at a particular time. A need becomes a motive when it is aroused to a level where it becomes intense. This intensity of motive drives the person to act in a way that could satisfy the needs. Similarly, some form of needs that the consumer will strive to satisfy motivates consumer buying behaviours.

According to Abraham Maslow (1970) people are driven by specific needs at different times of their lives. Maslow constructed his hierarchy of needs to explain the different levels of needs that exist within an individual. At the bottom of the hierarchy, Maslow identified *physiological* needs (such as hunger and thirst) as being the most basic and most important needs that individuals strive for. Once these needs have been satisfied, they cease to become a motivator and individuals move to the next level – *safety* needs, followed by *social* needs. Social needs are those where the sense of belonging and love are considered as important motivating elements. *Esteem* needs come next, where individuals hope to achieve recognition and self-esteem. The top level of Maslow's hierarchy is *self-actualization*, where individuals are motivated by the need to achieve self-development. Thus, Maslow's motivational theory explains the levels of motivation experienced by individuals as they go through the different stages of life. To a marketer, understanding the motivating factor of target markets is important in order to develop suitable marketing strategies capable of satisfying their current needs. **RM-R**

References

Maslow, A. H. (1970) *Motivation and Personality*, 2nd edn, New York: Harper and Row.
Mowen, John C. (1995) *Consumer Behaviour*, 4th edn, Englewood Cliffs, NJ: Prentice Hall.

Measurement

Measurement is used to assist the analysis and evaluation process, the nature of measurement being governed by what is being investigated. Measurement techniques are becoming more sophisticated, with statistics being employed in such fields as econometric modelling, analysis of media effectiveness, brand positioning and cluster analysis for customer profiling and geodemographics. Questionnaires may be used, databases interrogated, interviews and group discussions held and surveys conducted. Rather than eliciting verbal responses, methods may be employed to measure autonomic responses such as pupil dilation, eye movement, skin response, brain wave patterns and pulse rates, all of which indicate the effects of marketing communications by measuring individuals' physiological changes.

Campaigns may be measured across a variety of outcomes to elicit their impact on such things as levels of awareness, recognition, recall, attitude and opinion change, sales response, trial and adoption, brand associations, coverage, reach, trade response, shelf footage, enquiries and competitive positioning. However, when determining whether a campaign is working or has worked, it is important that any measurement is made against the objectives set for the campaign. For this reason, objectives should be clearly stated and be measurable wherever possible. This is the basis of the DAGMAR approach (**d**efining **a**dvertising **g**oals for **m**easured **a**dvertising **r**esults) advocated by Colley (1961). Pickton and Broderick (2001) suggest that the SMARRTT acronym can be used to help determine suitable objectives which (even if this is not always feasible) should aim to be **s**pecific, **m**easurable, **a**ctionable, **r**ealistic, **r**elevant, **t**argeted and **t**imed.

Measurement can be taken in three broad areas to assess if campaigns are efficient, effective and economical. Efficiency is a measure of 'doing things right' (not wastefully), effectiveness is a measure of 'doing the right things', (achieving the right outcomes), and economy is a measure of doing them within resource constraints (least cost). To undertake a comprehensive assessment of marketing communications, consideration should be given to measuring any and all of its various aspects. This includes the quality of initial analysis, each element of the marketing communications mix, the media used, the audience reached, budget allocations and resourcing, the appropriateness of objectives set, timing and scheduling, the message and imagery used, the management of the marketing communications effort and the quality of integration and synergy achieved. **DWP**

References

Colley, R. (1961) *Defining Advertising Goals for Measured Advertising Results*, New York: Association of National Advertisers.

Pickton, D. W. and Broderick, A. (2001) *Integrated Marketing Communications*, London: Financial Times Prentice Hall.

Media

The media are the 'vehicles', 'channels' or 'carriers' of marketing communications messages. Without the media, marketing communications cannot be effective.

The term 'media' is usually applied to the 'mass' media – press, TV, cinema, radio, posters and the Internet. Some also include direct mail as a mass medium. But, for marketing communications, this would be unnecessarily limiting. As carriers of messages, media are much more numerous and varied. Marketing communications media are anything capable of carrying marketing communications messages. As such, this includes packaging, company stationery, signs, shop displays, promotional giftware and merchandise items, leaflets and brochures, vehicle livery, people/word of mouth, video games, CD-ROMS and DVDs, uniforms, etc. Even the Houses of Parliament, the White Cliffs of Dover, corn fields and the athlete Linford

Cristie's contact lenses have been used as 'ambient' media to carry marketing communications messages.

Huge sums are spent each year in the media. Ensuring both effectiveness and efficiency are paramount if money is not to be wasted. For the effective use of media, key requirements are to ensure reach, impact and frequency.

- *Reach* is the ability of the medium to be seen and heard by as many of the target audience as possible. This is usually expressed as a percentage of target audience reached.
- *Impact* has to do with the effect created by the marketing communication. Although this will be a function of the content of the marketing communications, the medium used also has a role to play.
- *Frequency* is a necessary part of the process as, usually, receiving the marketing communications once will not be sufficient to create impact. So the media have to carry the message numerous times. This increases the reach and increases the opportunities to see (OTS) or hear (OTH) the message, so that more people (particularly within the target audience) see the message more often.

Fundamentally, media planning is the task of managing reach, impact and frequency cost efficiently so that media objectives are achieved within budget constraints. A measure of cost efficiency is cost per thousand (CPT), which is used to compare the cost of reaching one thousand members of the target audience in each medium. Media planners and buyers need market and media information to assist their decisions. **DWP**

Reference

Pickton, D.W. and Broderick, A. (2001) *Integrated Marketing Communications*, London: Financial Times Prentice Hall, chs 11, 12 and 32.

Media commission

This is the discount received by advertising agencies from media owners, as of right, on the price of advertising time or space bought. It may in practice be called 'agency commission', or simply 'commission'. The rate varied in the early days of the 'commission system' (explained in 'Advertising commission system'), but eventually stabilized at 15 per cent of the published list price. That figure is today the standard in most countries and across most media, though some lesser media vehicles offer only 10 per cent. List prices are published in the media owner's rate cards, and in the independent compendium British Rate and Data ('Brad'), or its equivalent elsewhere.

For this system to work properly, media owners must deny commission to advertisers and restrict it to bona fide advertising agencies. Non-experts understandably find it hard to believe that they would in fact refuse a demand for direct commission from an advertiser with the spending muscle of those in the table in 'Advertisers', but historical precedent and professional etiquette have so far maintained the convention intact. To qualify for the discount, an agency would apply for formal 'recognition' by one or more of several representative bodies. In the late 1970s, pressure from media-buying specialists spinning off from conventional agencies ('media independents') led to the abandonment of those universal agreements, but individual media owners' sales contracts still stipulate standards relating to status and creditworthiness as preconditions for commission.

Suppose that advertiser ABC delivers a brief to advertising agency XYZ, and in due course approves a proposal that includes a poster campaign taking advantage of a package deal from an outdoor advertising contractor. XYZ places the order, not ABC, at a rate card cost of £10 000. The advertising starts to run, and the contractor renders an invoice to XYZ for £10 000 minus (15 per cent of £10 000), or £8 500. XYZ in turn bills ABC for the full package price, verifiable in Brad. When both accounts have been settled, the media owner has received £8 500, XYZ's bottom line is £1 500 healthier than it would have been, and ABC has remained totally unaffected, financially. **KC & BZE**

Reference

Crosier, K. (1999) 'The argument for advertising agency remuneration' in P.J. Kitchen (ed.), *Marketing Communications: Principles and Practice*, London: Thomson Learning, ch. 25.

Media owners

These are not actually the owners of 'the media', but the organizations holding the rights to sell advertising space and time in mass media vehicles. In Britain, the media mix they collectively make available to advertisers comprises five so-called 'major media'. No one ever identifies the implied 'minor' variants, but an industry handbook lists as many as 18 'other advertising media' (Advertising Association, 1999), one of which – the Internet – is widely expected to become major during this century. The table below shows the share of total national advertising expenditure held by the conventional five. It is clear that there are in fact two major and three minor advertising media. This is true of all European countries and the USA (where cinema advertising is not generally available at all).

Table: The UK media mix in 1998

	per cent of total advertising expenditure
Press	59.2
Television	31.9
Outdoor	4.4
Radio	3.7
Cinema	0.8

Source: Advertising Association (1999)

Crosier (1999) describes each ingredient of this mix in more detail than is possible here, with references to other authors who treat them in even greater detail. Belch and Belch (1998) provide an authoritative review of the American situation.

Press owes its dominance to its diversity: regional and local newspapers account for a third of its total share, national newspapers contribute almost a quarter, magazines the same, and 'directories' account for a tenth. *Commercial television* is steadily becoming equally fragmented: 14 regional ITV stations, national Channels 4 and 5, GMTV, six cable channels and 33 on-shore satellite services – before the advent of digital broadcasting adds hundreds of new terrestrial and satellite stations. That network shares the total audience 50:50 with the BBC. The *outdoor medium* is conventionally divided into sites targeting motorists and public transport users, and all others, a distinction based on presumed differences in viewing behaviour. *Commercial radio* was dubbed 'the 2 per cent medium' until the mid-1990s, when several initiatives turned it into the fastest growing of the five, at last attracting national brands. Like commercial television, it shares the audience 50:50 with the BBC and is in the midst of a massive digital expansion. *Cinema* was on its last legs until the advent of multiplexes produced the first rise in total audiences for half a century. Advertisers since attracted to the unique audience profile of the revitalized medium have included brewers, Levi's and DeBeers.

British media planners are well provided with reliable research data for all but the smallest subdivisions of the media mix. Media buyers deal with a manageable number of sales consortia, rather than literally hundreds of separate owners – the practical problem that gave rise to advertising agencies in the first place. **KC & BZE**

References

Advertising Association (1999) *Marketing Pocket Book 2000*, Henley-on-Thames: NTC Publications.

Belch, G. and Belch, M (1998) *Advertising and Promotion: an Integrated Marketing Communications Perspective*, 4th edn, New York: McGraw-Hill.

Crosier, K. (1999) 'The relationship among advertising, agencies, media, and target audiences', in P.J. Kitchen (ed.), *Marketing Communications: Principles and Practice*, London: Thomson Learning, pp. 430–432.

Media strategy

The formulation of media strategy is a matter of allocating a fixed advertising appropriation among the large variety of media vehicles available, with the aim of delivering the advertising message to the target audiences, cost-effectively. The task is almost always delegated by advertisers to the media department of their advertising agency or to 'media independents'. The classic British textbook on media strategy is Broadbent and Jacobs (1984), in which general principles remain valid despite great changes in the UK media mix since it was published. More recent but less comprehensive is an authoritative review of media planning in times of rapid change, in Butterfield (1997). British readers should treat American alternatives with caution; there are crucial differences in the availability and use of media between the two countries.

Media strategy development begins with a clear 'psychographic' description of the audiences to be reached, for the sophisticated and comprehensive databases built up by industry-wide media research over many years can tell planners a great deal about their associated media-consumption characteristics. The next step is to search for ground in the media landscape unoccupied by competing advertisers. Audience specifications are then matched with the 'coverage', 'reach' and 'penetration' offered by media vehicles surviving preliminary filtering, to yield a broad-brush strategic plan. Reduction to a manageable number of options is nowadays routinely entrusted to widely available on-line media selection programs or desktop software packages. Though media planning has become a highly numerate and technologically sophisticated discipline, the final decision-making process remains susceptible to the influence of routine, past experience and industry folklore.

The resulting operational plan is converted into a campaign schedule by 'media buyers', specialists with an encyclopaedic knowledge of 'their' media and the disposition needed to haggle successfully with the media owners' hard-nosed salespeople. Brierley (1995) provides a clear explanation of this complicated process. Once the campaign has run, the planning team will assess its cost effectiveness and retain their findings as an input to future cycles of media strategy development. **KC & BZE**

References

Brierley, S. (1995) *The Advertising Handbook*, London: Routledge, ch. 8.

Broadbent, S. and Jacobs, B. (1984) *Spending Advertising Money*, 4th edn, London: Business Books.

Butterfield, L. (ed.) (1997) *Excellence in Advertising: The IPA Guide to Best Practice*, Oxford: Butterworth-Heinemann, ch. 11.

Multiple functions of mix instruments

The metaphor of the marketing mix rightly suggests that the combination of elements may yield a result that far exceeds the sum of the components. It also leaves room for opposite situations, where awkward combinations lead to negative interactions amongst the elements and poor if not catastrophic end results.

To look at mix instruments from the perspective of marketing mix functions is one way to realize their unavoidable interaction. Indeed a solid axiom of the marketing mix is that any instrument mainly fulfils one function but at the same time affects all other functions. Put another way, any marketing mix instrument serves (or hampers) a primary function but also affects several secondary functions.

Take the simple example of a manufacturer of fashion clothes and more in particular their choice of outlets. The primary mix function of these outlets is clearly the distribution function. But at the same time the other marketing mix functions are also affected. If the outlets are, for example, upmarket boutiques versus downmarket department stores and clothes departments of hypermarkets, the communication function will be affected. In the first case it would be much easier to convey an exclusive image. In the second case quite naturally a much less exclusive image would be created, even if the garments ranges were identical. Image reasons alone would squeeze the pricing function into a completely different price bracket. The negotiating position and pricing policy of mass retailers themselves would also affect the pricing function of the manufacturer's marketing mix. The communication function might also be affected as these mass retailers might invite the manufacturer to participate in their retail advertisements. The choice of retail outlets would also affect the need fulfilment function of the manufacturer's marketing mix. Upmarket boutiques provide extra service and status, but on the other hand they may be reluctant to carry the full range of the manufacturer's garments, etc.

A second example is temporary price discounts. Their primary function is the current situational or promotional function. Suppose, however, that the temporary price discounts make customers more price conscious and also make them expect lower prices on a more permanent basis. This would mean that the generic pricing function is affected. Suppose also that the use of temporary price discounts reflects badly on the image of the product. Consequently the communication function would be affected. Suppose for the same reason that more upmarket retailers become reluctant to carry the brand, then clearly the distribution function is affected as well.

WvW & JDH

Reference

Van Waterschoot, W. (1999) 'The marketing mix', in M.J. Baker (ed.) *The IEBM Encyclopaedia of Marketing*, London: Thomson Learning.

Netiquette

One interesting site for readers to access is the 'blacklist of Internet advertisers' (math-www.uni-paderborn.de blacklist). The sections include web developers, billing companies, affiliate partners, Internet promotion, web sites, Internet service providers, resources, in other words a hall of shame and news. Probably, the last two are the most interesting. The Internet does, therefore, have a culture of behaviour referred to as 'netiquette' or 'net-etiquette' in relation to newsgroups. Notably, observing netiquette is not optional, it is a 'must do' activity. The inability to follow guidelines will not only create a bored, bemused or annoyed group of accessors, or even just an adverse reputation; it could also lead to a company being 'flamed' or at worst 'shamed' or blacklisted. Often the shaming and naming, when promoting the company to a specific group, should be done in order to contribute positively to group discussions, thus underpinning corporate image (see Hamill and Kitchen, 1999; Kennedy, 1999). **PJK**

References
Hamill, J. and Kitchen, P.J. (1999) 'The Internet', in P.J. Kitchen (ed.) *Marketing Communications: Principles and Practice*, London: Thomson Learning, ch. 22.
Kennedy, A.J. (1999) *The Rough Guide to the Internet*, London: Rough Guides Ltd.

Networks, alliances, and joint ventures

Organizations are trying to break down walls between themselves and their stake-holders by treating them as business partners. Kotler (1997) argues that relationship marketing will ultimately result in building a *marketing network*. A marketing net-work consists of the company and all its supporting stakeholders – for example customers, employees, suppliers, distributors, retailers and others with whom it needs to build mutually profitable business relationships.

Since it is extremely difficult for one supplier alone always to offer the highest quality product accompanied by the most superior service at the lowest price, build-ing strategic alliances is vital. A *strategic alliance* is an enduring relationship between an organization and its supporting stakeholders that involves a mutual effort to solve problems and meet customers' needs. The ultimate aim in building a strategic alliance is the creation of a long-term competitive advantage for the partners, often globally. Companies form strategic alliances with domestic and/or multinational organizations in an attempt to improve their capabilities and resources. Proctor (1996) argues that 'Joint ventures involve inter-organizational pooling of strengths for the effective delivery of product market strategies.'

The creation of a strong relationship is beneficial for both parties. The partners collaborate by forming a joint venture (a jointly owned company), licensing agreements, long-term purchasing and supply arrangements, or joint research and development programmes (Jobber 1995). There are several types of strategic alliance. Some take the form of new ventures between sellers and customers in order to secure the continuous supply of components and services into the customers' manufacturing operations; others are formed between potential competitors in order to develop a new market (Proctor, 1996).

Joint ventures have several drawbacks. There might be disagreement between the partners regarding marketing, investment, reinvesting the earnings for growth and other policies (Kotler, 1997). **IPD**

References

Jobber, D. (1995) *Principles and Practice of Marketing*, Maidenhead: McGraw-Hill.
Kotler, P. (1997) *Marketing Management: Analysis, Planning, Implementation, and Control*, 9th edn, Englewood Cliffs, NJ: Prentice Hall International Editions.
Proctor, T. (1996) *Marketing Management: Integrating Theory and Practice*, London: Thomson Learning.

New developments in marketing

The only new development in marketing is the realization that there's nothing new in marketing. All the available ideas have been tried, all possible theories tested, all matrices abandoned. Every advertising treatment, promotional tactic, pricing policy and competitive strategy has had its day. There's nothing left to do but recycle the old favourites, relaunch passé products, stretch long-established brand names to their elastic limit and beyond, or combine existing concepts in the hope that any ensuing amalgam can somehow be presented as new and improved.

Many academic authorities, admittedly, are unwilling to accept that marketing is finished, since the progressive, ever-onward-ever-upward mindset is very strongly marked in our field (Brown 1996, 1999). The evidence, however, is irrefutable. Retro goods and services are everywhere apparent (*retro-marketing*). Antiquated ideas, wrapped in new terminology, are making a comeback (*Art of marketing*). The giants of pre-modern marketing are being recuperated, after a fashion (*Barnumarketing*). And, the principal philosophical position of the present time maintains that originality is impossible (*postmodernism*). Marketing, in short, has become so ubiquitous – and the much-vaunted 'concept' broadened so much – that it no longer exists as a separate entity. It is all but indefinable (*postmodern marketing*), it is here, there and everywhere (*globalization*), it is a perfect imitation of a non-existent original (*hyperreality*). **SFX**

References

Brown, S. (1996), 'Trinitarianism, the eternal evangel and the three eras schema', in S. Brown *et al.* (eds), *Marketing Apocalypse: Eschatology, Escapology and the Illusion of the End*, London: Routledge, pp. 23–43.
Brown, S. (1999), 'Marketing and literature: the anxiety of academic influence', *Journal of Marketing*, 63(1):1–15.

New product development (NPD)

This relates to products or services that might be new, innovative and unique; replacement products that are substantially different to existing offerings or imitative products (termed 'me too' products) that might be new to a particular company, but not new to the market place. As well as completely new products, the process of NPD also covers product improvements, product modifications and new brands. Relaunched products also fall into this categorization, and this refers to original products that have gone into decline, but where the company sees that there is enough market potential left if the image of the product is changed through manipulating the marketing mix and giving the product a new 'image'.

In some companies a small, often elite, 'new product department' oversees all such activity. Its work covers the control of a number of activities from R&D through to marketing. When a new product looks viable a 'product' or 'project' champion is appointed to oversee development from design to launch (see also 'New product development process'). **GL**

References
Lancaster, G. and Massingham, L. (1999) *Essentials of Marketing*, 3rd edn, Maidenhead: McGraw-Hill, pp. 203–208.

New product development (NPD) process

The process of new product development goes through a number of logical sequences from the inception of the idea to its launch. The stages were conceptualized by Booz-Allen, Hamilton Company (1982) and consist of: idea generation, screening, business analysis, development, market testing and commercialization.

Ideas are first *generated* and these can come from a number of sources such as marketing research, brainstorming, research and development, the sales force, company employees or customers. In a marketing orientated company, the culture should encourage new product ideas and this should be linked to some kind of reward to those bringing successful new ideas forward.

Initial screening is the first stage of sifting good ideas from less viable ones, and it is at this stage that 'go' or 'drop' decisions should be made, as little expenditure has been incurred at this point. This process should consider matters such as whether the idea will be suitable alongside the current product range.

Business analysis investigates the new product's potential viability in terms of its market potential and its financial prospects. At the end of this stage, costs will increase considerably, so only potentially successful ideas should remain.

Development is the point at which the company is committed to taking the product to market. This involves research, design and development that should be coordinated with views from the marketplace, so close liaison with marketing research is essential. This is also a good point at which to abandon the product if it is not deemed to be viable, rather than risk a high profile failure in the marketplace.

Market testing can involve product placement tests with customers or indeed a full test market through a product launch in a closely defined geographical area.

Commercialization is the final phase, where the product is launched. Various filters that have been provided should reduce the possibility of failure at this stage, but even so many products still fail at this final hurdle. **GL**

References
Booz-Allen, Hamilton Inc (1982), *New Product Management for the 1980's*, USA: Booz-Allen, Hamilton.
Lancaster, G. and Reynolds, P. (1998) *Marketing*, Basingstoke: Macmillan, pp. 126.

Niche marketing

Niche marketing occurs when an organization concentrates its marketing effort on a small group of customers that exhibit specific needs and wants. These customers may be a sub-group of a larger, more easily recognizable market segment. The niche will require narrower targeting by the organization as customers within it are likely to be more demanding about receiving precisely the product or service they require. It is the opposite of mass marketing, where the company expects one product to be suitable for large numbers of customers.

Niche marketing is practised by both large and small companies, indeed the beauty of niching is that a very small company is able to compete equally with a multinational. The smaller the niche, the fewer competitors there are likely to be. This means that niche markets will often pay premium prices for the products or services they specifically require, making it a profitable market for the organization.

Niche markets can develop into mainstream markets over time, for example safari holidays to Africa were long the preserve of the wealthier customer but are now accessible to package holiday tourists as the cost of international travel has reduced.

Examples of larger companies involved in niche marketing are the car manufacturers. BMW produce its 'M' series cars, which are very powerful, more sporting versions of its standard customer offering. These specialist products are based on saloon cars but retail for double the price of the standard vehicle. An example of small firm niche marketing is Eastern Bikes who produce hand-built frames for BMX bikes. Retailing at prices 500 per cent higher than a mass manufacturer, Eastern Bikes, will sell 250 frames per annum as opposed to the tens of thousands manufactured by, for example, Raleigh. **SR**

Reference
Linneman, R.E., (1991) *Making Niche Marketing Work: How to Grow Bigger by Acting Smaller,* Maidenhead: McGraw-Hill.

Non-store and online retailing

Non-store retailing involves selling to the consumer through channels other than traditional shop premises. Options include mail order, television, party plan, telephone/fax based ordering, CD-ROM, the use of interactive retail kiosks and online Internet shopping. Around 60 per cent of UK adult consumers have shopped from home.

Developments of non-store retailing reflect the needs of time-poor consumers who are looking for increased choice and greater control. In particular, retailers are increasingly utilizing the convergence of technologies of Internet, TV and mobile telephones to attract the growing online market. In 1999, online trading directories listed over 1000 UK retail sites, approximately half transactional, and exponential growth is predicted.

Retailers can employ a variety of strategic options for the Internet, ranging from not getting involved with 'information only' to fully transactional websites. For those with a high financial investment in stores the new channel can pose a threat if it reduces store sales. However, margins of up to 25 per cent for electronic selling compare favourably with 2-6 per cent for stores. The Internet also offers direct selling opportunities to manufacturers and makes globalization achievable for small retailers.

The online shopping market is currently biased towards younger affluent males; however, access across all consumer groups is rapidly growing. Benefits to consumers include competitive prices, with intelligent search agents carrying out price comparisons and opportunities for the participation in consumer buying clubs. However, security of payment over the Internet is still questioned by many. Consumer familiarity with the brand and confidence and trust in the retailer are important for Internet retailing, which is less well suited for purchase decisions that rely on the senses of touch, smell or taste. The most popular categories for Internet shopping are computer software and hardware, books, music and entertainment products. All UK grocery multiples are experimenting with Internet selling, and clothing is also an important development area. Pioneers have included Dell, Tesco Direct and Amazon.com. **RAS**

References

De Kare-Silver (1999) *e-Shock 2000, The Electronic Shopping Revolution*, Basingstoke: Macmillan Business.

Dadomo, S. and Soars, B. (1999) *A Guide to E-Commerce – Business to Consumer*, Watford: Institute of Grocery Distribution Business Publication.

Mintel (1999) *Online Shopping*, London: Mintel International Group.

Ody, P. (1998) *Non-Store Retailing: Exploiting Interactive Media and Electronic Commerce*, London: Financial Times Retail and Consumer.

Objectives

An objective is a measurable outcome of strategic or tactical activity that can be targeted by planners. An objective is not an aim: aims might be targeted, but are not necessarily measurable.

For example, a firm might aim 'to sell as much as possible'. This is a useful aim, but cannot be measured because there is no way of knowing in advance how much can be sold. An objective might be 'to sell 10 per cent more than we did last year'. This is measurable, since presumably the planner knows how much was sold last year.

Objectives are the strategic statements of where the managers would like the firm to be. Objectives might be financial and therefore expressed in terms of profits, market share, return on investment or other quantitative measures. Objectives might be philosophical, expressed as a mission statement, or they might be qualitative, perhaps in terms of service levels, rate of introducing new products, level of staff turnover or other non-financial issues.

Weinberg proposed eight dichotomies for objective setting.

1. Short-term profit vs. long-term growth.
2. Profit margin vs. market position.
3. Direct sales effort vs. market development.
4. Penetrating existing markets vs. developing new ones.
5. Profit vs. non-profit goals.
6. Growth vs. stability.
7. Change vs. stability.
8. Low-risk vs. high-risk situations. **JWDB**

Reference
Weinberg, R (1969) 'Developing marketing strategies for short-term profits and long-term growth' Paper presented at the Advanced Management Research Inc. seminar, New York.

Odd pricing

Odd pricing or 'the practice of ending prices in odd numbers (1, 3, 5, 7, 9) and of pricing just below a 0 (.49, .99, ...)' has become widespread in many categories. It is believed that 'odd' price endings may affect price perceptions beyond the monetary price value and may generate higher sales. Recent studies provide factual evidence of this phenomenon (see Stiving and Winer, 1997; Wedel and Leeflang, 1998). The price ending effect may stem from an 'underestimation mechanism'. Psychological factors explaining the underestimation of odd prices are the consumers' tendency to round prices down and to compare prices from left to right. Consumers are also bound to ignore rightmost digits as a result of limited information processing and memory capacity: they consider additional price digits until the marginal costs of processing and recalling exceeds the expected marginal benefits, which again leads to underestimation (Huston and Kamdar, 1996). In addition, an 'association mechanism' may be at work. Odd price endings may implicitly present a fair price (being the odd price rounded up to the next integer) and therefore be perceived as discounted price levels. This promotional connotation could be an incentive to buy the product.

However, it appears that not all consumers react in the same way to odd prices, and that odd price endings might not work at all price levels (Wedel and Leeflang, 1998). Moreover, odd prices are not recommended for all products: in particular, they are not appropriate for products that require thought (e.g. cars) and for products for which an upmarket image is pursued (Levy and Weitz, 1995). **KCa, BF, EG**

References

Huston, J. and Kamdar, N. (1996) '$9.99: can 'just-below' pricing be reconciled with rationality?', *Eastern Economic Journal*, 22(2):137–145.

Levy, M. and Weitz, B. (1995), *Retailing Management*, Chicago: Irwin.

Nagle, T.T. and Holden, R.K. (1995) *The Strategy and Tactics of Pricing: A Guide to Profitable Decision Making*, Englewood Cliffs, NJ: Prentice Hall.

Stiving, M. and Winer, R.S. (1997) 'An empirical analysis of price endings with scanner data', *Journal of Consumer Research*, 24(June): 57–67.

Wedel, M. and Leeflang, P.S.H. (1998) 'A model for the effects of psychological pricing in Gabor-Granger price studies', *Journal of Economic Psychology*, 19:237–260.

Opinion leaders

It is common for consumers to seek information by asking the advice of another person whom they consider knowledgeable or whose opinion they value. This individual is known as an 'opinion leader'. Opinion leaders are people who are frequently able to influence the attitudes and behaviours of others. Generally, opinion leaders are people who have some expertise in certain areas and to whom others can refer. They also tend to be socially active and to share the same values and beliefs as the consumers who refer to them for advice. Often opinion leaders are friends or acquaintances who are able to impart relevant information about products or services to others.

Identifying and understanding opinion leaders is important to marketers because of the extent of influence such people exert over other consumers. Influential personalities have been known to create strong followers who imitate their purchasing and consumption patterns. Opinion leaders are usually innovators and among the first to buy new products. They also have very high self-confidence and are often willing to share information about products or services. Because their actions are often watched by others who strive to follow them, they can usually impart both positive and negative information about product performance. Their opinions are often accepted because they are considered as credible and have no vested interest. However, opinion leaders can be quite difficult to identify because they are not necessarily celebrities. Despite the difficulty, it is still worth the effort to try and locate dominant opinion leaders because they may hold the key to influencing other consumers' purchasing and consumption patterns. **RM-R**

References
Williams, K.C. (1984) *Behavioural Aspects of Marketing*, Oxford: Heinemann Professional Publishing.

Organizational buying: overview

Organizational buying decisions can be seen from three interrelated perspectives. These are the stages through which companies go when buying the product or service *(the buying process,)* the range of participants involved in the buying decisions *(the buying centre),* and the influences on the buying process *(choice criteria).* Effective industrial marketing decisions depend on developing a thorough understanding of each of these aspects of buying behaviour. **SP**

References
Eckles, R.W. (1990) *Business Marketing Management*, Englewood Cliffs, NJ: Prentice Hall.

Organizational buying: process

There are several distinct stages in the organizational buying process. These can be seen in terms of the purchase of fuel oil. A company becomes aware of the need, when it compares its fuel usage with the amount of oil remaining in the storage tanks. The specification of the type of oil was made when the heating system was first installed. The re-order quantity will be determined by the consumption rate and possibly a pre-negotiated discount for bulk purchases or loyalty to one supplier. The buyer may not look very far for suppliers if there is a contract in place to buy from one source. There will be little or no evaluation of alternatives in this situation. Orders could be placed over the telephone, with little or no direct contact with the supplier. The contract may only be reviewed once per year.

Each of these elements of the buying process present different opportunities for a supplier to influence the buying decision. At the initial pre-purchase stage the key problem is to create an awareness of the company's capability to supply. It may also be possible to increase the buyer's awareness of the need. For example by stressing that fuel prices can rise as well as fall the suppler could make companies aware of the need to enter into a longer term supply contract, which could even out the price of fuel. This type of long term contract to supply is typical of many industrial commodity products.

Equally a new supplier may be able to enter the market by providing new services. Typically companies will review a range of quotes before renewing existing commitments to suppliers. There are opportunities at the contract review stage to provide new and more competitive offers. In the case of fuel oil this could include automatic monitoring and replenishment before the oil runs out. **SP**

References
Johnston, W.J. and Lewin, J.E. (1996) 'Organizational buying behaviour', *Journal of Business Research*, 35(1):1–16.
Weiss, A.M. and Heide, J.B. (1993) 'The nature of organizational search in high technology markets', *Journal Of Marketing Research*, 30(2):220–234.

Organizational buying proposals

Organizational buyers are likely to seek proposals in a range of different buying situations. The proposals can range from a verbal quote over the telephone to an extensive written response to a customer's enquiry. The latter is typical of high cost purchases where there may be a considerable degree of uncertainty in the buyer's mind as to the best solution to the problem.

For example, a company may believe that it requires a new organizational structure to reflect its new chosen business strategy. However, it is uncertain about the best way to put this strategy into place. It could contact several different firms of management consultants. Each of these consultancy companies may have a different way of dealing with the re-structuring process. By asking for proposals the buying company is seeking to draw out the expertise of the supplier.

Proposals are also an effective way of reducing the quoted price, where the buyer has already developed a specification. By asking for proposals against a specification the buyer is able to compare the relative competitiveness of individual suppliers and achieve a better price. Frequently suppliers are asked to itemize individual areas of cost in the proposal, so that buyers can do a detailed comparison between alternatives. Buyers may frequently ask suppliers to produce a revised quotation based on the first round of quotes received from potential suppliers. The quotation process is used to manage suppliers.

It can frequently be a very expensive and time consuming process to develop proposals for a potential client. There is often no guarantee that the company's bid will be successful. However there is often no alternative. In some markets (for example government contracts), the buyer must be able to demonstrate that several competitive quotes were obtained before the contract was placed. **SP**

Reference
Eckles, R.W. (1990) *Business Marketing Management*, Englewood Cliffs, NJ: Prentice Hall.

Organizing for international marketing

This is a large and potentially dangerous topic because change is the order of the day and new forms of organization for international marketing are being invented as I write. I will deal with the topic at three levels.

Level 1: moving from export to international
Historically, certainly for much of the 20th century, my examination of the history of internationalization would reveal what might be called incremental internationalization. The path followed by many companies is:

Licensing ➔ Export via agent or distributor ➔ Export through own sales representatives or sale subsidiary ➔ Local packaging or assembly ➔ Foreign direct investment (FDI) in factory production.

This represents a learning curve and was entirely appropriate in the pre Information Age technology period.

Level 2: internationalization begins
When sales through agents or distributors or through a sales subsidiary become significant, internationalization begins to occur. The overseas business of the company is differentiated from its domestic sales, management is differentiated and specialization begins to occur. Then, new organizational challenges appear.

There are five main groups of international company organization.

- *Type 1 – the geographical type*: The company, seeing diversity in its markets overseas, may focus on a geographical area, using regional managers, to whom local country managers report.
- *Type 2 – the product type*: Where products are more diverse than markets, specialization may occur at the product level, i.e. product divisions have responsibility for marketing their own products internationally.

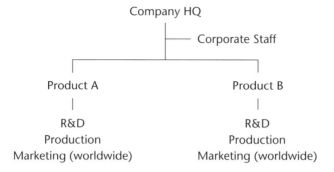

- *Type 3 – the matrix type*: Subsidiary managers report along both geographical lines and product groups. A type with a poor track record.

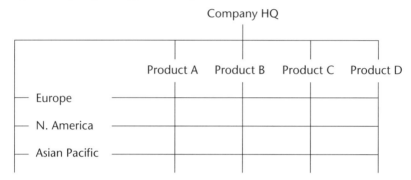

- *Type 4 – the project type*: Large-scale assembly operations such as dam, bridge and power station projects may utilize project group management for the duration of the project.
- *Type 5 – the mixed structure*: Combines a product division with an international division, appearing on a chart like this:

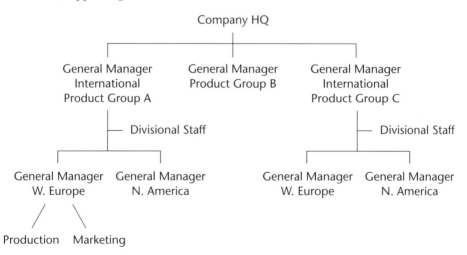

The functional managers have direct relationships with all foreign subsidiaries, i.e. home-based functional managers are directly responsible for all international business. SKF, the Swedish ball bearings company, still uses this form of organization.

Level 3: the transnational corporation
Perhaps the mature form of international organization, it is best defined and positioned as shown in the following table.

Table: **The transnational corporation**

Organizational characteristics	Multinational	Global	International	Transnational
Configuration of assets and capabilities	Decentralized and nationally self sufficient	Centralized and globally scaled	Sources of core competences centralized, other decentralized	Dispersed interdependent and specialized
Role of overseas operations	Sensing and exploiting local opportunities	Implementing parent company strategies	Adapting and leveraging parent company competences	Differentiated contributions by national units to integrated worldwide operations
Development and diffusion of knowledge	Knowledge developed and retained within each unit	Knowledge developed and retained at the centre	Knowledge developed at centre and transferred to overseas units	Knowledge developed jointly and shared worldwide

Information technology will continue to facilitate information exchange, and extend the span of control. Predictions about the demise of middle managers proliferate, suggesting that organizations will continue to evolve, making possible virtual companies, characterized by global operations and reach, managed by a small core of senior managers. **MJT**

Reference
Bartlett, C. and Ghoshal, S. (1989) *Managing Across Borders: The Transnational Frontier*, Boston: Harvard University Press.

Outsourcing
Outsourcing is the decision to seek a supplier for a particular product or service rather than provide it 'in house'. This is a 'make or buy' decision. The main factors on outsourcing are the relative costs of producing the product or service internally compared with those of the external market, and the degree of control over the purchasing situation. This choice is frequently an important strategic one for the company. Some companies have deliberately chosen to outsource as much as possible of the business, retaining only the essential elements that give it a competitive edge.

Some products or services are strategically important to the survival of the business and the company would never seek to find an outside supplier. For example the company may have technical know how in terms of knowledge of materials or production processes. This knowledge gives it a comparative advantage which it would not wish to give up. Therefore it would never seek to find an external supplier.

By comparison, catering and cleaning services are frequently outsourced to specialist companies which are able to supply these services more efficiently because of specialist expertise. Personal computers are made from many standard items (for example the Intel processor is widely used by a range of manufacturers).

Make or buy choices can also focus the attention of the company on the efficiencies of its own operations. If the company conducts an analysis of the alternative costs of supplying a product or service in-house with the costs of getting that service from an outside supplier, this can provide a good indication of the relative efficiency of the in-house activity. Such a review may not lead to outsourcing. This activity is sometimes referred to as 'market testing'. **SP**

References

Giunipero, L.C. and Monczka, R.M. (1990) 'Organizational approaches to managing international sources' *International Journal Of Physical Distribution and Logistics Management*, 20(4):3–13.

Matthyssens, P. and Van den Bulte, C. (1994) 'Getting closer and nicer: partnerships in the supply chain', *Long Range Planning*, 27(1):72–84.

Packaging

When a product has been developed, it is important that strategies are devised that add to its value. An important element here, especially for fast moving consumer goods, is packaging, which is an important aid to selling along with branding. In addition to appealing to consumers, packaging must also appeal to retailers and this includes bulk 'outers' in which individual packages for sale are packed. Well packaged products in relation to both 'inners' and 'outers' can thus induce offtake by both the trade and individual consumers.

The function of packaging is basically to preserve and protect the contents and to help to sell the product inside in terms of the package's promotional appeal. This is a function of design and the information that is conveyed on the pack itself. Its design should also relate to the package's storage qualities and its convenience in use. GL

Reference
Kotler, P. (1994) *Marketing Management, Analysis, Planning, Implementation and Control*, 8th edn, New Jersey: Prentice Hall, pp. 457–461.

Packaging as a marketing tool

Packaging is a very significant, yet often under-represented part of the marketing communications mix. It is said to have two main functions: to protect the product and to display and communicate. Compliance with certain commercial and legal requirements means that packaging and labelling frequently need to specify particular information such as details of contents, sell and use-by date, bar code and manufacturer's registered address.

Packaging may be referred to as 'a silent salesman' in that it attracts attention, creates appeal and helps sell the product. It is widely thought of as the visual identity of the brand (Danton de Rouffignac, 1990). It embodies brand values and differentiates one brand from the others using a medium that is virtually free (Cowley, 1991). An ideal package, according to Lewis (1991), is one that brings to the customer's mind the essence of what the brand is all about whenever and wherever it is seen. It influences customer choice at the point of sale and acts as a reminder in the home. For fast moving consumer goods, a virtual war of packaging display is fought daily on supermarket, pharmacy and other retailer shelves and display units.

Although packaging contains basic information about the product, it also makes extensive use of promotional designs and offers. Colour, shape, typography, copywriting, layout, feel and sometimes smell, are all examples of elements that are carefully considered in packaging design. Packaging is also a primary medium for carrying sales promotion offers. It is an effective and extremely efficient means of communication. Offers might include details of price deals, competitions, free gifts and coupons, and special packaging might be used to provide trial sizes, extra contents, banded packs with other products or two-for-one deals, and so on.

Packaging, today, is a mixture of art and science combining, as it does, creativity and technology. New packaging materials and printing techniques are constantly being developed, giving the goods that they clothe extra protection and offering designers new and exciting creative opportunities. **DWP**

References
Cowley, D. (ed.) (1991) *Understanding Brands: By 10 People Who Do,* London: Kogan Page.
Danton de Rouffignac, P. (1990) *Packaging in the Marketing Mix*, Oxford: Butterworth-Heinemann.
Lewis, M. (1991) 'Brand packaging', in D. Cowley, *Understanding Brands: By 10 People Who Do,* London: Kogan Page.

Penetration pricing and experience curve pricing

Penetration pricing and experience curve pricing are pricing strategies in which new products are introduced at low prices. For both strategies, the objective is to exploit pioneer advantages and pre-empt competition.

Penetration pricing is justified by the presence of a number of price sensitive customers in the market – low prices attract and capture the price sensitive consumer segment. Charging a low entry price implies that the company loses money initially on customers willing to pay more, but this may be made up for by a larger loyal customer base by the time new entrants show up.

Experience curve pricing is based on the 'experience effect', which implies that as cumulative production quantity increases, manufacturing procedures become more efficient ('learning by doing', technological improvements) and so allow similar output levels at lower unit cost. With a low initial price, the company can quickly realize a high sales volume and thus build up economies of experience – in other words, realize a cost advantage – before competitors enter. Though experience effects are potentially important, they are not obtained automatically. A thorough effort may be needed to exploit the benefits of experience. This is especially true in an international setting, where experience effects are conditional upon an efficient transfer of skills and knowledge between business units throughout the world (Phillips *et al.*, 1994).

For penetration and experience curve pricing, the company must decide on the initial price level as well as the pattern of price adaptations over time. Crucial ingredients in these decisions are the reservation prices for various customers and the magnitude of loyalty or experience effects. Also, the company must make sure that there is not a strong perceptual association between price and quality (see also Dolan and Simon, 1996; Hanna and Dodge, 1997). **KCa, BF, EG**

References
Dolan, R. J. and Simon, H. (1996), *Power Pricing: How Managing Price Transforms the Bottom Line*, New York: The Free Press.
Hanna, N. and Dodge, H.R. (1997) *Pricing: Policies and Procedures*, London: Macmillan Press.
Monroe, K. (1990) *Pricing: Making Profitable Decisions*, New York: McGraw-Hill International Editions.

Nagle, T.T. and Holden, R.K. (1995) *The Strategy and Tactics of Pricing: A Guide to Profitable Decision Making*, Englewood Cliffs, NJ: Prentice Hall.

Phillips, C., Doole, I. and Lowe, R. (1994), *International Marketing Strategy*, London and New York: Routledge.

Tellis, G.J. (1986) 'Beyond the many faces of price: an integration of pricing strategies', *Journal of Marketing*, 50(October): 46–60.

Performance analysis

Performance analysis is the process of examining the implementation process in terms of its outcomes. The performance of the various activities required by the marketing plan is analysed according to their success (or otherwise) in achieving the expected outcomes. The analysis is useful in designing corrective measures to ensure that the activities do not deviate from the original plan, unless a deliberate change of direction becomes necessary because of changes in the external environment.

Analysing performance means that there must be a suitable monitoring system in place. This means that suitable performance criteria must be established; in most cases this will follow on automatically from the marketing plan, which will normally include targets and the dates by which they should be reached. Information on progress towards targets should be included; for most objectives it should be feasible to create criteria by which progress can be judged – stages which need to be passed, and so forth.

Information needs stem from the establishment of criteria. The information collected should be minimized if possible; not only is staff time too valuable to waste collecting irrelevant information, but the plan loses credibility if it involves overburdening staff. Furthermore, staff become aware very quickly if they are collecting information which serves no useful purpose, and will not cooperate with collecting the information in future. Information falls into two categories: information regularly collected and supplied to management and information which is collected as needed for specific purposes. Internal information systems commonly fall into the first category, but may also become involved in one-off information gathering; otherwise, external agencies or specially-commissioned research projects might provide the necessary information for the particular problem.

The performance of a given task will be judged on the expected performance. The judgement is not entirely mechanical, however; the manager needs to take account of any extenuating circumstances and may need to allow for overperformance in another area of implementation. **JWDB**

Reference
Thompson, J.L. (1997) *Strategic Management, Awareness and Change* London: Thomson, ch. 6.

Performance indices

Performance indices are measures of the outcomes of planned activities. Typically there are three types of performance indicator: financial indices, market indices and marketing measures (Gross *et al.*, 1993).

Financial indices are based around profit and loss accounts, net income, balance sheet valuations of marketing assets such as brands or intellectual property (patents and copyrights), returns on investment in promotional campaigns, and so forth. Financial indices are most commonly quoted in company reports and in the business press, and therefore acquire a higher prominence than they might deserve.

Market indices are concerned with issues such as growth in sales, market share, market stability and competitive advantage. Sometimes these are measured in financial terms, but more commonly they would be measured using unit sales (number of products sold).

Marketing measures are based on issues such as customer satisfaction, export orientation, product quality and corporate image. These areas are difficult to measure, but in some cases trade bodies or other outside organizations make awards to companies which show excellence in such areas. These awards are often regarded as prestigious, and can be used for publicity purposes. During the late 1990s marketers showed an increasing interest in establishing industry-wide standard measures for marketing indices, partly as a way of ensuring that marketing as a profession acquired greater status and credibility with the business press and partly because marketing measures are likely to give a better indication of the long-term health of a company than would be the case with financial indices. **JWDB**

Reference
Gross, A.C., Banting, P.M., Meredith, L, N. and Ford, I.D. (1993) *Business Marketing*, Boston: Houghton Mifflin.

Personal selling and marketing communications

Personal selling is one of the major categories of the marketing communications mix. In many respects, it is the most powerful and influential in that direct communications between sales staff and customers permit the greatest opportunity for dialogue, problem solution and objection and complaints handling. But personal selling is also the most expensive form of marketing communications. Advertising and PR, which make use of the mass media rather than one-to-one communications, can reach many millions of people for the cost of running a sales force.

Because of the way it is organized in most companies, personal selling is generally thought of as a separate function from the rest of marketing communications. It is usually the case that 'sales' is given a separate department under its own management and with its own budgets. This need not always be the case as it can be more fully integrated within a broader 'marketing' or 'sales and marketing' section. Personal selling may be undertaken by industrial and business-to-business sales forces, but it is also typified by the retail sales representative within consumer marketing. Telemarketing, the use of the telephone for personal selling, is becoming increasingly popular as companies search for improved cost efficiency.

The roles of selling are varied and are changing in prominence over time as the nature of business is moving from transactional to relationship marketing (see 'Relationship marketing'). This is leading to greater emphasis being placed on negotiation, building relationships and key account management (Starkey and Harwood, 2001). Traditional views of personal selling have highlighted it as a seven-stage process (the level of activity in each being dependent upon the sales situation) involving:

- prospecting and evaluating customers
- preparing for customer contact
- approaching the customer
- making the presentation
- overcoming customer objections
- closing
- follow-up.

Chonko *et al.* (1992) have classified sales jobs into two broad categories; 'service selling' – increasing sales from the existing customer base, and 'development selling' – converting new prospects into sales. Anderson (1995) has identified three basic roles: 'order taking', order supporting' and 'order getting'. Lancaster and Jobber (1997) similarly split the selling function into three: 'order-takers', 'order-creators' and 'order-getters'.

In considering the wider jobs of salespeople, Wilson (1993) has identified nine sales roles, while Donaldson (1998) has classified selling according to different sales situations as shown in the table below. **DWP**

Table: **Roles in personal selling**

Wilson's sales roles	Donaldson's sales situations
• Customer partner	• Consumer direct
• Buyer/seller team coordinator	• Industrial direct
• Customer service provider	• Government/institutional direct
• Buyer behaviour expert	• Consumer indirect
• Information gatherer	• Industrial indirect
• Market analyst and planner	• Food brokers
• Sales forecaster	• 'Specifier' sales
• Market cost analyser	• Key account sales
• Technologist	• Telesales
	• Systems selling/team selling
	• Franchise selling
	• International selling

References
Anderson, R. (1995) *Essentials of Personal Selling*, Englewood Cliffs: Prentice Hall.

Chonko, L., Ennis, B.M. and Tanner, J.F. (1992) *Managing Sales People*, Boston: Allyn and Bacon.

Donaldson, W. (1998) *Sales Management: Theory and Practice*, London: Macmillan.

Lancaster, G. and Jobber, D. (1997) *Selling and Sales Management,* 4th edn, London: Pitman Publishing.

Starkey, M. and Harwood, T. (2001) 'Personal selling and sales management', in D. Pickton and A. Broderick, *Integrated Marketing Communications*, London: Financial Times Prentice Hall, ch. 27.

Wilson, K.J. (1993) 'Managing the industrial salesforce of the 1990s', *Journal of Marketing Management*, 9:123–139.

Personal selling defined

Personal selling is personal contact with one or more purchasers for the purpose of making a sale.

Personal selling is an essential element in marketing. It is the promotional means involving face-to-face contact with buyers and must be performed by salespeople who are customer oriented, who seek solutions to customers' problems in the long-term interests of their company and their customers. Personal selling is most effective when combined and integrated with other elements in the marketing mix so as to represent a total communications package.

The most significant difference between selling and other elements in marketing communications is the personal contact. The need for personal contact varies depending on a number of factors such as the type of customer, the frequency of purchase, the newness of the product, technical advice required and sales and service support. In some situations, communications is achieved more effectively by impersonal means such as advertising, and the skill in marketing management is to deploy resources so that the communications result is both effective and efficient. For example, personal selling costs may be as high as 70 per cent of marketing expenditure for industrial products and less than 20 per cent of marketing expenditure for fast moving consumer goods.

The tasks in personal selling can vary but are likely to involve the following key elements: customer problem solving, retaining and increasing existing business, finding new business, providing buyers with service and information and complaint handling. The role also involves representing the company and providing internal coordination within the supply firm and external linkages between firms. Hence, the salesperson may be described more accurately as customer accounts manager, business development manager or customer service representative. **WGD**

Reference
Donaldson, B. (1998) *Sales Management: Theory and Practice* 2nd edn, Basingstoke: Macmillan.

Personal selling, role of

The role of personal selling in a market-driven organization has three essential components – information, persuasion and relationship management. First, the information role: salespeople, in conjunction with others such as market researchers, need to be able to identify opportunities in their markets and the specific needs and wants of their customers and potential customers and to be able to mobilize their personal and corporate resources behind customer solutions. These solutions may be the product/service package offered in a particular way to highlight the uniqueness of your offer. At various stages in the buying process this communication is most effectively achieved by face-to-face personal contact. This information role is a two-way communications process from salespeople to customers and with the needs of prospective and satisfied customers being conveyed via salespeople back to management responsible for marketing decisions. Increasingly, this is combined with a customer support or service role to look after customers and protect their on-going relationship. This is the information task of salespeople.

A second role salespeople must perform is that of persuasion. In a competitive economy most commercial enterprises appeal to prospective customers faced with an abundance of choice. As a result adoption of marketing-oriented activities is no guarantee of a sustained competitive advantage. Prospective customers will have to be convinced that their needs have been identified correctly and that the product/service/information mix provided by salespeople and the supply firm represent the best deal to their benefit over any competing alternative.

Third, the role of salespeople is creating, building and sustaining relationships. Salespeople provide a link in the exchange process between buyer and seller based on oral communication rather than by impersonal or electronic means. This role involves the salesperson being conductor, coordinator and collaborator to reflect the competencies of the firm. The salesperson is also an ambassador, adviser and enabler on behalf of the supply organization. In practice, we can observe that the role of the salesperson is continuing to move away from a traditional and frequently perceived role of aggressive and persuasive selling to a new role of relationship manager. **WGD**

Reference
Grikscheit, G. M., Cash, H.C. and Young, C.E. *Handbook of Selling*, 2nd edn, New York: Wiley.

Place and product classes

The development of distribution channel structures may be influenced by the different product classes that are going to be distributed. Products that are classified as 'convenience goods' are likely to be distributed through conventional marketing channels or through an intensive distribution strategy. For such goods, gaining maximum accessibility is often the main distribution objective since convenience goods are those which the consumers buy frequently, immediately and with minimum comparison and buying effort. They are usually low priced and are therefore widely available. As such, the distribution channels for this type of goods are likely to be characterized by the existence of layers of different distributors specializing in specific channel functions.

In contrast, goods or services classified as 'shopping goods' may require a more selective distribution strategy where selected distributors may act as agents or distributors with assigned territories to cater for consumer demands within the geographic locations. Shopping goods are those where the consumers usually go through the process of comparing and searching for the best alternative before making the final purchase. This would include products such as furniture, electrical goods and clothing. For this type of product, a few selected distributors with specialized functions serving a specific geographical location are usually involved in the distribution process.

Consumer products classified as 'speciality' goods require a more exclusive distribution strategy. Speciality goods are those that consumers seek without much need to compare in terms of pricing and suitability but which they are inclined to buy because of the goods' unique characteristics. These include products such as luxury cars, high-priced electrical goods and branded, custom-made clothing. For these types of goods, an exclusive distribution strategy may be necessary where only one distributor is allocated in a particular geographic location to serve the needs of target consumers. The exclusive nature of such a distribution channel is in line with the type of goods that are being offered. The distribution channel structure may be a simple one where very few intermediaries are involved in the distribution functions. **RM-R**

References

Rosenbloom, B. (1995) *Marketing Channels – A Management View*, 5th edn, Fort Worth Texas: Dryden Press.

Stern, L.W., El-Ansary, A.I. and Brown, J.R. (1994) *Management in Marketing Channels*, 2nd edn, New Jersey: Prentice Hall International Editions.

Place or channel, definition

Place or channel of distribution refers to the development of distribution structures where relevant interdependent organizations undertake the tasks of moving goods (or services) from the point of inception to the point of consumption. The channel of distribution of a product or service is essentially its distribution structure, where goods from the manufacturer (or service from the service provider) are made available to end-users for final consumption. The distribution structures are made up of sets of institutions, agencies and establishments – often called 'intermediaries' – that are responsible for carrying out specific activities which facilitate the movement of goods through the channel. The activities undertaken by channel intermediaries are often considered as flows which depict the movement of the functions in the distribution channel. All the flows, within the channel structures are indispensable, meaning that at least one intermediary must undertake the responsibility for each of the flows in order to ensure that the distribution channel will operate effectively.

From a managerial perspective, distribution channels are viewed as the involvement of external organizations in distributing the goods and services of the manufacturer or producer. These external organizations are the intermediaries or the firms which are involved in executing channel functions including buying, selling and transferring title to products or services. Thus, managing the distribution channels is an important responsibility undertaken by the firm assuming the role of the channel leader in order to ensure that distribution objectives are achieved. Management of the distribution channel requires an inter-organizational management perspective since firms that are involved in a distribution channel are external organizations which may have differing roles and objectives. In effect, this may complicate the task of managing distribution channels. Developing effective channels of distribution is often considered a challenging task requiring a thorough perspective of distribution requirements. **RM-R**

References

Bucklin, L.P. (1967) 'The economic structure of marketing channels', in Mallen, B.E. (ed.), *The Marketing Channel*, New York: John Wiley & Sons.

Gattorna, J. (1978) 'Channels of distribution conceptualisation: a state of the art review', *European Journal of Marketing*, 12(7);471–512.

Stern, L.W., Ellansary, A.I. and Brown, J.R. (1994) *Management in Marketing Channels* Englewood Cliffs, N.J.: Prentice Hall International Editions.

Planning and control combined

Combining planning and control means that the system has automatic checks and balances built into it, in other words, the plan is self-correcting.

All marketing plans should have provision for control of the process. Deviations from the plan need to be compensated for and corrections applied; combining these with automatic changes to the plan requires a higher level of sophistication. The planners need to consider fall-back positions in the event of objectives not being attained or in the event of more promising objectives presenting themselves in the course of the plan.

For example, a failure to achieve an objective through a promotional campaign might automatically trigger an increase in budget, an alternative promotional device or even a change of objective. The advantage of building in fail-safe policies is that decision making is quicker, corrective action is taken as soon as a control mechanism indicates that there is a problem, rather than having to be left until the planners are able to meet to formulate a new plan. The closer the evaluation and control mechanisms are to the planning process, the quicker the organization can respond to changing circumstances (Goldschlager, 1993). **JWDB**

Reference

Goldschlager, A. (1993) 'Improving the marketing process is a continuous commitment', *Marketing News* 27, June.

Planning and implementing marketing programmes

Planning and implementation are the linked processes of forecasting the future business environment and needs and ensuring that appropriate actions are taken to enable the firm to meet its marketing objectives within the context of that environment.

The process goes in three stages: preparing the marketing plan and budget; implementing the plan; and monitoring and controlling the plan throughout the timespan that it covers. Preparing the plan includes deciding on the frequency of the planning cycle, the nature and scope of the plan and the situational analysis (Macdonald, 1995).

The planning process is intended to provide a systematic structure for decision making about the future. The resulting plan is, first, about the firm's marketing strategy. Strategy is concerned with the firm's long-term aims and objectives: the overall direction the business is going in. Secondly, the planning phase will consider tactics – the shorter-term activities which determine how the firm is to achieve the strategic objectives.

The marketing plan is developed to cover specifically the organization's relationships with its customers, competitors and publics. It will state exactly what is to be done in respect of each of the 7Ps – product, price, place, promotion, people, process and physical evidence (Booms and Bitner, 1981). Implementation guidelines should include all the activities to be undertaken, who is responsible for ensuring that they are undertaken and the timescale for their completion.

Monitoring processes will need to be included, but (perhaps more importantly) control systems should be in place to ensure that corrective action is taken if results deviate from the plan. Having said that, the plan will need to include a degree of flexibility to allow for unexpected events. **JWDB**

References

Booms, B.H. and Bitner, M.J. (1981) 'Marketing strategies and organisation structures for service firms' in J. Donnelly and W.R. George (eds) *Marketing of Services*, Chicago Ill.: American Marketing Association.

Macdonald, H.B. (1995) *Marketing Plans; How to Prepare and Use Them*, Oxford: Butterworth-Heinemann.

Political factors

Political factors are those issues which stem from government policies and public opinion. Public opinion colours the environment in which marketers must operate; the rise in environmental awareness during the 1990s caused many firms to change their policies, even when they were not affected by legislation. The furore in the UK over genetic modification of food crops demonstrated that public opinion is important to firms, both in the production and in the distribution areas.

Government policies affect businesses in the following ways.

- Legislation may create opportunities or represent threats to existing businesses.
- Government expenditure is a substantial proportion of many markets (or even the entirety of it, in the case of defence manufacturers). Changes of policy may mean that expenditure is diverted away from some areas, and towards others. (Maucher, 1993).
- Implementation of legislation can create burdens because of 'red tape', even when the legislation itself is not particular onerous.
- Governments may seek to develop agreements with industries or trades unions to develop joint initiatives, without resorting to the force of legislation to back them up.

For most firms, political factors remain part of the macro environment; in other words, most firms have to accept government policy and public opinion and work within their constraints. For very large or very influential firms, political factors can be manipulated and opinion changed, or governments influenced, to make the business environment easier. **JWDB**

Reference

Maucher, H.O. (1993) 'The impact of the single European market on regional product and price differentiation – the example of the European food industry' in C. Halliburton, and R. Huneberg (eds) *European Marketing: Readings and Cases*, Wokingham: Addison-Wesley.

Positioning

As identified by many academics and practitioners, positioning is the key to marketing strategy. Marketers need to consider decisions about the positioning or perceptions of the product or service within the mind of the customer. The adaptation of the marketing mix in determining the desired positioning of the product or service should endeavour to ensure the achievement of a unique place in a competitive market.

Positioning is the process of designing an image and value so that customers within the target segment understand what the organization, product or brand stands for in relation to the competition – in other words, how it is differentiated. Therefore, position is a fundamental element of marketing planning.

The process involves a number of stages: identifying the key criteria or attributes which customers will use to judge the product or service; establishing the product's competitive advantage; deciding on those benefits/characteristics that are to be emphasized; implementing the positioning concept using the marketing mix.

To assist in this process, researchers undertake surveys to find out how consumers perceive each of the different brands on the market in terms of the relevant criteria. This is then plotted using pairs of criteria such as quality and performance or price and taste, to determine the position of the ideal product and the actual position of the products surveyed. This technique leads to the construction of perceptual maps which help to identify the current positioning of competitor's products and the existing position of the product. Once an image that sets the product apart from the competing products is identified, the desired position must be communicated to the target consumers. Although this is a promotional issue, it is also important that the product is made available and the price, product and packaging are all developed to communicate the desired positioning.

During 1998, the UK repositioning of the Italian drink Campari was undertaken, to position it as an upmarket drink for fashionable young men. The target segment/audience was seen as City boys, who had high earnings, car owners, two holidays a year and read the men's style press. There was a strong promotional push in terms of a £3 million television campaign, supported by poster, sampling activity and advertorials within GQ magazine.

The repositioning was to emphasize a 'really cool, distinctive drink'. The campaign was described as 'strong man's communication' with the emphasis on mixing bitterness with pleasure, which pushed the idea of mixing the spirit with orange juice rather than soda. The television execution featured a 'cool' bar owner getting the better of a burglar who turns up wearing his stolen jacket. **RAA**

References

Ashford, R, (1999) 'Segmentation, targeting and positioning', *Business Review*, 5(3):27–29.
Baker, M. J., (1996) *Marketing: An Introductory Text*, London: Macmillan Press, pp. 63–67.
Piercy, N., (1997) *Market-Led Strategic Change*, Oxford: Butterworth-Heinemann, pp. 194–211.

Postmodern marketing

Paradox, they say, is one of the characteristic features of postmodernism and marketing is one of most characteristic incongruities. For many cultural commentators, marketing represents the epitome of the postmodern condition. Consider shopping centres. The typical Arndale developments of the 1960s – all reinforced concrete, flat roofs, straight lines, low ceilings and oozing mastic – have been eclipsed by postmodern shopping malls, which are bright, airy, eclectic, ornamented, themed, unashamedly kitsch and invariably welcoming. In advertising, likewise, the straightforward marketing pitch of tradition ('this product is good, buy it!') is almost unheard of these days. Contemporary commercials are incorrigibly sly, subtle, allusive, indirect, clever, parodic, irreverent, self-referential (ads about ads), cross-referential (ads that cite other cultural forms – soap operas, movies, etc.) and made with staggeringly expensive, para-cinematic production values. Consumers, too, are changing. The certainties of the modern era, where mass marketing mediated between mass production and mass consumption, are a dim and distant memory. Today, there are no rules, only choices, no fashion only fashions, the Joneses are avoided at all costs, and anything not only goes but has long since gone (Brown, 1995, 1997).

The paradox, however, is that such patently postmodern examples of marketing practice have not been paralleled by postmodern marketing scholarship. As a general rule, the voluminous published literature on postmodern marketing is not the work of marketing academics, commentators or researchers. Within marketing, postmodernism is widely considered inconsequential, incomprehensible, incorrigible, the preserve of the lunatic fringe, a distraction from the discipline's model-building ambitions, something that is defined by its rejection of definitions. I ask you! At most, 'postmodern marketing' features in the final, tucked-well-out-of-the-way, sure-no-one-reads-it-anyway chapters of marketing readers and anthologies, usually under a catch-all title such as 'marketing miscellany', 'pot pourri' or 'new directions'. Be that as it may, there is some evidence of a sea change in marketing scholarship. The logic, order, rationality and model-building modalities of the modern research tradition are being enriched by manifold qualitative, literary, humanities-based and aesthetics-led research procedures, many of which can be considered 'postmodern'. Perhaps the clearest indication of postmodernist-at-work, however, is the unconventional way in which their papers, books and research reports are written. Exaggeration, hyperbole, humour, flights of literary fancy and lots of big words are their principal trademarks, as is their hopeless addiction to self-citation. Present company excepted... **SFX**

References
Brown, S. (1995), *Postmodern Marketing*, London: Thomson Learning.
Brown, S. (1997), *Postmodern Marketing 2: Telling Tales*, London: Thomson Learning.

Postmodernism

Postmodernism is one of *the* buzzwords of the late twentieth-century. It has been applied to everything from making love (over the Internet, by means of teledildonic body-suits) to making war (as in the Gulf or Kosovo, where virtual attacks were mounted and western casualties avoided at all costs). In many ways, indeed, postmodernism is a kind of make-work scheme for underemployed intellectuals, since an enormous number of scholars – in every conceivable academic discipline – seem to be engaged in explaining, applying, interpreting and codifying the concept, if it is a concept (Sim, 1998).

Perhaps the most important thing to note about postmodernism, however, is that it is a portmanteau or umbrella term, which is often used in a broad, all-encompassing sense. Nevertheless, four main sub-divisions can be discerned: postmodernity, postmodernism ('proper'), post-structuralism and, for want of a better neologism, posture.

Postmodernity pertains to latter-day developments in the socio-economic environment. The world, according to this viewpoint, has entered a new historical epoch, where traditional ways of working, producing, consumption and exchange have given way to a computer-driven, sound-bitten, pick 'n' mixed, ever-faster, 24-hour, totally fragmented, increasingly interdependent, unstable verging on chaotic marketing milieu. It is a world where the beating of a butterfly's wings in South America can cause a stock market crash in Hong Kong, the lowering of hem-lines in Paris or yet another malfunction in the hapless Hubble telescope. Paradox is everywhere, incongruous juxtapositions abound, acceleration is all.

Postmodernism, strictly speaking, is an artistic movement, a revolt against the once shocking, but subsequently tamed, 'modern' tradition of the early- to mid-20th century. In architecture, for example, postmodernism is characterized by the eschewal of the austere, unembellished, 'glass box' International Style of Le Corbusier and Mies van der Rohe, and a return to the populist, ornamented, kitsch's kissing cousin mannerisms of Portman, Sterling, Venturi and Gehry. Broadly similar trends are discernible in most other areas of artistic endeavour – literature, music, poetry, fine art, film, drama and so on (see Connor, 1997).

Post-structuralism is an enormously influential school of literary theory that emerged in the early- to mid-1970s. Although it is often associated with a group of leading French thinkers including Jacques Derrida, Roland Barthes and, to some extent, Michel Foucault, the designation is also applied to today's anti-Enlightenment turn in western philosophy. The *philosophes'* search for objective knowledge, universal laws and meaningful generalizations has been superseded by an appreciation of the boundedness of knowledge, the limits to generalization and the absence of universal laws. Post-structuralism, in effect, maintains that reality is not an objective fact, to be discovered, measured and classified, but akin to a text, which is interpretable in many different, yet equally valid, ways.

Posture refers to the typically postmodern attitude, orientation or mood, its way of looking at the world. Irony, parody, playfulness, irreverence, insolence, couldn't-care-less cynicism, tongue-in-cheek insouciance and absolute unwillingness to accept the accepted are its principal distinguishing features. The progressive, optimistic, things-can-only-get-better, washes-whiter-than-white worldview of the 'modern' era has been replaced by a combination of impertinence, scepticism, lassitude and bang-or-whimper apocalypticism. The postmodern is suffused with an air of finitude, ending, transition, crisis and impending, possibly calamitous change. There is nothing new. There can be nothing new. All that remains is to play with the pieces in the Legoland of late modernity (Brown, 1998). **SFX**

References

Brown, S. (1996) 'Art or science?: fifty years of marketing debate', *Journal of Marketing Management* 12(4):243–267.

Connor, S. (1997) *Postmodernist Culture: An Introduction to Theories of the Contemporary*, Oxford: Blackwell.

Sim, S. (ed.) (1998) *The Icon Critical Dictionary of Postmodern Thought*, London: Icon.

Power relationships on the Internet

In the presence of higher information exchange or intensity, channel power shifts in favour of customers and consumers (Glazer, 1991). Distinctions between producers, distributors and consumer(s) start to break down. It is not a matter of transmitting messages, as would be the case for advertising, direct marketing, marketing public relations – i.e. single linear messages to many [potential] customers. Instead the firm or company more appropriately tailors messages to suit the needs, wants and desires of recipients. This is done through the process of web site navigation in which customers choose which information or data they wish to receive from a company. Thus what has occurred and will occur more and more over time is a shift in the balance of power in favour of customers and consumers. The old selling and marketing process has changed to potential collaboration of consumers in terms of idea generation, product design, price to be negotiated, distribution arrangements and in the communication effort itself. For example, in the USA and to a lesser extent in the UK, purchase of automobiles may come about as a result of consumers broadcasting their interests over the Internet and soliciting bids from different firms. Digital, as a further example, enjoyed significant success in making the Alpha AXP computer system available to customer for a test drive over the Internet.

Over the past 30 years the control of information transitioned from manufacturers to distributors. The dominant form of information control (and thus marketing) is now in the hands of distributors. It is only in the last ten years that information is transitioning further into the hands of customers and consumers. The most obvious change is in the ways in which consumers can access information that enables them to purchase required products and services. Rather than being at the mercy of manufacturers or distributors in geographic or time-constrained marketplaces, in the Internet's interactive marketspace, buyers and consumers initiate searches for what they want or need. In many cases the search procedure is international or global (Schultz and Kitchen, 2000)

The power relationship represents a revision to the traditional linear marketing systems personified in most leading textbooks. Instead of goods and services flowing from manufacturers to distributors to consumers they can flow through the interactive marketplace in any direction. Consumers can contact manufacturers or distributors directly. Manufacturers, distributors and consumers can interface with each other. The new power relationship is personified by give and take, interaction, and a flowing of informational exchange – up, down, horizontally, vertically and throughout the process. **PJK**

References

Glazer, R. (1991) 'Marketing in an information-intensive environment: strategic implications of knowledge as an asset', *Journal of Marketing*, 55 (October).

Schultz, D.E. and Kitchen, P.J. (2000) *Communicating Globally: An Integrated Marketing Approach*, Macmillan Business, London.

Pressure groups and watchdogs

A 'pressure group' is a formal organization, usually of a voluntary nature, which exists to promote a specific issue and cause changes in organizational, governmental or individual behaviour. For example, environmental pressure groups use a range of tactics to cause changes in corporate behaviour. Such groups might write letters to the firm, organize boycotts of the firm's goods, generate negative publicity about the firm, or seek to lobby government to introduce legislation to curb the firm's activities.

Confrontation with pressure groups is rarely effective; although their power is usually minimal, their influence can be strong and they are often able to cause damage to the firm's public relations efforts. Pressure groups are best dealt with by consulting them about the issues of concern; this can often defuse difficult situations, and turn the situation to the firm's advantage in terms of PR. (McDonagh, 1998)

A 'watchdog' is a paid individual or organization, usually governmental, with statutory powers enabling it to force changes in the behaviour of firms and other organizations within the industry it has responsibility for. It acts as a regulatory body. Since the widespread (and worldwide) privatization of former State enterprises, watchdogs have been created in response to public concerns about the monopoly power of the new organizations. For example, OFTEL is the UK's watchdog with responsibility for the telecommunications industry; OFWAT is the equivalent for the water industry. Watchdogs are not confined to privatized industries, however; they exist for financial services such as banking and insurance and for service industries such as package holidays and tourism.

Watchdogs often have powers which enable them to enforce decisions, but will usually prefer to arrive at compromises and mutually-agreed solutions to problems. The key to success in dealing with watchdogs is to keep them informed of forthcoming changes in policy. Some industries have established their own regulatory bodies, thus pre-empting government action and retaining some control over the situation. **JWDB**

Reference

McDonagh, P. (1998) 'Towards a theory of sustainable communication in risk society: relating issues of sustainability to marketing communications', *Journal of Marketing Management*, 14: 591–622.

Price dimensions

Next to the narrow perspective of prices as 'the number of monetary units to be paid', a more comprehensive view is gaining way, in which price is considered as 'what is given up, from the customer's point of view, to obtain the product or service' (see Zeithaml, 1988; Keegan, 1995).

This broader interpretation extends the 'traditional' price notion along three dimensions. First, it recognizes the possible discrepancy between objective and perceived prices. It is unrealistic to assume that all customers have complete information on amounts to be paid, and psychological processes may affect how price information is assimilated. Decision makers have to account for these disparities between real and perceived prices in targeted customer segments.

Second, prices need not exclusively be specified in monetary terms at the time the product is acquired. Product usage may entail additional costs of repair, maintenance and energy consumption that should be accounted for. Also, price in a general sense encompasses non-monetary efforts of product acquisition. A typical example in consumer markets is 'time prices' as a result of travel, shopping, waiting, search and transaction time. In industrial markets, installation, transportation, order handling and inventory carrying represent examples of non-monetary efforts.

Third, price also includes a 'risk' component. The risk associated with product adoption may be functional, such as the risk of product failure or of poor technical and delivery support. It may also be social or psychological in nature, an example being the risk of signalling low social status when driving around in a Lada. Because of the two latter dimensions, setting prices may encompass the specification of 'purchase and use conditions' associated with monetary price, over the product's life cycle (Hutt and Speh, 1992). **KCa, BF, EG**

References

Gijsbrechts, E. (1993) 'Prices and pricing research in consumer marketing: some recent developments', *International Journal of Research in Marketing*, 10(2):115–151.

Hutt, M.D. and Speh, T.W. (1992) *Business Marketing Management*, Fort Worth: The Dryden Press.

Keegan, W. (1995) *Global Marketing Management*, Englewood Cliffs, NJ: Prentice Hall.

Zeithaml, V. (1988) 'Consumer perceptions of price, quality and value: a means-end model and synthesis of evidence', *Journal of Marketing*, 52 (July): 2–22.

Price discounting

A price discount is any price reduction (stated as a percentage or monetary value) that can be perceived as temporary or exceptional. Price discounts differ in the criteria that are used for granting them. These criteria can be time, customer or quantity specific.

Time-based discounts are often part of a promotional action. In *random discounting*, the company offers temporary price cuts at random points in time. It exploits consumer heterogeneity in price knowledge and search costs: knowledgeable consumers search for bargains and buy the product at the low price, while others usually pay the regular price. *Periodic discounting* implies that prices systematically change over time to exploit consumers' different willingness to pay related to purchase period. A typical example is seasonal discounting, where lower prices are charged in off-season or end-of-season periods.

Second market discounting explicitly stipulates different prices for different customer segments: while most customers are charged a 'regular' rate, others (those in the 'second' market) benefit from a discount. A typical example is dumping, where the same product is offered at a high price in one market, and at a much lower price (often below average cost) in other (more price sensitive) markets. Trade discounts offered by manufacturers to distributors performing specific functions (e.g. ware-housing), are also illustrations of second market discounting. Since second market discounting is a more direct form of price discrimination, it is often subject to legal restrictions. Also, the company should ensure the presence of barriers hindering resale among consumers or diversion of products from one market to another (Kahn and McAlister, 1997).

Finally, with *quantity discounts* (i.e. charging lower unit prices if larger amounts are purchased, see, for example, Dolan, 1987), a company tries to attract heavy users with higher price sensitivity and lower holding costs. By selling in larger quantities, the seller can save on inventory and transaction costs (see also Hanna and Dodge, 1997). **KCa, BF, EG**

References

Dolan, R.J. (1987) 'Quantity discounts: managerial issues and research opportunities', *Marketing Science*, 6(1):1–23.

Dolan, R. J. and Simon, H. (1996) *Power Pricing: How Managing Price Transforms the Bottom Line*, New York: The Free Press.

Hanna, N. and Dodge, H.R. (1997) *Pricing: Policies and Procedures*, London: Macmillan Press.

Kahn, B. E. and McAlister, L. (1997), *Grocery Revolution: The New Focus on the Consumer*, Reading, MA: Addison Wesley Educational Publishers.

Monroe, K. (1990) *Pricing: Making Profitable Decisions*, New York: McGraw-Hill International Editions.

Nagle, T.T. and Holden, R.K. (1995) *The Strategy and Tactics of Pricing: A Guide to Profitable Decision Making*, Englewood Cliffs, NJ: Prentice Hall.

Tellis, G.J. (1986) 'Beyond the many faces of price: an integration of pricing strategies', *Journal of Marketing*, 50(October): 46–60.

Price discrimination

When a company adopts price discrimination, it tries to exploit differences in willingness to pay between customers. In the case of *direct price discrimination*, the company explicitly charges higher prices to consumers who are prepared to pay more, and lower prices to those with a lower willingness to pay (see Hanna and Dodge, 1997; Lilien and Rangaswamy, 1998). For instance, publishers charge higher subscription rates for their journals to libraries than to private subscribers.

However, since the customers' price sensitivities are not always apparent and since direct price discrimination often causes legal problems, companies may resort to *indirect forms of price discrimination*. Indirect price discrimination is based on self-selection, i.e. customers themselves select the price regime that best matches their needs. Typical examples are random discounting, periodic discounting and quantity discounts. In *random discounting*, the company indirectly discriminates among customers with low search costs and customers with high search costs by lowering the price randomly and infrequently. Price-sensitive customers with low search costs will be knowledgeable about prices and will therefore buy when prices are discounted, while other customers are more likely to buy at the regular price (Tellis, 1986). In *periodic discounting*, prices systematically change over time to exploit customers' different willingness to pay related to purchase period (e.g. some consumers are willing to pay the full price for fashion products early in the season, while others wait for end of season sales) (Tellis, 1986). Finally, *quantity discounts* exploit the differences in willingness to pay for a first, second (etc.) unit of the same product, by granting a discount when larger quantities are purchased (see, e.g. Dolan, 1987). **KCa, BF, EG**

References

Dolan, R.J. (1987) 'Quantity discounts: managerial issues and research opportunities', *Marketing Science*, 6(1):1–23.

Hanna, N. and Dodge, H.R. (1997) *Pricing: Policies and Procedures*, London: Macmillan Press.

Lilien, G. L. and Rangaswamy, A. (1998) *Marketing Engineering: Computer-Assisted Marketing Analysis and Planning*, Reading, MA: Addison-Wesley.

Nagle, T.T. and Holden, R.K. (1995) *The Strategy and Tactics of Pricing: A Guide to Profitable Decision Making*, Englewood Cliffs, NJ: Prentice Hall.

Tellis, G.J. (1986) 'Beyond the many faces of price: an integration of pricing strategies', *Journal of Marketing*, 50(October): 46–60.

Price flexibility and price boundaries

A key consideration in pricing is that of 'pricing flexibility', or the extent to which the company has freedom in setting prices. Pricing flexibility can be assessed through the analysis of price boundaries: minimum and maximum price levels that the company could charge for a product. Some factors set a 'price floor'. This is true for costs: typically, price should allow the company to cover the various costs incurred to provide customers with the product. Other aspects such as legal constraints, or the fact that customers associate low price with low quality, may also prevent the company from charging prices below a minimum level. Keeping prices sufficiently high may also help avoid competitive reactions leading to a downward price spiral and, eventually, a price war. Other elements constitute an 'upper bound' on price. The maximum price a company can charge predominantly depends on customers' willingness to pay for the product and on prices charged by current competitors. The threat of market entry by new competitors may also be a reason for keeping prices sufficiently low. Again, government regulations may impose an upper bound on price in certain markets (e.g. pharmaceuticals).

From the company's perspective, the difference between lower bound and upper bound constitutes the company's 'latitude in pricing', and is an indicator of importance of price as strategic instrument. Pricing latitude varies strongly between markets and companies and basically depends on the 'market structure': the number of buyers and sellers and the degree of product differentiation. In commodity markets such as paper pulp or steel, characterized by many sellers compared with the number of buyers and little or no product differentiation, companies have virtually no freedom in setting prices. They can only charge prevailing market prices, which are mainly driven by cost. Conversely, in high-tech markets such as PCs or specialized consulting services, where competitors offer differentiated products to a broad customer base, pricing flexibility is typically substantial. **KCa, BF, EG**

References

Dolan, R. J. and Simon, H. (1996) *Power Pricing: How Managing Price Transforms the Bottom Line*, New York: The Free Press.

Hanna, N. and Dodge, H.R. (1997) *Pricing: Policies and Procedures*, London: Macmillan Press.

Price level determination

Price level determination refers to the assessment of the absolute price that customers will have to pay for a product in 'normal' circumstances (i.e. apart from specials or temporary offers). The major techniques for price level determination are discussed below.

In *optimization* and *simulation* methods, prices are set with the aid of models made up of demand and cost functions and, if relevant, competitive reaction functions. While optimization methods derive an 'optimal' price by means of mathematical techniques (see e.g. Feichtinger, Luhmer and Sorger, 1988; Bultez *et al.*, 1995), simulation techniques simulate and compare different pricing scenarios and select the scenario that generates the 'best' results (e.g. simulation on the basis of conjoint models: cf. Goldberg *et al.*, 1984; Kohli and Mahajan, 1991).

When the information needed to apply optimization and simulation methods is unavailable or too costly, simple rules of thumb can be used. These rules, however, are based on partial information – most of them are cost-based – and therefore often yield far from optimal results. In *mark-up pricing*, the company determines unit price by applying a pre-specified 'mark-up' (usually in terms of percentage) to unit cost. In the case of *target return pricing*, the company calculates the premium to be charged over unit cost to realize a desired return on investment (ROI) (see Levy and Weitz, 1995; Kotler, 1997). *Going-rate pricing* bases prices largely on competitors' price levels, in order to maintain the competitive (price) position. In *perceived value pricing*, the basic idea is to set price in such a way that the ratio of perceived value to price for the company's product equals that of competitors (see e.g. Kijewski and Yoon, 1990; Kortge and Okonkwo, 1993).

The previous techniques are useful if prices are set unilaterally by the company. In some (especially industrial) markets, though, prices are the result of an interactive process between buyer(s) and seller(s). In price negotiation, sellers and buyers make a number of proposals and counterproposals before a price is agreed upon (Reeder *et al.*, 1991). In competitive bidding, sellers submit bids, specifying the characteristics and price of the offer, to a potential buyer (e.g. a government agency). After a specified deadline, the latter then selects the most appealing bid (Nagle and Holden, 1995). **KCa, BF, EG**

References

Bultez, A., Gijsbrechts, E. and Naert. P. (1995) 'A theormen on the optimal margin mix', *Zeitschrift für Betriebswirtschaftswissenschaft*, 4:151–173.

Feichtinger, G., Luhmer, A. and Sorger, G. (1988) 'Optimal price and advertising policy for a convenience goods retailer', *Marketing Science*, 7(2):187–201.

Goldberg, S.M., Green, P.E. and Wind, Y. (1984) 'Conjoint analysis of price premiums for hotel amenities', *Journal of Business*, 57(1) part 2 :s111–s132.

Hanna, N. and Dodge, H.R. (1997) *Pricing: Policies and Procedures*, London: Macmillan Press.

Kijewski, V. and Yoon. E. (1990) 'Market based pricing: beyond price performance curves', *Industrial Marketing Management*, 19:11–19.

Kohli, R. and Mahajan, V. (1991) 'A reservation price model for optimal pricing of multi-attribute products in conjoint analysis', *Journal of Marketing Research*, 28(August): 347–454.

Kortge, G.D. and Okonkwo, P.A. (1993) 'Perceived value approach to pricing', *Industrial Marketing Management*, 22:133–140.

Kotler, P. (1997) *Marketing Management: Analysis, Planning, Implementation and Control*, 9th edn, London: Prentice Hall.

Levy, M. and Weitz, B. (1995) *Retailing Management*, Chicago: Irwin.

Lilien, G. L. and Rangaswamy, A. (1998) *Marketing Engineering: Computer-Assisted Marketing Analysis and Planning*, Reading, MA: Addison-Wesley.

Nagle, T.T. and Holden, R.K. (1995*) The Strategy and Tactics of Pricing: A Guide to Profitable Decision Making*, Englewood Cliffs, NJ: Prentice Hall.

Reeder, R.R., Brierty, E.G. and Reeder. B.H. (1991) *Industrial Marketing*, Englewood Cliffs, NJ: Prentice Hall.

Price perceptions

Following traditional microeconomics, consumers correctly register prices and use them as input for purely rational purchase decisions. Yet a myriad of studies on price perceptions undermine these assumptions.

First, many consumers have low awareness of products' absolute price levels. This may be due to the complexity of price information and the limited price variation in specific product categories. Other factors explaining this limited price knowledge are consumers' time pressure and/or low involvement with the product category, the inference of prices from non-price cues (e.g. product's appearance) or from the store's overall (price) image (see Dickson and Sawyer, 1990; Grewal and Baker, 1994;

Berné *et al.*, 1999) and the fact that prices are often encoded in a relative way ('cheaper' or 'more expensive' than other products in the same category).

Second, when evaluating prices consumers often resort to simplified decision rules and undergo several psychological processes. For one, consumers may evaluate a price by determining its relative position vis-à-vis other prices in the market they are aware of at that moment (their 'evoked range of prices') (see e.g. Janiszewski and Lichtenstein, 1999). Alternatively, consumers are thought to consider only the products with a price that lies within their 'range of acceptable prices' (see e.g. Petroshius and Monroe, 1987). The upper limit of the range represents the maximum amount consumers are willing to spend, while the lower limit stems from the required minimum quality. Consumers then evaluate the accepted prices by comparing them with a 'reference price' derived from, for example, competitive prices, advertised 'regular' prices, past prices and price expectations. Prices exceeding the reference price are less likely to lead to a purchase, and vice versa. However, when actual prices considerably deviate from the reference price and lie outside the 'latitude of acceptance' (see e.g. Kalyanaram and Little, 1994) they induce an adjustment of the reference price itself. Another psychological phenomenon involved in the price evaluation process relates to 'mental accounting' (Thaler, 1985), which implies, among other things, that consumers perceive a loss (e.g. a price increase of £1) as larger than a gain of equal value (e.g. price discount of £1) (see also Heath *et al.*, 1995). **KCa, BF, EG**

References

Berné, C., Múgica, J.M., Pedraja, M. and Rivera, P. (1999) 'The use of consumer's price information search behaviour for pricing differentiation in retailing', *The International Review of Retail, Distribution and Consumer Research*, 9(2):127–146.

Blattberg, R.C. and Neslin, S.A. (1990) *Sales Promotion: Concepts, Methods, and Strategies*, Englewood Cliffs, NJ: Prentice Hall.

Dickson, P. and Sawyer, A.G. (1990) 'The price knowledge and search of supermarket shoppers', *Journal of Marketing*, 54(July): 42–53.

Grewal, D. and J. Baker (1994) 'Do retail store environmental factors affect consumers' price acceptability? An empirical examination', *International Journal of Research in Marketing*, 11(2):107–115.

Heath, T.B., Chatterjee, S. and France, K.S. (1995) 'Mental accounting and changes in price: the frame dependence of reference dependence', *Journal of Consumer Research*, 22(June): 90–97.

Janiszewski, C. and Lichtenstein, D.R. (1999) 'A range theory account of price perception', *Journal of Consumer Research*, 25(March): 353–368.

Kalyanaram, G. and Little, J.D.C. (1994), 'An empirical analysis of latitude of price acceptance in consumer package goods', *Journal of Consumer Research*, 21(December): 408–418.

Petroshius, S.M. and Monroe, K.B. (1987) 'Effect of product-line pricing characteristics on product evaluations', *Journal of Consumer Research*, 13(March): 511–519.

Thaler, R. (1985) 'Mental accounting and consumer choice', *Marketing Science*, 4 (3):199–214.

Zeithaml, V. (1988) 'Consumer perceptions of price, quality and value: a means-end model and synthesis of evidence', *Journal of Marketing*, 52(July): 2–22.

Price sensitivity and price elasticity

Price sensitivity, or the impact of price on demand and sales volume, constitutes a core element for pricing. Typically, the price of a product acts as a 'constraint' that prevents consumers from spending their income elsewhere. A price increase, or a price exceeding an economical or psychological threshold, induces consumers not to buy any more or to purchase in smaller quantities. At the market level, this leads to a 'downward sloping demand curve': market demand (total quantity sold in marketplace) declines as the price is set at a higher level.

Price elasticity is a typical measure of price sensitivity. It is defined as the relative change in demand resulting from a relative change in price. For instance: an elasticity of –2 implies that a price increase of 1 per cent (say: from 10 to 10.1 euro) would trigger a decrease in quantity sold of 2 per cent (say: from 1000 to 980 units). Price elasticities vary strongly between markets and product categories. In a meta-analysis of consumer markets, Tellis found elasticities to range between approximately –10 and +2.5, with an average value of –1.76 (Tellis, 1988). Consumer price sensitivities depend on product characteristics such as brand uniqueness, price complexity, whether price is used as a quality cue, whether payment is shared or the product is used in combination with other items, product importance in the total budget, switching costs, storability and availability of substitutes (Nagle and Holden, 1995). In industrial settings, buyers' willingness to pay for a product primarily depends on the extent to which it allows them to serve their own customers cheaper, faster or better.

Even for a given product and within a given market, price sensitivities may vary strongly. Instead of setting its prices based on aggregate indicators of price sensitivity at the market level, a company may find it profitable to account for differences in price response across customers and adopt a price discrimination approach, tailoring its pricing strategies to distinct market segments. **KCa, BF, EG**

References

Dolan, R. J. and Simon, H. (1996) *Power Pricing: How Managing Price Transforms the Bottom Line*, New York: The Free Press.

Nagle, T.T. and Holden, R.K. (1995*) The Strategy and Tactics of Pricing: A Guide to Profitable Decision Making*, Englewood Cliffs, NJ: Prentice Hall.

Tellis, G. J. (1988) 'The price elasticity of selective demand: a meta analysis of econometric models of sale', *Journal of Marketing Research*, 25(November): 331–341.

Price signalling

In price signalling, a seller uses the price of a product to convey additional information to non-knowledgeable consumers. Price signalling has typically been used to reveal information about product quality. Since price and quality are often related, consumers may use price as a quality indicator. This strategy might even work if there is no objective link between price and quality for any firm, e.g. if none of the suppliers is 'honest' about product quality. This is true in markets with extreme information asymmetry between the supplier (manufacturer or retailer) and all customers, and where prices are driven up by advertising claims concentrating on certain (irrelevant) quality aspects. Signalling high quality is especially effective when (i) consumers are able to get information on price more easily than information about quality, (ii) buyers want the high quality enough to risk buying the high priced product even without certainty of high quality and (iii) there are a large number of uninformed consumers. Skin moisturizers are an illustration of a market satisfying those conditions (see Tellis, 1986; Alpert *et al.*, 1993; Parker, 1995).

Alternatively, in a retailer context, price signalling can be used to inform consumers about the prices of other products in the store. In this case, consumers derive a global store price image from the few advertised prices. This type of price signalling will be most effective if it is hard for consumers (i) to obtain a complete picture of price levels in a store (e.g. because of store size or infrequent visits) and (ii) to compare prices across stores (e.g. when competing stores are in distant locations) (see Simester, 1995). **KCa, BF, EG**

References

Alpert *et al.* (1993) 'Price signalling: does it ever work?', *Journal of Consumer Marketing*, (10)4:4–14.

Parker, P. M. (1995) '"Sweet lemons": illusory quality, self-deceivers, advertising and price', *Journal of Marketing Research*, 32(August): 291–307.

Simester, D. (1995) 'Signalling price image using advertised prices', *Marketing Science*, 14(2):166–188.

Tellis, G.J. (1986) 'Beyond the many faces of price: an integration of pricing strategies', *Journal of Marketing*, 50(October): 46–60.

Pricing

Traditionally, the price of a product or service is defined as 'the number of monetary units a customer has to pay to receive one unit of that product or service' (Simon, 1989).

Setting prices is one of the most important marketing mix decisions, since price is the only marketing mix variable that generates revenues, and tends to have an immediate effect on buyer behaviour. Yet, in practice, pricing decisions are often made arbitrarily or merely on the basis of cost-related criteria, with no or limited pricing research to guide them. As a result, prices often fail to capture the value realized by other marketing mix instruments (Rao, 1984; Nagle and Holden, 1995). The figure below provides a schematic overview of the steps involved in effective pricing.

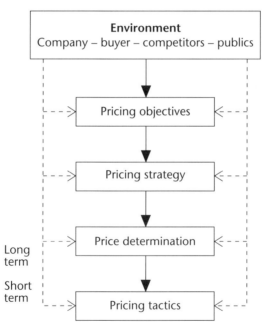

Figure: **The different stages in pricing**

Obviously, thorough analysis of the environment is a prerequisite for proper strategy selection. Company objectives and costs, buyer behaviour, characteristics of competitors and of other publics may strongly affect relevant pricing options. Environmental analysis is a building block for the specification of pricing objectives, which must – on top of being consistent with the environment – be attainable and operational. The next step is to specify which pricing strategies will result in obtaining the objectives and to select the alternative most appropriate for the pricing environment. To implement the selected strategy, a price structure and price level(s) have to be determined. These price structure and level(s) need to be supplemented with short term oriented, tactical price manipulations.

It goes without saying that the process just described is not a purely chronological one. As the dotted lines in the figure indicate, environmental characteristics influence each subsequent step. Also, feedback loops within one decision period and over time are bound to occur. **KCa, BF, EG**

References

Monroe, K. (1990) *Pricing: Making Profitable Decisions*, New York: McGraw-Hill International Editions.

Nagle, T.T. and Holden, R.K. (1995) *The Strategy and Tactics of Pricing: A Guide to Profitable Decision Making*, Englewood Cliffs, NJ: Prentice Hall.

Rao, V.R. (1984) 'Pricing research in marketing: the state of the art', *Journal of Business*, 57(1)part 2: S39–S60.

Simon, H. (1989) *Price Management*, Amsterdam: Elsevier.

Pricing and legal issues

When setting prices, managers should ensure that their pricing policy fits the legal framework they operate in.

Several national or international regulations mainly aim to preserve competition. *Predatory pricing*, where a price is set at a low, unprofitable level to drive out competition, is prohibited by the Sherman and Robinson-Patman Act in the US (Nagle and Holden, 1995). In an international setting, the same restrictions hold for dumping, i.e. selling a product at a much lower price, often below average cost, in the foreign market (see e.g. Keegan, 1995). Price fixing arrangements among competitors or channel members (see Sheffet and Scammon, 1985; Fabricant, 1990) may reduce competition and raise consumer prices, and are therefore prohibited by the Sherman Act in the US and by Article 85 of the Treaty of Rome in the EU. Price discrimination is illegal under the Robinson-Patman Act if it has the effect of reducing competition, except when prices reflect differences in costs or need to adjust to the low prices of local competitors. Tie-in sales, where customers are allowed to buy a product only if purchased in combination with another product, are also subject to the Robinson-Patman Act. In the EU similar regulations are valid (Treaty of Rome).

Other regulations primarily focus on the protection of consumer interests. Unit pricing laws, for example, compel retailers to indicate clearly price levels on product units or by means of shop-window lists. Also, consumers are protected against deceptive pricing, the general rule being that price information should not misrepresent the true nature of the firm's prices (Kaufman *et al.*, 1994; Hanna and Dodge, 1997). Further, governments can restrict the range of legally accepted price levels. This can be done in a direct fashion, by imposing price ceilings or price floors, or in an indirect way, by means of VAT rates or excises (see also Levy and Weitz, 1995; Nagle and Holden, 1995).

Finally, in international markets, protectionist regulations such as import duties may affect prices in an indirect way. Usually they result in price differences between domestic and export markets. Since import duties could induce a company to charge lower transfer prices to its foreign subsidiaries, admissible transfer price levels are further restricted by government regulations aimed at preventing tax evasion. **KCa, BF, EG**

References

Fabricant, R. A. (1990) 'Special retail services and resale price maintenance', *Journal of Retailing*, 66(1):101–18.

Hanna, N. and Dodge, H.R. (1997) *Pricing: Policies and Procedures*, London: Macmillan Press.

Kaufman, P.J., Smith, N.C. and Ortmeyer, G.K. (1994) 'Deception in retailer high-low pricing', *Journal of Retailing*, 70(2):115–138.

Keegan, W. (1995) *Global Marketing Management*, Englewood Cliffs, NJ: Prentice Hall.

Levy, M. and Weitz, B. (1995) *Retailing Management*, Chicago: Irwin.

Monroe, K. (1990) *Pricing: Making Profitable Decisions*, New York: McGraw-Hill International Editions.

Nagle, T.T. and R.K. Holden (1995) *The Strategy and Tactics of Pricing: A Guide to Profitable Decision Making*, Englewood Cliffs, NJ: Prentice Hall.

Sheffet, M.J. and Scammon, D.L. (1985) 'Resale price maintenance: is it safe to suggest retail prices?', *Journal of Marketing*, 49(Fall): 82–91.

Pricing, creative approaches to

On the face of it pricing would seem an area where creative thinking is least applicable. However, special price deals and the use of the price mechanism as a means of promoting the sales of products lend support to the argument that it is an area where there must be scope for creativity. It is perhaps where price changes are contemplated that there is most scope for creative thinking. Sooner or later organizations have to adjust their prices. When it is in a downward direction this usually pleases the customer and the firm does not need to disguise its actions. However, when an upward adjustment in price is required consumer resistance is often felt quite strongly.

Organizations can often disguise price rises, permanent or temporary, by making it appear that no price rise is in fact occurring. This can be achieved in any one of the following ways.

- The discount structure can be altered so that the total profit to the company is increased but the list price to customers remains the same.
- The minimum order size is increased so that small orders are eliminated and overall costs thereby reduced.
- Delivery and special services are charged for.
- Invoices are raised for repairs on purchased equipment.
- Charges are made for engineering, installation and supervision.
- Customers are made to pay for overtime required to get out rush orders.
- Interest is collected on overdue accounts.
- Lower margin models in the product line are eliminated and more profitable ones sold in their place.
- Escalator clauses are built into bids for contracts.
- The physical characteristics of the product are changed – e.g. it is made smaller.

Pricing then has a psychological dimension to it and wherever this exhibits itself there is scope for creativity. **TP**

Reference

Proctor, T. (2000) *Strategic Marketing*, London: Routledge, pp. 223–224.

Pricing objectives

Pricing objectives set the stage for all subsequent pricing decisions and constitute a benchmark for evaluating them. They should, in line with general company objectives, exploit the possibilities of the marketplace. Pricing objectives can be classified in a number of ways (see Tellis, 1986; Levy and Weitz, 1995; Ansari *et al.*, 1996). A typical classification distinguishes between objectives that are (i) profit oriented, (ii) volume oriented, (iii) cost oriented and (iv) competition oriented. The examples in the table below demonstrate that pricing objectives may coincide with overall company objectives (e.g. profit maximization), or be directly related to pricing decisions (e.g. price leadership).

Table: **The different types of pricing objectives**

Profit oriented	Volume oriented	Cost oriented	Competition oriented
Maximize profit Reach target return on investment Maximize market skimming	Sales growth or maintenance Market share growth or maintenance Market penetration Increase usage, participation or store traffic	Pursue economies of scale Exploit experience effects Recover investment costs	Price leadership Entry deterrence Market stabilization Meet competition

While profit maximization is the most often cited pricing objective, most companies do not pursue a single objective. A series of objectives can be specified with weights or priorities attached to them. In other cases, one objective is to be 'optimized' subject to a minimum performance on other dimensions (e.g. maximize market share without incurring a loss). In both cases, subobjectives should be mutually consistent.

Formulating pricing objectives further requires the specification of deadlines and units to which the objectives apply. The period in which one wants to obtain results crucially affects further price decisions: different strategies may be needed to maximize short term profit versus long term profit. Concerning the unit of analysis, several options could be contrasted. Within the confines of the company, results could be pursued for single products versus product lines. From a channel perspective, decisions could stimulate profit for the channel as a whole, or concentrate on one level. In international settings, local or global profits may be strived for. **KCa, BF, EG**

References

Ansari, A., Siddarth, S. and Weinberg. C.B. (1996), 'Pricing a bundle of products or services: the case of nonprofits', *Journal of Marketing Research*, 33(February): 86–93.

Hanna, N. and Dodge, H.R. (1997) *Pricing: Policies and Procedures*, London: Macmillan Press.

Levy, M. and Weitz, B. (1995) *Retailing Management*, Chicago: Irwin.

Nagle, T.T. and Holden, R.K.(1995) *The Strategy and Tactics of Pricing: A Guide to Profitable Decision Making*, Englewood Cliffs, NJ: Prentice Hall.

Tellis, G.J. (1986), 'Beyond the many faces of price: an integration of pricing strategies', *Journal of Marketing*, 50(October): 46–60.

Pricing research

Knowledge of customer reactions to prices is a crucial input for sound pricing. To assess customers' price response, managers can choose between several methods. *Surveys* constitute an important way of obtaining information on customer price perceptions, preferences and purchase intentions. Various approaches have been developed to obtain such information, examples being the 'Price Sensitivity Meter' approach, where respondents are shown a range of price levels for a product and must indicate which ones are too expensive, expensive, cheap and too cheap, and the 'Buy Scale' where they express whether they intend to buy a product at a preselected price (see Nagle and Holden, 1995). A drawback of these procedures is that they only reveal what consumers claim they would do in hypothetical purchase situations.

Actual purchase behaviour in response to price changes can be quantified using *econometric analysis of historical data* on sales and prices, at the market level, the store level, or the level of the individual. Major limitations of this approach, however, are that it cannot be used for new products (for which no historical data are available), and that it may be difficult to isolate the price effect form other influences on consumer behaviour.

Controlled experiments, either in the form of simulated purchase surveys and trade off analysis, in-store experiments, or laboratory purchase experiments, help overcome these difficulties but are typically costly and time consuming. Selecting the most appropriate technique for price sensitivity measures is therefore not an easy issue. When selecting a technique and drawing inferences for pricing decisions, managers should pay attention to key issues such as price dynamics, the impact of the choice context, interactions between price effects and those of other marketing variables, the impact of psychological factors and customer heterogeneity in price response. **KCa, BF, EG**

References

Lilien, G. L. and Rangaswamy. A. (1998) *Marketing Engineering: Computer-Assisted Marketing Analysis and Planning*, Reading, MA: Addison-Wesley.

Monroe, K. (1990) *Pricing: Making Profitable Decisions*, New York: McGraw-Hill International Editions.

Nagle, T.T. and Holden, R.K. (1995) *The Strategy and Tactics of Pricing: A Guide to Profitable Decision Making*, Englewood Cliffs, NJ: Prentice Hall.

Pricing strategies

A pricing strategy generally describes the course of prices within a planning period and across the target market(s), given the company's objectives and the characteristics of the environment. The most important strategies are highlighted below (see Tellis, 1986; Hanna and Dodge, 1997).

Differential pricing strategies charge different prices across consumer segments or over time. In *peak-load pricing*, lower prices are charged in off-season periods. *Price skimming* involves the introduction of new products at a high price level directed at the price-insensitive consumer segment, followed by a gradual price decrease to capture the (more) price-sensitive consumer groups. In *random discounting* temporary price cuts are offered at random points in time. When consumer segments can be easily identified, more *direct price discrimination* schemes can be used, if legal (e.g. charging lower prices for public transportation to senior citizens).

Other strategies crucially rely on competitive differences. In *price signalling*, a company uses 'price' as a cue for unrevealed (product, store) attributes (e.g. price as quality indicator). *Geographic pricing* relates to the way a company deals with transportation costs, when the target market covers geographically distant regions with different competitive situations. *Experience curve pricing* as well as *penetration pricing* refer to the introduction of new products at low prices to pre-empt competition.

A number of strategies are relevant for companies offering a line of products. *Premium pricing* implies that a premium is charged for superior versions in a line of substitute products, but that lower quality versions are priced below cost. In *image pricing*, an identical version of the original product is marketed with another name and a higher price, in order to signal quality. In *price bundling*, a company sells two or more products in a single package at a special price. *Complementary pricing* is adopted when some items in a line of complementary products are sold at a low price, while a premium is charged on other items. **KCa, BF, EG**

References

Hanna, N. and Dodge, H.R. (1997) *Pricing: Policies and Procedures*, London: Macmillan Press.

Levy, M. and Weitz, B. (1995) *Retailing Management*, Chicago: Irwin.

Nagle, T.T. and Holden, R.K. (1995) *The Strategy and Tactics of Pricing: A Guide to Profitable Decision Making*, Englewood Cliffs, NJ: Prentice Hall.

Tellis, G.J. (1986), 'Beyond the many faces of price: an integration of pricing strategies', *Journal of Marketing*, 50(October): 46–60.

Pricing tactics

Pricing tactics refer to short term price decisions to realize short term objectives or respond to short term changes in the environment (Morris and Calantone, 1990; van Waterschoot and Van Den Bulte, 1992). Sudden changes in consumer demand (taste, weather), trading conditions and operational inefficiencies, can incite a company to offer temporary discounts. An example is a price discount aimed at liquidating excess stocks. In their purest form, tactical price changes – often referred to as 'price promotions' – involve offering straight price reductions on the product's regular price. Besides direct price cuts, more indirect tactical price changes can be adopted, such as coupons, or 'banded packs' (e.g. two packs offered for the price of one).

Pricing tactics can be used by, or addressed at, different parties in the marketing channel. In the case of 'consumer promotions' and 'retailer promotions', the price cut is offered by the manufacturer and retailer, respectively, to consumers. Temporary price reductions offered by manufacturers to retailers fall under the heading of 'trade promotions'.

Pricing tactics, which are often of a 'correctional' nature, supplement the company's pricing strategies. Pricing strategies set the basic price structure in accordance with long term objectives and environmental conditions. Pricing tactics involve decisions such as selection of the items on which price cuts will be offered, the depth of the discount (e.g. should there be a 10 per cent or a 15 per cent reduction off the regular price?), the duration of the offer and the way it will be communicated to the target group (e.g. will it be announced in a flier or receive specific display support in retail outlets?). These decisions have a major impact on the effect of the temporary price change.

The effects triggered by pricing tactics are multiple. Temporary price cuts typically lead to a substantial immediate sales increase for the promoted item and can also positively (or negatively) impact on the sales of complementary (substitute) items. In addition, their impact may extend beyond the promotion period, because of phenomena such as purchase acceleration or stockpiling or changes in the consumer's attitude towards the brand. To appreciate fully the impact of tactical price changes, it is necessary to account for both their short and long term implications on sales and profits. **KCa, BF, EG**

References

Blattberg, R.C. and Neslin. S.A. (1990) *Sales Promotion: Concepts, Methods, and Strategies*, Englewood Cliffs, NJ: Prentice Hall.

Gijsbrechts, E. (1993) 'Prices and pricing research in consumer marketing: some recent developments', *International Journal of Research in Marketing*, 10(2):115–151.

Lilien, G.L. and Rangaswamy, A. (1998) *Marketing Engineering: Computer-Assisted Marketing Analysis and Planning*, Reading, MA: Addison-Wesley.

Morris, M.H. and Calantone, R.J. (1990) 'Four components of effective pricing', *Industrial Marketing Management*, 19:321–329.

Nagle, T.T. and Holden, R.K. (1995) *The Strategy and Tactics of Pricing: A Guide to Profitable Decision Making*, Englewood Cliffs, NJ: Prentice Hall.

Van Waterschoot, W. and Van Den Bulte, C. (1992) 'The 4 P classification of the marketing mix revisited', *Journal of Marketing*, 56(October): 83–93.

Primary research

Primary research essentially involves primary data collection, where the researcher goes out in the field and collects relevant data by means of questionnaire surveys, interviews or observations. The main purpose of primary research is to collect first-hand data that will answer the research objectives. Using primary sources, the researchers can collect precisely the information that they want. They can also specify the operational definitions used in collecting the data and can eliminate or monitor and record extraneous influences on the data as they are being collected. Some of the most common types of primary data collected through primary research are i) *attitudinal data,* which reflects respondents' feelings and convictions towards a subject, ii) *awareness data*, which assesses level of respondents' knowledge of some phenomenon under study, iii) *motivational data,* which helps explore the underlying reasons as to why respondents behave in the way they do, iv) *behavioural data,* which assesses respondents past behaviours that can be used to predict future actions, and v) *classification data,* which are essentially demographic information including classification information such as age, sex, race or education. **RM-R**

Reference
Cooper, D.R. and Schindler, P.S. (1998) *Business Research Methods*, Boston: McGraw-Hill International Editions.

Problem definition

Defining a problem is part of the research process whereby the researcher assesses whether a gap exists between the actual and the desired state. Based on the broad outline of the research, issues that are of interest to the researcher are further defined so that they become very clear. A problem definition is, therefore, a precise statement outlining the issues that are going to be investigated by the researcher. Without a concise problem definition, the researcher may not be able to direct all his or her efforts towards solving the problem at hand. However, it should be noted that a problem does not necessarily mean that something is seriously wrong with a current situation, but it *does* indicate that there is an interest in an issue in which identifying the right answers might help to improve the situation. Therefore, a problem definition could identify existing problems or it could be a quest by the researcher to achieve better situations.

Defining the problem at the early part of the research process ensures that the researcher is clear about the issue at hand. This helps in developing a precise research framework, which would allow the researcher to formulate relationships between specific variables that are to be investigated. Problem definition is sometimes called 'problem statements' and these form an important part of a research. These are usually precise and succinct statements, which guide the researcher towards developing the appropriate research methods for investigation. Indeed the problem definition serves as a basis for the researcher to proceed deeper into the research process. **RM-R**

Reference
Sekaran, U. (1996) *Research Methods for Business*, 2rd edn, New York: John Wiley & Sons.

Problem identification and definition

Techniques for divergent generation of ideas tend to adopt the following approach:

- fact-finding
- problem/opportunity finding (or redefinition)
- idea finding
- solution finding or evaluation
- acceptance finding (putting solutions into practice).

Executives can identify problems in one of a number of ways, which include: comparison of current experiences with past experiences; comparison of current experiences with current objectives or plans; comparison of performance with models of desirable outcomes; and comparison of performance with that of other organizations or sub-units. Redefining a problem can unlock a new viewpoint leading to many creative solutions. Since different executives may have different perspectives of the problem there is need to consult everyone concerned before the problem is finally fully specified.

A structured approach involves generating relevant data to improve understanding of the problem. This in turn allows one to consider different problem perspectives. Techniques involve asking such questions as: 'who?' 'what?' 'where?' 'when?'. Much information can be obtained from scanning documents and reports and attending meetings. In addition, many of those involved in the problem solving will have this information in their heads. Producing a checklist for use during pre-problem solving acts as a general guide for prefacing the use of some other analytic method. Defining the limits or boundaries and dimensions of a problem are important.

One useful approach to problem definition is a technique called 'laddering'. Perspectives can come in varying degrees of complexity. One can think of them as occupying different heights on a ladder. It is often useful to consider where you are on a ladder and whether it would be worthwhile going up to higher levels of generality or down to levels of specifics. The ladder can have many rungs but we can think of it as having a top portion, a middle portion and a bottom portion. At the top we find the *strategic* or *conceptual level,* in the middle we find the *operational* and *managerial level*, while at the bottom we find the *immediate* and *fix it quick level.*

Asking the question 'why?' moves one up the ladder while asking the question 'how?' helps one to move down the ladder. **TP**

Reference

Proctor, T. (1999) *Creative Problem Solving for Managers*, London: Routledge.

Problem solving

The process of problem solving involves a systematic and organized effort to investigate a specific problem that needs a solution. A series of well-planned and carefully executed activities are normally conducted to solve specific identified problems. This is essentially the process of conducting research. When the problem identification process has uncovered a problem or opportunity, problem-solving research is undertaken to determine the solution to the problem: it tries to find the most viable ways of solving specific marketing problems.

In conducting problem solving research, the researcher is required to carry out a series of carefully planned and executed activities that will enable them to know how marketing problems can be solved or at least minimized. Problem solving research includes pricing, promotion, distribution and product research. Each of these requires the researcher to carry out the research process systematically, diligently, objectively and logically. At the end of the research process, it is hoped that new facts or information will be discovered to help solve the problem. **RM-R**

Reference

McDaniel, C. and Gates, R. (1999) *Contemporary Marketing Research*, 4th edn, St Paul: South-Western College Publishing.
Sekaran, U. (1996) *Research Methods for Business*, 2nd edn, New York: John Wiley & Sons.

Problem solving (simple and complex)

The process of problem solving in consumer buying behaviour typically refers to the pre-purchase process when consumers are deciding on the types of products and brands to purchase and other buying related matters. Such buying decisions are influenced by several important factors. The type of decisions and the complexity of the decision process will determine the extent of problem solving required. Some decisions are simple to make whilst others are complex. Basically, the level of involvement is an important determinant of the type of decision process a consumer will adopt. High involvement decisions imply that the consumer will put much effort into the decision and consider this to be important. In such cases, extensive comparison of stores, brands and prices will be carried out. This is typical of complex problem solving, where the mode of decision making requires much effort and can take a long time.

On the other hand, with low involvement decisions, much less effort will be expended prior to purchase. Generally, in such cases, consumers are less attentive to marketing stimuli and less effort will be given to the overall decision-making process. Impulse purchase is quite common in this situation. Low involvement decisions are typical of simple problem solving. A limited amount of effort is given to deciding on the purchase and buying decisions can be made quickly. Consumers who are already familiar with a product or service or who have routinely purchased the same product or service in the past are very likely to undertake a simple problem solving approach in deciding on their purchase.

It is important for marketers to understand both simple and complex problem solving approaches undertaken by consumers because this will help them to plan appropriate marketing strategies to meet the needs of both types of decision-making process. In a complex problem-solving situation marketers may develop marketing stimuli that can help consumers to assess information about the product or brand and make comparisons. However, in a simple problem-solving situation, marketers may want to develop marketing stimuli that can perhaps induce consumers towards impulse purchase or trial purchases. **RM-R**

References
Solomon, M.R. (1996) *Consumer Behavior*, Englewood Cliffs, NJ: Prentice Hall Inc.
Wilkie, W.L. (1994) *Consumer Behavior*, 3rd edn, New York: John Wiley & Sons.

Product class

Product class relates to both industrial and consumer goods, and this entry describes categories of goods and services.

'Industrial goods' include the following.

- *Installations* or the plant and machinery required for the manufacturing process, usually involving complex decision-making criteria in their specification and purchase.
- *Accessories*, which are also capital goods, but are less critical and depreciate over a shorter period, for example items such as computing equipment and materials handling equipment.
- *Raw materials* are a major part of purchasing activity and this describes material in its raw state and upon which no secondary work has been done, examples being steel plate, wool and timber.
- *Components* are similar to raw materials, and this classification is sometimes called 'part-manufactured goods'. In this case some work has been done already, and the components are used in the production process that goes to make up the finished product. Examples are valves and flanges.
- *Materials* are items required in the production process, but are not a component part of finished products. This includes items such as packaging, drill bits, fuel and cutting oil.

- *Supplies* includes items such as cleaning and maintenance materials and stationery that are not used in the production process. Purchasing tends to be more routine and it is often simply a matter of reordering from a regular supplier, with price being the major purchasing criterion.

'Consumer goods' include the following.

- 'Convenience goods' (see 'Convenience goods').
- 'Shopping goods' (see 'Fast moving consumer goods').
- 'Speciality goods' or major purchases made at infrequent intervals where much investigation in the marketplace is undertaken by consumers prior to purchase.
- 'Unsought goods' (see 'Unsought products'). **GL**

References
Kotler, P. (1994) *Marketing Management, Analysis, Planning, Implementation and Control*, 8th edn, New Jersey: Prentice Hall, p. 434.

Product classes and marketing mixes

The marketing mix (see 'Marketing mix') relates to how the variables under the control of marketing can be manipulated in terms of targeting predetermined groups of customers. Product classes (see 'Product class') relate to both industrial goods and consumer products. The two interrelate through manipulating the marketing mix to suit the type of product class being marketed. In the case of fast moving consumer products there will often be an emphasis upon promotional techniques such as advertising and sales promotion. In business to business marketing there will tend to be more of an emphasis upon selling. It is the task and skill of marketing management to determine how this marketing mix is manipulated to best suit specific circumstances. **GL**

Reference
Kotler, P. (1994) *Marketing Management, Analysis, Planning, Implementation and Control*, 8th edn, New Jersey: Prentice Hall, p. 434.

Product defined

The product, which includes services, is sometime defined as a 'bundle of satisfactions', which includes the physical product or service (or the 'core product') and intangible factors such as the service offering, which is called the 'augmented product' or the 'extended product'.

At a tangible level, the concept of what physically comprises a product is what most customers think of when considering which product to purchase. Marketers think principally of the benefits of the core product and this is emphasized in terms of demonstrating its benefits to customers. However, this appeal can also extend to features such as packaging or servicing arrangements that supplement the core product.

The augmented product includes those benefits over and above those related to the tangible product. This includes factors such as the level of service that will be provided, and this is particularly important for products that need to be serviced quickly (e.g. cars). Indeed, it is often the availability and levels of after-sales service that is a principal factor in purchasing decisions. Theodore Levitt first documented this augmented product concept when he suggested that marketers should consider 'what market they were really in'. Rather than take a narrow, product orientated view, he suggested that they should expand this to include factors such as the provision of customer finance, availability when required and attractive packaging as being a better basis for competing in the marketplace. He also contended that marketers should look beyond the simple notion of what the product or service conveyed and he illustrated the example of railways, which he extended from the simple notion of rail transport to the wider notion of movement of goods and people. **GL**

References

Levitt, T. (1960) 'Marketing myopia', *Harvard Business Review*, 18(1).

Levitt, T. (1981) 'Marketing intangible products and product intangibles', *Harvard Business Review*, May/June: 94–102.

Product differentiation

This is an attempt by a manufacturer to distinguish its products from that of competitors in a market where all product or service offerings are similar. In this situation an undifferentiated marketing strategy pertains within the marketplace. Product differentiation occurs when it is perceived that one product offering is distinguished from other similar product offerings.

Successful product differentiation occurs when customers perceive a particular product to be better or superior to other similar offerings. Differentiation is, therefore, a perception that is created in the mind of the customer. This might involve changing the style, packaging, design or colour of the product or through the use of advertising and other types of promotion. For instance, all washing detergents are basically similar. Product differentiation is attempted by detergent manufacturers through the emphasis of criteria such as being more powerful, being softer, attacking ground-in stains and being good at 'deep down' cleaning. **GL**

Reference

Kotler, P. (1994) *Marketing Management, Analysis, Planning, Implementation and Control*, 8th edn, New Jersey: Prentice Hall, pp. 295–302.

Product innovation and adoption process

When an entirely new product is introduced to the marketplace it passes through a number of stages in a manner first proposed by Everett Rogers. This is explained in the following figure.

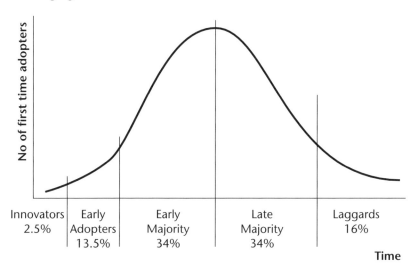

Figure: **Number of first time adopters**

The first category is called 'innovators', representing 2.5 per cent of the population, who eventually adopt the product. They have a low level of perceived risk and probably such as the 'adventure' of being associated with the purchase of something that is innovative.

The next category of 13.5 per cent is 'early adopters', who are adventurous purchasers and who have a low level of perceived risk.

The next two groups comprise 34 per cent each of the market and they are the 'early majority' and the 'late majority'. The former adopt before average adoption and rely principally upon marketing information before making their purchase. The late majority are a more cautious group, but they are still prone to social pressures to adopt the product for the first time.

The final 16 per cent represents 'laggards', who are not really interested in the new product, but eventually adopt when they see the advantages that the innovation offers.

Rogers also proposed an Innovation/Adoption model whereby consumers go through a number of phases before purchasing a new innovative product. It is a hierarchical model that takes the purchaser through the various sequential stages from simple awareness, ultimately to final adoption. The stages in this model are as follows:

Awareness → Interest → Evaluation → Trial → Adoption

Marketers classify innovations into a number of categories.

- *Innovative* products are entirely new to the market.
- *Re-launched* products occur where there are sufficient sales left in a declining market, but where the image is revamped.
- *Replacement* products provide a modified alternative to the existing product in terms of new features or a new design.
- *Imitative* products are copies of successful innovative products. **GL**

Reference
Rogers, E.M. (1983) *Diffusion of Innovations*, 3rd edn, New York: Macmillan.

Product life cycle

The notion of the product life cycle (PLC) asserts that once products are developed and launched they are then subject to a pattern of demand that starts slowly during 'introduction'. This grows quickly during 'growth' and then stabilizes during 'maturity'. This maturity period is sometimes divided into 'maturity' and 'saturation'. Sales have stabilized, but the rise to the peak is termed 'maturity', and 'saturation' is where demand begins to tail off and competition is intense. This phase tends to be the longest phase in the PLC. Demand gradually diminishes during the final stage, during which period the product is normally deleted.

The following figure illustrates a product life cycle curve for a hypothetical product. In reality, the process will never be as 'neat' as this, but the following pattern is a generalization of what normally happens. The notion of the PLC has come in for considerable criticism as a planning tool. It is, however, sometimes taken too literally by product managers because a sales glitch during the 'growth' phase is sometimes interpreted as the onset of 'decline', and the product is deleted prematurely.

The scale break during the 'maturity' and 'saturation' period is meant to signify that this period can take up considerable period compared with the other phases, depending upon the product being considered. In the case of a fashion product, this period might only be for a season, whereas for a new model of car it might well be for five years or more.

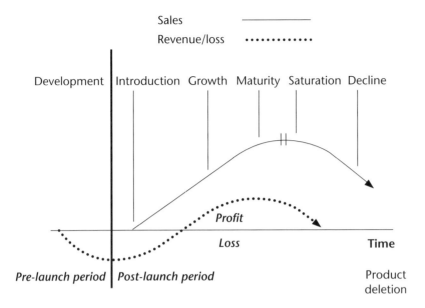

Figure: **Product life cycle curve**

In normal commercial circumstances a decision will be taken to delete the product during the 'decline' phase once profits decline steeply. **GL**

Reference
Lancaster, G. and Reynolds, P. (1998) *Marketing*, Basingstoke: Macmillan, pp. 128–133.

Product life cycle stages, planning for

Using the figure in 'Product life cycle' (above), each of the stages is now described in terms of planning implications.

- *Development* is where no sales are made, but research and development and marketing research costs mount as these are incurred prior to launch. During this phase, critical decisions are made in relation to whether to 'drop' or 'go' (see 'New product development').
- *Introduction* is the launch period and the product or service slowly gains acceptance. It is likely that only 'innovators' will purchase during this period (see 'Product innovation and adaption process') and the launch price will be high as the company may be engaging in a 'skimming' price policy. There are few, if any, competitors and distribution will be 'exclusive' and not widespread. The expense of launching the product might be costly owing to the fact that advertising and sales promotional costs will be high, as consumers have to be informed of the product's existence. It is a stage where many new products fail.
- *Growth* is sometimes termed 'exponential' and it is when sales take off and competitors start to offer similar products. Competitors might have been conducting concurrent research, but may have been slower in bringing such products to market. During this phase, promotional activity changes from the creation of awareness to creating a brand image. Distribution moves from exclusive to selective distribution as more sales outlets begin to stock the product. The first round of skimming will probably take place, which begins to depress profits.
- *Maturity* and *Saturation* are where sales peak and during this period demand tends to reflect replacement and not new demand. Attempts are made to differentiate

products with the addition of features. Towards the saturation phase competition is fierce and the final round of skimming takes place meaning that there is little by way of profit margins. More imitative products will come onto the market, with the principal appeal being low price.

- *Decline* is the final stage, which is epitomized by steadily falling sales and price cutting. This is often a function of a new product or process replacing the old one. Many producers exit from the market, but those who stay in can sometimes make a profit for a time as there is less competition. **GL**

Reference
Lancaster, G. and Reynolds, P. (1998) *Marketing*, Basingstoke: Macmillan, pp. 128–133.

Product life cycle value and use

The product life cycle (PLC) is a theoretical model which describes the stages a product goes through from introduction and early growth, through maturity and finally decline and obsolescence (see 'Product life cycle'). It is thought that most products follow a similar pattern, but the timescale of the PLC varies greatly from one product to another; it is difficult to predict how long the maturity phase will last, for example. Some products, such as computer games, may go through the entire life cycle in a matter of months, others, such as pitta bread, have a life cycle measured in thousands of years. The theory suffers from a number of flaws (Blythe, 1998).

- It assumes that there is no reversion to earlier consumer preferences; in other words, the movement is all one-way. Occasionally, old-fashioned products become popular again because of nostalgia; the PLC does not take account of this.
- The model assumes that no marketing activities take place to revive the product when it is in the decline phase (or that no strategic decision is taken to take the product off the market).
- The model considers only one product, whereas most marketers have to balance the demands of several products.

The product life cycle model is useful to describe what is happening to product sales, but is not much help in predicting what will happen. It is virtually impossible to predict how long the maturity phase will continue, since the PLC is dependent on technological changes, and these might happen at any time. In other words a new product on the market might trigger a rapid decline. **JWDB**

Reference
Blythe, J. (1998) *Essentials of Marketing*, London: Pitman.

Product line

Products that are closely related in terms of possessing similar physical characteristics are classed as 'product lines'. Strategic decisions involve marketers deciding how many models or products should go into a particular line. For instance, a coffee manufacturer can have a number of product lines including instant coffee, ground coffee and coffee bags. The instant coffee line might then contain six individual brands, the ground coffee line five brands and coffee bags two brands. The number of brands in an individual product line is referred to as the 'depth of the product line'. The number of related product lines a manufacturer carries is referred to as the 'width of the product mix' (see also 'Product mix'). **GL**

Reference
Lancaster, G. and Reynolds, P. (1998) *Marketing*, Basingstoke: Macmillan, p. 126.

Product line pricing

Product line pricing can be used by multi-product firms, and involves balancing prices over different products in the assortment. The relevance of product line pricing is mostly due to the existence of demand interdependencies and economies of scope (Tellis, 1986; Dolan and Simon, 1996; Hanna and Dodge, 1997).

In *complementary pricing*, some products in the line (e.g. computer hardware) are sold at a low price, but a 'premium' is charged on complementary products (e.g. software) in the line. Having bought the low-priced product, consumers incur transaction costs to switch to other (competitive) product lines. The presence of these transaction costs allows the company to charge more for the second (complementary) product. A variant of complementary pricing is 'loss-leadership' by retailers.

The adoption of *premium pricing* implies that high quality products in a line (e.g. 'luxury' hotel rooms) are sold at a high price, which compensates for the 'loss' incurred on the low-priced, low quality products (e.g. regular hotel rooms). The appropriateness of this strategy depends on the presence of economies of scale and differences in willingness to pay between consumers.

Firms that apply *image pricing* sell two identical versions of a product (e.g. wine, cosmetics) under different names and at different prices. The expensive version targets consumers who consider price as a quality cue while the cheaper version attracts consumers knowledgeable about the product quality.

In *price bundling*, two or more products (e.g. automobile options) are sold together at a single price (see Guiltinan, 1987; Venkatesh and Mahajan, 1993; Ansari *et al.*, 1996). A bundling strategy can be 'pure' (products are only available as a package) or 'mixed' (products are available as a package or separately). Bundling is typically an appropriate strategy when the bundled components are complements and when consumers have inverse preferences for the respective components. **KCa, BF, EG**

References

Ansari, A., Siddarth, S. and Weinberg, C.B. (1996), 'Pricing a bundle of products or services: the case of nonprofits', *Journal of Marketing Research*, 33(February): 86–93.

Dolan, R. J. and Simon, H. (1996) *Power Pricing: How Managing Price Transforms the Bottom Line*, New York: The Free Press.

Guiltinan, J. P. (1987), 'The price bundling of services: a normative framework', *Journal of Marketing*, 51:74–85.

Hanna, N. and Dodge, H.R. (1997) *Pricing: Policies and Procedures*, London: Macmillan Press.

Nagle, T.T. and Holden, R.K. (1995) *The Strategy and Tactics of Pricing: A Guide to Profitable Decision Making*, Englewood Cliffs, NJ: Prentice Hall.

Tellis, G.J. (1986) 'Beyond the many faces of price: an integration of pricing strategies', *Journal of Marketing*, 50(October): 46–60.

Venkatesh, R. and Mahajan, V. (1993), 'A probabilistic approach to pricing a bundle of products or services', *Journal of Marketing Research*, 30(November): 494–508.

Product managers

Product management is part of a marketing organizational structure whereby marketing management is split into sub-divisions that oversee two individual aspects of the marketing function. This type of organizational structure is particularly appropriate for fast moving consumer goods. One of the functions is 'sales management' This aspect of marketing is responsible for the sales of products or services and in large organizations it can be organized in a hierarchy from sales management to regional management levels and then to area management and finally down to individual sales representation.

The other part of the structure is 'product management' and this is the term that is normally used in business to business marketing. In fast moving consumer goods

(FMCG) type structures the person who is in charge of a particular brand is called a 'brand manager' and the person in charge of all the company's brands or products is called the 'product manager' or sometimes the 'brand manager'. The function of product (or brand) management is to plan all the marketing activity that goes into a particular brand. This includes advertising, sales promotion, marketing research and all other non-selling marketing activity associated with the brand.

It is important that there is a close liaison between product or brand management and sales management. This is in order to ensure that all product plans are communicated to individual members of the sales force. They will then have the information and tools at their disposal to be able to communicate the company's tactical plans to their customers (e.g. the timing and content of a specific advertising campaign in support of a particular brand that the company markets). It is the task of marketing management to ensure there is coordination between product and brand management. **GL**

Reference

Lancaster, G. and Reynolds, P. (1998) *Marketing*, Basingstoke: Macmillan, pp. 122–123.

Product mix

The product mix refers to all the products offered for sale by a company. Strategic assessments must be made about which of the company's products should be offered and which should be deleted. When considering the addition of new products or product deletions, strategic decisions should reflect a consistency with the company's marketing objectives. Additions to and deletions from the width and depth of the product mix should be taken in conjunction with decisions about how such additions and deletions might relate to the company's product range in general. Analysis of the product mix questions every aspect of the company as any decision has financial, technical and marketing implications. The critical nature of product strategy becomes apparent when one considers the consequences of failure and the necessity for success.

Product mix decisions are complex and multi-faceted as they need to be consistent with, and in support of, overall company objectives and strategies. They need to be evaluated in relation to both the strengths and weaknesses of the company itself, and to the opportunities and threats that are prevalent and likely in the future. **GL**

Reference

Lancaster, G. and Reynolds, P. (1998) *Marketing*, Basingstoke: Macmillan, p. 127.

Product portfolio models

Product portfolio models are an attempt to classify products and services along two dimensions. They are used as strategic marketing planning tools and have proved to be very successful in their application.

An early application of a portfolio model was introduced by the Boston Consulting Group, and this is still very popular today. This is sometimes called the 'Boston Box', although it is more popularly referred to as the BCG Matrix. It measures relative market share from 'low' to 'high' along the 'X' axis and then measures market growth rate from 'low' to 'high' along the 'Y' axis. This results in a quadrant wherein products (or strategic business units) are categorized as being one of: 'stars', 'cash cows', 'question marks' (or 'problem children' or 'wildcats') and 'dogs'. Descriptors are given to each of these quadrants in terms of what it represents for particular strategic business units (SBUs) that fall into a particular box. This forms the basis of strategic marketing planning that deals with the movement of products from less successful into more successful boxes of the quadrant.

Another popular portfolio model was developed by the management consultants, McKinsey for General Electric, USA. This is now called the 'GE Matrix'. It produces more information than the BCG matrix as it produces nine boxes along the axes: 'business strength' (from low to high) and 'industry attractiveness' (from low to high).

A number of other matrices exist, namely: 'The Shell Directional Policy' matrix, 'The Industry maturity/competitive position' matrix, developed by management consultants Arthur D Little, and Michael Porter's 'Strategic position in industry life-cycle' matrix. These are the most popular ones, but there are many more that are suited to specific applications. **GL**

Reference
Lancaster, G. and Massingham, L. (1999) *Essentials of Marketing*, 3rd edn, Maidenhead: McGraw-Hill, pp. 88–104.

Product quality

Consumers regard quality as meaning the entire package of the service or product, which includes any additional features that sustain its capability to fulfil its indicated performance in the mind of customers.

The concept of 'total quality management' has superseded that of the production-based notion of 'quality control'. It now extends right through the organization to meeting customer expectations satisfactorily. This is achieved through 'benchmarking' which means looking at competitive offerings against the company's own offerings and identifying the best standards of performance in areas such as delivery, and the elimination of defects, and ensuring that the company matches up to these benchmarks. This means examining internal factors such as management and workforce relations. Employees must consistently seek to achieve better ways of performing work tasks. This is coupled with the formation of supplier and customer partnerships. The success of this benchmarking is through the measurement of quality from the viewpoint of customer satisfaction. **GL**

Reference
Kotler, P. (1994) *Marketing Management, Analysis, Planning, Implementation and Control*, 8th edn, New Jersey: Prentice Hall, pp. 731–733.

Product-market scope

The term 'product-market scope' refers to the organization's range of product lines and its presence in different types of markets. In other words, it refers to the strategic decisions that underpin the management of the breadth and depth of product lines offered in selected or different types of markets.

A product line is a group of brands or products which are similar in their performance or the benefits they produce for the consumer or customer. The depth of this product line depends on the customer requirements and the competition in different markets. Thus an organization may prefer to concentrate or focus on a small number of products or brands, but market these in a wide range of different types of markets or vice versa (i.e. a wide range of products marketed in a limited market).

For example, Rolls Royce and Bentley Motor Cars are constantly developing the two marques the Rolls Royce and the Bentley. These brands are targeted at the super-premium luxury niche markets of the world. The product scope therefore, is narrow, however, the organization only operates in these niche markets so the market scope (although international) is also fairly limited.

In contrast, the marketing strategy adopted by the Virgin group illustrates a wide range of products and services in a wide range of markets.

Table: **Virgin companies by market sector**

Sector	Businesses
Travel and tourism	Virgin Atlantic, Virgin Express, Virgin Hotels
Retail and cinema	Virgin Retail, Virgin Cinemas
Media	V2 Music Group, Virgin Communications
Consumer products	Virgin Cola, Virgin Jeans, Virgin Cosmetics

Kingfisher is a further example of an organization with a diverse range of products which are offered in different markets. The group has acquired a number of companies such as B&Q, Darty, Comet, Woolworth's, Superdrug, Chartwell Land (a leading investor in the retail property sector), Entertainment UK and MVC, thus a wide product-market scope is achieved by this organization. **RA**

References
Aaker, D. (1998) *Strategic Market Management*, New York: John Wiley and Son.
Gillespie, A. (1998) 'Virgin territory', *Business Review*, 5(1):4–6.
Jobber, D. (1998) *Principles and Practice of Marketing*, London: McGraw-Hill.
Lowes, B., Pass, C. and Sanderson, S., (1994) *Companies and Markets*, Oxford: Blackwell.

Product selection and buying

Buying is the process of translating the retailer's strategy into a concrete product assortment, and obtaining merchandise for resale to the customer. For independents, buying is usually carried out by the owner or manager; in large multiples buying is a specialist function, using large buyer teams or committees. The central aim is to maximize the profitability of the total range stocked.

Typically buyers are involved in decisions concerning selection of suppliers and products, pricing, merchandising and promotion, as well as quality control. They make use of retailer buyer power in negotiating the terms of trade (including cost prices, discounts, credit terms, discounts, advertising allowances, delivery conditions). The buying function carries responsibility for sales forecasting and stock decisions, for both the introduction of new products and the reordering of existing lines. A centralized buying function generates economies of scale. The quality of buying decisions can be greatly enhanced through the timely analysis of market trends and use of bought in market information.

Where new product lines are to be selected, as is frequently the case in fashion retailing, the principles of 'open to buy' are applied, where the buyer is given a budget for a particular period. Reordering decisions make use of the principles of the 'economic order quantity technique' which aims for an optimum balance between the costs of ordering and stock holding. Most large-scale retailers are now able to support such decisions with electronic point of sale (EPoS) data and the use of sales based ordering systems and electronic data interchange (EDI) links to suppliers. Increasingly, buyers act as link persons in ongoing partnerships with suppliers. Such collaboration is fostered by the development of retailer own brands, which may need considerable technical input, as well as by manufacturer drives towards the use of category management and efficient consumer response systems (ECR), which are demand driven and emphasize profit maximization for the whole category (e.g. washing powder) rather than individual product lines (e.g. Persil). **RAS**

References
Baron, S., Davies, B. and Swindley, D. (1991) *Macmillan Dictionary of Retailing*, London: Macmillan Reference Books.
Diamond, J. and Pintel, G. (1997) *Retail Buying*, London: Prentice Hall International.
McGoldrick, P.J. (1990) *Retail Marketing*, London: McGraw-Hill.

Production and fulfilment

The figure below summarizes the flow of the production process for a direct mailing.

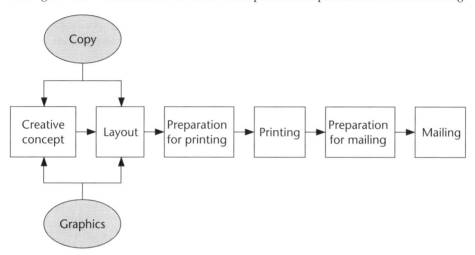

Figure: **The production flow**
Source: Roberts and Berger (1989)

Improvements in printing technology mean that it is now possible for campaigns to be personalized. Although improvements in database technology have promised the possibility of one-to-one marketing, print and production techniques have traditionally lagged behind. However, with the advent of digital printing one-to-one marketing is now firmly on the agenda. After printing, some items will need binding and finishing (e.g. folding, embossing, trimming and laminating, depending on the requirements of the mailing). Also, before mailing, items will be folded and inserted, envelopes will be labelled, personalized and sorted by postcode or other targeting variable and bagged for the mail deliverer.

Fulfilment is concerned with receiving and dealing with orders or enquiries via the mail, telephone, Internet or interactive TV. As with all 'contact opportunities', fulfilment offers an opportunity to capture data on potential customers. Systems must be set up to deal with receipt of customer mail or calls, then to capture their details, produce personalized response output, enclose and mail information or products (which in turn involves order picking, packing and dispatch), analyse the statistics on enquiry nature, level, timing profiles, bank monies for orders and update stock control systems.

Fulfilment is not the end of the process; rather it is a potential beginning of a relationship. As more attention is paid to the quality of service as well as to products, it is important for the direct marketer to ensure that responses to direct response TV, mailings and telephone contacts are appropriate for the customer. In the past there were two industries: one catering for handling responses from sales promotions such as coupons and competitions and the other for direct marketing. These are now becoming increasingly integrated. **MJE**

Reference
Roberts, M.L. and Berger, P.D. (1989) *Direct Marketing Management*, Englewood Cliffs, NJ: Prentice Hall, p. 250.

Programme implementation

Programme implementation is the process of putting the marketing plan into effect. Implementing the programme presents problems of its own; it is all too easy for planners to imagine that preparing the plan is sufficient and that implementation will follow as a natural consequence.

Implementation involves three stages: identifying who will be responsible for the activities, ensuring that resources are available for the activities and monitoring the outcomes of the activities. Factors which contribute to the effectiveness of implementation include the skills of the people involved, organizational design, incentives for those involved and communication effectiveness within the organization.

Implementation strategies can be developed by analysing the forces for and against implementation (Piercy, 1992). When any new initiative is implemented, there will be resistance; the organization needs to be moved from its current situation towards a target situation, and this will impact unfavourably on some individuals, who will be likely to resist the changes. Implementation usually involves a few key strategies that must be accomplished if the changes are to be achieved; if the strategies are high priority but low acceptability, conflicts will result. These conflicts will need to be addressed and resolved. If the priority is high, and the acceptability of the change is high, the implementation will go through easily because all those concerned will have an interest in seeing that it does so.

The earlier these problems are addressed, the better; implementation problems should be addressed at the planning stage. If this is not done, the plan may include strategies which have to be abandoned in the face of opposition from within the organization, which will render the original plan useless. Also, input at an early stage from those who will have to carry out the tasks outlined in the plan will mean that the strategies will be more acceptable, and conflicts are less likely to occur. JWDB

Reference
Piercy, N. (1992) *Market-Led Strategic Change* Oxford: Butterworth-Heinemann.

Promotion management

The task of managing promotions and marketing communications often revolves around a specific product or brand and is handled by the product or brand manager. Other corporate communications and corporate marketing communications may be handled by a corporate communications manager working within a specific strategic business unit or for the organization as a whole. The actual titles of the people responsible will vary between organizations. They will reflect the type of business they are in, their seniority, and the area of promotions they are responsible for: marketing manager, public relations director, sales manager, advertising executive, product group manager, corporate communications director, merchandising manager, sales promotions manager, and many more. One of the most challenging tasks they face is in trying to ensure all forms of marketing communications are integrated successfully. This is an area of growing concern to organizations and one that many companies have not achieved in the past.

The tasks of management are many and varied and this is no less true of promotions management. Perhaps one of the easiest ways to conceptualize it (Kotler, 1991) is to suggest that it involves the process of:

- *Analysis* – the collection, interpretation and use of relevant information that can be used for planning and management.
- *Planning* – the decision-making process involved in producing marketing communications plans.
- *Implementation* – the task of turning plans into action and making sure they work.
- *Control* – the process of checking if the marketing communications are likely to work, are working or have worked.

Above all, promotion management is about managing people. It is typically the case that large numbers of people are involved who do not come under the direct control of the manager – personnel from numerous promotional agencies, printers, other internal employees, researchers, etc. This presents a particular challenge for promotions managers. **DWP**

Reference
Kotler, P. (1991), *Marketing Management: Analysis, Planning, Implementation and Control*, 7th edn, Englewood Cliffs, NJ: Prentice Hall.

Psychological environment

Organizational buying decisions are mainly concerned with satisfying the needs of the organization. Therefore the main influences on the buying decision are the extent to which the product or service meets technical or commercial requirements. However, whilst this is the most important consideration it is also clear that there can be a wide range of influences on the buying decision beyond technical and commercial considerations. These influences form part of the psychological environment.

For example, the principal reason for purchase of a car for a sales representative is to provide a means of transport. The cost of purchase and the cost of running the vehicle are key factors in the choice of a vehicle. However, since there is a major element of personal consumption involved in the use of a company vehicle, the organizational buyer is subject to as many different personal influences as the consumer faced with the same choice.

Marques such as Mercedes, BMW and Audi stress the fact that their vehicles retain their value over the period of ownership. They also stress safety and low overall running costs because of the quality of the vehicle. However each of these vehicles also stresses other less tangible aspects in their product promotion. These include status, performance, technical sophistication and safety, each of which is designed to appeal to a specific psychological profile.

Psychological influences on organizational buying include personal demographics such as age, previous experience and training and level of seniority. They also include personality traits such as attitudes to risk, extroversion or introversion and self-confidence. Each of these factors will influence the organizational buying decision in different ways. Effective marketing anticipates the influence of these factors and uses careful analysis of buying motivation to develop appropriate marketing programmes. **SP**

References
Bunn, M.D. (1994) 'Key aspects of organizational buying: conceptualization and measurement, *Academy of Marketing Science Journal*, 22(2):160–170.

Draper, A. (1994) 'Organizational buyers as workers: the key to their behaviour, *European Journal of Marketing*, 28(11):50–66.

Psychological processes

Psychological processes refer to the internal processes individuals use to interact with the world. In trying to understand the environment and its influence, individuals use several psychological stimuli. The level of motivation, perception, attitude formation and the learning process are all psychological factors that will influence consumer buying behaviours. Psychology focuses on the internal processes that consumers use to buy and consume products or services. The psychological processes reflect consumers' thoughts, feelings and attitudes towards a product or service or a brand. They also accentuate the importance of personality and personal experiences. Psychology assesses the level of comprehension that an individual has towards a product or service.

Understanding of key psychological processes is indeed important to marketers because it serves as input in explaining consumer behaviour outcomes. How consumers react to marketing stimuli is dependent on their psychological processes. Consumers are often bombarded with a multitude of stimuli and their sensory organs are unable to accept all the stimuli at once. Essentially, the process of receiving and interpreting information is very dynamic and is influenced by consumers' attitudes and beliefs, motives and past learning, which are essentially psychological factors. In addition, the character of the stimuli themselves may influence consumers' acceptance of them. As such, marketers need to be aware of the impact of the psychological processes in planning their marketing stimuli. **RM-R**

References
Wells, W.D. and Prensky, D. (1996) *Consumer Behavior*, New York: John Wiley & Sons.

Williams, K.C. (1984) *Behavioural Aspects of Marketing*, Oxford: Heinemann Professional Publishing.

Public policy

Despite a widely-held view that companies should prioritize the increasing of their profits or the enhancing of shareholder value, this is now seen by many to be rather myopic in the marketing environment of the 21st century, when companies are being exhorted to manage their affairs in ways which are not detrimental to the public interest (i.e. to society).

The development of societal marketing, marketing ethics and green marketing have contributed much to broadening the conception of marketing to include public policy aspects.

Public policy embraces issues relating to public management and the external impact of companies' marketing actions – e.g. ethical, legal, environmental – which might be reflected in:

- *product* (e.g. the impact of cigarettes on smokers' and non-smokers' health; risks to women from silicone breast implants; cosmetics developed by testing on live animals)
- *place* (e.g. the impact of out-of-town shopping centres on inner-city decay; the risks of fraud associated with e-commerce)
- *promotion* (e.g. below-the-line promotion, such as sponsorship by tobacco companies of sporting events; and above-the-line promotion, such as advertising contraceptive products on television)
- *price* (e.g. price discrimination by car manufacturers/dealers in the UK involving the setting of prices at levels which are much higher than in other EU countries; bribery as an element in placing contracts – especially in the context of public sector projects).

Additional public policy themes include competition (e.g. avoidance of collusion;

the regulation of monopolies, utilities and financial markets) and consumerism (e.g. truth in advertising) which all give scope for government-sponsored restrictions on the unconstrained freedom of marketing activities to impact on the public interest in a negative way. **RMSW & CTG**

References

Carrigan, M. (1995) 'POSIT-ive and negative aspects of the societal marketing concept: stakeholder conflicts for the tobacco industry', *Journal of Marketing Management*, 11(5)(July): 469–485.

Dunfee, T.W., Smith, N.C. and Ross Jr., W.T. (1999) 'Social contracts and marketing ethics', *Journal of Marketing*, 63(3)(July): 14–32.

Journal of Marketing Management (1998) Special issue on contemporary issues in green marketing, 14(6)(July).

Journal of Public Policy and Marketing.

Purchase scenarios influence

Consumer purchasing decisions are influenced by the situations surrounding consumers. An in-store situation, for example, is a scenario that can influence consumer purchasing decisions. In-store stimuli such as merchandising display, shelf positions, pricing promotions, product assortment and store ambience are important in influencing purchasing decisions, especially unplanned purchases. The physical surroundings can have a strong pulling power in getting consumers to purchase. The in-store environment has been shown to induce purchasing by consumers who had no earlier plan to shop. It is important for marketers to identify various influential in-store situations because of the implications associated with unplanned purchasing responses.

Social surroundings can also influence consumers' purchase behaviour. Social occasions such as birthdays and weddings where gifts are bought are ideal situations for influencing consumers to purchase more 'self-involvement' products. Selecting products as gifts for others usually entails more self-involvement and requires purchasers to put more thought into the buying process. In such a situation, consumers may spend more time in searching for relevant information and are more likely to visit more stores in selecting the most suitable gifts.

A situation where consumers are exposed to marketing information is another scenario that influences purchasing decisions. If consumers remember information from advertisements or are told of some news about a product by friends or are approached by salespeople and are given information on products, this is likely to influence their purchasing decisions. Such situations are important factors for marketers to take into consideration when planning their communication strategies. Marketers are interested in identifying the medium of communication most effective in persuading people to buy a product or service. **RM-R**

References

Hoyner, W. and MacInnis, D. J. (1997) *Consumer Behavior*, Boston: Houghton Mifflin Company.

Mowen, J.C. (1995) *Consumer Behaviour*, 4th edn, Englewood Cliffs, NJ: Prentice Hall.

Qualitative research

Qualitative research is a research technique that probes into consumers' minds and how they view a particular issue. The objective is to acquire an understanding of people's motivations, attitudes, preferences and behaviours. It is often used to gain a qualitative understanding of the underlying reasons and motivations of consumers in order to develop an initial understanding of a situation. Hence, qualitative research is exploratory in nature and is often conducted in an unstructured manner in comparison with quantitative research.

Qualitative data is collected so that the researcher is able to understand more about issues that cannot be directly observed and measured. Consumers' feelings, thoughts and intentions, which can influence their behaviours, are examples of information that are of interest to a qualitative researcher. Essentially, qualitative research tends to be more intensive than standardized questionnaire-based interviews. There is a longer, more flexible relationship with the respondents, which provides more depth and greater richness of context. As such, it is often possible to gain new insights and perspectives through qualitative research. Because of the time that is normally spent with respondents, the number of respondents is small and they are selected specifically for the research purpose. The most common methods used in collecting data include in-depth interviews and focus group discussions. In in-depth interviews, face-to-face interviews are conducted with respondents to explore particular subject in detail. The interview can be unstructured, where respondents are given maximum freedom to respond within the bounds of topics of interest to the interviewer, or they can be asked semi-structured questions. Focus group discussions are conducted by selecting appropriate participants to sit in a group and discuss selected topics relating to the issue of interest. Each participant in a group of five or more is encouraged to express views on each topic, and to elaborate on or react to the views of other participants. **RM-R**

Reference
Ghauri, P. Gronhaug, K. and Kristianlund, I. (1995) *Research Methods in Business Studies*, New York: Prentice Hall.

Quantitative research

Quantitative research seeks to quantify the data gathered, and typically applies some form of statistical tools in analysing the data. It is often done in a very structured manner and samples selected are often large and representative of the population. Quantitative research ensures that the research is conducted scientifically where characteristics such as purposiveness, rigour, testability, replicability, precision, confidence, objectivity and generalizability are observed. By using statistical tools, data obtained from quantitative research are analysed to ensure that the findings can be generalized to the total population that is being studied.

Quantitative research often develops hypotheses about specific variables that will be tested by using statistical tools. A hypothesis is an educated guess about the solution to a research problem. Hypotheses are statements which, expressed logically, define relationships between two or more variables. They are tentative statements that need to be tested with empirical data. A good hypothesis will contain clear implications for testing relationships among variables. In hypothesis testing, the researcher determines whether a hypothesis concerning some characteristics of a given population is true, based on the evidence generated from the statistical analysis. The use of hypotheses characterizes most quantitative research. **RM-R**

Reference
Sekaran U. (1996) *Research Methods for Business*, 2nd edn, New York: John Wiley & Sons.

Questionnaires

A questionnaire is a preformulated written set of questions to assess respondents' views towards a particular subject. The questionnaire is presented to the respondents, who record their answers, usually within closely defined alternatives. It is a tool for collecting data and should be used to gather relevant data that can answer the research objectives. Each questionnaire must be designed with the specific research objectives in mind and must be developed following specific logical steps. It is important that the researcher plans what to measure, formulates relevant questions to get the required information, decides on the order and wording of questions, designs the layout, then tests the questionnaire on a small sample of respondents to minimize ambiguity of questions. This pre-testing should provide some idea of relevancy of questions and ambiguity and, where necessary, appropriate changes should be made before the questionnaires are distributed to the total target respondents.

A good questionnaire design should focus on three main areas: the wording of the questions, how the variables in the questions are categorized, scaled, and coded after receiving the responses, and its appearance. These are important issues to consider in designing a questionnaire because they can minimize biases in research. Questionnaires can be administered personally or mailed to respondents. When they are administered personally, they can usually be completed within a short time and respondents may have the chance to clarify any queries about the questions on the spot. When questionnaires are mailed to respondents, the possibility of respondents not answering them is much greater. Mailed questionnaires often have low response rates. In addition, respondents are not able to clarify any doubts that they may have with particular questions. Some effective techniques, however, have been formulated to increase the response rates of mailed questionnaires. These include sending follow-up letters, enclosing small monetary or non-monetary incentives and providing respondents with self-addressed, stamped return envelopes. **RM-R**

References
Chisnall, P.M. (1986) *Marketing Research*, London: McGraw-Hill.
Kumar, V., Aaker, D.A. and Day, G.S. (1999) *Essentials of Marketing Research*, New York: John Wiley & Sons.
Sekaran, U. (1996) *Research Methods for Business*, 2nd edn, New York: John Wiley & Sons.

Reference groups

A reference group is a set of people to whom individuals look for guidance in terms of their attitudes, knowledge, behaviours and norms. Individuals often compare themselves with these reference groups and they also look to them in guiding their consumption behaviours. Reference groups may be informal or formal: family, friends and colleagues are informal groups, whilst groups that are set up formally such as church groups, schools or clubs are a form of formal reference groups.

The most common types of reference groups are aspirational, associative and dissociative. *Aspirational* reference groups are those that are admired and which individuals wish to be like but of which they are not currently members. A good example is a pop group or rock band. *Associative* reference groups are those that one belongs to, such as churches or a club. *Dissociative* groups are groups whose attitudes, values and behaviours are disapproved by others and to which people do *not* aspire to become members.

Identifying the different reference groups is important to marketers because of the marketing implications. Understanding the aspirational reference groups of the target market is important because marketers can then associate their brands with these reference groups. Also, the consumption patterns or the purchasing habits of members of aspirational or associative reference groups are likely to be emulated by others. Thus, planning the right marketing strategies in line with these reference groups is important. On the other hand, identifying and understanding dissociative reference groups is also crucial to ensure that any marketing efforts that may not be well accepted by others are prevented. Thus it is important for marketers to understand the influence that reference groups have on their target consumers. **RM-R**

Reference
Schiffman, L.G. and Kanuk, L.L. (1983) *Consumer Behaviour*, New Jersey: Prentice Hall.
Solomon, M.R. (1996) *Consumer Behavior*, Englewood Cliffs, NJ: Prentice Hall.

Regionalization

As we enter the 21st century, a visitor from another planet (particularly if he/she landed in Geneva or Seattle) might observe that world trade was organized in the following way.

At the top of the pyramid is something called WTO (World Trade Organisation), set up in Geneva in 1994, formerly known as GATT (the General Agreement on Tariffs and Trade). GATT was founded in 1948, and acted as a sort of referee in the game of world trade. It operated with four basic principles.

1. Trade should be conducted on the basis of 'the most favoured nation', i.e. there should be no discrimination in trade.
2. Domestic trade should not be protected by tariffs; the goal was a zero tariff regime.
3. Measures such as dumping and subsidy should not interfere with fair, global competition.
4. Tariffs should be reduced through multilateral negotiations and 'bound' against future increases.

It must be said that GATT, over almost 20 years, had an excellent trade record in reducing tariff barriers, although it failed to deal as effectively with so-called 'non-tariff barriers' such as quotas, discriminatory procurement practices, restrictive customs procedures, selective monetary controls and exchange rates and restrictive administrative arrangements. The WTO, the successor organization, has a principal mandate of demolishing non-tariff barriers and dealing with the restrictive dimensions of regionalisation.

Our visitor from another planet would see that the flow of world trade involves four principal regions, or trade areas.

1. The *European Union*: currently embraces 350 million people, all the nations of Western Europe, excluding Switzerland and Norway. No internal trade barriers, a common external tariff, a common market (free movement of factors of production), eventual unification of monetary and fiscal policy. Potential new members include Poland, Hungary, the Czech Republic and Slovenia.
2. *NAFTA*, a free trade association, embracing the USA, Canada and Mexico; population 380 million.
3. *MERCOSUR*, a Latin America free trade area, embracing Argentina, Brazil, Paraguay and Uruguay; population 198 million.
4. APEC, Asia Pacific Economic Cooperation zone: 18 countries, potentially covering 60 per cent of the world's population, including Japan, China, Singapore, Taiwan, South Korea. Singapore is the centre of *ASEAN* (Association of South East Asian Nations – Singapore, Malaysia, Indonesia, the Philippines, Thailand and Brunei).

These four trading blocs will in the 21st century account for the majority of world trade movements. That is why they are important to international marketers. **MJT**

References
Paliwoda, S.J. and Ryans, J.K., (eds) (1995) *International Marketing Reader*, London: Routledge.
World Bank (1996) *World Development Report: From Plan to Market*, Oxford: Oxford University Press.
Useful web sites
WTO – www.unicc.org//wto/Welcome.html
EU BASICS – HTTP://eubasics.allmanstand.com/general.html
APEC – www.apecsec.org.sg.apecnet.html
NAFTANET – www.nafta.net
UNCTAD (UN Conference on Trade and Development) –
    www.unicc.org/unctad/en/enhome.html

Regulation and ethics (codes of practice)

Marketing communications are regulated by voluntary codes of practice and by the law. These codes and legal constraints reflect the ethical and moral views of society and vary from country to country. However, regulation systems tend to follow the objective that marketing communications should be legal, decent, honest and truthful, a practice first determined by the International Chamber of Commerce. The challenge is to allow freedom of speech and expression whilst, at the same time, protecting society without recourse to unwieldy or over-cumbersome regulations and laws. Some countries rely almost entirely on voluntary codes, others on extensive legal constraints, and others on a balance between the two. The UK system falls into the latter category, but great reliance is placed on the voluntary system as the first line of control.

In the UK, the Advertising Standards Authority (ASA) is responsible for codes of practice covering non-broadcast advertising (press, posters and cinema), direct mail, sales promotions and Internet advertising. Broadcast advertising – television and radio – is covered by the Independent Television Commission (ITC), the Broadcast Standards Commission (BSC) and the Radio Authority (RA). Broadcast advertising is pre-vetted (checked before broadcast) but this is not generally required for other marketing communications.

A confederation of similar bodies throughout Europe, the European Advertising Standards Alliance (EASA), endeavours to ensure a degree of consistency and continuity in the European Community and beyond. While these bodies are responsible for administering the codes, their sanctions tend to be limited. Where necessary, legal proceedings can be pursued.

Ethical practices dictate that marketing communications should not tell lies, deliberately mislead, misinform or go beyond the bounds of decency. Specific codes of practice require that certain promotions are not permitted, are heavily restricted or are confined in particular ways. Ingredients on foodstuffs have to be shown in descending order of quantity, cigarette advertising is not permitted on television in the UK and must appear with a health warning in other media and on packaging. There are limits placed on nudity, strong language and the use of shock tactics. Some advertisers try to test the limits of regulation but where they do, they run the risk of censure. It is in the area of decency that most difficulty is caused, as no universal agreement exists about what is and is not decent, it is something that is constantly changing in line with changing ethics, morals and levels of public acceptance. **DWP**

Reference

Pickton, D.W. and Broderick, A. (2001) *Integrated Marketing Communications*, London: Financial Times Prentice Hall, ch. 9.

Relationship building

Marketing is moving away from focusing on individual transactions towards building value-laden relationships and value delivery networks. Gronroos (1990) stipulates that the relationship approach to marketing involves the creation, maintenance, and enhancement of relationships with customers and other partners, at a profit, in order to meet the objectives of the parties involved. Parasuraman *et al.* (1991) postulate that relationship building is 'process intensive'. It requires time, money, and commitment that may not produce immediate results.

There are different strategies for developing relationships with customers. Berry and Parasuraman (1991) suggest that an organization can adopt any of three customer value-building approaches: financial, social and structural. The first value-building approach centres on adding financial benefits to the customer relationship. For example, airlines reward frequent business passengers with free or reduced-price leisure tickets and manufacturers offer money-back guarantees. Wulf (1998) postulates that reward programmes are the first step in the process of building a close customer relationship, which is however not a sustainable long-term strategy. The second approach is to add social benefits as well as financial benefits. In this case, company personnel concentrate their efforts on enhancing their social bonds with customers by individualizing or personalizing their customer relationships. That is, they learn individual customers' needs and wants and then they individualize and personalize the company's products and services. The third approach to building customer relationships is to add structural ties in addition to financial and social benefits. The organization may supply customers with special equipment, such as software programs, and/or computer linkages to enable their customers to manage their orders and inventory.

Service organizations can customize the customer relationship and hence more easily achieve long-term customer relationships. Service providers have many opportunities to learn about the specific characteristics and requirements of individual customers and can utilize these data to precisely tailor service to the situation at hand.

Relationship marketing demands continuous attention to the needs of customers and constant development of products and services to match their evolving needs and build long-term relationships. **IPD**

References

Berry, L.L. and Parasuraman, A. (1991) *Marketing Services: Competing Through Quality*, New York: The Free Press.

Gronroos, C. (1990) *Service Management and Marketing: Managing the Moments of Truth in Service Competition*, Lexington MA: Lexington Books.

Parasuraman, A., Berry, L.L. and Zeithaml, V.A. (1991) 'Understanding customer expectations of service', *Sloan Management Review*, Spring: 39–48.

Wulf, K.D. (1998) *Relationship Marketing*, in B.V. Loovy, R.V. Dierdonck and P. Gemmel (eds) *Services Management: An Integrated Approach*, London: Financial Times – Pitman Publishing, pp. 61–78.

Relationship marketing

More and more companies are recognizing the importance of practising relationship marketing, which focuses on the importance of building and sustaining long-term relationships with customers through an emphasis on the creation of superior customer value and satisfaction. In addition to customer relationships, the success of marketing performance depends on the creation and retention of long-term relationships with other parties, for example suppliers, retailers, and distributors. Kotler and Armstrong (1996) define relationship marketing as: 'The process of creating, maintaining, and enhancing strong, value-laden relationships with customers and other stakeholders'(p. 550).

Traditional marketing focuses on creating transactions rather than relationships. Relationship marketing shifts the focus from merely selling to customers to serving them effectively. As competition intensifies and markets mature, organizations recognize the importance of retaining their customers by emphasizing customer satisfaction and value and hence creating customer loyalty. A key aim of relationship marketing is the achievement of long-term customer retention. The provision of superior customer service is a prerequisite for effective relationship marketing.

In relationship marketing the focus shifts away from transactions to relationships: 'Customers become partners and the firm must make long-term commitments to maintaining those relationships with quality, service and innovation' (Webster, 1992). As it is usually cheaper to retain a current customer than to attract a new one, successful organizations focus their efforts on the creation of effective strategies for retaining customers. Two key strategies for retaining customers are regularly to monitor and evaluate the quality of customer relationships over time, and continuously develop services and products that match the changing needs of customers (Zeithaml and Bitner, 1996).

The growing importance of relationship marketing has been followed by a wide acknowledgement of the contribution of customer service to building effective long-term customer relationships. Bateson (1995) stipulates that relationship marketing highlights the importance of customer retention, product benefits, establishing long-term relationships with customers, customer service, increased commitment to the customer, increased level of customer contact and high quality. **IPD**

References

Bateson, J.E.G. (1995) *Managing Services Marketing: Text and Readings,* 3rd edn, Orlando: Dryden Press.

Kotler, P. and Armstrong, G. (1996) *Principles of Marketing,* 7th edn, Upper Saddle River, New Jersey: Prentice Hall International Edition.

Webster, F.E. (1992) 'The changing role of marketing in the corporation', *Journal of Marketing,* October: 1–17.

Zeithaml, V.A. and Bitner, M.J. (1996) *Services Marketing,* Singapore: McGraw-Hill International Editions.

Relationship marketing and marketing communications

Although marketing has been around for thousands of years (product development, advertising, pricing and distribution can all be traced back to early civilization), marketing as a coherent discipline and body of knowledge is a very recent phenomenon. Early attempts to conceptualize marketing emphasized the transactions or exchanges between organizations and their customers as though they were a series of one-off activities. Partly because of a changing business environment and partly because of new insights into the marketing process, more emphasis today is placed on continuing transactions and the relationships that are consequently forged (Christopher *et al.*, 1991; Buttle, 1996; Brodie *et al.*, 1997). This has been termed 'relationship marketing'.

Relationship marketing is viewed as a new marketing paradigm by some, but for others it is simply a better representation of what they have seen happening for years. There is also increasing recognition of the importance, not just of customer relationships, but also of relationships with *all* relevant parties involved in the marketing process, from suppliers and agents to intermediaries, consumer groups and end users. Relationship marketing extends the single-minded emphasis on customers to embrace relationships with all stakeholders and publics (Brodie *et al.*, 1997; Hunt, 1997). This is not a new phenomena to many marketing communications practitioners. The public relations profession has for many years long extolled the virtues of building relationships with a range of publics, and direct marketing has emphasized the need for database and relationship management. Likewise, successful salespeople, especially in industrial markets, develop a deep understanding of the importance of building and maintaining customer relationships.

It is clear that the move from a transactional to a relationship emphasis in marketing has significant implications for marketing communications. Relationship marketing requires that they should be better harmonized and integrated and that they are focused towards a greater range of target audiences (Hutton 1996). Emphasis should not be on one-off communications but, instead, on on-going communications. **DWP**

References

Brodie, R., Coviello, N., Brookes, R. and Little, V. (1997), 'Towards a paradigm shift in marketing? An examination of current marketing practices', *Journal of Marketing Management,* 13(5):383–406.

Buttle, F. (ed) (1996), *Relationship Marketing: Theory and Practice*, London: Paul Chapman Publishing.

Christopher, M., Payne, A. and Ballantine, D. (1991), *Relationship Marketing*, Oxford: Butterworth-Heinemann.

Hunt, S. (1997), 'Competing through relationships: grounding relationship marketing in resource-advantage theory', *Journal of Marketing Management*, 13(5):431–445.

Hutton, J. (1996), 'Integrated relationship marketing communications: a key opportunity for IMC', *Journal of Marketing Communications*, 2(3):191–199.

Relationship marketing and the marketing continuum

Relationship marketing is concerned with all activities directed towards attracting, developing and retaining customer relationships. Gronroos (1994, 1996) indicates that there are a number of strategies open to marketers, along what he calls the 'marketing strategy continuum'. At its extreme, 'transactional' exchange involves single, short-term exchange events encompassing a distinct beginning and ending. On the other hand, 'relational' exchange involves transactions linked over an extended time frame.

Gronroos suggests that most consumer goods companies, with mass markets and little contact with their ultimate customers, are more likely to be on the transaction end. Despite this, there have been several attempts to apply relationship marketing concepts to consumer markets. The main elements come from research in industrial marketing, which indicates that relationships are complex, long-term in nature and mutually beneficial. They are characterized by trust, commitment, mutual benefit, adaptation, respect and regard for privacy. If relationship marketing is to be successfully applied within consumer markets, then such 'relationships' should incorporate these integral elements (O'Malley *et al.*, 1999).

It is probably more complex in practice because it is not merely a case of whether an individual wants a relationship with a company but whether the company wants a relationship with that individual (some customers being deselected because they do not contribute sufficiently to profitability). Furthermore, the type of relationship needs to be determined, after all we all have unique relationships with everyone we know and meet, so the conceptual ideal of relationship marketing might lack pragmatism. **MJE**

References
Gronroos, C. (1994) 'From marketing mix to relationship marketing', *Management Decision* 32(2):4–20.

Gronroos, C. (1996) 'Relationship marketing in consumer markets', *Management Decision* 43(3):5–14.

O'Malley, L., Patterson, M. and Evans, M. (1999) *Exploring Direct Marketing*, London: Thomson Learning, ch. 7.

Relationship to corporate plan

The relationship the marketing plan has to the corporate plan is a description of the degree of fit between overall corporate strategies and those which relate directly to the firm's relationship with its customers and publics.

The corporate plan is usually much greater in scope than the marketing plan. The corporate plan will include statements about the reasons for the company's existence, its responsibilities to stakeholders, the customer needs that are met by the firm's products, the amount of product diversification the company expects to encompass, the role of research and development in the corporate future, and so forth. Not all these issues are strictly marketing-related, although all will impinge directly or indirectly on marketing activities.

The marketing plan is often seen as being subsidiary to the corporate plan, as stemming from it as a functional part of the overall corporate strategy (Macdonald, 1995). This is because the corporate plan will typically be broken down into departmental responsibilities: marketing, innovation, resources, productivity, social responsibility and finance. In fact the two operate in parallel; the corporate plan should, in any good market-led firm, be designed around the needs of customers and other publics. The difference between the two is that the corporate plan is operating with a broader focus.

At a more mundane and practical level, the corporate plan is usually drawn up by the firm's top management, whereas the marketing plan will be drawn up by the marketers alone. **JWDB**

Reference

Macdonald, H.B. (1995) *Marketing Plans: How to Prepare and Use Them*, Oxford: Butterworth-Heinemann.

Research and development

Research and development (R&D) is a major department in most organizations and it usually reports directly to general management. It is thus on a par with marketing in terms of its intra-company importance. In innovative companies that are product led, this function tends to be extremely important and senior within the organization. R&D is normally a continuous activity, with certain projects having a lot of resources devoted to them. Once the project has reached the marketplace in terms of it becoming a tangible product, it is then handed over to production. Production will produce it in accordance with a production schedule that is agreed with marketing as determined by potential customer demand.

In a marketing orientated company, R&D and marketing should work in close liaison, for it is the marketplace that should be the starting point for new product ideas, and customers should also be canvassed about their views in relation to existing products. This activity is part of marketing and is covered under the heading 'marketing research'. Many traditional R&D departments are now putting 'design' into their title to show that they regard customer aesthetics as being as important as pure research and development. The new departmental name then becomes 'research, design and development' (R,D&D).

R&D sometimes initiates new product ideas, and liaison then takes place with marketing research to see whether the concept is acceptable to consumers. This process can continue through a number of stages until a tangible product is produced, and this is finally tested out on consumers through the process of product testing. Marketing research is thus the link between consumers and R&D. Marketing research techniques such as brainstorming, test marketing and product testing feature in this continuous relationship. **GL**

Reference

Kotler, P. (1994) *Marketing Management, Analysis, Planning, Implementation and Control*, 8th edn, New Jersey: Prentice Hall, pp. 731–733.

Retail advertising

Advertising forms part of the retailer's 'promotion mix' and consists of paid for, sponsored media messages that must be coordinated with the rest of the marketing mix and other store activities.

Whereas manufacturers advertise to a market, retailers target a geographical trading area, therefore retail advertising is often a local activity, used to inform, persuade and reinforce loyalty. Retailers essentially have two 'brands' to advertise, i.e. products and stores, which may necessitate differences in communications objectives and media mix. Because of this two main types of advertising are employed – indirect action and direct action. The former is institutional advertising, concerned with the creation or transformation of the corporate brand positioning and store image. This type of advertising creates goodwill for the store by emphasizing prestige and services. It aims to attract potential customers and focuses on recall and purchase intentions. In contrast, direct action advertising aims to sell products by focusing either on their attractiveness or on price, such as bargain and clearance sale advertising. Consumers can be categorized as store-loyal or store-switching: the latter are responsive to price, which makes price-focused advertising important.

In 1997, 50 large UK retailers spent £2.6 billion on advertising, also called 'above the line expenditure'. Each advert must be crafted to specific objectives and contain a clear 'unique selling proposition'. The reading matter of the advert is called 'copy' and must be carefully coordinated with the visual features. Media expenditure is allocated within the overall advertising budget. TV, radio and national newspapers are deemed most effective for corporate campaigns and adverts featuring a wide product mix aimed at a large customer base.

Cooperative advertising with manufacturers is on the increase, with a £2 million manufacturer annual spend. Also, trends in grocery retailing indicate that, with the introduction of loyalty cards, which facilitate the individualization of promotional activities, retailers tend to scale down advertising expenditure, partly because advertising effectiveness is very difficult to measure. **RAS**

References

Baron, S., Davies, B. and Swindley, D. (1991) *Macmillan Dictionary of Retailing*, London: Macmillan Reference Books.

Davies, G. (1990) *Advertising in Retailing*, Harlow: Longman.

Rossiter, J.R. and Percy, L. (1997) *Advertising Communications and Promotion Management*, 2nd edn, New York: McGraw-Hill.

Retail brands

Retailer 'own brand' products are goods developed or purchased by a retailer exclusively for sale through its outlets. The 'label' may bear the same name as the retailer (e.g. Tesco Value) or it may bear another title (e.g. Marks and Spencer's St. Michael and Autograph clothing). Advantages of own brands are higher profit margins and a competitive edge, as well as the creation of a distinctive store image and enhanced retailer power over manufacturers.

Originally developed in the grocery sector, UK own brands are growing rapidly in the DIY and retail chemist trades. A high degree of concentration among leading multiples and the market share taken by own brands are related, which accounts for the strength of own brand sales in grocery retailing. Considerable economies of scale in advertising arise as the company and the own brand can be promoted simultaneously. The leading retail grocery brands developed from being an undifferentiated product alternative to a manufacturer brand to being brand alternatives in their own right. Rapid growth was further driven by intense price competition fuelled by the advent of the continental discounters in the early 1990s. This prompted the widespread introduction of generic 'tertiary budget own brands', which were used to reduce the cost of a shopping basket. Retail brands are used to stimulate customer loyalty, often in conjunction with loyalty card schemes such as the CWS dividend card scheme, which links points exclusively to expenditure on Co-op branded goods, at a very generous rate.

For the manufacturer, savings arise from not having to promote own brand goods, however, supplying own branded goods is generally less profitable. This may be redressed by forming close long-term retailer–manufacturer partnerships, which aim to maximize overall profitability. The majority of branded manufacturers were forced to enter the own brand market despite a growth in lawsuits concerning brand theft and copy-catting. **RAS**

References

Burt, S. and Davis, S. (1999) 'Follow my leader? Lookalike retailer brands in non-manufacturer-dominated product markets in the UK', *The International Review of Retail, Distribution and Consumer Research*, 9(2).

Key Note (1997*) Own Brands*, Hampton: Key Note Ltd.

Mintel (1998) 'Customer loyalty in retailing', special report, London: Mintel International Group.

Wileman, A. and Jary, M. (1997) *Retail Power Plays: From Trading to Brand Leadership: Strategies for Building Retail Brand Value*, Basingstoke: Macmillan.

Retail change theories

Theories of retail change can be divided into cyclical, conflict and environmental theories and combinations thereof. *Cyclical theories,* including the wheel of retailing, the retail accordion and the retail life cycle, are centred on the concept of trading up, whereby retail institutions, commencing as low-cost, cut-price, narrow-margin operations metamorphose into high-cost, conservative, top-heavy organizations based on quality goods and services, thus making room for potential newcomers at the bottom end. *Conflict theories* conceptualize change as the outcome of inter- and intra institutional strife. An action–reaction sequence of a four stage institutional change process is proposed: shock and defensive retreat are followed by acknowledgement and finally adaptation; the latter initiating further crisis and conflict. Both cyclical and conflict theories have been criticized for overemphasizing inter-institutional strife with broader environmental issues (such as culture and demand structures) not being considered. In contrast, *environmental theories* see institutional innovations as responses to either sociological forces, legal constraints or technological developments. Survival and prosperity depend on adaptability to alterations in the trading milieu. Combination models can be subdivided into cycle-environment concepts, cycle-conflict configurations and environmental-conflict approaches, plus further models incorporating all three aspects.

All the above theories tend to neglect the dynamic interaction between retailers and contemporary consumption activities. The 'new geography' perspective addresses this and links retail change and consumption practices. However, studies within this tradition often focus on single sites and individual consumers or consumer groups, thus neglecting the impact the dynamic interactions between consumers and retail sites have on broader retail market structures and thus retail change. Alternatively a neo-Marxist perspective may be used to conceptualize retailing as a mediating system between production and consumption. In this, retail capital's primary aim is accumulation by maximizing the exchange value of goods, whereas for consumers, the use value of commodities is the dominant factor. Retail change processes occur because of the strains within the capitalist system, driven by inter-firm competition and changing consumption practices. **RAS**

References

Brown, S. (1987) 'The wheel of the wheel of retailing', *International Journal of Retailing*, 3(1):3–36.

Pioch, E.A. and Schmidt, R. A. (2000) 'Consumption and the retail change process: a comparative analysis of toy retailing in Italy and France', *The International Review of Retail, Distribution and Consumer Research*, 10(2).

Wrigley, N. and Lowe, M. (eds) (1996) *Retailing, Consumption and Capital. Towards the new retail geography*, Harlow: Longman.

Retail functions

Whilst many small independent retail businesses are organized in a web design with the owner/manager at the centre coordinating all activities, most large retailers follow a functional format. Typically, retail organizations feature the standard business functions, adapted to their specific context. These include buying, merchandising and operations, logistics and supply chain management, personnel, internal and customer services, administration, information systems, location planning and promotion. However, this list is not exhaustive and varies considerably between different retail organizations. Functions can also be merged and integrated, for example, distribution and information systems, and there are many possible inter-functional overlaps and links.

A commonality for many large retailers is a hierarchical business structure, which can be split into head office and store functions, with varying ladders of coordination at, for example, district and regional level, in between. The different parts of the retail industry vary considerably in the extent to which functional responsibilities are devolved down to the individual outlet level. For example, in public house retailing decision making is often quite decentralized, with a great deal of management empowerment at district and even public house level. This has the advantage of encouraging initiative and boosting morale, but can result in a lack of coordination. In the grocery trade, highly centralized decision making is the norm, with head office controlling and coordinating the functions, and stores largely implementing head office decisions, with minimal adaptation to local conditions. Key advantages lie in economies of scale and a higher degree of control, but this approach may also sacrifice local responsiveness and flexibility.

Historically, for many retailers marketing has been viewed as a distinct function within the business, combining advertising, promotions and selling. There is now a trend for retailers to move away from this traditional trading orientation towards a customer focused marketing orientation, where the principles of marketing serve as an overarching framework and underpinning philosophy for the whole business of retailing. **RAS**

References
Hart, C., Kirkup, M., Preston, D., Rafiq, M. and Walley, P. (1997) *Cases in Retailing: Operational Perspectives*, Oxford: Blackwell.
Oldfield, B.M., Schmidt, R.A., Clarke, I., Hart, C. and Kirkup, M. (eds) (2000) *Contemporary Cases in Retail Operations Management*, Basingstoke: Macmillan Business.
Oldfield, B.M., Schmidt, R.A, Kirkup, M., Hart, C. and Clarke, I. (eds) (1998) 'Retail Operations management', special issue *Management Case Quarterly* 3(1).

Retail marketing

Retail marketing is concerned with the application of marketing tools within the operating context of the retail organization. Despite the increasing globalization of supply chains and the growing internationalization of UK retailing, this is still typically the national environment, with its culture, institutions and regulatory framework.

In the UK, retailing is a highly dynamic industry, reflecting changes in the rest of society. Consumer demand patterns are affected by changing demographics (e.g. the growth in singles households, an ageing population, increases in the number of working women) and growth in part-time labour, changes in disposable incomes and consumer credit. Consumers are relatively affluent, sophisticated and time-pressured and therefore demanding of service.

Structurally, relatively limited government intervention with the growing industry concentration has supported a transformation of the patterns of dominant organizational forms, replacing small independents with multiples. This has resulted in economies of scale, centralization of decison making, buying and financial management. Retailers have increased their buying power and expanded their product ranges, often including the development of their own retail brands.

The UK planning system and its changing approach towards town centre locations has had a strong impact on the location and development of formats. Numerous new outlet types and formats have emerged, to fit the requirements of both large scale out-of-town developments (e.g. warehouse clubs, hypermarkets and category killers) and the regeneration of local neighbourhoods and the High Street (e.g. convenience formats and non-store retailing).

The 1990s saw a revival of price competition, accompanied by a strong service emphasis. There has also been an increase in retailer diversification (e.g. grocers moving into non-food products and High Street fashion retailers into catalogue selling). At the end of the century, many retail organizations were developing a range of parallel formats and channels. Increasingly, retailers are forging strategic partnerships with their suppliers and are utilizing information technology to streamline business processes throughout the supply chain in order to meet consumer demand.
RAS

References

Baron, S., Davies, B. and Swindley, D. (1991) *Macmillan Dictionary of Retailing*, London: Macmillan Reference Books.

Burt, S., Hallsworth, A. and Reynolds, J. (1997) *The Structure of the British Retail System*, Toronto: Centre for the Study of Commercial Activity, Ryerson Polytechnic University.

Findlay, A. and Sparks, L. (1999) *A Bibliography of Retail Planning*, Stirling: The National Retail Planning Forum, Institute for Retail Studies.

Key Note (1998) *Retailing in the UK*, Hampton: Key Note Ltd.

McGoldrick, P.J. (1990) *Retail Marketing*, London: McGraw-Hill.

Omar, O. (1999) *Retail Marketing*, London: Pearson.

Sternquist, B. (1998) *International Retailing*, New York: Fairchild Publications.

Retail marketing definition and scope

Retail marketing encompasses the activities involved in facilitating mutually beneficial exchange relationships between business organizations supplying goods and services and consumers. Retailers strive to gain competitive advantage by manipulating and coordinating the marketing mix variables to match strategic objectives.

The 'product' encompasses goods and services, determined by consumer demand and market positioning. Many retailers sell both own labels and manufacturers' brands, in a mix determined via the buying function. Consumer perceptions of value for money are informed by a combination of price and quality. Pricing strategies include discounting, 'every-day-low-pricing' and premium pricing. Location, or place decisions are crucial determinants of retail success. Retailers compete for sites in large scale out-of-town shopping centre developments, but there is also a trend to revive competition in the High Street and within local communities through investment in convenience formats, and virtual locations are developed on the Internet. Retail promotion aims to create strong retail brands through a dual focus on both own label goods and store image. Locally, retailers often focus on price promotions. Loyalty cards serve as a tool to capture customer information, thus facilitating individualized promotions. Retailers increasingly make use of service provision, such as baby changing facilities, car rescue schemes, checkout packing services and loyalty rewards to provide physical evidence of their engagement with consumer concerns. The participants in retail marketing are customers, staff and supply side partners. Retailers with a true marketing orientation carefully monitor and match consumer trends and expectations. Staff training is crucial, since retail employees are the retailers' human interface with the customer and wages are one of the highest costs at store level. Cooperation with manufacturers at all levels of the marketing effort has become increasingly important. Arguably, rather than retailers competing with each other, the trend is towards competition between integrated supply chains. This is facilitated by extensive use of information technology, which aids knowledge sharing. Thus the processes of supply chain management and retailing are becoming increasingly streamlined, cost effective and demand driven. **RAS**

References

Baron, S., Davies, B. and Swindley, D. (1991) *Macmillan Dictionary of Retailing*, London: Macmillan Reference Books.

McGoldrick, P.J. (1990) *Retail Marketing*, London: McGraw-Hill.

Omar, O. (1999) *Retail Marketing*, London: Pearson.

Retail marketing formats

A 'format' is a distinct way of presenting the retailer's offering to the consumer. Retailers make use of a multitude of formats to achieve differentiation and to target different market segments.

Very small scale retailers make use of casual formats, such as car boot sales and market stalls. Small independent retailers with more permanent businesses have historically been very active in serving local communities via convenience outlets, however, this has recently also attracted the multiples. Other traditional formats include small shops, supermarkets and superstores. The development of department stores also facilitated the development of concessions (i.e. shops within the store, often representing major cosmetics or designer clothing brands). Petrol forecourt shops and airport retailing are further symbiotic formats which are currently on the increase.

The out-of-town shopping centre developments of the 1990s spawned additional formats, such as the hypermarket, which is much larger than the comparable superstore, and so-called 'new formats'. The latter are typically very large-scale stores located in out-of-town locations, with a range of unique selling propositions. Warehouse outlets typically offer no-frills displays, limited customer service and value for money. Price clubs operate on a membership basis and offer excellent discounts for bulk buying. Factory outlets sell surplus stock direct from factories. 'Big box' category killers offer a very wide and deep assortment of merchandise in their chosen category, at below industry-average prices. Most new format retailers originated in the US where they have been very successful. Their introduction into European markets is part of the retail internationalization process. In recent years, UK government policy aimed to put a curb on large-scale out-of-town developments, encouraging town centre retail developments instead. Whilst it is recognized that out-of-town locations may be more suitable for the type of merchandise sold by the new format retailers, this has created a less favourable climate for the creation of further retail parks to accommodate new formats. **RAS**

References

Fernie, J. (1995) 'The coming of the fourth wave: new forms of retail out-of-town development', *International Journal of Retail and Distribution Management*, 23(1):4–11.

Hallsworth, A., Jones, K. and Muncaster, R. (1995) 'The planning implications of new retail format introductions in Canada and Britain', *Service Industries Journal*, 15(4):148–163.

Verdict (1993) *Warehouse Clubs*, London: Verdict Research Limited.

Retail parks

A retail park is an area in excess of 50 000 square feet in an edge-of-town or out-of-town location, incorporating a wide range of goods and service retailers and ample car parking. Whilst in the 1980s and early 1990s there was an emphasis on retail warehouse parks, the turn of the century has seen a reorientation towards combined retail and leisure facilities.

The first UK retail warehouse park was opened in 1981. This type of development typically features a cluster of free-standing, single-storey industrial type buildings ('sheds') each occupying a minimum floorspace of 1 000 square metres, selling non-food goods. Retail warehouses are a common format for multiple retailers selling carpets and furniture, electrical goods and do-it-yourself home improvement products, as well as toys, children's goods and motor accessories.

Recently the term retail park has been increasingly applied to 'destination sites', combining catering, leisure, retail shops and services and attracting consumers from a very wide catchment area. The USA is at the forefront of the development of true leisure/retail hybrids, such as those developed by Galyan Trading, whose sites feature ski slopes and canoe runs and are in many ways similar to theme parks.

UK shopping parks usually feature a more modest offering of leisure facilities. However, consumer research indicates that nearly half of adult consumers are happy to go shopping even if they have no particular purchases to make, indicating the vast scope for attracting leisure spending and potential impulse purchasers. In the mid-1990s the UK property developer P&O Shopping Centres created CentrO, the largest European shopping mall. Located in Germany, near Oberhausen, it features a range of retail and leisure outlets and 11 000 car parking spaces. However, legal restrictions on shop opening hours may hinder the exploration of the full potential of the concept. Whilst retail parks may have an adverse impact on trade in the centres of nearby towns, they can also spearhead the development of new communities around them. **RAS**

References

Baron, S., Davies, B. and Swindley, D. (1991) *Macmillan Dictionary of Retailing*, London: Macmillan Reference Books.

Brown, S. (1990) 'Innovation and evolution in UK retailing: the retail warehouse', *European Journal of Marketing*, 24(9):39–54.

Fernie, J. (1995) 'The coming of the fourth wave: new forms of retail out-of-town development', *International Journal of Retail and Distribution Management*, 23(1):4–11.

Retail pricing

Retail pricing is the process of determining the charge to the customer for a product purchased. Potential strategic objectives include maximization of sales or profit and establishing and maintaining competitive and market position.

Classical economic theory on the price/sales volume (i.e. demand) relationship does not generally apply to retail pricing. Retailers often have to set prices for 30 000 plus items and therefore an approach suited to 'multi-product profit maximization' is needed. A clear strategic direction is vital, and pricing must be coordinated with the rest of the marketing mix to create consistent image. Consumer value perceptions are based on the price/quality relationship and brand loyalty decreases price sensitivity. Overt price competition has a powerful impact on longer-term consumer impression of the retailer's price image. Promotional price comparisons often focus on the cost of an average shopping basket as an indicator of overall prices.

Approaches to the pricing of individual product lines can be guided by costs (e.g. 'cost plus', where a percentage mark-up is applied to cost prices) or demand factors (e.g. discounting and premium pricing, where the competitive position is key). In practice, mark-up levels for individual products are based on a bundle of information, including previous prices, local average prices and competitor price comparisons. 'Category management' techniques can help identify the best price and product mix within a category.

A limited number of different price points can be used as focal points, either by direct application ('price lining'), or by grouping prices around them ('price clustering'). The use of psychological prices, such as £4.99, is also popular. Price differentials between a retailer's own brands and manufacturers' brands can build market share for the former. During price wars, for grocery retailers the sale of generic budget own brand items at virtually cost prices is an alternative to across-the-board discounting. For fashion retailers, during seasonal sales periods heavy mark-downs on previous prices are used to generate sales volume. **RAS**

References

Gedenk, K. and Sattler, I. (1999) 'The impact of price thresholds on profit contribution – should retailers set 9-ending prices?' *Journal of Retailing*, 75(1):33–57.

McGoldrick, P.J. (1990) *Retail Marketing*, London: McGraw-Hill.

McIntyre, S. and Miller, C.M. (1999) 'The selection and pricing of retail assortments: an empirical approach – empirical tests in a retail situation', *Journal of Retailing*, 75(3):295–318.

Schmidt, R.A. and Wright, H. (1996) *Financial Aspects of Marketing*, Basingstoke: Macmillan.

Retail pricing strategies

In deciding upon their positioning and pricing, retailers typically adopt one of two strategies: every-day-low-pricing (EDLP) or high-low pricing (HILO).

An EDLP approach resembles a uniform pricing strategy, where the retailer permanently charges low prices. This strategy emphasizes the continuity of prices at a level somewhere between a regular non-sale price and a deep discount sale price (Levy and Weitz, 1995). It is for this reason also referred to as 'every-day-stable-prices'. The HILO strategy, in contrast, is characterized by higher regular prices, but which are accompanied by frequent temporary price cuts on selected items. Retailers adopting a HILO approach (sometimes referred to as 'promo stores') often buy their merchandise on deal. EDLP and HILO are not merely pricing, but overall positioning strategies, i.e. unique combinations of advertising, pricing and service. Promo stores offer a high service level and larger assortments to attract service sensitive, large basket consumers (with higher time constraints). They use the promotions to appeal to cherry pickers for the promoted items, eventually even convincing them to buy non-promoted merchandise from the store. The HILO strategy therefore combines principles of random discounting (selling promoted items to price sensitive consumers through irregular promotions) and of complementary pricing (convincing consumers to buy other items at regular prices once they are in the store). EDLP stores, in turn, try to secure a sufficiently large customer base through low basket prices but offer a lower service level. They attract price sensitive and time constrained shoppers (Lal and Rao, 1997; Bell and Lattin, 1998).

Various authors have discussed the advantages and disadvantages of EDLP versus HILO approaches (see e.g. Levy and Weitz, 1995). While EDLP leads to reduced price and advertising wars, improved inventory management, and lower operating costs, HILO allows for more emphasis on quality and service, creates excitement, and helps move merchandise. **KCa, BF, EG**

References

Bell, D. R. and Lattin, J.M. (1998) 'Shopping behavior and consumer preference for store price format: why 'large basket' shoppers prefer EDLP', *Marketing Science*, 17(1):66–88.

Lal, R. and Rao, R. (1997) 'Supermarket competition: the case of every-day-low-pricing', *Marketing Science*, 16(1):60–80.

Levy, M. and Weitz, B. (1995) *Retailing Management*, Chicago: Irwin.

Retail sector

The retail sector is one of the most rapidly developing sectors within the distribution channel structure. Within it lie diverse firms offering various retail goods and services including food and grocery, clothes, footwear, household goods, banking and financial services, hotels and hospitality services, and many more. In addition, there is a diversity of retail stores ranging from small, specialized shops to large retail chains offering a huge assortment of merchandise and services. In recent years, there has been a growing interest in non-store retailing where retail shopping can be done without the need to visit retail outlets. There is a growing trend towards adopting technology into the formation of retail entities and in the execution of retail operations. E-commerce, for example, is making its presence felt significantly within the retail sector.

Trends within the retail sector have brought about several changes in the development of retailing worldwide. Over the years, the sector has moved into international boundaries where more and more retailers are expanding beyond their domestic markets. The saturation of domestic markets is encouraging retailers to expand into international markets. This has increased competition to the extent that those who failed to meet the standards at the international level are forced to retreat. This was a common scenario in the early 1990s in many countries worldwide including most of the European countries, the United States and Japan. It is expected that the retail sector will expand even further in the new millennium with technology aiding the advancement of this sector worldwide. **RM-R**

References

Lusch, R.F., Dunne, P. and Gable, M. (1990) *Retail Management*, Cincinnati, OH: South-Western Publishing.
Rosenbloom, B. (1981) *Retail Marketing*, New York: Random House.

Retailers as channel participants

Retailers are channel intermediaries involved with the distribution of goods and services. The main target market of retailers is the ultimate consumer rather than business purchaser. Retailers therefore play an important role in breaking bulk where goods bought in large quantities from the wholesalers or manufacturers are broken down into smaller units. Retailers also provide product assortment to consumers when they sell goods from more than one manufacturer.

Retailers represent the final link in the distribution channel where goods and services are made available to final consumers. It is therefore important for retailers to understand consumer needs well as they are the closest to end-users and manufacturers often depend on them for consumer information. Retail managers often make decisions on merchandise assortment, pricing, store atmosphere and customer services in order to achieve a competitive retail strategy that appeals to target customers.

Retailing today has become a very competitive and innovative industry where new forms of retail formats have emerged to meet the changing needs of consumers. Typical retailers such as supermarkets, convenience stores and speciality shops are existing side by side with new forms of non-store retailing including e-commerce and various forms of direct retailing using electronic formats. Direct retailing is expanding since consumers today are looking for more convenient ways of shopping. **RM-R**

References

Berman, B. and Evans, J.R. (1992) *Retail Management – A Strategic Approach*, New York: Macmillan.
Mason, J.B., Mayer, M.L. and Ezell, H.F. (1991) *Retailing*, 4th edn, Boston, MA: Irwin.

Retailing evolution

Retailing has been an important force in the UK economy since the first emergence of market towns, as illustrated by Napoleon, who called England a nation of shop-keepers. For every new generation of consumers, both consumption and retailing practices are transformed in a reflection of broader societal changes, as illustrated by the table, below.

In an agricultural society local markets and small shops dominated. The 19th century industrial revolution created both a working and middle class town popu-lation with regular and growing incomes, resulting in steady demand for mass consumer goods. International export trade and mass manufacturing technology made a wider range of goods available, and retail outlets aided distribution. Also the cooperative movement emerged and became important in grocery retailing. National manufacturer brands grew, and retailers began reaping economies of scale through the introduction of chain stores and self-service. After World War II, retail concentration increased. The second half of the 20th century saw the growth of shopping centres, out-of-town developments and the influx of new formats from the USA. At the end of the century, information technology brought about further transformations. Joined through knowledge sharing and partnership arrangements, supply chains rather than retailers are competing and multiple channel operations are becoming popular. A *trading orientation* is replaced by a *marketing orientation*. **RAS**

Table: **Retail evolution**

	Pre-modern	Modern	Post-modern
Type of retailers	Specialists	One-stop shops	Alliances
Dominant outlet types	Small shops	Supermarkets, superstores, retail warehouses	Parallel channels, mixed portfolio of formats
Location preferences	Town centre	Out-of-town	Parallel investment in town centre, out-of-town and virtual locations
Degree of concentration	Low	High	High
Product range	Narrow	Wide	Very wide
Demand factors	Basic necessities	Mass consumer goods	Very wide range of customized consumer goods
Product sourcing	Local	National/ international	Global
Service	Counter service	Self-service	Wide range of customized service options
Mode of transport	Walking and home delivery	Car	Car and home delivery
Efficiency factors	Relatively inefficient small scale operations	Economies of scale through multiple creation	Economies of scale at supply chain level
Technology	Not essential	Supporting operations	Crucial, at heart of operations
Competition	Between shops	Between multiples and between brands	Between supply chains

References

Bromley, R.D.F. and Thomas, C.J. (eds) (1993) *Retail Change: Contemporary Issues,* London: UCL Press.

Fernie, J. (ed.) (1998) *The Future for UK Retailing: Change, Growth and Competition,* London: Financial Times Business.

Seth, A. and Randall, G. (1999) *The Grocers, the Rise and Rise of the Supermarket Chains,* London: Kogan Page.

Wrigley, N. and Lowe, M. (eds) (1996) *Retailing, Consumption and Capital. Towards the New Retail Geography,* Harlow: Longman.

Retention and loyalty schemes

Marketing is keen to acquire customers, but even keener to retain them because retention costs are significantly lower than acquisition costs. Also, if retained customers can be moved into a meaningful relationship the lifetime values of these customers can be extremely lucrative.

Loyalty should go beyond regular purchasing. Dick and Basu (1994) in their conceptualizing of the loyalty phenomenon argue that 'relative attitudes' are also important. That is, loyalty depends not only on positive attitudes toward the store or brand, but also on differentiated attitudes toward the alternatives (see the figure, below). In other words if a consumer is positive toward store A, and not very positive towards B and C then the consumer might indeed develop loyalty toward A. On the other hand if there are fairly similar positive attitudes toward A, B and C, then there is unlikely to be real loyalty. In this case the consumer might patronize a particular store regularly but because of factors such as convenience and familiarity.

This analysis is useful because it is an explanation of why apparent loyalty (at least regular patronage) might not be true loyalty. Conversely, it contributes to our understanding of why some consumers exhibit aspects of real loyalty without holding particularly strong positive attitudes toward that store. In this latter case the argument would be that a positive but weak attitude toward A might be accentuated by even weaker positive attitudes towards B and C.

Dick and Basu (1994) describe a situation in which relative attitude is low (little to choose between the alternatives) but which is also characterized by high store patronage and they describe this as 'spurious loyalty'. Where, alternatively, there is low patronage but strongly differentiated and positive attitudes toward A, this is 'latent loyalty'. Otherwise expected high patronage in this case might be inhibited by co-shoppers' preferences, for example.

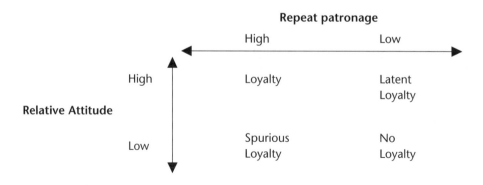

Figure: **Loyalty**
Source: Dick and Basu (1994)

When it comes to real loyalty itself, it is clear by now that they see this as where there is both high patronage and a positive attitude toward the store which is not matched by similarly positive attitudes toward alternative stores. **MJE**

Reference
Dick, A. and Basu, K. (1994) 'Customer loyalty: toward an integrated conceptual framework' *Journal of the Academy of Marketing Science* 22(2):99–113.

Retro marketing

In January 1998, the 'new' Volkswagen Beetle was launched in the United States, to resounding critical acclaim and unalloyed customer approval. Designed by leading automobile imagineer, J. Mays, and manufactured at a state-of-the-art plant in Pueblo, Mexico, the new Beetle combines the distinctive bubble shape of the old VW Bug with the latest automotive technology to produce the perfect retro product, a brilliant combination of past style and present content. The neo-VW, admittedly, is not alone. Apart from the host of automotive imitations – the Chrysler PT Cruiser, the BMW Z9, the new Ford T-Bird and suchlike – retro marketing is de rigueur in numerous product categories including motor cycles, coffee makers, cameras, radios, refrigerators, telephones, toasters and perfumes, to name but a few. Retro, moreover, is apparent across the various components of the marketing mix, from faux-antique packaging and repro retail stores to on-line auctions, which represent an hi-tech throwback to pre-modern pricing policies. Such is its ubiquity, indeed, that most 'new' products these days seem to be line extensions of long-established brand names, be it chunky Kit-Kat, Levi's stay-pressed jeans, Virgin personal pensions or Harley Davidson deodorant (Brown 1999, 2000).

Marketing's latter-day retro orientation has been attributed to all manner of factors, including demographic trends (ageing baby boomers look back), socio-economic turmoil (which stimulates yearning for simpler, less stressful times), the *fin de siècle* effect (end of the century gives rise to retrospection) and the so-called 'postmodern' condition (with its assumption that originality is not only impossible but unnecessary). Regardless of the underlying causes, there are at least three major variations on the retro theme: repro, neo and neo-repro. *Repro* involves reproducing the old pretty much as was, albeit meanings may have changed in the meantime (as, for example, when old products such as Spam and Spangles are relaunched, or ancient black-and-white advertisements are rebroadcast). *Neo* refers to combinations of old and new, usually in the form of old-style styling and hi-tech technology (new Beetle, 1950s Box Brownie with auto-focus and motor wind, etc.). *Neo-repro*, on the other hand, involves second helpings of the past, insofar as it revives or reproduces something that traded on nostalgia to start with (Laura Ashley's recent revamp, *Star Wars Part 1*, new houses built in the mock Tudor style of the late 19th century). Retro marketing, in point of fact, is not confined to goods and services. It is no less evident in the world of ideas, most notably the much-vaunted Relationship Marketing paradigm. Like today's toothpaste and washing powder manufacturers, who promise to 'restore' the natural whiteness of our teeth and 'protect' the colour of our clothes, relationship marketers attempt to retain existing customers rather than create them anew. Despite its proponents' claims to the contrary, relationship marketing is not a new paradigm, a revolution, a breakthrough, the be-all-and-end-all, but an old-fashioned idea with go-faster stripes. So now you know. **SFX**

References
Brown, S. (1999), 'Retro-marketing: yesterday's tomorrows, today!', *Marketing Intelligence and Planning*, 17(7):363–376.
Brown, S. (2000), *Marketing – the Retro Revolution*, London: Sage.

Reverse marketing

Reverse marketing is a new term that indicates the changing role of selling in commercial transactions. Traditionally sellers have tended to be the people who have initiated commercial transactions, and the term 'travelling salesman' is now part of the English vocabulary.

The following figure illustrates what this means. It can be seen that salespeople have traditionally sought out buyers, especially in business to business marketing situations, and visited them on a regular 'sales journey cycle'. In the context of the diagram this is referred to as 'traditional marketing'. In a traditional marketing situation, negotiation tends to reflect a transactional approach to selling, with price being the major criterion. 'Winning individual orders' is important to the salesperson, who is normally remunerated on a basic salary plus commission. Obtaining orders tends to be viewed on a transaction by transaction basis.

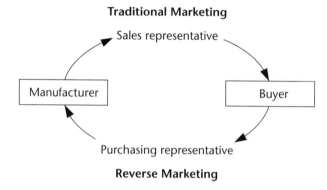

Figure: **Traditional marketing vs. reverse marketing**

The notion of 'relationship marketing' has stemmed from the fact that buyers are increasingly seeking to source their materials and components from a single supplier and form long term relationships. This has been brought about by the adoption of 'just in time' (or 'lean manufacturing') methods of production. Here, standards of quality and reliability of delivery are in many cases more important than price. In order to ensure that they source from the type of manufacturer who can fulfil these quality and reliability criteria, purchasing representatives seek out manufacturers and enter into long term manufacturing arrangements. This switch in initiative in the commercial transaction from seller to buyer is termed 'reverse marketing'. The role of the manufacturer's salesperson then becomes more one of providing liaison between the company's production department and customers, and the task of customer retention becomes as important as winning new customers. **GL**

Reference

Jobber, D. and Lancaster, G. (2000) *Selling and sales management*, 5th edn, Harlow: Prentice Hall, pp. 157–163.

S

Sales analysis

Sales analysis is the process of determining the sources of business according to region, customer type, product type or other classification in order to discover weaknesses or identify patterns in marketing results.

In many cases, a firm might be making satisfactory sales and profits overall, but may have particular products, regions, customer types or even salespeople who are unprofitable or even loss-making (Small Business Report, 1988). Sales analysis enables the firm to identify the good performers and the poor performers, and either stop doing business with the poor performers or try to use the experience gained from good performers to improve the results from the poor performers. Typical bases for sales analysis are as follows.

- Geographical region.
- Customer type.
- Product type.
- Size of customer.
- Sales representative or sales team.
- Type of marketing approach taken.
- Intermediary type.

Comparison of sales from the different sources enables the marketer to decide whether, for example, to continue servicing a particular group of customers or whether to continue distributing through a particular type of intermediary.

Software packages for carrying out sales analysis are widely available. **JWDB**

Reference
Small Business Report (1988) 'Sales analysis: a revealing look at company performance', 13(March): 52–57.

Sales environment

The *sales environment* is created through an integrated approach on store design, merchandising, product placement and space allocation, with the aim of maximizing store attractiveness and profitability.

Increasingly retailers apply the concept of 'retail theatre' and aim to create added value by integrating entertainment with store design. Designers draw on environmental psychology and make use of atmospherics to stimulate the senses (sight, sound, smell and touch). By generating pleasure and arousal in this way, consumers are encouraged in approach and ultimately purchase behaviour. Different kinds of layout can be used to guide the consumer through the store to minimize dead areas and encourage impulse purchases. However, to appeal across all age groups care must be taken not to alienate the older consumer who tends to be less favourably inclined to innovations such as the introduction of music and multimedia.

Developed in collaboration between retailers and manufacturers 'category management' offers a tool for the optimum allocation of display space. It makes use of the knowledge that consumers shop by the category rather than the product and aims to maximize profitability for the category as a whole by using the ideas of 'direct product profitability' (profit after all storage, handling and space costs have been paid for) and 'space elasticity' (the relationship between sales volume and space allocation) in conjunction with space management software. The use of integrated computer based communications between designers and retailers, supported by computer aided design (CAD) packages and 3D modelling and drawing tools has greatly aided improvements in the shopping environment.

Store design is used to create a branded image of the whole retail offering, thus positioning the store and differentiating it from competitors. This aids the introduction of new formats, refurbishments and also globalization. The design and refit cycle is accelerating, and design consultancies take a lead role, integrating all aspects of store image, visual communications and corporate identity. **RAS**

References

Bitner, M.J. (1990) 'Evaluating service encounters: the effects of physical surroundings and employee responses' *Journal of Marketing* 54(April): 69–82.

Clarke, I., Kell, I., Schmidt, R.A. and Vignali, C. (1998) 'Symbolism and meaning in the consumer experience: a semiotic analysis of the "British pub"', *Qualitative Market Research*, 1(2):132–144.

Mintel (1999) *Retail Store Design*, London: Mintel International Group Ltd.

Oldroyd, M. (1998) *Sales and Marketing Environment*, CIM work book series, Oxford: Butterworth-Heinemann.

Sales forecasting

The aim of a sales forecast is to produce an accurate figure for the company's future sales; in practice, this is extremely difficult to do, and all forecasting suffers from a greater or lesser degree of inaccuracy. Because of this, sales forecasting is better carried out as a continuous process rather than a once-a-year exercise; the figure below illustrates the elements in the process.

Forecast calculations are based on conditions within the industry, within the country and within the firm. The forecast is then compared on an ongoing basis with actual results, and the findings are fed back into the company conditions and the forecasting calculation. It should be noted that the forecast itself will affect performance; once a forecast has been made, the salesforce will feel under pressure to achieve it (or if the forecast is perceived as being too easy to achieve, the salesforce may relax a little).

The conditions within the industry, country and firm are themselves the results of other forecasts, which can also become self-fulfilling, particularly in the case of large firms with substantial market shares.

Forecasts may be short-term, (two or three months ahead), medium-term (a year or two ahead) or long-term (for periods of three years or more). Short-term forecasts are usually used for tactical planning, for example to schedule production or to plan leave allowances for salespeople. Medium-term forecasts are of most use in budgeting; accuracy is important because an underestimate of demand might leave the company unprepared to meet customer needs and an overestimate might leave the company with unsold stocks. Some company directors do not understand that salespeople are there to manage and direct demand rather than create it; therefore some sales 'forecasts' are actually generated by directors who want to force salespeople to sell goods whether there is a need for them or not.

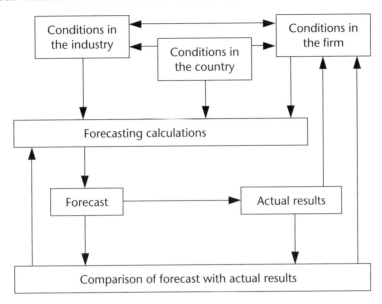

Figure: **Sales forecasting as a process**

Long-term forecasts are used to develop strategic plans. Some industries habitually predict demand for 10 years or more into the future, particularly those industries which rely on large investments in capital equipment; some fast-changing industries may not predict demand for a given product more than three years or so in advance. In general, these concerns belong with the board of directors; the sales manager might have the task of contributing to a long-term forecasting exercise, but is unlikely to have sole responsibility for it (Lancaster and Jobber, 1997). **JWDB**

Reference
Lancaster, G. and Jobber, D. (1997) *Selling and Sales Management*, London: Pitman.

Salesforce organization

Here we refer to the structure and deployment of salespeople, or groups of salespeople, to achieve organizational sales goals. This is most effective where duplication of effort is eliminated, where internal conflicts are minimized and co-operation maximized. This means setting clear objectives, specifying the role for salespeople and the tasks to be performed and organizing them into an effective unit.

The first issue in sales organization decisions is whether to use agents or an internal salesforce. This decision will depend on market characteristics and potential, company characteristics and resources and the degree of specialist product or market knowledge required by salespeople. A second issue is how to deploy salespeople, and this is normally done by geographical, product or market specialization, or by a combination of these methods. The third issue concerns how best to allocate salespeople to sales tasks.

The principles of good organizational design are:

- organizations should be market oriented and customer focused
- organizations should be based around activities rather than people
- authority should be delegated and responsibilities clearly defined
- reasonable span of control
- organizations should be stable yet flexible
- organizations should be balanced and coordinated in terms of activities.

Although the principles of good organizational design remain the same over time, the implication is that to survive in today's dynamic and competitive environment, organizations will have to restructure their communications to be sufficiently flexible and responsive to their customer's demands. Business has become more relationship based, more international, more diverse and more technologically dependent than hitherto. Salesforce organizations must reflect this so that the integration of technology, information and service is adequate for customers and cost effective for the organization. **WGD**

Reference
Futrell, C.M. (1998) *Sales Management: Teamwork, Leadership, and Technology,* 5th edn, Fort Worth TX: Dryden Press.

Salesforce size

This refers to the number of people, approved by management, to perform sales tasks to achieve the organization's selling goals.

There is no one correct way of determining salesforce size although it is possible to reduce waste and increase efficiency by more appropriate deployment of personnel. Key issues concern the type of selling, the nature of the product and the relationship between buyer and supplier.

The first task is to identify the time required for different sales activities and tasks. These include demonstration and presentation time, the proportion of new potential accounts to existing accounts, the time needed for negotiating on price and other aspects of the offer, merchandising and stock management issues. Technical advice, complaint handling, credit and cash collection and paper work, including marketing information and other tasks, increase the time spent on non face-to-face selling thus increasing overhead costs.

Generally, there are three methods for determining salesforce size. First, there is the workload method, based on the premise that salespeople have similar numbers and size of accounts, that the number of calls and travel time is relatively even and therefore the workload can be equalized. This is rarely the case and the most serious defect in this approach is the lack of compatibility between sales potential and workload. The second method is the incremental approach, where salespeople are added as sales per territory increases. The main flaw in this approach is that salespeople follow sales rather than the other way round. Finally, there is the sales potential method that attempts to allocate sales effort to the identified sales potential. Although this is an appropriate principle, the problem is that of accurately forecasting potential at the territory level. **WGD**

Reference
Cooper, S. (1997) *Selling Principles, Practice and Management,* London: Pitman.

Salesforce structure

In this entry we refer to the means by which salesforce effort is allocated to specific sales tasks, to groups of customers, to geographical regions or to specific products or product groups. Initially, the management decision is the degree of centralization required. To be customer driven suggests a high degree of decentralization but this decision must depend upon the market coverage required, the level of service, the costs of service and other situational factors.

Geographic specialization is appropriate in larger rather than smaller organizations, where there is a widely spread customer base rather than only a few, where regional variations are more important than national standards and where personal contact between buyer and seller is frequent rather than occasional. The advantages of a geographical split are likely to be that travel time and expense is lower. Each salesperson can build good customer and area knowledge which itself is a motivating factor in that salespeople manage their territory. There is less confusion, since multiple calling on a single customer is avoided, customers know who is the point of contact. Additionally, management control and evaluation is more easily administered. These advantages are important but the complexity of today's selling job and the dynamics of the business environment may require specialization.

Hence, product specialization is more appropriate where a firm has product lines which differ in technical complexity, end users and profitability. Each salesperson can then attain the necessary expertise in product knowledge to handle different customer requirements more effectively. With this type of organization problems can arise with duplication of effort and multiple calling on one customer. This requires management to promote co-operation between salespeople with minimum conflict and confusion as to who does what job.

Market specialization tends to exist where customers can be segmented or allocated on an individual or group basis. This may be the ultimate in customer orientation but is also a high cost solution. The salesforce structure must be linked to the markets to be served, the characteristics of customers and prospects and specific issues concerning buyer behaviour and buyer processes. This is a complex organizational problem. **WGD**

Reference
Noonan, C. (1998) *Sales Management*, Oxford: Butterworth Heinemann.

Sales management role

The sales manager's role varies with the position held and their level in the organization. These can be classified as 'strategic', 'tactical' and 'operational'. This classification seems to typify the way most sales organizations operate with director, middle managers and first line supervisors. In smaller organizations one person may embrace all three decision levels. At the *strategic* level, sales managers should be concerned with definition of the firm's existing and future business in terms of the markets to be served now and in the future, the types of products which satisfy customers in these markets and the areas of business the company does not want. The strategic decision stage is crucial to long-term business success and is linked to the marketing strategy of the firm.

At the *tactical* level sales management decisions are conducted following marketing and sales strategy decisions. That is, where the market and sales potential is known and the identity and location of customers and prospects has been established. The balance between personal selling and other marketing variables is clear, the role salespeople are to perform is determined and management tasks fall into three areas. First, structuring the salesforce in terms of its size and organizational design. Secondly, developing the salesforce in areas such as recruitment, selection and training. Thirdly, motivating the salesforce through effective supervision, leadership and remuneration and also by means of evaluation and control.

Management concern at the *operational* level is to get people to do the job it wants done in the correct way. Management skills must encourage salespeople to manage themselves and their territories as far as possible. Responsibilities of the manager include the type of person to be recruited in terms of personality, knowledge, skills and motivation. First-line managers must also understand the needs and characteristics of the customers they serve. They must be able to evaluate and react to competitors' sales strategies and other environmental factors. Finally, they must be aware of organizational policies and procedures as they apply to the sales organization and implement rules and regulations for their salespeople. The way this is done can be a strong motivating factor in sales performance. **WGD**

Reference

Grikscheit, G.M., Cash, H.C. and Young, C.E. *Handbook of Selling*, 2nd edn, New York: Wiley.

Sales promotion

Sales promotion is often defined as those marketing communications activities not included under the headings of sales, advertising or public relations (PR). However, this is slightly misleading, because it implies that sales promotion is simply an alternative to these as a marketing communications medium. Although usually discussed within marketing communication, sales promotion represents a customization of the standard marketing mix, which typically aims to influence existing or potential customers. To do this, a promotion may alter the nature of the price, the product or its distribution arrangements and to be successful it may need to be supported by salesforce, advertising or PR activity. Perhaps the shortest way to encapsulate sales promotions is to describe them as 'special offers', but a definition which captures the variety and versatility of the activities included within sales promotion would describe them as: 'marketing activities, usually specific to a time period, place or customer group, which encourage a direct response from customers or marketing intermediaries, through the offer of additional benefits.'

This definition highlights that sales promotions are:

- *non-standard* – promotions are usually specific to a time (e.g. January sales), a place (e.g. offers run jointly between manufacturers and specific retailers) or a customer group (e.g. discount interest rates offered by lenders to new mortgage customers)
- *response-orientated* – while activities such as advertising and PR seek to shape attitudes and to build an image for a company or brand, promotions aim to generate much more specific responses, such as making a purchase, sampling a product, or sending for information about it
- *benefit-orientated* – promotions offer their targets something extra in order to gain a response from them; these benefits may be received instantly (e.g. a free sample), after a delay (e.g. money-off-next-purchase coupons), or they may be cumulative (e.g. supermarket loyalty card schemes).

The definitions of sales promotion that are used are many and varied. For example direct mail is sometimes included as a sales promotion tool, when it is actually one potential means of delivering sales promotions to customers. The line between the conventional market offering and the customized promotional market offering can also become blurred, particularly if promotions conceived as temporary become permanent fixtures, as has happened with many airline frequent-flier schemes. **KP**

References

Peattie, K. and Peattie, S. (1993) 'Sales promotion: playing to win?', *Journal of Marketing Management*, 9(3):255–270.

Peattie, S. and Peattie, K. (1999) Sales promotion, in M.J. Baker, *The Marketing Book*, 3rd edn, London: Butterworth-Heinemann, pp. 418–442.

Sales promotion and consumer behaviour

Sales promotions can influence consumer behaviour in many ways. In many cases a promotion will influence the consumer's choice of product category, brand or retail outlet. They can also influence the pre-purchase stages of the consumption process by encouraging customers to gather product information, try a free sample or product test or visit the point of sale. They can affect the timing of purchases, either by accelerating purchase decisions or moving them to specific times. This can be important in seasonal markets where demand smoothing is desirable. They can affect the volume of consumers' purchasing. Brand-loyal consumers may stockpile while their preferred brand offers a promotion, and brand-switchers may stockpile while any brand is being promoted. Promotions can also be used to influence consumer behaviour post-purchase, for example by using sweepstake prizes to encourage consumers to return completed guarantee cards or customer satisfaction questionnaires. So the narrow view of sales promotion held by some as something which 'rents' short-term increases in sales volume at the expense of building long-term brand loyalty, is clearly misconceived. Sales promotion provides a range of tools, which are varied, often sophisticated and potentially creative. However, in an era when marketing managers are under increasing pressure to produce short-term results, the tactical price-based promotion will remain commonplace.

One issue that should be considered, particularly for price-based promotions, is the danger of changing the consumers' reference price. A reference price represents what customers see as the 'normal' or 'right' price for a product. Excessive discounting can lead to consumers' reference prices being lowered to the extent that they view a return to normal prices as a price rise, and resist it. This provides a lesson that sales promotions, such as other competitive weapons, can have their effectiveness blunted by overuse or careless use. Used thoughtfully, with proper planning, and with careful integration with the rest of the marketing mix, sales promotion can contribute a great deal to the process of communicating with consumers and influencing their attitudes and behaviour. **KP**

References

Chandon, P. (1995) 'Consumer research on sales promotion: a state-of-the-art literature review', *Journal of Marketing Management*, 11:419–441.

Fraser, C. and Hite, R. (1990) 'Varied consumer responses to promotions: a case for response based decision making', *Journal of the Market Research Society*, 32(3):349–375.

Lattin, J.M. and Bucklin, R.E. (1989) 'Reference effects of price and promotion on brand choice behaviour', *Journal of Marketing Research*, 26(4):299–310.

Sales promotion and marketing communications

Sales promotion, a main category area of marketing communications, is a diverse set of promotional activities. People often refer to it as 'below-the-line' promotion although this term actually applies to an even wider group of marketing communications activities (technically, all but advertising).

The economic incentive aspect of sales promotion, such as price deals, are widely recognized. However, sales promotions also embrace communication initiatives such as product leaflets, merchandising and point of sale. Crosier and Bureau (1990) make this point when they describe sales promotion as 'a highly elastic term, embracing a host of marketing tactics'. They suggest 'a fundamental distinction can now be proposed between economic-incentive sales promotions, such as free samples, premium offers, money-off deals … and communication-initiative sales promotions, such as product literature.' Although, these authors refer to sales promotion as a 'host of tactics', Cummins (1998) points out that it can be used strategically as well if it 'enhances the firm's distinctive capabilities, increases competitive advantages and builds long-term relationships'.

Pickton and Broderick (2001) define sales promotion as 'activities used to encourage the trade and/or end customers to purchase or take other relevant action by affecting the perceived value of the product being promoted or to otherwise motivate action to be taken'. They recognize this might be through incentives or through information and that such promotions can be targeted towards employees, investors, the trade, etc., as well as end customers. They can, thus, be used for both 'push' and 'pull' promotions (see 'Trade and consumer promotions'). **DWP**

References

Crosier, K. and Bureau, J.R. (1990), 'Definition of sales promotion' in M.J. Baker, *Dictionary of Marketing and Advertising*, 2nd edn, London: Macmillan.

Cummins, J. (1998), *Sales Promotion: How to Create and Implement Campaigns That Really Work*, 2nd edn, London: Kogan Page.

Pickton, D.W. and Broderick, A. (2001), *Integrated Marketing Communications*, London: Financial Times Prentice Hall.

Sales promotion effectiveness

The effectiveness of sales promotion has often been underestimated. Academic research for many years concentrated heavily on value-increasing promotions, and on their impact on consumers' perception of prices and on purchasing patterns. Practitioners have also mostly limited their evaluation of promotions' effectiveness to studying sales patterns before, during and after a promotion is run. These two factors have combined to focus attention on the rational-economic aspects of promotions, and on their short-term tactical impact on sales. More recent research has suggested that sales promotions can be very effective in meeting more strategic marketing objectives such as raising brand awareness, broadening product use, assisting in brand repositioning, supporting advertising themes and improving customer attitudes towards brands and producers.

Although advertising and sales promotion are often portrayed as rivals for the largest share of the marketing communications budget, it is clear that both techniques work best as components of integrated marketing communications programmes. Sales promotions can take advantage of advertising themes to be easily recognized and understood by consumers. Promotions can also make an effective focus for advertisements highlighting sales, competitions to win exotic prizes and a host of other special offers.

Unlike most advertising, sales promotions can be interactive and can be effective in gathering information about customers as well as communicating information to them. Promotions can create interaction with customers by requiring them to fill in forms, answer questions or visit retail outlets. This information can be used to build customer databases or to explore customers' perceptions of products and their benefits. Guinness, for example, used information gathered from a competition to pinpoint its competitors in the take-home beer market.

Sales promotions are strongly associated with markets such as packaged foods and drinks. They are also sometimes wrongly viewed as effective only as an aid for mature and struggling brands. The list of the Institute of Sales Promotions award winning promotions for 1999 demonstrates the diversity of companies taking advantage of sales promotions and the extent to which they feature in the strategies of leading brands, including: Barclays Bank, Carlsberg-Tetley Brewing, Peperami, Marlboro, Pepsi, National Car Rental, Sainsbury's Supermarkets, One-2-One Telecoms, Kraft-Jacobs-Suchard, Tango and Volvo. **KP**

References
Bemmaor, A.C. and Mouchoux, D. (1991) 'Measuring the short-term effect of in-store promo-
tion and retail advertising on brand sales: a factorial experiment', *Journal of Marketing
Research*, 28(2):202–214.
Tellis, G.J. (1998) *Advertising and Sales Promotion Strategy*, Reading MA: Addison Wesley.

Sales promotion: importance and growth

Measuring the level of marketing expenditure on sales promotion is made difficult
by the inconsistencies in the way it is defined. There is a consensus that promotion
has grown steadily over the last 20 years, comfortably to exceed spending on advertising. The Institute of Sales Promotion estimates that the value of sales promotion
in the UK for 1999 was around £10 billion. For many fast moving consumer goods
companies, promotions account for up to 75 per cent of the marketing communications budget.

Several factors have driven this growth in sales promotion. In part it reflects concern about the cost-effectiveness of traditional 'brand-sell' advertising in the face of
rising advertising costs, increasing advertising 'clutter' and technologies such as
'smart' video recorders, which edit TV commercials out of video recordings. In comparison with these growing doubts about advertising, sales promotion has grown in
credibility, particularly with the widespread use made of promotions by leading
brands such as McDonalds and Coca-Cola. The growth also reflects changes within
industries, where intense competition and the narrowing of differences between
producers make promotions important as tie-breakers in the quest to clinch sales.
Often companies have little choice but to match competitors' promotional offers,
which leads to proliferation. Power balances have also shifted away from manufacturers and towards retailers in key markets for sales promotion such as packaged
foods and drinks. Retailers are increasingly interested in running promotions with
manufacturers to attract increased sales volumes. Finally, customers have changed.
They are no longer willing to congeal into mass markets that can conveniently be
targeted with a single product and single advertising message. Today's consumer is
more individualistic than ever, faced with a wider choice of products and brands
than ever, and is increasingly cynical and 'savvy' in respect to advertising and its
ability to influence them. Sales promotions can offer humour, novelty and tangible
benefits, and reach the customer at the point of sale, where purchases can be
instantly prompted.

Technological advances are also promoting more variety and creativity in sales
promotion. New packaging technologies are allowing a wider range of products to
take advantage of sampling. Electronic commerce has seen a boom in on-line
coupon offers and loyalty schemes. Smart card technology is allowing coupon information to be stored and its value to be encashed automatically. **KP**

References
Peattie, S. and Peattie, K. (1999) 'Sales promotion', in M.J. Baker *The Marketing Book* 4th edn
London: Butterworth-Heinemann, pp. 418–442.
Toop, A. (1992) *European Sales Promotion: Great Campaigns in Action*, London: Kogan Page.

Sales promotion objectives

It might be assumed that the aim of sales promotion is simply the promotion of
sales by encouraging product trial or stimulating additional purchases. However,
there is a range of strategic and tactical objectives that promotions can seek to fulfil, including the following.

- *Creating awareness or interest*: the 1999 Barclays/Cadburys Creme Egg 'How Will

You Save Yours?' promotion generated 85 per cent customer awareness and a sales increase of 190 per cent over forecast.

- *Assisting in the launch of a new brand*: sampling programmes are often used to support product introductions.
- *Reinvigorating a mature brand*: merchandise collections such as the Kodak Gold Collection or Pepsi 'Stuff' been used to attract attention to familiar brands.
- *Deflecting attention away from price competition*: garage forecourt promotions (such as the ubiquitous free glasses) were used for many years to escape straightforward price competition in a largely undifferentiated market.
- *Counteracting competitor actions*: discount coupons can rapidly be issued to boost demand temporarily to respond to competitor initiatives.
- *Reinforcing advertising themes*: the Peperami 'Fanimal' promotion offered toy mascots based on the animated star of their advertisements, leading to a 17 per cent sales increase.
- *Gathering consumer information*: competition entry forms can be used to gather information about consumers and their preferences.
- *Developing relationships with consumers*: loyalty programmes can be used as a basis for relationship marketing.

Typical objectives for a trade promotion would be to:

- encourage sales efforts from intermediaries
- increase shelf space for products
- increase intermediaries' stock levels
- gain support for in-store displays or other promotions
- gain access to new outlets
- counteract pressure from sales downturns or competitor actions
- reinforce communication with, or education of, intermediaries.

A single promotion can often contribute to a number of objectives and can involve more than one company. Joint promotions are increasingly popular and can allow manufacturers and retailers, manufacturers and services companies, or different types of manufacturer to combine in ways that would be infeasible for joint advertising. For example, a promotion run in America by Procter and Gamble offered 750 Cadillac cars as prizes at a cost of $9 million. The seven key P&G brands involved gave General Motors a direct communication channel into 98 per cent of American homes, while the chance of winning a car acted as an incentive to buy P&G products, and provided a useful quality 'cue'. **KP**

References

Cummins, J. (1998) *Sales Promotion: How to Create and Implement Campaigns that Really Work,* 2nd edn, London: Kogan Page.

Peattie, K., Peattie, S. and Emafo, E.B. (1997) 'Promotional competitions as a strategic marketing weapon', *Journal of Marketing Management,* 13(8):777–789.

Sales promotion planning

Despite the level of marketing expenditure being invested in promotions, they have often not enjoyed the level of careful planning that is afforded to advertising campaigns. It is therefore not surprising that mismanaged sales promotions can create problems, which in certain famous cases have proved disastrous. Unexpectedly high redemption rates for premiums or cash-back offers can prove very expensive, as demonstrated by the Hoover Free Flights offer. Coupons can be used fraudulently. Children's toys placed inside food products have led to choking incidents, and delays in fulfilling mail-in offers can lead to consumer dissatisfaction and consumer group involvement.

Good promotional planning can help to avoid such problems, and should consider:

- which of the objectives outlined above the promotion is intended to achieve or contribute to
- the targets for the promotion – how they should be influenced by the promotion, and what response is required from them
- the practical constraints of the promotion such as budget, timings, location, logistics and insurance
- the choice of media used to deliver the promotion, which could be in-store, on-pack, via direct mail or in printed media
- by whom and how the promotion should be managed and evaluated
- how the promotion will relate to the overall marketing strategy for the product or brand, including its positioning, stage in the product life-cycle and communication strategy.

It is also important for promoters to consider the laws governing promotions. This varies between countries, even within the European Union, and the harmonization of European promotional law may threaten several techniques popular in the UK, such as BOGOF (buy-one-get-one-free) offers and prize draws.

The planning and execution of promotions may be conducted by companies themselves, or with the aid of specialist agencies and 'handling houses'. Today there is a trend towards integrated marketing communications agencies, which can help companies to develop advertising campaigns, sales promotions, PR or direct mail campaigns. Such agencies can provide the skills of creativity, design, artwork and purchasing needed to create a promotional campaign. Handling houses act as an interface with consumers by processing information (such as coupons or competition entries) and dispatching premiums, brochures, vouchers and payments. **KP**

References

Cummins, J. (1998) *Sales Promotion: How to Create and Implement Campaigns that Really Work*, 2nd edn, London: Kogan Page.
Quelch, J.A. (1989) *Sales Promotion Management*, Englewood Cliffs, NJ: Prentice Hall.
Strang, R.A. (1976) 'Sales promotion: fast growth, faulty management', *Harvard Business Review*, 54(1):115–124.

Sales promotion types

Sales promotion can be seen as a toolkit encompassing a wide variety of marketing techniques. This toolkit can be sub-divided in many ways, but the most fundamental distinction is between 'value-increasing' and 'value-adding' promotions. Value increasing promotions alter the basic 'deal' (the relationship between the product and its price) by increasing the quantity or quality of the product on offer, or by reducing its price. Price reductions can be direct (e.g. sale or discount), or indirect (e.g. coupon or refund offers). Value adding promotions leave the product/price relationship intact, and instead add something new into the market offering, such as a free gift, an entry into a competition or an extended guarantee.

Promotions vary in terms of their targets. Most target customers, usually with the aim of providing them with an additional incentive to purchase and a reason for buying the promoted brand rather than its competitors. These are known as 'pull' promotions. There are also trade or 'push' promotions, which usually involve offering retailers and other marketing intermediaries incentives to stock and promote particular products. Typical trade promotions include:

- special discounts (known as 'allowances')
- extra product

- gifts
- contests
- the provision of free marketing information, management training, or inventory control assistance
- point-of-sale displays.

A company's own salesforce can also be a target for promotional contests aimed at improving motivation and performance. At their simplest these could be considered as just an element of salesforce remuneration and management. They can, however, be very creative. National Car Rental's 1999 promotion offering film-themed prizes to branch personnel, to encourage them to boost weekend car rental sales, yielded a 456 per cent sales increase.

Although sales promotion is usually associated with consumer markets, it is also an important aspect of business-to-business marketing. Exhibitions stands giving out free gifts and competition entry forms, negotiating special deals for key customers, product samples, and promotional merchandise such as calendars, pens and mugs can all help to promote the company and win business.

Another way of differentiating between promotions is in terms of the benefits that they offer their targets. There are many different types of benefit offered including:

- *simple economic benefits* – from promotions such as discounts, coupons and two-for-the-price-of-one offers
- *risk reduction benefits* – from free samples, product tests, product information and extended guarantees
- *convenience benefits* – from free delivery, free gift-wrapping or free wedding-list services
- *psychological benefits* – from charity-related promotions and from the feeling of being a 'smart shopper' that comes from taking advantage of special offers
- *'fun' benefits* – from competitions, clubs and collectible merchandise. **KP**

References
Diamond, W. and Johnson, R.R. (1990) 'The framing of sales promotions: An approach to classification', *Advances in Consumer Research*, 17:494–500.
Tellis, G.J. (1998) *Advertising and Sales Promotion Strategy*, Reading MA: Addison Wesley.

Sampling

Sampling is the process of selecting a sufficient number of elements from the population so that it becomes a sample for the research. By studying the sample and understanding the properties or the characteristics of the sample subjects, it would be possible to generalize the characteristics of the population. Sampling is one of the major tools of research, which involves the study, in considerable detail, of a relatively small number of informants taken from a larger group. Ideally, the sample should be a good example of the defined universe or population so that the corresponding values of the population such as age, income, percentage of users and non-users can be estimated.

In carrying out research, it would be difficult and impractical to study the whole population. Therefore samples are determined as representations of the population. Studying a sample rather than a whole population is sometimes likely to lead to more reliable results since there is likely to be less error in collecting data, especially when a large number of elements are involved. The required sample size normally depends on the desired level of data precision, the degree and nature of data analyses, the extent of homogeneity of population elements, the amount of research funds available and the time allowed in the study. Since surveys have different objectives, it is necessary to distinguish clearly the aims of the particular survey so that the sample can be designed specifically to obtain the right quantity and quality of information. **RM-R**

References

Lehmann, D. Gupta, S. and Steckel, J. (1998) *Marketing Research*, Massachusetts: Addison-Wesley.
Proctor, T. (1997) *Essentials of Marketing Research*, London: Pitman Publishing.

Scientific method

Research can adopt a scientific method of enquiry. Scientific research has the focused goal of problem solving and takes a step by step approach in its investigation. It is a method of research where the process of identifying problems, gathering data and analysing data are conducted logically and organized systematically. The emphasis of scientific research is objectivity and rigour in the investigative process. Because of the rigour, scientific research allows other researchers to test similar situations and come up with comparable findings. The scientific method of research requires researchers to state their findings accurately, thus allowing a high level of precision and confidence.

Scientific method of research essentially tries to incorporate the precision of science into the methodology and analytical processes, thus allowing for the development of objective conclusions. This method of gathering information also allows for findings to be applicable in other research settings. There is a need to ensure that meticulous details of the research process are taken into consideration. For example, research sampling design has to be logically developed or the theoretical framework needs to be worked out logically and many other details require proper research planned prior to data collection.

It should also be pointed out it is not always possible to conduct research that is totally scientific. There are instances when we may be dealing with more subjective matters such as human feelings, emotions or attitudes. In marketing it is quite common for researchers to require information on consumer attitudes or consumer perceptions, which can be quite difficult to quantify. In such situations, limitations have to be acknowledged. Still, to the extent that the research can be designed to ensure objectivity, rigour, precision and testability, then scientific investigation methods would have been followed. **RM-R**

Reference

Sekaran U. (1996) *Research Methods for Business*, 2nd edn, New York: John Wiley & Sons.

Secondary research

Secondary research is research that focuses on secondary data or data that is already available. It may be obtained from internal and external data sources. Internal data sources include sales records, cost information, distributors' report and consumers' report. This is information that is readily available within a marketing firm. External sources include reports from government agencies and trade associations, books, periodicals, newspapers, companies' annual reports, syndicated commercial reports and computer retrievable databases. The main benefit of secondary data in comparison with primary data is that it is less costly and usually takes less time to collect. However, the main limitation is that it may have been previously collected for some other purpose and so may not meet the needs of the existing research exactly. In addition, there is a possibility that it may be outdated.

Secondary data does have several uses that can be beneficial to researchers. It may actually provide enough information to resolve the problem being investigated without the need for further primary data. It can also be a valuable source of new ideas that can be explained later through primary data. In addition, secondary data helps to define the problem and assists in the formulation of hypotheses. With secondary information, a better understanding of the research problem is possible. **RM-R**

References
Proctor, T. (1997) *Essentials of Marketing Research*, London: Pitman Publishing.

Segmentation

Market segmentation involves subdividing a market into distinct and increasingly homogeneous subgroups of customers, where any subgroup can conceivably be selected as a target to be met with a distinct marketing mix.

A segment is a group of customers or potential customers who share some common characteristics that make them different from other groups of customers. Segmentation is a fundamental area of market strategy, although it is commonly only considered from a tactical perspective within many organizations.

Essential data is required before decisions can be made about the variables on which to segment the market. This data includes an understanding of how the market works, its size, descriptors for the different customers found within the market, the key product and service requirements from the customer's perspective and the consequential benefits.

There is a wide number of variables that can be considered for consumer segments, where often two or more bases might be valid:

- *geographic* – regions, density, population (e.g. different countries with different cultural differences and tastes)
- *geodemographic* – systems such as ACORN and MOSAIC
- *demographic* – sex, age, nationality, family life cycle
- *behavioural* – benefits sought, usage rate, loyalty status, attitudes (e.g. toothpaste for smokers)
- *psychographic* – personality, Mitchell's VALs (lifestyle groups), Young and Rubicam's 4Cs (cross-cultural consumer characterization); a major UK theme park uses lifestyle groups to segment the market and categorizes them as 'Cash Rich' and ''Ere We Go's'

However, in relation to today's postmodern culture, it can be considered that markets are more fluid than stable, with consumers or customers representing a fragmented set of variables. This therefore has implications when trying to consider the market segments as homogeneous, indeed, these fragmented markets may mean that some of the traditional segmentation techniques such as demographics are not being effective. Therefore, marketers may need to consider smaller and smaller segments, which may result in considering customers' individual requirements, and mass customization or tailor-made products may be more appropriate.

Approaches or variables for segmenting business to business markets can be more complex, such as demographic issues relating to the type of industry, geographic concerns in relation to regions and territories, operating variables such as technology, user status (e.g. heavy – key accounts), purchasing approaches which are related to buying criteria and policies (e.g. the National Health Service seeks quality at a low price and mainly buys centrally), situational factors such as the urgency or size of orders. **RA**

References
Firat, A.F. and Shultz II, C.J. (1997) 'From segmentation to fragmentation: markets and marketing strategy in the postmodern era', *European Journal of Marketing*, 31(3/4):183–207.

McDonald, M., and Dunbar, I. (1998) *Market Segmentation: How to Do It, How to Profit From It*, London: Macmillan Press.

Tapp, A. (1998) *Principles of Direct and Database Marketing*, London: Financial Times/Pitman Publishing, pp. 55–77.

Segmentation, targeting and positioning

Because customers differ, often in a wide variety of ways, a single product or marketing approach is rarely capable of appealing to the needs and wants of all buyers within a particular market. Given this, the marketing planner needs to categorize buyers on the basis both of their characteristics and their specific marketing needs with a view to adapting the product and/or the marketing programme to satisfy these different needs and demands.

Market segmentation, targeting and positioning (STP) consists of three stages:

- the *segmentation* or sub-dividing of a market into smaller groups within which there are broadly homogeneous patterns of need
- the selection by the strategist of those segments which the organization will then *target* or focus upon
- the development of an offer within each of these segments that is most likely to appeal to the targeted customer groups (*positioning*).

Via the first of these steps, the marketing manager seeks to break the market into strategically manageable parts on the basis of demographic, geographic, psychographic, life style and/or purchasing differences and similarities.

Having decided how best to segment the market, the marketing manager then faces a series of decisions on how many and which segments to approach or target. In doing this four factors need to be considered:

- the size and growth potential of each segment
- the overall structural attractiveness of favoured segments
- the organization's objectives and resources
- the ability of the organization to establish itself within its chosen segments and operate effectively.

The final strand of STP marketing involves selecting the position the product is to occupy within the segment. In doing this, the organization is informing customers what the product means, the values that are associated with it and how it differs from competitive offers. **CTG & RMSW**

References

Hooley, G.J., Saunders, J. and Piercy, N.F. (1998) *Marketing Strategy and Competitive Positioning*, 2nd edn, Hemel Hempstead: Prentice Hall Europe.

McDonald, M.H.B. and Dunbar, I. (1998) *Market Segmentation: How to Do It, How to Profit From It*, Basingstoke: Macmillan Press.

Rapp, S. and Collins, T. (1990) *The Great Marketing Turnaround – the Age of the Individual and How to Profit From It*, Englewood Cliffs, NJ: Prentice Hall.

Semiotics

Signs and symbols are all around us. They help us to understand our lives. They can appeal to any of our senses (sight, sound, smell, taste and touch). A sign is 'anything that stands for something (its object) to somebody (its interpreter) in some respect (its context)' (Mick, 1986). The study of these is known as 'semiotics', from the Greek *sema*, meaning marks or signs. The subject matter of semiotics has been described as 'the exchange of any messages whatever and the system of signs which underlie them' (Sebok, 1991). Peirce (Hartshon *et al.*, 1975) regarded semiotics as 'super-ordinate' to all other human social sciences. We even make extensive use of signs in our everyday conversations and interactions, consider those in the figure below.

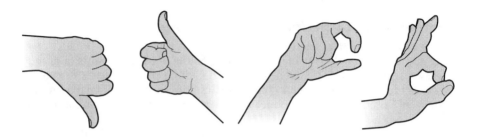

Figure: **Hand signs**

Signs are 'shorthand' communication tools because they convey a great deal of meaning efficiently and, usually, very effectively. To indicate how powerfully they can communicate, consider the shapes and words in the figure below. The shapes and words are meaningless, yet when asked to pair them together, the vast majority of people associate the left hand figure with Omlaru and the right hand figure with Katati.

Omlaru

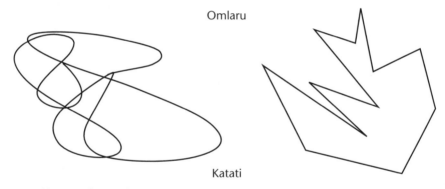

Katati

Figure: **Signs and meanings**

And this is how signs work, by association, these associations being made as part of our growing up, our language, religion and culture. It is not surprising, then, that some signs and symbols, shapes and colours are relatively universal, whereas others vary from country to country. Reds, yellows and oranges are associated with warmth, blues with cold, but the meaning of black and white vary. In some societies black is associated with death whereas in others, white is the colour of funerals and mourning, although, as Danesi (1993) points out, colours (and other signs) have different meanings depending upon the context in which they appear.

Marketing communications make extensive use of signs, symbols, colours and shapes, not least because a great deal has to be conveyed in a short time and space. In particular, use is made of logos, company colours, packaging, musical phrases, faces of personalities or cartoons (consider Disney's Mickey Mouse and Kentucky Fried Chicken's Colonel Sanders), and so on. Over time, these become closely associated with particular companies. Some of the best known throughout the world are the logos for Shell, McDonalds, Nike and Coca Cola. Wherever they appear, there is immediate recognition and associations are made. **DWP**

References

Danesi, M. (1993) *Messages and Meaning: An Introduction to Semiotics*, Toronto: Canadian Scholar's Press.

Hartshon, C., Weiss, P. and Burks, A.W. (eds) (1975) *Collected Papers of Charles Sanders Peirce*, Cambridge: Harvard University Press.

Mick, D.G. (1986), quote from C.S. Peirce in 'Consumer research and semiotics: exploring the morphology of signs, symbols and significance', *Journal of Consumer Research* 13(September): 196–213.

Sebok, T.A. (1991) *A Sign is Just a Sign*, Bloomington: Indiana University Press.

Service quality

Because of the intangibility of service it is important that it is delivered to a consistently high standard so customers can recount the experience in a positive manner. This can result in word of mouth recommendation to colleagues, family and friends. A service is perceived to be provided at a certain level, and if expectations are exceeded then the likelihood is that the customer will become a repeat purchaser. Parasuraman *et al.* (1985) have devised a 'SERVQUAL' model, which identified a number of gaps that can result in ineffectual service provision.

- *The gap between management perception and customer expectations* – which means that management does not appreciate the customers' needs.
- *The gap between service quality specifications and management perception* – which means that management does not set standards of performance.
- *The gap between service quality specifications and the delivery of service* – which means that operational personnel may be inadequately trained to meet the standards expected.
- *The gap between service delivery and external communications* – where the expectations from promotional activity are not matched in practice.
- *The gap between perceived and expected service* – where customers envisage a better service than the one that has been provided.

A service that is well managed means that board level management is committed to quality, high standards of service and a system for monitoring the level of service performance (see 'Service quality measurement'). **GL**

Reference

Parasuraman, A., Zeithaml, V.A. and Berry, L.L. (1985) 'A conceptual model of service quality and its implications for future research' *Journal of Marketing*, (Fall): 44.

Service quality measurement

In practical terms this means the process of auditing the levels of service performance of both the company's offerings and those of its competitors.

There are a number of marketing research techniques that can measure comparative performance, including 'mystery shopping', whereby purchases are made anonymously in chosen service outlets to ascertain whether what happens in practice matches up to that which is planned and expected. An example is certain franchise food establishments that employ researchers to test regularly the quality of service in their outlets. A number of criteria are investigated, including the way the customer is met and greeted, how long they are kept waiting before they were seated and how the ordering process is conducted. It even goes into details such as the number of staff on duty and extends to matters such as the table layout and the condition of toilet facilities.

Another method is to employ regular customer feedback measures whereby service provision is measured anonymously against those of competitors through an independent marketing research agency. This can measure criteria such as how complaints are dealt with, how responsive the company is to customers' needs and how the company's service matches up to those of competitors. **GL**

References
Berry, L.I. and Parasuraman, A. (1991) *Marketing Services: Competing through quality*, New York: Free Press.

Services

A service is an intangible satisfaction that a company offers to customers. Services are often linked to the provision of goods. In the case of cars, goods are the principal element of the sale, and the after sales service, although important, is a lesser component of the commercial transaction. In the case of a train journey, the principal element is the service of transportation. Sometimes tangible goods are associated with the service such as the on-train restaurant service or a timetable. A pure service is where no goods are associated with the purchase of the service, such as cleaning and garden care.

Services such as vending equipment are purely impersonal, whilst others, such as restaurants, involve people – and in this case is it primarily people that make the service successful. Similarly, some services, such as restaurants, require the presence of the customer, whereas others, such as the servicing of a car, do not.

A number of features distinguish services from physical products.

- *Intangibility* – where the service cannot be seen or examined prior to purchase, and the purchaser has to envisage it through prior description or experience.
- *Inseparability* – where the service is usually produced and consumed at the same time (e.g. a meal in a restaurant), which is different to physical products.
- *Variability* – where because each service depends upon the personnel who produce it and the customers who use it, the circumstances surrounding the sale will vary from sale to sale, so the service will vary between transactions. Service companies will seek to obviate this by attempting to standardize service performance throughout the organization.
- *Perishability* – refers to the fact that some services such as rail services cannot be stored. If a train runs with a low volume of passengers on one journey, the spare seats cannot be stored for a future occasion. **GL**

References
Lancaster, G. and Massingham, L. (1999) *Essentials of Marketing*, 3rd edn, Maidenhead: McGraw-Hill, pp. 231–235.

Services brands

Services brands face challenges beyond those of product brands, because of their form. However, the concept of the brand is common between services and products; it is the brand's execution that is different. It is therefore necessary to appreciate the services brand's execution.

The first challenge is intangibility. To overcome this many services brands emphasize their distinctive logos, providing tangible clues. Reputation and size of a service brand are used by consumers as proxies for quality, and organizations frequently link their services brands with the corporate brand to facilitate associations.

The inseparability of production and consumption is another challenge. Consumers' expectations may differ between service encounters because of the extent to which they interact with staff. This can be partially resolved by care in selecting and training staff. It can also be resolved by ensuring consumers are aware of their roles as, for example, McDonald's ensures through the signage and design of its outlets. By focusing on building brand relationships in consumer-staff interactions, services brands can be tailored more to individuals' needs.

Owing to the difficulty of ensuring consistent staff behaviour, this impacts on perceived quality. Some argue for careful planning, automation and regular performance reviews to reduce this problem, in essence leaving little discretion to staff and where possible replacing any staff activities with technology. An alternative perspective argues that if the organization has a strong corporate culture, this signals to staff the type of behaviour expected and then allows them a little latitude when dealing with consumers to tailor the service brand.

Services brands face the challenge not only of developing an image to attract consumers, but then stopping competitors from alluring them. This is typically faced by pensions and life assurance brands, where the brand promise is bought long before the benefit is realized. Regular consumer communication helps reinforce loyalty, as does the development of a respected reputation. **LdeC**

References
Blankson, C. and Kalafatis, S. (1999) 'Issues and challenges in the positioning of service brands: a review', *Journal of Product and Brand Management* 8(2):106–118.

Camp, L. (1996) 'Latest thinking on the optimization of brand use in financial services', *The Journal of Brand Management* 3(4):241–247.

de Chernatony, L. and Dall'Olmo Riley, F. (1999) 'Experts' views about defining services brands and the principles of services branding', *Journal of Business Research* 46(2):181–192.

de Chernatony, L. and McDonald, M. (1998) *Creating Powerful Brands in Consumer, Service and Industrial Marketing*, Oxford: Butterworth-Heinemann.

Levitt, T. (1972) 'Production line approach to services', *Harvard Business Review* 50(September–October): 41–52.

Shopping centres

A shopping centre is a planned scheme for a particular retail location, usually owned by a property development company (e.g. Capital Shopping Centre or P&O Shopping Centres) and incorporating a managed mix of tenants and outlet types. Named department and variety stores (such as Selfridges, Marks & Spencer, Debenhams) are typically featured as anchors.

Shopping centre numbers and floor space have consistently grown for the last 30 years, and at present there are approximately 800 shopping centres in the UK. Completed in 1986, the Metro Centre was the first major out-of-town development, since then the trend has been for retailers to develop sites within out-of-town and regional centres rather than the High Street. From a retailer point of view, advantages of shopping centre locations include better coordination of management and promotion, larger, more flexible units and higher levels of pedestrian flow. Higher rentals and service charges, combined with long leases, pose some disadvantages. Also, a very long planning horizon is needed, since planning applications for new out-of-town developments can take up to 10 years to process.

For the consumer, shopping centres can offer a more attractive, safer and user-friendly shopping environment, combined with a more cohesive retail offer and a larger choice of shops. Consumers are increasingly mobile and time poor; with three quarters of households owning a car, convenience, free parking, speedy access and Sunday and late opening hours are important attractions. Occasional complaints of overcrowding are no real deterrent. Large out-of-town shopping centres are most popular with affluent shoppers under the age of 35.

Metro Centre, Merry Hill, Meadowhall and Lakeside are the most successful UK retail locations by both turnover and profitability. Current planning guidelines aim to slow down out-of-town developments and strengthen town centres. However, shopping centres may provide the focal point for the development of newly evolving communities, as illustrated by the fact that both Merry Hill and the Metro Centre have been redesignated town centres in their own right. **RAS**

References

Baron, S., Davies, B. and Swindley, D. (1991) *Macmillan Dictionary of Retailing*, London: Macmillan Reference Books.

McGoldrick, P.J. (1992) *Regional Shopping Centres: Out-Of-Town vs. In-Town*, Aldershot: Avebury.

Miller, D., Jackson, P. and Thrift, N. (1998) *Shopping, Place and Identity*, London: Routledge.

Mintel (1997) *Shopping Centres*, Special Report, London: Mintel International Group.

Situational analysis

Relevant information must be gathered in order to assist marketing managers in the development of strategies. Marketing management is a continuous process of collecting and assessing relevant information that may help improve the firm's marketing operations. The more rigorous the process of collecting this information, the better the decisions made. In many instances, managers make decisions without prior analysis of the situation. The likely outcome of this is a bad effect on sales and profitability since decisions made were not based on quality information. Therefore, situational analysis is necessary in order to ensure that concrete procedures are set up for assessing the environment and the marketing system. In addition, a situation analysis evaluates the internal strength and weaknesses of the firm to ensure that the right information is fed into the system for effective decision making.

A situation analysis is essentially a continuing process of gathering and analysing environmental and internal information. Environmental information consists of data gathered from the environment. It identifies the threats and opportunities within the marketing environment and assesses the competitive situations. In addition, trends that affect demands are also evaluated to provide marketing decision makers with the right input to plan their marketing strategies. A major responsibility of the marketing research function is to provide relevant information that will help detect problems and opportunities. At the internal level, information on resource availability, sales data and performance indicators are assessed and then matched with information relating to issues external to the organization. In this way, marketing decision makers are likely to have an effective pool of information to make the right decision. **RM-R**

Reference

Kumar, V., Aaker, D.A. and Day, G.S. (1999) *Essentials of Marketing Research*, New York: John Wiley & Sons.

Social class

In almost every society, there is a form of structure that divides the people within it. Social classes are divisions that exist within a society that are permanent and are structured in some orderly manner. Combining a number of factors such as income level, occupation, education, wealth and other variables may form social classes. In most societies, it is common to group social classes into upper, middle and lower classes. The upper class of most societies includes the aristocracy, the new social elite and the professionals. These groups of consumers often view themselves as intellectual, liberal, political and socially conscious (Hoyer and MacInnis, 1997). The middle class consists of white-collar workers and often they look at the upper class for guidance on certain behaviours, for example, proper etiquette, fashion selections and leisure activities. The lower classes are the working class consumers, generally represented by the blue-collar workers. The working class tends to be more resistant to change and they exhibit distinct patterns of consumption.

Members within a social class share similar values, interests and behaviours. This is important because they tend to share the same purchasing and consumption patterns. Social classes show distinct product and brand preferences, especially for goods considered as luxuries such as cars, furnishings and leisure activities. People who are grouped within the same social class are approximately equal in terms of their social standing and they tend to socialize with people within the same social structure. In essence, social class structures are important because they strongly affect norms and values and this in turn affects behaviours. Such behaviours exert strong influence on decisions of acquisitions, consumption and disposition. Thus, a consumer's buying behaviour will be greatly affected by their social class and the extent of influence exerted by the social classes. **RM-R**

Reference
Hoyner, W. and MacInnis, D.J. (1997) *Consumer Behavior*, Boston: Houghton Mifflin Company.

Social influences

Social groups have been known to exert strong influence over their members. The process of social influence can take place in several ways. For instance, a person may imitate the behaviour of others whom he or she believes are behaving the correct way. There are situations when members of a group are not sure of the correct way to behave and therefore will follow the way the group behaves as a guide to the 'right' behaviour. Sometimes social influence occurs when a person conforms to meet the expectations of another person or the group. Conformity may occur because of cultural pressures, fear of deviance or commitment or dedication to the group.

Social influence may be divided into 'normative social influence' and 'informational social influence' (Wilkie, 1994). *Normative social influence* exists when there is a strong social pressure in the decisions that consumers make, for example, when a consumer buys a brand only to please, gain others' approval or avoid disapproval. When consumers learn relevant information about products or services from other people or groups and are influenced by these sources of information, *informational social influence* exists. The content of the information is an influencing factor that may get consumers to behave in a certain manner.

It is quite common to look at the behaviour of others to provide a yardstick to reality (Solomon, 1996). As a means of increasing confidence, consumers tend to look at the behaviour of others as a benchmark for self-evaluation. This form of comparison often occurs with people who may share some similarities with the consumer. To marketers, the process of social influence should be well noted because targeting appropriate marketing efforts at the person or group exerting the social influence may be worth the effort because of the impact they have on consumers' buying behaviours. **RM-R**

References
Solomon, M.R. (1996) *Consumer Behavior*, Englewood Cliffs, NJ: Prentice Hall.
Wilkie, W.L. (1994) *Consumer Behavior*, New York: John Wiley & Sons.

Social responsibility and privacy

Whether an individual perceives there to be any infringement of privacy resulting from direct marketing activity is of course an individual matter, but the potential concerns include the following.

- *Physical privacy,* which relates to the volume of direct marketing that, after a certain level, consumers might see as a physical intrusion.
- *Inaccuracy:* here the use of inaccurate data results in negative consumer reactions.

- *Information privacy*, which refers to the ability of individuals to determine the nature and extent of information about them being communicated to others. Once a database has been compiled many direct marketers sell mailing lists to interested parties on the basis of various profiling exercises on the data. The dilemma therefore is one of balancing consumers' rights to control access to their personal information and companies' rights to information access for business purposes. A recent debate that epitomizes many of the issues involved concerned the use of the electoral roll. This was not collated for marketing purposes and perhaps should not therefore be used in this way. On the other hand, without the electoral roll it would be difficult to identify individual households from census data and therefore individualized accurate targeting might be jeopardized, resulting in more rather than less unwelcome targeting.
- *Environmental* concerns: even though many consumers think there might be a depletion of natural (forest) resources as a result of large quantities of direct mailings, most of the paper is actually derived from managed and renewed plantations.
- *Wider social responsibilities* include debating whether the acquisition by marketing of 'state' data (such as the census) is unethical and similarly the ethics involved in the acquisition by the state of marketing data (such as the Inland Revenue wanting to have loyalty scheme data to check those whose tax affairs they are investigating). There might also be concerns that criminals could access personal details of customers from databases, for example for targeting burglaries. MJE

References

O'Malley, L., Patterson, M. and Evans, M. (1997) 'Intimacy or intrusion? The privacy dilemma for relationship marketing in consumer markets', *Journal of Marketing Management*, 13.

Patterson, L., O' Malley, M. and Evans, M. (1997) 'Database marketing: exploring consumer concerns' *Journal of Marketing Communications*, 3(3):151–174.

Sponsorship

Sponsorship is often considered to be an element of public relations although it is a specialist field in its own right. It is a rapidly growing area of marketing communications and can take many forms, from the sponsorship of individuals to the sponsorship of companies and events. Although common practice in the USA for many years, elsewhere it has only been during the 1990s that there has been any significant sponsorship of films, television programmes, product placement and cause-related activities.

The most prolific areas of sponsorship are in sports and the arts; sponsors often relying on television coverage to extend their target audience reach. A more subtle form is product placement, arranging for a company's product to be included in film and TV programme production so that it may be seen being used in favourable situations. Ford and Chrysler cars have provided vehicles for film sets for many years. It is widely used by drinks companies such as Perrier and Coca Cola. Ray-Ban gained wide recognition for their 'Aviator' sunglasses after they were used in the film 'Top Gun' staring Tom Cruise. BMW supplied the makers of the film, 'Tomorrow Never Dies' with 17 750iL cars in order to have their product associated with the James Bond character (Oakes, 1997).

Berrett (1993) defines sponsorship as 'a contribution to an activity by a commercial organization in cash or in kind, with the expectation of achieving corporate and marketing objectives.' It is not the same as charitable giving (although charities may well be the beneficiaries) in that a commercial benefit is expected by the sponsor. It is used by some organizations to overcome regulatory barriers that otherwise restrict other forms of promotion. This has been especially true in the tobacco industry. Sponsorship is less explicit than other promotional tools in that the sales message is usually less direct and relies instead on the development of favourable associations between the sponsor and what is being sponsored. **DWP**

References
Berrett, T. (1993), 'The sponsorship of amateur sport – government, national sport organisation, and corporate perspectives', *Society and Leisure*, 16:323–346.
Oakes, P. (1997), 'Licensed to sell', *The Guardian*, 19th December, p. 13.

Stages of economic development and marketing

An examination of international trade statistics will reveal a pattern of trade that will surprise no one, namely that economic development is one key to understanding marketing opportunities. Most trade takes place between the nations that are most developed. It must follow that there is a link between economic development and marketing. This is not to say that no trade takes place between the most developed and the least developed, but the nature of this exchange is different. For example, undeveloped countries' natural resources are needed by the most developed economies, providing a basis for exchange.

A methodology for handling the issue of economic development has been developed, and it is of interest to marketers because it throws light on both qualitative as well as quantitative factors that will define marketing opportunity. Seven environmental factors are analysed and graded on a scale of hot to cold. The methodology looks such as this:

Degree of environmental characteristics	Hot country	Moderate country	Cold country
Political stability	High	Medium	Low
Market opportunity	High	Medium	Low
Economic development and performance	High	Medium	Low
Cultural unity	High	Medium	Low
Legal barriers	Low	Medium	High
Physiographic barriers	Low	Medium	High
Geo-cultural barriers	Low	Medium	High

Clearly the methodology is crude, the threefold classification judgemental. However, the methodology has been empirically applied by Sheth and Lutz (1973), and the resulting league table appears to have meaning. It is useful in so far as it suggests that it is possible to classify countries as having market potential at an aggregate level, although this type of analysis may conceal market opportunities at a particular industry or product specific level.

In general, advanced countries have hot values (USA, UK, West Germany, France, Netherlands, Canada, Belgium, Denmark, Italy, Taiwan are the top 10) and the least developed have cold values (Yemen, Laos, Afghanistan, Nepal, North Vietnam, Israel, Burma, Pakistan, Iraq and Jordan constitute the bottom 10).

I do not particularly like this type of analysis because the effective marketer is looking for particular opportunities and this type of general analysis may obscure such opportunity. **MJT**

Reference
Sheth, J.N. and Lutz, R.J. (1973) 'A multivariate model of multinational business expansion', in S.P. Sethi, and J.N. Sheth, (eds), *Multinational Business Operations* in *Marketing Management*, California: Goodyear Publications.

Store location

Despite the growth of non-store retailing, store location remains vital to retail success. Location strategy must reflect overall corporate strategy and trading policies, achieving its objectives via acquisitions or new store development. In a climate of rising property and land costs, and with 25 year leases the norm, location decisions imply a substantial long-term financial commitment to investment in fixed assets.

An array of sophisticated site evaluation techniques is available, but often only the large multiples have the expertise to apply them all. The *analogue method* uses data on comparison stores with similar characteristics to forecast potential sales for new locations. The *checklist technique* makes use of numerous internal (e.g. historical data) and external data sources (e.g. Experian postcode data on the population) to construct lists of relevant factors, such as information on local consumers and competitor stores within the catchment area, accessibility of the proposed site, and projected costs of the development. *Multiple regression models* make use of spreadsheet technology and known relationships between store sales volume and other variables, such as selling area and number of competitors within a certain radius, to predict likely sales for a proposed new store. *Spatial interaction* or *gravity models* make predictions based on the assumption that future sales are likely to be influenced by the store or centre attractiveness and travel distance.

In the UK planning policy guidance notes inform local authority land-use plans which determine whether planning permission for proposed development is granted. In making this decision local authorities take into account the need for consumer choice, sustainability, the desirability of protecting greenfield sites and maintaining a healthy High Street and the likely impact of the new development on the environment, traffic and other retailers. Following a prolonged trend towards out-of-town developments, retailers are now successfully diversifying by format and location, simultaneously investing in large scale out-of-town developments and small scale High Street convenience stores. **RAS**

References

Fernie, J. (ed.) (1998) *The Future for UK Retailing: Change, Growth and Competition*, London: Financial Times Business.

Findlay, A. and Sparks, L. (1999) *A Bibliography of Retail Planning*, Stirling: The National Retail Planning Forum, Institute for Retail Studies.

Guy, C. (1994) *The Retail Development Process: Location, Property and Planning*, London: Routledge.

Medway, D., Alexander, A., Bennison, D. and Warnaby, G. (1998) *Retailer Involvement in Town Centre Management*, MMU research report 98/1.

Pal, J., Bennison, D. and Clarke, I. (1995) 'Location decision making: an exploratory framework for analysis', *International Review of Retail, Consumer and Distribution Research*, 5(1):1–20.

Wrigley, N. and Lowe, M. (eds.) (1996) *Retailing, Consumption and Capital. Towards The New Retail Geography*, Harlow: Longman.

Strategic alliances

Alliances are bonds or connections between families, states, parties or, in this case, commercial organizations. In business, an alliance is normally strategic in nature and forms an association of two or more organizations united by a formal contract or treaty for some agreed-upon purpose, usually to increase the competitiveness of both organizations or parties by combining their value chain activities. Most alliances are by their very nature defensive in form, as their purpose is to counter the threat of competition – frequently two companies who might in other circumstances be competitors or common enemies unite to form a strategic alliance. This formality requires that at least two parties pledge mutual assistance against an actual or potential competitor. The basis for an alliance frequently stems from the advantages gained by collaboration between organizations and commonly takes the form of the exchange of technology, research and development, distribution and supplier relationships, and other market related benefits. It is often the nature of markets, viz. the difficulty of entry, that provides a major incentive for the formation of a strategic alliance.

For most organizations, reaching global markets and realizing their full global potential is relatively hard without some form of partnership or licensing arrangement. In some markets, for example Japan, forming a partnership with one of the major Japanese organizations is often a precursor to market entry. The pace of technology and the diffusion of new products requires short lead times and highly efficient distribution and promotional capabilities. In other markets, such as Europe, governments may unite to fund expensive projects rather than allow outsiders to dominate. The development of the European airbus project, for example, brought together the resources of Britain, Germany and France in the face of the threat from Boeing. In the main, insufficient resources and/or supply chain issues are sufficient incentive for companies to form strategic alliances. AJN

References

Bronder, C. and Pritzel, R. (1992) 'Developing strategic alliances: a conceptual framework for successful co-operation', *European Management Journal*, 10(4).

Gugler, P. (1992) 'Building transnational alliances to create competitive advantage', *Long Range Planning*, 25(1):90–99.

Strategic and tactical direct marketing

Although the marketing database can merely be used as a list from which to target customers via direct marketing activity, it can also provide information for both planning and analysis purposes.

Shaw and Stone (1988), for example, propose a four stage process of development of the marketing database. In *phase one* they suggest the database is merely a sales database originating from accounting systems and focusing more on product sales than on customers. The *second phase* is where there are often multiple databases for different sales territories or retailers and, although they can be well used within the sector they cover, there can often be overlapping effort due to lack of communication and coordination – customers might receive direct mailings from the same company, but different and even conflicting mailings from different parts of that company. *Phase three* sees more of a customer focus and one database coordinates all communication with customers. Analysis is according to profiles, transactions and other relevant factors in order to determine how to target segments and individuals. In *phase four* there is true integration, when different organizational functions, not just marketing, are linked with the marketing database.

If the organization is not truly customer orientated then there will only be a tactical role for the marketing database, but if used strategically, then it has a central role to play – as DeTienne and Thompson (1996) imply in their definition of database marketing:

'Database marketing is the process of systematically collecting, in electronic or optical form, data about past, current and/or potential customers, maintaining the integrity of the data by continually monitoring customer purchases and/or by inquiring about changing status and using the data to formulate marketing strategy and foster personalized relationships with customers'.

On the other hand, if used merely tactically, the nature of the marketing database does not need to make much reference to corporate strategy or organizational structure and under such circumstances is more concerned with 'the next event' than with a longer term view of customers. MJE

References
DeTienne, K.B. and Thompson, J.A. (1996) 'Database marketing and organizational learning theory', *Journal of Consumer Marketing*, 13(5):12–34.
Shaw, R. and Stone, M. (1988) *Database Marketing*, Aldershot: Gower.

Strategic groups

One of the forms of analysis a company must undertake is to identify who it believes are its competitors. Sometimes, referring to an 'industry' analysis is too broad, since an industry may be made up of many companies, some of which are more natural direct competitors than others.

The basis of strategic group analysis is to identify companies with similar strategic characteristics. These companies may have similar strategies, product ranges, technical capabilities, distribution channels, customer groups etc. In attempting to determine which characteristics are the most appropriate for strategic group analysis, it is necessary to understand the history of the industry, the forces at work in the environment and the underlying strategies of the companies within the industry.

The analysis of strategic groups can be useful in a number of ways. First, it enables companies to identify their closest competitors and to assess on what basis competitive rivalry is likely to take place. Secondly it can indicate how likely it is for one company to move from one strategic group to another. Movement between strategic groups is usually only successfully achieved through acquisition, since many of the skills and capabilities required are difficult to build internally. Thirdly, by analysing different groups within the industry, it is easy to identify gaps which are not catered for or which have become vacant. In the UK, the German food retailer Aldi has displaced Kwik Save as the main food discounter, as the latter attempted somewhat unsuccessfully to shift into another strategic group. Finally, the analysis can also highlight potential problem areas within an industry, which could ultimately impact more on certain strategic groups than others. Despite this, companies must not completely ignore the activities of other strategic groups, since over time, competitive boundaries can merge and distant competitors can become very close. **PBB**

References
McGee, J. and Segal-Horn, S. (1990) 'Strategic space and industry dynamics', *Journal of Marketing Management*, 6(3):175–193.
McGee, J. and Thomas, J. (1986) 'Strategic groups, theory, research and taxonomy', *Strategic Management Journal*, 7(2):141–160.

Strategic marketing management

Strategic marketing management is primarily concerned with the development of the direction of the organization and the alignment of the business with the environment. The strategic marketing management process, which needs to be developed within the overall framework, constraints and expectations of the corporate plan, consists of five distinct stages, which involve the identification of the following.

1. Where the organization is currently– *strategic and marketing analysis*.
2. Where it wants to go – *strategic direction and strategy formulation*.
3. How it might get there – *strategic choice*.
4. Which way is best – *strategic evaluation*.
5. How the management team might best ensure arrival – *strategic implementation and control*.

The first of these five stages involves the marketing manager in identifying the organization's current market position. Included within this is the analysis of the organization's existing performance levels, its assets, competencies and overall levels of capability, its competitors and its customers.

The second stage involves the development of the organizational vision and mission, together with short and long term objectives. This is done against the background of a detailed analysis of the environment and the development of the competitive position and stance that will be pursued. In essence, this represents a choice among market leadership, market challenger, market follower and market niching.

From here, the marketing manager focuses upon the detail of the strategy and *how* the organization might operate through the framework of the marketing mix. This then leads to the fourth stage and to the application of the criteria that are to be used for evaluating the options open to the organization. The fifth and final stage is that of the implementation and control of the strategy and the feedback into the ongoing cycle of planning and strategy development. **CTG & RMSW**

References

Doyle, P. (1998) *Marketing Management and Strategy*, 2nd edn, Hemel Hempstead: Prentice Hall.
Ferrell, O.C., Hartline, M.D., Lucas, G.H. and Luck, D. (1999) *Marketing Strategy*, Orlando: Harcourt Brace.
Fifield, P. (1998) *Marketing Strategy*, 2nd end, Oxford: Butterworth-Heinemann.
Piercy, N. (1997) *Market-Led Strategic Change: Transforming the Process of Going to Market*, 2nd edn, Oxford: Butterworth-Heinemann.
Wilson, R.M.S. and Gilligan, C.T. (1997) *Strategic Marketing Management: Planning, Implementation and Control*, 2nd edn, Oxford: Butterworth-Heinemann.

Strategic window

Marketing strategy can be defined as a process of strategically analysing environmental, competitive and business factors affecting business units and forecasting future trends in business areas of interest to the enterprise. Strategic windows are the strategic opportunities that the organization will need to consider in terms of identifying options for its marketing strategy.

An example of this may be the consideration of Hong Kong as a strategic window on Asia. The Hong Kong economy in 1999 stabilized and growth in this area was stimulated by the government, which earmarked billions of dollars for infrastructure construction. Indeed, Hong Kong's economy was expected to grow by 2.2 per cent by the end of 2000 and stronger overseas demand was expected to lift exports. Private consumption is anticipated to expand in future as the threat of growing unemployment lessens and real estate prices recover. The previous slow growth was generated by several of its major trading partners, in particular Singapore, Korea and Japan. Therefore, it may be appropriate for an organization to consider market entry into Hong Kong as a potential strategic opening to Asia.

Indeed, some organizations may need to consider geographic areas as strategic windows to develop their growth strategies or organizational capabilities. For example, the Global TransPark Region of North Carolina is currently marketing itself as 'the strategic window to the world's marketplace'. The justification for this statement is that 700 manufacturing companies are profiting from the economic advantages and resources which are found in the area. It boasts that the Region's employment base is more manufacturing intensive than the US national average, which includes some of the highest rates of manufacturing employment growth in stone, clay and glass products. With no telephone monitoring restriction legislation and no sales tax on long distance calls and 800 numbers, it considers itself a prime location for organizations that wish to position themselves strategically in order to prosper in business.

However, the strategic window of opportunity will need to be considered by the organization in terms of a spectrum of factors, which include the existence of competitive advantage when pursuing this strategy, perceptions of risk, objectives of management, competitors, desired image and the link with the current strategy.

Indeed, many organizations are currently considering the search for the strategic technology window. With the growth of information technology and e-business, strategic investments in technology are a potential opportunity for many organizations to 'get in first'. **RAA**

References
http://www.gtp.net/strategic.html
North Carolina's Global TransPark Region, 27 February, 2000.
http://www.aquality.com/hongkong.html
Hong Kong: A Strategic Window on Asia, 27 February, 2000.

Strategy formulation

The formulation of strategy refers to the process by which strategies come about – how they are made, dreamt up or emerge over time. The question of how strategy is or should be best formulated has been the subject of ongoing debate amongst strategists and strategy scholars. Traditional views of strategy formulation see the process as one in which senior management determine strategy through a deliberate, rational planning process. The elements of this process comprise: systematic analysis of the external environment and marketplace; identification of alternative strategic options; selection of the most attractive options that will achieve the most valued ends; development of detailed implementation plans.

While this rational planning view of strategy making dominated early thinking about strategy formulation, this perspective has been strongly challenged in recent years on a number of grounds. For example, behaviourists have challenged the assumptions of rationality on the part of decision makers, arguing that individuals and organizations tend to act in only a bounded-rational manner. Others question whether strategy making should be seen as a pattern of *decisions* or a pattern of *actions*. Here the distinction is drawn between an organization's *intended* strategy and its *realized* strategy, the former being the patterns of decisions that organizations plan to execute, and the latter being the pattern of actions that have been accomplished. Here a further question arises – whether all realized strategies are necessarily intended. In some cases, strategies may emerge unintentionally as organizations advance step by step, seeking out the most appropriate way forward.

Challenges to such prescriptive perspectives of strategy formulation have emerged which suggest that, in reality, strategy often only emerges over time and often through a rather messy and fragmented process. Here, for example, strategy formulation has been described in terms of an entrepreneurial, cognitive, learning, evolutionary, political or cultural process. A characteristic of these so-called descriptive schools of thought about strategy making is their recognition that strategy often develops, not as some form of 'grand strategy', but rather incrementally, as organizations respond to, and learn how to cope with, the external environment in which they operate. This incrementalism perspective rejects the idea of planners developing deliberate strategies, favouring instead a view of the strategy making process which involves sense-making, reflection, learning and experimentation as strategists gradually discover appropriate strategic solutions to the challenges their organizations face. Incrementalism does not, however, reject the value of planning per se, rather planning is viewed as a valuable means of organizing and controlling routine activities concerned with the implementation of strategies.

Thus, strategy formulation needs to be recognized as a complex human process which may be underpinned by planning, but which may involve other less deliberate and not entirely rational processes as organizations struggle to determine how best to respond the external challenges and opportunities they face. **DM**

References
Chafee, E.E. (1985) 'Three models of strategy', *Academy of Management Review*, 10(1):89–96.
DeWitt, B. and Meyer, R. (1999) *Strategy: Process, Content, Context*, 2nd edn, London: Thomson Learning.
Hart, S.L. (1992) 'An integrative framework for strategy-making processes', *Academy of Management Review*, 17(2):327–351.
Mintzberg, H. and Lampel, J. (1999) 'Reflecting on the strategy process', *Sloane Management Review*, Spring: 21–30.

Supermarkets and superstores

Supermarkets and superstores are self-service retail outlets with selling areas of between 2500 and 25 000 square feet (supermarkets) and in excess of 25 000 square feet (superstores). The latter are often located on a free-standing site with associated car parking, at the edge of town or out of town. Globally, supermarkets are increasingly dominant in food retailing.

In the UK, 75 per cent of grocery purchases take place in supermarkets and superstores, and their share has been growing, largely at the expense of independent convenience outlets. Historically most UK operators started as independent grocers or dairies and rapidly expanded during the 1970s and 1980s. Growth in disposable incomes, increased ownership of cars and freezers, plus growing pressures on time led to changing shopping patterns, thereby increasing demand for large one-stop shops.

In 1998 supermarket and superstore sales came to £70.79 billion (i.e. nearly 40 per cent increase on 1993). Following the price wars of the early 1990s, the expansion of discounters has levelled off and other competitors such as Marks & Spencer are experiencing problems. Concentration of supermarkets and superstores among the 'big four', i.e. Tesco, Sainsbury's, ASDA and Safeway has been increasing, but further openings are restricted by the lack of new planning permissions.. Responses to the dangers of price sensitive core products and potential market saturation have included diversification into higher margin non-food products, as well as financial services, and international expansion (e.g. Sainsbury's move into the US and Tesco's Eastern European activities). Competition for customer retention takes the form of enhanced services, e.g. Sunday and 24-hour opening, Internet ordering and home deliveries, take-away services and in-store crèche and baby changing facilities. The introduction of loyalty cards facilitates data gathering with a view to individualized promotions.

UK operating margins of 4–7.5 per cent are above average compared with Europe and the USA, sparking off the recent Office of Fair Trading inquiry into the profitability of supermarkets. The recent Somerfield/Kwik Save and Walmart/ASDA mergers are likely to increase competition considerably. **RAS**

References
Baron, S., Davies, B. and Swindley, D. (1991) *Macmillan Dictionary of Retailing*, London: Macmillan Reference Books.
Gray, D. (1999) *Hypermarkets and Supermarkets in Europe*, London: Financial Times Business.
Key Note (1999) *Supermarkets and Superstores*, 16th edn, Hampton: Key Note Ltd.

Suppliers

A supplier is any individual or firm that provides a service, raw materials or finished products for use or resale in a business. Suppliers are not only those firms that provide raw materials for use in manufacturing or stock for retail shops and wholesalers; they might equally be the firm's accountants or solicitors.

Suppliers form part of the firm's micro-environment; at first sight, they would appear to be outside the scope of marketing, but since they form part of the firm's publics there are public relations implications in the firm's dealings with its suppliers. Also, most firms are suppliers for somebody else, whether it be another firm or the final consumers.

Suppliers can cause problems for a firm in several ways; they might supply shoddy goods, miss delivery dates, supply the wrong items or cause problems with invoices and credit facilities. The interface between suppliers and customers is handled by the suppliers' salespeople and the customers' buyers, but ultimately most of the people involved in the supplier's business have some degree of responsibility, and all those involved in the customer's business are affected in some way.

The relationship between suppliers and customers should be as close as it is possible to make it; the logistics approach to supply dictates that each firm is a link in a chain which reaches from the raw materials extraction through to the final consumer, and each link in the chain needs to connect with all the others if the process is to operate efficiently. Ultimately, the greater the efficiency of the supply chain, the more rewarding and profitable it is for all concerned – raw materials producers, manufacturers, wholesalers, retailers and consumers (Buchanan, 1992). **JWDB**

Reference

Buchanan, L. (1992) 'Vertical trade relationships; the role of dependence balancing and symmetry in attaining organizational goals', *Journal of Marketing Research* 29, February, pp. 65–75.

Surveys

Surveys are essentially the main choice of collecting primary data. The main advantage of this method in collecting data is that a great deal of information can be collected about an individual respondent at one time. The survey method is also versatile, whereby any settings can be used and adapted to the research objectives. Surveys can be designed to capture a wide array of information on diverse topics and research subjects. Attitudes can be measured through surveys, especially those that assess consumers' awareness, knowledge and perceptions about products or services. Surveys can also be used to determine the lifestyles of respondents. By assessing consumers' lifestyles, it would be possible for marketers to identify and segment the market.

There are five basic types of survey methods: personal interview, telephone interview, mail survey, fax survey and computer survey. Generally the choice of survey methods to use is dependent on factors such as the sampling procedure to be used in the research, the type of population, the question form and the content as well as the costs involved in carrying out the survey.

It is likely that surveys will continue to be one of the dominant methods of data collection for marketing research. The advancement of technology has brought about new ways of conducting surveys, for example, computers and interactive technology, which are likely to be widely used by marketing researchers. **RM-R**

Reference

Chisnall, P. (1992) *Marketing Research*, 4th edn, London: McGraw-Hill.

SWOT analysis

SWOT analysis is a tool for assessing the current strategic position of the company in terms of its strengths, weaknesses, opportunities and threats. SWOT combines internal and external features of the company's situation.

SWOT helps to create a decision making model for the firm's strategic planning, but in common with most models it is a drastic simplification and it relies heavily on the knowledge and judgement of the individuals who carry it out. The planner's view of the company's strengths and weaknesses may not coincide with the consumer's view, for example. Also, what may be a weakness in one context could be a strength in another; a small firm may see its size as a weakness compared with larger firms, but this may be a strength in terms of responding quickly to consumer needs.

A further problem is that threats can easily turn into opportunities and vice-versa, for example, new restrictive legislation might seem such as a threat, but may instead make life difficult for the firm's competitors and, in time, easier for the firm (Blythe, 1998).

As with other planning tools, SWOT may encourage managers to make lists rather than address problems, also the SWOT analysis does not, of itself, prioritize the factors. This means that a minor weakness might assume the same importance as a major strength or a major opportunity may be balanced out by a weak threat.

Having said that, SWOT analysis is one of the most widely-used tools of strategic planning, and is certainly an extremely useful starting-point for most managers.
JWDB

Reference
Blythe, J. (1998) *Essentials of Marketing*, London: Pitman.

Target market potential, forecasting

Target market potential is the maximum sales that could be achieved for a given product class from a given group of customers. The total market potential assumes that every potential customer in the market will buy the product, that they will use it at every opportunity and that they will use the product fully on each occasion.

The overall target market may be broken down into segments, each with its own congruent set of needs and each with its own version of the product class or its own favourite brand (Doyle, 1998).

The first step in forecasting target market potential is to calculate the maximum level of demand – the demand if all possible buyers were to buy to the maximum realistic extent, in both frequency and quantity. Maximum level of demand is an interesting theoretical concept, but is, in practice, rather difficult to measure; for example, the definition of 'realistic extent' is difficult to arrive at. Another problem is that marketing activities affect the individual's propensity to buy and use products.

The second stage is to factor in competitive activity. Again, this is difficult because competitors will often change tactics, introduce new products or generally behave in an unpredictable manner. New competitors may enter the market or products that have previously not been identified as competition may make inroads into the market.

The third stage is to examine trends in the external environment. Market potential is affected by all the factors within the environmental mix (see 'Environment for marketing communication').

An alternative method of calculating target market potential is the build-up approach, in which data about individual segments is aggregated to produce an overall figure. In some respects this method is easier, since the existing customers can be surveyed about their purchasing intentions and an overall picture constructed. The method will not work in the case of new products, and environmental and competitive issues still need to be factored in. **JWDB**

Reference
Doyle, P. (1998) *Marketing Management and Strategy*, 2nd edn, Hemel Hempstead: Prentice Hall.

Target marketing

Target marketing is the process of selecting an appropriate segment to aim the marketing effort towards. Normally marketers would choose the most profitable segment to target, but other corporate objectives (for example competitive issues) might cause marketers to target less profitable segments in order to achieve a longer-term goal.

Market coverage strategies are outlined below.

Table: **Market coverage strategies**

Market specialization	The firm aims to meet all the needs of a specific segment.
Selective specialization	The firm aims to satisfy the needs of several separate segments which do not relate closely.
Product specialization	The firm produces a full line of a single product class, for example potato crisps.
Full coverage	The firm targets every possible segment of the market.
Product/market concentration	Often called 'niche marketing', this is where the firm takes over one small corner of the market, fulfilling needs in depth.

Concentrated marketing covers a single segment; differentiated marketing concentrates on two or more segments, offering a different package of benefits to each, and undifferentiated marketing offers a similar product to a very wide market. Undifferentiated marketing is relatively rare, since products rarely suit all types of customer; a commonly used example is petrol, but even here several different types of petrol are available to different market segments (Schorsch, 1994).

The marketing strategy needs to consider all aspects of the segment. This means not only that the product needs to be right, but also the promotion strategy, the pricing, the distribution and all other aspects of the marketing effort need to be tailored to the targeted consumers or customers. The three key questions that the marketer needs to ask are: 'what are the needs of the members of the segment?', 'what is already available to them?' and 'what can the firm offer that is better than what is currently available?' **JWDB**

Reference
Schorsch, L.J. (1994) 'You can market steel' *McKinsey Quarterly*, January, pp. 111–120.

Target marketing, forecasting

A target market consists of a group of potential customers with similar characteristics (e.g. similar needs). Similarity can be defined broadly or narrowly, and on such a spectrum, segmentation analysis will be applied (see 'Targeting').

Target marketing requires three questions to be asked about potential customers.

- Who are they?
- What are their choice criteria?
- What do they think of us?

The reader of this entry needs to understand the nature of the buying decision in marketing, and also why target marketing is critical to international marketers.

Both in organizational markets (business to business) and consumer markets, buying decisions are in the hands of the decision making unit (DMU). The DMU may consist of the initiator, an influencer, the decider, the buyer and the user. In consumer markets an individual may perform all five roles; in some organizational markets, different individuals or even different groups may perform each role. Why is this important? Because we need to be able to identify and communicate with the person or people taking on these roles – we must be able to target each role and role player. Market segmentation is a concept and a research technique that enables us to do this.

In international marketing, target marketing has a special relevance. Studies of the exporting behaviour of British companies have, over a long period (1976 was when the phenomenon was first analysed – see BETRO, 1976), demonstrated a widespread failure to employ target marketing. Too often companies enter foreign markets with virtually no research, perhaps in response to an order or an enquiry from an overseas buyer, or because a company manager holidayed abroad and saw a business opportunity. Some companies respond to 'industry talk'. The BETRO report concluded that the majority of British exporters spread their resources too thinly over too many markets. It recommended that exporters concentrate their resources on their best markets. Market segmentation follows the rationale of concentrating resources on the best prospects. MJT

References

BETRO Trust Committee (1976) *Concentration on Key Markets*, London: British Overseas Trade Board.
Paliwoda, S.J. and Thomas, M.J., (1998) *International Marketing*, 3rd edn, Oxford: Butterworth Heinemann.
Piercy, N., (1982) *Export Strategy: Markets and Competition*, London: Allen and Unwin.

Targeting

Having decided the approach or variables to use to segment the market (segmentation), the number of segments to enter must be considered. Targeting is the decision about which segment or segments to prioritize for adapting the marketing mix and marketing efforts.

The market segments must be researched and considered in terms of their characteristics, where the task of building up a fuller picture of the target segments is undertaken. This is known as 'profiling' and the descriptors or variables are used to formulate the characteristics of each segment. An example of a profile relating to the segment demographics of the antique doll collector market may be related to the age range (30-45), education level (mainly graduate), employment and income (part-time or full time professional with family income of £20 000–£40 000), family (married with one or no children).

Marketers must assess the attractiveness of the segments to target. Ideally market segments should exhibit four characteristics: measurability and rate of change (the size and purchasing power of any segment must be measurable and the rate of any changes within that segment must be identified); substantiality (the segment must be large enough and profitable enough to warrant a different marketing mix); accessibility (the segment must be able to be reached); and actionability (the degree to which effective mixes can be formulated for attracting and serving the segment).

When considering the targeting strategy the organization will need to assess the optimum market coverage patterns: the single segment concentration or niching – where the company can develop a strong market position; the selective specialization – rather than just selecting one segment the organization targets several; product specialization – this is where the organization concentrates on marketing a specific product type to a variety of target markets; market specialization – the organization concentrates on satisfying the range of needs of a particular target group; or full market coverage – this is an expensive choice, serving the whole market with a full range of products.

These decisions will be made taking into consideration the organization's resources and capabilities, the position of the product in its life cycle, the homogeneity of the market, the intensity of competition, production economies of scale, brand share, market size and structure and the customer's requirements in terms of product and service.

The targeting of a segment leads the marketer to consider the positioning decisions for the product or service in relation to the characteristics and profile of the target segments. **RAA**

References

McDonald, M. and Dunbar, I. (1998) *Market Segmentation: How to Do It, How to Profit From It,* London: Macmillan Press.

Sleight, P., (1997) *Targeting Customers: How to use Geodemographic and Lifestyle Data in Your Business*, Oxford: NTC Publication.

Technological factors

Technology refers to techniques of engineering and the new products that application of such techniques have developed. It refers to such areas as new manufacturing techniques, new communications media and new products.

Changes in technology have a marked effect on business practice and the business environment. The effects fall into the following categories.

- Changes in markets due to new ways of doing things, for example, the advent of automobiles signalled the collapse of the market for horsewhips.
- Changes in business practice. Communications technology such as the Internet has changed the way many firms do business, in the same way as the invention of the fax machine or, even earlier the telephone, revolutionized business practice (Grey, 1996).
- Changes in manufacturing techniques. The widespread use of automation has resulted in a dramatic fall in employment in factories, as well as a dramatic reduction in manufacturing costs.
- Creation of new market opportunities. The widespread distribution of home computers has led to much-increased opportunities for firms selling computer peripherals, games and so forth.

The pace of technological change has increased and appears set to continue to increase; this will mean an ever-growing need for firms to adapt their thinking to meet the changes. Developments are often hard to predict, since the impact of a new technology might not be immediately apparent. For example, home video recorders were originally thought of as an extension to existing entertainment facilities; few observers would have predicted that the ability to record favourite programmes would encourage families to spend more time together, and would lead to easier access to distance-learning organizations such as the Open University. **JWDB**

References

Grey, R. (1996) 'Untangling the Web', *Marketing* 25 January pp. 25–26.

Telemarketing

Telemarketing is a term used to describe the use of the telephone for sales and marketing purposes. It can be used for a variety of research, pre- and post-selling activities as well as for selling itself. Starkey (1997) has identified four main aspects: lead generation, telesales, building and maintaining databases and customer care (use of customer carelines and crisis management control). Telesales tends to be the area of telemarketing with which most people are familiar. The impetus for its growth is the increasing cost of running a salesforce compared with that of operating telesales teams, particularly as a way of keeping in contact with, and selling to, lower value accounts. Telemarketing can be 'inbound' (people phoning in) or 'outbound' (employees phoning out) and, increasingly, companies are making use of free phone, low cost call and premium lines to encourage direct response, 'inbound' telemarketing.

Call centres run either by the company itself or by professional agencies are being used to facilitate telemarketing activities. With eight integrated call centres around the UK serving 20 million customers with access at local call rates, British Gas has the fifth largest call centre network in Europe handling 800 000 calls per week (Wisdom, 1997). Modern call centres usually provide a mix of automated and personal service features, but many inbound telemarketing calls may only be connected to a computer to handle standard enquiries so that actual telephone operators may not even be used. Full-service call centres will be a complex interaction of telephone exchanges, automated call distributors, computers and software for handling calls, with links to databases, other computer applications and people.

The use of the phone for telemarketing purposes is not without criticism and as customers become increasingly sensitive and sophisticated, telemarketing will have to follow suit. Badly handled phone calls can reduce sales rather than encourage sales, with 68 per cent of people preferring not to deal with an organization again if a single call is handled poorly (Henley Centre, 1996). **DWP**

References

Henley Centre (1996) *Teleculture 2000*, The Henley Centre Report.

Starkey, M. (1997) 'Telemarketing' in D. Jobber (ed.), *CIM Handbook of Selling and Sales Strategy*, Oxford: Butterworth Heinemann.

Wisdom, R. (ed.) (1997), *Focus: The Newsletter of Brite Voice Systems Europe, Middle East and Africa*, Cambridge, UK: Brite Voice Systems.

Telemarketing and call centres

The use of the telephone in direct marketing grew very rapidly during the 1990s in particular, with an associated proliferation of call centres. The number of call centre 'seats' rose from 173 000 in 1996 to 503 000 in 2000. Overall, by the end of the 1990s more was spent on telemarketing than on direct mail.

Recent legislation means that if an individual registers with the Telephone Preference Service that they do not want to receive unsolicited telephone calls, then such calls are illegal. This was probably timely because unsolicited calls have been heavily criticized by annoyed recipients on the grounds of intrusion.

However, it is clear that many people are more comfortable using the telephone than in previous eras, the tremendous increase in mobile 'phone use is but one reflection of this trend. As a result, time constrained consumers are increasingly turning to the telephone to order goods and services, for telephone banking and for making many other forms of contact with companies. Direct marketers are increasingly facilitating these contacts by including telephone (often freephone) numbers in their press, TV, outdoor and radio advertising.

Even with the heavy investment in call centres to handle the massive increase in telephone contact, companies are finding enormous cost savings over the 'retail branch' approach. The cost of a financial transaction in person at a bank branch might be in the region of 68p whereas via the telephone it might be nearer 38p.

The use of automation in telemarketing has been widely and rapidly adopted. Calls can be handled by computer rather than by real people, which means consistency of approach through 24-hour days and 365-day years. One problem, of course, is the dislike many consumers have of the impersonal and artificial nature of automated telephony.

Even where real people handle calls there can be problems. The call centre industry pays operatives poorly and empowers then minimally, meaning that some callers are left frustrated if their enquiry would result in any deviation from the telephonist's 'script' or domain of expertise.

The progression to e-commerce via the Internet is likely to lead to an early decline in call centres and telemarketing unless they respond to these market pressures and perhaps move from merely handling calls to being customer management centres within more strategic relationship marketing programmes. **MJE**

Reference
O'Malley, L., Patterson, M. and Evans, M. (1999) *Exploring Direct Marketing*, London: Thomson Learning, ch. 8.

Territory deployment

Territory deployment is the means of allocating customers or groups of customers as a basis for assigning a salesperson to achieve their sales objectives. This is usually on a geographical, product or market basis or a combination of these.

Arguably, this is one of the most crucial aspects of decision making for sales managers. That is, how to obtain maximum revenue for minimum cost to achieve marketing and sales objectives? Many models and, today, computerized systems have been devised to improve this resource allocation problem.

Territories are established for several reasons. First, to gain adequate coverage of the market. Secondly, to define salespeople's responsibilities and facilitate performance evaluation. Thirdly, to improve customer relationships and provide better service and support to ensure customers' needs are adequately met. Finally, to reduce selling expenses.

The procedure for establishing sales territories is to select a base unit, evaluate accounts and sales potential within the territory, analyse the salesperson workload, design basic territories and assign salespeople to these designated territories.

As noted, a number of models and systems have been suggested for maximizing the time allocation problem of salespeople. Indeed a whole industry has emerged to sell computerized solutions. These have not produced the performance improvement hoped for but there is merit in this approach. We will restrict comment to the key issues. These include the variables to be included in the time management allocation problem. For example, the volatility of the markets being served, the characteristics of the account and the geographical territory, the salesperson's experience and effort, the competition and the effort and experience of the company in these markets. We conclude that the most effective and efficient territories are those where effort is allocated where the sales potential is greatest. **WGD**

Reference
Rackham, N. and De Vincentis, J. (1999) *Rethinking the Sales Force: Redefining Selling to Create and Capture Customer Value*, Chicago Ill: American Marketing Association.

Test marketing

Test marketing is the stage where the product or service and relevant marketing programme are introduced into more realistic settings. Test marketing allows the company to test and experience marketing the product before spending a lot of money fully introducing it to the market. This provides the marketer with a feel of how the product will fare in the market prior to its full introduction. It is set in a real market context as opposed to an artificial one.

Test marketing has two primary functions: it functions as a tool for gathering information and helps to predict the outcome of the marketing programme when it is applied to the real market. When a company conducts a test marketing, it is able to assess whether its marketing programme, including the positioning strategy, advertising, distribution, pricing, branding and packaging strategies are appropriate for the needs of the market.

Generally, marketers use three types of test markets. In *standard test markets*, a small number of representative cities or markets are selected for the marketing campaigns. The results from the marketing campaigns are used as inputs in the development of the real marketing programmes. In *controlled test markets,* panels of stores that have agreed to carry the new products for a fee are monitored by research firms. Sales results are tracked to determine the impact of marketing strategies on demand. In *simulated test markets*, marketers test the new products in a simulated shopping environment. This method usually costs much less and keeps the new product out of competitors' view.

Whichever method is selected, the most important consideration is that enough feedback is obtained to guide marketers in developing their marketing strategies. Test marketing is really a tool of testing the ground before launching the product or service to the mass market. As such, getting the right information is crucial. **RM-R**

Reference
Kotler, P. and Armstrong, G. (1996) *Principles of Marketing*, 7th edn, Englewood Cliffs, NJ: Prentice Hall.

Kumar, V., Aaker, D.A. and Day, G.S. (1999) *Essentials of Marketing Research*, New York: John Wiley & Sons.

Trade and consumer promotions

One of the greatest advantages of studying marketing communications is that there are examples all around for everyone to see and, for the most part, enjoy. At least this is true of consumer promotions – marketing communications primarily targeted at end customers and consumers. We associate these promotions, for example, with television, radio, cinema, press and poster advertising, publicity in the news media, point of sale displays and merchandising, direct mail to our homes and sales promotion competitions. They are referred to as 'pull' promotions because of the way in which they attempt to 'pull' the product through the distribution chain by encouraging demand from the end market.

Rather more behind the scenes, however, is a wealth of other marketing communications and promotional activity targeted at the trade, the majority of which is hidden or goes unnoticed by most consumers. These trade promotions are of two broad types. First, there are promotions of industrial or business-to-business goods and services intended for purchase and use by the trade. Second, there are promotions that encourage the trade to stock and provide goods and services for the consumer market. Such promotions are carried out by manufacturers, service providers and trade members themselves and are called 'push' promotions because it is as though they are encouraging products to be pushed through the distribution chain.

Trade promotions are an exceptionally important part of the total marketing communications effort. They involve all aspects of the marketing communications mix although personal selling often plays a bigger role. Not appreciated by many people, consumer companies are as heavily involved in trade promotions as they are in consumer promotions in their attempts to get their products to market. **DWP**

Reference
Pickton, D.W. and Broderick, A. (2001) *Integrated Marketing Communications*, London: Financial Times Prentice Hall, ch. 21.

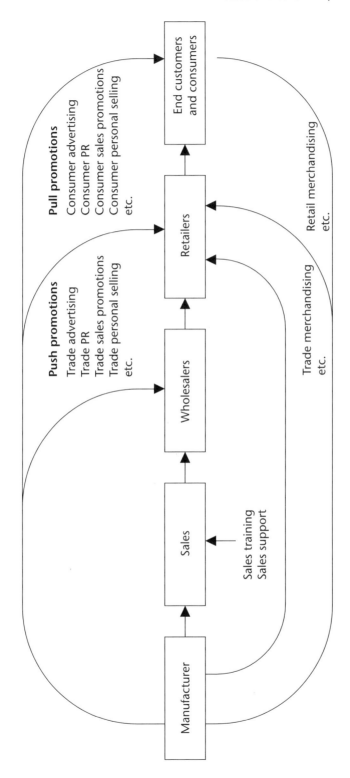

Figure: **Push and pull promotional strategies**

Transactional data and lists

Transactional data is now a major source of data for many direct marketers. This has been facilitated by the widespread use by retailers Electronic Point of Sale (EPoS) terminals and also by the development of product codes which are standardized between manufacturers, distributors and retailers. European Article Number (EAN) is compatible with the Universal Product Code (UPC) in the USA. This implies that any retailer with an EPOS system can access information.

The direct marketing application of bar-codes (EAN/UPC) in retailing includes the ability to record who buys what. Products can be matched with customers via credit, debit (switch) and loyalty card numbers. Retailers will therefore be able to match special offers with individual customers.

As an example of transactional data, an inspection of a resulting retail loyalty scheme database might reveal, for a certain Mrs Smith, her address and a variety of behavioural information including: she shops once per week, usually on a Friday, has a baby (because she buys nappies), spends £85 per week on average and usually buys three bottles of wine a week. By knowing what individual consumers buy, the retailer might be able to target them with relevant offers whilst the consumer saves money in the process (Evans, 1999).

The direct marketer is also able to analyse transactional data to identify recency, frequency and monetary values of each customer. These can then be segmented and those contributing the most to profitability can be targeted more heavily than others. An issue for debate is the policy of 'deselecting' those customers who do not buy much or very often. Is this merely good business practice or is the resulting 'exclusion' a concern in terms of marketing's wider social responsibility? **MJE**

References

Evans, M. (1999) 'Food retailing loyalty schemes and the Orwellian millennium?' *British Food Journal*, 101(2):132–147.

U

Uncontrollable environments

Uncontrollable environments include those aspects of the external or internal threats and opportunities which the organization's management must deal with but is powerless to change. Although the precise factors will vary from one organization to the next (and from one country to the next), the uncontrollable environment typically includes government legislation, the economic boom-and-bust cycle, cultural and demographic shifts, changes in technology and climatic or seismic incidents.

Small firms may not be able to control the actions of large firms who are their customers, suppliers or competitors; conversely, very large firms (for example, the giant American fruit companies) have sufficient power in Third World countries to be able to dictate to governments (Kotler, 1986).

If firms are to deal effectively with the uncontrollable environment, they need to be prepared to respond efficiently to environmental changes. This usually means an emphasis on forward planning and preparation, including an assumption that the environment will change. The uncontrollable environment offers opportunities as well as threats; legislation might hamper an unscrupulous competitor, for example, or a climatic change might stimulate demand for the firm's products.

Some areas of the uncontrollable environment might be subject to influence, for example, although government legislation might not be subject to control, Members of Parliament are susceptible to lobbying and are often influenced by pressure groups. Proactive managers work on the assumption that most environmental factors can be influenced if sufficient numbers of those affected can become involved. **JWDB**

Reference
Kotler, P. (1986) 'Megamarketing', *Harvard Business Review*, March–April: 117–24.

Unsought products

These are goods or services that the potential purchaser has not actively considered buying. They are associated with sales orientated tactics. 'Unsolicited Goods and Services' legislation has been passed in the UK to restrict its application, and this means that goods sent by post that were not ordered by the recipient can be retained. This is called 'inertia selling' and it is the kind of tactic that reflects the unsavoury side of marketing, as the notion is that consumers need to be forcibly per-suaded to purchase products they would never actively consider buying.

Some life assurance salespeople have also been accused of employing dubious practices to push their products (i.e. insurance policies). Potential customers do not always see the necessity of a life policy, so they are targeted by direct marketing approaches such as direct mail, telephone selling or even through door-to-door 'cold calling', often on the pretext of conducting a survey. This 'softening up' process then 'qualifies' respondents as 'prospects' and it is followed by a personal visit from a sales representative. Methods of selling insurance policies often amount to noth-ing more than the application of the 'hard sell' or putting the facts to customers so that when asked if they want to take the transaction further, they cannot say 'no'. This situation is usually compounded by the remuneration structure that in many cases depends solely on commission or a retainer based salary plus commission. **GL**

Reference
Kotler, P. (1994) *Marketing Management, Analysis, Planning, Implementation and Control*, 8th edn, New Jersey: Prentice Hall, pp. 432–436.

Vertical integration

Many industries have a number of discrete processes, ranging from raw material extraction to processing, manufacturing, distribution, retailing and after sales service. Each of these stages can in effect be undertaken by separate and quite distinct companies. 'Vertical integration' is the term used to describe the acquisition of a company that supplies a firm with inputs of raw materials or serves as a customer for the firm's products or services, (e.g. a distributor).

If, for example, a furniture manufacturer was to acquire a timber company this would be referred to as 'backward vertical integration', since the furniture company is in effect moving backwards down the industry supply chain. Alternatively, if a manufacturer of furniture were to open a range of retail outlets to sell its own products, this would be referred to as 'forward vertical integration'.

Companies will assess the degree to which either backward or forward vertical integration brings appropriate benefits to the business. Backward vertical integration aims to secure supplies at a lower cost than the competition, but after the merger or acquisition it is crucial to keep pace with technological developments and innovation on the supply side or the benefits may be lost. Similarly, forward vertical integration secures customers or outlets and to some extent guarantees customer preference for the product. If, however, the manufacturing and retailing processes require distinct and separate skills, the benefits of forward vertical integration may be elusive.

Ford, the US based car manufacturer, has over recent years continued a policy of forward vertical integration, and now not only manufactures cars, but also finances them and provides after sales service (it purchased the UK-based Kwik Fit company in 1999). The prime reason for this is that Ford acquires a larger proportion of its profits away from mainstream manufacturing, particularly in the financing and after sales service.

It is also benefiting by acquiring larger amounts of customer data, something which has been denied manufacturers in the past because of their distance from the end consumer. **PBB**

References

Chandler, A.D. (1990) 'The enduring logic of industrial success', *Harvard Business Review*, March–April.
Porter, M.E. (1985) *Competitive Advantage* New York: Free Press.

Kay, J. (1997) *Foundations of Corporate Success*, Oxford: Oxford University Press.

Vertical Market Networks

Vertical market networks are characterized by centralized management systems where distribution functions are coordinated by one firm that owns the network. A vertical market network is a network of horizontally coordinated and vertically aligned establishments which are managed as a system. The main aim of such a network is to achieve distribution economies through integrating and synchronizing marketing flows within the distribution channel.

In a vertical market network, the controlling firm manages distribution operations where issues such as channel leadership, division of work, control and conflict management are decided at the central level. Centralized decision making ensures that all channel operations carried out by diverse channel members are well coordinated and are moving towards the accomplishment of common distribution objectives. Common types of vertical market networks include administered marketing channel systems, contractual marketing channels and corporate vertical market networks. Administered marketing channel systems are essentially conventional marketing channels where independent firms carrying out distribution functions are coordinated through specific programmes developed by the managing firm. Although distribution channel members within an administered system have no formal organizational structure that binds them together, they are being coordinated through the implementation of distribution or marketing programmes that are agreed by all the parties concerned. In contrast, the contractual marketing channel systems are characterized by the existence of formal contractual agreements that bind channel members together. Such contracts specify precisely the job functions and responsibilities of each channel member. The controlling channel member that holds the contract is therefore the channel leader coordinating all channel functions.

In a corporate vertical market network, one firm holds ownership to the whole distribution network. For example, when a manufacturing firm owns the wholesaling and/or retailing operations, this is known as 'corporate forward integration', while 'corporate backward integration' occurs when either a retailer or a wholesaler owns its supplying firms. One of the main reasons for channel members to integrate either forward or backward is to maximize their degree of control of the total distribution functions. Often, corporate vertical marketing systems offer the highest degree of control because one controlling firm owns all firms within the distribution network. In such a system, emphasis is on intra-organizational rather than inter-organizational management. **RM-R**

References
Etgar, M. (1976) 'Effects of administrative control on efficiency of vertical market systems', *Journal of Marketing Research*, XIII(February): 12–24.
Heide, J.B. (1994) 'Interorganizational governance in marketing channels', *Journal of Marketing*, 58(January): 71–85.
Rosenbloom, B. (1995) *Marketing Channels – A Management View*, Fort Worth, Texas: Dryden Press.

Voluntary groups

A voluntary or 'symbol' group is a contractual association of retailers working towards mutual benefits without losing autonomy. Cooperation can involve a shared image through common fascia, uniform pricing structures, joint own brands and collaborative buying. The resulting increased turnover leads to lower selling costs and higher labour and space productivity. In addition the group can use its power to negotiate discounts for bulk buying. Further advantages lie in enhanced control of supply chain, logistics and IT support, which is particularly significant for small shops which often do not have the resources to invest in scanning systems if operating independently. A weakness may arise from inconsistent execution at store level.

UK voluntary groups date back to the 1950s, and in 1998 they had approximately 5500 outlets and turnover of £3150 million. Their presence is most significant in grocery retailing and for retail chemists.

In the grocery sector, voluntary groups (such as Costcutter, Spar, Mace and Londis) focus on the convenience trade, where the number of non-affiliated retailers is decreasing. The group's customer base is dominated by females in the lower socio-economic groups. Each group aims for specialization, for example via the introduction of automatic teller machines (ATMs), special member discount schemes, petrol forecourt partnerships and differential internationalization experience. Spar is the largest, backed by six regional wholesalers, operating in 28 countries and through 35 000 stores. Nisa-Today's coordinates a number of voluntary groups and facilitates national distribution and advantageous buying terms.

The 1990s saw the emergence of pan-European retail alliances and buying groups, e.g. Associated Marketing Services, with membership from 14 countries and a turnover of 85.6 billion ecu, and European Marketing Distribution, with a turnover of 103.9 billion ecu and incorporating Nisa-Today's. Such groups combine both multiple retailers and national buying groups with the aim of increasing supply chain efficiency, facilitating collective purchasing and the development of euro-brands, introducing suppliers to other members and new markets and investigating joint marketing opportunities. **RAS**

References

Baron, S., Davies, B. and Swindley, D. (1991) *Macmillan Dictionary of Retailing*, London: Macmillan Reference Books.

Beard, J., Gordon, D., Spillard, L., Walton, J. and Webb, S. (1999) *Grocery Retailing 1999, The Market Review*, Watford: Institute of Grocery Distribution.

Gordon, D. and Wilson, S. (1999) *Convenience Tracking Programme Market Review 1999*, Watford: Institute of Grocery Distribution.

Web site design and web site marketing

One of the most visible elements of organizational marketing communication – and indeed corporate communications – is the organization's web site. The table below indicates some well known web sites.

Table: **Illustrative web site and marketing data**

Company	URL	Traffic (monthly)	Target audience	Advertising
Yahoo	www.yahoo.co.uk	22-24 million	General Internet users	Banners, keyword searches, content sponsorship
BT	www.bt.com www.telfort.nl www.viaginterkom.de	3-5 million	General Internet and corporate users	Banners, micros, classified
Microsoft	www.msn.co.uk	9 million	UK population	Banners, sponsorship, microsites, promotion
De Beers	www.edata.co.za/debeers	Not known	General Internet users	Banners, keyword searches, content sponsorship
Scoot	www.scoot.co.uk	Over 1 million	Everyone who wants to buy something	Banners, sponsorship

Source: Hamill and Kitchen, 1999; Schultz and Kitchen, 2000

Note that the primary purpose of the web site may not be to sell something to someone. In other words web site design goes well beyond selling online.

The key to achieving marketing or other purposes is a well-designed site and effective marketing of the site to achieve a large number of hits. Ellsworth and Ellsworth (1994) suggest that good web site design can be accommodated by adhering to two basic principles:

- delegate to html experts: DIY works well in the home, but not here
- use the *nifty* acronym – navigability, interactivity, functionality (or features), testability, and your 'customerability' (or visibility) to aid the design process.
  - *Navigability*: Can the visitor/user find his/her way around the website? Does the site contain signposts? Is there an opening menu? Are these navigable? The firm should test navigability on a regular basis. A recent experience shared by both editors is accessing sites where one is simply lost in a short time and navigating out is difficult and laborious. This simply should not happen as it creates bad feeling and a negative image for the company/organization.
  - *Interactivity:* Is the web site more than a form of electronic yellow pages? Visitors will soon get bored flipping over page after uninteresting page. The firm/organization is not just broadcasting messages in a fixed traditional mode (i.e. like a brochure or sales message), instead it is intended to be *inter-active* – to allow visitors to dig deeper and deeper for the information or data they require. It is not a passive, 'keep turning the page' medium. Hypertext links should be available, as should e-mail interchange and a mechanisms for encouraging response as a means of gathering market research data and building a relationship.
  - *Functionality/features*: This refers to page design and/or authoring. The visit to a web site needs to confer something of value, if only the entertainment value or the information obtained. Delivery before selling is an essential part of marketing features or functions. Moreover, the functionality and service provided does not end when a sale occurs. A recent and annoying illustration is a major academic text book distributor. Despite knowing when, for example, a book is adopted for a specific course or module, no attempt is made to apprise lecturers when a new edition is forthcoming or when a book is out of print. And yet, a simple e-mail would help build and retain customers instead of annoying dissonance.
  - *Testability*: The literature suggests testing the web site locally before posting it on the Internet. However, marketing practice would suggest testing on a regular basis, ensuring the site is up-to-date, working well, and that it is innovative, interesting, and offers value. A recent test of a well-known, well-ranked business school (not named or flamed here) provided an interesting example of what was happening in 1998, but was of little relevance to today. Here the tester needs apply the electronic equivalent of a duster and polish.
  - *[Your] Customerability/visitorability:* In a text on marketing, the need for a customer oriented approach is vital in terms of web site design. It is not really what the company/organization wants to say, but what customers want to hear, see, or access that is important.

Sterne (1995) suggested that web site design and marketing can be expressed in poetic form:

Shout it from the roof tops. Write it in the sky
Promote until your budget pops, until they all surf by.
Announce in proper newsgroups, Mail directly through the post.
Fire up the sales troops. Televise the most.
A 1-800 number won't get you any calls.
Unless you advertise it, and paint it on the walls.
Put it on your letterhead. Put it on your cards.
A web site will be left for dead unless it's known on Mars.

> Your web site can be funny, pretty, useful, crisp, and clean,
> But if you don't promote it, its message won't be seen.

The poem (however derisory) suggests that web site design, and *inter alia* internet communications, does not operate in stand-alone mode. 'Build it and they will come' did not apply to Emerson's mousetrap, and it does not apply here. Instead, the Internet is part of an overarching and coherent marketing strategy, linked to the annual marketing planning structure, and is integrated and stands alongside all other facets of marketing communication activity. **PJK**

References

Ellsworth, J.H. and Ellsworth, M.V. (1994) *The Internet Business Book*, New York: John Wiley.

Hamill, J. and Kitchen, P.J. (1999) 'The Internet' in Kitchen, P.J. (ed.) *Marketing Communications: Principles and Practice*, London: Thomson Learning, ch. 22.

Schultz, D.E. and Kitchen, P.J. (2000) *Communicating Globally: An Integrated Marketing Approach*, London: Macmillan Business.

Sterne, T. (1995) Message posted to the inet-marketing @ einet.net discussion group.

Wholesalers as channel participants

One of the most significant intermediaries in the distribution channel is the wholesaler. Wholesalers consist of businesses that are engaged in the distribution of goods and services in large quantities for resale or business use to other organizations such as retailers, industrial, commercial, institutional and professional firms as well as to other wholesalers. Wholesalers play an important role in the distribution function by bridging the gap between manufacturer and consumer. They provide services such as financing, negotiating and ordering and they may also take physical possession of goods when they provide storage and warehousing facilities. Many wholesalers also take title of the goods they store, which reduces the inventory costs for their customers.

There are many different types of wholesaling institutions emerging as the result of their target markets' varying needs. These institutions can be grouped into three major types of wholesalers: merchant wholesalers, agent wholesalers and manufacturers' sales branches and offices. *Merchant wholesalers* take ownership of the goods they are dealing in and they are often independently owned. They are paid for their services on a profit margin basis. They can either be full-function or limited function wholesalers. Full-function merchant wholesalers perform all or most of the marketing functions required by their customers, whilst limited function wholesalers provide only specific wholesaling services. Cash-and-carry distributors, rack jobbers and drop shippers are some of the more common examples of these wholesalers.

Agent wholesalers are somewhat different from merchant wholesalers in that they do not take ownership and rarely take possession of the goods they are handling. They are primarily involved in negotiation and dissemination of market information and they provide ordering services. In payment for these services, agents are given commission. Typical types of agent wholesalers are brokers, commission merchants, and auctioneers.

When manufacturers opt to undertake wholesaling activities on their own, they will be opening their sales branches and offices. *Manufacturers' sales branches* and offices are wholesaling operations owned and operated by a manufacturer when they feel that independent wholesalers are unable to provide necessary services required by customers. For example, when technical expertise is required or when customers buy in large quantities which cannot be handled effectively by intermediaries. Manufacturers also tend to have more control of the distribution function when they open their own sales branches and offices. **RM-R**

References

McCalley, R.W. (1992) *Marketing Channel Development and Management*, Westport, CT: Quorum Books.

Sweeney, D.J. (1992) 'Warehouse clubs! Hypermarkets! Supercenters!', *Retail Business Review*, November: 8–22.

World Wide Web (WWW)

The World Wide Web (WWW) is simply the area – known as the Internet – where commercial operations occur and where users go for information. Increasingly consumer-centric or consumer-friendly, most users access the Internet through search mechanisms such as Netscape, or by paying for services such as AOL or CompuServe (Shimp, 1997) Notably, the USA is far more advanced in terms of accessibility, simply because the diffusion rate of personal computers with modems attached is significantly higher than in Europe (see Donaton and Mussey, 1995). The Web, or the Internet, is both a medium and a market – a 'marketspace' – in which relationships can be built, image enhanced and exchanges transacted. Its success or otherwise will depend on freeing consumers, responding to their needs, wants and desires, adapting to their expressed preferences and modes of doing business. **PJK**

References

Donaton, S. and Mussey, D. (1995) 'Online's next battlefront: Europe' *Advertising Age*, March 6th, p. 18.

Shimp, T.A. (1997) *Advertising, Promotion, and Supplemental Aspects of Integrated Marketing Communication*, Orlando: The Dryden Press.

DAY WALKS

Bay of Plenty
& Rotorua

Also by Marios Gavalas:

Day Walks of the Coromandel
Day Walks of Northland
101 Top North Island Beaches
Day Walks of Greater Auckland (with Peter Janssen)

DAY WALKS OF THE
Bay of Plenty
& Rotorua

Marios Gavalas

REED

Cover image: The clear waters of Lake Okataina, including the pa at Te Koutu, are fringed by a ribbon of forested hills.
Back cover image: From the summit of Mt Maunganui, the endless sweep of the Bay of Plenty beaches recedes to the horizon.

Disclaimer

Although every effort has been made to ensure the accuracy of information contained in this book, the publisher and author hold no responsibility for any accident or misfortune that may occur during its use. The Department of Conservation (DoC) is continually upgrading and altering tracks. For up-to-date information, DoC should be consulted before attempting any walk.

Reed Publishing (NZ) Ltd
Te Karuhi tā tāpui o Reed (Aotearoa)

Established in 1907, Reed is New Zealand's largest book publisher, with over 300 titles in print.

For details on all these books visit our website:
www.reed.co.nz

Published by Reed Books, a division of Reed Publishing (NZ) Ltd, 39 Rawene Rd, Birkenhead, Auckland 10. Associated companies, branches and representatives throughout the world.

National Library of New Zealand Cataloguing-in-Publication Date
Gavalas, Marios.
Day walks of the Bay of Plenty and Rotorua / Marios Gavalas.
ISBN 0-7900-0898-X
1. Trails—New Zealand—Bay of Plenty Region—Guidebooks.
2. Bay of Plenty Region—Guideboks. I. Title.
796.51099342—dc 21

ISBN 0 7900 0898 X
First published 2003

© 2003 Marios Gavalas
The author asserts his moral rights in this work.

Edited by Sam Hill
Maps by Nick Keenleyside

Printed in New Zealand

Contents

Rotorua Lakes

Maps

Preface

This guide is intended for the holidaymaker, local resident or tramper looking for a day walk in one of Rotorua or the Bay of Plenty's many areas of scenic splendour. With so many options, this guide aims to help you select the most rewarding walks.

For each walk, information on access to the start of the walk, notes on the state of the track and a short narrative on points of interest are provided.

Track grades are subjective and are provided to help you choose a suitable walk. Please refer to the section on track grades for an explanation of the system.

Approximate completion times are provided as a guide. They may vary according to the track conditions and your walking speed.

Some walks involve stream crossings and tidal sections. Make sure you are aware of tide times and consult DoC on stream levels before attempting these walks.

Other walks quote one-way times. You should arrange appropriate transport to meet you at the other end or embark on the walk suitably prepared.

The Department of Conservation has an information centre in Tauranga, and can also be contacted in Rotorua. They administer all walks, unless otherwise stated.

Most walks described in this book are not suitable for dogs. They traverse ecologically sensitive areas, which are prone to disturbance. Some walks not administered by DoC may be suitable. Contact the appropriate council for up-to-date information on dog restrictions.

The prevalence of thieves is an unfortunate nuisance, especially at quiet road-ends. The surest way to deter them is to immobilise your vehicle and take all valuables with you.

If this guide enables you to visit somewhere you might not have otherwise discovered, or enhances your enjoyment of a morning walk along a deserted beach or in a lush green forest, then it has succeeded in its aim. Happy walking!

Acknowledgements

Thanks to Keren, who, as always, supported me throughout the project.

Our trusty 1971 VW Kombi 'Betty' must be mentioned, as she was our reliable vehicle and home for the duration of the research.

At Reed, thanks to Peter Janssen for his support of the project and also to my editor, Sam Hill.

A thank you to all the DoC staff, including Reg Phillips, without whose assistance the project could not have been completed. Kate Ackers' comments on the manuscript were much appreciated.

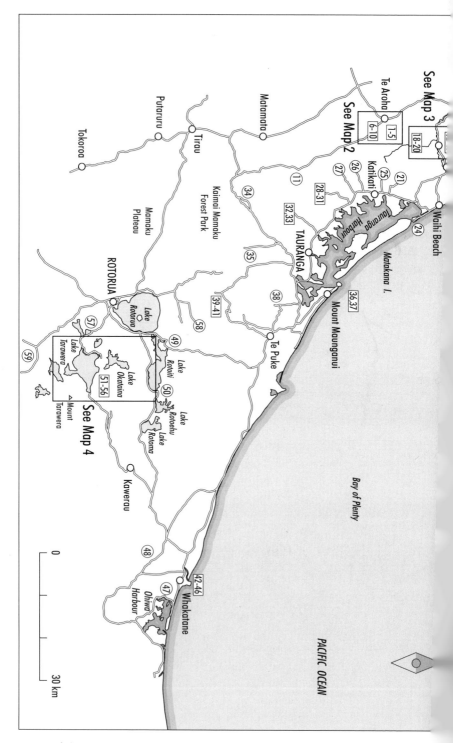

Bay of Plenty & Rotorua walks

Introduction

While discovering the walks in the Bay of Plenty and Rotorua region, you could be relaxing by the calming mystique of a lake, enjoying the views from a lofty peak, appreciating the sweeping coastline or standing amid the relics of old goldmining operations.

Maori have occupied the region for at least 600 years. A large proportion of the migratory canoes landed in the Bay of Plenty, which developed into an important centre for Maori culture.

According to one Maori legend, Ngatoro-i-rangi, a great tohunga from Hawaiki, climbed Tongariro and caught a chill. He appealed to the gods to send him warmth. His sisters came from Hawaiki with fire, travelling under the land and sea, resurfacing occasionally to check their direction. They left a trail of fire, as directional indicators, from White Island to Tongariro, forming the present-day chain of volcanoes.

The Taupo Volcanic Zone extends for 240 km from White Island to Ruapehu. Over 15,000 cubic km of lava, ash, ignimbrite and rhyolite have been ejected over two million years. Active volcanism is still shaping the landscape.

Dormant volcanic systems provide a majesty and splendour to the scenery. The touch of humans abounds in the goldmining and logging histories of the region. The dense network of tracks is ripe for exploration and enables historic artefacts, lush forest, twinkling lakes and coastal drama to be witnessed.

Birds of the Bay of Plenty and Rotorua

The songs of native birds can be conspicuously absent and an eerie quietness often presides over the forest interior. Introduced predators and habitat clearance have kept populations low and the forest devoid of its most tuneful residents.

Occasionally your attention may be caught by the sudden appearance of a fantail perched on a nearby branch. The whistling sound of kereru wings may cause your attention to turn skywards. Perhaps the dulcet calls of a tui or bellbird may even cause you to stop and search the canopy in an attempt to catch a glimpse of the musical genius.

These encounters occur with unfortunate rarity. With the introduction of humans, and especially Pakeha, came the arrival of mammalian predators. Rats, mice and feral cats climb trunks and negotiate the branches to feed on eggs and chicks. Stoats, ferrets and weasels are attracted to nestlings, and prey on the defenceless chicks while the parents are away feeding.

Vast tracts of forest have been cleared for agricultural purposes. The diminished habitat has resulted in declining populations of many New Zealand birds, including kiwi, kaka and kokako.

On the coast, the habitat and breeding areas of terns, oystercatchers and dotterels have been decimated by building and competitive land use. Shallow, exposed nests fall prey to feral cats, domestic dogs and vehicles. Some species, such as the New Zealand dotterel, are now very rare.

Predator control programs implemented by DoC are aimed at reversing this decline and are meeting with some success. The fencing off of coastal breeding grounds and increasing public awareness are allowing populations to recover. Where warning signs are posted, heed their advice and keep away, especially during the spring and summer breeding seasons.

Here are some forest residents you will meet:

Fantail/Piwakawaka (*Rhipidura fuliginosa*)

The friendly fantail will greet you with an energetic 'cheep' as you pause to rest. Performing aerial acrobatics between perches and displaying its livery on alighting, the fantail will always succeed in attracting your attention. Fantails will often follow you, preying on the insects disturbed as you pass.

The fantail feeds from dawn to dusk, executing skilful movements in mid-air to catch flying insects. Males will show off to visitors by dropping their wings and fanning their tails.

Bellbird/Korimako (*Anthornis melanura*)

The bellbird is often heard, but rarely seen, as its sweet song is carried through the vegetation. Its bell-like notes are learned from neighbouring adults of the same sex or from parents.

Often bellbirds are heard in tandem, singing and counter-singing to determine territorial spacing. Pairs are monogamous and may sing a duet.

These honey-eaters take nectar from many native trees. By feeding on berries in autumn, they act as important seed-dispersing agents in the ecology of the forest.

Tui/Parson bird (*Prosthemadera novaeseelandiae*)

The melodic tones of the tui often penetrate the forest interior. Singing from dawn to dusk, the tui resonates a formidable repertoire of pure bell-like notes. These virtuoso musicians can compose a symphonic range of songs.

Distinguished by an aristocratic white throat patch, the tui is an important member of the forest community. By eating nectar and fruit and often travelling large distances to abundant food sources, the tui helps disperse seeds and pollinate plants.

Kereru/New Zealand Wood pigeon (*Hemiphaga novaeseelandiae*)

The herbivorous kereru will be seen either feeding voraciously on a variety of native fruits or resting on a sunny perch digesting its meal. It will give itself away by causing berries to drop from the canopy while gorging on a feast of fruit.

Its preferred diet is composed of the larger-fruited podocarps such as miro and matai. Species such as tawa, taraire and karaka rely heavily on the kereru for the dispersal of their seeds.

Because of its wide gape, the kereru can eat large fruit. Little abrasion of the seed occurs in the gizzard, allowing seeds to pass through the digestive system intact. In this way the kereru ensures the perpetuation of its food source.

On the coast look for:

New Zealand dotterel (*Charadrius obscurus*)

The shy and reserved cheeps of the New Zealand dotterel accompany a walk along many Bay of Plenty beaches. Pairs of birds are loyal and usually stay within sight of each other. They step lightly like ballerinas over the sand and keep a safe distance from humans. They may fake a broken wing to discourage you from passing too close to their nests.

They lay camouflaged eggs in shallow hollows in the dune. As their nests are prone to disturbance, keep dogs under control and keep out of fenced areas during the breeding season.

Variable oystercatcher (*Haematopus unicolour*)

These black and white birds are normally seen in pairs and kick up a vociferous racket when approached. They sound their whistling cheeps at the slightest chance of intrusion, and will often walk a considerable distance up the beach before taking flight.

Oystercatchers fly low to the water with a powerful wing flap, and feed at the mouths of rivers and estuaries. Often their footprints can be traced to encircle a bivalve, whose shells they prise open with their long red beaks.

Caspian Tern (*Hydroprogne caspia*)

Distinguished from the more boisterous red-billed gull by pointed wings and a more erratic wing flap, the Caspian tern is an expert diver.

Deftly spying fish by hovering above the water, they can dive with accomplished aerobatic skills to capture their prey.

Their red beak and black facial markings contrast with their white bodies. Caspian terns will often be seen in flocks resting on offshore stacks or coastal rocky outcrops.

Safety when walking in the Bay of Plenty and Rotorua

- It can rain with unabated ferocity any time of the year in the Bay of Plenty and Rotorua. If it has been raining previous to or during your walk, streams may be at flood level. Do not attempt to cross a stream in flood. Wait until it subsides.
- Some walks involve crossing streams and rivers. Make sure the water level is safe to cross and check tide times for tidal walks along the coast.
- Always check the weather forecast before departing. Weather can change very quickly.
- Always take enough water, food and, if necessary, shelter for your walk. Make sure you are fit enough for the grade of walk you are attempting.
- Possum trappers use many tracks through the forest. They mark their routes with pink triangles. Do not follow these. Follow orange triangles only. Other common track markers include orange rectangles that look like pieces of Venetian blinds. Take care as sometimes markers can be sporadic. If in doubt, return to your last known point and proceed from there.
- Walks around Karangahake and the Wairongomai Valley traverse old goldmining areas. These are peppered with shafts and tunnels, which are generally unsafe to enter unless they form part of a formal track.

Stay close to the marked tracks, as vertical shafts can be concealed by vegetation.
- Inform a friend, relative or DoC of your intended itinerary before departing on walks into rugged backcountry.
- Take a detailed map and compass. These will not only aid navigation, but also inform you of interesting features in the area. *The NZ 260 Map Series* 1:50,000 Topomaps are useful. *The Kaimai Mamaku Forest Park Map*, also 1:50,000, is invaluable for its detailed representation of all the walking tracks in the park.
- Many walks pass through concealed valleys and remote coastal areas. Cell phone repeater stations are scarce. Do not rely on cell phones as safety devices, even on the summits of hills.

Track Grades

Please note that these grades are subjective and are provided as a guide only.

Tracks are graded according to length, gradient and surface.

Grade 1: Track surface is metalled or even with only minor undulations. Directions are clearly signposted. Walks usually take less than half an hour.

Grade 2: Track may be metalled or unmetalled. It is clearly marked and well formed but usually involves some inclines.

Grade 3: Track is unmetalled but well formed and usually marked. Can be uneven and boggy with frequent inclines.

Grade 4: Track is usually formed but may be marked or unmarked. It may be very steep, uneven or boggy. Walks of this grade are more appropriate for people of good fitness with some outdoor experience.

For walks graded 2 and above, you should be adequately prepared with food and water. It is advisable to wear strong shoes, preferably sturdy boots, and take a detailed map (e.g. 1:50,000 Topomap or Parkmap).

Where a track can be attempted from two directions, the descriptions given in the book apply to one direction only. If you attempt a walk in one direction only, make sure there is suitable transport for you at the conclusion of your walk.

Marked tracks usually have orange triangles or rectangles nailed to trees. Each marker is usually visible from the previous one, but marking can be sporadic. If you think you have strayed from the track, retrace your steps to the last reference marker. Do not follow pink, blue or yellow triangles; they are there to guide possum trappers and managers of bait stations and drop lines.

New Zealand Environmental Care Code

When walking in the Bay of Plenty and Rotorua, follow the Environmental Care Code:

- Protect rare and endangered plants and animals.
- Take rubbish with you when you leave.
- Bury toilet waste in a shallow hole away from waterways, tracks, campsites and huts.
- Keep streams clean.
- Take care with fires. If you must build a fire, keep it small, use dead wood, douse it with water and remove evidence of it when you leave. Portable stoves are preferable, as they are more efficient and pose less risk to the environment.
- After camping, leave the site as you found it, if not a little better.
- Keep to the track. This minimises the chance of treading on fragile seedlings.
- Respect the cultural heritage.
- Enjoy yourself.
- Consider others and respect their reasons for wanting to enjoy Rotorua and the Bay of Plenty's beauty.

Kaimai Mamaku Forest Park

The Kaimai Mamaku Forest Park is split into two distinct geographical and geological areas. To the south, the vast rolling sea of soft ignimbrite with the dissected valleys of the Mamaku Plateau contrasts the high forested volcanic hills of the Kaimai Range to the north.

The park covers approximately 37,000 ha and was gazetted in 1974. The peaks of the range, with an average altitude of 800 m, receive a rainfall of between 2000 and 3000 mm per year. On its western flank is the

Hauraki Fault, which has upthrown the eastern ranges of volcanic andesite, ignimbrite and pumice breccia.

Most of the volcanic rocks were erupted between 2 and 20 million years ago. The volcanic activity contributed to the auriferous reefs, which attracted prospectors in the late 1800s. Nearly all the gold was found underground in veins of quartz. The gold was formed by rising hydrothermal water, heated from deep in the earth's crust. As it rose through cracks and fissures, it inherited minerals and metals from the rock surrounding it. On mixing with cooler groundwater near the surface, it deposited quartz and any other metals such as gold and silver onto the walls of the cavities.

An underground reef was accessed by tunnelling horizontal adits, or drives, at various depths. Vertical shafts were sunk to connect the levels. Within the reef, vertical rises were dug to excavate a portion of the reef. These methods were employed at Mt Karangahake, which is now riddled with a labyrinth of tunnels. The ore was then removed from the mine by wheelbarrow, railway truck, or lifted up the shaft in a cage.

Once out of the mine, the ore was processed. A stamper battery crushed the ore into a fine powder by pounding it with a series of heavy stamps. The crushed ore was then washed over amalgamating tables. The gold (and silver) was trapped by a thin layer of mercury to form an amalgam, which was scoured off and heated. This separated the mercury from the bullion. The Karangahake Gorge Walkway and Wairongomai Valley contain abundant relics of the goldmining heyday and make interesting exploration.

The impenetrable peaks of the Kaimai Range were tamed by early Maori, who used a number of tracks traversing the hills. The Wairere Track, arising from the conspicuous Wairere Falls, is the most famous and was also used by early Europeans and traders.

The highest peak of the range is Mt Te Aroha (952 m). The summit

Jagged bluffs and steep pinnacles are features of the Kaimai Range, which is a chain of weathered volcanic peaks.

is cloaked in a goblin forest, where the wind-blasted, stunted vegetation of silver beech, mountain cabbage tree and kaikawaka is shrouded in a palimpsest of green mosses, lichens and liverworts. There is fog on the summit around 190 days per year.

The kauri forests of the upper North Island reach their southern limit near Katikati, which also demarcates the northern limit of silver beech and kamahi. The tracks around the Waitawheta Valley allow you to explore the relics of the kauri logging industry, which devastated the once-magnificent forests further north in the Coromandel and Northland.

At least 20 forest types are recognised in the park, and some of the mid-high altitude forests resemble those of ranges further south. Podocarp hardwood forest mainly consists of rimu, miro and rata, tawa, hinau and kamahi. There are also restricted distributions of rewarewa, pukatea, mangeao, kahikatea, puriri and tawari. Nearly all podocarps have been logged and the forest has been highly modified by fire and mining. The Henderson Tramline Loop Track, Lindemann Loop Track and Puketoki Scenic Reserve tracks are some of the places where evidence of earlier logging still exists.

The Waihou River snakes through the flat plains of the Hauraki and Waikato. This river is fed by the innumerable streams, which flow from the hills and caused devastating floods before the construction of stopbanks and other flood prevention measures. The entire Kaimai Range is adorned with waterfalls and cascades, which add scenic jewels to the forest walks.

The Mamaku is a broad dissected plateau around 600 m above sea level and is deeply entrenched by streams, mostly flowing to the Wairoa River and tributaries of the Waihou. Ignimbrite sheets were erupted between 1 million and 250,000 years ago.

The Kaimai Range forms a prominent barrier between the Waikato and Bay of Plenty regions. The Whakamaramara Plateau slopes gently to the east, incised by many streams flowing to Tauranga Harbour. Around the perimeter of the range are numerous access points to the lengthy track network, which forms a walker's paradise.

Te Aroha

Mt Te Aroha is a remnant volcano, part of a large chain of extinct volcanic cones that erupted between 2 and 24 million years ago. The focus of volcanic activity started near Great Barrier Island and migrated south, leaving the Coromandel and Kaimai Ranges in its wake.

The weathered remnants of Mt Te Aroha are composed mainly of andesite and dacite lavas. The Hauraki Fault runs roughly parallel with the western side of the Mt Te Aroha and the Kaimai Range, causing the abrupt gradient characteristic of the range's western flank.

The Arawa version of the naming of Mt Te Aroha relates to Kahu-mata-momoe, a son of Tama-te-Kapua, who is buried on Mt Moehau. In one legend, the range between Mt Moehau in the north and Te Aroha in the south is likened to a waka, with Moehau being the bow and Te Aroha the stern. The many peaks embody the people of the canoe.

On scaling the mountain's heights, Kahu-mata-momoe felt the warm sea breeze, which induced a melancholy mood, and caused him to murmur the words 'Muri-Aroha' (a love for those left behind). He thought of his distant kin on the seashore and gazed to the coast, saying the peak should be called 'Aroha-tai-o-Kahu' (a love towards the sea). He then climbed further along the ridge and looked inland, naming the peaks nearby 'Aroha-uta-o-Kahu' (Kahu's landward love).

According to a Ngati Maniapoto and Tainui narrative, Rakatara, the priest of Tainui, explored the region where his tribe had settled around Kawhia and came to the great peak. On surveying the land he named the inland and seaward-facing peaks.

As altitude increases, the vegetation changes according to the different environmental conditions.

Sitting atop the 952 m Mt Te Aroha is a TV mast shrouded in mist nearly 200 days per year.

19

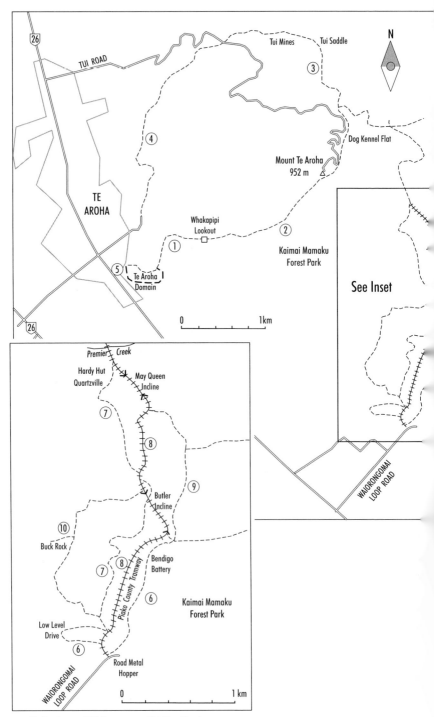

Te Aroha and Waiorongomai Valley Tracks

Below 200 m the forest shows similarities to coastal vegetation, with species such as kohekohe, puriri and tawa present. Above 400 m, mid-altitude forest of rimu and miro gives way, through a transition zone of tawari and tawa, to the distinctive goblin forest characteristic of high altitude zones.

The summit is shrouded in cloud for nearly 200 days of the year. The abundant moisture provides conditions for mosses and liverworts to cloak the vegetation with a mantle of green. The height that stunted silver beech, tawari and tawheowheo forest can reach is limited by colder temperatures, high winds and occasional snow.

Mt Te Aroha is the northernmost limit for silver beech and kamahi, which is replaced by towai further north in the Coromandel.

The black-coloured Te Aroha stag beetle (*Geodorcus auriculatus*) was first identified on the slopes of Te Aroha in 1903, but its distribution is very limited. The name comes from the mandibles on the male, which resemble stag's antlers. The rare and endangered Hochstetter's frog is known to inhabit shaded locations on the mountain.

The Whakapipi Lookout Track, Te Aroha Mountain Track, Tui Link and Ridge tracks and Tui Domain Track can be combined to form a circuit. This grade 4 walk is suitable for fit, well-equipped trampers and takes approximately 6–7 hours.

The tracks up Mt Te Aroha are well-formed, but the 952 m peak should be treated as a mountain. The temperature at the summit can be ten degrees cooler than the town. Weather can change quickly and snow can occur. You should be suitably equipped and adequately prepared with food, drink and warm clothing before attempting the walk. Check the weather forecast and seek local advice.

1 Whakapipi Lookout Track

GRADE 3

TIME 45 minutes one-way

ACCESS The start of the track is signposted from near the Mokena Geyser, by Number 8 spring in Te Aroha Domain.

TRACK NOTES

- The walk is administered by Matamata-Piako District Council.
- The track is wide but occasionally uneven. The climb is a steady one, zigzagging to the lookout platform.

21

POINTS OF INTEREST
- There are extensive views of the Waikato and Hauraki plains and the Kaimai Range.
- During Te Aroha's heyday as a spa town, the walk was prescribed to convalescing patients on the recommendation of Dr Wohlmann. In 1903, the Oertel Treatment recognised the positive cardiac benefits of hill climbing.
- The hill was also known as Bald Spur because it was devoid of vegetation, most of which had been cut down during the days of gold prospecting.

2 Te Aroha Mountain Track

GRADE 4

TIME 1¾–2¼ hours one-way

ACCESS The track starts from the Whakapipi Lookout and is a continuation of the same track.

TRACK NOTES The track continues to climb steadily to the TV mast and lookout at the summit trig (952 m).

POINTS OF INTEREST
- An interpretive panel found on the track shows the geography of most of the upper region of the North Island, including Mts Ruapehu, Ngauruhoe and Taranaki, all of which are visible on a clear day. The Hauraki and Waikato plains stretch to the hazy southern horizon, while to the north, the Firth of Thames flanks the Coromandel Range.
- There is a variety of vegetation on the journey to the summit, with a change in altitude contributing to differing humidity, temperature and wind conditions.

The ascent of Mt Te Aroha passes through varied vegetation. At higher altitudes, the abundant moisture feeds ferns and mosses which cloak every available surface.

3 Tui Link Track and Ridge Track

GRADE 4

TIME 1¾ hours one-way

ACCESS The track starts from the junction with Tui Domain Track, ten minutes from the top carpark on Tui Road. Alternatively, if you complete a circuit of Mt Te Aroha, the track is signposted from the southern side of the summit area.

TRACK NOTES

- This description applies from the junction with the Tui Domain Track.
- For 30 minutes the track is marked with orange rectangles, and climbs gently to cross Mountain Road and the remains of Tui Mine.
- Veer left for five minutes over the tailings to the remains of the Tui Mine mill.
- Turning right, the track follows the old road for 15 minutes over the tailings to the top of the mine and is marked with orange triangles.
- Re-entering the forest, it is a 30 minute climb to the Tui Saddle and the junction with the Mangakino Pack Track. For the next 30 minutes, the track climbs through sometimes open forest to Dog Kennel Flat and the junction, with links to the Wairongomai Valley.
- The final 30-minute ascent to Te Aroha summit passes through more moss-covered montane forest.

POINTS OF INTEREST

- Tui Mine was initially worked from 1884, but because of the high concentration of lead and zinc in the ore, processing was quickly abandoned.
- In 1964 renewed interest led to the discovery of lead, copper and zinc. In 1967 the Norpac Mining Company was formed and a crushing and treatment plant was constructed, costing £100,000. The plant crushed 1000 tonnes per week and the ore was shipped to Japan. The ore from the Tui Mine was later discovered to be contaminated with mercury and was thus rejected by overseas buyers. The mine closed in 1973 and the vast wasteland of contaminated tailings is a lasting legacy.
- The huge conical concrete hoppers used to funnel the ore to the crushing plant are still visible, along with the remains of rusting machinery and tramlines.
- Dog Kennel Flat was named during the era of goat culling, when kennels were kept on the grassed area.

4 Tui Domain Track

GRADE 2 to Hamilton Street
       3 to Tui Road top carpark

TIME 1¼ hours one-way to Hamilton Street
      2 hours one-way to Tui Road top carpark

ACCESS The track heads north from the Mokena Geyser in Te Aroha Domain. Hamilton Street is off East Avenue, which runs parallel with Centennial Avenue (SH26) north of the town centre.

Tui Road (unsealed) is on the right just before leaving Te Aroha along SH26 north.

TRACK NOTES

- This track is administered by Matamata-Piako District Council.
- This track links with the Tui Link Track and Ridge Track to complete a circuit of Mt Te Aroha. The description applies from the Mokena Geyser in Te Aroha Domain.
- To Hamilton Street, the track is mostly even and undulates, crossing two shallow streams. After passing the Water Treatment Station (15 minutes) and the Mountain Bike Track (15 minutes), there is a five minute return detour to a lookout over the town.
- It is a further 30 minutes to the junction with Hamilton Street, which takes 15 minutes one-way to the road-end and involves crossing the Tunakohoia Stream. The rocky bed usually prevents a wet crossing.
- Bearing right, the track crosses the Tunakohoia Stream after ten minutes, climbing steeply past an adit of the Mayflower Claim.
- A ten minute return detour to a waterfall lookout comes shortly after on the right.
- The track crosses two footbridges on its way to a junction with the Tui Link Track and Ridge Track, leading to Te Aroha summit.
- From the junction it is ten minutes to the top carpark on Tui Road (unsealed), with the track passing the remains of a water race and the old reservoirs.

POINTS OF INTEREST

- The impressive waterfall tumbles in a series of cascades down a steep gorge.
- The water race was gravity-fed from the Tui and Tunakohoia streams to the reservoirs, which contributed to the generation of Te Aroha's first electric power supply.

5 Te Aroha Domain Loop Walk

GRADE 2

TIME Domain Lower Walk 15 minutes one-way
   Domain Upper Walk 15 minutes one-way

ACCESS The track starts from the Mokena Geyser in Te Aroha Domain.

TRACK NOTES

- This track is administered by Matamata-Piako District Council.
- The Domain Upper Walk climbs gently, passing the junction with the Whakapipi Lookout Track after five minutes. It undulates through forest to meet the junction with the track to Wyborn Pool.
- Continue right on the Domain Lower Walk to return to the Mokena Geyser. This track is mostly sealed and has a more gentle gradient than the Upper Walk.

POINTS OF INTEREST

- The 44 ha Te Aroha Domain was gazetted as a recreation ground in 1881, and has been restored with such painstaking attention to detail that you almost expect a sophisticated Edwardian lady to glide past at any moment, her voluminous dress and whalebone corset shaded beneath a parasol. The Domain still exudes the tranquillity that made it a preferred destination for the 'carriage trade' so people could 'take the waters'.
- The taking of regular exercise was a popular treatment in Edwardian times, and a shaded walk through the forest provided the perfect tonic. Patients convalescing at Te Aroha would stop at numerous drinking taps, which bordered the present-day walk.
- Each tap was serviced by a different spring, all with differing mineral compositions and healing qualities. The water with a high concentration of bicarbonate of soda was often prescribed to prim and well-mannered ladies suffering from a 'lack of regularity'. Constipation was caused by low fibre diets, hard physical labour and uncomfortable whalebone corsets. Despite interminable flatulence, the cure was well proven. The taps still border the path, although the dragonheads and statuettes of the ornamental surroundings have disappeared. Also lost and overgrown are the secret gardens, which led off from the main track.
- During Te Aroha's heyday of the late 1800s, it received wide publicity in the tourist literature and attracted more bathers than Rotorua. Visitors much preferred a trip to Te Aroha, as the journey from Auckland allowed relaxation aboard a boat to Thames, then a leisurely and dignified cruise aboard the steamship *Kotuku*, which plied

the Waihou River. A trip to Rotorua involved bumping and rattling a further 64 km over the Mamakus in a Cobb and Co. carriage.

- During the mid-1900s, public attitudes towards spas shifted. As the motorcar developed and people became more mobile, the beach became the preferred setting for relaxation. Pharmaceutical 'cures' and improving diet diminished the need for lengthy periods of convalescence at a spa. Te Aroha, like many other New Zealand spa resorts, fell into partial decline.
- The Mokena Geyser is the only natural hot soda-spring geyser in the world and erupts in a five m jet every 40 minutes.

The Waiorongomai Valley

In 1880 Hone Werahiko discovered gold on the western slopes of Mt Te Aroha. After continued prospecting, there seemed to be the potential to extract substantial quantities of gold around Buck Reef.

In 1882 Jesiah Firth, one of New Zealand's richest men at the time, with James Clarke, formed the Te Aroha Battery Company and bought the 40-stamp Piako Battery to the Waiorongomai from Thames. They constructed two water races and spent £20,000 constructing one of the largest crushing plants in the country.

Initially, encouraging prospects from assaying the available ore prompted the Piako County Council to help construct a tramway. In 1883, after an eventual cost of £19,000, the tramway started operating. It was five km long, fell 426 m and included three bridges, two tunnels and three self-acting inclines. Horses, and later a steam hauler, were used to pull the trucks. Ore chutes or aerial tramways were used to link claims away from the main line.

The burgeoning town of Waiorongomai developed apace with the goldfield and attracted a population of approximately 3000. The inhabitants were serviced by three hotels and a dozen shops, some of which made deliveries 'up the hill' to the miners' camps. With the influx of tourists to nearby Te Aroha for mineral spas, the goldfield became part of the tourist experience.

After the huge initial investments in infrastructure, further excavations did not live up to expectations. The hard quartz, a high degree of impurities from base metals and inefficiencies in the processing prompted new claims to be pegged.

In 1886 the New Era Battery was constructed but was soon deemed unprofitable. Poor gold recoveries and summer droughts caused water shortages for the Firth and Clarke Battery.

After various changes in the battery's ownership, an ambitious project to drive a low-level tunnel along Buck Reef was attempted. It was planned to be large enough for a locomotive, but finances became scarce and the tunnel was downsized. After 500 m of the intended four km was completed, the project was abandoned.

In 1898 E.H. Hardy acquired the Firth and Clarke Battery and operated it at a profit, mainly because the existing infrastructure was already in place.

In 1908 the Bendigo Company started working the Silver King Reef on the lower slopes of the valley. An aerial ropeway connected it to the Piako County Tramway. Most of the plant was removed following disappointing results.

In 1912 the Firth and Clarke Battery burned down. The plant of the rebuilt battery was used for road metal production from 1920–27. The concrete bins evident today are relics of that operation.

In 1935, Mines Inspector J.F. Downey described the history of mining on the Waiorongomai goldfield as 'one long chapter of disaster'.

Today, many of the old pack tracks used by horses delivering goods around the goldfield and the Piako County Tramway are used as tracks to explore the valley. Most are well-formed, wide and even. All tracks cross side streams with waterfalls. These usually allow a dry crossing.

It is a steady climb up the valley past the many artefacts of the goldmining heyday. The Department of Conservation has recently undertaken a huge restoration project, and many artefacts now enrich the imagination with visions of the valley's stories.

The Waiorongomai Valley is signposted along Waiorongomai Road, four km south of Te Aroha

This pipeline carried water, which powered a water wheel in the Bendigo Battery.

along Te Aroha Gordon Road. There is a parking bay, from where the tracks to the valley begin.

6 Low Level Loop Track

GRADE 3

TIME 2 hours return

ACCESS The start of the track is signposted just above the Waiorongomai carpark.

TRACK NOTES

- The track is wide and climbs gently to a side track on the right leading to the Bendigo Battery. This ten-minute detour is steep and accesses the old battery site.
- Shortly after, a two minute link track on the left leads to the bottom of the Butler Incline. The loop track follows the Piako County Tramway on a gentle gradient for 40 minutes to the junction with the High Level Pack Track.
- Continue straight ahead for ten minutes to the Low Level Drive, where a short loop takes you to the beginnings of the tunnel. After ten minutes, the main track rejoins the High Level Pack Track, five minutes from the carpark.

POINTS OF INTEREST

- The walk is liberally marked with information panels explaining the history of individual areas.
- In 1908 Thomas Gavin formed the Bendigo Company and started working the Silver King Reef near the Waiorongomai Stream. By 1911 the small crushing plant was connected to the Piako County Tramway by an aerial ropeway. Poor early yields of low-grade ore necessitated the plant's upgrade, and the unprofitable operation ceased in 1912. The remains of stamps, water race, cyanide vats and ore hoppers are still evident.
- The Low Level Drive, started in 1896, was an ambitious project designed to eliminate the need for vertical shafts further up the valley, and thus obviate the need for double handling of ore. The aim was to penetrate nearly four km into the reef at an estimated cost of £30,000.
- A rimu box drain lay under a tunnel 3.3 m high and 2.4 m wide. Workers intended to use a compressed air drill to speed up construction,

so a 390 m long water race was constructed from steel pipes to drive a pelton (water) wheel to power the air compressor. By 1898 the compressor was complete but the waterpower was unavailable. The project was abandoned when the tunnel was only 370 m long.

7 High Level Pack Track

GRADE 3

TIME 2 hours one-way

ACCESS From Waiorongomai carpark, head up the initial track for two minutes. The High Level Pack Track is signposted to the left.

TRACK NOTES

- The track climbs for 20 minutes, passing both intersections of the Low Level Loop Track and the start of the Buck Rock Track. It continues for 45 minutes, crossing the Butler Incline via a footbridge and joins the Piako County Tramway past the top of the Butler Incline.
- Follow the tramway for a minute and veer left at the signpost. Continue for 45 minutes, passing the site of Quartzville and Hardy's Hut until you meet the Piako County Tramway, ten minutes above the top of the May Queen Incline and ten minutes below Premier Creek.

POINTS OF INTEREST

- During Waiorongomai's heyday, stores in the township included bakeries, hardware and ironmongers, a butchery and grocers. All the supplies were delivered to the upper workings of the goldfield by packhorses, which followed the track used today.
- Quartzville was the site of a small miners' settlement, established in 1882 by miners who wanted to live closer to the mine workings.
- Malcolm Hardy was the last miner in the valley. He lived in the derelict hut, the vandalised remains of which are still visible.

8 Piako County Tramway

GRADE 3

TIME 2 hours one-way

ACCESS Follow the High Level Pack Track for 15 minutes to the intersection where the Low Level Loop Track leads to the Low Level Drive. The Piako County Tramway is on the right.

TRACK NOTES

- The lower section of the Piako County Tramway, from the junction of the Low Level Loop Track and Low Level Drive to the bottom of the Butler Incline, forms part of the Low Level Loop Track.
- The track is wide and follows the old route of the Piako County Tramway. In many places the restored rails and sleepers are evident.
- The track follows a gentle gradient for 45 minutes, reaching the bottom of the Butler Incline and a two minute link track, on the right, with the Low Level Loop Track.
- Butler Incline is very steep (25 degree slope), 400 m long and takes approximately 25 minutes to climb. At the top on the left is the junction with the Buck Rock Track.
- Butler Incline is prone to erosion and has been back-breakingly restored by DoC staff. It is better for your bones and the incline if you walk up rather than down it. Please return by either the Buck Rock Track or High Level Pack Track.
- The tramway continues on a gentle gradient, passing the intersection with the High Level Pack Track and, after 20 minutes, the New Era Branch on the right by the compressor. It then crosses Diamond Creek and climbs the very steep May Queen Incline.
- The track ends after a further 20 minutes at Premier Creek, having passed the junction with the High Level Pack Track.

Back-breaking restoration of mining infrastructure by DoC allows walkers to imagine a time when trucks were pulled along the Piako County Tramway.

- The final ten minutes involves a stream crossing and a short dark tunnel.

POINTS OF INTEREST

- After initial assaying, the encouraging estimates of payable gold in the Waiorongomai goldfield persuaded the Piako County Council to help build a tramway to connect the many disparate claims to the Firth and Clarke Battery.
- In 1882, after three months of surveying and planning the specifications, construction commenced and a year later the tramway opened. It cost £18,000, of which the Government contributed £19,000, and used 140 tonnes of iron rails.
- The three level sections were linked by three self-acting inclines. Full carts of ore dragged empty carts up the inclines by means of the double-drum winding gear at the top. At the middle of each incline, the three rails split into four, allowing the trucks to pass. On the level sections, trucks of ore were pulled by horses, and later, by steam locomotive.
- The remains of winding gear are still evident at the top of the Butler Incline. Many rails have been removed, restored and replaced. Berdans, truck wheels and cuttings still engage our sense of nostalgia.
- The Rand Drill Company compressor was used to pump air and water uphill to the mines. It was salvaged from the streambed in the 1990s to aid its preservation.

he winding gear at the top of the Butler Incline was used to aid trucks mount the 25° slope.

9 New Era Branch

GRADE 4

TIME 50 minutes one-way

ACCESS The New Era Branch starts from the top of the Low Level Loop Track, at the junction where the link track to the bottom of the Butler Incline departs.

TRACK NOTES The track crosses two streams then climbs very steeply up the snout of a spur. The track is marked with orange rectangles and continues steeply to the base of the May Queen Incline on the Piako County Tramway.

POINTS OF INTEREST Construction of the New Era Battery started in 1884. The structure was carried piece by piece to the site on packhorses. The battery was connected to the Piako County Tramway by the New Era Branch, which was constructed in 1886. It was 400 m long and cost £1500 to construct, but by the time construction ceased, most of the nearby claims the battery relied on had been abandoned. After only six years the plant was closed.

10 Buck Rock Track

GRADE 4

TIME 50 minutes one-way, not including 30 minutes return to Buck Rock

ACCESS The Buck Rock Track branches from the High Level Pack Track, 20 minutes from the carpark.

TRACK NOTES

- For 20 minutes the track is wide, but after the junction with the side track to Buck Rock, becomes narrower.
- The sidetrack to Buck Rock is very steep, uneven, poorly formed and occasionally marked with orange triangles. After exiting the forest, you will need to skirt behind the outcrop to reach the summit. Be very careful of rogue gusts as the cliffs are sheer.

POINTS OF INTEREST

- Buck Rock is a 60 m-high exposed outcrop of quartz, first noted by gold prosectors on the southern side of Mt Te Aroha. Initial assaying proved promising and led to the development of goldmining infrastructure in the Waiorongomai Valley.

The exposed outcrop of Buck Rock first attracted gold prospectors to the Waiorongomai area.

- Buck Reef, the wider vein of quartz of which Buck Rock is an exposed outcrop, has been traced for five km and is 40 m wide in places.

11 Wairere Falls Track

Note: The main track to Wairere Falls is currently closed. This description follows the Old Maori Trail.

GRADE 4

TIME 2½ hours return

ACCESS Wairere Falls are signposted along Goodwin Road off Old Te Aroha Road, 17 km north of SH24 and 27 km south of Te Aroha.

TRACK NOTES

- The alternative route via the Old Maori Trail is marked with orange triangles and is signposted after following the main track for 15 minutes.
- The Old Maori Trail crosses a fence, then climbs very steeply on a slippery, uneven surface for 45 minutes before rejoining the main track. It is a further 15 minutes to the lookout at the top of the falls.

POINTS OF INTEREST

- The Wairere Falls cascade over 150 m and form a visible feature over much of the Hauraki and Waikato plains. It was this conspicuous presence that gained them notoriety as a landmark for navigation in the days when the only mode of travel was by foot. Travellers were drawn to the falls, as they indicated the start of the Wairere Track.

The Wairere Track was one of the most commonly used routes over the Kaimai Range and was noted in the journals of early European travellers.

- Ngauhue, an early Polynesian explorer from Rarotonga, was said to have killed a moa at the base of the falls and taken the flesh back to his homeland.
- Following Hongi Hika's devastating musket raids in the 1820s, many Ngati Maru became firmly encamped in the traditional tribal areas of Waikato peoples. Tensions mounted and, under the leadership of Te Waharoa, muskets, men and flax were brought over the Wairere Track for the ensuing battles.
- Later, Ngati Haua prevented Ngati Maru from using the Hauraki Gulf as a port, so the main seaport became Tauranga and all goods were carried over the Wairere Track. Traders carting sacks of flax and kumara often caused the route to degenerate into a quagmire, especially in winter.
- During the period of early European occupation, many missionaries, traders, explorers, tourists, prospectors and travellers passed over the Wairere Track. Archdeacon Alfred Brown, the pioneer missionary of Matamata, walked the track many times between 1834 and 1858. His travels were described in journals.
- E. Dieffenbach, F. Hochstetter, William Colenso, and Bishop Pompallier were among the early travellers who traversed the route.

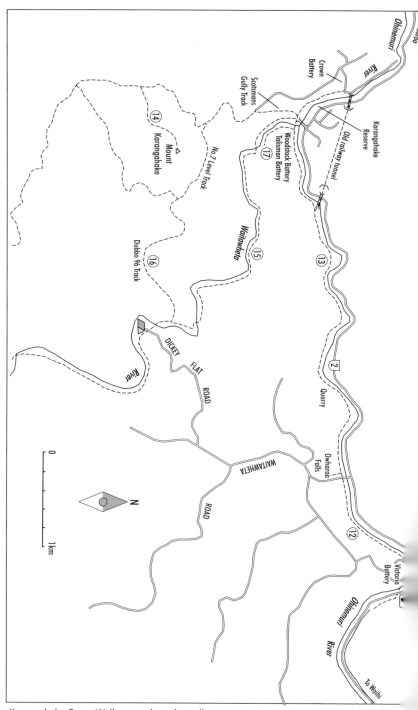

Karangahake Gorge Walkway and nearby walks

Waihi

The Karangahake Gorge Walkway

The Karangahake Gorge Walkway starts from the Waikino Visitors Centre and follows the southern bank of the Ohinemuri River to the carpark opposite the remains of the Crown Battery.

The track follows the route of the old Paeroa to Waihi railway line, which linked the main mining centres of the Karangahake Gorge. The area is rich in goldmining history and many of the relics are well preserved and accessible.

Gold was first mined from the Karangahake area in 1875 and continued until the closure of the Victoria Battery at Waikino in 1955. At peak production in 1909, the Karangahake goldfields accounted for nearly two-thirds of all gold produced in New Zealand.

In 1889 the McArthur-Forrest cyanide process was first trialled at Karangahake. This substantially increased the efficiency of gold recovery from low-grade ores in the region.

During the 1890s, the Crown, Talisman and Woodstock Batteries were constructed. These processed the ore mined from Karangahake Mountain. The Victoria Battery serviced the Martha Mine at Waikino. The impressive foundations and structures of this goldmining infrastructure are still in evidence. All are linked by the Karangahake Gorge Walkway.

The walkway is serviced by four carparks located at the Waikino Visitor's Centre, Waitawheta Road (Owharoa), Karangahake Reserve (opposite the Talisman Tearooms) and Crown Hill Road (Karangahake). Toilet facilities are available at the Waikino Visitors Centre, Karangahake Reserve and the Crown Hill Road carpark.

Further information is available from the Waikino Visitor's Centre, seven km from Waihi and 15 km from Paeroa along SH2.

12 Waikino Visitor's Centre to Owharoa Falls
(VIA THE VICTORIA BATTERY)

GRADE 2

TIME 30 minutes one-way

ACCESS From the Visitor's Centre at Waikino, follow the tunnel under SH2 and the footbridge over the Ohinemuri River. There is parking for Owharoa Falls at the Karangahake Walkway carpark on Waitawheta Road.

TRACK NOTES

- After passing through the Victoria Battery site, the wide metalled path follows the old railway line. It is suitable for wheelchairs.
- To reach Owharoa Falls, cross Waitawheta Road and turn left. The falls are approximately three minutes further up the road on the right. Descend the metalled track, where those in wheelchairs will require assistance.

POINTS OF INTEREST

- Construction of the Victoria Battery by the Waihi Goldmining Company started in 1896. As technologies in ore processing changed, the battery was modified to keep up with improvements.
- The turbines were driven by water from the Waitekauri River and the Ohinemuri River Dam. By 1903, 200 stamps had been installed, capable of crushing 800 tonnes of ore per day. This made the Victoria Battery the largest facility of its kind in New Zealand.
- With the introduction of the McArthur-Forrest cyanide process in the early 1900s came the construction of hexagonal concrete foundations. These supported 40 cylindrical steel tanks. Each vat was 4.5 m in diameter and 15 m high. The crushed ore and cyanide solution was agitated with compressed air to recover the gold and silver. This method increased the efficiency of the recovery process.
- The battery was closed in 1955. Many of the building's foundations are still in existence and accessible via a network of informal walking tracks. Alternatively, there is a tour given by the Victoria Battery Tramway Society. Check at the Old Transformer House, which is now a small museum and information centre.
- The Owharoa Falls empty into a bubbling swimming hole.

13 Owharoa Falls to Karangahake

GRADE 2

TIME 1½ hours one-way

ACCESS Owharoa Falls is two km from the Waikino Visitors Centre on the left. There is parking at the Karangahake Walkway carpark at the bottom of Waitawheta Road.

Another carpark is situated opposite the Crown Battery in Karangahake, 7.5 km from the Waikino Visitors Centre and 8.5 km from Paeroa. The walkway starts from the Crown Battery.

You can also join the walkway from the Karangahake Reserve, 600 m east of the Crown Battery and overbridge.

TRACK NOTES

- From Owharoa Falls the track continues to follow the railway line. The surface is metalled and even.
- Some 40 minutes from Owharoa, a short detour arrives at a stone quarry and waterfall.
- After a further 20 minutes you can pass through the old railway tunnel (one km long and illuminated). Alternatively, continue past the Woodstock and Talisman batteries via a winding concrete track to the Crown Battery.

POINTS OF INTEREST

- The railway tunnel was excavated as part of the Paeroa-Waihi railway line. This was constructed between 1900 and 1905 and aided the transportation of mining machinery and coal.
- The Woodstock and Talisman batteries were built and remodelled in the 1890s. The Talisman had 50 stamps and the Woodstock 40 stamps. In 1904 the Talisman Consolidated Gold Mining Company took over the Woodstock Mine. These workings had produced nearly 100,000 kg of bullion by 1920.
- The impressive remains of the Crown Battery, constructed in 1892, used to house 60 stamps. The gradient of the hill and the foundation structures give a good impression of how gravity was used in the ore processing.

14 Karangahake Mountain Track

GRADE 4

TIME 4½ hours return

ACCESS Near the western end of Karangahake Gorge at the overbridge on SH2, turn into Crown Hill Road. Head uphill and turn left, continuing along Crown Hill Road to a parking bay on the right at the road-end.

The start of the track is signposted through the gate.

TRACK NOTES

- This description follows an anticlockwise loop around the mountain.
- Timings and directions given here may vary considerably from those posted on the track.
- After 15 minutes a signpost shows Number 7 Level to the left. This is where you will rejoin the track, having completed the loop.
- Head right, along the wide rocky track on a steady gradient, ignoring the track on the left after 25 minutes. The track becomes grassier through low scrub, and after 30 minutes reaches a five minute return detour to a lookout on the right.

Views north from the summit of Mt Karangahake stretch over the Hauraki Plains to the Firth of Thames.

- The track is muddier, more slippery and rutted as it climbs steadily for 45 minutes to a junction. To the left along a narrow track is the 20 minute return track to the antenna near the summit.
- Retrace your steps to the junction and continue downhill for 20 minutes to another signposted junction.
- Head left for 15 minutes until you reach the junction with the track to Mangakino Stream and Number 7 Level.
- For the next 1½ hours the track descends Number 7 Level, passing the junction with the Dubbo 96 Track after one hour and many old mining tunnels.
- Horizontal mine tunnels (adits) and vertical shafts pepper the slopes of the mountain. Stay close to the marked tracks.

POINTS OF INTEREST

- By the mid-1880s, the Woodstock Company, New Zealand Crown Mines and Talisman Goldmining Company had acquired all the claims on Karangahake Mountain.
- The Maria Reef was the main reef of Mt Karangahake, and was traced 700 m vertically over 16 levels to 150 m below sea level. Four main shoots were known as Woodstock, Talisman, Bonanza and Dubbo.
- The views of the lower Waitawheta Gorge from the Number 7 Level Track are spectacular. The wooden footbridge of the Crown Tramway Track pales into insignificance against the majestic backdrop of the sheer walls of the gorge.

15 Crown Tramway Track

GRADE 1 to pump house
2 to Dickey Flat
TIME 45 minutes return to pump house
1½ hours one-way to Dickey Flat
ACCESS The start of the walk is signposted from the Karangahake Reserve, 600 m east of the railway overbridge on SH2, at the western end of the Karangahake Gorge.

To reach Dickey Flat from SH2, follow Waitawheta Road 1.5 km and turn right into Kennedy Road. Dickey Flat Road is on the right after 400 m and continues to a parking area with a DoC campground (piped river water and composting toilets).

TRACK NOTES

- From Karangahake Reserve, cross the footbridge and continue straight ahead. The metalled and even track is cut into the side of the rock face and perches above the Waitawheta River.
- After 15 minutes you can continue straight ahead to the underground pump house. You will need a torch in the tunnel, which bears right and descends a steep bank to rejoin the main track. You can return by the same tunnel entrance.
- To continue to Dickey Flat, cross the footbridge over the Waitawheta River. The track becomes unmetalled and, in a few places, is muddy and requires short descents to cross narrow side streams.
- After approximately an hour, there is a 100 m long tunnel, where you will need a torch. Shortly after, a footbridge recrosses the Waitawheta River to join the Dubbo 96 Track.
- Continue straight ahead for ten minutes, crossing another footbridge to the carpark and campground at Dickey Flat.

A short walk up the Crown Tramway track allows a view of the deep ravine of the lower Waitawheta Gorge.

POINTS OF INTEREST

- The scenically spectacular initial sections of the walk through the lower reaches of the Waitawheta River are complemented by the extensive mining history of the area.
- The track is perched on the rock face and hovers above the rushing waters of the Waitawheta River. The river has deeply incised the watershed, forming sheer canyon walls.
- The Crown Mine was situated on both sides of the Waitawheta River, which formed a natural crosscut through the reefs. The initial claim was made in 1883 and extensive workings started further up the Waitawheta River. The Crown Tramway was constructed to transport ore from Railey's Battery 2.5 km up the river.
- This was dismantled in 1888, and a crushing plant was erected on the same site. The Crown Mine ore was the first in the world to be treated by the patented McArthur Forrest potassium cyanide process in 1889. The patent for the process was held by the Cassell Company.
- The Crown Battery was constructed in 1891 and by 1898 there were 60 stamps. It ceased operation in 1916.
- The Paeroa water supply pipeline, which follows the route of the Crown Tramway, lines the side of the track.

16 Crown Tramway Track / Dubbo 96 Track / Number 7 Level Track / Scotsmans Gully Track

GRADE 3

TIME 3½ hours return

ACCESS The start of the Crown Tramway Track is at the Karangahake Reserve, 600 m east of the railway overbridge on SH2 at the western end of the Karangahake Gorge.

Alternatively, you can join the track from Dickey Flat carpark. To reach Dickey Flat from SH2, follow Waitawheta Road 1.5 km and turn right into Kennedy Road. Dickey Flat Road is on the right after 400 m and continues to a parking area with a DoC campground (piped river water and composting toilets).

You can also join the track from Crown Hill Road. At the railway overbridge on SH2 near the western end of Karangahake Gorge, turn into Crown Hill Road. Head uphill and turn left, continuing along Crown

Hill Road to a parking bay on the right at the road-end. Scotsmans Gully is signposted on the left after passing through the gate.

TRACK NOTES

- Proceed as for the Crown Tramway Track, then after the tunnel cross the footbridge over the Waitawheta River to the Dubbo 96 Track. Dickey Flat is a further ten minutes over another footbridge along the Crown Tramway Track.
- Dubbo 96 Track is marked with orange rectangles and climbs through forest for 30 minutes before crossing a small stream. Continue climbing to the junction with the Number 7 Level.
- The track descends for 30 minutes on a wide, metalled but uneven surface, passing the junction with the Karangahake Mountain Track. It continues to the carpark at Crown Hill Road.
- Shortly before the carpark, Scotsmans Gully is signposted on the right. This 15-minute link crosses and follows a small stream and exits by the footbridge over the Ohinemuri River.

POINTS OF INTEREST

- The Maria Reef was the main reef of Mt Karangahake, and was traced 700 m downwards over 16 levels to 150 m below sea level. The four main shoots were known as Woodstock, Talisman, Bonanza and Dubbo. The names of the tracks echo those of the reefs.
- The views of the lower reaches of the Waitawheta Gorge from the Number 7 Level are spectacular.

Water cascades from a tunnel near Dickey Flat at the junction of the Crown Tramway and Dubbo 96 tracks.

17 Windows Walk

GRADE 2

TIME 45 minutes return

ACCESS The walk starts from the Karangahake Reserve, 600 m east of the overbridge at the western end of the Karangahake Gorge.

Cross the footbridge over the Ohinemuri River, then cross the footbridge on the left over the Waitawheta River. The start of the walk is immediately signposted.

TRACK NOTES

- The track climbs for a short, steep section on an uneven surface to an intersection, where it levels off. The left fork passes some old ore-roasting kilns. Take care supervising children in the vicinity.
- Right takes you to the tunnels, where you will need a torch. The track is uneven in places. Return by the same track

POINTS OF INTEREST

- The walk is named because of the 'windows' looking out to the Waitawheta Gorge. These are sculpted breaks in the tunnel wall, which allow viewing of the rocks and river below.
- The extensive tunnels are associated with the Woodstock Mine.

- The Woodstock Battery originally crushed ore dry, but after being enlarged to 40 stamps in 1897, it changed to wet crushing. Roasting the ore in large kilns was common practice in the early 1890s, and was done to improve the percentage of recovered bullion. When the McArthur-Forrest cyanide process was introduced, it eliminated the need for the costly and dusty roasting process.
- The ore-roasting pits are now covered in vegetation at their bases, but you can still gain an impression of their size by the immensity of the holes.

The breaks in the tunnels are the 'windows' above the Waitawheta River.

The Waitawheta Valley

The Waitawheta Valley provides an impressive combination of spectacular scenery, varied forest and historical artefacts. The valley was virtually stripped of its kauri forest, which grows here near its southern limit. The extensive logging has left a legacy, including the remains of the tramway, which can be explored by walkers visiting the valley.

During the late 1800s, the thriving Ohinemuri goldfields of Mackaytown, Waitekauri and Karangahake fuelled a huge demand for timber.

In 1896 the Waitawheta Valley was surveyed and divided into three blocks, one of which was bought by the Kauri Timber Company. For the next 14 years, huge investments were made with the Waihi Gold Mining Company to construct a tramline through the Waitawheta Gorge.

Sheer-walled cliffs and a notoriously flood-prone river made work on the 19 km tramway both hazardous and expensive. When completed, horse teams were used to pull the logs onto trucks. At Owharoa Falls, a railway siding was used to lower logs onto carriages for transportation along the Paeroa-to-Waihi railway line. The Kauri Timber Company's operation ceased in 1915 having removed 9.4 million metres of kauri timber.

In 1922 an entrepreneur named Bob Joughin, who traded as the Waitawheta Timber Company, secured the cutting rights and the use of the tramway to extract the valley's final block of timber. Joughin built a mill at the head of the tramway and ingeniously converted a Fordson tractor to haul the sawn timber to the railway siding at Owharoa. His operation ceased in 1927 and the tramway was dismantled shortly after.

Today the route of the old tramway forms a walking track through the spectacular cliffs and bluffs of the gorge.

Access to the Waitawheta Valley from Waihi is along SH2 towards Paeroa. Turn left into Waitwheta Road two km past the Waikino Visitor's Centre. From Paeroa, Waitawheta Road is 13 km along SH2 on the right.

Continue along Waitawheta Road for 4.3 km and turn right into Franklin Road. After 200 m, Franklin Road bears right over a one-lane bridge. The road-end is a further 2.2 km. Access to the Waitawheta Valley is over farmland, 200 m past the carpark at the road-end.

All tracks (except the Dalys Clearing Loop Track) start from just inside the Kaimai Mamaku Forest Park boundary. To reach the park boundary, follow the yellow-ringed bollards for approximately 30 minutes across farmland.

The Waitawheta Valley is serviced by two huts. The Dalys Clearing Hut is located on Dalys Clearing Track and sleeps 20 people. Mattresses toilets and water are provided. The Waitawheta Hut, near the head of the Waitawheta Tramway Track, has 16 bunks without mattresses. There are toilet facilities and water. Both huts require tickets, pre-purchased from DoC field centres.

18 Waitawheta Tramway

GRADE 3

TIME 6–7 hours return

ACCESS The start of the track is signposted from the Kaimai Mamaku Forest Park boundary.

TRACK NOTES

- After periods of rain, the river level can rise rapidly and trap the unwary visitor between river crossings. Do not attempt the walk if conditions are unfavourable.
- The track is uneven and boggy in places.
- The Waitawheta River has six crossings in total. Wet feet are unavoidable at each crossing. The first crossing is encountered approximately an hour after entering the forest. From here it is possible to gain an impression of the immensity of the Waitawheta Gorge. The first four crossings occur in relatively quick succession.
- The track follows the old Waitawheta Tramway on a gentle gradient. The river crossings generally take place where once there were bridges. On the second crossing you will need to walk upstream approximately 20 m and cross the braid. The track is rejoined a few metres upstream from the final bridge footing.
- Bridges are provided over side streams after the sixth crossing. Occasionally the track becomes overgrown, but is always well formed.
- Approximately 30 minutes past the Waitawheta Hut is a series of informal tracks, some of which are overgrown. These cross the remains of the Waitawheta Timber Company's mill site.

POINTS OF INTEREST

- The Waitawheta Tramway was constructed between 1896 and 1910. It was financed by the Kauri Timber Company and the Waihi Gold Mining Company. The Waitawheta River was crossed in six places and the footings of the bridges are still evident.
- Many old sleepers are present on the track. There are also cuttings after the third and fourth crossings. Rusting lengths of tramline and

discarded truck axles allow walkers to recall a time when huge kauri logs were hauled 19 km to the Paeroa-to-Waihi railway line.

- The Waitawheta Timber Company's mill operated between 1924 and 1927. Today there are numerous remains of timber structures, and rusting cables as well as a consolidated sawdust heap.
- The Waitawheta Gorge is a spectacular feature of 100 m high cliffs. The vertical faces of hexagonally jointed andesite lava are so sheer that vegetation cannot find purchase. The riverside forest includes lush groves of ferns, red and silver beech and the occasional stand of kauri.
- About 20 minutes after entering the forest, there is a small waterfall on the right. This is framed with paritaniwha, which cascades to the trackside.

19 Kauri Loop Track

GRADE 3

TIME 2 hours return (from Forest Park boundary)

ACCESS The track is signposted to the left, immediately on entering the Kaimai Mamaku Forest Park.

TRACK NOTES

- This track requires a crossing of the Waitawheta River. After periods of rain, the river level can rise rapidly and trap the unwary visitor. Do not attempt the walk if conditions are unfavourable.
- The track loops and rejoins the Waitawheta Tramway 20 minutes upstream of the starting point. The track is well-formed but uneven and is marked with red rectangles.
- Near the end of the walk, on descending to the valley floor, cross Bluff Stream and head approximately 30 m up the Waitawheta River. A line of markers on a tree on the opposite bank indicates the point at which to rejoin the Waitawheta Tramway.

POINTS OF INTEREST

- The highlights of this walk are the magnificent kauri perched on the ridge top. The larger of the two has a diameter in excess of three m and is thought to be over 600 years old. These majestic trees provide a reminder of the forest's former glory.
- Stay on the boardwalk provided, as it protects the fragile root system of the kauri.

Numerous cascades are a feature of walks in the Waiorongomai Valley (11).

This compressor was salvaged by DoC from certain decay in the streambed and placed longside the Piako County Tramway in the Waiorongomai Valley (8).

Clumps of toetoe adorn the edge of the track on the way to Orokawa Bay (22).

A circuit around the base of Mt Maunganui encompasses a variety of scenery, including views of the beach (37).

Kaiate Falls (Te Rerekawau) are a series of picturesque cascades a short drive from Tauranga (38).

The force of the Waitawheta River has carved a chasm in the underlying volcanic rocks (18).

The 150 m high Wairere Falls are a distinctive landmark bordering the Waikato Plains, and indicated the start of the old Wairere Track (11) to early travellers.

An orange moss encrusts remnants of the Tui Mine (4), on the western slopes of Mt Te Aroha.

The Whataroa Waterfall (40) is the scenic highlight of a walk around the forest near Otanewainuku.

From the lookout at the end of Lindemann Road there are views to Tauranga Harbour and Mt Maunganui (25).

The Kaimai Range is adorned with boulder-strewn streams, such as those in the upper reaches of the Aongatete River (28).

Otarawairere Bay makes a pleasant spot for a swim or picnic during a walk along the Kohi Point Walkway (42).

he track to Humphries Bay (53) orders the idyllic and serene waters f Lake Tarawera.

A dense forest edges placid Lake Tarawera (51).

From the Kaimai Range near the Henderson Tramline Track (34) spring many small streams, bordered by lush green vegetation.

20 Dalys Clearing Loop Track

GRADE 3

TIME 3½ hours return

ACCESS The start of the track is signposted on the right, 150 m from the Franklin Road carpark.

Alternatively, if attempting the walk in reverse, follow the Waitawheta Tramway for about 20 minutes after entering the Kaimai Mamaku Forest Park. The start of the Dalys Clearing Track is signposted on the right.

TRACK NOTES

- This walk is a combination of three separate tracks — Dean's Track, the Mangakino Pack Track and the Dalys Clearing Track.
- The tracks are well-formed but uneven. They are marked with red rectangles, except for the Dalys Clearing Track, which is unmarked.
- From the start of the track near Franklin Road carpark, follow the marker posts over farmland for approximately 30 minutes. Take care crossing the stiles as some of the fences are electrified.
- On reaching the park boundary, follow the red markers through the forest along Dean's Track. After approximately 30 minutes, turn left onto the Mangakino Pack Track. The track climbs to a low saddle.
- After approximately 45 minutes, follow the signpost to the Waitawheta Tramway. This is along the Dalys Clearing Track via the Dalys Clearing Hut.

POINTS OF INTEREST

- The track is named after the Daly brothers, who were contractors during the kauri-logging era.

21 Ananui Falls Track

GRADE 4

TIME 4½ hours return

ACCESS Travelling four km north of Katikati, turn into Woodlands Road. Be careful, as there is another Woodlands Road to the north nearer Waihi.

Continue six km to the parking bay at the road-end, from where access to the Kaimai Forest Park is signposted.

TRACK NOTES

- Follow the fence and the Waitengaue Stream to the swing bridge. On the far side, head right at the junction with the Wairoa Track towards the Waitengaue Hut (which burned down in early 2002).

- There are two river crossings in the first 25 minutes. Wet feet are unavoidable during both.
- On the return, there is an alternative wet weather track, which can be used if the stream is in flood. It leaves from before the first river crossing (on the outward leg) and finishes after the second. The track is rough but marked with orange rectangles. It is signposted after the second river crossing.
- Follow the old tramway, crossing the narrow, shallow stream five times to the site of the Waitengaue Hut (1¼ hours from road-end).
- After 15 minutes you reach a junction. Ananui Falls are signposted straight ahead. The track climbs, at times steeply, for 45 minutes to near the top of the falls, where a signpost indicates the track to the top of the falls.
- Views of the falls on the ascent are tantalisingly hidden behind the vegetation, with only occasional breaks allowing glimpses.

From the top of the Ananui Falls, the expanse of the Kaimai forest reaches over the surrounding watersheds.

- Be careful around the top of the falls, as it can be slippery and is a long way down.

POINTS OF INTEREST

- Ananui Falls are hidden deep in the interlocking watersheds of the Upper Kaimai Range. They drop 106 m over a hexagonally jointed volcanic bluff into an abyssal chasm they have relentlessly carved.
- Logging of the Wairoa Stream catchment commenced in 1901, with the construction of several kauri dams. B.L. Knight was the main contractor, whose operations ceased in 1914.
- Between 1939–42, renewed interest in the many logs left abandoned in the stream beds prompted further efforts, which culminated in a drive of nearly 300 logs. The sheer weight of timber broke the booms at the junction with the Waitengaue Stream, and the logs floated to Tauranga Harbour. Most were recovered.

22 Orokawa Bay Walk

GRADE 2

TIME 1½ hours return

ACCESS The start of the track is signposted from the northern end of Waihi Beach.

TRACK NOTES

- To avoid wet feet at the start of the track, you may have to dodge the breakers.
- The track is wide and, for the most part, even. Where the track forks, follow the arrows. There are some uphill sections where the track rises over headlands.
- There is a 45 minute return detour to the William Wright Falls from Orokawa Bay. The track crosses the narrow Orokawa Stream on numerous occasions, often with convenient stepping-stones.
- Toilets are provided behind Orokawa Bay.
- This track can be extended to form a longer walk to Homunga Bay.

POINTS OF INTEREST

- This colourful coastline walk leads to a secluded, pohutukawa-fringed beach. Rocky headlands and fern-dominated bush are part of the dramatic coastal views.
- The William Wright Falls are 28 m high and cascade scenically in two stages.

23 Orokawa Bay to Homunga Bay Walk

GRADE 3

TIME 2¾ hours return

ACCESS The track starts from the bank behind the mouth of the creek at the northern end of Orokawa Bay.

TRACK NOTES

- A natural extension to the Orokawa Bay Walk, the track is steeper and more overgrown in places. Where the track crosses grassland, watch for the marker posts.

POINTS OF INTEREST

- The dramatic coastal scenery is offset by the rhythmical pounding of the waves on the rocks below.

24 Bowentown Heads

GRADE 2

TIME 1½ hours return

ACCESS From SH2, follow the signs along Athenree Road and at the beach turn right along Seaforth Road. Bowentown Heads are a further five km.

There are two carparks. The lower has toilets and both have picnic tables.

TRACK NOTES

- The tracks are administered by Tauranga District Council.
- Tracks around Bowentown Heads are mown strips of grass through native coastal vegetation and scrub. Occasionally the grass and soil have been eroded and washed away to reveal the rock beneath. This can be dangerously slippery when wet.
- There are two heads at Bowentown. The upper carpark accesses Te Ho and Te Kura a Maia pa sites. To explore Te Ho pa (the easternmost of the two) takes approximately 30 minutes return. Climb the wide grass track to the summit trig and loop around the northern section of the hill to meet the road.
- Te Kura a Maia pa can be explored from both carparks. A network of tracks follow the terraces and you can easily make your own way between carparks.
- From the northern end of the bottom carpark at Anzac Bay, follow

the wide track. The first five minutes are treacherously slippery when wet, as the grass cover has been removed.

- At the crossroads there are four options: the first two tracks on the left lead to a track that loops around the headland to Shelly Bay (ten minutes); the track straight ahead leads to Shelly Bay (five minutes); the track to the right takes you to the summit.
- From the far side of Shelly Bay continue along the track, which forks after five minutes. Right leads to the summit, from where you can return to Anzac Bay along the initial track to the left.
- From the upper carpark there is also a steep-stepped track to Cave Bay.

POINTS OF INTEREST

- From the summit of the head above Shelly Bay there are views of the upper reaches of Tauranga Harbour, Athenree and the Kaimai Range. From the trig at Te Ho pa there are views right up the beach through Bowentown to Waihi Beach. South past Matakana Island is Mt Maunganui and the whole sweep of the Bay of Plenty.
- Te Kura a Maia is one of the best-preserved and most accessible pa in the region. The topography and layout are still reasonably intact, so you can deduce how the pa functioned. The terraces on the southern part of the headland were probably used for dwellings, food storage pits and cooking areas. From the upper carpark you can also cross the defensive ditch to access the terraces. Middens litter the area. The pa had a chequered history because its strategic location was envied by competing tribes. Its name belies the many battles that were fought here and means 'training ground for a young warrior'. Originally it is thought to have been occupied by the Nga Marama tribe, but Ngati Maru from the Hauraki Plains later occupied the site.
- Bowentown Heads were formed around five million years ago from the extrusion of viscous rhyolite lava. The steep-sided domes have since been severely eroded to form the structures evident today. Originally the heads would have been islands, but since the stabilisation of sea levels around 6500 years ago, a neck of sand, or tombolo, has connected them to the mainland.
- Pohutukawa dominate the shoreline but unfortunately introduced wattle and gorse are prevalent.
- Cave Bay is a cosy stretch of sand at the foot of the heads. Huge rhyolite boulders are jumbled in heaps at the base of the cliffs.

Tauranga

25 Lindemann Loop Track

GRADE 3

TIME 4 hours return

ACCESS Turn into Lindemann Road two km north of Katikati and follow it uphill four km to a carpark, lookout and toilet at the road-end. The track starts through the gate and is signposted on the left.

TRACK NOTES

- The easiest route is an anticlockwise loop. Take the right fork, where the track is wide, formed and marked with orange rectangles. It climbs steadily for two hours to the junction with the Wairoa Pack Track.
- Fork left along the narrow, uneven track for 45 minutes to the junction with the Lindemann Ridge Track. A five minute return detour leads to the remains of a kauri dam and is signposted to the south.
- Return along the Lindemann Ridge track for 1¼ hours, passing the timber of an old kauri dam. This track is marked with orange triangles and can be steep and muddy in places.

POINTS OF INTEREST

- The most southerly kauri sawmill in New Zealand was constructed in the nearby Wharawhara Valley in 1902 by the Bond Brothers. Milling was later continued by the Cashmore Brothers.
- A three km bush tramway operated with a log chute higher up the watershed until 1909, when all available timber had been cut. Driving dams were also used to hold stocks of water. During times of flood, the dams were 'tripped' and the torrent of water would capture the logs in the streambed.
- The views from the lookout at the start of the track and occasional glimpses through the forest encompass the whole of Tauranga Harbour, with Mt Maunganui a distant speck on the horizon.
- Tauranga Harbour is a drowned river valley, with its many tentacles being the former valleys between ridges. The rising sea levels at the waning of the last Ice Age caused the present coastline to take shape. Matakana Island has since been built up from moving sands.

The remains of driving dams are still evident from the logging era near the Lindemann Loop Track.

26 Tuahu Kauri Track

GRADE 2

TIME 45 minutes return

ACCESS Some 3.5 km south of Katikati, turn into Hot Springs Road and continue to the road-end (unsealed), where the start of the track is signposted.

TRACK NOTES The track is wide, metalled and even. It climbs gently to the Tuahu Kauri, then veers left along a narrower, more uneven track (three minutes). You can continue along the main track for a further minute to another track on the left, which leads to the Tuahu Kauri along a metalled and more even surface. Both lead to a boardwalk by the tree.

POINTS OF INTEREST

- The Tuahu kauri is a rare remnant of the kauri forests that once cloaked the ranges. It is 12.6 m to the first branch and 2.7 m in diameter.

- The kauri (*Agathis australis*) reaches the southern limit of its distribution near here. The hammer-marked trunk of flaking bark is used to keep the trunk free of creeping epiphytes. In the branch clefts of the crown are whole communities of epiphytes, perched and sustained by the tree's enormous bulk.

27 Sentinel Track

GRADE 4

TIME 3½ hours return

ACCESS Travelling 3.5km south of Katikati, turn into Hot Springs Road and continue to the road-end (unsealed), where the start of the Tuahu Walkway is signposted. Continue to the Tuahu kauri, from where a sidetrack departs.

The bulbous protrusion of Sentinel Rock is thought to be a volcanic plug, the weathered remnant of a volcanic cone.

TRACK NOTES

- From the Tuahu kauri, the track climbs steeply along a formed but uneven track marked with orange rectangles. It levels out before climbing steeply again to an open clearing, where the track stops.
- It is not possible to continue to the top of Sentinel Rock, as the track is unsafe.

POINTS OF INTEREST

- Sentinel Rock is believed to be a volcanic plug, the eroded remnant of a volcanic cone. A volcanic plug is the solidified throat of a volcanic cone, whose less-resistant layers of ash, pumice and mud have been removed over time to leave the spectacular skeleton seen today.
- The entire Kaimai Range is a chain of extinct volcanoes, which have since been eroded and weathered so they appear jagged on the skyline, as seen today from the clearing below Sentinel Rock.

Aongatete Tracks

ACCESS From SH2 at Aongatete, turn into Wright Road, which becomes unsealed. Bear right after 8.5 km and the parking area is a further 200 m. Access to all tracks is from behind the toilet block in the Aongatete Lodge grounds.

You will need to walk up the gravel driveway for five minutes from the parking area and pass through the lodge buildings to the signpost.

28 Nature Trail

GRADE 2

TIME 15 minutes return

TRACK NOTES

- The track loops and is marked with orange rectangles. It is occasionally uneven. The interpretation panels are organised so they can be viewed when you complete the loop clockwise.

POINTS OF INTEREST

- The numerous identification signs aid species recognition for the uninitiated.

29 Swimming Holes Walk

GRADE 3

TIME 45 minutes return

ACCESS The start of the track is signposted to the right of the other tracks.

TRACK NOTES

- The track is wide, but can be slippery over clay and muddy in places. After 15 minutes, fork left at the signpost, from where the track descends to the Aongatete River. You will have to scramble down banks to reach the river.

POINTS OF INTEREST

- A delightful set of cascades tumble down the rocky river course and empty into a series of swimming holes. Head upstream for the larger pools.

A series of swimming holes and cascades are reward for the Swimming Holes Walk.

30 Short Loop Track

GRADE 3

TIME 45 minutes return

TRACK NOTES

- The track is marked with orange rectangles.
- After one minute, the track veers left at the signpost and continues for 15 minutes to the junction with the Long Loop Track. Head left for 15 minutes to another signpost with the Long Loop Track.
- Head left and after ten minutes the track exits the forest, descending through farmland to the parking area.

31 Long Loop Track

GRADE 3

TIME 2½ hours return

TRACK NOTES

- Veer left at the signpost after one minute and continue right after 15 minutes at the junction with the Short Loop Track. The track is now marked with orange triangles.
- After ten minutes you reach the Aongatete River. Head upstream for five minutes and make two stream crossings in quick succession before climbing a spur.
- After 45 minutes the track descends to another stream before veering back towards the junction with the Short Loop Track (one hour). It is a further 15 minutes to the parking area, with the final section crossing farmland.

POINTS OF INTEREST

- The lush greenery and moss-encrusted rocks around the Aongatete River lend a tranquillity to this section of the walk.
- The spur is capped in fields of kiekie, with rimu dominating the canopy.

Puketoki Scenic Reserve

ACCESS From SH2 turn into Barrett Road near Whakamaramara shops and service station. After 500 m turn left into Old Highway (also signposted Whakamaramara Road) then 300 metres further, turn right into Whakamaramara Road and follow it 6.5 km to Leyland Road.

Turn left and Puketoki Scenic Reserve is on the right after 800 m. On the opposite side of the road there is a large grass parking area with picnic tables.

32 Short Loop Walk

GRADE 1

TIME 15 minutes return

TRACK NOTES

- The track is wide, metalled and even. Bear left at the signpost and after five minutes you come to a three-way junction. Head right along the old tramline, passing the junction where the Long Loop Track begins.

33 Long Loop Walk

GRADE 2

TIME 45 minutes return

TRACK NOTES

- Bear left at the initial junction and after five minutes continue straight ahead at the junction with the Short Loop Track and old tramline. The track becomes more uneven and occasional tree roots protrude.
- After 15 minutes cross the bridge over the stream, and 15 minutes later there is a three minute return detour to a large rimu tree on the left. After recrossing the stream, the track rejoins the Short Loop Track before returning to the carpark.

POINTS OF INTEREST

- The dense foliage is topped by a canopy of tawa, rewarewa and the occasional large rimu. There are some dense stands of ponga in the understorey.
- In the early 1900s the Whakamaramara Land and Timber Company built a bush tramline, which crosses the reserve and now forms an evident section of the track network.

- The steel tramway was aided with bridges and extended 10.5 km to Plummers Point on the coast. Timber was loaded onto scows for transportation to Tauranga and Auckland. At first bullock teams were used to haul the trucks, but these proved too slow so steam haulers were later employed.
- The mill manager Henry Havelock Sharplin donated the reserve in 1926. He originally migrated from Canterbury with his wife, seven sons and three daughters. He employed 60 people in his mill and provided a school. The mill was later sold and ceased operation in 1946.

34 Henderson Tramline Loop Track

GRADE 4

TIME 4 hours return

ACCESS East of the Kaimai Summit, turn into Old Kaimai Road. The West Henderson Tram Track starts from a parking area by the Tuakopae Stream Bridge, 2.4 km from the southern end and 3.7 km from the northern end of Old Kaimai Road.

The North Henderson Tram Track starts from a signposted parking bay on the roadside, 1.9 km from the northern end and 4.2 km from the southern end of Old Kaimai Road.

TRACK NOTES

- Both branches of the track link with the North South Track, which traverses the Kaimai Range. To complete the loop, you will need to walk 20 minutes along Old Kaimai Road. Both tracks are marked with orange triangles.
- The West Henderson Tram Track takes 1¼ hours to reach the North South Track, and the tramline is evident after 25 minutes. Watch for the short detour to a waterfall and swimming hole after five minutes.
- The North Henderson Tram Track takes 1½ hours to reach the North South Track. After briefly crossing farmland, there are two stream crossings within five minutes (wet feet are unavoidable). Follow the old deer fence to another two stream crossings. The track then follows the old tram route and can be waterlogged after periods of rain.
- The section of the North South Track takes 40 minutes. It is narrow and occasionally overgrown. After rain, sections of the track can be waterlogged.

POINTS OF INTEREST

- The southern Mangatotara Forest was logged from 1936 by the Henderson Timber Company. Podocarp and hardwood species were extracted using the bush tramline in evidence today. Haulers were later replaced by tractors, which were used to hoist the logs onto trucks.
- The rimu extracted grew at altitude and was noted as being of high quality, especially useful for building and furniture. The mill closed in 1957, when all available resources had been used up.

35 Omanawa Falls

GRADE 2

TIME 30 minutes return

ACCESS From SH29 between Tauriko and Lower Kaimai, turn south into Omanawa Road. Follow it 10.7 km to a signposted parking area on the left. The track starts through the gate.

Omanawa Falls empty into a plunge pool that the water has relentlessly sculpted.

TRACK NOTES
- The walk follows an old vehicle track for ten minutes. It can be slippery where the rock surface is exposed, wet or covered in forest litter.
- It then passes through a cutting and runs alongside a ledge cut into the rock face above the Omanawa Falls and River.
- You can only view the falls from above, as the track ends at a locked metal door into the old power station.

POINTS OF INTEREST
- The Omanawa Falls tumble into a sizeable plunge pool at the head of the gorge, steadily carved by the Omanawa River.
- The Omanawa Falls' hydroelectric power station was planned in 1915 and was named after the pioneering engineer/salesman, Lloyd Mandeno. Before construction could begin, Mandeno was given the task of persuading the public of the benefits of electric power. The 150 kW power station was enlarged in the early 1920s.
- Lloyd Mandeno changed the lives of Tauranga wives, who were relieved of tiredness and household drudgery by the 'latest perfection in [electric] household appliances'. Advertisements told the gentlemen that if they cared for their wives (that is, converted to electricity), they would have a more comfortable home and a happier wife.

Mt Maunganui Walks

36 Base Track

GRADE 2
TIME 45 minutes return
ACCESS The track starts from the northern end of Pilot Bay, or from behind the campground below the Mount.

TRACK NOTES
- The track is administered by Tauranga District Council.
- The track is wide, metalled and well-used. It loops around the base of the mountain and is connected on the townward side by Adams Avenue.

POINTS OF INTEREST
- The walk is an eclectic mix of urban and natural views. The developed resort behind Mt Maunganui Beach, the industrial areas and port of

Tauranga, the estuary and city, Matakana Island and open ocean all appear as you complete the loop. The atmosphere changes noticeably according to your outlook.

- The track is shaded beneath a coastal forest of pohutukawa and whau, and during the walk you can hear the waves crashing on the rocks.

37 Summit Track

GRADE 3

TIME 1½ hours return

ACCESS From behind the campground at the north-western end of Marine Parade on the beach side of the town. For the 4WD track, access is from the northern end of Pilot Bay, on the estuary side of Mt Maunganui.

TRACK NOTES

- The track is administered by Tauranga District Council.
- A network of steep tracks weaves and crisscrosses the mountain to the summit. Familiarise yourself with the track layout on the noticeboards at the start of the tracks, as navigation can sometimes be confusing.

From the northern side of Mt Maunganui, there are views of Tauranga Harbour's southern entrance and Matakana Island.

- The easiest and quickest route is to follow the 4WD track from the northern end of Pilot Bay (45 minutes one-way). This is wide and metalled.
- The Oruahire Track departs from the northwestern end of Mt Maunganui Beach and climbs via the historic stone steps across pasture. After approximately 15 minutes there is an option to turn left along the Waikorere Track (20 minutes one-way to the summit), or continue right along the Oruahire Track (30 minutes one-way to the summit). The Oruahire track joins the 4WD track on the northwestern side of the mountain.
- A signpost to the Waikorere Track below the summit climbs steeply on a stepped, but uneven track to the summit.
- You can also join the Oruahire Track from an access track, which climbs from the Base Track near North-West Rock.

POINTS OF INTEREST

- According to one Maori legend, there were once three hills at the foot of the Kaimai Range. The beautiful Puwhenua was in love with Otanewainuku, a mighty hill nearby. The third hill, which was nameless, was also stricken by Puwhenua's beauty, but was rejected by her because he was nameless. In despair, he asked the patupaiarehe (mystical bush fairies) to cast him to sea. Working under cover of darkness, the patupaiarehe dragged him to the coast, forming the Waimapu Valley and Te Awanui (Tauranga Harbour). At first light, the patupaiarehe had to abandon the hill to its final lonely resting place. Through the ordeal he was named 'Mauao', which means 'trapped by the light'.
- The 232 m high rhyolite dome was erupted around four million years ago. Since it is a solitary piece of high ground, it commands spectacular views to distant horizons.
- Each tide, an estimated 180 million tonnes of water flow through the Tauranga Entrance of Tauranga Harbour, at the base of Mt Maunganui.

88 Te Rerekawau (Kaiate Falls)

GRADE 3

TIME 45 minutes return

ACCESS From Welcome Bay, follow Welcome Bay Road. Kaiate Falls are signposted along Waitao Road after 6.5 km. Continue for five km and turn left into Upper Papamoa Road. Te Rerekawau Scenic Reserve is signposted on the left after one km.

From Te Puke, follow Te Puke Quarry Road and Upper Papamoa Road for 9.3 km.

The track starts from the parking area, which has toilets.

TRACK NOTES

- The track is administered by Tauranga District Council.
- The track is mostly metalled, even and aided with steps on steeper sections.
- The main track loops around the falls and interconnects with several link tracks between opposite sides of the loop.
- From the carpark, bear left, ignoring the first track coming in on the left, which leads to Upper Papamoa Road. Continue left to the footbridge at the base of the upper falls (seven minutes), passing two junctions with tracks to opposite sides of the loop. A track connects to the return side of the loop. Be very careful of the slippery rocks.
- The descent to the lower falls is quite steep and exits at the base of the falls. The rocks here can be extremely slippery (five minutes).
- It takes approximately 20 minutes to climb to the carpark, passing the three link tracks.

POINTS OF INTEREST

- The upper falls are a series of small cascades, framed by ferns and dense vegetation. There is a choice of swimming holes at the upper falls and a larger hole at the lower falls.
- The ten m high lower falls have formed a substantial plunge pool and have eaten back the ignimbrite cliffs to form a shaded basin.
- Views of Tauranga and Mt Maunganui from near the carpark appear through a gap at the mouth of the valley.

Otanewainuku

Otanewainuku Forest covers 1220 ha and is dominated by the rhyolite dome of Otanewainuku. This protrudes above the flat ignimbrite sheet surrounding it to form a prominent point of high relief. A concealed fault extends north towards Papamoa Beach from the base of the hill.

To access Otanewainuku from Te Puke, follow Boucher Avenue until it turns into Number 2 Road. This becomes unsealed and leads to

Mountain Road. Turn right and 200 m on there is a small parking bay to your left.

From Greerton, follow Pyes Pa Road and turn left at Pyes Pa into Oropi Gorge Road. In Oropi, turn right into Oropi Road, then left into Mountain Road. The walks start from 200 m before Number 2 Road.

There are toilets and a picnic shelter near the carpark.

39 Rimu Loop Walk

GRADE 2

TIME 30 minutes return

ACCESS The start of the track is signposted from 30 m north of the parking bay. The completion of the loop exits at the southern end of the parking bay.

TRACK NOTES

- The track is well-formed, even and marked with orange rectangles. After 15 minutes the junction with the Whataroa Waterfall Track is signposted. The track undulates gently through the dense forest canopy.

POINTS OF INTEREST

- Monolithic rimu tower over mature tawa, and curtains of supplejack entwine the understorey.
- Rimu (*Dacrydium cupressinum*) can attain heights of up to 60 m and is a regal tree of lowland and lower mountain forests of New Zealand. The rich red timber has been highly sought after for house building and furniture making.

40 Whataroa Waterfall Track

GRADE 3

TIME 2 hours return

ACCESS As for Rimu Loop Walk.

TRACK NOTES

- Follow the Rimu Loop Walk in either direction and after 15 minutes the Whataroa Waterfall Track is signposted.
- The track undulates and is marked with orange rectangles. There are a few short steep descents and uneven sections.

- After 40 minutes, cross the side stream over rocks, and the waterfall is a further three minutes.

POINTS OF INTEREST

- The delightful 8 m high waterfall cascades down the Whataroa Stream, tumbling to an inviting swimming hole.
- The tawa-dominated forest is hung with supplejack, which weaves a dense curtain through the sparse understorey.

41 Otanewainuku Lookout Track

GRADE 3

TIME 1½ hours return

ACCESS The track starts from behind the shelter opposite the parking area.

TRACK NOTES

- Shortly after the start of the walk, the track forks. Both routes take about 45 minutes, although the left fork, via the kahikatea, may be a little shorter. The right fork, via the ridge, has a gentler but steadier gradient.
- Both tracks are well formed, even and occasionally marked with orange rectangles and triangles. The kahikatea is five minutes from the start of the track, after which it bears sharp right.
- Both tracks exit at an elevated lookout and trig, 640 m above sea level. The carpark is at 450 m above sea level.

POINTS OF INTEREST

- Otanewainuku was the favoured love of Puwhenua, a beautiful nearby hill. Her choice forced a nameless and rejected hill (later known as Mauao) to flee the area in despair, aided by the nocturnal patupaiarehe. Carving the Waimapu Valley (Tauranga Harbour), Mauao was abandoned at dawn in his present resting place, Mt Maunganui.
- According to one Maori legend, Tutanekai, the lover of Hinemoa, jumped off the summit of Otanewainuku, having fled from his pursuing Rotorua enemies.
- From the elevated summit you can see the Waimapu Valley, Tauranga Harbour and the entire sweep of the Bay of Plenty. White Island is at the hub and Cape Runaway is visible through the haze on a clear day. Orientation panels are posted on the lookout platform.

- The flat, forested expanse of the Mamaku Plateau dominates the scenery to the southwest. The even-contoured sheet of ignimbrite contrasts starkly with the nearby Kaimai Range.
- The forest is mainly composed of a high canopy of rimu and rata with a sub-canopy of tawari, tawa and kohekohe. With increased altitude the tawa/kohekohe sub-canopy blends with a miro/tawai sub-canopy.

The massive ignimbrite sheet forming the Mamaku Plateau is evident from the summit of Otanewainuku.

Whakatane

Nga Tapuwae O Toi

Known as 'The Footprints of Toi', the walkway can be completed in sections or attempted as a loop. The walk is a sumptuous combination of extensive coastal views, secluded bays, open beaches, pa remains, forested ridges and gullies.

Toi is thought to have arrived in New Zealand around 1150 AD, searching for his lost grandson, Whatonga, whose canoe was blown off course during a regatta in Polynesia. It is said Toi lived at Kapu-te-rangi pa, a commanding position above the entrance to the Whakatane River.

Toi was the eponymous ancestor and progenitor of many sub-tribes that collectively became known as Te Tini o Toi (the multitude of Toi).

The usual place to start is in Whakatane, from where the track follows the Kohi Point Walkway past the remains of Kapu-te-rangi pa and through Otarawairere Bay to Ohope West End.

After treading the sands of Ohope Beach, the track follows the mainly forested routes of Ohope Scenic Reserve and Mokoroa Bush Scenic Reserve back to Whakatane.

The complete loop will take around seven hours. The following description has divided the walk into sections, with details given for each.

42 Kohi Point Walkway

GRADE 3
TIME 3 hours one-way
ACCESS From the information centre in Whakatane, follow the path to the left of the Council offices. Turn left into Commerce Street and then immediately right into Canning Place. Approximately 50 m further on are a set of steeply climbing concrete steps, which start from behind Pohaturoa Rock (the rock with the hole in it).

Kapu-te-rangi pa and the trig station at the summit can also be reached from a parking area at the end of Kohi Point Lookout Road. Turn left into

Otarawairere Road from Ohope Road, and Kohi Point Lookout Road (unsealed) is on the left.

Access to Otarawairere Bay is also from a 45 minute return track that drops steeply from Otarawairere Bay Road. This is 1.3 km from the junction with West End Road in Ohope and 3.8 km from the start of Hillcrest Road in Whakatane.

The walk finishes at Ohope West End. At the entrance to Ohope, turn into West End Road and follow it to the end, where there are toilets.

TRACK NOTES

- Continue up Hillcrest Road on the footpath for 100 m. There is a worthwhile ten minute return detour to Papaka Redoubt Historic Reserve. This well-formed grass track leads to a lookout with panoramic views over Mt Tarawera, Whakatane, White Island and the Rangitaiki Plains to Mt Edgecumbe.
- To access Kohi Point Walkway, turn left opposite Papaka Redoubt Historic Reserve along Seaview Road. There is a parking bay with a bench and a five minute return detour along a well-formed track with a handrail to another lookout with ocean views. Follow Seaview Road another 200 m and turn left at the signpost marking the start of the Kohi Point Walkway.
- After five minutes the track reaches a wooden footbridge. To the left is a lookout at the top of the Wairere Falls.

The finger-like sandspit of Ohope stretches from its base at the end of the Kohi Point Walkway.

- After a 15-minute climb along a steep but well-formed track, there is a five minute return sidetrack to Kapu-te-Rangi Pa, also known as Toi's pa.
- Shortly after, the track runs through the Taumata Kahawai Pa. The defensive ditch is on the left and the bank where the palisade fence would have been is on the right. Look also for the kumara pits near the side of the track.
- The track then weaves through coastal forest and scrub, with panoramic views from Whale Island to White Island and Cape Runaway.
- After approximately 2¼ hours, the track drops into Otarawairere Bay. The track continues to the carpark at West End Road in Ohope.
- The rocks at the northern end of Otarawairere Bay are not negotiable around high tide. Check tide times at the Whakatane Information Centre before attempting the walk.

POINTS OF INTEREST

- Papaka Redoubt is the site of an armed constabulary base, constructed to help the town weather the raids of Te Kooti in 1869.
- Kapu-te-Rangi (kapu means 'reaching up to space' and rangi means 'heavens') is said to have been occupied by Toi-te-huatahi, a notable chief from whom many New Zealand tribes are descended. After visits to Great Barrier Island, Coromandel Peninsula and Tuhua (Mayor Island), he eventually settled in Whakatane. It is said he lived here with his grandson, Whatonga.
- The site has two distinct parts which are probably attributable to different periods of occupation. The main area of the pa was probably occupied during the late 1700s. Defensive ditches and banks were constructed to repel invaders.
- Oven stones were found on the lower terraces of the site, indicating human occupation that probably predated 1350 AD. The pa may have been deserted several times during its history.
- Taumata Kahawai Pa was the largest of the pa on Kohi Point and the defensive ditch is over 250 m long. At the highest points, houses and open meeting spaces were probably constructed. Cooking would have taken place on the lower terraces. The defences of the pa were virtually impregnable. The steep slopes of the headland, unencumbered views and large defensive ditch across the boundary of the pa allowed retreat to a central high point if needed. Next to the track you can still see the kumara pits.

- Otarawairere Bay is a secluded cove, which shelves gently and is generally safe for swimming. You can enjoy lunch and feel the tranquillity of this isolated setting from the shade of a pohutukawa tree.

43 Ohope West End to Ohope Scenic Reserve Entrance

GRADE 1

TIME 20 minutes one-way

ACCESS There is a large parking area with toilets at the road-end of Ohope West End. Ohope Scenic Reserve entrance is signposted at the junction with West End Road, Ohope Road and Pohutukawa Avenue.

TRACK NOTES

- The best way to complete this section of the walk is to walk along the beach. Alternatively, there is a footpath along West End Road.

POINTS OF INTEREST

- Ohope Beach stretches 11 km to the mouth of the Ohiwa Harbour. The long, finger-like sandspit is often decorated with shells.

44 Fairbrother Loop Walk

GRADE 3

TIME 1 hour return

ACCESS The track starts from the entrance of Ohope Scenic Reserve, which is signposted at the junction with West End Road, Ohope Road and Pohutukawa Avenue. This is at the bottom of the hill entering Ohope. If attempting Nga Tapuwai O Toi, you may wish to only walk one leg of the loop.

TRACK NOTES

- The track is wide, even and well-formed.
- After five minutes, the track forks, having reached the foundations of an old pump house. Both tracks climb to a summit junction and take approximately 25 minutes one-way, although the sections of gradient on the left fork are shorter and steeper.

POINTS OF INTEREST

- The track passes through regenerating coastal forest, with kawakawa, rangiora and hangehange in the understorey.

45 Ohope Scenic Reserve to White Horse Drive Junction via Burma Road

GRADE 3

TIME 2 hours one-way

ACCESS The track starts from the entrance of Ohope Scenic Reserve, which is signposted at the junction with West End Road, Ohope Road and Pohutukawa Avenue. This is at the bottom of the hill entering Ohope.

Burma Road is 2.3 km from Ohope and 1.6 km from White Horse Drive. The unsealed road does not have parking, but can be used as a pick-up point.

White Horse Drive is 300 m from the junction of Hillcrest Road, Gorge Road and Ohope Road and 1.3 km from the bottom of Gorge Road. There is limited parking at the end of White Horse Drive, which is a residential street.

TRACK NOTES

- The track is wide, even and well-formed and undulates through forest.
- It takes an hour to reach Burma Road, after which there is a ten minute climb before crossing two farmland stiles.
- Entering a densely forested area of private land, the track then skirts farmland and pine plantations. It is occasionally marked with posts.
- It is a further ten minutes to White Horse Drive Junction after the track forks to the right. If attempting Nga Tapuwai O Toi, take the left fork.

POINTS OF INTEREST

- The highlight of this section of the walk is the shaded forest in the Melville's private estate. The towering mature pukatea, with their buttressing roots, share the canopy with tawa and puriri. This is a memorable forest.

46 White Horse Drive Junction to Mokorua Bush Scenic Reserve

GRADE 3

TIME 1 hour one-way

ACCESS White Horse Drive is 300 m from the junction of Hillcrest Road, Gorge Road and Ohope Road and 1.3 km from the bottom of Gorge Road. There is limited parking at the end of White Horse Drive, which is a residential street.

Mokorua Bush Scenic Reserve is at the bottom of Gorge Road, where there is a carpark.

TRACK NOTES

- The track is wide, well-formed and even. It climbs to a ridge above Whakatane, before dropping to the bottom of Mokorua Gorge. The descent is steep and aided by steps.
- To complete Nga Tapuwai O Toi, turn right at the bottom of Gorge Road and walk 20 minutes along Commerce Street to central Whakatane.

POINTS OF INTEREST

- In the early 1900s, the land now occupied by the reserve was cleared for farming. The removal of the forest cover shortened the run-off time for water collected by the watershed during storms, increasing the frequency and power of flash floods. In 1948 a particularly devastating flood, which swamped the town of Whakatane, prompted acquisition of the land by the Council and Crown.
- The vigorously regenerating forest has been saved from grazing stock and now shows a combination of rangiora, kawakawa and pittosporums. An emerging canopy of rewarewa overlooks this verdant understorey.

47 Tauwhare Pa Walk

GRADE 2

TIME 30 minutes return

ACCESS The walk departs from the parking bay on the left, 500 m after the junction with Harbour Road at Ohope.

TRACK NOTES

- The track is metalled and even, and climbs to the pa on the hill. Wide, mown grass tracks lead around the remains, allowing for extensive exploration of the site.

POINTS OF INTEREST

- Tauwhare Pa occupied a prominent position on the western arm of the fertile waters of the Ohiwa Harbour.
- The harbour was known as 'the food basket of many hands'. Inhabitants would have fished for kahawai and snapper and collected oysters, cockles and whelks in kete (baskets woven from flax).
- The remains of the pa, which was probably built around 1700 AD, still shows the defensive ditches that would have protected the three-tiered

platforms. Interpretive panels at the site show how the village mig|
have functioned, aiding you to imaginatively recreate the structure •
the pa.

- The location was frequently contested between Ngati Awa in the we
and Whakatohea in the east.

The name 'food basket of many hands' is conferred on Ohiwa Harbour, which provided sustenance for the inhabitants of Tauwhare Pa.

48 White Pine Bush Scenic Reserve

GRADE 1

TIME 15 minutes return

ACCESS From Whakatane, follow Valley Road from Commerce Street t
the junction with SH2 (White Pine Bush Road). The walk starts froı
the parking bay seven km further on the left. It is a further 5.5 km to th
junction with SH30.

TRACK NOTES

- The track is wide, even and suitable for wheelchairs, although falle
branches and fronds may require removal from the track.

POINTS OF INTEREST

- The white pine, kahikatea (*Dacrycorpus dacrydioides*) is New Zealand
tallest native tree. Its straight trunk was much prized for use as spaı
and masts.

- Most timber was felled to make butter boxes, as the wood did not impart an odour to the butter.
- Kahikatea predominates in wetter sites and is the dominant tree in a dense forest of pukatea and tawa. A verdant understorey is lavishly carpeted with ferns and nikau palms. It is a rare remnant of this forest type, which once grew in the valleys and lowlands all over the Bay of Plenty.

Kahikatea forest was once abundant on the swampy valley floors of the Bay of Plenty.

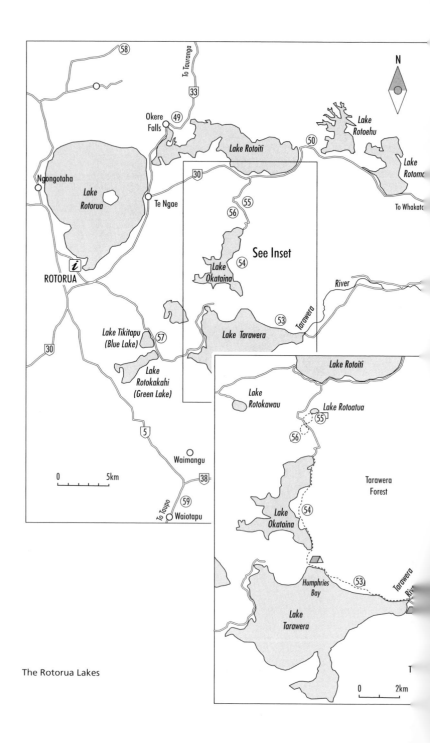

The Rotorua Lakes

Rotorua Lakes

The Rotorua Lakes

The Taupo Volcanic Zone or Volcanic Belt extends 240 km from Mt Ruapehu to White Island and passes through the Rotorua Lakes area. The region is sprinkled with hot springs and geysers, and studded with active and inactive volcanoes. The 1886 Mt Tarawera eruption is a recent reminder of the awesome forces still at work, unceasingly reshaping the landscape.

Rock throughout the Rotorua region is in a constant process of recycling through tectonic movement. Molten magma, from deep below the earth's crust, rises through cracks and fissures in the overlying mantle and materialises in a bewildering array of geothermal manifestations. The Rotorua lakes area is world-renowned for its geothermal attractions, and some, such as Rainbow Mountain, are easily explored.

The Rotorua lakes lie on a raised area at the edge of the volcanic plateau, which covers approximately 25,000 square km. The region is composed of ignimbrite sheets, the product of a succession of violent eruptions. Ash and pumice were spewed out in vast quantities and sometimes fused to form solid lumps.

Large ignimbrite floods erupted around 500,000 years ago, possibly from the Rotorua area, and flowed northwest towards Tauranga, forming the crest of the Mamaku Plateau. Fractures around Okataina also flowed to Rotoiti and Maketu.

Pumice and ash deposits were probably formed by eruptions of cataclysmic proportions, which ejected the debris high into the air from where it was blown by the wind to fall over vast areas. Hot gases would have fuelled convective currents to keep the ash aloft. The edges of many Rotorua lakes are rimmed with a fine matrix of reworked pumice.

When an empty magma chamber collapses after an eruption, a depression called a caldera forms. The craters can later be filled with water, forming lakes such as Lake Rotorua.

Rhyolite lava is another product of the region's volcanic eruptions. The sticky, viscous lava flows slowly from its source and forms hills with steep sides. The features of rhyolite lava are concentrated around Lake Okataina.

The Okataina volcanic centre is a large caldera in which a cluster of rhyolite domes and flows have formed. Around 64,000 years ago, the final phase of eruption caused the land to collapse and form a basin known as the Haroharo Caldera. The north shore of Lake Rotoiti is the preserved wall of the caldera. Its western boundary is less distinct, but is near the Blue and Green lakes (Tikitapu and Rotokakahi). Lake Okataina was formed when the northern arm of Lake Tarawera was cut off by a further rhyolite flow.

Lakes Rotoma, Rotoehu and Rotoiti were formed when the northern end of the caldera was blocked by Haroharo rhyolitic lavas. For a time they were linked to Lake Rotorua, until a col in the ridge caused an overflow and the birth of the Kaituna River. This chiselled a lower notch, reducing lakes Rotorua and Rotoiti to their present levels and separating lakes Rotoehu and Rotoma. Lakes Okareka, Rotokakahi and Tikitapu were isolated to the west by other rhyolite flows.

Landforms are constantly reworked by erosive powers. Valleys are carved by rivers such as the Kaituna River, which flows through the Okere Falls Scenic Reserve. These rivers then transport sediment to the coast, where it is deposited to form alluvial plains and wetlands, such as those at the lower reaches of the Rangitaiki River.

The large lake areas provide a habitat for a wide variety of birdlife, especially waterfowl. These include rare New Zealand scaups, black swans and the ubiquitous mallard duck.

Before the advent of Europeans, most of the land in the Rotorua Lakes area was smothered in a dense podocarp/hardwood forest. Towering rimu, totara, rata and kahikatea would have cloaked the land and edged the lakes in a mosaic of innumerable green hues. Much of the original forest has been removed to convert the land to pasture and to plant exotic species. Periodic burning sparked by volcanic eruptions has

Serene Korokitewao Bay, Lake Rotoiti.

also contributed to a steady process of forest renewal and regeneration. However, large pockets of forest remain, especially around lakes Okataina and Tarawera.

The Rotorua region is home to the Arawa people, whose history can be traced back to the landing of the *Arawa* at Maketu. The ancestors of the waka settled the area, making use of the hot pools for cooking and keeping warm in the cool winters. The abundance of fish and eels in the rivers supplemented a diet of cultivated kumara and taro. These were grown on the fertile soils, which were liberally renewed with nutrients after showers of volcanic ash.

Lakes were used as navigation routes, and portage routes for example along Hinehopu/Hongi's Track, were common. The bountiful resources of the area and the density of population led to contest between tribes and has contributed to a rich and colourful pre-European regional history.

The Department of Conservation administers most tracks in the Rotorua Lakes area. They are usually well-formed and occasionally marked with orange triangles.

The geothermal landscape is extremely fragile and prone to human disturbance. It can also be dangerous. You should keep to marked tracks and supervise children at all times.

49 Okere Falls Scenic Reserve

GRADE 2

TIME 1 hour return

ACCESS Turn into Trout Pool Road at the Okere Falls settlement, 8.2 km north of the SH30 and SH33 junction. The large parking area with toilets is a further 500 m on the right.

TRACK NOTES

- The track is wide metalled and even.
- From the carpark there is a one minute return walk down steps to a lookout, that is level with Okere Falls. These steps are often wet and slippery.
- At the turbine by the toilets, there is one minute return detour to a lookout above Okere Falls.
- The main track continues for ten minutes to a side track on the right, down Hinemoa's Steps to Tutea Caves (five minutes return) and a lookout above a further set of falls.

- It is a further 15 minutes to the Trout Pool and another parking area, 1.3 km north of the first carpark. Networks of informal tracks weave around the small series of rapids and falls in the vicinity of the placid Trout Pool. Rotorua District Council administers this area.

POINTS OF INTEREST

- The area was the traditional homeland of Ngati Pikiao. The Okere River was also known as the Kaituna River, which served as an abundant food source, especially the eel holes at the base of the falls.
- The turbine at the entrance to the track was salvaged from Okere Falls Power Station, which was constructed in 1901 to fuel the burgeoning demands of an expanding Rotorua. From 1902, with power connections to the Palace and Grand Hotels, demand outstripped the capabilities of the single generator and a second 50 kW Waverley Horizontal turbine was installed. By 1907 there was a need to double the output so a side dam was constructed to increase the head of water. It was not until 1913 that a 24-hour service was introduced. The station closed in 1939.

The rotting metal detritus at the base of Okere Falls was once part of a power station.

- Tutea's Caves are named after a local chief. During times of war, women and children hid in the secluded caverns, sheltered by steep forested hills and the river.
- The name 'Hinemoa's Steps' was an invention to lure tourists, who visited the area from the early 1900s. They were cut in 1907 under the supervision of Mr Beal, the engineer in charge of the power station construction.

50 Hinehopu/Hongi's Track

GRADE 2

TIME 2 hours return

ACCESS Around 18 km from the junction of SH30 and SH33 at the eastern end of Lake Rotoiti, turn into Tamatea Street. Continue 600 m along the lake edge, where there are toilets.

The start of the track departs from the opposite side of the lake's parking area. There is another parking area by Hinehopu's Tree. There is only limited parking at the Lake Rotoehu end of the track, 500 m past Hinehopu's Tree.

TRACK NOTES

- The track is wide and mostly metalled, with a few uneven sections. It undulates gently through mature forest at the foot of high bluffs between lakes Rotoiti and Rotoehu.
- Continue 30 minutes to a junction. The right fork takes three minutes to Hinehopu's Tree. The left fork takes five minutes to reach another junction to Hinehopu's Tree (two minutes one-way), from where it is 15 minutes to the western edge of Lake Rotoehu.

POINTS OF INTEREST

- The dense tawa forest with buttress-rooted pukatea and vine wrapped rimu is netted with convoluted braids of supplejack.
- From around 1620, Te Ara-o-Hinehopu ('Hinehopu's Track') has passed through the forest to Ko te Whaka-maru-ra o Hinehopu ('The sunshade of Hinehopu'). As a baby chieftainess, Hinehopu was hidden by her mother under the matai tree to avoid being found by an enemy. Hinehopu grew fond of the trees and creatures of the forest.
- Under the tree she met Pikiao II, and many hapu of Ngati Pikiao sprung from their union.

- It is said the matai has powers that can influence the weather in favour of the traveller.
- Hongi Hika, the famous Ngapuhi warrior, used the track as a portage between Lake Rotoiti and Lake Rotoehu. The name 'Hongi's Track' is sometimes conferred on the link between the lakes.

51 Tarawera Falls Track

GRADE 1

TIME 30 minutes return

ACCESS To reach Tarawera Falls you must obtain a vehicle permit from Fletcher Challenge Forests. These can be arranged for no charge at their office on Long Mile Drive in Rotorua. Turn into Tarawera Road off Te Ngae Road (SH30; signposted Lake Tarawera) and take the second turn on the right. The visitor centre is a further kilometre on the left.

Be extremely careful when approaching Tarawera Falls.

Alternatively, permits can be obtained from the Kawerau Information Centre for a small fee.

Access to Tarawera Falls is sporadically signposted and passes through forestry roads, which are mostly unsealed. Be extremely careful, drive with your lights on and watch for logging trucks.

From SH34 in Kawerau, turn into River Road and then Waterhouse Street. After one km turn left then right into Rotoiti Road (unsealed) and continue 13 km to the junction with Tarawera Road. After 4.5 km turn left into Waterfall Road. The road-end is a further 5.3 km, where there is a parking area and toilets.

TRACK NOTES
- The track is wide, metalled, even and suitable for those with wheelchairs.
- It climbs gently to a lookout below the falls.

POINTS OF INTEREST
- The waterfall spews from a hole in the rhyolite bluff and tumbles over huge boulders at its base, leaving a white veil in its wake. This curious geologic feature stems from cracks and fissures in the huge block of rhyolite lava ejected by Mt Tarawera around 11,000 years ago. These weaknesses in the rock capture the course of the river, approximately 30 m behind the cliff face, and weave an underground network of watercourses that re-emerge through the hole in the cliff.
- Rarely do the falls flow over the top of the bluff, but have done so recently in times of extreme flood, when the deep canyon is also sculpted.

52 Tarawera Falls to Tarawera Outlet

GRADE 3

TIME 1½ hours one-way

ACCESS As for the Tarawera Falls Track.

Alternatively, to reach Tarawera Outlet at the junction of Rotoiti and Tarawera roads, continue along Tarawera Road for 500 m and turn right. The DoC campground with toilets and piped water (from the lake) is a further 11.5 km at Tarawera Outlet.

RACK NOTES
- The track is well-formed but unmarked for 15 minutes to a signposted junction. The right fork is a shortcut that rejoins the main track, but it is better to fork left to view the Disappearing River (ten minutes).

- The area around the Disappearing River can be slippery, and there are no rails to prevent falls. Be vigilant supervising children.
- The track passes through a series of small but roaring cascades (unsuitable for swimming) before reaching a wide, more placid stretch of water. At the head of the watershed the forest becomes more open, from where it is 45 minutes to a footbridge at Tarawera Outlet and the junction with the track to Humphries Bay and Lake Okataina.

POINTS OF INTEREST

- The Disappearing River is the beginning chapter of the same story that concludes with the Tarawera Falls. The water gurgles down a cavity in the rock and winds its way through a series of

Disappearing River is not suitable for swimming.

subterranean cracks to re-emerge at the falls. In places the sound of running water seems to emanate from the rocks, even where there is no water to be seen.

53 Tarawera Outlet to Humphries Bay

GRADE 3

TIME 2¾ hours one-way

ACCESS As for the Tarawera Falls Track.

To reach Tarawera Outlet, continue along Tarawera Road at the junction of Rotoiti and Tarawera roads, and after 500 m turn right. The DoC campground with toilets and piped water is a further 11.5 km at Tarawera Outlet.

TRACK NOTES

- Cross the swing bridge from the campground at Tarawera Outlet and turn left. The track mostly passes through shaded forest.

- The track follows the lake edge for an hour, before climbing inland. It then becomes narrower and more uneven, but is marked with orange triangles. On descending to the lakeshore again, it is a further 30 minutes to Humphries Bay.

POINTS OF INTEREST

- The views across the eastern arm of Lake Tarawera to Mt Tarawera are composed of dense green forest, placid, rippling water and the sombre hulk of the dormant volcano.
- Volcanic eruptions have occurred in the region of Mt Tarawera for approximately 400,000 years, but most information is recorded from the last 21,000 years.
- Between 400,000 and 50,000 years ago, there were five or six huge eruptions in the region, ejecting approximately 500 cubic km of magma. This caused a collapse of overlying ground to form an 18 by 25 km caldera. A 10–50 m thick layer of ash and pumice coated the entire region and welded to form an ignimbrite sheet.
- There were eight smaller eruptions of ash and pumice 50,000–24,000 years ago.
- During the last 21,000 years, 80 cubic km of magma has been ejected in 11 separate episodes, which have built up the Haroharo and Tarawera craters. Around 40 vents have erupted rhyolite magma with pyroclastic explosions of ash and pumice.
- Eruptions 18,000 years ago began to form the present Mt Tarawera, and other rhyolite eruptions 15,000, 11,000 and 800 years ago have contributed to the present form.
- On 10 June 1886 the largest volcanic eruption in New Zealand's recorded history formed a gash the full length of the crater, and spurted a column of ash ten km into the air.
- Basalt scoria and mud were spread over a large area of the Bay of Plenty, and ash fell onto ships 220 km from the source. Over 100 fatalities were recorded from nearby settlements in Rotomahana. Lightning in the eruption cloud sent fireballs that set light to buildings in Te Wairoa Bay. There was daylight darkness over the Bay of Plenty and East Cape regions.

54 Eastern Okataina Walkway

GRADE 3

TIME 3½ hours one-way

ACCESS The track is signposted from the western side of the carpark at the end of Okataina Road. There is a lodge and parking area behind the beach at Tauranganui Bay.

TRACK NOTES

- The track is well-formed and occasionally marked with orange triangles. It passes through shaded forest for its entire length.
- The track meanders above the lakeshore for 15 minutes to a fork. The right fork is a 20 minute return detour to the beach at Te Koutu and the pa. You can follow the track right before the beach, cross the stile and wander around the pa to view the food storage caverns. Please respect the burial site and do not enter the caverns.

The jetty, lodge and carpark at Tauranganui Bay are at the start of the Eastern Okataina Walkway.

- The main track continues to hover above the lake, descending to Kaiwaka Bay after 30 minutes.
- For the next 1½ hours, the track traverses a protrusion into the lake through varied forest types before returning to the lake edge.
- It is 45 minutes to Otangimoana Bay, from where the track climbs a narrow neck between Lake Okataina and Humphries Bay on Lake Tarawera.
- To continue to Tarawera Outlet takes a further 2¾ hours via the Tarawera Outlet to Humphries Bay Track.

POINTS OF INTEREST

- One translation of the name 'Okataina', a shortened form of 'Te Moana-i-Kataina-a-Te Rangitakaroro', means 'Lake of Laughter'. It echoes the story of Chief Rangitakaroro, who was resting with his warriors near the lake. One young warrior exclaimed how the lake resembled a sea, a comment that caused great amusement amongst his fellow tribesmen. Their laughter was carried around the lake and remains in its name.

The entrance to a kumara storage pit at Te Koutu pa.

- The natural amphitheatre around the headland at Te Koutu pa is known as 'the soundshell' as noise echoes in its vicinity.
- The headland was the site of Lake Okataina's most prominent pa. The numerous caverns hewn into the hillside were probably used for the storage of kumara.
- The track was used as a portage route between lakes Okataina and Tarawera.
- Seepage from Otangimoana Bay into Lake Tarawera is the main outlet for Lake Okataina, which is approximately 20 m higher than Lake Tarawera.

55 Ngahopua (Twin Lakes Track)

GRADE 2

TIME 45 minutes return

ACCESS The start of the track is signposted directly opposite the turn-off to the Okataina Outdoor Education Centre, 4.3 km down Okataina Road from SH30. Ample parking is provided in the grounds near the education centre.

Lake Rotongata occupies a volcanic crater.

TRACK NOTES

- Walk the access road from the education centre to Okataina Road.
- The track is marked with orange triangles and climbs for 25 minutes over a leafy forest floor to a lookout above Lake Rotongata. Take care supervising children, as the lookouts are perched above steep drops and some areas are unfenced.
- A series of lookouts above Lake Rotoatua are on the left before you reach a junction with the Anaha Track. Head right for five minutes to rejoin the road one km south of the education centre.

POINTS OF INTEREST

- Lakes Rotongata and Rotoatua occupy a bisected volcanic crater, formed around 3,500 years ago. The tranquil Lake Rotongata is ringed with a thatch of raupo, which provides a habitat for scaup and dabchicks. The larger Lake Rotoatua is a clearer lake with dense podocarp forests descending steeply to its shores.

56 Tarawhai Track

GRADE 2

TIME 50 minutes return

ACCESS The start of the track is signposted 100 m before the Okataina

The dense podocarp forest near the Okataina Outdoor Education Centre is easily explored via the Tarawhai Track.

Outdoor Education Centre on the southern side of the access road. There is parking at the education centre.

TRACK NOTES

- The wide leafy track weaves through dense forest for 40 minutes and joins the Western Okataina Track ten minutes south of the education centre.
- Head right to return to the start of the track.

POINTS OF INTEREST

- This unlogged block of podocarp forest has some fine examples of towering rimu and matai, with a kahikatea fringe.
- A dense green mat of ferns carpets the forest floor, which is otherwise sparse because of browsing deer, pigs and wallabies. Near the southern end of the track, a fenced area shows how the forest floor looks when it is saved from these introduced browsers.
- Panels of conspicuous specimens aid species identification for the uninitiated.

57 Lake Tikitapu (Blue Lake Track)

GRADE 2

TIME 1¾ hours return

ACCESS The track starts from the northwest corner of the lake at the western end of the beach.

There are large parking areas with toilets behind the beach at the northern end of the lake.

TRACK NOTES

- The track is generally wide and uneven with a few undulations and muddy sections. It is unmarked, but follows the perimeter of the lake.
- Following the track in an anticlockwise direction: After 40 minutes of skirting the western side, there is a five minute return detour to a beach on the southern side of the lake.
- After a further ten minutes there is a crossroads. Veer left for 20 minutes to another parking area, where steps descend to another beach. Follow the lake edge track for 30 minutes to the road, where the track ends.

Pumice beaches border Lake Tikitapu's pristine waters.

Renowned for its clear blue waters, Lake Tikitapu is circumnavigated by a wide track.

- Take extreme care on the final ten minutes along the roadside footpath back to the carpark.
- The track is jointly managed by DoC, Fletcher Challenge Forests and Rotorua District Council.

POINTS OF INTEREST

- The shaded walk passes through fern-dominated native forest and exotic plantations of the Whakarewarewa Forest. All the while, the serene blue waters of Lake Tikitapu, which are suitable for swimming, lap the fine pumice beaches.
- One story of Lake Tikitapu's naming relates to a daughter of a high-born chief, who bathed in the waters while wearing Tikitapu — a sacred heirloom ornament worn around the neck. It was usually attached with a flax chord, but as she swam, it became detached and is still lost.

58 Kaharoa Kokako Track

GRADE 3

TIME 1½ hours return

ACCESS From Rotorua, follow Fairysprings Road, Ngongotaha Road and Hamurana Road, then turn left into Tauranga Direct Road. Kaharoa Road is a further five km on the right. Turn left into Kapukapu Road after 3.4

km, which becomes unsealed. The track is a further 8.3 km.

You will need to park in the large parking area on the right and walk ten minutes along the road to the signposted start of the track.

TRACK NOTES

- After ten minutes of walking along the road, the formed, unmarked and uneven track follows the ridge of a spur to the Onaia Stream.
- Return by the same route after exploring the edge of the stream. Take care, as the mossy rocks can be very slippery.

POINTS OF INTEREST

- The haunting melody of the kokako's song is an unfortunate rarity in the New Zealand

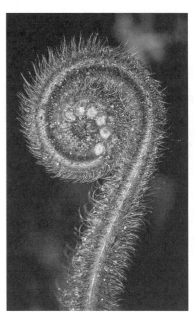

Fern fronds unfurl near the Onaia Stream on the Kaharoa Kokako Track.

forest. Since the introduction of predators such as rats and possums, competition for food and predation of chicks has led to a worrying decline in numbers. The total population is now estimated to be 1500 individuals.

- If you attempt this walk in the morning, you may be fortunate enough to hear the dawn chorus or catch a glimpse of the kokako's steely grey colourings and striking blue wattle below the black mask of facial feathers.
- The efforts of the Kaharoa Kokako Trust, DoC, Environment Bay of Plenty and volunteers have been rewarded with an increase in bird numbers in the Kaharoa Conservation Area, and a commensurate improvement in the health and diversity of the forest.
- Since the Trust's formation in 1997, 47 kokako have been successfully bred.

59 Rainbow Mountain Track (Maungakaramea)

Note: Maungakaramea is an active geothermal area with a fragile ecosystem. You MUST stay on the track at all times.

GRADE 2 to Crater Lake

   3 to summit

TIME 20 minutes return to Crater Lake

   3 hours return to summit

ACCESS Rainbow Mountain is signposted 500 m after the turnoff to SH38, 29 km south of Rotorua on SH5.

TRACK NOTES

- The track to the Crater Lake is narrow and even. It climbs gently for ten minutes to a junction, one minute from the Crater Lake lookout.
- The main track climbs steadily, on a mostly even surface, for 1¼ hours to a junction with the metalled road. The summit is a further five minutes.

POINTS OF INTEREST

- Rainbow Mountain has been an active geothermal area for several hundred years and a reserve since 1903. The surface features are a manifestation of the extensive Waimangu/Waiotapu hydrothermal field.
- The Crater lakes nestle at the foot of scarlet and white cliffs, encrusted with sporadic clumps of tenacious vegetation. The colours arise from the hydrothermal activity, which cooks the rock to release minerals and chemically alters their composition. The lakes harbour a biota very restricted in distribution, which includes thermophyllic bacteria and enzymes.
- The lake visible from the lookout is a milky peppermint colour and nearby there are bubbling hydrothermal outlets. Steaming fumaroles vent wisps of cloudy vapour on the hilltop above.
- Rare vegetation on the warm slopes includes kanuka, endangered orchids and tropical ferns. Much of the vegetation on the mountain is directly related to the thermal conditions, with periods of cooling interspersed with episodes of burning. A mosaic of tall shrubland, low forest and isolated stands of kamahi forest cloak the slopes.